Reason in Action

Works of John Finnis available from
Oxford University Press

Reason in Action
Collected Essays: Volume I

Intention and Identity
Collected Essays: Volume II

Human Rights and Common Good
Collected Essays: Volume III

Philosophy of Law
Collected Essays: Volume IV

Religion and Public Reasons
Collected Essays: Volume V

Natural Law and Natural Rights
Second Edition

Aquinas
Moral, Political, and Legal Theory

Nuclear Deterrence, Morality and Realism
with Joseph Boyle and Germain Grisez

REASON IN ACTION

Collected Essays: Volume I

John Finnis

UNIVERSITY PRESS

OXFORD
UNIVERSITY PRESS

Great Clarendon Street, Oxford ox2 6DP

Oxford University Press is a department of the University of Oxford.
It furthers the University's objective of excellence in research, scholarship,
and education by publishing worldwide in

Oxford New York

Auckland Cape Town Dar es Salaam Hong Kong Karachi
Kuala Lumpur Madrid Melbourne Mexico City Nairobi
New Delhi Shanghai Taipei Toronto

With offices in

Argentina Austria Brazil Chile Czech Republic France Greece
Guatemala Hungary Italy Japan Poland Portugal Singapore
South Korea Switzerland Thailand Turkey Ukraine Vietnam

Oxford is a registered trade mark of Oxford University Press
in the UK and in certain other countries

Published in the United States
by Oxford University Press Inc., New York

© J. M. Finnis, 2011

The moral rights of the author have been asserted

Crown Copyright material reproduced with the permission of the
Controller, HMSO (under the terms of the Click Use licence)

Database right Oxford University Press (maker)

First published 2011

All rights reserved. No part of this publication may be reproduced,
stored in a retrieval system, or transmitted, in any form or by any means,
without the prior permission in writing of Oxford University Press,
or as expressly permitted by law, or under terms agreed with the appropriate
reprographics rights organization. Enquiries concerning reproduction
outside the scope of the above should be sent to the Rights Department,
Oxford University Press, at the address above

You must not circulate this book in any other binding or cover
and you must impose the same condition on any acquirer

British Library Cataloguing in Publication Data

Data available

Library of Congress Cataloging in Publication Data

Data available

Typeset by Newgen Imaging Systems (P) Ltd, Chennai, India
Printed in Great Britain
on acid-free paper by
CPI Antony Rowe

ISBN 978–0–19–958005–7

1 3 5 7 9 10 8 6 4 2

PREFACE

The earliest of the essays collected in these five volumes dates from 1967, the latest from 2010. The chronological Bibliography of my publications, near the end of each volume, shows how the collected essays are distributed across the volumes. But each volume also contains some essays previously unpublished.

Many of the essays appear with new titles. When the change is substantial, the original published title is noted at the beginning of the essay; the original can of course always also be found in the Bibliography.

Revision of previously published work has been restricted to clarification. Where there seems need for substantive qualification or retractation, I have said so in an endnote to the essay or, occasionally, in a bracketed footnote. Unless the context otherwise indicates, square brackets signify an insertion made for this Collection. Endnotes to particular essays have also been used for some updating, especially of relevant law. In general, each essay speaks from the time of its writing, though the dates given in the Table of Contents are dates of publication (where applicable) not composition—which sometimes was one or two years earlier.

I have tried to group the selected essays by theme, both across and within the volumes. But there is a good deal of overlapping, and something of each volume's theme will be found in each of the other volumes. The Index, which like the Bibliography (but not the 'Other Works Cited') is common to all volumes, gives some further indication of this, though it aspires to completeness only as to names of persons. Each volume's own Introduction serves to amplify and explain that volume's title, and the bearing of its essays on that theme.

CONTENTS

List of Abbreviations   ix
The Cover Picture   xi

Introduction   1

Part One   *Foundations*   17

1. Practical Reason's Foundations (2005)   19
2. Discourse, Truth, and Friendship (1999)   41
3. Scepticism's Self-Refutation (1977)   62
4. Self-Refutation Revisited (2005)   81
5. Bernard Williams on Truth's Values (2008)   92
6. Reason, Authority, and Friendship (1970)   104
7. Reason, Universality, and Moral Thought (1971)   125
8. Objectivity and Content in Ethics (1975)   130
9. *Is* and *Ought* in Aquinas (1987)   144

Part Two   *Building on the Foundations*   157

10. Action's Most Ultimate End (1984)   159
11. Prudence about Ends (1997)   173
12. Moral Absolutes in Aristotle and Aquinas (1990)   187
13. 'Natural Law' (1996)   199
14. Legal Reasoning as Practical Reason (1992)   212

Part Three   *Public Reason and Unreason*   231

15. Commensuration and Public Reason (1997)   233
16. 'Public Reason' and Moral Debate (1998)   256
17. Reason, Passions, and Free Speech (1967)   277
18. Freedom of Speech (1970)   298
19. Pornography (1973)   312

Bibliography of the Works of John Finnis   325
Other Works Cited   337
Acknowledgements   345
Index   347

LIST OF ABBREVIATIONS

AJJ	American Journal of Jurisprudence
Aquinas	1998d: John Finnis, *Aquinas: Moral, Political and Legal Theory* (OUP)
CL	H.L.A. Hart, *The Concept of Law* [1961] (2nd edn, OUP, 1994)
CUP	Cambridge: Cambridge University Press
FoE	1983b: John Finnis, *Fundamentals of Ethics* (OUP; Washington, DC: Georgetown University Press)
HUP	Cambridge, Mass.: Harvard University Press
In Eth.	Aquinas, *Sententia Libri Ethicorum* [Commentary on *NE*] (ed. Gauthier) (1969)
In Pol.	Aquinas, *Sententia Libri Politicorum* [Commentary on *Pol.* I to III.5] (ed. Gauthier) (1971)
LCL	Germain Grisez, *The Way of the Lord Jesus*, vol. 2 *Living a Christian Life* (Quincy: Franciscan Press, 1993)
MA	1991c: John Finnis, *Moral Absolutes: Tradition, Revision, and Truth* (Washington, DC: Catholic University of America Press)
NE	Aristotle, *Nicomachean Ethics*
NDMR	1987g: John Finnis, Joseph Boyle, and Germain Grisez, *Nuclear Deterrence, Morality and Realism* (OUP)
NLNR	1980a: John Finnis, *Natural Law and Natural Rights* (2nd edn, OUP, 2011)
OUP	Oxford: Oxford University Press (including Clarendon Press)
Pol.	Aristotle, *Politics*
ScG	Aquinas, *Summa contra Gentiles* [A Summary against the Pagans] (c. 1259–65?)
Sent.	Aquinas, *Scriptum super Libros Sententiarum Petri Lombardiensis* [Commentary on the Sentences [Opinions or Positions of the Church Fathers] of Peter Lombard] (c. 1255)
ST	Aquinas, *Summa Theologiae* [A Summary of Theology] (c. 1265–73)
TRS	Ronald Dworkin, *Taking Rights Seriously* ([1977] rev edn with Reply to Critics) (HUP; London: Duckworth, 1978)

THE COVER PICTURE

Wreck of the Admella, 1859; oil on canvas by Charles Hill (1860).

The *SS Admella* was a steam-powered 400-ton sailing ship built in Glasgow in 1857 for the inter-colonial trade between, as its name lamely signified, Adelaide, Melbourne, and Launceston. In mid-winter 1859, not long before dawn on Saturday 6 August, currents drove it onto a reef nearly a mile off the deserted coast of southernmost South Australia. Special bulkheads designed to prevent flooding of the holds caused it to break apart into three sections within fifteen minutes of running aground. Most of the passengers found themselves on its bow section, and perished when that sank on the second day, not long after about a dozen of them had hazardously made their way by rope to the aft section, depicted in the painting. Meanwhile, after a number of the crew had lost their lives attempting to reach shore, two sailors succeeded and on Saturday night made their way fifteen miles across swamps and sandhills to a lighthouse, whose keeper immediately set out for the nearest post-office town; after the keeper had been thrown from his horse, a stockman completed the journey and telegraphed for rescue ships.

The painting may give a synoptic view of a number of life-saving efforts made by boatmen from the *SS Lady Bird* and *SS Ant* on the seventh and eighth days after the wreck. None of these succeeded on Friday 12th, and more lives were lost among the rescuers; already over eighty passengers and crew had perished, by drowning, thirst, and exhaustion. On the eighth day, Saturday 13 August, the rescuers were able to approach in three boats and, with great difficulty, take off the surviving eleven passengers and thirteen crew.

INTRODUCTION

Deliberating about what to do is itself already an action. True, it is internal and, in a sense, procedural. But it is voluntary and intentional, even if not deliberate, and is already to some extent self-shaping. Philosophers of more or less Humean persuasion hold that it is one's reason's service to desire. Judgments based more closely on evidence will hold, instead, that deliberating extends to, and is guided by, discerning what is desirable, beneficial, worth desiring. This discerning is a matter of *understanding* what gives *reason for* desiring ends (the more or less far-reaching purposes one has in mind) as well as for fashioning the ways and means one chooses in order to pursue and attain them.

Reason as a capacity, an aspect of one's natural constitution, and reason's responsiveness to the intelligible products of its own activity—the decisive and self-determining responsiveness (to projects and proposals for action) that is called *will*, willingness, and so forth—is the subject of Volume II. In the present volume, reason is considered not so much as a capacity or activity, an element of one's make-up as a person, but rather in the intelligible *content* of its activities. Reason is the capacity to understand and work with *reasons*. Reasons are reasons for judging a thought, a proposition, to be true (or false, or doubtful). Some reasons are reasons for judging it to be true (or not certainly true) that some state of affairs that one might help bring about *by doing* something would be beneficial, worth bringing about. Call these reasons *practical*. They include principles picking out possible states of affairs as beneficial (desirable), and propositions (plans, proposals) for pursuing such opportunities effectively and in other ways reasonably. This volume is about such *reasons for action*. Volume III deals with the relatively specific kinds of reason for action that we call rights and, more compendiously, common good. Volume IV deals with the kinds of reasons that are systematically and publicly adopted—in some cases simply ratified, in others created, 'posited'—by persons acting in and for a political community, to articulate and supplement the principles which pick out *human* rights and standing elements of political common good. And Volume V locates reasons for action in the context of their deepest sources, considers their intelligible content in its furthest reaches, and proposes them as public when sound.

I. FOUNDATIONS

Before reasoning is understanding—those acts of insight, mostly humdrum and inconspicuous, by which one gains the concepts and words with which one thinks, communicates, and gets to know the world far more broadly and deeply than senses alone enable one to experience it. We do not understand without prior experiences of the world we can see, hear, touch, taste, smell, and correspondingly imagine it; but when we do understand, we go beyond those data of experience. The propositions, explicit and implicit, in which alone our concepts and words have their full meaning, take us beyond the particulars given in experience to the more or less universals, the types, the general; to the true as opposed to the mistaken; and, by reasoning, from the caused to the cause; and so forth.

At least after it has first begun to supervene upon bare experience, understanding is preceded and occasioned by questions. The young child's questions ask for data ('What happens if you…?' 'What's a "…"?') to supplement what is given it by its own experiences. Children ask also for names; and for the understanding that comes by location of the named in types and the typical, and in relationships such as the causal in any of its varieties; and before long they ask for assurance about what is real and true as opposed to what is just a picture or a story. The child notices that questions can get answers, that answers can suggest further questions, that answers—at any rate those which make sense and do not contradict other answers and the data of its senses—hang together. By an act of insight—of understanding which is not reasoned to—the child (you or me) gets the idea (concept) of *knowledge*, of a whole set, indeed *the* whole set, of correct answers to all the questions that could be asked, of a possible access to all that is real and not just a picture or a story. More precisely, the child gains, more or less clearly and explicitly, the proposition that *knowledge is possible*.

That insight is not, properly speaking, an inference, a deduction from premises, or even a *conclusion* from data or experience. *Knowledge* is, for the child, a new concept, and acquiring the concept is an essentially simple insight. The acquisition brings into view (that is, into one's understanding) a double reality: a world, so to speak, of knowables, of truths, and of realities, getting the truth about which is or would be knowledge; and among those realities are me, the child, and my parents and teachers and playmates, all of whom are or can be anticipated to be bearers—*knowers*—and sources of knowledge. And this is not a bare concept, but a proposition incorporating it: knowledge is possible and to some extent also actual. Getting into the position where some such proposition is not only understandable but also affirmable will have included some encounter with negation: statements that lacked meaning, or coherence, or correspondence with obvious realities, and statements that were disowned by their makers as 'only a story' and such like. Knowledge comes into one's childish and maturing intellectual life as counterpart to mistakes, deceptions, and illusions or fantasies.

The knowledge—warranted and true belief—that knowledge is possible is knowledge of a kind that in a reflective, philosophical categorization can be called 'theoretical' or, even less satisfactorily, 'speculative' or even 'contemplative': knowledge about the way things are—*Is*-knowledge. But these names make little or no sense except by contrast with knowledge that is 'practical'—directed and directing towards deliberation, choice, and action. But what is practical understanding and knowledge? The child begins to acquire it almost as soon as it begins to acquire non-practical understanding and knowledge, which along with other experience provides a 'basis' for the getting of practical understanding. But the acquisition of practical understanding is no more an inference from non-practical understanding than the acquisition of a new, foundational concept such as 'knowledge' was an inference from the experience of questions being answered.

Take the example that lies to hand. Understanding that knowledge is not only possible but *desirable*, a benefit, a good *to be pursued*, and that being ignorant or mistaken is undesirable, a lack, deficiency, a bad *to be avoided*, is another simple, original, and foundational act of insight. It adds to the *Is*-knowledge that knowledge is possible a new concept and category of concepts: *Ought*-knowledge. This is not the 'ought' that is part of non-practical knowledge's stock of information about regularities: 'It's the equinox, so the tides ought to be higher'; 'It's spring, so the roses should be budding'; and so forth. Rather, it is an ought that directs me to the good I *am to* (should, even if in fact I don't) choose and try to achieve—an 'am to' which is not predictive but normative, not future indicative but gerundive, action-guiding by making sense of action by making it intelligible as the means to an intelligible purpose. And the purpose or objective is intelligible precisely as *beneficial*, as the attaining, instantiating, actualizing of an intelligible good: knowledge, moving from ignorance to knowing. Ignorance is bad, so it's good to listen to the teacher, read the work assigned, ask questions, and so forth—oughts that are truly directive or normative, even though they have to be reconciled with other oughts that I come to understand, and none of them directs to action regardless of circumstances.

The proposition that knowledge is a good worthy of being pursued is a proposition of a kind so foundational and original that it can be called a practical *principle*, indeed a practical first principle. But this one is not the only first principle of practical reasoning. Among the others is the one that essay 2 pairs with it, in discourse about 'discourse ethics' with Jürgen Habermas: friendship, in various forms and strengths, is intelligibly desirable, choice-worthy, and to be pursued. Only reflectively and philosophically are this good and practical principle clearly distinguishable from a feature of all the basic human goods and all the first practical principles: that they are good also for *others like us* and that the principles direct each of us to have an interest in the attaining and instantiating of the relevant good not only in our own life but in the lives of *anyone*. The boundaries of 'anyone' and 'others like us', doubtless quite hazy in the young child's initial grasp of the basic goods and first practical principles, eventually get clarified in terms of the human: all human persons. This universality of the practical principles, and of their normativity for each of us, both reinforces the normativity of the good of friendship, and is capable of qualifying and limiting that normativity.

Here practical reasonableness comes into view as a further basic intelligible good to which a distinct practical first principle directs us. For it is obvious, or soon obvious, that one might respond to one or other or all of these basic human goods and practical first principles unreasonably. The limitations and vulnerabilities of one's life and capacities not only occasion in us an understanding of a further basic good—human life (one's very existence) and health—but also demand that one adjudicate between the normative claims of each and all of the first practical principles in their bearing on the ways one's own choices and actions might affect the future existence and flourishing of oneself and others. That such an adjudication be reasonable is obviously good not only as a means to realizing any of the other intrinsic goods but also in itself. This architectonic good—of pursuing the other goods in one's own and others' lives *well*, fully reasonably, without deflection or distortion by sub-rational motivations—is the matrix of all normativity that is not merely practical but specifically *moral* (ethical). The principle that adequately articulates its content and directiveness is not successfully identified in, say, essays 7 and 8 or in *Natural Law and Natural Rights*, but can be found in *Fundamentals of Ethics* and many later works such as, in this volume, essay 14, sec. II and essay 15, sec. IV. Its formal demand is that one be reasonable. But since the good of practical reasonableness, like the corresponding principle articulated as that formal demand to be reasonable, is only one of a number of equally fundamental and obvious basic goods and corresponding first principles, 'be reasonable' is not left with Kantian thinness as a demand merely for non-contradiction (universalizability). It has instead the substantive content provided by those other first principles, picking out and directing us to promote and respect the basic aspects of human flourishing.

That last sentence could have ended with the word 'nature'. For in identifying flourishing, well-being, fulfilment, one is implicitly identifying the nature of the being which is (or might in propitious circumstances be) flourishing. The storm of 'conservative' objections with which essay 9 contends would never have blown up if the objectors had appreciated how central to the thought of their philosophical masters, and how sound, is this axiom: you know something's nature when you know its capacities/ potentialities, and these you know when you know their actualizations, and these activities/actions you understand and know only when you know their objects. The axiom applies analogically across the various fields of knowable subject-matter, and its terms, such as 'object', are analogical: their meaning shifts systematically according to the kind of subject-matter, while never becoming a mere pun. When the shift of meaning is allowed the scope that evidence of reality's complexity suggests, the axiom survives the emergence of modern experimental and mathematicized natural science from its Aristotelian forerunner. And the axiom's applicability to the field of human existence, freedom, and action is clear enough. The objects of human action are the intelligible goods picked out and directed to by practical reason's first principles. These goods when realized by freely chosen actions in propitious circumstances go to make up the flourishing of human beings and their communities. That flourishing is the manifesting of human capacities at their fullest. It is the adequately full unfolding and disclosing of human nature. Of course, we can only flourish because we have the capacities to do so—because we have the nature we have, prior to any choices we might make. But none of us knows, adequately, what human flourishing is and what its component goods are, by first knowing that nature. In the order of coming to know (the epistemological order), knowledge of the goods, as intelligible, desirable, pursuit-worthy, comes before knowledge of our nature as such. True, one cannot gain the practical insight that knowledge is good and pursuit-worthy unless one first knows that it is possible. But one also knows that ignorance is possible, and death (as opposed to life), and folly (as opposed to practical reasonableness), and a loner's self-sufficiency (as opposed to friendship). It is the original, underived insight into which in these pairs of possibilities is *good* and *to-be-pursued* that enables us to know what human flourishing is and, reflectively and theoretically ('speculatively', 'contemplatively'), to give an adequate account of human nature.

So the rationally available standard for our deliberating, choosing, and acting is not 'Follow (your) nature', or even the Suarezian/Grotian 'Follow rational nature'. Those are not false standards, but they are rationally available only once their content has been supplied by following out the available, true, and sufficient standard: 'Reason is to be followed'—that is, reason's first principles, the foundational *reasons* for action.

The *mainstream* in ethics, which runs from Plato through Aristotle and Aquinas and then to the various more or less Suarezian or Grotian thinkers against whom Hobbes, Hume, and Bentham react with more confidence than care, lacked clarity—at least at its textual surface—on the matters about which these critics proved most influential. Aristotle remarks that *phronēsis* ('prudence' in the sense of practical reasonableness as the virtue that integrates one's whole character and deliberation) concerns means, not ends. And then, having left hanging the question how we identify and ratify our ends, the ultimate purposes that provide all practical reasoning with its starting points (its principles), he made matters worse by saying—in the course of a taxonomy of reason's elements and functions—that *nous*, understanding and insight, is concerned with the particular, with the judgment made about a particular option in its particular circumstances. All the elements of the answer to the hanging question about practical reason's first principles are provided by Aquinas; but he was a theologian, never wrote a philosophical treatise to expound the philosophical (not theological) positions which he had in mind in his treatment of moral theology, and left the elements scattered about in his vast writings. And instead of repudiating the Aristotelian dictum that prudence is about means not ends, he employed the dictum in his own work, leaving his interpreters to sort out the resulting confusion: see essay 1 n. 16, and essay 11. Even some of his earliest followers succumbed to the temptation to treat reason as fundamentally contemplative; for them, reason becomes practical not—as Aquinas held and this Introduction argues—by further insights into what is not merely attainable but would be *good* to attain, as an *intelligibly* desirable kind of end; rather (as the scholar wrote who finished his unfinished commentary on the *Politics*) reason becomes practical, end-pursuing, by the addition of some act of *will* preferring some kinds of practical possibility over others. But one's 'will' is either one's responsiveness to reasons, or one's responsiveness to the urges of emotions, passions, and 'desires', sub- and pre-rational. The Humean picture of practical reason—reason in deliberation—as the slave of the passions was in a sense prepared for by the Aristotelian sayings about *phronēsis* and *nous*, and by scholastic sliding away from Aquinas's quite fundamental grasp that will is at bottom responsiveness to reasons, to the intelligibility of intrinsic human goods.

The critical response to Hume which Kant intended and attempted to carry through miscarried by its failure to question Hume's assumption that reason cannot do what, we should be clear, every modestly intelligent child can do. The neo-scholastic response to Hume similarly failed to bring to bear a philosophically clarified and contextualized showing of the first principles of practical reason; the response conflated them with the moral norms for which they are the principles, put forward a doctrine of human nature which though sound enough was not critically grounded, and left the transition from *Is* to *Ought* in an obscurity which minimized or even eliminated the differences between free but reasonable, ought-aware choice and compliance with either sheerly given instincts (inclinations) or the commands and prohibitions of a source threateningly superior in power.

That is the context, then, not only of the already mentioned fairly early essays 7 (on reason's normativity, against Hume) and 8 (on foundations, against radical sceptics), but also of the even earlier essay 6 (on reason and one of its first principles, friendship, as potential sources of an exit from the sequence of unsustainable positions in twentieth-century English moral philosophy). Essay 1 has pride of place because the Humean problematic about reason and sub-rational motivations remains central to our philosophical culture and atmosphere, and is itself radically and fruitfully problematized by Christine Korsgaard, even if, as the essay goes on to argue, she is prevented from harvesting most of the fruits by her own Kantianism. Korsgaard's critique of Hume and Humean assumptions about practical reason is carried through by her into critique of sophisticated contemporary versions which disclaim descent from Hume. Bernard Williams's distinction between 'internal' and 'external' reasons for action is a good instance of such a covertly Humean position, as essay 5 recalls in the course of a wider exploration of flaws in this representative late-twentieth-century philosopher's appropriation both of the tradition, and of truth and reasonableness itself.

One's philosophical or other 'theoretical', 'speculative', or 'contemplative' thinking—for example, on natural scientific, or historical questions—is directed 'formally' (that is, regardless of its 'content', its subject-matter) by a normative standard or consideration: that one's reasoning be responsive to all the relevant data or evidence, free from fallacies, and coherent both with itself and with other positions one judges sound and for present purposes unrevisable. This normativity internal to non-practical reason is also internal to practical reason. Indeed, practical reason includes among its concerns one's non-practical reasoning, as an activity at least partly subject to one's will and therefore a substantive matter for deliberation and choice. Reason is not a little person inside oneself, and practical reason and non-practical reason are not two entities. One's reason is an aspect of one's undivided reality, and the distinction between theoretical and practical reason is a distinction between two different functions of one's reason, that is, of one's own understanding and reasoning. And these functions overlap and include each other, primarily because making use of each or either is a voluntary activity guided by an at least implicit judgment that it is worthwhile, a good purpose one has reason to choose, and to choose to do well; secondarily, because practical reason's activities in directing this or any other activity are subjects for reflective scrutiny and philosophical contextualization. The normativity of logic precisely as such—paradigmatically, the necessitation of conclusions by premises—is normativity within the logical order, not the natural, the practical-technical, or the practical-moral.[1] But the demand to respect that normativity conscientiously in one's thinking is a requirement of the practical-moral order, a requirement of the same kind as that one assemble all relevant evidence and follow evidence where it leads, that one not deceive oneself, that one not deceive one's collaborators in scientific projects or one's students, that one not use human beings as mere material for one's scientific purposes, and so forth.

The arguments about self-refutation in essays 3 and 4 give a kind of particularity to these reflections on theoretical reason's practical character (all questions of utility aside), and on practical reason's integrity as the slave of truth, not the passions. For the point of respect for evidence and coherence and logical validity is that they are requirements of truth attaining. Practical truth is truth. Like non-practical truth it is found by critical attention to all relevant data and questions, coherence with all other truths, and correspondence, not to reality in the same sense as non-practical truth's correspondence (since practical principles and the propositions derived from them concern what is not yet real but might be made real by the actions they direct), but rather correspondence to fulfilment. That is, practical principles have their truth by anticipating—being in an anticipatory correspondence to—the fulfilment whose realization is possible through actions in accordance with them.[2]

---

[1] On these four kinds of order, see e.g. essay 14, sec. III.
[2] See *Aquinas* 99–101; also 1987f at 115–20.

As it happens, the essays in this volume say relatively little about the content of an adequate inventory of practical reason's first principles; essay 14's summary list, structured around the concept of harmony, is a somewhat over-synthesized construct. Better is the brief account in footnote 25 of essay 15 (see further essay III.5 (1996a), sec. III), with its clear inclusion of the human good whose omission from the account in *Natural Law and Natural Rights* and essay 14 (and from 1987f) could not fail to be puzzling to anthropologists and social historians, but whose inclusion is unsettling, embarrassing, and 'controversial' to many in our strangely ideologized generation: marriage, the commitment and institution fully adequate to living out a loving and equal joint and several parenthood (fatherhood and motherhood). As sympathetic a philosophical critic as Timothy Chappell argues that marriage cannot be a basic human good:

> We do not complete any action-explanation by saying that the action to be explained is aimed *at marriage*. It is perfectly intelligible to go on and ask why marriage is a good thing, in a way that it is arguably not intelligible to go on and ask why friendship and knowledge are good things. Moreover, what makes marriage a good thing is nothing separate from its instantiation of other basic goods, such as, say, friendship, self-integration, play, aesthetic good..., physical health and well-being—and even, dare one say it, *physical pleasure*.[3]

Chappell's list of goods he thinks explain the good of marriage conspicuously omits the very good which gives the friendship of spouses its *marital* point and its commitment to permanent exclusiveness in sharing of sexual pleasure: its orientation to procreation and parenthood. And it is just a mistake to say that no action-explanation is completed by stating that marriage is the action's end. The action of marrying (which in a certain sense extends through the entire marriage and everything done for the sake of it: essay III.20 (2008c), sec. I) is sufficiently explained by saying that it is the beginning of the actualizing of this intrinsic good itself. Knowledge and friendship have all sorts of benefits as means to other goods, benefits which can usefully be explained while leaving unexplained the *intrinsic* good (knowledge, or friendship, for its own sake and in spite of every cost and disappointment)—unexplained because in need not of explanation but only of some exemplification(s) sufficiently unencumbered by distractions to allow the intrinsic desirability to be manifestly intelligible. So too the benefits of bringing into being, and then into maturity, children who will maintain their elders and contemporaries can usefully be explained while leaving unexplained—and again in need of no explanation but only clear exemplification—the intrinsic good of parenting by joint and equal

---

[3] Chappell, 'Natural Law Theory and Contemporary Moral Philosophy' at 38–9.

procreating and by appropriately dedicated providing for and nurturing: the central case[4] of marriage.[5]

My failure to have identified marriage as the basic good it is (leaving it divided between procreation and friendship) reinforces the reflective question whether the inventory is the right one, and an inventory of the right components. Studying criteria for assessing human development in the context of international aid, Sabina Alkire tackled the question from two of the various relevant directions: theoretical reflections of philosophically minded scholars, and the practical experience of recipients of aid whose lives and circumstances are close to basic. Her book, *Valuing Freedoms: Sen's Capability Approach and Poverty Reduction*, surveys over thirty attempts at an inventory, and gives prominence, as its title witnesses, to the terms with which Amartya Sen's theory of welfare and justice is constructed: freedom, capability, and functioning. She shows that Sen wavers between these terms because each is meant by him to signify something which it does not quite articulate: human good or value, a way of flourishing, of being fulfilled by chosen actions and cooperation. Capabilities, functionings, and 'substantive' freedoms are intelligible as the Aristotelian 'capacities' and 'actualizations' of capacity in their application to the specifically human, characterized as it is by the fact of freedom of choice and the opportunity (with its many economic, cultural, and political preconditions) of self-determination, valuable if used for truly intelligible goods. She concludes that Sen's terms, in his use of them, get their sense as ways of speaking about (aspects of) *basic reasons for action* and *basic dimensions of human flourishing* or development or, negatively, of poverty reduction.[6]

Sen himself has avoided making any kind of inventory, expressing doubts about its appropriateness yet seemingly inviting others to the task and pointing, appreciatively but without commitment, to Martha Nussbaum's explorations and taxonomies.[7] Nussbaum builds these on a sound critique

---

[4] Chappell's final argument is summarized in the question 'Was Solomon partaking of the basic good of marriage when he took his seven-hundredth wife?' Yes, and No—rather as one who today devotes his life to astrology or necromancy does and does not partake of the basic good of knowledge, and as the wary friendship between Mafia killers (like members of Stalin's Politburo in 1937) does and does not partake of the good of friendship.

[5] Alkire, 'The Basic Dimensions of Human Flourishing: A Comparison of Accounts' at 93 concludes 'One could go part of the way towards addressing the above problems by proposing "family" as a distinctive reason for action'. But the problems arose because she was not clear that the central case, that gives what intelligibility they have to non-central cases (both reasonable and unreasonable/ immoral), is precisely the one in which marriage is understood and lived as both the instituting of a new family and the continuing of earlier ones. It is this (in brief) that makes unsatisfactory the position adopted in *NLNR* and maintained in Alkire's list of nine basic reasons for action (*ibid.*, 99), namely that 'reproduction' is simply an aspect of life.

[6] Alkire *Valuing Freedoms*, e.g. 51–2, 76–7.

[7] *Ibid.*, 28–31. For the developed inventory, see Nussbaum, *Women and Human Development*, 78–80. Sen, 'The Place of Capability in a Theory of Justice' at 248–9, hints that, whereas Nussbaum

of scepticism, and to emphasize the significance she rightly attributes to self-determining choice[8] focuses not on 'actual functions' but on 'central human functional capabilities': each item on the list begins 'being able to...'. But though the goods that are the objects of capabilities and the point of 'functions' (better: freely chosen actions) are thus kept out of focus, her conceptions of flourishing give the list an evaluative quality that in many instances removes it from the level of first principles to the level of an already at least partly moralized set of conclusions from them—and moralized, in some instances, quite questionably. Thus *Life* is said to include 'not dying... before one's life is so reduced as to be not worth living'.[9] Knowledge appears not as a basic human good concerned with truth and reality but rather, if at all, as an aspect of a capability to use *Sense, Imagination, and Thought* 'in a "truly human" way, a way informed and cultivated by an adequate education, including... literacy and basic mathematical and scientific training'.[10] *Practical Reason* appears as 'Being able to form a conception of the good and to engage in critical reflection about the planning of one's life'; that the conception of the good, and the plan of life, be not only self-formed but also reasonable is a value—indeed a basic value—left in silence. Yet into the tenth and last item, *Control over One's Environment*, enter the overt moral and political judgments involved in specifying the content of that phrase as: 'Being able to participate effectively in political choices that govern one's life...' and 'Being able to hold property (both land and movable goods)...'. The political judgments are not (on certain factual assumptions) unreasonable, but their reasonableness is not the intelligibility of first principles or basic aspects of human flourishing. The good of handing on one's life and culture procreatively and familially (that is, maritally) nowhere appears, despite the references to 'reproductive health' and 'choice in matters of reproduction' and the allusions to a satisfying sex life or opportunities for sexual satisfaction which appear under both *Bodily Health* and *Bodily Integrity*. Relationship to the transcendent: not envisaged. It is a list dateable to within a decade.

The preceding paragraph's analysis and comment are mine, not Alkire's. Her own critique of Nussbaum's list and of the many others she surveys, and her own testing of the categories with women subjects of development aid in northern Pakistan, led her to a list[11] essentially the same as that

---

seems to think that a list of minimally needed capabilities 'can be arrived at directly on the basis of foundational theory', he himself envisages such a list emerging only 'as outcome of participatory public discussion'. But only by making a 'foundational' judgment about its *content* could such a discussion (unlikely enough in itself) be reasonably said to have had such an 'outcome'.

[8] *Women and Human Development*, 74. [9] *Ibid.*, 78. [10] *Ibid.*
[11] Alkire, 'Basic Dimensions of Human Flourishing' at 99; cf. *Valuing Freedoms*, 72–3.

in essay 14, to which she adds 'harmony with the natural world' (which I think more a matter of aesthetic appreciation, acknowledgement of the transcendent's larger purposes, and a prudent concern for sustainability), while remaining open to the possibility that under some other description the marital-familial might find a place. Her work repays reflection in its own right, and is a reminder that the dialectical, exploratory, and clarifying philosophical vindication of practical reason's foundations has dimensions which I have scarcely revisited systematically since *NLNR*, Chapter IV.

II. BUILDING ON THE FOUNDATIONS

The essays in this part relate more or less closely and centrally to the movement from first principles to moral standards and moral judgments. In this movement the first principles, in themselves intelligible as pre-moral and lending intelligibility to immoral plans and decisions, take on their fullest range and true implications—as moral principles. Essay 11, as indicated above, is also concerned with the vindication of first principles even independently of their moral implications. But it is prudence, the supreme moral-philosophical virtue, that is accomplishing this vindication, and since prudence's goal is not only philosophic clarity and truth but also moral truth and morally sound choices and actions, the essay is involved in that movement up and out from first principles into morality.

Essay 10 is a response to Aristotelians and Thomists who found difficulty in recognizing *NLNR*'s account of practical reason and ethics as a continuation rather than a betrayal of the tradition. Though the essay's last sections, and touches here and there in earlier sections, are theological, the essay's purpose is to show how a strictly philosophical moral philosophy (ethics) needs and has a unifying 'last end'. This turns out to be, not an end-state whether in this world or the next, but an ideal of practical reason—integral human fulfilment, not as goal of any plan or project, but as an ideal against which options can be measured as open to such fulfilment or not open to it, and thus as fully reasonable (morally sound) or more or less unreasonable (immoral). For this ideal is the conceptual counterpart or resultant of the idea that the directiveness of each and all of the first practical principles must not be deflected or cut down by sub-rational motivations. That their integral directiveness involves prioritizing and specializations of many kinds is evident, but the true measure of such prioritization is not emotional even when, as in the application of the Golden Rule (fairness), the application of a rational standard for prioritizing legitimizes resort to emotionally shaped preferences (and de-legitimizes an inhuman Kantian or Stoic exaltation of rationality or moral law above spontaneous love and affection). Integral human fulfilment is the fulfilment of all human persons and their communities, precisely because each of the first practical principles picks out and directs one towards a basic human good which is as good in the lives of others as in one's own. Essay 10's intimations of this ideal of practical reason, intimations tailored to showing how far Aquinas employs it as the working integrator of his philosophical ethics, are elaborated with some care and specificity, in their own philosophical right, in essay 14, sec. II (and essay 15, sec. IV).

Essay 12, whose discussion of Strauss is revisited in essay III.5 (1996a), sec. II, itself supplements the more foundational philosophical treatment in Chapter V ('"Kantian Principles" and Ethics') of *FoE*, by questioning the easy assumption of contemporary Oxford scholars that Aristotle had no time for moral absolutes, that is, for exceptionless negative moral norms/rules/standards. Those who find it embarrassing to consider the issue in the context of the basic good of marriage, as Aristotle did, can profitably transpose the discussion to the matter of torture (in response to the ticking bomb). The possibility of absolute moral rights, which an organ of modern conscience such as the European Convention of Human Rights acknowledges and juridically adopts, is dependent on a successful critique of consequentialist ethical theories. Essay 13, sec. V, locates the issues briefly. Their place in any sound and central-case legal system is shown and exemplified a bit in essay 14, secs VI and VII. The purpose of this essay, which gives it its place in this volume rather than in Volume IV (where it would have been quite fitting), is to explore the various different ways in which a decent system of positive law will derive from morality and thus, most ultimately, from the first principles of practical reason and the vision of human good that they outline.

III. PUBLIC REASON AND UNREASON

The critique of consequentialist conceptions of moral life and judgment is set out, briefly, in some of its fundamental aspects, in essay 15 ('Commensuration and Public Reason'), secs I and II. Section IV of that essay is a synoptic presentation of the morality that results from the integration of practical reason's first principles by the master moral principle of openness to integral human fulfilment. The essay's title and prologue speak of *public reason* in the straightforward sense, unconcerned with the restrictions promoted by Rawls with his misappropriation of that phrase.[12] Those restrictions are discussed in some detail in essay 16,

---

[12] My use of 'public reason' here—as in essay 2 at 58—is equally unconcerned with the various particular ways in which the phrase was deployed by Hobbes, Milton, and Rousseau, as mentioned in the first endnote to essay 16.

both at large and in the context of the issue which Rawls himself chose to illustrate his conception of public reason.

The volume ends with three essays written nearer in time than we now are to the tipping point at which our culture abandoned the serious attempt of many centuries to protect practical reason's civil rule over the passions in the domain where they are most practised in enslaving it to their destructive sway. This abandonment coincided, not coincidentally, with the blurring of understanding of, and much diminished institutional support for, the good of marriage and maritally structured family. The old law, dealing with the issue in the context of an individual reader of pornography, expressed this sort of blurring and loss of grip with the colourful phrase 'deprave and corrupt', and it seems too quick and superficial to dismiss such terms as mere 'moralizing' when applied to the culture as a whole. Essay 19 challenges the sophisticated lightness with which Jonathan Miller shrugged off the problem. Essay 17 does not reach the moral-cultural problem, but explores some of the psychological context in which practical reason(ing) as an activity is carried through, reasonably or unreasonably. Essay 18 ('Freedom of Speech'), forty years on, seems both right in its opening sketch of the social-conventional restrictions on freedom of speech, and wrong in its inattention to the risk that the law of the land, and the rules of private-public association such as universities, would repress the very kinds of intellectual discourse—on matters of fact, or practical truth, and public importance—that 'freedom of speech and the press' was institutionally proclaimed to protect and public reason, straightforwardly understood, requires.

In a number of this volume's essays, the good of practical reasonableness has been explained as inner integrity and outer authenticity: authenticity in that one's actions carry out one's own choice that one made in line with one's own deliberations; integrity, in that one's emotions—passions—and sensibilities are integrated with one's reason's judgments and choices. No one can expect to be immune to unsettling emotions such as fear; but in one's awareness of oneself as a practical reasoner one can and should aspire to a balance of dispositions such that one's reasonable judgments are not deflected by contrary emotional drives, but rather are supported by the emotions that one can use one's imagination and memory and knowledge of the world to summon up to counteract the emotions that conflict with one's reasonable judgment. Just as it is virtually impossible for even the most sophisticated mathematicians to think mathematically without some support from images (diagrams and the like) which they know perfectly well are partly false to mathematical reality, so it is impossible for bodily beings such as us to act without some support from our emotions and therefore from our imagination and memory. The reasonable ideal is that one's understanding and reasoning rules over one's emotions civilly and constitutionally, not tyrannically but cooperatively, as civil leaders cooperate with those willing (not supine or slavish) free citizens whom they direct. Those who on the unstable fore-part of the *Admella* could not master their fears and attempt the rope crossing to the stable aft-section soon perished. Some of those sailors who mastered their fears and volunteered to swim for help perished too, as did some of the lifeboatmen who braved ferocious seas to approach the wreck. But the rescue attempts succeeded, so far as they could and did, because many were able to engage emotions—the emotions associated with ideals and reasonable traditions of honour, loyalty, fellow-feeling, and cooperation in common enterprise—in the service of reason. The acts of reason they brought to bear in the action of rescue will have included logical and scientific reasoning about cause and effect, technical reasoning about boat-handling, and practical-moral reasoning about the human goods of life and that friendship which, as the tradition has always taught, extends even to unthreatening human *strangers* encountered in the wilds.

Part One
Foundations

1
PRACTICAL REASON'S FOUNDATIONS*

One's investigations, reflections, and communications are actions. Sometimes they are simply spontaneous, but very often, as with other kinds of action, one needs to opt into them by deliberation, choice, and continued effort, all of which make noticeable one's responsiveness to opportunities. This essay revisits some main elements in that responsiveness.

I

Doing law immerses one both in practical reason's activities, thinking about what to choose and do, and in a certain amount of reflection on the content and structure of that thinking. As Aquinas says, laws whether highly general or very specific are all 'universal propositions of practical reason'.[1] From the beginning of one's legal studies, especially in a common law jurisdiction, one is working to identify the propositions of law that are correct for the jurisdiction (let us say, 'valid'). To oneself and others, one shows both the content and the correctness of these propositions by referring to further propositions, picking out conditions for the validity of a proposition of law—conditions some of which jurists call sources of (this jurisdiction's) law and others of which they call principles of interpretation. Some nineteenth- and twentieth-century legal theories, such as those of John Austin and Hans Kelsen, could be taken to imply that the conditions for legal validity all concern *form* and *originating fact*: forms of transaction or process, such as enactment by the dateable activities of a particular legislature. And that position has initial appeal to lawyers, used as they are to seeking the 'root of title' in forms of dateable transaction such as sale, conveyance, registration, and the like. But it has turned out to be both mistaken and self-defeating to deny that criteria or premises for

---
* 2005a; read at a conference in September 2005 at Princeton University, at which the commentators included Terence Irwin and Patrick Lee.
[1] *ST* I–II q.90 a.1 ad 2.

judging propositions of law valid or not valid, correct or not correct, characteristically refer (and need to refer) also to *content*, to considerations concerning the kind of conduct that the proposition whose validity is in question purports to direct or authorize, or concerning the ways in which other propositions of law may or do direct or authorize such conduct.

Theories making that denial err in supposing that an account of law's validation would succeed in describing or explicating something recognizable—or worth having—as legal thought and practice while failing to acknowledge the centrality to legal thought and practice of such content-based criteria as that (i) purportedly valid propositions of law must not contradict or be practically inconsistent with each other, and (ii) the propositions validated by particular, dateable legal transactions *remain* valid unless and until some invalidating event, and (iii) later transactions and their normative products prevail over earlier transactions and their products of the same kind. None of those criteria is entailed by any factual propositions or originating events, and none is a requirement of logic (for no requirement of logic excludes the sober judgment that such-and-such a community, and indeed each of its members, is simply confused, and/or that its rulers enact contradictory rules in order to confuse their subjects).

And theories seeking to expel from 'juristic science' all non-formal criteria of validation defeat their own descriptive-explanatory purposes. In any community the criteria of validation employed by its law will be found to make reference to such content-based considerations as that the law's subjects need to be given coherent and practicable directions, that the law needs to change from time to time, that the law's requirements and authorizations should be ascertainable by its subjects in advance, that disputes should be settled, transactions and their putting into effect be facilitated, wrongs righted, reasonable expectations respected, fraud discouraged, and so forth. Criteria of content such as the general principles of law I have just mentioned are sometimes, and reasonably, called principles of interpretation. They shape any jurist's understanding of statements and other originating events purporting to validate propositions of law in this or that particular jurisdiction, and equally shape any juristic assessment of that purported validity. All these general criteria, and even more so the more specified institutions and rules giving effect to them in the different ways we find in different communities, presuppose positions about what would be good for the community in question, and what would be harmful to it (instability, uncertainty, irresolvable disputes, absence of opportunity to make arrangements that will order future events, unresponsiveness to new threats and opportunities, and so forth).

In short: the law's sources include not only relevant judgments of the higher courts, applicable statutes and constitutional documents, writings of jurists, and principles and structures of logic, but also general principles articulating what seem to one, in one's legal thinking—as they have seemed to many others—to be requirements of civilized, decent, humanly appropriate behaviour. And even to understand a legal system, let alone to participate in upholding, applying, and developing one, is to engage with practical reason, in a manner that invites awareness of, and opportunity for reflection upon, its structure, shape, process, criteria, and logic as a set of reasons for action that count as (legal) reasons because of their place in that legal system's overall project of directively picking out prospective goods and ways to attain them, prospective harms and ways to avoid them. Sometimes, indeed, this reference to goods and harms is direct and immediate; more commonly, I think, it is to be discerned only by 'tracing back' the specific proposition of law to the principles from which it is 'derived', principles articulating such a reference as a part of the rational process of interpretation and validation by which, as good lawyers, we can make clear the justification for affirming that such-and-such ('*p*', and 'It is part of our law that *p*') is indeed a valid or true proposition of law (that is, of the law of this jurisdiction at least).

II

So a lawyer, particularly in the common law tradition,[2] can readily find congenial an account of practical reason such as Aquinas offered in his discussion of law, treating every human positive law as a proposition derived from practical reason's very first principles, whether by way of

---

[2] Jurists in the modern civilian (Roman Law-based) tradition are inclined to call the subject-matter of their discipline *droit* or *derecho* or *diritto*, *Recht*, *ius*, 'right', terms which their tradition of interpretative theory contrasts with *lex* and its derivatives *loi*, *ley*, 'law'. Undeniably, *what is just* as between persons in relation to some matter is law's direct concern. But such relationships are not so fundamental that they cannot be explicated and shown to be just(ified) by reference to the principles of practical reason—the most universal true propositions about what is or is not to be done. Unfortunately, even the English tradition of translating and interpreting Aquinas became corrupted on this point, as is indicated by the quite erroneous Dominican translation of Aquinas's statement that *lex* is *aliqualis ratio iuris* as 'law is an expression of right' when the obvious and correct translation is something like 'law is (in the nature of) a *foundation* of or informing idea behind right(s)'—just as, Aquinas's preceding sentences explain, the *ratio* of a building is what pre-exists in the mind of the builder and *regulates* (provides the 'rule' for) the building work. *ST* II–II q.57 a.1 ad 2: '... *sicut eorum quae per artem exterius fiunt quaedam ratio in mente artificis praeexistit quae dicitur regula artis, ita* etiam *illius operis iusti quod ratio determinat quaedam ratio praeexistit in mente, quasi quaedam prudentiae regula*.... Et *ideo lex* non est ipsum ius, proprie loquendo, sed *aliqualis ratio iuris*.' The sentence here replaced by ellipses muddies the waters by recalling the specialized Roman Law sense of *lex* as something written, but the argument as a whole is clear, and should control any translation of *ratio iuris*.

'conclusion' or, much more commonly, by the non-deductive but rational specification that he calls *determinatio*.[3]

But there can be no question of simply accepting Aquinas's account, whether because it is his, or because it incorporates Aristotle's (and Plato's), or because it fits some main aspects of one's lawyerly habits of thought. Everything in it has been challenged, and needs to be reappropriated—if and to the extent that it deserves to be—by thinking through the challenges and denials it confronts.

It is commonly supposed that the easy way to show what is meant by 'practical reason' or 'rationally required' is to point to cases where opting for and doing or achieving X will get one what one wants—will satisfy one's desire, or one's here and now dominant desire. The necessity of means to an end established in and by one's desiring it is taken to be paradigmatic practical necessity, practical rationality, and normativity (at least practical as distinct from, say, logical normativity). Such thoughts can be given the label Humean, or neo-Humean, and so they are,[4] but Hume himself gives disconcerting voice to their implication for the very idea of practical reason:

> *'Tis not contrary to reason* for me to prefer the destruction of the whole world to the scratching of my finger. 'Tis not contrary to reason for me to choose my total ruin to prevent the least uneasiness of an Indian or person wholly unknown to me. 'Tis as little contrary to reason to prefer even my own acknowledged lesser good to my greater, and have a more ardent affection for the former than the latter. A trivial good may, from certain circumstances, produce a desire superior to what arises from the greatest and most valuable enjoyment....[5]

Hume's claim here struck me long ago as more like an admission about what his account of reason entails. It is that my being deflected by this desire for a trivial good from doing what is required to get the greatest and most valuable enjoyment for myself, or to save everyone (or the whole world) from destruction, is *not contrary to reason*. That is to say, 'prudence', in the thin modern sense of self-interest, is no more rationally required, or even *rationally* motivated, than morality in the thin modern sense that gets its content by an implied contrast with self-interest.

Nor is this a matter of Hume being carried away by love of paradox or rhetorical effect. This is just one of several ways in which Hume denies or

---

[3] On *determinatio* see *ST* I–II q.96 a.4c; *NLNR* 282–90, 295–6; essay IV.7 (1996c) and IV.13 (1985c).
[4] They are also more than neo-Humean, so pervasive are their sources and influence; for the neo-Kantian and Weberian (not to mention Nietzschean) elements in 'the modern fact-value distinction' and the alleged 'positivity of values', see my reflections on Kronman, *Max Weber* in essay IV.9 (1985b).
[5] Hume, *A Treatise of Human Nature*, 416 (Book 2, Part 3, sec. III, para. 6) (emphasis added).

is committed to denying that there is practical *reason*, in favour of a picture in which we simply *do* whatever we do, and what one *actually does*, in each successive situation, shows what it was that one was desiring (wanting) most—shows what was one's (dominant) end *and* the means one judged available and sufficiently efficacious. In such a picture there is simply no room for normativity, for being *guided* or *directed* to adopt certain means (by reason of their efficacy for one's end(s)) which, however, one might (irrationally or at least unreasonably) fail to adopt. All that counts is one's current dominant desire, which may well be the desire to avoid the burdens and/or bad side effects of the means necessary to attain what *was*, until a moment ago, one's dominant desire. The *is* of 'is what I at this moment most desire', like the *is* of 'is what I was most desirous of until a moment ago' (and, for that matter, the *is* of 'my intelligence is of the kind that finds means to ends'), provides no ground for an *ought*. Thus a mechanics of desire (in the end reducible to something as crude as Hobbes depicts) has eliminated all the conceptual space which might have been occupied by practical reason. A reason that is slave to desire can indicate canny ways to satisfy some of one's desires but gives no *reasons* for action.

These implications of the Humean position were methodically and effectively traced in Christine Korsgaard's critique (1997) of the standard assumptions about the normativity of instrumental reason, and more particularly about the normativity or practical rationality of (self-interested) prudence.[6] There she reached a strong but, I think, justified conclusion. There can be no practical rationality at all—no even hypothetical *imperatives*, no rationally *required* means—unless there are 'some rational principles determining which ends are worthy of preference or pursuit',[7] 'normative principles directing the adoption of ends', 'something which gives normative status to our ends'[8] by giving 'unconditional reasons for having certain ends, and, it seems, unconditional principles from which those reasons are derived'.[9] (One might put it like this: if reasons did not go all the way down, there is no way they could enter directively into our deliberations at all.) For 'unless something attaches normativity to our ends, there can be no requirement to take the means to them'.[10] Such ends, moreover, have to be '*good*, in some sense that goes beyond the locally desirable'.[11] For 'I must have something to *say to myself* about why I am [willing an end, and am committed and remain committed to it, even in

---

[6] Korsgaard, 'The Normativity of Instrumental Reason'.   [7] *Ibid.*, 230.   [8] *Ibid.*, 250.
[9] *Ibid.*, 252.   [10] *Ibid.*, 251.
[11] *Ibid.*, 250–1. Korsgaard, at 251, 252, is tempted to resile from this to allow for a 'heroic existentialist act' of 'just tak[ing] one's will at a certain moment to be normative, and commit[ting] oneself forever to the end selected at that moment', 'for no other reason that that [one] wills it so'. But she should concede that unless such a person considers that there is something worthwhile in doing

the face of desires that would distract and weaknesses that would dissuade me]—something better [to say to myself], moreover, than the fact that this is what I wanted yesterday'[12] (or indeed a moment ago or even, in the struggle of feelings, 'locally', want now).

We might summarize Korsgaard's observations by saying: basic reasons for willing—for choosing and carrying out one's choice—state *what is good about* what the action intends, and good in a way that could be said to give unconditional reason for acting in pursuit of such good(s) or at least with an eye to avoiding what would negate such good(s). Such good-identifying reasons are unconditional, I take her to mean, not in the sense that they are 'categorical' or 'moral' but in the sense that they are non-dependent, not in need of justificatory or validating explanation—primary, intrinsic, basic.

III

Still, the question whether we are in a position to specify the basic reasons for willing and doing and consider them together, as a set, is one that (so far as I am aware) Korsgaard, like most other contemporary philosophers, abstains from framing or answering. In her case, the abstinence may be connected with the philosophical tradition within which she explicitly places herself. The influence of this tradition—so important if we are to understand much modern theology, too—can be seen when in her Oxford lectures of 2002 she takes up the question whether or not (as she formulates it)

desires and inclinations are simply responses to the good-making properties of objects, and it is only the good-making properties of objects that we need to talk about when we talk about our reasons, not the desires and inclinations themselves.

Her answer is: 'as a Kantian, I disagree' with that picture in two ways. First,

in Kant's view [i] the features of the objects we desire that we mention when we explain why we value those objects would not give those objects value were it not for the way in which those features are related to human physiology and psychology. [ii] At the basis of every desire or inclination, no matter how articulately we can defend it, is a basic suitableness-to-us that is a matter of nature and not of reason. [iii] Value is relational and what it is related to is our nature.[13]

---

so, some good in or reason for doing so, such an 'act of commitment' and of subsequent 'taking as normative' is not rational but irrational.

[12] *Ibid.*, 250.   [13] Korsgaard, *Self-Constitution*, 122 (numbering added).

As to this first way of disagreeing, I would remark that the three propositions she here identifies as Kant's view all seem to me, as they are stated, sound, save for the contrast implied in 'of nature and not of reason'; and none of them gives a sufficient reason for doubting that intelligent desires and inclinations are responses to the good-making properties of possible objects of desire, deliberation, and choice. As to her second way, it again appeals directly to that specific tradition and its master:

> As a Kantian I believe that it is our own choices that ultimately confer value on objects, even though our choices are responsive to certain features of those objects.[14]

I interject to suggest that part of the problem Korsgaard is making for herself arises from the ambiguity of 'object'. In the older tradition which Kantian (or at least Kant's) thought seeks both to support and to contest, the objects of one's choice are (i) one's actions, (ii) the states of affairs that actions can instantiate or otherwise bring about, and (iii) the consequent fulfilment (in part if not in whole) of persons that is the ultimate point of actions and their intended effects. In such an understanding of the term 'object', there is no plausibility to the thought that our choices, in responding to some feature of an object, confer value upon it. Still less would there be plausibility to it if the term *object* is taken to include a person who might be benefited or harmed by my choice and action. But to return to Korsgaard's second point:

> In choosing objects, in conferring value on things that answer to our nature in welcome ways, an agent is affirming her own value. She takes what matters *to her* to matter absolutely and so to be worthy of her choice.

[We can return to these questionable sentences in a moment, after letting Korsgaard add her own well-judged caveats.]

> But even if the agent herself believes this Kantian theory, it doesn't follow that she must think of herself as choosing objects simply because she wants or likes them. She can still talk to herself, and to others, about what she likes about them, and why. So even though there is a sense, on my account, in which we choose things 'because we want them', a sense in which the inclination provides the reason, it doesn't follow that when someone asks you

[and that someone might well be 'the agent herself', as Korsgaard's earlier rendering of the point recalled: 'I must have something to say to myself...']

---

[14] *Ibid.*, 123.

[when someone asks you] why you chose something, [it doesn't follow that] 'I wanted it' is the right answer.... [W]hen you are explaining your values to another person, it is quite uninformative to mention the fact that you have an inclination for the object as the basis of the value. He knows that... [H]e wants to know *which* inclination you are having, what is drawing you to the object. And you specify that by describing, as far as you can, the incentive [that is, by giving a motivationally loaded representation of the object, presenting the object as desirable or aversive in some specific way].[15]

Taking the passage as a whole, and giving full weight to the well-judged caveats that are its concern after its first three sentences, I wonder if there is not here another instance of what one finds in the full shadow of the Enlightenment: Hume founding everything in (what we innocently think of as) practical reason on desires that happen to be built into our nature, our 'human physiology and psychology'; Kant denying that that can account for the rational force, the normativity (prescriptivity or directiveness), of any *reasons* for action, and ascribing that normativity to reason's self-legislation; Korsgaard taking this to be a matter of 'committing oneself' to ends, but like Kant being unable to give any fundamental account of which ends it is intelligent and reasonable to commit oneself to. And all the while the late-Aristotelians of the time (like some still today) are unable to provide the help that flickers momentarily into view with Korsgaard's idea of 'a basic suitableness-to-us that is a matter of nature'; for, not unlike the passage from her Oxford lecture, they treat this as 'a matter of nature *and not of reason*',[16] having lost touch with the foundational epistemological insight of Aristotle and Aquinas that I regret not articulating as such in *NLNR*: a nature such as ours is *known* by understanding the objects that make

---

[15] Ibid.

[16] For another, complementary statement of some deficiencies in the neo-Aristotelean tradition, see *FoE* 32 where, having shown Anthony Kenny advancing the view that there are 'some desires which are beyond questioning, which simply exist as "natural facts" about me or about everyone, and which make practical reasoning and reasonableness possible *without themselves being matters of reason or understanding at all*', I went on:

Here we obviously have rejoined Hobbes and Hume. But not just Hobbes and Hume. A whole school of interpreters of Aristotle has claimed that when Aristotle said 'deliberation is of means not ends' he meant to ally himself with those who maintain that the basic ends of our action are provided not by our intelligent grasp of certain objectives as truly good, but rather by the desires with which human nature equips us, or which we simply happen to have. And that school of interpreters has found supporters among the many neo-scholastics who thought they were following Aquinas when they said that *prudentia* concerns means not ends, and that *synderesis* (the other aspect of reason mentioned by Aquinas in this connection) is a matter not of understanding ends but of intuiting moral truths about the fitting or the obligatory, i.e. about certain *conditions on* the pursuit of ends (the ends of human action being then supposed to be given by subrational 'inclinations'). (Emphases in original.)

sense of the acts by which the capacities of a being of such a nature are realized.[17]

The resulting Enlightened confusion is epitomized by the oscillation in this passage of Korsgaard's, between (a) the idea of 'conferring value [by our choices] on things that answer to our nature in welcome ways', (b) the contrary idea that their answering to our nature makes them valuable prior to our choice, and makes our choice of them intelligent and (in principle) reasonable, and (c) the idea that as agents we have a value of our own that is to be 'affirmed'—which might mean merely alleged (freely asserted and therefore freely deniable), but may more naturally mean judged to be what it truly is.

What is to be made of the thought that in action one is 'affirming one's own value'? First: as I am sure she takes for granted, it would be unreasonable of me simply to assert, without reason, that while I have my own value, and what matters to me matters 'absolutely and *so* [is] worthy of my choice', nevertheless you and everyone else do not have that kind of value, and what matters to you and others does not matter in the same kind of way. So if it were not evident—self-evidently assertable—that others, at least some others, and what matters to them, are of value in a way that counts as giving *me* unconditional (if not categorical or obligatory) reason for acting in favour of *them*, the thought that I and my concerns have such value would have no purchase. Second: Korsgaard's own sound arguments against Humean misconstruals, with the resultant willy-nilly overthrow, of practical reason show well enough that no mere desire or resolve of mine to treat *myself* and what matters to *me* as of inherent ('absolute') value or worth can provide any *reason* for my so treating myself and my attitudes and inclinations or, indeed, their objects.

Third: to say (or think) that I and the objects of my choice have *value* is to invite the question whether this says anything of interest, anything worthy of belief, unless it implies conditions and exclusions. To be choiceworthy, mustn't the objects of my choices have a value *not* predicable of the object of a drunk searching for a lamppost to serenade, or—to shift the nature of the doubt—of the object of a ruthlessly selfish and cruel conman, habitually flattering to deceive, rape, rob, and for the pleasure of it to kill? And can my value count for anything, in deliberation or reflection, unless it is *other* than that of such *agents* as a vigorous cancer, or a crocodile diving to its lair with its still living booty, someone's child, between its jaws? More pertinently still, isn't it clear that one's thoughts about the value of one's objectives, and of the personal identity one will ineluctably shape for oneself by pursuing

---

[17] See *FoE* 20–2; *Aquinas* 29–34, 90–4, 102; [and Introduction at 5 above].

them, cannot be reasonably affirmed unless they could be mistaken? That they can be mistaken is something we have all learned, or at least come to presume, from experience, by the very dawn of the age of reason—by 6 or 7 or whenever it was.

IV

Following Aquinas, and Germain Grisez's rethinking of Aquinas, and the evidence of (inter alia) empirical anthropology, *NLNR* offered a list of basic reasons for willing (*intelligent* wanting) and doing. Jurisprudential discussions of the book have tended to focus too exclusively on the list, as if the answers to all decisive questions are here. Philosophers have tended to ignore them; many perhaps assume that so straightforward a recital could not possibly be a true response to the issues considered by Hobbes, Hume, Kant, or Nietzsche, though others like Martha Nussbaum and Amartya Sen have rejected the assumption and proposed their own comparably brief and substantive lists.[18] In 1995–7, Sabina Alkire put the resultant alternative though partially overlapping lists to the test of consonance with the self-understanding of women in the village of Arabsolangi in far upcountry Pakistan, as she describes in her doctoral book *Valuing Freedoms*.

Aquinas thought of these basic reasons as the first practical principles or principles of practical reason—'principles' both as *propositions* of high generality and comprehensiveness, and as *sources* of all intelligent thinking about what to do. They are the 'principles of natural law or natural right' that lawyers are in search of. But though they are justly thought of as a kind of *ending* place in a lawyer-like search for the roots of law's claims, what I want to stress in the rest of this essay is that identifying and affirming them is only a beginning.

What qualities of thought and response are involved in getting from the first principles to the relatively specific judgments of a kind fit to be laws in a just political community? Some of the issues around this question have been explored by Terence Irwin in 'The Scope of Deliberation: A Conflict in Aquinas' (1990) and 'Practical Reason Divided: Aquinas and his Critics' (1997). His earlier article suggested that Aquinas inconsistently holds both (A) that deliberation is always about means, not ends, and the intellectual virtue of deliberating well—*prudentia*—has *no role* in the virtuous person's identification (and adoption) of the right end or ends, which is rather a matter of that non-deliberative grasp of basic ends and first practical principles that Aquinas calls *synderesis* and says is shared by the virtuous

---

[18] See Alkire, *Valuing Freedoms* [and Introduction at 10–12 above].

and vicious alike, and at the same time (B) that *prudentia* does (necessarily) have a role in that identification (and adoption) of the right end or ends which distinguishes the virtuous person from the vicious. In his later article, Irwin tacitly abandons this claim about Aquinas's inconsistency, and finds the needed reconciliation in the thought that there is a 'macro-prudence', the governing virtue of deliberating well about everything to do with what happiness consists in, in general (so to speak) (206); the *synderesis* that virtuous and vicious share tells us no more and no less (according to Irwin's synthesis) than that there is for each and all of us a 'universal end' (203, 204), 'the final good of human beings with the nature they have' (202); it is for macro-prudence to set us on the path to right action by determining that universal end and final good.

But this is not, I think, the right way to synthesize Aquinas's statements—whose inconsistency (at the level of *statements*) has interested his friends for many centuries[19]—into a coherent set of *propositions* about the role of intellectual (but not the less moral) virtues (summarily, *prudentia*) in establishing the content of practical reason (and thus of ethics and sound politics).[20] The 'ultimate first principle of natural law' (202), does not articulate, even generically, the concept of a universal end or final good of beings with our nature.[21] Aquinas's vigorous explorations of such a final end, in launching the *Prima Secundae*—explorations driven both by specifically theological concerns and premises, and by the model of Aristotle's *Ethics*—yield for a philosophical ethics little or no fruit beyond the paradoxical notion that there is an *imperfecta beatitudo*, an incomplete complete-fulfilment, which consists in living in line with the virtues. What it is to have these virtues, and how one's responsive understanding can advance from the first principles grasped in *synderesis* to the distinctions

---

[19] See Cajetan's commentary (Aquinas, *Omnia Opera* [Leonine edition], VI, p. 433) on *ST* I–II q.66 a.3 ad 3. And see essay 11, written in response to Irwin's 1990 article.

[20] Irwin, 'Practical Reason Divided' at 210 shows well how 'a virtuous agent must understand (perhaps without formulating) the sorts of considerations that concern the theorist'.

[21] Having quoted the central part of *ST* I–II q.94 a.2 on the first principles of practical reason, Irwin says (*ibid.*, 202): 'In this passage Aquinas refers back to his discussion of the final good (I–II qq.1–5).' But I see in q.94 a.2 no reference, even implicit, to that discussion of 'the final good'. The connection that q.94 a.2 makes between *good* and *aiming* is indeed 'not tautologous or trivially analytic'; but that is not because, in affirming the connection, Aquinas 'is claiming that rational agents, in acting for the sake of the good, seek to achieve a rational structure in their aims'—or at least he is not here making or in need of an assertion about 'rational structure in [one's] aims' under the description *rational ordering of aims to one single final aim*. The fact that qq.1–5 seem to argue that anyone who has rationality cannot but have some such single final aim is important to Aquinas but not, I think, to q.94 a.2 nor even to its development in the structure of secondary principles of practical reason which are the *ratio* of the moral virtues and the most general principles of (for) positive law. The link affirmed in q.94 a.2 goes through the concepts of the desirable (*appetibile*) and the perfective [that which makes better-off and is thus opportunity], and the tight link between these is, in the *Summa Theologiae*, most clearly asserted in I q.5 a.1 (see *NLNR* 78–9).

between morally good and bad, and virtuous and vicious choices, is left by the early sections of the *Prima Secundae* in as much obscurity as Aristotle leaves the question how his discussions of *eudaimonia* in *Ethics* I and X illuminate the virtue of justice in *Ethics* V.

No, the 'ultimate first principle of natural law', occupying the same sort of place in practical thinking as the principle of non-contradiction in all thinking,[22] directs only that we act to *some intelligible point*, and the substantive first principles have their directiveness precisely in and by picking out the kinds of point (end, good, value) that have the requisite intelligibility—intelligibility as desirable because beneficial for anyone: life, marriage, knowledge, friendship, practical reasonableness, and likeness to and harmony (indeed, *assimilatio*) with the transcendent source of all reality and value.[23]

Anyone who has the prerequisite knowledge of cause and effect and of what is attainably possible (for example, that questions can be answered, and answers hang together as fields of knowledge) can understand both the content and the directiveness of the propositions which pick out and direct us to favour following these basic human goods. But one cannot respond concretely to that directiveness without considering these ends in their relationship both to each other and to what might instantiate and/or effect them intelligently. For one cannot *intend* any kind of end, however ultimate or 'macro-', without understanding it in relationship to means—to something that would promote or realize and instantiate an end of that kind: *ST* I–II q.12 a.4. So everything about how these basic intelligible human goods hang together and are sensibly (reasonably) realizable is matter for practical reasonableness, that is, for *prudentia*.[24] There is no 'special faculty' called *synderesis*.[25] Rather, from end to end of practical

---

[22] *ST* I–II q.94 a.2c ('Hoc est ergo primum principium legis, quod bonum est faciendum et prosequendum, et malum vitandum'); *Aquinas* 79–80, 86–7.

[23] Here I slightly adjust Aquinas's list in *ST* I–II q.94 aa. 2 and 3, changing 'knowledge of God' to accommodate the tight relationship he sees between the desirability of knowing God and the desirability of, in understanding him, being *like* him: *ScG* III, c.25 n.1; *Aquinas* 308, 311, and 315.

[24] When Philippa Foot shook free from the neo-Humeanism which I pointed out as fundamental to her moral thought in essay 6 at 120–1 (and see her dismissive comment on the page after 1970a's last page (in the same edited volume)) and *FoE* 28–9, 62, an important part of her self-liberation was coming to see the mistake of holding, as so many have and do, that 'we come first to a theory of rational action, and then try as best we can to slot in the rationality of acts of justice and charity': 'Does Moral Subjectivism Rest on a Mistake?' [her 1994 Hart Lecture at Oxford] at 4–5. On the mistake in what Sidgwick named and upheld as 'the modern ethical view', see e.g. my remarks in *Aquinas* 111, on the theories 'constructed to expound the rationality and/or natural primacy of egoistic "prudence", and to explore the question how we may "bridge the gap" between such prudence (on the near bank) and morality (on the farther shore).' Cf. *NLNR* 134.

[25] Aquinas's very first proposition about *synderesis* is that it is *not* a *potentia* (but rather a *habitus* [a dispositional ability somewhat like one's ability to *use* multiplication tables]): *ST* I q.79 a.12c [and *Aquinas* 89 n. 138]; cf. Irwin, 'Practical Reason Divided', 201. [See essay 11 at 175, 178 below.]

reason(ing) there is simply one's understanding (*intellectus, intelligere*) with its beginnings or roots or foundation in non-deductive acts of insight into, understanding of, the data of experience, and then the effort and discipline of reasonable judgment—as in 'a person of judgment'. 'Judgment'[26] is indeed the idiomatic practical English for *prudentia*, which itself is nothing other than one's extending one's intelligence into mastering—by *informing* and guiding, with the basic goods' integral intelligibility—one's deliberations, judgments, choices, and the carrying out of one's choices in actions and the fulfilment possible in the circumstances for oneself and those whom one's actions benefit.

I agree with Irwin (and Aristotle and Aquinas) that the principles which are picked out by a philosophical ethics and which shape both that ethical theory and political/legal theory worthy of the name cannot be other than a reflectively self-aware and appropriately extended version of *prudentia*—of right-minded thinking about what to do with one's life including one's life as a citizen. I mention this here because the thought that one cannot do ethical/political theory well without having the moral (and intellectual) virtue of practical reasonableness can seem arrogant, but really is a recognition that in *this* kind of theorizing one has a special and unavoidable vulnerability to theoretical error, namely to theoretical error arising precisely because of some regrettable defect in one's character, which entails some want of *prudentia*. (Of course, one can be, so to say, 'academically' adept at articulating and finding one's way around an ethical system which one accepts as propositions already articulated by others, whether by a single *magister* or by a community, 'school', or tradition, rather as if it were a legal system—just as we nowadays can be adepts of the Roman Law of, say, slavery. This needs no well-developed practical reasonableness, no *prudentia* or other virtues. But nor is it theory, properly speaking.)

Still, it does not follow that every error or weakness in one's theorizing must be ascribed to one's moral flaws. Failure to reflect accurately upon one's deliberations and dispositions, and/or to reason from one's reflections correctly and energetically, can be the cause of oversights and errors of theoretical judgment. The account of ethics given in *NLNR* fails to identify what unifies and validates the intelligibility of the eight or nine principles with which its chapter on the 'methodological requirements of practical

---

[26] 'My salad days, / When I was green in judgment...': *Anthony & Cleopatra* 1.5.607; see also 1.4.555: '...boys, who, being mature in knowledge, / Pawn their experience to their present pleasure, / And so rebel to judgment'; likewise 2.2.754, 3.13.2279; and countless other places in Shakespeare's characters' reflections on character and action. It matters not at all that Cleopatra may be wrong, or merely playful, in claiming to be now less immature, less lacking in practical reasonableness.

reasonableness' is concerned. It should have explicated those proto-ethical principles as specifications of morality's master principle (that one should remain open, in all one's deliberating and willing, to integral fulfilment—fulfilment which is not one's own, nor indifferent to one's own, but is to be located in the fulfilment of all human persons in all their communities). Such specifications give us something properly decisive to 'say to [one] self' (as Korsgaard put it) in the face of those emotional motivations which would deflect us from—as distinct from those that support us in—responding with integral reasonableness to the directiveness of the basic reasons. And thus we move from the understanding, in itself pre-moral,[27] of the basic human goods, the basic practical reasons, to moral distinctions and reasons—from, for example, the goods of life-in-health, and emotional-rational integrity, with their correlative bads or harms of bodily or psychosomatic loss, disharmony, and suffering, to the *moral* distinction between cruelty and the beneficent infliction of suffering as a side effect of, for example, healing or rescuing.

V

This essay stays with the foundations and goes no further into either the further, intermediate principles which structure specifically moral (and properly legal) thought or the dialectic with ethical methods such as the utilitarian, consequentialist, or proportionalist and their legal-theoretical counterparts.[28] Its theme is the first practical principles in their own progressively discoverable, unfolding content. One motive for staying with this theme is to underline one's reason's unity. Though reason directed towards deliberation and choice has its truly first and undeducible first principles, theoretical or speculative reason and practical reason are nowise two powers. In one's thinking soundly about what it would be good to do, to attain, or to become, one draws upon all one believes about what can be, is, has been, or is probable. And the understanding of such basic truths as 'Knowledge is good and desirable and to be valued and pursued'—an understanding available even to those who will not deploy it appropriately—presupposes an awareness ('theoretical' if you like) of the *possibility* (attainability) of overcoming ignorance, an awareness which is

---

[27] 'Pre-moral' does not mean 'non-moral': see *Aquinas* 87:

The moral sense of 'ought', understood critically, not merely conventionally, is reached...when the absolutely first practical principle is followed through, in its relationship to all the other first principles, with a reasonableness which is unrestricted and undeflected by any subrational factor such as distracting emotion. In that sense, the 'ought' of the first principles is incipiently or 'virtually', but not yet actually, moral in its directiveness or normativity.

[28] See *NLNR* 111–24; *FoE* 80–135; *NDMR* 177–272; *MA* 13–83; and essay 15.

being supplemented by the new, original, logically underived (undeduced) 'practical' insight articulated in that true practical proposition. Equally, in one's thinking soundly about what kind of being we human beings are, one is drawing upon that stock of original, primary practical principles, which are thus not only the source (*principium*) of the normativity[29] articulated in legal[30] and moral thinking but a source also of our knowledge of human nature. For, to repeat, we know the nature of a dynamic reality such as ours by knowing the capacities of this kind of being, and the capacities in their turn by knowing the activities of which such beings are capable, and we understand those activities only by understanding their point—and that point is precisely what one is identifying in identifying each of the basic forms of human good.

'Identifying' is hardly an adequate term, however. What we are here concerned with is an understanding of each of these kinds of opportunity, of these desirable aspects or ways of being a human person and a human community. As I have been saying, such an understanding of opportunity is equally a perception, a becoming aware, of the normativity that, when its content and force is elaborated, we call moral—a becoming aware of the content as well as the rational force (normativity, directiveness) of moral propositions. The most specific and hard-edged of moral norms will be no more than a specification of what was (is) generically contained as directive in the principles that pick out the basic forms of human opportunity/ perfection. So: what these basic principles contain, what these basic forms of human well-being truly are, is to be inquired into with zeal and care— with effort—and with all the resources of reflection, including what we lamely call fiction (say, *King Lear*).

What we call *will* is essentially one's responsiveness to one's understanding of such opportunities. (Whether Hume's teaching about reason's incapacity to motivate was the result more of his misunderstanding understanding, or of his misunderstanding human appetition's multiple layers of resource, scarcely matters: the teaching is thoroughly mistaken.[31]) In seeking to expand one's understanding of the basic kinds of opportunity open to us, one

---

[29] There are other sources of normativity: logical, technical, and natural. But in as much as one's thinking in logic, technology, and art, and in natural sciences as much as in the ethical and legal domains, is an *action* subject to one's choices, the actual conduct of thought and argument is always dependent in part upon the practical normativity entailed by the good(ness) and pursuit-worthiness of *knowledge*.

[30] Of course, there is plenty of legal thinking that de facto merely imitates without participating in acknowledgement of the moral normativity which makes best sense of having law; but such legal thinking is non-central, however frequent it may happen to be.

[31] To criticism such as Korsgaard's summarized in sec. III above add, e.g., George, 'A Defense of the New Natural Law Theory' in his *In Defense of Natural Law*, 17–30; Boyle, 'Reasons for Action: Evaluative Cognitions that Underlie Motivations'.

is responding—with that kind of generic interest or pro-attitude Aquinas calls *voluntas simplex*—to the intelligible goodness of whichever kind of good is presently the focus of one's inquiry, but one is also responding with something more focused and closer to choice, that is, with *intent*, to the intelligible good of knowledge, and to the *bonum rationis*, the good of extending reason's motivating sway, its existential, more than merely propositional, normativity in one's own life (one's deliberating, choosing, and doing).[32]

In the last twenty-five years, those of us engaged in the reflective practical undertakings of which *NLNR* was a manifestation have tried various such explorations of basic human goods. Marriage, for example: it was not properly identified in *NLNR*, where life, transmission of life, and friendship were left in an uncertain relation.[33] Reflection on the complementarity of the two sexes, and on the way that in marital acts the couple can each actualize, express, and experience their chosen commitment to marriage as the form of friendship oriented and appropriate to procreation, has provided a good example, I think, of the sort of enhancement of understanding that I am wanting to point to here.[34] And then there is that good which can be called harmony between persons, or friendship, or sociability, or even justice. The radical (foundational) equality between persons that turns out to be its very core can become understood by reflections upon such extremes in human opportunity or peril as we considered in inquiring whether final retaliation against the inhabitants of an enemy state, or strategic intra-war attack on the inhabitants of a city or other region, or the production of human beings by technical manipulation of materials, are indeed opportunities or mere temptations.

The good which occasion has prompted us to consider perhaps most closely is that of human life itself. From its beginning to its end it is nothing less or other than the very existing of the person, the human being. Aquinas, precisely when giving his fullest but not quite exhaustive list of the basic human goods, says that *this* good is, as existence, one that we share with all other creatures whatever.[35] Though true, this would be very misleading if it made one overlook the vast differences between the existing of a molecule (or of a lake) of water, the life of a carrot, the life of a

---

[32] On *bonum rationis*, widely neglected in accounts and attempted reiterations of Aquinas's moral theory even though it is precisely the good to which *prudentia* is directly the adequate response, see *ST* I–II q.94 aa. 3 and 4; also q.91 a.2c; q.93 a.6c; *Aquinas* 83–5, 98–9.

[33] See *NLNR* 86–7. Editors and translators of Aquinas's consideration of the basic practical principles in *ST* I–II q.94 a.2c have shown a similar failure of understanding on the matter: see *Aquinas* 82, 97–8.

[34] See e.g., *LCL* ch. 9 especially sec. E; and essay III.22 (1997d). To some extent it is rather a recovery by philosophy of an enhanced understanding already attained in other domains of thought.

[35] *ST* I–II q.94 a.2c.

cat, and the life of a human being. For human life is the existence of a being with the radical capacities—real in their dynamism towards action even when they are prevented from actuation by immaturity, sleep, sickness, or other injury, or decay—to live in sanctity, heroism, shame, guilt...

But those are moral if not also legal categories of human character, so I will restrict my articulation of the point to more foundational categories such as meaning, truth, and freedom. Our nature as human creatures, the array of radical capacities we all have from the outset, is exemplified by how we do things with words. Certain sounds or marks, sheerly physical even when retained in imagination and memory as brain-states, convey by a kind of embodiment both understanding and intention (will to communicate *this* and not *that* or *not-this*)[36] between persons utterly separated in every physical dimension. This communicating displays, both as effect displays cause and as an exemplary analogy, how in the being, make-up, and existence of their human authors, materiality or bodiliness (physical, chemical, biological, and psycho-somatic) is united with that which is as immaterial as a meaning—a notion, a proposition, a question, a purpose—shareable across continents or centuries (or the dinner table or the courtroom). As Aquinas argued, this kind of unity is best signified by taking one's soul to be the very form and act(uality) of one's body, such that it can even be said to 'contain' the body and be the body's very basis.[37] Here we reach the metaphysical foundation of human equality, which entails the inequality with us of all other creatures of which we have experience, all of them in truth not merely non- but sub-human, or lacking the dignity of the human because lacking a radical capacity foundational to our reality.[38]

In practical thinking the metaphysics of the human person—such as I have just sketchily articulated—is normally left unarticulated, outside the focus of advertence. In its place is, first, the understanding, intrinsic to the initial grasp of first practical principles, that basic goods such as knowledge, life, and friendship are good not only for me or thee, but for 'anyone'; and second, the awareness or assumption that our choices and therefore our actions matter, and that we are responsible in all the four senses Hart distinguished:[39] we *cause* effects, have at least radical *capacity*

---

[36] This dual sense of 'meaning' is one of the realities being subtly evoked at *The Tempest* 1.2. 496–9:

When thou didst not, savage,
Know thine owne meaning; but wouldst gabble like
A thing most brutish, I endow'd thy purposes
With words that made them known...

[37] See *Aquinas* 177–9; and essay II.2 (2005c), sec. 2.
[38] On 'radical capacity', see essay III.14 at 219–20, 227, 238–40 (1995b at 30–1, 68–70).
[39] Hart, *Punishment and Responsibility*, ch. 10.

for care and choice, can have *roles* and duties of care and conduct, and consequently *liability* to praise or blame, for merit or guilt, which make no sense unless our unrepented free choices last in us as the intransitive, self-shaping, identity-constituting dimension of chosen action or inaction. Our interest in such multiply-grounded attributions of responsibility signifies this sort of practical-cum-theoretical understanding that our existence is as beings capable of mattering now because of our subsisting individual identities each with a past as well as a future. Such transcendence of the material, in both the benefit(s) we envisage and the personal subjects we know are open to being so benefited, is part of what warrants the thought that each of us matters—matters in our life or death, health or ill health, our knowledge or our ignorance, our reasonableness or unreasonableness, our friendship or self-centredness. It is part of what warranted Elizabeth Anscombe in referring, philosophically, to 'the mystical value of the human being'.[40] Even though she was always ready to treat a word like *mystical* in the way she treated Aristotle's talk of the bloom on the face of youth (talk offered to explicate the relation between pleasure and the objective of reasonable choice)—'babbling', she called it—it is I think a better word to try to convey what needs to be acknowledged about the value of the existence of each human being than the word 'absolute', which someone might take Korsgaard's account to be asserting.

We need some such awareness of human value if we are to make sense of the normative force, the directiveness of the principles of practical reason, the directiveness which they have when taken, not one first principle after another in isolation from each other and from the need to make particular choices, but in their integral directiveness under the architectonic, regulatory directiveness of the good of practical reasonableness itself—that is, when taken as *morally* normative. Sometimes the death of someone known to us reinforces for us that awareness. Shakespeare, who makes present to us incomparably the actuality, the sheer vitality of human lives, and whose intentions were at the same time more knowingly philosophical than is often assumed, took some real individual's death as the occasion for articulating (amongst other things!) the dependence of practical reason and its directiveness upon a responsive awareness of the value that human beings have and can enhance and diminish by their own responsiveness to it. In an enigmatic and unparalleled poem first published in 1601 and commonly known as 'Phoenix and Turtle', he memorializes, as Patrick Martin and I have I think shown,[41] the marriage and death

---

[40] Anscombe, *Human Life, Action and Ethics*, 260 [and see essay II.3 (2009a)].
[41] 2003e; see also essay II.2 at 54–5 (2005c at 267–70).

of a young woman, shortly after her public execution for religion in late February 1601; he memorializes, that is to say, not only the union of wife and husband (phoenix and turtle[dove]) with each other through years of separation by the husband's exile for religion, but also her constancy through the years after his death. The poem's term for this constancy and fidelity to commitment is, as was then a more common use of the words, 'truth' and 'true'. Despite the extreme abstractness of its central 'anthem', and its rigorous structuring by formalities of reasoning and of religion, what the poem centrally articulates is a grief that seems unmistakably the author's own, and a kind of awe at the costly and active loyalty of the spouses to each other (as well as to what they each held most dear, held in common, and each died in miserable solitude for upholding). This couple's closeness and constancy in love, especially while divided and *parted* by exile, are celebrated in a series of virtuoso quasi-mathematical, quasi-metaphysical paradoxes over seven stanzas, culminating in the structure of cause-and-effect, evidence-and-inference, antecedent-and-consequent that is introduced along with the poem's last quasi-personal subject, Reason itself:

> Reason in itself confounded,
> Saw Division grow together,
> To themselves yet either neither,
> Simple were so well compounded
>
> That it cried, how true a twain,
> Seemeth this concordant one,
> Love hath Reason, Reason none,
> If what parts can so remain.[42]

'Love hath Reason' is here most carefully presented as expressing Reason's own insightful judgment. Anyone who accepts a position like the one I have been arguing for or re-presenting in this essay will want to take this statement in a sense that corresponds neither to the Humean/Weberian 'desire creates reason' and 'confers value upon its object', nor to the Pascalian 'the heart has its reasons, which are unknown to reason'. May not this poet's 'Love hath Reason' be compatible with and perhaps even affirm the position that love of persons, each precisely for his or her own sake, has the reasons which the first practical principles pick out, the human goods

---

[42] Lines 41–8. The poem's anthem began in line 22 with 'Love and constancy is dead,' and its lament ('Threnos') will reach a not quite final conclusion in line 64 with 'Truth and beauty buried be.' That lament began in line 53 with 'Beauty, truth and rarity, / Grace in all simplicity, / Here enclos'd in cinders lie,' and ends (lines 65–8) 'To this urn let those repair / That are either true or fair: / For these dead birds sigh a prayer.'—thus affirming that the death of this exemplary couple is neither an oblivion nor extermination.

towards which those principles direct us, each of these goods an aspect of the worth (in deprivation or fulfilment) of each human being?

Practical reason's first principles are, so to speak, transparent for the persons who can flourish in the kinds of way to which those principles direct us—so transparent that it is, in truth, those persons for whose sake we are responding when we respond at all to those reasons' summons. Such love goes all the way from the truly all-embracing 'Love your neighbour as yourself' to particular commitment to another[43]—for example the uniquely exclusive while outward-looking commitment constitutive of marital love—and is of the essence of all the practical normativity we call moral and, in proper case, legal. And for backsliders like us, the relatively few persons of heroic virtue can be a reminder, inspiring rather than depressing, that *but for* one's own—one's 'love's' and 'will's'—responsiveness to what these reasons summon us to, rational capacity would and will be for each of us nothing more than what Hume pretended it cannot but be for all, a slave of the passions that thus is, gives, and has 'reason none'. If the poet who was a self-effacing maestro of judgment, and whose artistry gets its deepest force in enactments of reconciliation and fellowship, concurs in denying that the highest or deepest *imperium* belongs to sightless desire or aversion, we have a telling witness or advocate (not precisely an argument); but whether his work is properly understood as such concurrence is obviously a *quaestio disputabilis* for another day. In any event, there may be some who find more persuasive the resonance of the articulated principles with lived experience, aspirations, and efforts, not least those of poor and far upcountry villagers.

POSTSCRIPT

A. Natural inclinations and first practical principles

Patrick Lee asks me to be more forthcoming or precise about what I called the dependence of practical reason and its directives on a responsive awareness of the value that human beings have and can enhance or diminish

---

[43] See *Aquinas* 127:

'One should love one's neighbour.' But to love a person volitionally (not simply emotionally) is to will that person's good. So, to love one's neighbour is to will the neighbour's good—and not just this or that good, but good somehow integrally; and nothing inconsistent with a harmonious whole which includes one's own good (likewise integrated in itself and with others' good). Thus the love of neighbour principle tends to unify one's goals. Moreover, the love of neighbour required by this principle need not be a 'particular friendship'. (FN: The love involved in a particular friendship {amor amicitiae} does have at its core, however, one's willingness as a friend to treat the friend as one treats oneself {amans se habet ad amatum, in amore amicitiae, ut ad seipsum}: II–II q.28 a.1 ad 2.)

by their own responsiveness to it.[44] This is linked with the question (in my mind) whether Lee is right to say that, according to Aquinas, our insights into human goods, the insights articulated in first practical principles, are insights 'into one's natural inclinations', inclinations which are 'data for the practical insight'. That is not the way I read Aquinas, nor, more importantly perhaps, is it the way things (so far as I can see) really are. Rather, I think that the practical insight, say, that knowledge is good and pursuitworthy, has as its data—the data to which the insight will add something original—the awareness not only of the urge (inclination) to question and the experience of satisfaction when a question is answered, but also the 'theoretical' insight that knowledge is possible. To the experience of a question getting an answer, another question getting an answer, and so on, this non-practical insight adds the original (new) understanding that there is a whole horizon of possibility (call it truth and knowledge) of which particular answers to particular questions are only instances. Only then does *practical* insight add the *further*, practical understanding that that field of possibility is also a field of opportunity, benefit, a perfection, etc. When that second, practical insight is followed through by chosen commitments to study, reflection, investigation, and so forth, one's original understandings both of knowledge's possibility and of its worth are greatly deepened and enhanced.

I think this mutual reinforcement of theoretical and practical insight is pervasive. So one's originally childish insight into the practical truth that those opportunities are opportunities for me *and anyone like me*, or into the opportunity of being a friend by valuing and willing the good of another or others for their own sake, is reinforced by knowledge of the *capacity* of myself and others to make the efforts, commitments, self-disposing devotion to others, and so forth, or to come up with the twisty rationalizations and evasions of betrayal, and so forth. On all this deepened knowledge of possibility there supervenes the enhanced practical understanding of the *worth* of the person for whom or by whom such acts of will and communication are possible.

B. Reason and love

Terence Irwin's commentary at our conference raised some searching questions about friendship and fulfilment or *eudaimonia*. He took up my explanation of 'Love hath Reason, Reason none' and said:

I take [Finnis] to mean that love of persons for their own sake helps to explain how facts about human fulfillment constitute reasons that guide our actions, and thereby helps to explain normativity.

[44] Lee, 'Comment on John Finnis's "Foundations of Practical Reason Revisited"'.

And later he said that:

As I understand Finnis's Shakespearean view, he assigns some sort of priority to love in the generation of reasons.

But I want to maintain, and I suggest that the poem maintains, the priority of insight and understanding of goods to every response of will, including the totalizing sort of response of friendship or *amor amicitiae*.

The Reason who/that is introduced in the poem is at first the theoretical reason which stands baffled or teased by the paradoxes of unity and difference, conceptual quasi-paradoxes such as that *one* is not a number, and so forth—and baffled too by the unity of friendship, a unity which is, I think, captured not so well by the Aristotelian notion of the friend as 'another self' as by the Aristotelian notion that in friendship there is in view a truly *common* good not reducible to my good or thy good, and completely beyond capture by a word or phrase such as 'self-interest'.

And finally what Reason finds baffling is the constancy of the poem's couple in their commitment to each other and to the good of the truth which each was looking to beyond themselves. What amazes Reason is (as it says) that their unity could survive what parted them—as the poem does not explicitly say but its deciphering enables readers to know: exile, poverty, and then a death.

So I take the poem to be saying—not that Love supplies motives unknown to reason, motives which then operate in place of Reason, in Reason's place—but rather (i) that the Love exemplified in the literally exemplary couple *has* the true reasons (fully acknowledgeable by Reason) that are given by the worth of the persons involved, their true loveableness; but (ii) that to live up to this takes more than the intelligibility of the loveable goods instantiated in these loveable persons; it takes the wholehearted response of those persons; and (iii) that to observe by example the possibility of such devoted, constant, 'true' responsiveness enables one to deepen and reinforce one's understanding of the goods of knowledge, friendship, and practical reasonableness and thus also one's understanding of the good/value of the persons whose whole lives instantiate and exemplify those goods so awesomely. Love *does have* reasons, but these would remain 'no reason' if they remained merely intelligibilities affirmable by reason, and were not taken up, out of the fungibility of goods that can be and are instantiable in countless people, and embodied in *commitment to this particular person*. (Something like the same issue arises in patriotism and other forms of loyalty.)

2

DISCOURSE, TRUTH, AND FRIENDSHIP*

I

In launching (or relaunching on a sound basis) the philosophical discourse about natural law which has continued to this day, Plato explored with still unsurpassed penetration the ethics of discourse itself. For the dialogue of the *Gorgias* facilitates its readers' meditative appropriation both of morality's deepest sources (*principia*) and of the conditions for very significant kinds of action: truth-seeking dialogue, discussion or discourse, and meditation or reflective deliberation.

The framework of the dialogue satisfies the procedural conditions for fruitful discourse. The parties—Socrates and Gorgias, Polus, Callicles, and Chaerophon—are equals in freedom of status and of speech,[1] unconstrained by any pressure for proximate decision and action, united in the mutual comprehension afforded by a shared and highly articulate and reflective culture, and assembled among free and equal fellow citizens who similarly are culturally united and (unlike, say, the audience for Socrates' *apologia*) unconstrained. And from the outset, and again and again, Socrates points to further conditions.

The first of those further conditions,[2] the one most overtly articulated, is that the parties to discourse shall set aside speech-making and engage only in *discussion*,[3] in which answer follows and responds to question and is not

---

* 1999a ('Natural Law and the Ethics of Discourse'); read at the European University in Florence in 1998, on a conference panel about and with Jürgen Habermas.

[1] They meet and discourse in the city where there is 'more freedom of speech than anywhere in Greece' (i.e. in the world): *Gorgias* 461e. Note: In general I quote from the translation by Allen, *The Dialogues of Plato*, vol. I. Allen's prefatory 'Comment' on the *Gorgias* (*ibid.*, 189–230) is valuable, not least his demonstration of the wide philosophical superiority of Plato's Callicles (not to mention Callicles' philosophical superior, Socrates!) to Nietzsche: *ibid.*, 219–21; and his showing (206) that the fallacies in Socrates' arguments often denounced by modern commentators (cf. Irwin, *Plato: Gorgias*, v) are liable to be in the eye of the beholder.

[2] *Gorgias* at 461d: 'observe one *condition*...bridle that long answer method'.

[3] Discussion: *dialegesthai* (447c—contrasted with 'a performance'; 449b—contrasted with 'that lengthy kind of discourse [*logōn*] Polus began'; 453c—discussion as discourse motivated by desire to *really know* its subject-matter).

employed to block further questions.[4] But there are other conditions, and Socrates, while indicating them here and there throughout the dialogue, states them most summarily on the occasion when he also articulates the formal relation between *truth* and *consensus under ideal conditions of discourse*. Under conditions we today would call 'ideal', Socrates/Plato affirms, persons engaged in discourse *will agree*: that is a mark of truth.[5] The conditions? 'Knowledge, good will, and frankness'[6]: (i) a sound, wide-ranging education; (ii) good will towards the other parties to the discourse/discussion (indeed, the kind regard one has towards one's friends); and (iii) willingness to speak frankly (even when that involves admitting one's mistakes, self-contradictions, and self-refutation), and not to feign agreement.[7] In the absence of these conditions, even universal assent to a proposition would be no evidence (let alone a guarantee) of its truth.[8] And when the conditions are fulfilled, the discussants' convergence is not a *criterion* of truth, a standard to which one can appeal to discriminate, *within* argument, between sound and unsound judgments. Rather it is a *mark* of truth, a welcome and confirmatory consequence of their common willingness to attend to what every truth-seeking discussion must have as its objective: 'things which are' (the truth of the matter) (*ta onta*),[9] what 'is so',[10] 'what is true and false concerning the matters of which we speak—for it is of common good to all that the thing itself become manifest'.[11] But this *reality* to which true propositions correspond is *not* something accessible or intelligible (still less is it adequately imaginable) otherwise than by question and answer, coherent, self-consistent thought, attention to all relevant evidence, all pertinent considerations.[12] Nor, therefore,

---

[4] Esp. 449b.
[5] 486e5–6; also 487e, 513d. On 'marks of truth', see the discussion of Wiggins in *FoE* 63–4.
[6] *Gorgias* 487a2–3: *epistēmē, eunoia, parrēsia*.
[7] 487a–e; see also 473a, 492d, 495a, 500b–c, 521a.
[8] See e.g. 472a, 475e. One must add what is not so often noted by those who speak of the 'burdens of judgment' and the 'fact of pluralism', that in non-ideal conditions (i.e. all actual and foreseeable conditions) the *absence* of universal assent to, and the existence of widespread dissent from, a proposition is no evidence of its falsity.
[9] 495a8.   [10] 509b1.   [11] 505e4–6.
[12] Plato is scarcely a 'Platonist' as that figure appears in Habermas's pages. Plato as I read him (and particularly the Plato/Socrates of the *Gorgias*) would assent without difficulty to the position which Habermas articulates thus (under the description 'pragmatism'):

'Real' is what can be represented in true statements, whereas 'true' can be explained in turn by reference to the claim one person raises before others by asserting a proposition. With the assertoric sense of her statement, a speaker raises a criticizable claim to the validity of the asserted proposition, and because no one has direct access to uninterpreted conditions of validity, 'validity' (*Gültigkeit*) must be understood in epistemic terms as 'validity (*Geltung*) proven for us.' A justified truth claim should allow its proponent to defend it with reasons against the objections of possible opponents; in the end she should be able to gain the rationally motivated agreement of the interpretation community as a whole. (Habermas, *Between Facts and Norms. Contributions to a Discourse Theory of Law and Democracy*, 14.)

can there be any other basis for rationally affirming or denying that 'correspondence', in relation to any particular subject-matter of discursive or reflective inquiry.[13]

The indispensable conditions on which discussion is worthwhile, then, can be reduced to respect-and-concern for the two human goods which Socrates/Plato keeps tirelessly before the attention of the reader of the *Gorgias*: truth (and knowledge of it), and friendship (goodwill towards other human persons). These conditions are rich and powerfully exclusive. The reader cannot fail to observe what Socrates never *explicitly* affirms: many of the participants in *actual* discourse-communities, not least (and not most) in wealthy democracies, do not meet those conditions. It is therefore impossible, I suggest, to justify a modern

> discourse ethics [which] adopts the intersubjective approach of pragmatism and conceives of practical discourse as a public practice of *shared, reciprocal perspective taking*: each individual finds himself compelled to adopt the perspective of everyone else in order to test whether a proposed regulation is also acceptable from *the perspective of every other person's understanding of himself and the world.*[14]

The proposal that in discourse, and equally in choosing 'regulations' of social life generally, we should 'adopt the perspective of every other person's understanding of himself and the world' is incoherent. That is, it refutes itself in the manner Socrates explores and comments upon.[15] For: some participants in discourse and in social life generally, perhaps many participants, *understand themselves* in more or less uncritical conventional patterns of thought picked up from the surrounding culture (perhaps under comforting descriptions such as 'pious', 'traditional', 'enlightened',

---

While assenting to all this, Plato, Aristotle, and the tradition would be inclined to add (quite reasonably) that there is a legitimate reflective inquiry into what it is about the world (including people) and rationality that makes possible this expectation that fully rational and reasonable people considering the relevant data would concur.

[13] The illusion which underpins most denials of the objectivity of ethics is this: that to which true judgments have their truth by corresponding ('the facts,' 'the world,' 'reality'...) somehow lies open to an inspection conducted otherwise than by rationally arriving at true judgments of the type in question (scientific, historical, cryptographic..., and, why not? evaluative...). That illusion is the root of all those reductive programmes which we call philosophical empiricism—programmes like those of Hobbes and Hume and successors of theirs...(*FoE* 64.)

Among those successors is, in his own curious way and despite his own intentions, Kant: see *FoE* 122–4. And, confronted by the assertion that, after an 'irreversible critique' of metaphysics, this is a 'postmetaphysical era', one should add 'metaphysical' to the parenthetical list of types of true judgment (for the reasons indicated by Rawls, 'Reply to Habermas' in *Political Liberalism*, 379n).

[14] Habermas, *Justification and Application: Remarks on Discourse Ethics*, 154 (emphases substituted). Habermas himself from time to time observes that 'discourse ethics' envisages 'ideal conditions...including...freedom of access, equal rights to participate, *truthfulness on the part of participants*, absence of coercion in taking positions, and so forth': *ibid.*, 56 (emphasis added), and (*ibid.*) a 'cooperative quest for the truth'.

[15] e.g. *Gorgias* 495a, 509a.

or 'modern').[16] And some, perhaps many, understand themselves just like Polus and Callicles, in their different ways: as more or less covert admirers and desirers of power's gratifications and rewards, which they prefer to any interest in truth or friendship; they understand themselves as unconcerned, *on principle* (so to say), with the interests or perspectives of other people as such. 'Perspectives' such as these should be, not adopted but rather rejected, for the sake of discourse (not demagoguery), truth (not mendacious or myth-ridden propaganda), friendship (not self-seeking flattery), and the *real* interests of all (including those wrongly interested in adhering to and acting upon their immoral 'perspectives').[17]

II

Does that entail that Plato/Socrates' own willingness to discourse on friendly terms with Polus and Callicles, these inward admirers of tyranny, is itself performatively inconsistent? By no means. While they are at all willing to listen, he can and will try to illustrate and explain, to them as well as to any bystanders of goodwill, the *worth*—the desirability—of a friendship (including a public politics) based on shared acknowledgement and respect for intrinsic human goods such as truth and (such) friendship. *Such* goods can be elements of a *common good*.

That the good of truth, and of getting to know it for its own sake, is one among these basic aspects of that human well-being which can be truly common (a *koinon agathon*)[18] is a truth which Socrates finds dozens of ways to assert. If his assertions leave Polus and Callicles unimpressed, they perhaps do not fail to move the old sophist Gorgias.[19] Indeed, as Plato intended and in some measure foresaw, they are appeals over the heads (and under the guard) of unreasonable people to anyone willing to listen. (And

---

[16] Habermas himself, of course, is well aware of this, and from time to time emphasizes it strongly. But I have failed to discover the basis on which he supposes that this fact is compatible with reaching moral conclusions by the method he recommends (sc. of adopting the perspective of every other person's understanding of himself and the world). It is one thing to favour the true interests of each and every person, quite another to favour or adopt the self-understanding of those who do not know or do not care what is truly in their interests.

[17] So we must read with due reserve Aquinas's (Aristotle's) generous-minded praise of his opponents in discourse; it is due only on the assumption of their goodwill, an assumption often falsified in other contexts: *Sententia super Metaphysicam* XII lect. 9 n.14—

Since, in choosing what to believe and what to reject, we ought to be guided more by truth's groundedness than by affection or illwill towards those who put forward an opinion, *so* (Aristotle says) we should love both those whose opinion we follow and those whose opinion we reject. For each of them were seeking to inquire after truth, and each assisted us to do so. [Sed *quia* in eligendis opinionibus vel repudiandis, non debet duci homo amore vel odio introducentis opinionem, sed magis ex certitudine veritatis *ideo* dicit quod oportet amare utrosque, scilicet eos quorum opinionem sequimur, et eos quorum opinionem repudiamus. Utrique enim studuerunt ad inquirendam veritatem, et nos in hoc adiuverunt.]

[18] *Gorgias* 505e6, quoted at n. 11 above.   [19] See 506a.

the division between unreasonable and reasonable people is also a division *within* one's own—in practice, everyone's—individual mind-and-will.)

Considered as the benefit to be gained or missed in a discussion (or a course of reflection), truth is a property of the judgments to be made by those (or the one) engaged in the common (or solitary) inquiry. So, existentially, it is the good of understanding and knowledge. Its intelligible goodness, its character as not merely a possibility but also an *opportunity*, is grasped, in practice, by anyone capable of grasping that the connectedness of answers with questions, and with further questions and further answers, is that general and inexhaustible possibility we call knowledge. This grasp of a field of possibility as a field of *opportunity* originates in an act of that kind of undeduced (though not data-free) understanding which C.S. Peirce, in common with the tradition originated by Plato, calls *insight*.[20]

If one set out to argue—to contend in discourse or in one's private reflections—that truth (and knowledge of it) is not an intrinsic good, desirable for its own sake as the avoidance and overcoming of ignorance, muddle, and error, one would refute oneself.[21] One's argumentative (seriously asserted) denial would be performatively inconsistent; what is asserted would be inconsistent with what is instantiated in and by the activity of seriously asserting it, arguing for it, proposing it for acceptance.[22] The bringing to

---

[20] See e.g. Buchler, *The Philosophy of Peirce*, 304, a passage in which Peirce, italicizing the word 'insight', speaks of 'the abductive suggestion [which] comes to us like a flash' as 'an act of *insight*'. Peirce's emphasis on the fallibility of the thought which thus emerges is entirely compatible with the Aristotelian thesis (e.g. *ST* I q.85 a.6) that insight (*nous, intellectus*) is intrinsically infallible; for in every particular instance, what strikes one as sheer insight (which could not but understand matters as they are) may in fact be a mere 'bright idea', distorted by oversight, imaginative fantasy, and/or prior or subsequent fallacious reasoning. Always, bearing this possibility of error in mind, one must go beyond simple insight to judgment (itself a matter of insight into the fulfilment of conditions of adequacy to the data, validity of argumentation, etc.). Even basic insights into first principles are appropriately reviewed and defended by what the tradition calls 'dialectic'. So 'wisdom' is a matter not only of drawing conclusions from, but also of making judgments about, indemonstrable first principles, and of rebutting (*disputando*) those who deny them: *ST* I–II q.66 a.5 ad 4; *Aquinas* 88. (Underlying Kant's allegedly 'good grounds for abandoning the Aristotelian concept of judgment' (Habermas, *Justification and Application*, 17) is 'the vestigial empiricism so often denounced in Kantian thought': Lonergan, *Insight*, 154, 339–42; cf. essay V.9 at 149 (1992d at 16). Allen, *The Dialogues of Plato*, vol. I, 220, puts the root of the matter straightforwardly—though 'insight' is a better term than 'intuition': 'Assuming without argument the nonexistence of intellectual intuition, on which the classical tradition in metaphysics is based, [Kant] undertook to prove that what he called theoretical reason is powerless in metaphysics and ethics....')

[21] Essay 3 [and essay 4].

[22] Essay 3 at 66–8, 70–2 and the works of Isaye, Mackie, and Boyle there cited. See also *NLNR* 73–5, 79–80; Boyle, Grisez, and Tollefsen, *Free Choice: A Self-Referential Argument*, 122–38. For an example of self-refutation in the attempt to exclude insights of the kind articulated in what the tradition called *principia per se nota* (general propositions foundational to reasoning in a given domain; self-evident [though neither data-less nor dialectically indefensible] principles), consider Habermas, *Between Facts and Norms*, 226:

Substantial reasons *can never* 'compel' in the sense of logical inference or conclusive evidence. The former does not suffice for justification, because it merely explicates the content of the premises, whereas the latter is not available except in the case of singular perceptual judgments, and even then it is not beyond question. *Hence* there is no 'natural' end to the chain of possible

light of such performative inconsistency is one, but only one, of the kinds of refutation (*elenchos*) which Socrates employs and which Callicles vainly urges him to abandon.[23] Refutation of this particular kind is not, to be sure, a strict demonstration of the truth which the self-refuting assertion denies;[24] it is rather a cogent defence of that truth—in this particular case the truth that knowledge is a basic human good—against any serious denial. And it is a form of defence peculiarly and appropriately unsettling for the self-refuting sceptic,[25] since what refutes his assertion is instantiated in his very own (inner or outward) act. This is not self-contradiction in the usual sense of asserting contradictory propositions (a contradiction from which one can escape by simply abandoning one or both of them). It is inconsistency, rather, between what one asserts (denies) and the data given, willy-nilly, by one's own very choosing to assert it.[26] One's position is ridiculous,[27] absurd;[28] it is a vivid manifestation of that 'discord with oneself'[29] which is involved in some measure in every kind of inconsistency, and which Callicles—testifying to its unacceptability—hopes to avoid by brutal frankness.[30]

In the logical domain of argumentation, self-refutation (whether by self-contradiction or performative inconsistency) is a mode of refutation. In the existential domain of *praxis* it is an unworthy condition of truncated appropriation of truth, a kind of self-mutilating, a notable way of leaving oneself 'limping and crooked' in *psychē* 'due to falsity and pretence'.[31] The

---

substantial reasons; one *cannot* exclude the possibility that new information and better reasons will be brought forward. (Emphases added.)

Here Humean empiricism and Vienna positivism take a new form, but remain as always incoherent both with their own claim and with the intelligence deployed in articulating them. In particular, Habermas is seeking to exclude *in advance* precisely what he says *cannot* be excluded, viz. the possibility that 'better reasons will be brought forward' to show that, e.g., truth and friendship have intrinsic worth and are constituents of the 'natural end to the chain of possible substantial reasons', and that this truth about truth and friendship is unrevisable. (Note: I am not denying that there are differences in the way in which various types of good-and-sufficient reasons 'compel' assent; in some types of instance, assent can (psychologically) be withheld and so depends upon one's dedication to truth. See *Aquinas* 11 n. 10, 87–8.)

[23] Dear friend [Socrates], be persuaded by me. Cease from refutation (*elenchōn*) and practise the music of affairs (*pragmatōn*). Practise that which will make you seem wise (*doxeis phronein*).... Do not emulate men who practise refutation (*elenchontas*) in these petty matters, but rather those who possess life and glory [reputation] (*doxa*) and many other goods. (*Gorgias* 486c–d)

[24] See e.g. Aquinas, *Sententia super Metaphysicam* IV lect. 6 n.14 [609]: elenchus or argumentatio (which Aquinas thinks would better have been called *redarguitio*, self-refutation: n. 3 [608]) is 'not demonstration *simpliciter*'.

[25] Much 'postmodernist' loquacity seeks to hide the irrationality, the surrender to evil, which persisting in performative inconsistency entails.

[26] So it is, in the last analysis, a denial of evidence (data), and thus is less a question of logical incoherence than of turning away from or blindness to *what is so*, such as Socrates begged to be saved from even when it involved him in no logical inconsistency: 'if I seem to any of you to *agree with myself in* something that is *not the case*, you must lay hold on it and refute me' (*Gorgias* 506a2–3). Illogicality is not the only, or even perhaps the most dangerous, obstacle to truth.

[27] Cf. *Gorgias* 509a7.   [28] 519c4.   [29] See 482b6. See also Plato, *Sophist* 252c.
[30] *Gorgias* 482d–483a.   [31] See 525a2–3.

Gorgias strenuously insists (as does Habermas in his own way) upon the moral significance of the existential choice between concerning oneself with soundness in argumentation, in the hope of overcoming one's ignorance, incoherence, or blindness to *what is so*, and concerning oneself with success in, say, erotic/political affairs.[32]

III

But in grasping the goodness, the intrinsic worth, of truth and knowledge of it, one grasps that it is a basic good not only for oneself but for anyone like oneself—a basic *human* good. Moreover, knowledge is not the only human possibility which, by insight into the data of one's inclinations and capacities, one grasps as an opportunity, an intrinsic good. Friendship, the sharing in goods with another or other persons each for their own sake,[33] is another such good. For each and both of these reasons, one cannot reasonably seek a fulfilment which is only one's own. Because there is more than one intrinsic good, and also because one's pursuit of any basic good is threatened by more or less chaotic sub-rational desires, aversions, and inertia ('licentiousness'[34]), one needs look to establishing and confirming order in one's soul: a temperate (including courageous)[35] will and character. Because one's pursuit of fulfilment would be unreasonable and self-mutilating if it were indifferent to friendship and to the worth of the instantiation of human goods in the lives of other people, one needs look to getting order into one's relations with one's fellows, one's communities. The name for that order, *and* for one's constant concern for it, is justice.[36]

---

[32] So Callicles loves and flatters both the *demos* and his lover Demos (481d, 513b–d), while Socrates takes care not to let the shifting opinions of his own beloved Alcibiades deflect him from the unchanging arguments of philosophy, his weightier love (482d). Or, as Callicles puts it, one should (and Socrates, he confidently—and, *we* know, mistakenly—thinks, in the end will) dismiss philosophy ('spending one's life whispering with three or four kids in a corner': 485e) in favour of the 'free, important, sufficient' affairs of the courts, public and private business, and 'human pleasures and desires', the whole voluptuous 'music of affairs': 484d, 485e, 486c. Consider also the admission wrenched from the soul of Callicles, late in the discourse: 'I don't know why, but you seem to me to make sense, Socrates. Yet I suffer the affection of the multitude. I don't quite believe you': 513c.

[33] Not to be confused with the unilateral 'altruism' introduced by Comte. Since friend A wills the good of friend B for B's sake, and B the good of A for A's sake, A must will also his own good (for B's sake) and B his own good (for A's sake), so that each is raised to a new standpoint, concern for a truly *common* good. See *NLNR* 142–4, 158; *Aquinas* 111–17.

[34] *Gorgias* 507d.   [35] 507b–c.

[36] I hold these things so and I say that they are true. But if true, then he who wishes to be happy must, it seems, pursue and practice temperance, and each of us must flee licentiousness as fast as our feet will carry us.... This seems to me the mark at which we ought to look and aim in living; so to act as to draw everything of our own and of the city toward this, that justice (*dikaiosynē*) and temperance (*sōphrosynē*) shall be present to him who is to be happy. He must not permit unchastened desires to exist or undertake to fulfil them, for then an endless, aimless evil will be his, and he will live the life of a robber...dear neither to god nor to any

The recognition of human equality which (as Plato/Socrates makes plain) is the core of a just will[37] is nothing other than the recognition that basic human goods are realizable as much in the lives of other human beings as in my own life. To refuse that recognition is to be buried in untruth. No one thus enslaved to error can intelligently think himself happy; to think so would be to bury oneself deeper in untruth, untruth about what fulfilment is. Properly (rationally) understood, knowledge, friendship, fulfilment, and justice are inter-defined. So it is a mistake, and one avoided by the tradition founded by Plato and his followers (say, Aristotle and Aquinas), to think that there is within practical reason an 'ethics' concerned just with 'how one sees oneself and who one would like to become' and thus in a different domain from the 'morality' of concern for 'the interests of all'.[38]

One cannot, then, have order in one's soul (will) without anticipating and doing what one reasonably can to promote and respect an order of equal justice in one's societies, one's associating or communion with one's fellows. And it would be folly to expect justice and friendship to exist in

man, for it is impossible to live in association (*koinōnein*) with him, and where there is no association (*koinōnia*), there is no friendship. (507c–e)

[37] See e.g. 489b1 (*dikaion to ison*); 508a6 on geometrical equality as informing principle of justice.

[38] Cf. Habermas, 'On the Pragmatic, the Ethical, and the Moral Employments of Practical Reason' in *Justification and Application*, 1–17; and n. 58 below. The incoherence of the distinction is made clear, it seems to me, by Habermas's exposition of it:

...ethical questions point in a different direction from moral questions: the regulation of interpersonal conflicts of action resulting from opposed interests is not yet an issue. Whether I would like to be someone who in case of acute need would be willing to defraud an anonymous insurance company just this one time is not a moral question, for it concerns my self-respect and possibly the respect that others show me, but not equal respect for all, and hence not the symmetrical respect that everyone should accord the integrity of all other persons. (*Ibid.*, 6.)

The compatibility of self-respect with this dealing with the insurance company cannot, I suggest, be rationally assessed without making 'moral' judgments about the conditions on which property rights are justly respected and justly overridden, and about the injustice of fraud, and so forth. There is just one question: 'how one ought to live' (492d4–5; 500c3–4) and one summary answer: temperately/courageously and justly (507d–e). (Nor, I believe, is it acceptable to assign Aristotle's ethics (*moralia*) to the supposed 'ethical' (as distinct from moral) domain of practical reason, even with the qualification that the supposed individual *ethos* is supposedly for Aristotle 'embedded in the *polis*' or in 'the life historical horizon of a customary *ethos*' (*ibid.*, 6, 10). Aristotle seems to me widely different from the 'neo-Aristotelians', e.g. MacIntyre, whom Habermas regularly criticizes under that title; the criticisms are more acceptable than the assimilation of their culture-relativism to Aristotle, whose *Nicomachean Ethics* soon makes clear that it is aimed *against* the view ('people think') that 'the question of the morally admirable (*to kalon*) and the question of the just are...the subject of such variety and fluctuation that...they are matters not of nature but of *mere convention*': *NE* I.3: 1094b14–17.) Likewise unacceptable, both as philosophy and as history of philosophy, is that *way* of distinguishing 'good' from 'right' which parallels Habermas's ethics/morality distinction and is presupposed in statements such as: 'an Aristotelian approach...views practical reason as limited essentially to ethical self-understanding and consequently to the sphere of the good' (*ibid.*, 21). Justice is a virtue (a good of the person), but the 'object', i.e. the very point of justice is the other person's *right* (*ius suum*), i.e. what as a matter of equality the other person—centrally (*proprie*), everyone alike (*indifferenter omnibus*)—is entitled to (*quod ei secundum proportionis aequalitatem debetur*): *ST* II–II q.57 a.4, q.58 a.1 and a.11, q.122 a.6.

any society whose members are not concerned to promote and maintain such rational, desire-integrating order in their individual souls (wills). Moreover, just as no one could intelligently call a society good whose members treat each other as robbers treat their victims, so no one could intelligently call good the life of an individual who is enslaved to his subrational desires for gratification and thus, too, cut off from the reality, as opposed to spurious imitations, of friendship. In each type of case—the individual and the society—the order in question is good because it is intelligent and reasonable and the corresponding forms of disorder are so far forth unreasonable and bad. And this appropriateness of good order in the individual and society is not something we just invent; rather, it *becomes clear to us* by experience, thought-experiment, discussion, rational judgment.

So, both because its desirability is discovered rather than dreamed up and because being reasonable is central to what we find ourselves to be (*in potentia*) and reasonably want to become and remain (in act), we can call this reasonable order in the soul and in society '*natural*'—something *naturally* good. And since in each type of case the good, reasonable, natural order can and must be picked out in the form of normative propositions directing one towards individual and social choices promotive and respectful of good order, the relevant directive propositions are appropriately called *laws*. (For law of any kind governs precisely by directiveness *within* the deliberations of its subjects.)

Thus Socrates/Plato transforms the Calliclean opposition between nature (*physis*) and law/convention (*nomos*) into the recognition of a *natural law*—the set of propositions which pick out (i) the goods (such as knowledge and friendship)[39] to be pursued and (ii) the principles of reasonableness in realizing goods in the life of oneself and one's fellows—the principles of justice and the other virtues.[40] The Calliclean/Nietzschean[41] proposal

---

[39] For attempts to identify a more or less full list of basic human goods and reasons for action, see *NLNR* 59–99; *Aquinas* 80–6; 1987f at 106–15; [and Introduction at p. 9 above].

[40] '... proper arrangement and good order of the soul have the name of lawfulness and law, whence souls become law-abiding and orderly; and this is justice and temperance ... [and] the rest of virtue....': *Gorgias* 504d, e. '... there is a certain order properly present in each thing, and akin to it, which provides a good naturally suited to it....' Any authentic exercise of practical reason, such as a true art (*technē*) like medicine as distinct from a mere pleasure-oriented knack (*empeiria*) like pastry-cooking (500e5) or cosmetics or rhetorical-sophistic politicking-by-flattery (463b), 'considers the nature (*physin*) of the person it serves and the cause [and nature (*physin*): 465a4] of what it does, and is able to render an account (*logon*) of each' (501a1–3).

[41] For a careful documentation of the close relationship between Callicles and Nietzsche, see Dodds, *Plato: Gorgias*, 387–91; for a brief but deeper philosophical assessment of Dodds's pages, and of the differences which are rooted in Nietzsche's post-Kantianism, see Allen, *The Dialogues of Plato*, vol. I, 220–1.

to consider natural and therefore choiceworthy ('just by nature')[42] the rule of the stronger, in ruthless pursuit of the desires they happen to find within themselves,[43] ends in incoherence and self-refutation. The weak, in concert, are naturally stronger than the strong and subject him to their law and conventional wisdom of equality-based justice.[44] Does their natural strength *entitle* them to rule? Does anyone's? The 'inference' from 'is' to 'ought' is obviously fallacious.

Again, proposing the 'principle' that a worthwhile life consists in freedom from subjection to others turns out to be performatively inconsistent, for (as Callicles is brought to admit) it implicitly proposes living by flattery and demagogy, conforming more or less slavishly (if only for personal safety) to the desires of the many.[45] And the 'principle' that the content of the emancipated life is the search for satisfaction of all one's desires deprives Callicles of any *basis for* his own judgment that, say, the catamite's pathetic slavery-to-desire is unworthy.[46] Its incompatibility, moreover, with the conditions of reasonable discussion (discourse) is made manifest, for readers of Plato's dialogue to contemplate at leisure, by the speech-making, the surliness, the sulky abdication from the to-and-fro of debate, and the not too veiled warnings that, outside the discussion, and after a trial by rhetoric not truth, Socrates' property may well be confiscated and he himself exterminated.

IV

In the discourse, of course, these warnings are merely argumentative, allusions to what, 'in principle', is liable to happen to you if you adhere to the principle that 'it is better to suffer wrong than to do it'. Plato's reader, as Plato intended, knows more than the parties to the discussion. Knowing that the warnings were verified, one learns again that discourse is seamlessly integrated with the rest of practical life, and that one's conduct in discourse is morally significant, to be assessed by ethical (that is, moral) as well as argumentative (that is, logical) criteria. When one hears Socrates/Plato affirm the worth of truth, justice, and friendship and the worthlessness of lies, of injustice, and of the Calliclean/Nietzschean resolve to 'be hard', one hears it knowing that Socrates chose to practise what Socrates/Plato discursively affirms. He did not lie in self-defence.[47]

---

[42] *kata physin...dikaiou*: 483e1 (and therefore *kata nomon...physeous*: e3); also 484b1 (*physeōs dikaion*), 488b2–3.
[43] 482e–484b.   [44] 488d.   [45] 521a–b with 518a–d.   [46] 494c–e.
[47] Cf. Habermas, *Justification and Application*, 63:

On closer inspection, however, we find that negative rights and duties can no more claim 'absolute' validity than can positive duties. An untruthful statement that saves the life of another is

(In taking that as exemplary, we need not so regard—nor, I think, did Plato so regard—every aspect of Socrates' trial advocacy.) And when we hear him affirm that doing injustice is worse than undergoing it, we know not only that he put this into practice but also that Polus and Callicles' allusions to this thought's unpopularity were to be verified in the event, and not just once:

> ...you decided to judge *as a group* the cases of the ten generals...—illegally, as later it seemed to all of you. But at the time, I alone of the Prytanies opposed doing a thing contrary to law, and cast my vote against it. And when the orators were ready to impeach me and have me arrested—you urging them on with your shouts—I thought that with law and justice on my side I must run the risk, rather than concur with you in an unjust decision through fear of bonds or death.
>
> Those things happened while the City was still under the Democracy. But when the oligarchy came, the Thirty in turn summoned me along with four others to the Rotunda and ordered us to bring back Leon the Salamanian from Salamis so that he might be executed, planning to implicate as many people as possible in their own guilt.... Strong as it was, that oligarchy did not so frighten me as to cause me to do a thing unjust, and when we departed from the Rotunda, *the other four went into Salamis and brought back Leon*, and *I left and went home*. I might have been killed for that, if the oligarchy had not shortly afterward been overthrown.[48]

Perhaps the four who went off to fetch Leon for liquidation rationalized their complicity in murder by an ethics of 'the situation', a 'principle of appropriateness (*Angemessenheit*)'.[49] Or perhaps with the zest for thuggery of a Polus; or just with a more lofty Calliclean shrug. Perhaps, rather, they were decent people ashamed of what they were doing, acknowledging each to himself—though not in 'discourse' with anyone else—the injustice, untruth, evil of their choice. And since the consequences of Socrates' choice to *go home* are continuing, quite strongly, to this very day (for example through the hearts of readers of so many eras), we can judge how unreasonable it is to try to guide moral (that is, ethical) judgment by an assessment of the 'overall net balance' of premoral good and bad consequences 'promised' by each of the options available in 'the situation'—a situation which in reality *includes* our situation, so far away and so many centuries later. An ethics of

---

no less morally commanded than killing in cases of self-defence.... Valid norms are valid only in a 'prima facie' sense.
See further, for this relaxed ethics of lying, *ibid.*, 66.

[48] *Apology* 32b–d (trans. Allen, *The Dialogues of Plato*, vol. I, 95) (emphases added).

[49] Cf. Habermas, *Justification and Application*, 14; see also 36–7, 63–4, and passim (note the book's title). For a critique of ethical methodologies which propose to subject all norms, negative as well as positive, to a 'test' of appropriateness to 'the situation', see e.g. *MA* 16–24, 101–5; *FoE* 80–108; *NDMR* 238–72.

'natural law' (rational principles) cannot embrace any moral methodology of the kinds proposed by utilitarianism (consequentialism, proportionalism) or by 'situation ethics'.

V

Plato speaks through, and in a sense over, the dialogue, discourse, discussion of the characters he has communicatively set in motion. He is addressing the reflection, meditation, and eventually the inner deliberation of his readers, one by one. More radically than its being carried forward *inter partes*, discourse is in the reason and will of the individual. Would it not be quite a mistake to treat as 'solipsism' the 'monologue' which indeed is at the heart of any worthwhile dialogue?[50] It is in the outwardly silent—perhaps only momentarily silent!—but intensely active contemplation of the reflective person that the worth of real friendship and the worthlessness of demagoguery and tyranny—and so too of inauthentic, flattering, or domineering discourse[51]—are understood and appreciated, and opportunities for participating in the one or the other are chosen or rejected. The will to seek advancement or protection by lying to one's fellows—and to become accomplice in their untruths—is preceded, commonly and 'naturally' enough, by the self-deception of rationalization (not least in Calliclean types who tell themselves and others about their ruthless frankness).[52]

Without the return to oneself of *reflection*—without, that is to say, the inner appropriation, however speedy, of one's understanding's enhancement of experience, and one's grasp that the conditions for judgment are or are not fulfilled—discourse is 'mere talk' or, worse, manipulation.[53] And without a very resolute philosophical appropriation of the whole content of this inwardness one can scarcely appropriate the metaphysical truth

---

[50] A sliding assimilation of 'monological' to 'solipsistic' seems to occur in the critique of Dworkin offered in Habermas, *Between Facts and Norms*, 224–5.

[51] On sophistic (*litigiosa*) discourse, which in part is badly motivated (e.g. by desire to seem wise) and partly irrational (e.g. in refusing to concede anything which cannot be demonstrated *stricto sensu*), see Aquinas, *Sententia in Metaphysicam* IV lect. 16 n.12; *In Pol.* II.2 n.1 [185]; *Commentarium in Libros Perihermeneias* I.9 n.9; *Expositio super Iob* VI and v.29.

[52] On inner evading (*subterfugere*) of truth, see *Aquinas* 11 n. 10.

[53] Moreover, as McInerny, *Aquinas against the Averroists*, 158 remarks:

However difficult philosophical inquiry may be, however scandalous the radical differences among sophisticated philosophical theories appear, the Aristotelian view is that communication and agreement are in principle possible because the discussants are human beings with common cognitive equipment and a common fund of experience.

The 'Aristotelian view' is also Plato's. And McInerny's point is valid even in discourse with those who (not without, it seems, some complacency) regard 'radical differences' not as 'scandalous but as a desirable and somehow in-built aspect of 'modern life'.

to which one is inescapably committed by any rational affirmation of 'the universalism of equal respect for all and of solidarity with everything that bears the mark of humanity'.[54] Without that appropriation one will capitulate (as I later observe) to a delimitation of the 'all', and of 'humanity', a delimitation that has all too evidently been constructed in the felt interests of the *strong*, at even the most dramatic expense of the weak. So a community, too, has the responsibility of scrutinizing the results of such reflection, and of making and embodying in its highest constitutional law a *correct* judgment—not simply a consensus or democratically or judicially approved judgment[55]—about *which beings are to be acknowledged to be members of the community*. On so fundamental a matter of right, the normal criteria of legitimacy are, I repeat, supplanted by the overriding duty to define the boundaries of legal 'personality' and right *correctly*.

We talk easily of Plato's authoritarianism. In part this marks our naïvety in reading dramatic explorations of the foundations of ethics as if they were political manifestos or treatises. In part it is a mark (as I shall later say) of Plato's incomplete appropriation of the democratic implications of his own radical grasp of human equality in substance and in right. We likewise talk easily and dismissively of Plato's dualism, and this talk, too, is partly justified by weaknesses in Plato's philosophical armoury,[56] but more surely is also a mark of our own materialist naïvety and fumbling inattention to reality. Most, perhaps everything the *Gorgias* says about soul as ground of human dignity and of an individual's most significant excellences or failures as a person is fully consistent with that personal body-soul unity which Aristotle and more resolutely Aquinas explicitly (and Plato surely, if not explicitly) brought to light by reflection on the experience, the inwardness-outwardness of being in action.

In the act of, say, speaking to my partner in discourse, I understand my utterance as the carrying out of a choice *which I made*, and in the same act I am aware of my audible uttering, see the hearers register their comprehension, feel, say, confidence or anxiety, remember a past

---

[54] Habermas, *Justification and Application*, 15.
[55] e.g. *Dred Scott v Sandford* 60 US 393 (1857). [See essay II.1 (2000a) at 26–7.]
[56] I have in mind the aspect of Plato's writings about soul which Aristotle criticizes in *De Anima*, in particular the criticisms which Aquinas, in his commentary, summarizes allusively (*In De Anima* I lect. 8 n.131):

> soul shapes a body fit for itself; it does not enter a ready-made body. Plato and other philosophers, speaking only about the nature of soul, have given an inadequate account, failing to define *which* body goes with a given soul.

This criticism can be summarized, again, as the complaint that Plato takes soul to be mover of body as sailors are movers of their ship, so that 'soul is united to body not as form but rather as mover and director' (Aquinas, *De Unitate Intellectus*, c. 1 para. 5 [McInerny, ed., *Aquinas against the Averroists*, 23]).

misunderstanding, and hope my statement will make my point. This experience of the *unity (including continuity)* of my being—as a feeling, willing, observing, remembering, understanding, physically active and effective mover or cause of physical effects and equally an undergoer and recipient of such effects—is a datum which philosophical exploration of human and other natural realities can adequately account for only with great difficulty and many a pitfall. Still, prior to all accounts of it, this intelligible presence of my many-faceted acting self to myself is a datum of *understanding*; one and the same I—this human being—who am understanding and choosing and carrying out my choice and sensing, etc., is a reality I already truly understand, albeit not yet fully (explanatorily, with elaboration). (Indeed, it is only given this primary understanding of one's understanding, willing, and so forth, that one can and typically does *value* such understanding, freedom, voluntariness, unity of being, and so forth.)

So, as Aristotle and (plainly) Aquinas argue more or less explicitly,[57] any account proposing to explain these realities must be consistent with the complex data it seeks to explain, a set of data which includes the proposer's performance, outward and inward, in proposing it. The only account which meets these conditions will be along the lines they argue for: the very *form* and lifelong *act(uality)* by which the matter of my bodily make-up is constituted the unified and active subject (me myself) is a factor, a reality, which Aristotle (after Plato) calls *psychē* and Aquinas calls soul (*anima*). In the human animal—the very same animal whose interests in every individual case are to be taken equally into account, in Plato's as in the hopefully 'postmetaphysical' ethics—from the very outset of his or her existence as human, it is this one essentially unchanging factor, unique to each individual, which explains (1) the unity and complexity of the individual's activities; (2) the dynamic unity in complexity—in one dimension, the programme—of the individual's growth as embryo, fetus, neonate, infant... and adult; (3) the relatively mature individual's understanding of universal (for example, generic) immaterial objects of thought (for example, classes, or truth and falsity, or soundness/unsoundness in reasoning); and (4) this unique individual's generic unity with every other member of the species. In members of our species the one factor unifying and activating the living reality of each individual is at once vegetative, animal (sentient and self-locomotive), and intellectual (understanding, self-understanding, and, even in thinking, self-determining by judging and choosing). Though the manifold activations of these bodily and rational powers are variously dependent upon the physical maturity and health of the individual,

---

[57] See Aquinas, *De Unitate Intellectus* III.3 [79]; *Aquinas* 177–9.

the essence and powers of the soul seem to be given to each individual complete (as wholly undeveloped, *radical* capacities) at the outset of his or her existence as such. This is the root of the dignity we all have as human beings. Without it, claims of equality of right would be untenable in face of the many ways in which people are unequal.

This metaphysics of the activity of discourse, which cannot rightly be pushed aside as an outmoded 'philosophy of subjectivity'—as if discourse could be undertaken or accounted for without the subjectivity of the deliberating and reflective subject—enables a theory of natural law to stabilize and clarify practical reason's undeduced grasp of first principles of the form 'knowledge [friendship...etc.] is a good for me and *anyone* (any being *like me*)'. The same metaphysics is the indispensable basis for rationally affirming the core of the 'natural law' account of right: one's choices and other acts and dispositions of will must be open always to *integral* human fulfilment, that is to the fulfilment of *all human* persons and communities. (This metaphysics is also the core of a fundamental account of *language*, in which intelligibility, corporeality, and sociality are uniquely unified as techniques and products available and perspicuous to spiritually organized living human organisms.)

VI

The distinction between ethics and morality turns out to be not merely (as I said) analytically unsound, a kind of category mistake[58] (and a curious relic, as it seems, of Kant's oversight of the basic *reasons for* action). It also has bad consequences for Habermas's political-legal theory. For, as deployed in that domain, it has much the same role as Rawls's untenable distinction between 'comprehensive doctrines' and 'public reasons'. In each case the author treats the distinction he has drawn as enabling him to set aside, but *without seeking to refute*, objections to legally permitting and authorizing the deliberate killing of very young or irreversibly damaged (unconscious?) human beings. Rawls, who in *Political Liberalism* introduced abortion as his one concrete illustration of how his 'political liberalism' actually applies, shunts the objections to killing young unborn babies aside as being not within the alleged 'overlapping consensus' or 'reasonable'. Habermas, who introduced the topics of abortion and euthanasia into a

---

[58] A rather serious mistake, I think; the bifurcation between these supposed domains of practical reason, and the thought that 'ethical' reason is naturally egocentric (unless ethnocentric) (see e.g. *Between Facts and Norms*, 97), are very damaging both to ethical/moral understanding in general and to the specifically vocational choices and commitments which one must make for oneself by choices between options none of which is ruled out by the general principles of morality.

'Reply to Critics', shunts similar objections aside as being merely 'ethical' and thus concerned, not with what is *required* by a morally indispensable respect for the *interests of all as equals*, but only with what is '*best* for *us*' (that is, for the partisans of this or that ethical opinion). Thus he cuts himself off from the very meaning of the discourse of his partners in discourse, or at least so radically misconceives their views that civil conversation with them is substantially obstructed. And above all he thus proposes a quite fallacious justification/rationalization for abandoning very many of our fellow human beings, by legally authorizing the intentional termination of their lives. In doing so, he abandons his own fundamental 'moral' thesis that decisions must be taken in the interests of *all*; he lays aside his own 'appeal to an ever-wider community'.[59] This, it seems to me, is a *diskursethische* debacle worth observing in some detail.

The killings in question are those involved in euthanasia and abortion. The examples are brought forward by Habermas without explication. I shall assume that by 'abortion' is meant cases of induced termination of pregnancy which on one view are wrongful because they intend the death of the unborn; and that by 'euthanasia' is meant killing on the ground that the life of the person to be killed is no longer worth living (say, because of irreversible unconsciousness).[60]

Notoriously, such killings and the question whether they are immoral and should be legally prohibited are the subject of a rather intense public discourse. Habermas contends, however, that this discourse concerns 'the ethical question of which regulation is respectively "best for us" from "our" point of view'.[61] This enables him to say that, when discussion has shown that the disagreement 'cannot be resolved either by discourse or by compromise', then the matter must be raised to a new 'level':

> Each participant must turn away from the ethical question.... They must, instead, take the moral point of view and examine which regulation is 'equally good for all' in view of the prior claim to an equal right to coexist.[62]

The 'all' for whom the regulation is to be 'equally good' do not, it appears, include the unborn or the irreversibly unconscious, but rather the 'all' comprising those who want or 'need' to choose these killings, all those who oppose them, and all who look on more or less indifferently. The 'equal right to coexist' is emphatically *not* the 'equal right of the unborn and the permanently unconscious' which those on one side of the so-called 'ethical'

---

[59] Habermas, 'Reply to Symposium Participants' at 1486.
[60] It should be observed that Habermas finds personally rather 'unbearable' the practice of euthanasia as it would—given certain assumptions about public opinion—be required by his position to be legally and socially permitted: *ibid.* at 1490.
[61] *Ibid.*   [62] *Ibid.*

debate had been asserting. No, indeed. Anyone on *that* side of the debate must now—in virtue of the other side's 'right to coexistence'—stand aside to let people on the other side opt for the killings they (often, no doubt, reluctantly) propose:

> ...the normative expectation connected with this—that when necessary we tolerate the members of another group whose behavior is ethically reprehensible to 'our' view—does not necessarily imply any damage to our integrity: 'we' (for instance, as Catholics confronted by a 'liberal' abortion law) may continue at an ethical level to abhor the legally permissible practice of others as we have in the past. Instead, what is legally required of us is tolerance for practices that in 'our' view are ethically deviant.[63]

But all this distorts almost beyond recognition the actual and historical *discourses* on abortion, euthanasia, and their legalization. When the most recent British parliamentary committee report on euthanasia explained its unanimous rejection of legalized euthanasia or assisting in suicide, it did so precisely on the ground of right:

> society's prohibition of intentional killing...is the cornerstone of law and social relationships. It protects each one of us impartially, embodying the belief that all are equal.[64]

When Peter Singer and I discoursed publicly on these matters at the Philosophy Society in Oxford in May 1998 [see essay II.18], it did not for a moment occur to us or, I daresay, to any of the many philosophers in the room that either of us was discussing what is 'respectively "best for me/my group" from "my/my group's point of view"' or what preserves or damages 'my integrity' conceived (absurdly, as Socrates showed) as separable from justice. The naïve relativism implicit in the claim that the ethical question is 'What is good (or right) *from my point of view?*' was decisively criticized and left behind by analytical philosophy by, at latest, 1960, with the demonstration that it makes ethical *discourse* (argument, *disputatio*) practically senseless.

Habermas's dismissal of unrefuted moral arguments by miscategorizing them as ethical is strategically parallel to Rawls's equally unargued dismissal of the very same arguments by miscategorizing them as 'not public' or 'not within public reason'. The nadir of misunderstanding is reached in a sentence of Rawls's directed at 'Catholics', strikingly similar to Habermas's invitation to 'for instance, Catholics' to stand aside and allow abortion and euthanasia because such 'behavior' 'does not necessarily imply any

---

[63] *Ibid.*
[64] Report of the House of Lords Select Committee on Medical Ethics (Chairman: Lord Walton), 31 January 1994, para. 237, reprinted in Keown, *Euthanasia Examined*, 102.

damage to [y]our integrity'. In Rawls's words: 'They [Catholics] need not exercise the right of abortion in their own case.'[65] So the position is this. Citizens opposed to abortion are claiming, with some good arguments, that abortion is rather like slave-owning. (The overwhelmingly secular British parliamentary committee saw essentially the same issue of basic equality rights at stake in euthanasia.) The argument of these citizens is that the killings whose legalization Rawls and Habermas defend are a radical, basic injustice imposed on people deprived or to be deprived of the protections of citizenship. The response(s) suggested by the argumentation of Rawls and Habermas would run something like:

You free citizens need not exercise the right to [own slaves] [abort your children] in your own case, so you can and must recognize our law as legitimate as it applies to the rest of us (and as we will enforce it against you if you interfere).

You people need not do any of this [killing] [slave owning] yourselves, so your integrity is undamaged and so you ought (and will be compelled) to stand aside to allow us, in the exercise of our prior right of coexistence with you, to ['coexist' with our slaves] [terminate our coexistence with these unborn children/fetuses and with people whose lives are not worth living].[66]

* * *

A sound 'natural law' theory has never been other than an appeal to public reasons—concerning kinds of choices consistent or incompatible with the real interests of all human persons—reasons that would command a universal consensus under ideal conditions of discourse and meanwhile are available to, and could be accepted by, anyone who is willing and able to give them fair and adequate attention, *including* those people whose immediate and partial interests (real or supposed) would be more or less damaged, and some or many of whose actual present beliefs would be negated, by accepting and acting upon those reasons as true. It has never been other than a theory which aspires to ensure that the content of its theses both coheres with and illuminates the natural, and the logical, and the technical (including linguistic-pragmatic), and the moral conditions under which those theses can be rationally adopted, affirmed in discourse, and acted upon in other forms of action. (It has always promoted precisely the discourse principle articulated today by Habermas.) It is therefore a

---

[65] *Political Liberalism*, lvi–lvii. See also Rawls, 'The Idea of Public Reason Revisited' at 798–9. On the relation between the paperback version of *Political Liberalism* and 'The Idea of Public Reason Revisited', see essay 16, esp. sec. IV at 266.

[66] The failure of Rawls's and Habermas's arguments does not entail that there are no grounds for coexisting with people who authorize and fund abortions of convenience, practice euthanasia, or intend the nuclear destruction—in certain eventualities—of entire cities with their inhabitants. I have explored these matters a bit further in *NDMR* ch. 13; and essay 16, at 265.

theory which goes far beyond the arbitrarily 'formal' and one-dimensional 'practical rationality' of Kant's attempt to save it from the ravages of empiricist-utilitarian incomprehension.

No one who has followed the course of theorizing from Plato through Aristotle to Aquinas and on to the contemporary discussion of natural law theory should, I think, be tempted by the periodization which locates practical rationality's effective emergence in the philosophy of 'the early modern' age—marked as it is by the long-exposed foundational mistakes of Hobbes, Hume, and (despite his best efforts) Kant. But nor should anyone think that the ethical and political theorizing of Plato, Aristotle, and Aquinas, which those early moderns so thoroughly misunderstood, needs no improvement or overhaul.

Their theorizings left in shadow the master principle of morality and the way in which it is specified in, for example, the Golden Rule[67] and in respect for every basic human good in every person and every act. They failed to follow through the implications of the fact that human life and health is one of these basic goods to be so respected and fairly promoted, and similarly the implications of the fact that religion as an appropriate harmony with the ultimate sources of existence, meaning, and value is another similarly basic good to be respected. They failed to follow through their own understanding of the equality and brotherhood of human beings with a critique of slavery properly distinguished from penal servitude. So their theorizings were disfigured with defences of capital punishment, and of punishment (even capital) for certain false beliefs on religious issues, and with either an acceptance of slavery or at least a rather complicitous silence about it (albeit in neither case unconditional). On these and a number of other matters the tradition has worked itself pure, or is somewhat closer to having done so. It has always been, essentially, a reflection on the inherent directiveness of the basic reasons for action, and a friendly *disputatio* grounded in reasons, not in mere appeals to the 'authority' of anyone, not even Aristotle or Plato.

---

[67] Following Kant, and here citing only the negative version of it, Habermas holds that the Golden Rule is egocentric: Habermas, 'Reconciliation through the Public Use of Reason: Remarks on John Rawls's Political Liberalism' at 117. He seems to forget that the Golden Rule, in classical ethics (e.g. Aquinas), takes its place as but one specification of the more universal demand that neighbour be loved as one loves oneself, and that, for the purposes of justice's basic demands, all members of the human race be treated as one's neighbours. In other words, the self-consciousness of the individual applying the Golden Rule was and is required by natural law theory (as indeed the very phrase 'natural law' connotes) to 'reflect a transcendental consciousness, that is, a universally valid view of the world' (*ibid.*), and to have been shaped also by morality's other high-level specifications of the master moral principle of openness to integral human fulfilment. Attention to what is 'in the interests of all' does not, however, exhaust the content of 'what I would wish others to do for me, or not do to me'; *part* of that content is a matter of sub-rational (but not per se unreasonable) motivating factors, such as degree of risk aversion. See essay 14, sec. VII.

VII

Reflecting on a body of work so close to natural law theory in intention and, in some respects, results, anyone may be oppressed by a renewed awareness of the non-ideal character of the discourse between theorists so near (even geographically and culturally) and yet so far apart.[68] The burden of history, pressing to convert each discussant into the mere voice of an 'ism', is great. History's burden on discourse is magnified in another way when some parties to the discussion seem concerned to derive from history (or their interpretation of it)[69] far more than others think possible without fallaciously inferring 'ought' or 'not-ought' from 'is' (was, has been, 'fact of pluralism', etc.).

Still, movement, even large movement, is possible,[70] as was learned at first hand by those of us who moved on from the lifeworld of Hume, Russell, et al. to take up friendly discursive residence with Plato, Aristotle, and Aquinas (alongside our respected twentieth-century teachers, whose interest in the ancients was of varying degree). Aristotle long ago taught the fruitfulness of dialogue and individual meditation in even very unpromising contexts, and the inseparable link between communicative action, inner reflection, and action of every other reasonable kind. He told, for example, of the Corinthian farmer who read the *Gorgias*, gave up his farm, and came to Athens to put his *psychē* under Plato's care.

NOTE

Jürgen Habermas responded briefly in 'A Short Reply' at 446–7. He thought that the essay proposes (i) a Platonist idea that 'some kind of contemplation...is the telos of knowledge', an end attained via discursive reasoning, and (ii) that ethical reasoning attains 'the contemplation or intuitive grasp of goods or hypergoods'—a proposal he thought raises (a) the 'usual question...how it might be possible for a knowing subject to grasp an independently existing order of moral values'; (b) the 'practical question of how to make this ontological assumption compatible with the "fact of pluralism" (cf. Rawls [*Political Liberalism*]) and the liberal demand of an equal right of everybody to pursue one's own conception of good'; and (c) the question 'whether moral insights depend on a privileged access to "the truth" and, if so, how this aristocratic epistemology would change a normative self-understanding of modernity that is best articulated in terms of egalitarian universalism'. Answers

---

[68] The same feelings will be evoked by engagement in discourse with ecclesiastical bureaucracies and 'liberal public opinion' (including its philosophically minded exponents) on matters close to people's hearts: see *NDMR* 367–70.

[69] Some of the history which forms the matrix of Habermas's theory of law (e.g. the account of the transition to modernity in *Between Facts and Norms*, 145–6) seems to me to have something of the same character as today's near-universal belief that even educated mediaeval people thought the world is flat (not a sphere)—sheer fiction, fabricated by secularist propagandists of the late eighteenth or early nineteenth centuries (see *Aquinas* 4, 16; Russell, *Inventing the Flat Earth*), and then handed down to educated twentieth-century people who accept it in entire innocence.

[70] And one can read with profit Habermas's explorations of the 'potential for self-transformation' of 'liberal public opinion': e.g. *Between Facts and Norms*, 374 et seq.

to these questions, and indications of why 'intuitive grasp' of basic human goods in first principles of practical reason is not to be confused with contemplation, can be found in this essay, and in the Introduction and essays 1 and 3–6. Since a 'liberal...equal right' and 'egalitarian universalism' are names for purported 'moral insights', Habermas's 'questions' tell against themselves: understood as intimating an argument or set of arguments, they are self-refutatory in a way that is characteristic of the (pervasive) style of thought they articulate as 'modernity'.

3

SCEPTICISM'S SELF-REFUTATION*

I

By inviting and inciting us to reflect on the implications of our own dispositions to act, *The Concept of Law* restored the theoretical vigour of jurisprudence and its openness to all the other philosophy and sciences of human affairs. Throughout that book, we are asked to reflect on what we would say when... But having been coaxed beyond the observation and correlation of external events and behavioural responses, we are asked not merely to relate such patterns of activity with patterns of language use, but also, and more fruitfully, to relate both external activity and use of language with the attitudes, dispositions, desires, interests, acceptances, presuppositions, and, indeed, the reasons, which we either have, or could understand having, in relation to such ways of acting and speaking. Patterns of behaviour and patterns of linguistic activity alike *display* patterns of reason(ing) and will(ingness); jurisprudence advances by going behind the display.

The present essay is a reflection on the implications of our willingness to further our understanding, to raise questions, to seek clarifications, and to make efforts to sharpen our perception. I do not take it for granted that the reader's desire is to further his understanding of law, coercion, or morality as social phenomena (though I digress, in sec. III, to tilt at a bad argument that has had some social success among lawyers). I assume no more than that the reader has sometime come across an assertion (or has himself entertained an idea) which he wished to dispute because it seemed disputable, to challenge because it seemed challengeable, to disagree with because it seemed to him foolish to agree.

My own reason for undertaking this reflection is my wish to dispute Hart's view that *knowledge* is more disputable and more debatable as an aspect of the good for man than *survival*.[1] By examining what is implied

---

* 1977a ('Scepticism, Self-Refutation, and the Good of Truth'), for a volume of essays in honour of H.L.A. Hart.
[1] *CL* 187 [citations use the first edition's pagination].

in any profound disagreement I wish to dispute Hart's assertion that 'men may profoundly disagree'[2] with the classical view that

> the specific human end or good is in part... a condition of biological maturity and developed physical powers, but... also includes... a development and excellence of mind manifested in thought and character.[3]

I do not wish to raise any objection about the course of argument on the relevant pages of *The Concept of Law* (pp. 186–8), pages which after all may be controlled by their author's desire to persuade hard-bitten lawyers and tough-minded social scientists to join him in seeing how far the *phenomena* of law and morality can be explained by reference to *at least* one, rather *minimal*, aim: survival. Nor do I wish merely to equivocate on a phrase such as 'men may profoundly disagree', which after all may have signified no more than that men violently or frequently disagree, or often act as if they disagreed. Nor will I speculate on the historical causes for the present situation of any philosophy or science of human affairs, in which the fact that values 'may be' (in some sense of 'may') 'and have been challenged' is explicitly or implicitly treated as methodologically controlling. Nor will I try to trace the ways in which that methodological decision controls the arguments and conclusions not only of a Hobbes (who first publicly rejected concern for any *summum bonum*)[4] but also of such apparently disparate enterprises as Hart's *The Concept of Law*, Rawls's *A Theory of Justice*, and Nozick's *Anarchy, State and Utopia*, and seriously obscures the purport of Fuller's *The Morality of Law*.

Rather, my concern is to contribute to a more exact understanding of a practical principle which Plato, Aristotle, and Aquinas regarded—rightly—as self-evident. What most sharply differentiates the classical from the modern philosophy of human affairs is that the one asserts while the other denies that truth (and knowledge of it) is as self-evidently and intrinsically good for man as life is. Not that I wish to defend any of the classical expositions of this principle and its self-evidence. Certainly I regard Aristotle's (apparent) view that truth is *more* self-evidently and fundamentally good than life[5] as more nearly correct than the modern view that knowledge is *less* self-evidently and fundamentally good than survival. But both views are wrong: self-evidently, both life and truth are intrinsically, underivatively, fundamentally good, and there is no priority, ranking, or hierarchy of the fundamental forms of human good.[†]

---

[2] *Ibid.*   [3] *Ibid.*, 186

[4] Hobbes, *The Elements of Law*, I c. 7 §6; c. 9 §21; c. 14 §6; c. 17 §14; II c. 9 §3; c. 10 §8; *Leviathan*, ch. XI (p. 49); ch. XLVI (pp. 366, 372).

[5] See *Eudemian Ethics* VII: 1244b23 ff.; cf. *NE* IX.9: 1170a26–b14. I leave aside the ambiguities in the notion of survival; they are underlined by Clark, *Aristotle's Man*, 19, 22, 172.

I consider (but cannot on this occasion argue) that life and truth are not the only fundamental aspects of human good. There are also such basic forms of good as may be summarily labelled play, aesthetic experience, friendship, practical reasonableness (including freedom and authenticity), and what may be with particular crudity labelled religion. In the usual senses of that modern and opaque word 'moral', not all of these are moral goods. They can best be described as the basic (underived) principles of practical reason. From them are derived (by an operation of practical reason which cannot be expounded here) conclusions which we would call moral principles, rules, obligations, counsels...

Aristotle had an explicit and definite account of the self-evidence and indemonstrability of fundamental principles,[6] but seems never to have applied it in working out an account of first principles of practical reason. As it happened, it was Thomas Aquinas who repaired the omission.[7] But his account of these principles, notwithstanding its clarity, has much more often than not been thoroughly misunderstood, by theologians in a hurry to claim for concrete moral rules the status of self-evidence, and by philosophers content to take it for granted that practical reason is just theoretical or speculative reason (misunderstood by them, moreover, as a kind of passive looking) supplemented by acts of will.[8] The present essay is a contribution to an investigation of the self-evidence and indemonstrability of fundamental practical principles. It relates to one particular practical principle, and it demonstrates that the principle can be defended against sceptical objections. But that demonstration is not to be understood as an attempt to demonstrate the principle itself.

The principle that truth (and knowledge of it) is a good objectively worthy of human pursuit cannot be demonstrated. But it stands in need of no demonstration and itself is presupposed, as we shall see, in all demonstrations whatsoever. It is self-evident. That does not mean that it is understood and accepted, even implicitly, by everyone. If it were understood and accepted by everyone, that fact would be neither ground for inferring the principle nor compelling evidence for its objectivity. Correspondingly, the fact that it is not universally accepted is neither a ground for denying it nor compelling evidence against its objectivity. Still, it is self-evident to anyone who has the experience and intelligence that are necessary to understand the terms in which it is formulated (though I am not implying that only those who formulate it act on it). To know that other people have valued knowledge for its own sake is relevant as a source of vicarious

---

[6] See *Posterior Analytics* B, 18: 99b16 et seq. [7] See *ST* I–II q.94 a.2; q.10 a.1; II–II q.47 a.6.
[8] For sound interpretation see Grisez, 'The First Principle of Practical Reason'.

experience, as a relevation or reminder of opportunities open to one. Taking it for granted that the reader has some knowledge of the opportunities for human knowing, the present essay eschews any attempt to evoke an understanding of those opportunities or their worth, and restricts itself to the negative role of refuting a form of sceptical doubt.

II

I shall use the terms 'retorsive argument' and 'argument from retorsion',[9] synonymously, to signify any argument which refutes a statement by showing that that statement[10] is self-refuting. That is a broad and rough characterization of the term, and will be refined by differentiating the types of self-refutation.

A first type of self-refutation is instanced by *propositions* which refute themselves either because they are directly self-contradictory or because they logically entail their contradictory.[11] Examples of this first type of self-refutation are such propositions as: 'I know that I know nothing'; 'It can be proved that nothing can be proved'; 'All propositions are false'. Slightly more subtle examples are: 'It is not the case that something is possible'; 'All propositions are true'. In the latter instances there is required some translation or logical manipulation and analysis before the self-refutation of the proposition is evident.[12] Nonetheless, the retorsive argument which makes the required translation or analysis should be clearly distinguished from all *ad hominem*[13] arguments which seek to show that one and the same speaker is here asserting that p and elsewhere asserting that not-p. There

---

[9] For want of any accepted English term I adopt this term from a continental usage. Isaye, 'La justification critique par rétorsion', introduces the topic as follows:

Nous appelons 'rétorsion' le procédé de discussion que saint Thomas nomme *redarguitio elenchica*. Il est essentiel à cette démarche d'être une *réponse*. Certaines objections sont ainsi faites que l'objectant, par le fait même de son objection, *in actu exercito*, concède la thèse qu'il voulait nier ou mettre en doute. Porter l'attention de l'objectant sur la concession qu'il vient de faire implicitement, c'est retourner l'objection en ma faveur, c'est rétorquer, c'est faire une rétorsion.

(Rétorquer: to retort, or to turn back.) [See also Moleski, 'Retortion'.]

[10] Throughout I adopt the following standard terminology (there are other standand usages, some of which are used by some of the authors cited): 'sentence' signifies a form of words, a grammatical entity, without reference to a particular utterance; 'statement' signifies an event in which a declarative or assertive sentence is uttered, an act of stating something, a kind of performance; 'proposition' signifies what is expressed by a sentence, e.g. what is stated by a statement.

[11] See Mackie, 'Self-Refutation—A Formal Analysis' at 195–6. I am following Mackie's taxonomy of types of self-refutation.

[12] For 'It is not the case that something is possible', see Mackie, op. cit., p. 195; for 'All propositions are true' see Aristotle, *Metaphysics*, IV.8: 1012b13; K 6.

[13] The term '*ad hominem* argument' is used very variously. A retorsive argument can be called '*ad hominem*', but only in a sense very different from arguments that point to inconsistency between different parts of a speaker's discourse, and *a fortiori* from arguments that undermine a speaker's assertions by demonstrating *his* unreliability, insincerity, etc.

is self-refutation of this first type only when one and the same proposition either is of the form 'both *p* and not-*p*', or is of the form '*p*' and logically entails 'not-*p*'.

A second type of self-refutation is instanced by statements whose occurrence happens to refute their content. I shall call this 'pragmatic self-refutation'.[14] An example of pragmatic self-refutation is afforded by someone singing 'I am not singing'. It might seem that pragmatic self-refutation is just a sort of trivial lie, of no philosophical interest. But the significance of pragmatic self-refutation is that it introduces us to the notion of performative inconsistency,[15] that is, inconsistency between what is asserted by a statement and facts that are given in and by the *making* of the statement.

The third type of self-refutation is instanced by propositions which cannot be coherently asserted, because they are inevitably falsified by *any* assertion of them. The proposition 'I am not singing' is not such a proposition, since it can be asserted, say, in writing. Similarly, the propositions 'Descartes cannot speak English' and 'Descartes does not exist' are not inevitably false, even though the first is pragmatically self-refuting when uttered by Descartes in English and, in that sense, cannot be coherently asserted by Descartes in English, while the second is pragmatically self-refuting when uttered by Descartes in any language or other mode of expression. But the proposition 'I do not exist' is inevitably falsified by *any* assertion of it: the sentence 'I do not exist', if uttered in a statement, inevitably states a false proposition. Equally incapable of being coherently asserted is the proposition 'No one can put words (or other symbols) together to form a sentence'. I shall call all propositions such as the last mentioned 'operationally self-refuting'.[16]

Operationally self-refuting propositions cannot be coherently asserted. But they are not, themselves, logically incoherent. Nor are they meaningless or empty, or *semantically* paradoxical. Examples of semantic emptiness or paradox are: 'This sentence is false', or the norm 'This norm may be repealed by a two-thirds majority' where 'this sentence' or 'this norm' in each case is not a colloquial reference to some other sentence or norm, but, rather is self-referential and fails to establish any definite reference.[17] Operationally self-refuting propositions have a quite definite reference and

---

[14] I follow Mackie's terminology, which has a more precise sense than the same phrase in, e.g. John Passmore, *Philosophical Reasoning*, ch. 4.

[15] For a useful review, see Boyle, 'Self-Referential Inconsistency, Inevitable Falsity and Metaphysical Argumentation', and works there cited.

[16] Following Mackie, 'Self-Refutation—A Formal Analysis' at 197.

[17] See Hart, 'Self-Referring Laws' at 174-5, 178; Ross, 'On Self-Reference and a Puzzle in Constitutional Law' at 7-17; Mackie, *Truth, Probability, and Paradox*, 242-7, 285-90.

hence can be (and inevitably are) false. Any such proposition is false because it is inconsistent with the facts that are given in and by any assertion of it. It itself is not self-refuting, but trying to assert it *is*.

A point similar to that made in the preceding sentences is made in more formally logical terms by J.L. Mackie. He prefers to say that any operationally self-refuting proposition either contradicts the proposition 'someone asserts that *p*' or else contradicts some proposition entailed by 'someone asserts that *p*'.[18] That is why the assertion of an operationally self-refuting proposition is said to be incoherent: one cannot coherently assert a self-contradiction; one who asserts a proposition *p* is implicitly committed to asserting, not merely whatever is entailed by *p*, but also any proposition entailed by 'someone asserts that *p*'; but where *p* is operationally self-refuting *p* contradicts one or more of those entailed propositions.

Hence the work to be done by a retorsive argument exploiting operational self-refutation consists in drawing out the 'implicit commitments' of the interlocutor, that is, the propositions entailed[19] by 'someone is asserting that...', that is, by the facts given in and by the interlocutor's statement. This is the most interesting and fruitful type of retorsive argument. Henceforward, references to self-refutation are (unless otherwise indicated) to operational self-refutation.

It is important to observe that, even where it is cast into logical form (as by J.L. Mackie, and as in sec. V of this essay), a retorsive argument from operational self-refutation achieves its effect by appealing to facts, which, of course, are not deduced by some logical operation but have to be recognized by the interlocutors in the ordinary 'empirical' ways. For '*p*' does not entail 'someone asserts that *p*'. Hence the peculiar force of a retorsive argument comes from the unavoidable *proximity* of the relevant facts. The self-refuting interlocutor is overlooking these facts, but is himself creating or instantiating them by and in his act of asserting (disputing). And here we may further observe that the interlocutor whom I refute retorsively may be either a person other than myself or, equally well, a voice of my own intelligence, a moment in that inner debate through which I pursue knowledge by raising questions, and supposing and rejecting or accepting hypotheses. So the self-refuting proposition may be expressed as an assertion, or as an argumentative hypothesis, or simply as an open question. One who asserts that *p* is implicitly committed to whatever is entailed by 'someone asserts that *p*'. One who considers *p* or asks whether *p* is not yet implicitly committed to asserting anything; but since he is

---

[18] Mackie, 'Self-Refutation—A Formal Analysis' at 196, 198.
[19] I follow Mackie's notion of entailment. One could also speak of implication: see Grant, 'Pragmatic Implication'.

considering whether or not he should assert p, he is implicitly committed to considering what would be entailed by 'someone asserts that p'. Moreover, most if not all that is entailed by 'someone asserts that p' is equally entailed by 'someone considers that p may be the case'.

What is entailed by 'someone asserts that p' very largely depends, of course, on what is meant by 'assert'. As Mackie's use of the notion of implicit commitment suggests, an assertion will be operationally self-refuting only if it is located in a universe of rational discourse and is (or is treated as) an authentic contribution to be assessed and judged at least primarily in terms of its correctness or rational justification and not (or not primarily) in terms of its utility as a conversation-filler, joke, ruse... nor for its euphony as a collection of vocables. As we shall see in sec. V of this essay, a retorsive argument when fully developed is in large part an analysis of the relevant sort of assertion, namely, that sort of assertion which would be *considerable* as a contribution to or solvent of some profound (but rational) disagreement about what is the case.

III

This section digresses, to illustrate a use of retorsive argument to expose self-refutation in a popular contention which, though legal, is not itself simply normative in form.

The contention may first be considered as it was expounded in Lord Birkenhead's defence of legislative 'sovereignty', that is, legislative freedom from the restraints of legal rules defining areas of legislative incapacity:

Some communities, and notably Great Britain, have not in framing constitutions felt it necessary, or thought it useful to shackle the complete independence of their successors. They have shrunk from the assumption that a degree of wisdom and foresight has been conceded to their generation which will be, or may be, wanting to their successors, in spite of the fact that those successors will possess more experience of the circumstances and necessities amid which their lives are lived.[20]

The polemical irony of the passage is a device for *expressing* (under the guise of reporting) *a claim to a degree of wisdom and foresight*, and for rhetorically asserting that claim against anybody who might doubt or deny that those who live at a given time will be as wise and far-seeing as the people of any other time and hence will know what it is best to do at and for their own time. But this claim of Lord Birkenhead's (unless it is a mere prediction that

[20] *McCawley v R* [1920] AC 691 at 703. This passage from the judgment of the Privy Council was much quoted in the great debate in the Indian Supreme Court about whether any parts of the Indian Constitution were immune from amendment: *Kesavananda v State of Kerala*, All India Reporter 1973 Supreme Court 1461 at 1592, 1835.

wisdom simply *will* not fail amongst certain peoples, a prediction always liable to be overturned by events) is significantly comparable with the implicitly but absolutely self-refuting claim that all claims are true. For it is certainly possible that amongst Lord Birkenhead's successors (call them S1) there might be some (perhaps the ruling class or party) holding and acting on the view that *their* successors (S2) were likely (for specifiable reasons, perhaps) to be unwise (perhaps generally, or perhaps just in relation to some specific question such as the question of the likely wisdom or unwisdom of their successors (S3)!). Is Lord Birkenhead committing himself to the contention that all his successors are going to be wise, even when they assert that some (or all) of their successors are going (or likely) to be unwise? If he is, he refutes himself, operationally as well as absolutely. For his contention (i) logically entails that his successors (S1) would be correct in thinking his contention incorrect and unwise, but (ii) implicitly commits him (by operational entailment) to the view that his contention is correct and wise.

What I am touching on here is, of course, what has often been called the paradox in the orthodox English view of parliamentary sovereignty. In Hart's conveniently precise rendering of it, that view stipulates that Parliament enjoys 'a *continuing* omnipotence in all matters not affecting the legislative competence of successive parliaments'.[21] Thus it rejects the alternative view 'that Parliament should *not* be incapable of limiting irrevocably the legislative competence of its successors'.[22] How would the orthodox view or doctrine be expressed or embodied in legal rules? For convenience (and without reference to Hart's distinction between primary and secondary rules), I describe as 'second-order rules' rules about the enactment of rules, and as 'first-order rules' rules about matters other than the enactment of rules. The second-order rule embodying the orthodox view of parliamentary sovereignty stipulates that the enactment of first-order rules is not restricted by reference to any subject-matter, and that the enactment of second-order rules *is* restricted by reference to subject-matter, namely, by the requirement that no second-order rule may (validly) be enacted which would contradict or limit the operation of the second-order rule embodying the orthodox view itself. Now this second-order rule is not itself self-contradictory or self-refuting. But any attempt to employ Lord Birkenhead's argument to support this rule (or the doctrine embodied by this rule) will fall into self-refutation. For those who attempt to defend the orthodox rule and doctrine by reference to *any* general principle (for example, Lord Birkenhead's principle about the temporal distribution of wisdom) are thereby implicitly committed to maintaining that they possess (in their principle) precisely 'a degree of wisdom and foresight' and that

---

[21] CL 146. (Hart is reporting the view, not supporting it.)   [22] *Ibid.*, 145.

this wisdom 'will be, or may be, wanting to their successors...' viz. to any successors who might wish to set aside the principle and the doctrine founded on it and (on the basis of 'the circumstances and necessities' amid which *their* lives will be lived) enact a second-order rule contradicting or limiting the operation of the second-order rule embodying the orthodox doctrine itself.

So my reason for making the present digression has been simply to point out that the oddity of the orthodox view lies deeper than the commonly identified verbal antinomies or semantic paradoxes about 'omnipotence', 'unrestricted' sovereignty, etc. Rather, the 'paradox' is the oddity—indeed, absurdity—of at time t_1 asserting (and acting on) the principle (*A*) that *all* decisions falling to be made at $t_2, t_3 \ldots t_n$ will be made more satisfactorily at $t_2, t_3 \ldots t_n$ than at t_1, while at t_1 also asserting (and acting on) the principle (*B*) that any decision at t_2 to restrict the range of decisions able to be made at $t_3 \ldots t_n$ would be a decision less satisfactory than the decision at t_1 to act upon principle *A*.

I am not claiming that the orthodox doctrine of parliamentary sovereignty inevitably involves the assertion of principle *A* as well as principle *B*. The doctrine might be defended as being, not a claim of principle, but simply a judgment, made at t_1 and contingently repeated at $t_2 \ldots$, that *now* is not the time (i.e. there is no good reason *now*) to restrict the competence of successor Parliaments. But this would be a very weak version of the doctrine, for it allows that in principle any moment might be a good time to adopt (or to authorize the adoption of) some restrictions on the competence of successor Parliaments.[23] And when anyone suggests that some such restrictions be adopted now, at t_1, the defender of the established doctrine is likely to fall back on some version of principle *A*, for example, Lord Birkenhead's.

IV

Retorsive arguments have been exploited against sceptics not only by Plato[24] and Aristotle,[25] the Stoics[26] and Augustine,[27] by Aquinas[28] (to a

---

[23] The doctrine might also be defended by drawing a sharp distinction between those who decide and act upon the doctrine (viz. the English establishment, officials or, if you prefer, 'the people') and the body whose powers of enactment the doctrine concerns (viz. Parliament). But then the 'paradox' reappears in the form, not of inconsistent (or at best arbitrary) attributions of wisdom and unwisdom as between a decision-maker and his successors, but of inconsistent (or at best arbitrary) attributions of wisdom and unwisdom as between one decision-maker (e.g. 'the people') and another (Parliament).

[24] *Theaetetus* 171.

[25] *Metaphysics* IV.4: 1005b35 et seq.; XI.4. See Aubenque, *Le Problème de l'être chez Aristote*, 124–6; Boyle, 'Self-Referential Inconsistency', 27.

[26] See the arguments assembled by Sextus Empiricus, *Pyrrhonean Hypotyposes* II. 185–6; *Adversus Mathematicos* VIII. 463.

[27] *De Civitate Dei* XI. 26; *De Libero Arbitrio* II. 3; *De Trinitate* X. 10, 16; XV. 12, 23; *Enchiridion* 20; *De Vera Religione* 39, 73; *Contra Academicos*, passim. Some of these texts are analysed by Matthews, 'Si Fallor, Sum', 151; he interprets them as (in our present terminology) retorsive.

[28] *De Veritate*, q.10 a.8 ad 2; a.12 ad 7; *ScG* II. 33. [And see pp. 89–90 below.]

much lesser extent), and perhaps by Descartes,[29] but also by latter-day philosophers as diverse as Lonergan[30] and Wittgenstein.[31] Can a retorsive argument be used against one who denies, not the objectivity of truth, identity, proof, meaning, or existence, but the objectivity of every value, every form of *good*?

There seem, in fact, to have been rather few attempts to develop retorsive argument in this direction. Augustine conjoined with his well-known 'Si fallor, sum' the further claim that one is secure from the arguments of the Academic sceptics, not only in respect of 'we are' and 'we know that we are', but also in respect of 'we love to be and to know that we are'—which, being translated out of Augustine's terminology of 'love', is to say: we are secure in affirming that our life is of value, and our knowledge of it likewise.[32] But he makes no attempt to work out any explicit argument for this.

Augustine had been profoundly affected by reading the now lost *Hortensius* of Cicero.[33] This work seems to have contained an argument in favour of philosophizing, along the lines that one who says that philosophizing is not worthwhile is himself philosophizing (since to argue about what is and is not worth doing is precisely to philosophize).[34] Now the *Hortensius* is assumed to have been based on Aristotle's also lost work, the *Protrepticus*, and certainly Aristotle's commentators between the second and sixth centuries AD constructed and, in many instances, attributed to the *Protrepticus* an argument of the form: (1) 'If we ought to philosophize then we ought to philosophize; and (2) if we say we ought not to philosophize then we ought to philosophize [in order to make out this assertion]; in any case, therefore, (3) we ought to philosophize'.[35] But a comparison of the various forms of this argument in the ancient sources reveals its obscurity. In particular, step (2) badly needs clarification, and, for want of clarification, is liable to be (and is) read in a non-normative sense. W.M. Kneale adopted this interpretation of step (2) when he said 'the most we can properly assert is "If *anyone says* there should be no philosophizing, then there must inevitably be some philosophizing, namely that which he

---

[29] See Mackie, 'Self-Refutation—A Formal Analysis' at 197–8, refining Passmore, *Philosophical Reasoning*, 60–4; Hintikka, '*Cogito, ergo sum*: Inference or Performance?'. Against this interpretation, see Kenny, *Descartes*, 42–8.

[30] Lonergan, *Insight*, ch. XI. [Cf. essay V. 9 at nn. 36–43.]

[31] Wittgenstein, *On Certainty*, paras.363, 459, 460; cf. also paras 506, 507, 514, and contrast para. 519. [Cf. pp. 131–7 below.]   [32] *De Civitate Dei* XI. 6.

[33] *Confessions* III. iv. 7; VIII. vii. 18; Brown, *Augustine of Hippo*, 40, 107.

[34] Lactantius, *Institutiones Divinae* III. 16 (Cicero, *Hortensius*, frag. 12 Müller; also in Ross, ed., *Aristotelis: Fragmenta Selecta*, 28).

[35] See the fragments from David and Elias in Ross, *The Works of Aristotle*, vol. xii, *Select Fragments*, 28. Kneale, 'Aristotle and the *Consequentia Mirabilis*', and Kneale, *The Development of Logic*, 97, accept that Aristotle is the author of this argument, but this view is vigorously rejected by Chroust, *Aristotle: Protrepticus: A Reconstruction*, 48–9.

has just begun"...'.[36] This reading deprives the argument of interest for anyone who, like us, is looking for retorsive support for a practical (that is, normative or at least evaluative) principle. For the following argument is quite obviously fallacious: (1) One who says philosophizing is worthwhile philosophizes; (2) one who says that philosophizing is not worthwhile philosophizes; therefore (3) philosophizing is worthwhile.

In recent times philosophers of such widely differing traditions as C.I. Lewis[37] and Gaston Isaye[38] have sketched retorsive arguments against scepticism about practical or normative or moral principles. But their presentations suffer from failure to distinguish between the different types of broadly retorsive argument, and from a too rapid assimilation of practical with moral principles. Hence there remains room for the present inquiry.

V

The retorsive argument which I wish to expound can be given the following rather extended formulation (among others):

For all p

(1) If I assert that p I am implicitly committed to 'I assert that p'.

(2) If I assert that p I am implicitly committed to anything entailed by 'I assert that p'.

(3) 'I assert that p' entails 'I believe that p [is true].'

(4) 'I assert that p' entails 'I believe that p is worth asserting'.

(5) 'I assert that p' entails 'I believe that p is worth asserting *qua* true'.

(6) 'I assert that p' entails 'I believe that truth is [a good] worth [pursuing or] knowing'.[39]

Therefore from (1)

(7) If I assert 'It is not the case that truth is [a good] worth [pursuing or] knowing' I am implicitly committed to 'I assert that it is not the case that truth is [a good] worth [pursuing or] knowing'.

And from (3) and (7)

(8) If I assert 'It is not the case that truth is [a good] worth [pursuing or] knowing' I am implicitly committed to 'I believe that it is not the case that truth is [a good] worth [pursuing or] knowing'.

But from (2) and (6)

---

[36] Kneale, 'Aristotle and the *Consequentia Mirabilis*'.

[37] Lewis, *Values and Imperatives*, esp. 64–74, 79–81, 123–5; cf. Carl Wellman, review, *Philosophical Review* 80 (1971), 398–9.

[38] Isaye, 'La justification critique par rétorsion' at 229–30 n. 9.

[39] The bracketed terms indicate alternative formulations (of which there are indeed many more. there need be and are no canonical formulations of first principles of reason).

(9) If I assert 'It is not the case that truth is [a good] worth [pursuing or] knowing' I am implicitly committed to 'I believe that truth is [a good] worth [pursuing or] knowing'.

So, from (8) and (9)

(10) If I assert 'It is not the case that truth is [a good] worth [pursuing or] knowing' I am implicitly committed *both* to 'I believe that truth is a good worth pursuing or knowing' *and* to 'I believe that it is not the case that truth is a good worth pursuing or knowing'.

Thus, if I assert that truth is not a good, I am implicitly committed to formally contradictory beliefs.

The argument (as I shall henceforth call it) indicates that I could never coherently deny that truth is a good. But if p seems to be the case (whether as self-evident or as warranted by evidence or reasons) *and* could never coherently be denied, p can reasonably be affirmed to be objectively the case.[40] Indeed, the argument can and should be read as if the term 'objectively' preceded each instance of the terms 'good' and 'worth'. (I return to this matter of objectivity later in the argumentation.)

Steps (1) to (6) of the argument elaborate the sense and force of 'assertion', as that term is employed here. So I explain them in turn.

Steps (1) and (2) may be taken together. As I remarked at the end of sec. II of this essay, to assert that p is not merely to utter 'p' (which might be by way of an elocution lesson, microphone testing, quotation, recitation, word-game or guessing-game...). One's utterance does not amount to asserting that p unless it implicitly commits one to denying that not-p, and to affirming whatever is entailed by p, and to denying whatever else would entail not-p. To say this is not only to draw attention to an obvious feature of the word 'assertion' and its cognates in ordinary philosophical usage; it also is to express one of the elementary conditions of rational thought and discourse: that it be coherent. Now 'X asserts that p' is, of course, *not* entailed by p. So step (1) is a substantive step. It states that if someone says that p, he is not to be counted as asserting that p unless he has at least the (rather minimal degree of) self-consciousness sufficient to recognize that it is also true that he is asserting that p is true. Without that degree of self-consciousness, connected rational thought is impossible and argumentative discourse not worth bothering about. This point does not need labouring. Step (2) is entailed by step (1), given the definitional relation (stated earlier in this paragraph) between asserting

---

[40] This is sometimes denied: e.g. Norman Malcolm, 'The Conceivability of Mechanism' at 71: 'The inconceivability of mechanism, in the two respects we have elucidated, does not establish that mechanism is false.' But there seem to be no good reasons for this denial: see Boyle, Grisez, and Tollefsen, 'Determinism, Freedom, and Self-Referential Arguments' at 34–5.

that p and implicit commitment to whatever is entailed by p. For 'I assert that p' is an instance of 'p'.

Step (3) states the generally accepted results of the intensive philosophical analysis (initiated by G.E. Moore) of assertions of the form 'p, but I don't believe that p'.[41] The reason why the present retorsive argument is not cast in the third person is that step (3) cannot be transposed directly into the third person. For 'X asserts that p' does not entail 'X believes that p', since X may be lying. (In discussing step (1) we have already excluded the possibility that X is merely reciting, joking, etc.) Of course, this possibility that X is insincere could be accommodated in a somewhat expanded (third-person) version of steps (3) and (8), yielding the conclusion that if X asserts that truth is not a good, he is either implicitly committed to contradictory beliefs (as in (10)) or is a liar. Such an expanded version would, I think, be equally serviceable as a retorsive argument.[42]

Steps (4) and (5) are indented because they are introduced into the argument only in order to prepare for step (6); together these three steps carry the whole argument out of the ordinary run of retorsive exposés of operational self-refutation, by stating an *evaluative* implication of assertion. Step (4) itself is, however, hardly controversial as it stands, prior to any analysis of the term 'worth'. For if 'I assert that p but I don't believe p' is an absurd, pointless, and (in *some* senses of 'self-contradictory') self-contradictory remark (unless it is to be taken in some non-straightforward sense), so equally is 'I assert that p but I don't believe that p is worth asserting'. Remember: 'asserting' is here not restricted to external utterances, but includes also, and even primarily, the internal operations of judgment, affirmation, assent, and the like.

Step (5) advances the analysis of the evaluative implications of assertion. It states that my thinking or saying that p does not count as an assertion of p unless I am thinking or saying that p (rather than either

---

[41] See Moore, 'Russell's Theory of Descriptions' at 203–4; MacDonald, *Philosophy and Analysis*, ch. IV; Grant, 'Pragmatic Implication' at 312–22; Mackie, 'Self-Refutation—A Formal Analysis' at 196.

[42] The possibility of lies, deceptions, and insincerities calls for more detailed attention than I can give it here. Gandhi, *Presuppositions of Human Communication*, argues 'that no account of assertion which was not also an account of *insincere* assertion could be regarded as satisfactory' (p. 15). But then, his book, unlike this essay, 'is very largely an attempt to understand the action of "telling" somebody something' (p. 141), and treats the role of a thinker as 'parasitic upon the roles of speaker and audience' (p. 140 n. 1). But his analysis has its value in indicating (as against H.P. Grice, and by way of subtle attention to the possibilities of deceit) that for a speaker (S) to assert to an audience (A) that p, is for S to perform communicatively an act which *both* (i) implies, prima facie, that S wants A to believe that p (or that S believes that p), but *also* (ii) does *not* imply, prima facie, that S is trying to get A to believe that p (since, if this second requirement is not met, S's action carries a prima facie implication of deceitfulness). As Gandhi argues, to understand assertion (in his wide sense) is to understand how these two apparently contradictory requirements are not really contradictory (pp. 141–2; 15–24).

(i) not thinking or saying that *p*, or (ii) thinking or saying that not-*p*) because *p* (so it seems to me) is true, that is, is correct, is-the-case.[43] For '*p* [is true] but [in asserting this] I don't care whether *p* is true or not' is absurd, pointless, and (in a sense) self-contradictory (except in some special sense or context). If readers have misgivings about this last point, they will at least grant that '*p*, but I don't care whether *p* is true or not' deprives the speaker's assertion that *p* of any claim to be regarded as a 'profound disagreement' with any assertion that not-*p*; it disqualifies the speaker from participation in any serious discussion of the question whether *p* or not-*p*.

Step (6) is the crucial step. Its meaning is quite ordinary and straightforward, and is standardly expressed when one exclaims 'good!' on successfully concluding an investigation. But because philosophical debate about these matters has a history that is not straightforward it is necessary to bracket out misunderstandings, as follows:

(i) 'truth is worth knowing' is to be understood as meaning that truth is a good to be pursued, and is good to attain in one's judgments; and ignorance and error are to be avoided.

(ii) 'truth is worth knowing' is not to be understood either as having a moral sense or implication or as incompatible with a moral sense, force, or implication. Similarly, in (i), 'truth is a good' is not to be understood as a moral proposition; and 'truth is to be pursued' is not to be understood as stating a moral obligation, requirement, prescription, or recommendation.

(iii) 'truth is worth knowing' is not to be understood as stating that knowledge is the only thing worth pursuing or having, i.e. is the only good; nor is it to be understood as stating that knowledge is to be pursued under all circumstances, or at all times.

(iv) 'truth is worth knowing' is not to be understood as claiming that knowledge is the supreme good, or that knowledge is to be pursued at all costs.

(v) 'truth is worth knowing' is not to be understood as claiming that every true proposition is equally worth knowing or that every subject-matter is equally worth investigating.

---

[43] Commenting on perhaps the earliest known instance of retorsive argument (Plato, *Theaetetus* 170a–171c), McDowell remarks:

> If all that Protagoras can say to us is '(P) is true *for me*; it may not be true *for you*', we are justified in wondering why we should find what he says interesting. It seemed to be interesting originally because he seemed to be asserting the truth *simpliciter*, not just the truth for himself, of (P). (McDowell, ed., *Plato: Theaetetus*, 171.)

(vi) 'truth is worth knowing' is to be understood as affirming that truth is an *intrinsic* good, in that

    (a) the correct answer to the question 'Is it the case that *p*, or is it the case that not-*p*?' is sought at least partly for its correctness as an answer, and not exclusively under some such description as 'whatever will satisfy my audience, whether or not they care for correctness or can distinguish correctness from error' or 'whatever answer first gives me satisfaction' or 'whatever position contributes to my survival'; and

    (b) *p* is considered worth asserting *qua* true, and is not merely the object of an *urge* to assert *p* for some reason other than that *p* is the case; the process of gathering data, raising hypotheses and testing them, and judging that there is sufficient evidence or argument to warrant affirming *p*, will be a rational process only if the man who is going through it remains open to the possibility that what in the end should be asserted is, not *p*, but not-*p*; furthermore, he must be willing to consider the truth or otherwise of any propositions *q*, *r*, *s*... that bear on the correctness of *p* or not-*p*, and in turn on the truth of *q*, *r*, *s*...

What has been said in (vi)(b) indicates a sense in which truth is a *general* form of good: truth is, so to speak, participated in by *all* correct propositions, judgments, and assertions, but is not exhaustively realized in (nor to be identified with) any of them.[44] But what is said in (vi)(b) also indicates why and in what sense the whole argument holds for all *p*, notwithstanding that we have countless casual beliefs (and thus make countless casual assertions) which we (casually) believe to be true but about whose truth we don't really care (except, perhaps, for some instrumental reason; consider, for example, the coffee-drinker's belief that coffee is cheap in the supermarket today). What determines whether *p* is or is not seriously asserted is not the content of *p*, but the dispositions and interests of particular persons. Provided we remember what was said in (v) above, we can say that there are no 'fields' in which truth in judgment is not a good. To say that truth is a good is to say that for any *p* it is better to believe (assert) *p* where *p* is true than to believe (assert) *p* where *p* is false, and than to disbelieve (deny) *p* where *p* is true.

---

[44] It is tempting to add to the analysis of 'assertion' completed in step (6) one further element, viz.: I assert *p* only if I consider truth (and knowledge of it) to be good not just for me but for any person (subject to the provisos in (iii) and (iv) above). For otherwise my asserting *p* would not be a real participation in truth-seeking discourse or debate with others. But it is probably clearer to handle this requirement in the way I have proposed handling the requirement of sincerity in relation to step (3), viz. as a distinct element in a third-person version of steps (6) and (9).

With these clarifications of its meaning, step (6) is, I believe, self-evidently true. The clarified meaning of step (6) has been fixed by reflecting on the conditions under which *assertions* are worth making, worth testing, worth evaluating as true or false (rather than as popular or satisfying), worth profoundly disagreeing with... This reflection makes it quite clear that truth is a good, that ignorance and error are to be avoided, that to attain to the truth is *pro tanto* to be well off while to remain in ignorance and error is *pro tanto* to be badly off, and that to lose one's desire for truth would be a bad thing. But at the same time, the reflection makes it clear that in seriously asserting that truth is a good (in the clarified sense), one is neither merely reporting nor merely expressing a desire one happens to have nor is one making a moral claim; nor is one reporting or relying on a universal or even a common belief of others. Still, the self-evidence of the proposition that truth is a good is no more queer or suspect than the self-evidence of, say, steps (1) or (3), or than the self-evidence of logical operations such as those which generate, say, step (8) from steps (3) and (7).

Once the meaning and force of step (6) are established by reflection on one's performance as a questioner and knower, there remains only the question whether the belief expressed in steps (6) and (9) (viz. 'truth is [a good] worth [pursuing and] knowing') is genuinely inconsistent with the sceptical belief expressed within steps (7) and (10) (viz. 'it is not the case that truth is a good worth pursuing or knowing'). For someone might exploit a distinction between 'factual' and 'evaluative' utterances to argue that the former belief is 'evaluative' while the latter (sceptical) belief is 'factual', so that the contradiction appearing in step (10) is only apparent.[45]

But in evaluating both the retorsive argument as a whole and the counter-argument just mentioned, it is important to bear in mind that the relevant question is not how to apply the problematic philosophical labels 'factual' and 'evaluative'. It is whether the belief expressed within step (6) is genuinely inconsistent with the sceptical denial within step (7). I have explained the meaning and force of the belief within step (6). So, if someone argues that there is no genuine inconsistency, he must show that the denial in step (7) has some other meaning. If he says that what is denied in step (7) is that truth is *objectively* a good, I reply that, in my understanding, what is

---

[45] A more extreme version of this move would be the claim that 'believe' is a term confined to factual assertions (so that the expressions of 'belief' in steps (4), (5), and (6) are ill-formed, and, where 'I assert that p' is evaluative, step (3) does not hold). But this claim involves a drastic stipulative restriction of ordinary usage, a restriction which could be justified only as a device for signalling the importance of the distinction which, in the less extreme version of the move, is alleged between evaluative and factual utterances. The same is true of a further version of the move, in which it might be claimed that the retorsive argument is ill-formed and unsound because 'assert' is confined to factual as opposed to evaluative assertions.

asserted in step (6) means that truth is objectively a good, as I understand 'objectively'. A judgment or belief is objective if it is correct; a proposition is objective if one is warranted in asserting it, whether because there is sufficient evidence, or because there are compelling grounds, or because (to one who has the experience and intelligence to understand the terms in which the proposition is expressed) it is obvious or self-evident that in asserting it one asserts what is the case.

Now the belief or judgment or assertion, in step (6), about the good of truth, can be described as 'evaluative' (or in classical terminology 'practical') while the sceptic's denial in step (7) may be intended to be 'factual' (or in classical terminology 'speculative'). I am quite content (as were Aristotle and Aquinas) to stress the difference between 'factual' and 'evaluative' judgments, and to affirm that the latter are not derived by inference from the former and are *sui generis*. But I see no reason to admit that evaluative judgments cannot state, in their own way, what they seem to state, viz. what is objectively the case (about the good of human beings, their opportunities, and their actions).[46] The *differences* between 'factual' judgments, such as 'this book is blue' or 'iron melts at 1535°C' and 'evaluative' judgments, such as 'truth is a good', do not warrant the conclusion that only the former class of judgments can be objective—any more than that conclusion would be warranted by the different but equally considerable differences between the aforementioned type of factual judgments and 'philosophical' ('second-order factual'?) judgments, such as the judgment expressed in the present sentence (or its contradictory).

Suppose someone objects that this all goes to show that I am assuming, in relating step (6) to step (7), that it is possible to have a coherent belief which is at once evaluative and factual (in the sense, now, of 'factual' corresponding to 'it is the case that', 'it is true that' and 'objective'), and that this assumption is both gratuitous and a *petitio principii* against the sceptic. I make two replies. First: my interpretation of step (6) is not gratuitous, but sets out a sober and straightforward analysis of what is involved in the rational activity of asserting that *p*; if this analysis turns out to be inconsistent with a philosophical thesis about the non-'factual' character of evaluative judgments, that is reason for denying or restricting the thesis (which characteristically was worked out in relation to moral exhortations and resolutions, and never adequately tested in relation to pre-moral 'evaluative' judgments such as that expressed within step (6)). Second: my interpretation of step (6) as both evaluative and objective does

---

[46] The logic of ascribing truth and objectivity to (some) value judgments has been well worked out by Kalinowski, *Le Problème de la verité en morale et en droit*, ch. IV.

not beg the question; the meaning of the proposition which the present retorsive argument defends is established not by the sceptic but by ourselves when we assert (as self-evident) what the sceptic *then* denies, viz. that (it is the case that) truth is a good worth pursuing. By showing only that that assertion straddles his distinction between the evaluative and the factual, the sceptic does not succeed in raising an objection.

Suppose, finally, the sceptic (a) grants that the belief expressed within step (6) not only expresses an evaluation which (*qua* evaluative) he does not contest but also, in *my* sense, is objective and states what is the case, but (b) says that his denial within step (7) is restricted to *his* sense of 'objective', 'factual', 'what is the case', etc. Then his denial can safely be ignored. For what he is denying now is not what was classically asserted about the good of truth. Indeed, his denial is now itself thoroughly obscure. What *does* he mean by 'objective', 'factual', 'what is the case', etc.? Usually, his meaning is indicated by the arguments he uses to defend his sceptical objections, viz. arguments from the diversity of moral beliefs, and from the impossibility of inferring evaluative from non-evaluative propositions. But those arguments simply do not apply to the belief expressed within step (6), as I have explained that belief.

Anyone, sceptic or not, who reflects on the whole argument and accompanying argumentation in this section might reasonably ask whether the retorsive argument set out in ten steps adds anything to what is asserted, without much argument, in step (6) and in the explanation of step (6). Well, any retorsive argument has its efficacy by testing the sceptic's objection against the facts (including implicit commitments to recognition and pursuit of values) that are provided in and by the sceptic's own performance as an objector. If the sceptic will not assent to the retorsive analysis of his own performance, he must be challenged to produce a more satisfactory analysis of his own performance as an objector (and, now, as an analyst of objections, too). The analysis will be satisfactory only if it shows that his objection is worth bothering about. And it will show this only if it departs from at least the most basic and radical sceptical tenets. The utility of retorsive argument is that it demonstrates that the sceptic is *bound* to produce this more satisfactory analysis (here, as an alternative to step (6)) if he is not to be involved in formal self-contradiction.

VI

Though one can toy with the notion that truth (and knowledge) is not a good worth pursuing, the retorsive argument should persuade the sceptic to cut short idle doubting. For the argument shows the irrationality of supposing that the doubt could ever mature into a correct affirmation that truth (and knowledge) is not an intrinsic good. The sceptic can always maintain coherence by *asserting* nothing (and so the ancient sceptics commended the *epochē* or suspension of judgment).[47] But the price of this is that he does not maintain a *position*, that is, any part in rational discourse or in a 'profound disagreement'. Coherence is not the only requirement of rationality (animals never fall into self-contradiction). Is there, then, any reason to make the effort which is required to maintain a complete suspension of judgment, a complete abstinence from affirmation and denial? (Mere idleness will hardly suffice!) Is not the sceptic's reason for this effort his strong (though misdirected) grasp of the value of truth (as we explained it in relation to step (6))? Is not his effort his tribute to the stringent and authoritative demands of a form of good which he sees corrupted by the conventionality, hastiness, prejudice, muddle, wishful thinking, and partisanship of dogmatists (including dogmatists who offer to defend the objective value of truth)?

And so, if someone were to claim that truth has its value, not for its own sake, but only instrumentally, as a means of survival, we should make a threefold reply. First, it is true that truth has instrumental as well as intrinsic value. Secondly, it is true (as martyrs who value truth for its own sake have always been aware) that there are occasions when treating or regarding truth as merely instrumentally good has survival value. But, thirdly, it would be incoherent (but also mistaken) to make the claim, or even tacitly to assume its validity, as part of one's commitment and contribution to scientific objectivity or philosophical reasonableness.

NOTE

Essay 8, from 1975, is an earlier exploration of this essay's main theme, in the light of Wittgenstein's *On Certainty*, together with an early attempt to deploy the general ethical theory better worked out in *NLNR* and, with ongoing further refinements, in *FoE*, *NDMR*, and *Aquinas*. Essay 4 revisits self-refutation more formally, and responds to some of the responses to the present essay.

† *'No hierarchy of basic goods'*...(p. 63). Better: none of the basic human goods is 'unqualifiedly commensurable as more or less valuable than the others' (p. 244 below). There are a number of hierarchies among them—e.g. life is a kind of presupposition of the others, and practical reasonableness presides over the realization of all of them—but no single hierarchy of value.

---

[47] Sextus Empiricus, *Pyrrhonean Hypotyposes* I, 8. But of course Sextus Empiricus goes on, and on, making judgments...

4

SELF-REFUTATION REVISITED*

If I am asked, or—more to the point—if I ask myself, what is the most strategic advice one might give to someone beginning philosophy, or what is the most important reason to be interested in the philosophical positions shared by Plato, Aristotle, Aquinas, and anyone who treats or has treated these philosophers as living masters, my shortest answer is: be sure that all the arguments you propose and defend are consistent with the fact that you are doing so, and with the fact that you judged it good to seek them out, test them, accept them, and therefore good to assert them or propose them for assent. For many, perhaps most, of the positions you will encounter, though widely accepted and of good repute among philosophers, refute themselves by their inconsistency with the fact that they are seriously proposed as worthy of acceptance by reason of their truth.

I

The senior philosopher at University College Oxford in the 1970s was a fellow-Australian, John Mackie, whose philosophical stance of common sense inflected by Lockean and Humean empiricism you can see depicted by our then colleague at the college—but since those days at Pittsburgh—John McDowell, in the *Oxford Dictionary of National Biography*. Mackie had earlier published a helpful and fairly sound formal taxonomy of types of self-refutation.[1] There are propositions that refute themselves because they are self-contradictory, or because they entail their contradictory: 'I know that I know nothing'; 'It can be proved that nothing is provable'; 'All propositions are false'; 'It is not the case that something is possible'; 'All propositions are true'. Then there are statements which are pragmatically self-refuting because their occurrence—the uttering of a declarative

---

* 2005b ('Self-Referential (or Performative) Inconsistency: Its Significance for Truth').
[1] Mackie, 'Self-Refutation—A Formal Analysis'.

or assertive sentence—*happens* to refute their content, as singing the assertion 'I am not singing' falsifies the assertion. Such merely pragmatic self-refutation is a more or less trivial kind of performative inconsistency— that is, inconsistency between what is asserted by a statement and facts that are given in and by the making of the statement. Much the more interesting kind of performative inconsistency is instantiated in the set of propositions that are self-refuting in that they *cannot* be coherently asserted because they are *inevitably* falsified by any assertion of them: for example 'I do not exist'; 'No one can put words (or other symbols) together to form a sentence'.

Performatively (or operationally) inconsistent, self-refuting propositions of this last kind are not logically incoherent, or meaningless, or empty, or *semantically* paradoxical like 'this sentence is false' or a statute consisting of nothing but one clause: 'This statute may be repealed by a two-thirds majority'. No, performatively self-refuting propositions have a quite definite reference, and hence can be (and inevitably are) false, because inconsistent with the facts that are given in and by any assertion of them. They are not in themselves self-refuting, but to try to assert any of them *is*.

Wanting to model the account of performatively or operationally self-refuting propositions as closely as possible on a logic template, Mackie preferred to say that any such proposition either contradicts the proposition 'someone asserts that p', or else contradicts some proposition entailed by that proposition. Such propositions, on this account, are incoherent in that one cannot coherently assert a self-contradiction, and anyone who asserts a proposition p is implicitly committed to asserting not only whatever is entailed by p, but also any proposition entailed by 'someone asserts that p'. On this account, the work to be done by an argument from self-referential inconsistency consists in bringing to light performative inconsistency by drawing out the 'implicit commitments' of the interlocutor. Or one can skip the machinery of implicit commitments, and the quest for *logical* incoherence or self-contradiction, and say instead that the work to be done consists in bringing to light the propositions entailed by 'someone is asserting that...', that is, the facts given in and by the interlocutor's statement. For even when it is cast into logical form, an argument from self-referential inconsistency achieves its effect by appealing to facts, which have to be recognized by the interlocutor(s) not by some purely logical operation but in the ordinary 'empirical' ways. For p does not entail 'someone asserts that p'. So the peculiar force of arguments from self-referential inconsistency comes from the unavoidable *proximity* of the relevant facts. Self-refuting interlocutors overlook those facts, but are themselves creating or instantiating them in and by their acts of asserting (disputing).

The interlocutor whose assertion I refute by pointing to the self-referential inconsistency of asserting it may be either a person other than myself or, equally well, a voice of my own intelligence, a moment in that inner debate through which I pursue understanding and knowledge by raising questions—putting them to myself—and supposing and rejecting or accepting hypotheses. So the performatively self-refuting proposition may be expressed as an assertion, or as an argumentative hypothesis, or simply as an (apparently) open question. In considering *p* or asking whether *p*, one is not yet implicitly committed to asserting *p* (or, for that matter, to asserting not-*p*), but since one is considering whether or not one should assert *p*, one *is* implicitly committed to considering what would be entailed by 'someone asserts that *p*'. Moreover, most if not all that is entailed by 'someone asserts that *p*' is equally entailed by 'someone considers that *p* may be the case'.

What is entailed by 'someone asserts that *p*' very largely depends, of course, on what is meant by 'assert'. As the talk of implicit commitment suggests, an assertion will be performatively inconsistent only if it is located in a universe of rational discourse and is (or is treated as) an authentic contribution to such discourse, to be assessed and judged at least primarily in terms of its correctness or rational justification and not (or not primarily) in terms of its utility as a conversation-filler, joke, or ruse, nor for its euphony as a collection of vocables. Arguments from self-referential inconsistency, when developed, turn in large measure on their success as accounts of the relevant sort of assertion, namely, the sort of assertion that would be *considerable* as a contribution to, or solvent of, some significant rational disagreement—or inner debate—about what is the case.

II

Central to the philosophical method of Plato's Socrates is the bringing to light of the interlocutor's inconsistency. Now showing an interlocutor's inconsistency does not entail the falsity of either of the inconsistent positions he proposes or has been brought to admit; it entails only that some one of them is false. But sometimes, as in the *Theaetetus*, what is shown is the kind of conclusion called by Socrates 'really exquisite' (171a): that the *proposition* asserted by the (imaginary) interlocutor (Protagoras) is self-refuting. This self-refutation is of the first type in Mackie's taxonomy, not, I think, true performative inconsistency: Protagoras's thesis about man being the measure amounts (as Socrates holds) to the thesis that every proposition asserted is true, which entails that every assertion of that thesis's falsity is correct. This demonstration seems formally to be a *reductio ad absurdum*—If it is the case that (If *p*, then not-*p*), then not-*p*. It is therefore very proximate to that complement to *reductio ad absurdum* which is known as the *consequentia mirabilis*: If it is the case that (If not-*p*, then *p*), then *p*. But as Plato has it, the demonstration that

If *p*, then not-*p*

seems to depend on the contingent fact that someone asserts that not-*p*. The difficulty can be circumvented, however, by noticing that interlocutors (who may or may not make assertions) can be replaced by the inner debate of considering whether *p* is true by reflecting that if it were true then not-*p* would be true: *reductio ad absurdum*.[2]

True and paradigmatic performative inconsistency is instantiated, as Aristotle's *Metaphysics* 4.4 shows, by the radical sceptic about contradiction, and the strategy of confuting more or less radical sceptics by showing their ineluctable self-referential inconsistency is carried forward by the Stoics, and then Augustine, who conjoined with his 'Si fallor, sum' (If I err, I exist) the further claim that we are secure from the arguments of the sceptics not only in respect of 'We exist' and 'We know that we exist', but also in respect of 'We love to exist and to know that we exist'. This further claim amounts to saying that we are secure in affirming that our life is itself of value, and our knowledge of it likewise. But Augustine makes no attempt to work out any explicit argument for this, and subsequent philosophical exploitations of arguments from self-referential inconsistency, such as those of Descartes (perhaps), Lonergan, Wittgenstein, and Grisez, did not attempt to put the strategy to use in relation to radical scepticism about value. Some such attempts were made in the mid-twentieth century by C.I. Lewis and Gaston Isaye, but each of these very different thinkers failed, I think, to distinguish between the different types of argument from self-refutation, and assimilated practical with moral principles much too quickly. So in the mid-1970s, encouraged by Joseph Boyle's careful exploration of 'Self-Referential Inconsistency, Inevitable Falsity and Metaphysical Argumentation', by the powerful application of the strategy by him, Grisez, and Tollefsen to determinism's denial(s) that there are any free choices,[3] and by the resolute, convincing and resourceful applications of the strategy in Grisez's book on the existence and nature of God,[4] I outlined and defended an argument that

---

[2] On the relation between *reductio ad absurdum* and *consequentia mirabilis*, see Nuchelmans, 'A 17th-Century Debate on the *Consequentia Mirabilis*' at 43, 57.

[3] Boyle, Grisez, and Tollefsen, *Free Choice: A Self-Referential Argument*, 122–38.

[4] Grisez, *Beyond the New Theism*, 111–13, 133–4, 172–80, 349–53.

it cannot be coherently denied that truth is a (not merely instrumental) good. A heavily abbreviated summary of the argument went like this:

> The sceptical assertion that knowledge is not a good is operationally [performatively] self-refuting. For if one makes such an assertion, intending it as a serious contribution to rational discussion, one is implicitly committed to the proposition that one believes one's assertion is worth making, and worth making *qua* true; one thus is committed to the proposition that one believes that truth is a good worth pursuing or knowing. But the sense of one's original assertion was precisely that truth is not a good worth pursuing or knowing. Thus one is implicitly committed to formally contradictory beliefs.[5]

But this Mackiean driving of the argument to a showing of formal self-contradiction rather veils its core, which is the bringing to light of what is entailed by one's *asserting* that *p*, namely that one is asserting also that one accepts (believes) that *p* is true (is correct, is the case). For '*p* but [in asserting this] I don't care whether *p* is true or not' is absurd, pointless, and (in a sense) self-contradictory (except in some special sense or context), or at least disqualifies one from treating one's assertion—or rather, 'assertion'—as a contribution to serious discussion of, or reflection upon, whether *p* or not-*p*.[6] It is of course possible to *suppose* that *p*, 'for the sake of argument', in order to explore its implications. But even such explorations, with their limited aims, are likely to miscarry unless those carrying them out are trying to reach a judgment, if not about the truth of *p*, then at least the truth of some other proposition epistemically related to *p*. And the willingness to leave the truth of *p* undecided, from the outset right through to the close of the discussion, entails that what is supposed or said about *p* will remain *unasserted*, even if various logical relations are asserted during the exploration.[7] In the domain of interpersonal discourse, it remains possible, of course, that the assertion that *p*, and the entailed assertion(s) that one believes *p* to be worthy of belief (and therefore fit to be asserted) *qua* true, are each lies. But a lie, too, makes no contribution

---

[5] *NLNR* 74–5 (recast in impersonal first-person syntax).

[6] Alexy, *The Argument from Injustice*, 38–9, argues that there is 'performative contradiction and, in this sense, a conceptual defect' in a judicial sentencing order pronounced in the following form: 'The accused is [hereby] sentenced to life imprisonment, which is an incorrect interpretation of prevailing law.' His thesis presupposes that the judge's authority is exhaustively describable as 'to apply the prevailing law interpreted correctly in accordance with legal norms of interpretation'.

[7] Kramer, 'What Good is Truth?' in his *In the Realm of Moral and Legal Philosophy*, 11–25 at 13, is mistaken in saying that, even if one has a 'lack of interest in the truth' about *p*, one nonetheless 'can assert a thesis quite honestly and accept whatever it entails, while defending it in order to grasp its implications...rather than to decide its truth' and equally mistaken in saying that this could amount to a 'serious discussion of [or earnest debate about] the question whether *p* or not-*p*'.

to serious discussion or reflection, no claim on anyone's attention to what it (purportedly)[8] asserts.

Matthew Kramer has tried to refute the argument from self-referential inconsistency to the intrinsic good of truth. He contends first that, for all the argument shows, truth could be merely instrumentally good, and even the sceptics' denial of truth's inherent goodness could avoid self-refutation by 'declaring *itself* to be valuable in an only instrumental way, the sceptical assertions themselves 'commend[ing] their own truth by having characterized themselves and their truth as [only] *instrumentally* good'.[9] This contention fails, since such declarations and self-characterizations of mere instrumentality are to no avail unless some end is identified to which *truth* is supposed to be instrumental (while falsehood, muddle, and ignorance are not), and Kramer's only gesture toward identifying such an end—'sav[ing] people from wasting time and effort on truths devoid of instrumental utility'—will not do: if truth is intrinsically good and knowledge of it intrinsically valuable, then there may be truths the knowledge of which it is no waste of time or effort to acquire even if they, and knowledge of them, are 'devoid of instrumental utility'. It makes good sense to regard ignorance or confusion about important and interesting matters as bad in itself, and the contrary as intrinsically good. Indeed, in view of the inter-connectedness of truths, it cannot be reasonable to suppose that there is any truth the knowledge of which we can *know* will never have any further value either for contemplation *as* true, or for some other end. For both these reasons, no one inquiring into the truth or falsity of scepticism about truth's value has reason to assume in advance that discovering and contemplating truths devoid of instrumental value would be a waste. As Kramer admits, a pure instrumentalism about truth 'may well be misguided and...profoundly riven by paradoxes'.

Kramer's second contention is that it was a non sequitur to conclude from (A): '"I assert that *p*" entails "I believe that *p* is worth asserting *qua* true"' to (B): '"I assert that *p*" entails "I believe that truth is a good worth pursuing or knowing"'. The value of the truth of one's statements may well consist only, says Kramer, in the value of 'the statements themselves'; and though one *may* perceive the value of truth-in-general, one's acknowledging the value of one's true statements does not 'logically bind' one to acknowledge the value of truth-in-general. This contention, too, misunderstands the argument, which does not attempt to deduce (B) from (A), and instead, as I formulated it, proposes (B) as a proposition which,

---

[8] Liars make an outward assertion that does not correspond to an inner assertion, that is, to any corresponding judgment. The judgment that *p* constitutes an inner assertion that *p*.

[9] Kramer, *In the Realm of Moral and Legal Philosophy*, 15.

when its meaning is fully clarified, 'is self-evidently true'.[10] Proposition (A) is no more than a preliminary exploration of 'the evaluative implications of assertion'.[11] Proposition (B) is clarified 'by reflecting on the conditions under which *assertions* are worth making, worth testing, worth evaluating as true or false (rather than as popular or satisfying), worth profoundly disagreeing with...'[12] The clarification involves a number of issues, including a recognition that 'truth is worth knowing' neither claims nor assumes that every truth is equally worth knowing or every subject-matter equally worth investigating.

To those issues I might have added one that Kramer takes up to exemplify this second objection of his when he argues that 'truth [as such, or in general] is worth knowing' is inconsistent with the duty to conceal from the axe murderer the truth about the whereabouts of his intended victim. I took it as going without saying that the duty not to inform the murderer of this truth[13] has no tendency whatever to show that truth and knowing it is not an intrinsic good. Like every other intrinsic good, from human life itself, or friendship or loyalty or authenticity, truth and knowledge of it can in its instantiations be misused and made destructive of other goods or other instances of the same good, and thus productive of evil, evil (Kramer speaks of 'obnoxious results')[14] which it can be one's duty under the Golden Rule or some other principle of fairness to prevent. And the goodness of an intrinsic good does not entail that there can be no circumstances in which it would be wrong to interest oneself in some instance of that good, or even to interest oneself in any instance of that good at the expense of some instance of another intrinsic good. Be all that as it may, the principal mistakes in Kramer's second objection, like those in his first, result from his focusing upon utterances, indeed the utterances of other people—what they declare or might declare—instead of on the primary locus of assertion: the judgment that is constituted by one's inner assent to a proposition which one's truth-and-knowledge-seeking inquiry, anticipating some such judgment, has identified as having the worth of truth and thus the assertability—the paradigmatic assertability—of truth.†

---

[10] Essay 3 at 77. To underline that (B) is not deduced from (A), I indented (A), and explained why I did so: see 72 and 74. But in reproducing the 'chain of reasoning' in which these 'steps' appear, Kramer eliminates the indenting and ignores the explanation—a sign of his inattention to the character of the argument.

[11] *Ibid.*, 74.   [12] *Ibid.*, 77.

[13] Kramer's argumentation assumes that there is no *tertium quid* between telling the murderer all one knows, and lying to him, and thus ignores the central moral tradition on lying, as to which see *Aquinas* 154–63.

[14] Kramer, *In the Realm of Moral and Legal Philosophy*, 17.

The same point holds for Kramer's third and most strenuously articulated objection: that one can bitterly regret discovering the truth, for example the truth (as he supposes) that God does not exist, and can even fall into a hatred of self and others which prompts one to share with others this same truth not as a good but as something that will wound or even destroy them too. I abbreviate a page or two of baroquely Nietzschean rhetoric. But the rhetoric gives the game away: those whom Jill, the resentment-fuelled *illuminata* of his scenario, desires 'demonically' to wound and wreck with truth are thought of by her (and thus by her puppet-master Kramer) as 'self-dec[eived]', 'delu[ded]', 'dupes' of the false ('arrantly delusive') beliefs they at present peacefully and happily hold.[15] The pejorativeness of those epithets signals, willy-nilly, the intrinsic good of being not self-deceived, not deluded, not the dupe of some falsehood however comforting and sustaining. To judge something an intrinsic good is, once again, not to judge or presume that its instantiation can never be inappropriate, or ever be altogether free of bad side effects. Still, that said, Kramer's rhetoric about the dupes of falsehood, unnecessary though it was for his scenario or for the objection and argument he was attempting to illustrate, is a nice example of unwitting self-refutation.

III

If arguments from self-referential inconsistency are misconstrued by objectors such as Kramer, they are not altogether dissimilarly misconstrued by some who deploy them. Bernard Lonergan's critique of empiricism, in *Insight*, has much of unsurpassed value, and helped me greatly at a crucial stage of my education. But he errs when he claims, in Chapter XI of *Insight*, that any attempt to revise his explanatory account of knowledge and its forms and structures would be 'necessarily fallacious' (because self-refuting).[16] It is in fact entirely possible to envisage revisions that would be entirely compatible with themselves and with the fact that they were being proposed and argued for. And such revisions might be quite substantial, revising the whole account—say, to make proper space for and articulation of *reasoning*, as an epistemologically crucial factor or element substantially overlooked in *Insight*. It is a mistake to say that

cognitional theory differs from other theory [because] other theory reaches explanation only by venturing into the merely supposed, but cognitional theory

---

[15] Ibid., 20–1.   [16] Lonergan, *Insight*, 336.

reaches explanation without any such venture; and since it contains no merely hypothetical element, it is not subject to radical revision.[17]

For the fact is that philosophical explanation of what is involved in coming to know, and in making assertions, has no special method. And, as Aquinas explains when analysing our knowledge of our coming to know (the very root of cognitional theory), we are not entitled to say that we understand unless and until we understand *something*, and this something—an *object* of cognition—cannot in the first instance be the act of cognition itself, and equally cannot be regarded as the 'merely supposed' if the understanding of understanding which is the root of cognitional theory is not itself to be 'merely hypothetical'. The truths that cognitional theory can attain have no special metaphysical necessity, no necessity of the kind that Karl Rahner called transcendental (and contrasted with the categorical, to the downgrading of the latter). They are not on some 'third level' or 'plateau of developing human meaning', transcending the levels of (i) mere doing and (ii) 'classical consciousness', in the later Lonergan's not too historically minded exaltation of (iii) historical consciousness.[18] What is special about truths of the kind that are, so to speak, warranted by arguments from self-referential inconsistency is just this—both much and not all one could desire—that their defence (making manifest their warrantedness) is peculiarly facilitated by the special *proximity* (so to speak) of the facts that are given in the performance of investigating them and of asserting *or denying* them.

Aquinas, well conscious of scepticisms but not pressed by the situation of his age to grapple with them extensively, deploys argument from self-refutation relatively rarely.[19] The most original and profound, so far as I can see, is his argument against those (often called Latin Averroists) who held that there is but one intellect and asserted that intellect is no more than something like a mover of, rather than a part of, indeed the shaping part of, the very form of, one's individual reality. And the fact with which that thesis is inconsistent is the very fact which, if I hold the thesis, I think of myself as instantiating: the fact asserted by 'I understand'.

---

[17] *Ibid.*, 342. This claim involves an arbitrary and indefensible use of the term 'mere supposition', and a devaluation of knowledge of matters other than the subject-matter of cognitional theory, a knowledge without which cognitional theory itself can make no justified assertions, or is reduced to solipsism.

[18] See the exposition and analysis of Lonergan's theory of historical consciousness in essay V.9 (1992d), sec. IV.

[19] See his *Sententia super Metaphysicam* IV.6 nn. 12–15 [607–10]; IV.17 nn. 7–8 [742–3]; XI.5 n. 13 [2223]; XI.6 n. 22 [2246]; *In Post. Anal.* I. 44 n. 10; *In Eth.* VI.5 n. 8 [1182]. It is important to note that neither Aristotle nor Aquinas claims that argument from self-referential inconsistency is original or novel; they seem to assume, surely rightly, that arguments from self-refutation are not only sound and important but also part of any educated common sense or simple and honest reflectiveness.

But that fact is understood and known in two ways, as Aquinas explains as early as *De Veritate*: (i) in an immediate non-explanatory but really understanding way, and (ii) in an explanatory way such that I understand at least something of the nature of what it is to understand.[20] The first of these ways is a kind of understanding presence of oneself to oneself (as understanding, and as wanting to understand, and as loving—or as we might say, valuing—this understanding).[21] This is not something one makes mistakes about. Mistakes are all too common, however, when one tries to give any kind of explanation of what kind of reality this understanding is. And it takes energetic philosophical work to display the self-referential inconsistency—the implicit denial that *I* the asserting person *understand*—which is involved in asserting that the intellect that comes to understand is to be explained as really one intellect somehow shared in by all who understand. So too it takes philosophical work to display, free from distractions like those I have been discussing, the sense in which anyone engaged in reflection, argument, and discourse—worthy of the name and of the attention of others—is implicitly acknowledging the intrinsic good of truth and knowledge of it as a good that is pursuit-worthy whether or not there is also prospect of other benefit to be gained by the pursuit or by discovering one of the possible answers to be true. Likewise, it took energetic philosophical work for Boyle, Grisez, and Tollefsen to show that rational inquiry into (and discourse about) whether anyone ever makes free choices presupposes norms of reasonableness in inquiry, norms which are normative precisely because it is possible to choose to ignore or violate them—so that those who argue that no free choices are ever made refute their own thesis.

IV

I did not directly answer one of the questions I framed at the outset: What is the most important methodological reassurance one can give to someone wondering whether to be interested in Plato, Aristotle, Aquinas, and those who have treated their works as masterly guidance? The answer I give that question is clear by now: these philosophies are in their main lines coherent with the facts instantiated and the evaluations presupposed in the philosophical work of articulating them, the fruitful work in prospect for all who, in developing their own free-standing pursuit of important

---

[20] *De Veritate* q.10 a.8c.
[21] *Sent.* I d.3 q.4 a.4c: 'ipsa anima [est] naturaliter sibi praesens… quantum se intelligit, tantum se vult et diligit'.

questions for the sake of answering them rightly, wish to learn what can and should be learned, directly or indirectly, from the grandmasters.

NOTE

† *Kramer's first two arguments*...(at nn. 7–13). Fish, 'Truth but No Consequences: Why Philosophy Doesn't Matter' at 390–7 lends his support to Kramer's first two arguments, drawing from them the radical conclusion (indicated in the sub-title) that philosophical truths hold (when they do) on a 'level' which is so entirely independent of 'the quotidian, mundane' level of historical or moral propositions that one *cannot get from* one level to the other (in either direction). Like Kramer, he focuses on utterances, to the neglect of judgments, and so fails to notice how the quotidian, mundane facts instantiated in the act of seeking to make one's judgments sound *count* in favour of philosophical propositions about the worth of truth, which in turn support propositions about the mundane moral responsibilities one has because truth—one's own and others' making *true* judgments—is one of the basic intelligible goods (responsibilities which of course do not include a duty to reveal truths to every inquirer however maliciously hostile to human good).

5
BERNARD WILLIAMS ON TRUTH'S VALUES[*]

I

Truth and Truthfulness: An Essay in Genealogy (2002) was the last book Bernard Williams published; on his death the following year, his obituarists widely judged him the leading British philosopher of his time. As it happened, H.L.A. Hart's last philosophical publication was his review[1] of Williams's most substantial work in moral philosophy, *Ethics and the Limits of Philosophy* (1985). Both men had studied philosophy in what was then the Oxford way: first Plato and Aristotle, firsthand, by close and critical argumentation, and only then the Enlightenment and the moderns. Each of them, though Williams much the more extensively, gave whole lecture courses on Plato. Though thus unusually familiar with the origins of our philosophy, each of them can be taken as representative of the methods and opinions characteristic of philosophy as it is being practised among us today. In that review of Williams's *Ethics* book, Hart endorsed Williams's opinion that ethics and morality have no rational foundations; for some 'thick' ethical predicates—such as 'is courageous' or 'was cruel'—a particular culture has defined what facts make it correct, within that culture, to predicate courage or cruelty of some person, deed, or disposition; but there are no more general, or universal, truths in ethics, nor any moral truths about what is obligatory or right or wrong.

The 'project' of Williams's *Truth and Truthfulness* is announced in these terms:

to see how far the values of truth could be revalued, how they might be understood in a perspective quite different from the Platonic and Christian metaphysics which had provided their principal source in the West up to now.[2]

---

[*] 2008a, secs I–II. For sec. III, see essay V.8; for secs IV–V, see essay II.7.
[1] Hart, 'Who Can Tell Right from Wrong?', discussed in essay IV.10 (2007b), sec. V.
[2] Williams, *Truth and Truthfulness*, 18.

I.5 BERNARD WILLIAMS ON TRUTH'S VALUES

The occasion for the 'revaluation' of the 'values of truth' is what Williams calls the 'pervasive suspicion about truth itself... [and about] whether we should bother about it', a suspicion that is 'very prominent in modern thought and culture'.[3] And so the book begins with a fairly vigorous and successful brief deployment of what is, though Williams does not say so, the classical dialectic against sceptical deniers of the existence (and therefore the value) of truth,[4] the dialectic which unfolds by showing how such denials refute themselves, rely upon what they deny, 'peck... into dust the only tree that will support them'.[5] The later chapters follow a method that Williams ascribes essentially to David Hume, and involve both imaginary and historical genealogies intended to show how 'very basic human needs and limitations, notably the need for cooperation',[6] are such that 'every society not only needs there to be dispositions of [the] kind [summed up by Williams as the virtues of Accuracy and Sincerity] but needs them to have a value that is not purely functional [but rather is intrinsic]'.[7] And in this argumentation, which is indeed, as Williams says, 'an example of philosophy',[8] there is embedded the striking and reiterated thesis that 'The concept of truth itself—that is to say, the quite basic role that truth plays in relation to language, meaning, and belief—is not culturally various, but always and everywhere the same.'[9] Everybody everywhere already has a concept of truth, indeed, they all have the same concept of truth.[10] (The fact that they may have very different theories of truth just shows how much people's theories of truth misrepresent their grasp of the concept.[11]) For instance, 'all human beings everywhere have understood that some statements about what has recently happened (for instance, what has *just* happened) are true', 'simply true'.[12] And this universal concept involves thinking of truth as valuable:

Genuinely asking a question, wondering how things stand, I aim at a true answer. Assertions can be assessed for truth, and they would not be assertions if they

---

[3] *Ibid.*, 1. [4] See *ibid.*, 5. [5] *Ibid.*, 19. [6] *Ibid.*, 38.
[7] *Ibid.*, 42, with 44 and 59. [8] *Ibid.*, 39. [9] *Ibid.*, 61.
[10] To avoid misunderstandings, note that *this* sense in which 'truth is a universal concept', while important to an understanding of human capacities, is of less interest to the questions considered in this essay than a sense which is quite different (even though it presupposes the universal human capacity to understand and predicate 'is true'), namely, that it is a 'mark of truth', one which we advert to when we understand that to assert that '*p* is true' is to imply one's belief that under ideal epistemic conditions everyone would concur in that judgment: see the discussion of David Wiggins's explorations of truth, in *FoE* 63–6.
[11] *Truth and Truthfulness*, 163. See also 276:

the richness and complexity of the archaic [Greek] truth vocabulary does not mean that the concept of truth, as we would recognize it, is absent. Indeed, it is only in the light of its presence, the fact that people in this culture stated things as true, questioned whether they were true, passed them on as true, and so on, that we can understand what this rich vocabulary means.

[12] *Ibid.*, 160.

94 PART ONE: FOUNDATIONS

could not. The assessment of beliefs and assertions as true is a favourable one... to that extent we can see that truth must be regarded as a value.[13]

Just to *what* extent truth is a value—whether it is of intrinsic value for its own sake, Williams leaves to later. For the moment let us stay with his dialectical critique of scepticism.

Part of it is an effort to minimize the scepticism of Friedrich Nietzsche, for whose ethical positions Williams had much sympathy, but whose wider position many of the postmodern deniers 'take...to be that we should give up on the value of truth altogether'.[14] Williams quotes late writings of Nietzsche to show that, even at 'the very end of his active life', he was dedicated to 'the value of truthfulness[, which] embraces the need to find out the truth, to hold on to it, and to tell it—in particular, to oneself'.[15] Williams's estimate of Nietzsche's dedication makes light of the counter-evidence afforded by Nietzsche's own frivolous playing, quite truculent about self-contradiction, with 'the value of truth' (Nietzsche's phrase before Williams) in the third part of *On the Genealogy of Morals* (1887),[16] the work from which Williams takes both the sub-title of his book on truth and the name (and not merely the name) for the method of his project.

And takes, indeed, his project itself. For Williams says it was Nietzsche's project, to which he, Williams, will 'in this book...try to contribute'.[17] The reason why Williams's statement of the project refers to 'the Platonic and Christian metaphysics' is found in the passage he had just quoted from Nietzsche:

...it is still a *metaphysical faith* upon which our faith in science rests...even we knowers of today, we godless anti-metaphysicians, still take *our* fire, too, from the flame lit by the thousand-year-old faith, the Christian faith which was also Plato's faith, that God is truth; that truth is divine.[18]

'Truth is divine' is a too high-flown and opaque formula for something that Plato takes care to articulate more soberly and intelligibly in the parts of his dialogue *Republic* that Williams discusses more than once in *Truth and Truthfulness*. These are the parts whose centre is the great parable or *eikōn* of the Cave in which one man is suddenly freed from a chained-up group who have all spent their lives looking at the shadows cast on the cave's back wall by artefacts which, unknown to the prisoners, are being carried back and forth between the prisoners and a fire which is burning far above and behind them, much nearer the cave's entrance. The man freed is turned

---

[13] Ibid., 84. Williams proceeds immediately to insist that this leaves entirely open the question whether telling the truth is a value.
[14] Ibid., 13. [15] Ibid. [16] See essay III.12 at 169–70 (1999b at 94).
[17] *Truth and Truthfulness*, 18. [18] Ibid., 14, quoting Nietzsche, *The Gay Science*, 344.

around and made to look first at the fire and then compelled to make his way right up to the cave's entrance and into the sunlight. There he sees for the first time the light of the sun, that is (says Socrates-Plato), of the ultimate source (a) of the shadows, and the fire, and artefacts that cast those shadows, and (b) of the earth, moon, and stars outside the cave—'somehow the cause', that is, of everything that this man and his fellows had ever seen (in any sense of seen).[19] And then Plato has Socrates make the decisive affirmation that is the point of the whole parable: just as the sun stands to sight and visible things, as source of their visibility but also of their coming to be, growth, nourishment, so 'the good itself', the very 'Form of the Good', stands to understanding and intelligible things, as source of the being (reality) of what we understand and source of all our understanding of it.[20] 'What gives truth to the things known and the power to know to the knower is the Form of the Good [*tou agathou idean*]' (one might say, to capture this use of 'Form', the very archetype of all goodness and reality).[21]

Now it is true that Plato sometimes—for example in the very next sentence—exaggerates the difference between what is purely intelligible, like geometry, and the empirical, material things that are 'mixed with obscurity' because they come to be and pass away. Aristotle had reason to insist more steadily on the extent to which material things are intelligible through the *forms* that are *intrinsic* to them. In doing so, he was only drawing out what Plato himself plainly implies in his last dialogue, *The Laws*, when he discusses the natural, empirical world as a domain not of mere brute fact and chance but of the art and providence of 'God who is supremely wise, and willing and able to superintend the world',[22] a world of beings whose movements are saturated in intelligibility, 'the cause of their changes lying within themselves'.[23]

But to Williams, though he is credibly reported to have regarded Plato as the greatest of all philosophers, the theses Plato was intimating with the Sun and the Cave are thoroughly objectionable. (i) Plato's 'account of the Form of the Good in the *Republic*' associated truth with goodness in a way which represents them as 'altogether prior to a human interest in them', indeed as 'in themselves entirely independent of our thoughts and attitudes',[24] so that (ii) Williams 'can only suppose, with Nietzsche, that such views, precisely in their obliteration of human interests, must

---

[19] *Rep.* VII 514a–517b, esp. 516c with VI 508b–509b.   [20] *Rep.* VI 508b.
[21] *Rep.* VI 508e.   [22] *Laws* X 902e–903a.
[23] *Laws* X 904c; the argument unfolds from 888e to 905d. And see *Rep.* VII 530a on 'the craftsman of the heavens' who 'arranged [the stars and their motions] and all that's in [the heavens]'.
[24] *Truth and Truthfulness*, 61.

be an expression of human interests'[25] (by which Nietzsche meant, of course, discreditable, twisted human interests such as self-lacerating guilt, malicious entrapment of the strong by the slavish, resentful weak, and so forth: the shameful, deflating genealogy of conscience and morality itself). (iii) To understand the intrinsic goodness of truth we should 'consider only certain human attitudes toward the truth, people's dispositions to discover it and express it', so that our inquiry has 'a naturalistic outlook' and so 'should be seen as an exercise in human self-understanding'.[26] It is only relative to such attitudes and dispositions which people happen to have that we can speak of human 'needs';[27] calling a need 'basic' and 'human' does not override this relativity to *desire*.[28] (iv) Instead, Plato's

> suggestion [with the Sun and the Cave and the *Republic* as a whole] is that real beauty and value are not to be found in this world at all, and that what is here is only some image or association of them; it is as though the world contained a photograph in place of a lover...[29]

These four claims quite misconceive a text that is foundational for our civilization and among the most important of Providence's preparations for the reception of Christian revelation 400 years later. Take point (iv). There are many good and beautiful things *in* this world, says Plato right here: start the list with knowledge and truth themselves.[30] Their source, what they are due to, is the Form of the Good—*the* good, divine[31] good— which is more beautiful and more valuable than they or any other good. So when Plato calls knowledge and truth images of *the* good—'good-like' or 'boniform' [*agathoeidē*]—the sense of 'image' is very remote from the static, lifeless photograph substituted for the lover. The images *he* is talking about are present particular realities, items, of knowing, rightness, justness, understanding, and so forth, each and all being *caused*—authored or 'controlled and provided'—by that of which they are likenesses.[32] By treating a photo as the relevant paradigm of an *image*, Williams shows how remote he and many like him have become from what Genesis and St Paul hold out to us as revealed: that human persons are each an image and likeness of their divine author,[33] and that indeed, as Aquinas explains,

---

[25] *Ibid.*   [26] *Ibid.*, 60.   [27] See text at n. 6 above.
[28] On the Humean character of Williams's conception of basic reasons for action and of basic values, see Rawls, *Political Liberalism*, 85 n. 33; Korsgaard, 'Skepticism about Practical Reason' at 19–23.
[29] *Truth and Truthfulness*, 143 with its endnote at 205. 'Elsewhere' than in the *Republic*, says Williams (143), pointing to the *Symposium*, Plato more truthfully suggests that real beauty and value are indeed to be found here in this world 'but only in an incomplete, never entirely satisfactory form'.
[30] *Rep.* VI 508e.   [31] See *Rep.* VII 516c.
[32] *Rep.* VII 516b ('cause of all that is correct and beautiful in anything').
[33] Genesis 1: 26–7; Acts 17: 28; Colossians 3: 10; cf. Romans 8: 29.

each created reality is a likeness of God, 'approaching that likeness more perfectly if it is not only good but also can act for the benefit of others'.[34]

So, although the divine cause, as point (i) asserts, is 'in itself entirely independent of our thoughts and attitudes', it is considered and discussed by Plato and the whole philosophical and theological tradition precisely as what causally enables us to think (most thoroughly when our thoughts are true) and supports and makes best sense of our attitudes when they are just and right. Even when Plato is most unbalanced in ways that Aristotle and Christianity correct, his account cannot truthfully be said (as point (ii) claims) to 'obliterate' human interests. His concern, in the *Republic*, with the divine things there envisaged and in some measure affirmed is with their significance as making sense of all the realities with which moral thought and political life are concerned—as providing a model [*paradeigma*] to those persons who 'see' these divine things, a model for the putting-in-order of their political community, of its citizens, and of themselves,[35] which these persons are to accomplish, or at least attempt, by sharing in their fellow citizens' labours, great and small,[36] including their law-making and above all their educative undertakings.[37]

So, as to point (iii), Plato will say that a truly 'naturalistic' attempt to understand truth and knowledge will indeed be 'an exercise in human self-understanding' which will only go well if it relates and extends self-understanding both to its sources, more and less remote, and (even before that) to the *objects* of human understanding. I have started with these difficult matters of divine causality and its dependent images and analogues because Williams's uncomprehending dismissal of them helps explain the oversights which facilitate the subjectivism or scepticism of his ethics, the ethics of so many whose truncated, 'naturalistic', self-understanding is that of 'we knowers of today, we godless anti-metaphysicians'.

II

'The values of truth', for Williams, are 'Sincerity and Accuracy', which he everywhere calls 'virtues of truth'. Here I shall say nothing about Sincerity, and look only to Accuracy. It is a great intellectual virtue. But, as Williams never recognizes, it is necessarily a secondary element in the disposition or desire to have true beliefs. More primary is curiosity, the desire to learn, to find out.[38] And most primary is the insight that knowledge is a good, pursuit-worthy for its own sake, and ignorance—not

---

[34] *ScG* II, c.45 n.2.   [35] *Rep.* VII 540a.   [36] *Rep.* VII 519d, 520d.
[37] *Rep.* VII 519e.
[38] And so Aristotle puts this first, in the opening sentence of the *Metaphysics* I.1: 980a21.

just error but also and more fundamentally *ignorance*—is something to be avoided. Having this insight is in every way prior to, and foundational for, intellectual virtues such as accuracy. And it is an insight we gain, not by reading books which like Aquinas's discourse on natural law identify this insight's content as a first and self-evident principle of practical reason and natural law, but by advancing from our own experience. What experience, and what advance?

As children, we ask questions, and they get answered.[39] Answers suggest further questions, which in turn elicit answers we can understand as *answers*, that is, satisfactory responses to the questions. At a certain point there comes a step change in our understanding; noticing how the answers hang together, we have the insight that together they constitute *knowledge*, that, in other words, our belief in these answers is justified and *what* we believe is *true*. It is part of the same insight that future answers to future possible questions will be further elements in this open-ended field, knowledge. So the core of the insight is that knowledge, our coming to know what up to then we did not know, is *possible*. This insight is not a deduction; in that sense it is not reasoned to, though it is grounded in the lived experience of (a) puzzling experience, (b) pertinent question, and (c) satisfying answer confirmed or at least not disconfirmed by experience. This insight, which becomes foundation and framework for many other insights and trains of reasoning, is itself a first, one of a number of such firsts, as we shall see. And usually, in the history of one's intellectual development (our biographies), this primary insight is accompanied or closely followed by another insight, equally in its own field a first, not a conclusion of any reasoning from deeper premises: the insight that knowledge is not simply a possibility but an *advantage*—a desirable, *beneficial* possibility, a good thing, a kind of benefit, a way of being that is better than being ignorant: one is better-off than if one's questions remained unanswered. And this kind of possibility is understood as sometimes beneficial even when no further or other purpose seems to be served, or even capable of being served, by gaining it. This first principle of practical reason, that knowledge is beneficial—a good that is worthy of pursuit, that is, in other words, *to be pursued*—is foundation (*principium, archē*) and framework for practical thought about how to make good on the opportunity, how to realize or actualize (achieve) it. The core of this thought is already normative: 'is to be pursued' means

---

[39] Here we could say a good deal more about the way in which (i) the answers given us ('It's hot! Careful!') are sufficiently often verified by our experience of or credible reports of confirmatory events or phenomena, and (ii) our belief in these answers is shown to be justified by those answers' coherence with each other and with the available answers to any further relevant questions, and (iii) this in turn lends credibility to other answers from the same or similar sources.

ought to be pursued, in a sense of 'ought' that is not yet moral (though it is incipiently moral). The desirability of this good, and sometimes attainable, possibility is the source of this normativity.

In this insight, one understands the advantage of knowing as good both *for me* and for anyone *like me*, anyone who like me asks or can or could ask questions—the girl or boy in the next desk, for example, or, come to think of it, girls or boys anywhere. As I say, this is not yet moral thinking. The normativity is not yet of the form 'they ought to be seeking knowledge', or 'I ought to be helping them overcome their ignorance or confusion', but it is an understanding, a recognition, that as I'm better-off overcoming my own ignorance so they are better-off overcoming theirs.[40]

That understanding can promptly be reinforced by another: it is good for each of us if we are in such a relationship to each other that each wants the other to be better-off, and finds some satisfaction or even joy in the other's (or others') success (say, in overcoming ignorance or confusion). This further insight, in other words, is that this sort of state of things between us really is better than the state of things which obtains when each is coldly indifferent to the other's (or others') success or failure, or when each of us wants the other's misery, as the playground bully wants the misery and humiliation of his victim. Like the insight into the good of knowledge, this further insight is neither a deduction from any proposition, nor a data-free 'intuition', but is harmonious with certain sub-rational inclinations and feelings. Gaining the insight stands, however, as a step-change in one's perception of reality and its possibilities, possibilities now understood as advantages and benefits and opportunities pursuit-worthy for their own sake. The intelligible good which is the object (subject-matter) of this further insight we can label the good of friendship, taking that term in its widest extension along the wide spectrum of relationships, from concern to protect a passing stranger from imminent peril in the bush all the way to the many-sided, stable, and loving friendship of good and true friends.

The good of friendship is a *common* good, not simply my good to which yours is good only as a means, nor your good to which mine is good only as a means, but the good of our each flourishing in and by concern for and promotion of the other's well-being for its own sake *and* for the sake of both of us. Each instance of this sort of particular common good, whether it involves two persons only or many more, is an instance of a

---

[40] As one learns that knowledge can be disturbing or distracting, and that many things are hardly worth knowing, one does not conclude that knowledge is not a good in itself, or good only for its utility as a means to satisfying other desires; rather, one concludes (or should conclude) that its bad side effects can be guarded against and/or worked around, and that knowledge which is strategic or fundamental is to be pursued in preference to trivialities that may arouse curiosity or win a game.

universal human opportunity, advantage, benefit: friendship. And the intelligibility of this kind of common good both exemplifies and reinforces the intelligibility of each of the other kinds of universal opportunity, each of the other aspects of human well-being. For there are other aspects of human well-being, other basic reasons for action, besides the two aspects and reasons I have been speaking of, knowledge and friendship. There is, for example, the intelligible good of human life and health, and there is the good of transmitting human life as parents of the offspring generated by that specific and specifically procreative friendship, the marriage of husband and wife, committed to being each of their children's father and mother, jointly progenitors, educators, and in due measure lifelong companions.

The reasons which all these and the few other basic human goods give for action cut across Bernard Williams's famous distinction between internal and external reasons. For of all and each of them it is right to say that it would give *reason* for action even to a person who happened to lack all (motivating) responsiveness to it, all 'subjective motivation' to pursue this kind of benefit, and even if such responsiveness to this kind of benefit could not be 'rationally arrived at'[41] from that person's existing motivations.[42] Williams's arguments against (what he calls) external reasons arbitrarily assume that there can be no originating practical insight into the intrinsic advantage (benefit, opportunity—intelligible good) offered by some kind(s) of possibility that experience and (non-practical) understanding show to be attainable; these arguments thus ally themselves with the unwarranted Humean dogma that reasons as such cannot motivate. That dogma is inattentive to the variety of kinds of reasons there are, and equally inattentive to the central human reality of human will as one's capacity to respond to, be motivated by, the intelligible goods one understands, including goods understood as good for their own sake and not only as means to something else, goods identified in the basic

---

[41] 'Internal and External Reasons' in Williams, *Moral Luck* at 109. On the distinction, see generally sec. 4 of Chappell, 'Bernard Williams'. A reason that fits the description given summarily in this sentence of my text is, in Williams's terminology, 'external' (and in his view impossible). Williams's point (i), text at n. 24 above, complained, in effect, that Plato treated the forms of the good as external reasons. For a decisive critique of Williams's categorization of reasons as internal or external, see Korsgaard, 'Skepticism about Practical Reason'.

[42] Here I part company with the critique of Williams's internal/external reasons arguments which is advanced by Christopher Tollefsen, 'Basic Goods, Practical Insight, and External Reasons', and later entertained also by Chappell, 'Bernard Williams', just insofar as Tollefsen relies on the position (which is Aquinas's) that 'the starting points of correct deliberation *are shared* by all agents—the basic goods, plus the recognition of well-being as the point of action'. I do not doubt that this thesis is true of all agents of sufficient intelligence and maturity. But I think it better not to try to explicate what a practical reason is by appealing to a fact such as universal sharing of starting points. Basic goods and reasons for action are *intelligible*, without reasoning, given only the experience and non-practical understanding of possibility which are *available* to virtually everyone.

reasons for action, reasons accessible to everyone able to deliberate and choose. It should be obvious that even though nothing is a practical reason if it could not motivate a rational person, and though no one is rational who lacks the capacity to be motivated by reasons, it by no means follows—nor is it the case—that such reasons do motivate everyone (or even anyone) on all occasions when they might have; or that there is no one who lacks the capacity to be motivated by such reasons.[43]

Ethical thought, morality itself, has as its shaping object the good of being directed in all one's choices and actions by the basic reasons for action, undeflected by sub-rational motivations that would, without reason, cut back on the directiveness of each and any of those basic reasons. That good of practical reasonableness has as its propositional core the master principle of morality (or ethics): that one have a will open to integral— one could say universal—human fulfilment, the fulfilment of all human persons and groups. Specific moral *principles*, such as the Golden Rule, have their intelligibility and force as specifications of that master principle: for example, just as one cannot have a will open to integral human fulfilment if one is willing to inflict harm on others for the sake of harming them, so one cannot have such a will if one is willing to do to others what one is not willing for others to do to you. More specifically still, moral *rules* pick out ways in which, for example, kinds of choice are wrong because, for example, such a choice intends the destruction, damaging, or impeding of a basic human good in the life of one or more persons. Moral rules of this kind, picking out kinds of act that are exceptionlessly wrong, identify those acts by their objects, that is their close-in objectives, not by reference to their consequences or other circumstances. Such rules are thus exceptions to the generalization[44] that moral reasoning becomes less certain as its propositions descend from high-level universal principles towards specific conclusions about particular options available in complex and imperfectly foreseeable or controllable circumstances. There are plenty of principles or rules identifying more or less specific affirmative responsibilities, but the relatively few exceptionless moral rules are all negative, identifying kinds of option always to be excluded from one's deliberations.[45] Wherever those

---

[43] The points made in this sentence are well made, against Williams, by Korsgaard, 'Skepticism about Practical Reason' at 11–25. See also Korsgaard, 'The Normativity of Instrumental Reason'; and essay 1, secs II and III, adopting Korsgaard's critique of Humeanism but criticizing her Kantian failure to move decisively beyond Humeanism, a failure to attend to the practical reasons which direct us to basic human goods besides practical reasonableness, goods such as knowledge, life, and friendship.

[44] See *ST* I–II q.94 a.4c; *Aquinas* 90–1.

[45] Affirmative moral rules, identifying choiceworthy kinds of option, apply *semper sed non ad semper* (always relevant but not in all circumstances to be chosen); only negative moral rules can be *semper et ad semper* (always relevant and in all circumstances to be followed). The exclusion of

inevitably wrong kinds of option bear on the acting person's relations to another person or persons, those same exceptionless negative norms, rules, or precepts pick out the content of a human right that is not only inalienable but also (to use the terminology of the European Court of Human Rights)[46] absolute, such as the right not to be tortured.[47]

The moral truths I have been recalling in these broad brushstrokes are a main part of what Bernard Williams called 'the morality system', which—in the book that Hart reviewed—he labelled scathingly 'the peculiar institution' (a euphemism once used in the American South to refer defensively to slavery). Morality has, on Williams's account of it, nine or ten defining features, each of which he attacks; his main criticisms have been assembled from his writings by Timothy Chappell, in the *Stanford Encyclopedia of Philosophy*,[48] and you can there see how strong in rhetoric and weak in refutatory force they are. Most if not all of them simply *assume* the absence of any substantive first principles of practical reason (and thus of moral reasonableness) such as are provided by the basic reasons for action that direct us towards realizing the basic human goods in our own life and the lives of others. In this assumption, nowhere (so far as I know) examined by Williams, he shares the same utter detachment from and apparent unawareness of the mainstream tradition (exemplified by Aquinas) as is displayed by Hobbes, Locke, Hume, the Utilitarians, Kant, and accordingly by most of yesterday's and today's English-speaking philosophers. But equally—I have been suggesting—what is missing is sufficient reflective awareness of certain primary workings, and the foundational content, of the practical understanding and reasoning available to all of us and

---

inevitably wrongful options will characteristically, if not always, leave open more than one option for choice, even if only the option of taking no action. See *Aquinas* 163–4.

[46] See e.g. *Saadi v Italy* [2008] ECHR 179, 49 EHRR 30. However, this unanimous decision of the Grand Chamber runs together an absolute prohibition (exceptionless norm) with an absolute duty not to do anything that might (as a matter of real risk) result in someone else violating that prohibition (or the equivalent exceptionless moral or natural law norm). That is, it obliterates the distinction between intended results and side effects which has been found necessary for the coherence of sets of moral teachings which include exceptionless (absolute) negative norms: see *MA* 67–74. The rule adopted in the case may be defensible on its merits (e.g. by a *Miranda*-like policy argument), at least in relation to 'torture' as distinct from 'degrading treatment', though in relation to deportation where there is a risk of later torture but no shadow of intent to subject the deportee to that risk or of collaboration with the potential torturers, the non-absolute rule in *Suresh v Canada*, 2002 SCC 1 (Supreme Court of Canada) at para. 78 seems preferable. What is certain is that the rule in *Saadi* is not defensible as an interpretation of the Convention's intended meaning or as an exposition of the logic of the interpretative gloss-term 'absolute'. In terms of the last paragraph of the section 'Absolute Rights' in *NLNR* 225–6, the Court's argumentation (if not its conclusory ruling) confuses a two-term with a three-term right.

[47] *NLNR* 224. For the derivation of a philosophically defensible natural (human) right not to be tortured, identifying with some precision the kind of act that counts as torture in warranted assertions of this right, and relating the right to basic human goods, see Lee, 'Interrogational Torture'.

[48] Chappell, 'Bernard Williams'.

manifested (though sometimes unreflectively) in the life of everyone who more or less rationally chooses. These substantive first principles, directing us to substantive goods such as life, knowledge, friendship, and so forth, provide genuinely 'thick' practical predicates between the wholly abstract or formal predicates 'ought', 'right', and 'good' and such morally laden and circumstance- and culture-relative predicates as those Williams called thick (courage, cruelty, and the like). But so far as I can see these first principles and basic goods and reasons for action don't get a mention, or a thought.

6
REASON, AUTHORITY, AND FRIENDSHIP*

> How should we explain to someone what a game is? I imagine that we should describe *games* to him, and we might add: 'This *and similar things* are called "games".' And do we know any more about it ourselves? Is it only other people whom we cannot tell exactly what a game is? But this is not ignorance. We do not know the boundaries because none have been drawn. To repeat, we can draw a boundary—for a special purpose. Does it take that to make the concept usable? Not at all! (Except for that special purpose.)
>
> (Wittgenstein, *Phil. Inv.* §69)

I

However, it is widely accepted that there is an enterprise called 'the theoretical or scientific study of law as a social phenomenon' (Hart, *CL* 205, vii; Kelsen, *Pure Theory of Law*, 1–2). This enterprise has been said on occasion to have a 'theoretical purpose', viz., 'to further the understanding of law, coercion and morality as different but related social phenomena' (*CL* vii [*CL²* vi]).

Before anyone begins the adumbrated 'theoretical study', the words 'law', 'the law', 'a law', 'legal', 'lawful', etc., are confidently used; it is in these terms that we formulate our intentions in making, obeying, disobeying, applying, evading, maintaining, enforcing, condemning, and praising what we call 'law', 'the law', etc.

But for the activity of making and maintaining law, there could be nothing for the intending theorist to consider as a 'social phenomenon'. Moreover, the boundaries of the 'phenomenon' of human positive law must (whether the theorist wants to speak of 'law' or to invent his own jargon)

---

* 1970a ('Reason, Authority and Friendship in Law and Morals').

be more or less closely determined by what people have intended and taken to be law (and not something else) in positing and reacting to law—that is, by what people have, for the practical purposes of making and maintaining law, been willing to call 'law', 'the law', 'a law', etc. (Of course, it may be that some societies have not wanted or bothered to distinguish between law, and say, morality—and yet the theorist might want to say that they had legal systems as well as morality; but he says that because he is willing to reinterpret the intentions and actions of people in those societies in terms used by people in our sort of society, where distinctions *are* drawn between law and morality, in the course of those decisions to act or react which, in sum, can seem to amount to a distinct 'social phenomenon'.)

Furthermore, it is evident that the relations between law and the activities of making, maintaining, applying, obeying, evading, etc., the law are, in the context of these activities, generally understood as relations between reason for action and action. To make a law is meant and taken as proposing a reason for acting in certain circumstances; to maintain, apply, obey a law is to treat it as in some way a reason for acting or for acting in a certain way; to evade a law is to treat it as an insufficient reason for acting in the way proposed.

Now, the relation between the categories, 'reason for acting' and 'social phenomenon', seems quite obscure, and the 'theorists' of law have not offered explicit accounts of it. To see what they regard as involved in 'the theoretical study of law as a social phenomenon', it is necessary to examine what they do.

Kelsen says that his scientific study of law as a social phenomenon describes the 'objective normative meaning' of sets of convergent acts of human willing in a given territory over a given time. Meaning is 'normative' (in the legal sense) when it can be expressed in propositions of the form: 'If A is done, then B, a coercive sanction, ought to be applied.' A normative meaning is 'objective' when the norm is one of a unitary system of norms deriving from a first norm or set of norms ('the historically first constitution') presupposed to be valid (that is, objective). A normative system is unitary if (i) all the norms are derived from one norm, and (ii) none of the norms so derived 'contradicts' any other norm in the system.

One is entitled to ask for Kelsen's 'theoretical' grounds for drawing the boundaries of the 'phenomenon' in the foregoing manner. One may inquire, for example, why the phenomenon described in the theory must contain no 'contradictory' or (to speak in a way perhaps less offensive to logicians) 'conflicting' norms. After all, an historian giving a description of what people in a given time and place regarded as 'the law' would not consider that *his description* was self-contradictory if he had to report that these people accepted as valid each of two 'conflicting' norms. He would consider these people, not his report, as muddled. Why? Because for people in a society to accept a law as valid is for them to count it as a reason for action; but a man does not regard his practical deliberations as in any way advanced by the proffering simply of two 'reasons for action' which conflict with, or in Kelsen's sense 'contradict', each other. And it seems that Kelsen's reason for insisting that 'the law' of a particular society be 'non-contradictory' must derive, at least in part,[1] from his initial description of law as 'the specific social technique which consists in bringing about the desired social conduct of men[2] through the threat of a measure of coercion which is to be applied in case of contrary conduct' (Kelsen, *General Theory of Law and State*, 19; *Pure Theory*, 33). (For, although a pair of conflicting rules might bring about *some* conduct desired by the ruler—e.g. fawning devotion to him, or widespread neurosis, or the avoidance of all situations which could bring a man within range of a pair of rules—and although this effect would be produced through the threat of a measure of coercion, it would not be through the threat of coercion *in case of contrary conduct*, but rather in case of venturing to be concerned in any way with the acts or facts mentioned in the pair of conflicting rules.)

But is Kelsen's a 'theoretically' adequate account of the function of law and of the sort of reason for acting that law constitutes? Hart thinks not. He does not deny that law has the function and *modus operandi* ascribed to it by Kelsen. A legal system, in Hart's view, certainly must contain 'primary rules' prescribing actions that must or must not be performed, generally on pain of sanction; and these rules must—here Hart goes beyond Kelsen—at least restrict the use of violence, theft, and fraud. But the system, if it is

---

[1] In part, Kelsen's insistence is based on his epistemological views on the relation between 'the law' and 'the science of the law'; these views make it impossible for him to admit that a scientific description of 'the law' of a particular society could report the simultaneous existence of valid conflicting norms. The complexity and oddity of these views are best seen in Kelsen, *The Communist Theory of Law*, 12–16. But the reason mentioned in the text is also operative in Kelsen's rejection of conflict between norms. Thus he says:

> It is not possible to describe a normative order by asserting the validity of the norm: 'A ought to be' and at the same time 'A ought not to be'...[We] cannot speak of both being valid at the same time. This is demonstrated by the relation between law and morals. Here, indeed, such conflicts are possible...In this dilemma, an individual who regards the law as a system of valid norms has to disregard morals as such a system, and one who regards morals as a system of valid norms has to disregard law as such a system...[N]o viewpoint exists from which both morals and law may simultaneously be regarded as valid normative-orders. No one can serve two masters. (*Pure Theory*, 328–9.)

Here, 'the epistemological postulate' is justified, at least in part, by reference to the 'dilemma' confronting 'an individual' in his practical deliberations about what to do, whom to serve. See also *Pure Theory*, 25. [See now essay IV.5 at 99–100.]

[2] Note that the men whose conduct is in question are primarily, for Kelsen, the officials charged with executing the coercive sanctions, rather than the other citizens: *Pure Theory*, 25. This complication, along with others—e.g. the basic norm—is ignored in the present discussion.

to function with certainty and predictability, if it is to provide for the efficient application of sanctions or other social pressure, and if it is to allow for regulated change, must also, says Hart, contain 'secondary rules' for recognizing rules as 'legal', for establishing adjudicatory and enforcement procedures, and for regulating change in legal rules and relationships. The class of rules of change is particularly important, since it includes rules providing facilities for individuals to plan their lives and trade and to realize their wishes by creating a structure of private rights within a framework facilitating the formation, proof, assessment, and enforcement of claims based on those rights (*CL* 27, 39, 89–96, 224). By way of these functional considerations, Hart arrives at the core of his account of law 'as a social phenomenon': it is a 'union of primary and secondary rules'.

This account needs some elaboration if it is not to be misunderstood. For there are not lacking those who suppose that to study social phenomena is, rather literally, to look and see what a people does as a rule, and then to describe its life 'in terms of observable regularities of conduct, predictions, probabilities, and signs' (*CL* 87). In Hart's account, on the other hand, a social rule exists if and only if a pattern of behaviour is regarded, in a critical reflective attitude, as a common standard of behaviour, as a common *reason for* acting, criticizing, demanding, claiming, admitting, etc., in willing accordance with the pattern of behaviour stipulated in the rule. Correspondingly, Hart on occasion shifts from speaking of law as a social phenomenon to speaking of it as a 'specific method of social control' (*CL* 205, 151, 39), viz., control by the making, recognition, and maintenance of 'standards for guidance' (38, 43)—we might say, control by the proffering and acceptance of specific types of reason for action. And then it is these 'standards for guidance' that constitute the 'legal system' as a 'union of primary and secondary rules'. (But note, incidentally, that if one says that the convergent making, maintenance, proffering, and acceptance constitute a 'social phenomenon', one risks equivocation if one says that the standards or reasons for acting so made, maintained, etc., constitute a 'social phenomenon'. This source of equivocation is very important, but I do not wish to pursue the matter here.)

But Kelsen too, as we saw, had something to say about law as a 'specific' means of social control by the creation of a 'specific' type of reason for action: the norm stipulating the conditions for the application of coercive sanctions. On what ground, Kelsen might object, is Hart's specification of the boundaries of the type to be preferred to Kelsen's? After all, there are many in every society who are controlled, not by the provision of useful standards for planning their lives and trade with predictability, but by the threat of coercive sanctions in case of conduct contrary to that desired by the rulers. For such people, law presents itself as a reason for acting only insofar as it is a sign of possible sanctions. And is not Kelsen in distinguished company? Aristotle's introduction of the topic of law, in Book X of the *Nicomachean Ethics* (1180a12), rather suggests that the point of having law is precisely to coerce the brutish many with threats of sanctions.

Hart replies, in effect, by way of a distinction drawn in many philosophical studies of law, for example those of Plato (*Laws* 722), Aristotle (*NE* X.9: 1179b4) and Aquinas (*ST* I–II q.96 a.5c). It is a distinction that Hart formulates variously; one of his versions is as follows:

> the existence of a legal system is a social phenomenon which always presents two aspects, to both of which we must attend if our view of it is to be realistic. It involves the attitudes and behaviour involved in voluntary acceptance of rules and also the simpler attitudes and behaviour involved in mere obedience or acquiescence. Hence a society with law contains those who look upon its rules from the internal point of view as accepted standards of behaviour, and not merely as reliable predictions of what will befall them, at the hands of officials, if they disobey. But it also comprises those upon whom, either because they are malefactors or mere helpless victims of the system, these legal standards have to be imposed by force or threat of force; they are concerned with the rules merely as a source of possible punishment (*CL* 197 [*CL*² 201]).

Thus, for Hart, a 'view' of a legal system as a 'social phenomenon' is 'realistic' only if it 'reproduces the way in which the rules function as rules' (88) in the lives of those members of society who voluntarily accept the rules as common standards of behaviour, who have an 'internal' attitude to the rules. For such persons, legal rules appear not only as threatening sanctions but also as offering conveniently determinate standards to follow in the conduct of transactions in which what is sought is not the evasion of penalties but mutual advantages of certainty, predictability, agreed conceptions of fair dealing, a short way with negotiation—what Aristotle compendiously calls, in commenting on what we call positive law, the convenience of common but context-specific measures, such as are established for wholesale or retail markets in corn and wine (*NE* V.7: 1134a35).

More important, however, than Aristotle's views about law are his views about 'theoretical method' in the philosophical study of human affairs. 'We hold that in all such cases the thing really is what it appears to be to the mature man, the *spoudaios*' (*NE* X.5: 1176a17). If Aristotle is asked for what purposes he draws a theoretical distinction or elaborates a theoretical concept, he will answer that he is seeking to show forth the concerns and self-understanding of the *spoudaios* and the categories relevant to the *spoudaia polis* (*Pol.* VII.12: 1332a33). In a radical sense, there is no distinct 'theoretical purpose' of the 'scientific observer' which could be set over against the 'practical purposes' that the *spoudaios* has in drawing the boundaries of concepts by using them in his life in society. 'Theory', in respect of human affairs, has no distinct *locus standi*. The difficulty of maintaining a distinct 'theoretical' ground or attitude is witnessed by Hart's reply to the objection which, as we have said, Kelsen might raise:

> It is sometimes urged in favour of theories like [Kelsen's] that, by recasting the law in a form of a direction to apply sanctions, an advance in clarity is made, since this *form* makes plain all that the 'bad man' wants to know about the law. This may be true but it seems an inadequate defence for the theory. Why should not *law* be equally if not more concerned with the 'puzzled man' or 'ignorant man' who is willing to do what is required, if only he can be told what it is? Or with the 'man who wishes to arrange his affairs' if only he can be told how to do it? (*CL* 39 [*CL*² 40]; emphasis added.)

The effortless shift, in this passage, from the concerns of 'theory' to the concerns of 'law' is startling only if one takes too literally the notion of a special 'pure theory' of law with peculiar 'theoretical purposes' of its own.

Still, Kelsen might further object against Hart (as Hart has objected against certain other theorists) that Kelsen's concept of law is wider than Hart's in that it includes, for example, 'primitive' legal orders without courts, legislatures, or centrally organized sanctions—for example, international law (*Pure Theory*, 38). Kelsen could use Hart's own words: 'the use of the narrower concept here must inevitably split, in a confusing way, our effort to understand both the development and potentialities of the specific method of social control' to be seen, Kelsen would say, in primitive, municipal, and international law alike (cf. *CL* 205 [*CL*² 210]).

Against this objection, Hart has, in effect, replied that

> the diverse range of cases of which the word 'law' is used are not linked by ... simple uniformity, but by less direct relations—often of analogy of either form or content to a central case (79 [*CL*² 81]).

International law he can then present as analogous in function and content, though hardly in form, to the union of primary and secondary rules which, for Hart, is the 'central case' of law. And to me this reply, so far as it goes, seems completely effective. However, Hart's express discussion of this type of analogy does nothing to suggest the criteria of centrality to be employed in such cases. He mentions Aristotle (234) and instances his stock-example of health—predicated first and centrally of a man, secondarily of his complexion, as a sign, and of his exercises, as a cause, of that health (15). But Hart does not mention Aristotle's applications of his concept of central or focal meaning to the concepts used in the philosophy of human affairs, such as 'citizenship', the 'order of the polis (*politeia*)', and 'friendship'. Yet these analyses of focal meaning illuminate Hart's procedure more than anything he says or cites. Perhaps the most explicit and accessible of these Aristotelian analyses is that of friendship (cf. *Eudemian Ethics* VII.2; *NE* VIII.2).

I am someone's friend, says Aristotle, if I feel goodwill towards him, or wish him well, on account of some lovable quality of his, and if each of us is known to the other to reciprocate these sentiments (*NE* 1156a1–5). But friendships vary according as the friends find lovable in each other (i) the other simply as a lovable man, or (ii) a capacity for giving pleasure, or (iii) a source of, say, business advantage. Now Aristotle says that the focal meaning of 'friendship' is friendship of the first category; the relationships of pleasure-seekers and business associates are friendship only in a related, secondary, extended, and qualified sense. There are two reasons, at least, that seem to weigh with Aristotle in determining that friendship of the first category embodies the primary or focal meaning of 'friendship'. First: if wishing my friend well is central to any form of friendship, it is only in friendship of the first category that my friend's good rather than my own is the primary, direct, and underivative object of my sentiments of goodwill. Secondly: stability of relationship is one of the greatest goods that I can bring my friend by being his friend; to be a fair-weather friend is one of the ways of not being a real friend but of merely seeming so; but only in friendship of the first category is stability of relationship either likely to be maintained or capable of being fostered for its own sake (that is, for one's friend's sake—as we say, 'for friendship's sake'); for in the other sorts of friendship, what is valued is my own pleasure or advantage, and as soon as the relationship ceases to offer prospects of affording pleasure or advantage, I have no further reason to foster the relationship. Pleasure-seeking and business relationships can only be called friendships insofar as they preserve in a qualified form the objects directly and unreservedly cultivated in friendship of the first category: mutual benevolence and aid and comfort, pleasant intercourse, and like-mindedness.

Aristotle expresses this, rather too starkly, in the *Eudemian Ethics*, when he says that the focal meaning of a term concerns the thing the definition of which is implied in the definition of all the other things bearing the same name (1236a20; Hardie, *Aristotle's Ethical Theory*, 64; Owen, 'Logic and Metaphysics in Some Early Works of Aristotle' at 188). Aristotle's point can perhaps be grasped by reflecting that friendship of the first category will ordinarily bring each friend pleasure and advantage for himself (not least because it is more pleasant to give than to receive; *NE* IX.7), though these pleasures and advantages are not what he seeks in the relationship.

So he can appreciate what it is to find pleasure and advantage in human communication; but the man who seeks only his own pleasure or advantage in such communication is not thereby enabled to appreciate what it is to love another for his own sake.

Thus for Aristotle the central case of friendship is the friendship of the *spoudaioi*, the mature men who can reasonably find each other lovable simply as such; the central case of the polis is the *spoudaia polis*; and the definition of citizenship applies centrally to the *spoudaioi* who are the citizens of the *spoudaia polis* (*Pol*. 1275a33, 1332a33).

Aristotle does not fail to add the necessary methodological note. Some people, perhaps, have no experience of real friendship, for example, because they are too immature ever to have been swayed by anything more than pleasure-seeking (cf. *NE* 1156a32) or because they are in the grip of *pleonexia*, the selfish desire for more than one's fair share of advantage (cf. *NE* 1179b15, 1095a1–6, 1167b9), and thus could make nothing of the philosophical analysis which differentiates the focal meaning of 'friendship', or of other like concepts. Or rather, such people could only make something of the analysis if they accepted that friendship really can be such on the authority of others. Aristotle characterizes the philosophical situation in a quotation from Hesiod:

> Far best is he, who knows all things himself:
> Good, he that hearkens when men counsel right;
> But he who neither knows, nor lays to heart
> Another's wisdom, is a useless wight.
>
> (*NE* I.4: 1095b10, trans. Ross)

That is, he is useless in respect of the acquisition of ethical knowledge (cf. Aquinas, *in loc*.). Now, of course, it is rather unlikely that people completely in the grip of *pleonexia* would recognize and respond to the authority of the mature man. But Aristotle's general point seems right: either you must have some experience of friendship, or else you must be capable of imaginative sympathy for such experience, if you are to carry out the philosophical analysis which is completely convincing and cogent to those who have the experience, but which is mere opining to those who have not had it and who are unwilling or unable to reconstruct it sympathetically (cf. *NE* 1179b27).

Thus, parallel to Hart's distinction between the two classes—those who voluntarily accept legal rules, and malefactors who attend to legal rules merely from self-interested fear of sanction—we have Aristotle's two classes—those who live to seek pleasure and avoid pain and who thus do not have even a notion of the really worthwhile (*kalon*) and truly delightful (such as friendship), and those who are open to a range of experiences which to them cannot but seem primary or focal, not by reference to any further 'value judgment' or 'moral principle', but simply as such (e.g. as friendship). But Aristotle subdivides the latter class of people into those who live these experiences, and those who in one way or another respect their example and more or less tag along (cf. also *Pol.* 1277b29). And this is merciful, since it means that to do moral or legal philosophy we do not actually have to be mature men, saints, or heroes; we only have to be able to recognize these for what they are.

Moreover, parallel to Aristotle's philosophical demarcations by explicit appeal to the experience and discriminations of the *spoudaios* are Hart's legal philosophical demarcations by appeal (not quite so confidently explicit) to the attitudes of those who willingly regard law as a specific type of guide to conduct. And parallel to Aristotle's elaborate analyses of secondary forms of friendship, of citizenship, of types of political order, etc., is Hart's willingness to discuss primitive and international law. Neither Aristotle nor Hart interprets his own demarcation of a central case as a proposal to banish the study of secondary cases to 'another discipline' (cf. *CL* 205 [read with 152], where 'the Thomist tradition' is accused of making such a proposal—wrongly, since Aquinas is soundly Aristotelian on this point: cf. *ST* I–II q.93 a.3 ad 2). In this way, the objection that we imagined Kelsen raising can finally be laid to rest.

Still, Hart's man with an 'internal viewpoint' is not yet Aristotle's *spoudaios*. Certainly, he is willing to do what is legally required; he wishes to arrange his affairs predictably (*CL* 39); he could see no reason for allegiance to a set of laws that provided no restrictions on the free use of violence, theft, and fraud (89, 189) or that did not back its restrictions with sanctions (193). Indeed, Hart does not allow that the internal viewpoint is consistent with every sort of motivation whatever; for example, to regard the law as a reason for acting simply out of one's short-term self-interest in avoiding sanctions is precisely *not* to have the internal attitude (88, 111–13, 197). But despite all this, it seems that Hart would deny that the internal attitude must standardly be based on the communal or civil friendship (*philia politikē*) that Plato, Aristotle, and Aquinas were inclined to identify as the standard motivation of law-making and law-maintenance in its central forms. Hart does indeed list 'disinterested interest in others' as one of the possible motives for allegiance to the law; but he insists that 'mere wish to do as others do' or 'an unreflecting inherited or traditional attitude' or 'calculations of long-term self-interest' will suffice (198, 226).

Doubtless these motives do all suffice. But is there any reason not to apply to the philosophical concept of the 'internal viewpoint' those philosophical techniques applied by Hart in his philosophical analysis of 'law'—viz., the identification of a central or standard instance among other recognizable but secondary instances? And in fact the listed types of reason for accepting law as a reason for action do not seem all equally appropriate as standards of relevance in philosophically determining the criteria of law as a specific type of reason for action. Both 'traditional attitudes' and 'desire to conform' seem derivative from, and thus secondary to, the attitudes of others (forebears and fellows) who have adopted the internal viewpoint for other reasons. Moreover, to accept law simply out of respect for tradition or, especially, out of long-term self-interest (in the narrow and colloquial sense of that term) would be to have no reason for obeying or applying it in a strictly legal fashion—even if by 'legal' is meant no more than what Hart is willing to count as the minimum functions and characteristics of a specifically legal 'means of social control': that it consist of rules, and that these provide for change, predictability, and certainty of application. For the aforementioned motives of tradition and self-interest do not provide any sufficient reason for 'taking seriously' (cf. 156) the policy—so central to the 'internal viewpoint' and allegiance to law—of applying in different cases, and against competing pressures and attractions, 'the same general rule, without prejudice, interest, or caprice' (157 [CL^2 161]).

Should we, then, adopt the position Hart was concerned to reject when he advanced his list of possible sufficient motivations for allegiance to law: the position that law can only be fully understood as it is understood by those who accept it in the way that gives it its most specific mode of operation as a type of reason for acting, viz. those who accept it as a specific type of moral reason for acting? Once Hart has abandoned the bad man's concerns as the criterion of relevance in legal philosophy, has he any reason for stopping short of accepting the morally good man's concerns as that criterion? We cannot leap to this conclusion, for the 'bad man' was not discounted as a standard of philosophical relevance because he was morally bad, but rather because he 'rejected' the law and attended to it only as a sign of possible punishment (88); so to speak of the 'morally' good is to introduce a new term in the debate. What does 'moral' mean?

II

That moral philosophy has to do with a type of reason for acting, a type of factor in deliberation, is the basis of Warnock's arguments against Intuitionism, Emotivism, and Prescriptivism (understood as three schools of twentieth-century English-speaking moral philosophy). Against the Intuitionists, Warnock complains that their theory leaves it unclear how moral information is related to other 'features of the world', how the truth of moral propositions can be evidenced, and how moral qualities (e.g. 'obligatory') provide a distinct type of reason for acting, choosing, criticizing, etc. (Warnock, *Contemporary Moral Philosophy*, 15–16). Against the Emotivists, he complains that they fail to distinguish *this* sort of reason for acting, assessable as good or bad reasons, from influences on action, such as propaganda and brainwashing, assessable as effective or ineffective (28–9). Against the Prescriptivists, he complains that they misrepresent moral reasons as reasons which we just *decide* to count as reasons (47). And at this point in Warnock's argument the standards of a kind of *spoudaios* are inescapably appealed to:

> there are people, I think, whose moral views do seem to be formed and defended in this way...who pick and choose not only on the question what is right and wrong, but also on the question what are even to be admitted as relevant considerations. But such a person, surely, is not so much a model as a menace; not an exemplar of moral reasoning, but a total abstainer from any serious concern with reason. (47)

Finally, this appeal to what 'we' would count as reasonable before 'we' start moral philosophy is the basis of Warnock's critique of what he calls the Anti-Naturalist thesis. It may be, he says, that there are 'no logical limits' to what a person may want, prefer, or adopt as a criterion of merit or evaluation; but there are limits to what 'we' could understand as a want, a preference, a criterion of merit or evaluation, or a reason for choosing. And similarly, 'not just anything can function as a criterion of *moral* evaluation', or as a moral reason for acting (66–7).

At this point we approach the fundamental problem of specifying the subject of moral philosophy, of drawing the boundaries of the specifically moral type of reason for acting. And at this point, Warnock and other contemporary moral philosophers seem to falter in their attention both (i) to the status of moral propositions as, or as ancillary to, reasons for acting, and (ii) to the necessity of arguing and discriminating, in moral philosophy, by appeal to the concerns and language of those who are 'models' and 'exemplars' of moral reasoning, rather than those who are moral 'menaces' or 'abstainers'.

Warnock insists repeatedly that the first question in moral philosophy is likely to turn out to be 'what it is to appraise things from the moral point of view, and what in particular that range of considerations is whose relevance is implicit in the adoption of that point of view' (68). The first investigation in moral philosophy should show, he says, this range of relevant considerations; if we know these, then and only then (60) can we usefully consider whether moral considerations are 'uniquely authoritative in issues of practical judgment' (76). Although he reserves a formal answer, Warnock leaves readers in no doubt that they should answer affirmatively the question: 'Is it true *a priori* that moral views are concerned with certain topics, and a matter for enquiry what role in life (or discourse) such views, in this instance or that, may be found to play?' (56). Warnock's impliedly affirmative answer to this question represents, it seems to me, a common opinion. Morality, it is said, gets its specific character from its subject-matter: the human good and harm we can work in the world—a range of topics, such as justice or the common good, which 'we' happen to take an interest in (cf. Philippa Foot, in her *Theories of Ethics*, 9, 92).

'A priori' it seems an implausible opinion. For the power and poignancy of the problem set Socrates by Glaucon in the *Republic* consists in this: that the unjust man can *seem* to be the just man; he can grasp the relevance of all moral 'considerations' and is 'concerned with' everything that in his society is accepted as a moral topic, and he differs from the just man simply in that he employs all these considerations and deals with all these topics *only* out of self-seeking (*Rep.* 361–2). And is not his 'viewpoint', that is, his mode of deliberation and appraisal, paradigmatically *not* a moral 'viewpoint', but rather a radically non-moral viewpoint, a toying with the topics which concern 'us' morally, an aping of 'our' moral discourse in pursuance of a thoroughly amoral style of reasoning?

To reach his suggested conclusion, Warnock first confronts the opinion that what is centrally characteristic of 'morality' is 'the way in which those who take a moral view feel about it'. Unfortunately, in considering the four 'factors' which have, he says, been taken to be centrally characteristic of morality, Warnock seems to forget his own initial remark that these factors may be taken either alone or in conjunction with one or more of the others (53). Thus he isolates the 'feeling', as he calls it, of being required to act in a certain way from the question of the importance of moral principles, thus distorting his account of both the 'feeling' and the importance. His objection to the view that a special feeling is characteristic of morality is that it is possible to have the feelings appropriate to morally objectionable behaviour and yet genuinely not believe that one's behaviour is morally objectionable. This objection seems to me to tell only against a crude view that, to use Warnock's phrase, a certain 'psychological penumbra' always accompanies moral belief. But the entertaining of a belief is, among other things, an experience of consciousness, especially in just those situations where acting or deciding according to one's beliefs—say, by following what one believes to be the only intelligent and reasonable course of action—involves overcoming one's emotions and sentiments, including those emotions and sentiments which, if one is psychologically normal, ordinarily accompany rather than contend against one's rationally determined beliefs. Freud was no doubt in just this situation when he decided, against the pull of shame and other such feelings, that to publish *The Interpretation of Dreams* was the only sensible and responsible thing to do. So it remains, for all that Warnock has said, that a central characteristic of a moral view of things is indeed a rather specific sense of being required to act in a certain way by one's own consciousness, not indeed of a 'sense of wrongdoing', but of unworthiness or guilt or wrongdoing or irrationality were one not so to act. And this specific sense will no doubt be found to be specific precisely because it is a sense or appreciation of the *importance* of performing in this way in this situation, regardless of one's emotions and sentiments, including one's normal moral emotions and sentiments.

Much more important here are the confusions of method that appear when Warnock turns to deal with the question of importance. He offers to attack the notion that a man's moral principles are to be identified as those which are in fact dominant in the conduct of his life. He passes over the ambiguity of 'dominant'. It is possible for a man to regard principles of conduct, for example demands of friendship, as the most important principles, even if, with a sense of failing and unworthiness, he sometimes fails to live up to them, or even if, with this sense of failing, he always fails to live up to them whenever they happen to conflict with another principle, such as 'me first'. (I shall say: for such a man the principles of friendship are *de jure* dominant in his deliberations.) To speak of principles as dominant simply because they are the principles most frequently followed by a man is to abandon the attempt to reproduce the way in which principles function in the deliberations (the antecedent conscience) of men who accept them as principles. In any event, against the undifferentiated and equivocal thesis that moral principles are dominant principles, Warnock raises two objections.

The first is that a man may regard considerations of some kind as more important than considerations of morality, in that he may take himself, on occasion, to be fully justified in not doing what he sincerely recognizes to be right from the moral point of view.[3] This is an argument that is commonly met with in one form or another. For example, it is said that in moral philosophy it is important to recognize that, while it *is* irrational to destroy, or to accept with complacency the destruction of, the object of

---

[3] But note that on p. 72 of *Contemporary Moral Philosophy*, Warnock seems to say that such a man would not be reasonable: he says that moral argument is not unlike other argument in that 'an argument offers reasons to people, and people are not always reasonable'. But if such a man is not reasonable, why bother about him, his sincerity, and his use of language?

one's affections (self, or friends), it is *not* irrational to admit, genuinely, that such-and-such is one's moral duty, and then to say 'So what?'

But this whole line of thought is a plausible move in moral philosophy only if one abandons the fundamental argument of Warnock and others against the Intuitionists, Emotivists, and Prescriptivists: viz., the argument that a philosophical account of moral reasoning is unacceptable if it misrepresents what would be accepted as reasonable moral reasoning by those who are moral models, not menaces—exemplars, not abstainers from serious concern with moral reasoning. *Of course* people exist of the type sketched by Warnock, and their sincerity need not be questioned. But there seems no good reason why moral philosophy should adapt its criterion of what is to count as 'moral' or as 'morally rational' simply to accommodate the moral eccentricity (not to say, degeneracy) of those for whom moral obligations are not *de jure* dominant (that is, violable only at the price of unworthiness or guilt); or of those for whom a moral argument simply gives no (or no sufficient) reason for acting; or of those for whom moral categories and standards are no more than a code written into the language of society, an external 'social standard'. Of course, if ethics were an historical account of the standards, principles, and opinions current in a given society in connection with certain topics accepted in that society as 'moral topics', then an account would solemnly have to be given of the role of these opinions in the life of this man (a saint) and that man (a struggler) and the other man (an amoralist). But recent moral philosophy has, rightly, been claiming to be something more than social history. Its claim has been wholly based on a claim to be able to show forth accurately what 'we' (who are concerned, for example, with the 'common good': cf. Foot, 9) could accept as a reason for acting, or count as a moral reason for acting. 'We' have been (rightly) contrasted with a motley throng of moral abstainers, Martians (Warnock, 66), people who think hand-clasping three times an hour is a virtue (Foot, 91), petitioners for saucers of mud and bits of straw, people who do not care a damn what happens to anyone but themselves, people who just *decide* what principles they are going to adopt and what evidence they are going to count as evidence, and so on and so on. The pith of the argument against the Prescriptivists and Anti-Naturalists has been that the wants, criteria, evaluations, modes of deliberation, etc. of that motley throng are to be regarded, in moral philosophy, as at best perversions of, and at worst not instances of, the wants, criteria, evaluations, modes of deliberation, etc., of which moral philosophy is an account, and which provide moral philosophy with its only available and relevant criteria for the specification of the concepts it employs: for example, 'moral', 'rational', 'good', etc. Warnock's man who regards himself as 'fully justified' in not doing what he sincerely recognizes to be 'right from the moral point of view' should be assigned to the category of moral eccentrics; his use of the terms 'fully justified' or 'right from the moral point of view' should be regarded as at best secondary or, perhaps, perverted or eccentric or (rather too rigidly) not 'moral' at all. That is, this man's point of view should not affect the problem of determining what are the specifying characteristics of the central case of 'a moral view of things' or of a 'rational' moral judgment—except perhaps reflexively, in that the moral oddity of this man's way of thinking of justification and obligation may help to point up, by contrast, the centrality, in the deliberations of the morally standard reasoner, of a sense of the importance and rationality of moral considerations (rather as reflection on deviant constitutions, such as tyrannies, helps to point up what is constitutional about more constitutional forms of government).

Warnock's second objection to the thesis that moral principles are dominant principles is simply that a man's dominant ideals may be such that we would not call them 'moral'. (Here I take it that 'dominant' clearly does refer to what I have called '*de jure* dominance'.) Warnock gives two examples to support this assertion:

(i) Homer, in approving the ferocity, guile and panache of the warrior chieftain, might be said to have been employing moral standards different from our own; but he might just as well, or better, be said not to have been applying moral standards at all (54).

(ii) it may well seem more natural to regard, say, Nietzsche...not as propounding an unusual system of moral principles, but rather as abandoning moral attitudes altogether and as preaching...an ideal of conduct and character of a quite different kind (50–1).

These remarks are a temptation to digression. I do not know how to describe, other than as 'moral', Homer's pervading concern to show the disorders worked in the soul and in society by *chōlos* and *erōs*, or his frequent meditations on the aetiology of evil and on the mechanics of guilt (*atē*) and right order (*themis*). And if Nietzsche's superman, who after all is not praised by Nietzsche simply as efficiently self-perfecting or self-satisfying, is to be denied the title of 'moral ideal', it should surely be because of Nietzsche's denunciation of conscience, responsibility, guilt, and merit as mere idols of *ressentiment*. But these are digressions. What is important is to observe that, once we have secured the philosophical technique of seeking focal meaning and central cases, we shall decline Warnock's invitation to declare Homeric and Nietzschean ethics 'not moral at all' but ideals of 'a quite different kind'. We shall not abandon the critique of these ideals to some discipline other than moral philosophy but shall simply be prepared to regard them as deviant or secondary forms of morality (Nietzsche's perhaps more radically deviant than Homer's). Warnock's whole objection stands and falls with a rigid dichotomy—moral: non-moral—which I see no reason to accept as adequate to handle the problems of classification in any moral, political, or legal philosophy.

The view that what makes moral concern 'moral' is its concern with certain topics underlies various oddities in the latter part of Warnock's valuable little book.

First, there is Warnock's view that the 'interesting business' of moral philosophy is 'investigating moral evaluation', 'enquiring, that is, what it is to appraise things "from the moral point of view"...' (68). Now if this is the business of moral philosophy, one will rather quickly discover that to evaluate or appraise, say, the *Iliad* from the moral point of view is a rather different matter from appraising one's own possible choices of action 'from the moral point of view'. One can feel free to appraise the *Iliad* from the moral point of view, or the historical, the pastoral, the tragic, the aesthetic...or not at all; but if one were to feel free to appraise or not to appraise one's own living from the moral point of view, one would no longer be even thinking of the paradigmatically moral 'point of view', but rather of something which one happened to call 'the moral point of view', in a secondary or deviant way—for example, the set of standards one learnt at one's mother's knee, or the code written into the language of one's society. A 'point of view' that does not have as an underlying theme a tension towards claims on one's actions (and, derivatively, on one's habits of deliberation and one's adoption of 'points of view') is not a (fully) moral point of view. From a fully moral point of view, all one's options, including the option of adopting or abandoning the moral point of view on one's own options, appear to be ordered or structured, and the character of this order or structure can be expressed by the contrasts which are the theme of the literature of moral alienation and struggle from earliest times: guilt and merit, right and wrong, worthy and unworthy, death and life...(It may be added that if, as I think, the heart of the Anti-Naturalist position in moral philosophy is that the existence and directions or forms of this tension in the soul are not explicable or justifiable by reference to any facts or 'features of the world', Warnock has not addressed himself to the heart of that position at all.)

Secondly, it is noticeable that, although Warnock has said, as against the Intuitionists, that 'we wish to know...what it is for an action to be obligatory, and we are not told' (16), the concept of obligation is quite missing from the exposition of his own views. This in itself is no ground for complaint against an exposition that is meant to be no more than exploratory. But it is a sign of a deeper problem. Warnock says that if certain kinds of 'facts' and 'features of the world' (e.g. 'human good and harm') are necessarily criteria of moral evaluation, moral arguments may in principle be logically demonstrative (69). One will inquire: Demonstrative of what? Warnock sketches an example of a 'logically cogent' argument: 'it could be shown... with this sort of conclusiveness that it would be morally wrong for me to induce in my children addiction to heroin'. Someone who denies this conclusion either has not followed the argument or does not know what 'morally wrong' means (70).

But from the premise that certain kinds of facts or features are necessarily criteria of moral evaluation (because, Warnock would say (67), of what the word 'moral' means), all, if anything, that can follow is a logically demonstrated conclusion of the form: such-and-such an issue is a moral issue, or of moral interest and relevance. From such a premise there cannot be demonstrated conclusions of the form: such-and-such is morally wrong, or bad, or shameful, or sinful, or undesirable, or undue, or illicit, or unrighteous. Not only is it impossible to derive conclusions in such form from premises about the topics relevant in moral deliberation; it also is rash to assume that the right and the good, the wrong and the bad, are synonyms in moral reasoning. Certainly, if the heroin argument had concluded: 'Thus, it is morally bad to addict one's children', there would have been those ready to inquire whether moral good is the highest good, moral evil the worst evil, and whether it is always (or here) obligatory to pursue the morally good or to avoid the morally bad—that is, the questions would be raised which Warnock upbraided the Intuitionists for failing to answer. Warnock's oversight is an oversight of the problem of the specific ways in which morally relevant considerations are relevant to human action.

Sometimes, however, I wonder whether it is an oversight. After all, Warnock seems on the whole to be following Philippa Foot's arguments, and she has proposed a far-reaching revision in the meaning of western moral language, perhaps the most far-reaching since Hobbes. For she has insisted (*Theories of Ethics*, 95, 9) that prudence is a cardinal virtue and that *it is obvious* that any man needs prudence, 'whatever his particular aims and desires'.[4] (And in her comments on this essay, she has said it

---

[4] [In the Introduction to *Theories of Ethics*, at 9, she says that 'someone who does not care a damn what happens to anyone but himself may truly say that he has no reason to be just'. She says this by way of explaining her more general remark that in writing 'Moral Beliefs' in 1958, reprinted in her *Theories of Ethics* at 83–100, 'It had not occurred to me to question the often repeated dictum that moral judgments give reasons for acting to each and every man. This now [1967] seems to me to be a mistake.' It is this Humean conception of reason, *and reasons*, as merely subservient to desires that was doing the work in the phase of Foot's thinking on which this essay is commenting. See further the endnote.]

again: prudence is a cardinal virtue 'quite apart from' its 'connection with justice'.) With one stroke the Platonic, Aristotelian, and Christian ranges of meaning of 'virtue' are abolished. For one of the great themes of western ethics is that it is *not* obvious that any man needs prudence, if by 'prudence' is meant the 'cardinal virtue'. Plato's *phronēsis* is the specific excellence (virtue, *aretē*) created in the soul of that *rare* man who has turned around and ascended to the vision of the Agathon: all men have the faculty for it, but few have it, and Plato distinguishes it sharply from the cleverness of the vicious (*Rep.* 518e–519a; *Theatetus* 176b). With, if possible, more emphasis, Aristotle distinguishes between the natural cleverness (*deinotēs*) that *obviously* any man needs, and the prudence (*phronēsis*) which cannot be acquired without virtue and which concerns a good which *seems pointless* to all save the *spoudaios*, the *phronimos* (*NE* 1144a24–36). Christians speak of the prudence of the flesh (Romans 8: 6), by which a man sinfully realizes only worldly goods; it is only the shadow of the cardinal virtue of prudence, which is the measure of all human virtues (*ST* II–II q.47 a.13). Again, would it not make nonsense of the *Republic* to suppose that a man could have true *phronēsis* (wisdom or prudence) without justice (and I mean 'justice' in our modern, and Mrs Foot's, sense)? Those who elaborated the concept of 'cardinal virtues', which Mrs Foot freely uses, were rather notably insistent on the necessary interdependence of the cardinal virtues (cf. *ST* I–II q.65 a.1; Lottin, 'Aristote et la connexion des vertus morales' at 344). Moreover, they were obviously right: a prudence 'quite apart from' justice is not a cardinal virtue but rather a facility in vice. In responding to this part of my essay, Mrs Foot has said that any man needs 'the wisdom to form good attachments'. But a man who forms 'attachments', 'whatever his particular aims and desires', without having the justice intrinsic to real friendship will not easily be distinguished (except perhaps in respect of energy and ruthlessness) from Glaucon's unjust man, nimbly pursuing the wholly selfish 'particular aims and desires' which he attains, as Glaucon says, 'thanks to his courage, his strength, and his resources of friends and wealth' (*Rep.* 361b, trans. Lindsay). 'Friends?' Rather: 'good attachments'; highly placed connections: cat's paws. It would be hard to know how to *argue* against a moral philosophy which refused to confront Glaucon's dilemma,[5] and which with open eyes proposed to abandon the classical attempts to differentiate the point of virtue, and of its central case (that of

---

[5] A dilemma which, after all, is not too fanciful: as Freud once said,
When I ask myself why I have always behaved honourably, ready to spare others and to be kind wherever possible, and why I did not give up doing so when I observed that in that way one harms oneself and becomes an anvil because other people are brutal and untrustworthy, then, it is true, I have no answer. Sensible it certainly was not. (Jones, *The Life and Work of Sigmund Freud*, 473.)

the man who is just by virtue of his prudence), from the point, and the role in deliberation, of other sorts of good.

It would be easy to conclude that I am arguing that the specifying characteristic of moral deliberation is that it proceeds in terms of, and arrives at an appreciation of, one's obligations. The conclusion would be too hasty. Reflection on obligation is not, I think, the best way of considering the specific features of moral reasons for acting. Among other things, such reflection is all too likely—in an effort perhaps to avoid 'religious beliefs which might complicate the matter' (Foot, *Theories of Ethics*, 97)—to derail into the conclusion that the force of obligation is the external pressure exerted in society by the 'just' upon the 'unjust' (cf. Foot, 9) (and thence, I suppose, that the voice of conscience is just the echo in the superego of society's urgings). Similarly, I am not sure that the moral mode of deliberation is best or most easily revealed by examining our reasonings about justice. If Aristotle is right, friendship is coextensive with justice, in respect of both subjects and objects; but it may be that in the claims of friendship both some of the content and all of the force of moral reasons for acting come more readily into view.

Friendship carries us, with Aristotle, beyond the contrast between egoistic flourishing and justice, the contrast which Mrs Foot has rightly identified as the beginning of our moral difficulties. For in real friendship one finds oneself in the situation in which friendship is seen to be necessary for one's own flourishing or self-perfection, but at the same time is seen to be something which, of its nature, cannot be cultivated for the sake of one's flourishing or self-perfection, but only out of a disinterested love of one's friend. (That, I think, is the specific mark of the moral good in general.) Again, friendship makes rigorous claims on one's actions, demands on pain of guilt and irrationality (it is irrational to accept with complacency the destruction of the object of one's love), demands which include all the demands of justice; but if one fulfils these obligations in order merely to spare oneself irrationality and breach of duty, one no longer is rising to the demands of friendship, for one no longer is acting simply out of friendship for the friend (cf. the transposition of this problem in *ST* II–II q.44 a.1 ad 2).

For Aristotle, the friendship between *spoudaioi* is the flowering of virtue; all the tools of his moral philosophy are assembled for his long, loving analysis of this virtue. The tools break in his hands. Right at the outset, the virtue of friendship escapes his schema: moral/dianoetic. Far more significant is Aristotle's failure to resolve the conflict between self-love and friendship. No one has sought a resolution more pertinaciously. True friends 'have in common' their *nous*, which in each of them is the finest and most lovable thing, the cultivation of which is the highest call on a man's choice, the virtue of *athanatizein*, of straining to immortalize, so to speak, in contemplation (*NE* X.7). But the equivocation on 'having in common', on *koinōnia*, is too evident to be escaped (cf. 1171b32). The *nous* is, after all, a 'part' of each of us (1166a16, 1168b28–35; 1178a2); so each man's moral effort ultimately collapses back into cultivation of self; the attempt to explicate self-sacrifice in friendship is hollow. Aristotle's ethics is defeated by his metaphysics; God, says Aristotle with great simplicity (1159a6), is too remote to be our friend. Aristotle cannot give an account consistent with the reasonableness of what he feels to be nobly rational and demanding. There could be no apparent reason to accept that one's friend had *even in 'justice'* a claim, in any respect equal to one's own, on one's rational choice, unless one saw in him the created image of the God who could seem more lovable than either one's friend or oneself.

III

The concerns of the players determine the boundaries of the game and generate a language to express its ins-and-outs. Law is the order of a game with many different types of players. But it lays down a *common* standard of action, as Hart says, not merely for the avoidance of evils but also in the pursuit of goods. So not only its nuances but also the precise role it can, centrally, play in human affairs are grasped, with the greatest specificity, by reference to the role it has for those who engage in it out of a discriminating concern for the demands of the common, the *koinōnia*—that is, out of civil or communal friendship, the central case of the 'internal attitude' to law. Such people's concerns with the law provide the criterion of relevance—the authoritative measure of adequacy and inadequacy—in legal philosophy. But the ethical analysis of the centrality of friendship in the moral life entitles us to go one step further. We can now say that recognition of legal obligation is centrally an appreciation of one's moral obligation; that legal obligation is thus a specific type of moral obligation; and that the enterprise of making and maintaining law is, centrally, a part of the moral form of life—which itself is lived in deviant and central forms.

NOTE

Philippa Foot, the commentator at the Jowett Society meeting where this essay was read, responded that when I said that she proposed '...the most far-reaching revision in the meaning of western moral language since Hobbes', I merely misunderstood her remarks 'on the cardinal virtues of courage, temperance, prudence and justice'. She had indeed said (in the 1958 essay on which I was commenting) that, while it could fairly easily be shown that anybody, whatever his particular aims and desires, needs courage, temperance, *and prudence*, some men might be able to argue that they would be better off without the restraints of justice. But (she said) I was mistaken in inferring that by 'prudence' she must mean the cleverness that Aristotle distinguished from *phronēsis* under the name of *deinotēs*:

> For any man needs, not only cleverness in the choice of means to the ends he happens to have, but also the wisdom to form good attachments. So the wise man does not, for instance, have the same values as one who is worldly or avaricious. In the context of a discussion of the cardinal virtues I took it for granted that 'prudence' would be understood as 'wisdom', and it is this that any man can be shown to need, whether or not he needs justice. I am not, of course, saying that a man who rejected the claims of justice would think the *same* acts to be against courage, temperance or prudence as the rest of the world; for his rule of conduct would be different, and he would not, for instance, think it cowardly to put another man in danger instead of himself. What I am saying is that *courage, temperance, and wisdom are moral virtues quite apart from their connection with justice*, and I do not know why Mr. Finnis finds this so startling. (Foot, 'Comment' at 124 (emphasis added).)

This comment of hers showed that the 'mistaken' inference was not so mistaken, since she did indeed hold that the 'prudence' or 'wisdom' of thoroughly unjust people is rightly called a virtue, just 'different from' the prudence (practical *wisdom* or *reasonableness*) which the 'rest of the world' count as that virtue. It was a little surprising to find her response so indifferent to the revision of moral language it entailed, and so dismissive of the classical thesis of the connection of the virtues. Essay 1 n. 24 mentioned her later change of mind, but her own *Natural Goodness*, in 2001, was even more forthcoming:

> ...I still [from 1958 through 1972] held a more or less Humean theory of reasons for action, taking it for granted that reasons had to be based on an agent's desires.[6]

As a result, of course, she had 'doubts about the rational status of morals' and was 'rather scandalously, inclined to restrict [the rationality of disinterested justice] to those whose desires were such as to allow them to be described as lovers of justice'.[7]

> In common with others, I took it for granted at that time that a discussion of the rationality of moral action would start from some theory or other about what a reason for action must be: rather favouring a desire-fulfilment theory with some special allowance for the force of considerations of self-interest. I now believe that both the self-interest theory of rationality and the theory of rationality as desire fulfilment are mistaken. Moreover, there seems to be a mistake of *strategy* involved in trying to fit the rationality of moral action into either theory: such an enterprise implying that we first come to a theory of rational action and then try as best we can to slot in the rationality of acts of justice and charity.[8]

See further her *Natural Goodness* chs 1 and 4. Cf. *Aquinas* 111.

---

[6] *Natural Goodness*, 10.   [7] *Ibid.*   [8] *Ibid.*

7

REASON, UNIVERSALITY, AND MORAL THOUGHT*

Hume's analysis of moral thought and discourse emerges from his critique of the rationalist tradition—Vasquez, Suarez, Grotius, Clarke, and Butler—for whom moral reasoning was a matter of *seeing* certain 'abstract relations of things', logically similar to, say, the mathematical relations between numbers. Aristotle would have applauded Hume's intention to discredit this tradition. For Hume, however, the upshot is that moral discourse 'indicates' (I choose a word poised between what Hume said and what his modern followers would like him to have said) the sentiments of sympathy and thence of approbation or disapprobation, which the speaker feels on contemplating some human deed or character. 'Now it is evident' (says Hume, *Treatise*, Part II, sec. 1):

> that those sentiments, whenever they are derived, must vary according to the distance or contiguity of the objects... [I]t is impossible we could ever converse together on any reasonable terms, were each of us to consider character and persons, only as they appear from his peculiar point of view. In order, therefore, to prevent continual contradictions, and arrive at a more stable judgment of things, we fix on some steady and general points of view....

Again:

> We know, that an alteration of fortune may render the [our] benevolent disposition entirely impotent; and therefore separate, as much as possible, the fortune from the disposition. The case is the same, as when we correct the different sentiments of virtue, which proceed from its different distances from ourselves. The passions do not always follow our corrections; but these corrections serve sufficiently to regulate our abstract notions, and are alone regarded, when we pronounce in general concerning the degrees of vice and virtue.

---

* Unpublished; read at a staff seminar in the Philosophy Department at Latrobe University, Melbourne, 14 September 1971.

And again, now in his *Enquiry concerning the Principles of Morals*, sec. 9 ('Conclusion of the Whole') Part I [para. 6]:

when [a man] bestows on any man the epithets of *vicious* or *odious* or *depraved*, he...expresses sentiments in which, he expects, all his audience are to concur with him. He must, therefore, depart from his private and particular situation, and must choose a point of view, common to him with others.

And this 'common point of view' is the foundation, for Hume, of 'any general system and established theory of blame or approbation' [para. 5].

Now it is obvious enough that in these passages *reason* both is doing, and is being portrayed as doing, more work than Hume's general theory of morals anywhere expressly allows for. The question has been raised: Why should we regulate our sympathy in a certain fashion? And Hume is willing to give reasons in response to this question: because your judgment will thus be stable, uniform, consistent, coherent, definite, communicable, and intelligible to others, and your discourse will thereby be *reasonable*. The desirability of these qualities of reasonableness in thought and discourse is taken by Hume as self-evident. In short, reasons are being given for adopting a policy, and the policy itself is that of being reasonable. In both respects, reasonableness, not sympathy, however important a constituent of the human constitution it may be, has taken up the final position in the analysis of moral thought and language—Hume's formal and vigorous protestations to the contrary notwithstanding.

The fact that all men have a certain range of feelings, and have a certain disposition to regulate those feelings in one way rather than another; or have a certain innate structure of the mind such that certain principles of deep grammar are universal (though still contingent—in that the class of possible grammars so defined is not the class of grammars that are logically possible as self-consistent and intelligible); or the fact that there can be detected in all social milieux a certain symbol-structure, expressed in totemism, myth, jokes, social organization, etc., in terms of binary correlation and oppositions between resemblances and differences—these and similar facts do not provide any good reason to judge that that range of feelings can reasonably be indulged, or that that manner of regulating them is the best one, or that those structures of the mind are principles of reason, or sources of knowledge, or that it is because the mind has the structures it has that analytic principles are true. The innateness, or in this sense universality, of an idea is never a reason for adopting the idea as reasonable, true or correct. 'I can't help thinking thus and thus' is a fact, not an appeal to reason or a contribution to rational discussion about what to do or what to think.

I.7 REASON, UNIVERSALITY, AND MORAL THOUGHT

Moreover, the need to judge reasonably is, in reason, more basic than the need to attain a common judgment. For (as each of us can say), for me:

my own present thinking, in contrast to the thinking of others, is transparent in the sense that I cannot distinguish the question 'Do I think that p?' from a question in which there is no essential reference to myself or my belief, viz. 'Is it the case that p?' [or from the question 'Is it right to think that p?'].[1]

This reveals the sense in which rational judgments are both common or universal and private or individual. They are common because for all who would judge reasonably the same transparency holds: for no one is there a distinct question, 'What do I think?', as distinct from 'What is the case?'. But judgments also are private, since the fact that some or all others think that p (or fail to think that p) is, for the same reasons, irrelevant to the question 'Do I think that p?'

Conversely, as the question '*Do* I think that p?' is transparent against the question 'Is it the case that p?', so this latter question is transparent against the question '*Is it right that* I should think that p?' All the questions require the same answer. But the form of the last question shows how that answer is in part an answer to a question about what should be *done* (in the sense of 'do' which comprehends questioning, supposing, considering, judging, reflecting...).

Reasoning, and coming to know by judging reasonably, is in all its forms and applications, an *opus*, a work, a deed, the attaining of an end by properly disposed means. We can say that since it is the deed with which philosophers are perhaps most familiar, it provides a good case by reference to which a philosopher can analyse the relationship between, on the one hand, moral language and thought, and on the other hand, the deeds to which moral language and thought relate.

Like other forms of action, rational inquiry and judgment makes sense by relation to its end, point, or guiding purpose, which in this case is the attainment by the inquirer of knowledge of what is the case, of truth and clarity about reality, in place of ignorance, error, misconception, muddle, illusion, and fantasy.

That truth and clarity about reality is to be preferred to ignorance, etc., that one is *better* than the other, is something presupposed by everybody willing to be a rational inquirer. And the reasonableness of the preference and of the implied judgment of value cannot reasonably be challenged or questioned; for to bother to question the preference and the presupposition itself only makes sense if the questioner himself presupposes that the

---

[1] Edgley, *Reason in Theory and Practice*, 90.

preference is sensible and that the implied judgment about desirability is warranted.

The virtue of reasonableness, as the concrete means or at least as the disposing condition for attaining the desired goal, is well known to everybody who has reflected on the problems of being a serious student, on the difference between scholarship and quackery, between obscurantism and enlightenment. Any account of the virtue will have to include impartiality, lack of prejudice and *parti pris*, a *just* appreciation of things, attentiveness, honesty in inquiry, refinement in consideration, patience, humility in the face of reality and logic as it is—and so on through the virtues.

These virtues are simply the *practical* implications, for anyone willing to be a rational inquirer, of the logical fact of the transparency of 'Do I think that *p*?' as against 'Should I think that *p*?' and 'Is it the case in reality that *p*?' For this logical truth entails that, for anyone who is reasonable, the truth about what is the case is not only something one can delight in attaining, but also a good-for-its-own-sake, sought for its truth and not for my delight. It is a good which has *authority* over and against one's self-love. That is no doubt why it also does not lose its desirability even when we realize that, in this world where everything does not lie open to immediate view, the truth is an *ideal* limit, a perfection to be sought but never fully attained.

I have been trying to describe and prescribe the way in which an Aristotelian moralist, or reasonable man, would break out of the circle Hume constructed for him. Moral philosophy is done, not by describing the opaque and brute facticity of universal structures of sympathy, feelings, or wants (nor, for that matter of codes, written into our or everybody's language, *à la* Kant and Hare), but by participating in and then reflectively describing the work of reasoning, in which a reason is not a fact about the way I do or shall think but a *guide to* thinking, a reason *for* thinking the way I do or shall—just as Hume, despite himself, thought that the end of attaining stable and universalized judgments gave good and sufficient reason for regulating one's feelings in a certain way. The starting point in moral thought will be, not certain truisms about human nature or facts common to all men, but certain things-obviously-to-be-sought-after—of which I have been discussing just one, viz. truth discovered by reasonable inquiry. The distinctively *moral* character of this seeking comes into view when one reflects on the *authoritativeness* of at least one of these ends-obviously-to-be-pursued—i.e., at least, the end of truth—where by 'authoritativeness' I mean to indicate the way in which seeking this end (logically) *cannot be a form of self-seeking* in some less than moral and merely individual sense. When egoism has been transcended in this way by the authoritativeness of an end, and thus by the 'obligatoriness' of the means to that end, the moral form of life and discourse begins to unfold.

In *friendship* there is the same sort of authoritativeness, the same sort of tension between self-love and that which is essential to my flourishing but which cannot (logically) be pursued for the sake of my flourishing but only for the sake of my friend's. When the demands of friendship and of truth-seeking are considered together, there begins to emerge (though I can only mention it, and not argue for it) the point of view commended, indeed commanded, by Hume[2] as the moral point of view, but commended by Aristotelians as the *reasonable* point of view—I mean the universal viewpoint of the participant in the human arena who seeks to act and judge as someone (as it were, a witness of the whole arena) who saw the whole arena, and had everyone's interests at heart, would wish him to act. For that witness, whose viewpoint it is only reasonable for us to adopt, is to be taken as impartial (as reason requires) but not as impassive and undesiring (for reason is a passion, and reasonableness one of the basic objects of reasonable desire).

NOTE

That 'reason is a passion' is more a Parthian shot than a thesis to propose and defend in its own right. Its defensible sense is that reason, properly understood, has the responsiveness and motivating capacity/activity that Hume reserves to the passions.

That the reasonable point of view is that of the universal spectator is the idea which, in my understanding of ethics ('the moral form of life') and the structure of practical reasonableness from about this time (1971) until the writing of *Fundamentals of Ethics* in 1983, was the inadequate though not wholly misleading or mistaken stand-in for the appropriate conception: the master moral principle that one's choices must be open to integral human fulfilment—that is, the fulfilment of all human persons and communities.

---

[2] 'He must, therefore, depart from his private and particular situation, and must choose a point of view, common to him with others': *Enquiry*, sec. 9, conclusion, Part 1.

8

OBJECTIVITY AND CONTENT IN ETHICS[*]

Wittgenstein's meditations on objectivity and reasonableness, in notes he wrote on certainty between late 1949 and two days before his death in April 1951, and now edited and translated by Elizabeth Anscombe (with von Wright and Denis Paul) as *On Certainty*, help undermine some common misunderstandings of objectivity and reasonableness.

What interests Wittgenstein, here, is not the state of complete conviction or total absence of doubt. That is 'subjective certainty', he says, and what interests him is, rather: 'when is something objectively certain?' (194; also 273). When Moore says that he *knows* that this is his hand, or that the earth has existed for a long time, he succeeds only in expressing his mental state of subjective certainty, of being sure. But something is objectively certain only 'when a mistake is not possible' (194). And whether one is incapable of being wrong or mistaken about something 'needs to be established objectively' (16, 15). It is compelling grounds that make certitude objective (270), and 'what is a telling ground for something is not anything I decide' (271). But what kind of possibility is in question when we say a mistake is not possible? 'Mustn't mistake be logically excluded?' (194). So Wittgenstein says:

> In certain circumstances a man cannot make a *mistake*. ('Can' is here used logically, and the proposition does not mean that a man cannot say anything false in those circumstances.) If Moore were to pronounce the opposite of those propositions which he declares, certain, we should not just not share his opinion: we should regard him as demented (155; also 217).

Denial of objectively certain propositions is not (he's saying) mistaken, it is crazy, senseless or insane, evidence of incompetence to judge or of mere misunderstanding of the language. Or it might be a joke. Correspondingly,

---

[*] Unpublished, 1 January 1975; for a priests' philosophy group (hence the scale of the reference to the priest-philosopher Bernard Lonergan). Unidentified parenthetical numbers refer to the enumerated notes or paragraphs in *On Certainty*.

I.8 OBJECTIVITY AND CONTENT IN ETHICS

about such propositions doubt is not possible. 'There are cases where doubt is unreasonable, but others where it seems logically impossible. And there seems to be no clear boundary between them' (454). The objective certainty of propositions correlates with the reasonableness of persons. So we say: 'There cannot be any doubt about [that proposition] for me as a reasonable person' (219). And 'when we say that we *know* that such and such..., we mean that any reasonable person in our position would also know it, that it would be a piece of unreason [madness: 281] to doubt it' (325).

But how does the reasonable person exclude doubt in any given case, and how is one to resist the sceptical philosopher's invitation to doubt in all cases? Wittgenstein's reflections on this proceed in several strands. In a first strand he reflects that some propositions are embedded in a vast system of propositions 'in which consequences and premises give one another mutual support' (142), a 'nest of propositions' (225), a 'host of interdependent propositions' (274) in which 'what stands fast is held fast by what lies around it' (144; also 234, 312, 594). However, within this system some propositions, though confirmed by some other propositions, are not like certain other propositions which Wittgenstein calls 'foundations' or 'fundamentals', a doubt about which 'would seem to drag *everything* with it and plunge it into chaos' (613). These foundations are carried by the whole house (248). Thus, for example, 'in the entire system of our language-games it belongs to the foundations' that the earth has existed for many years past (411). Such propositions may be empirical propositions, but 'it is clear that our empirical propositions do not all have the same status' (167), since some (such as the one just mentioned) form the basis of all our thought and are thus not merely (or at all?—308) empirical but also norms of description (167, 321; 634), rules (309, 319, 494).

But in a second strand of reflection, Wittgenstein is concerned to show that these certainties not only are rules or principles (124) of judgment but also are 'part of our method of doubt or inquiry' (151). This strand I find more interesting. Certain propositions are said to be 'exempt from doubt, are as it were like hinges on which [doubts] [and disputes: 657] turn' (341). 'It belongs to the logic of our scientific investigations that certain things are *in deed* not doubted' (342), *not* because 'we just can't investigate everything and for that reason are forced to rest content with assumptions' (343), but because 'if I want the door to turn, the hinges must stay put' (343).

Wittgenstein seems to have four points in mind here. First, that debate and dispute could not begin unless certain propositions were regarded by the disputants in common as incontrovertible—otherwise neither or none of the disputants could understand what the other or others meant to put in question. Second, that all testing of an hypothesis requires that some propositions be regarded as in need of no testing. Third, that doubt could not be formulated, and truth could not be sought through questioning, unless on the one hand the meaning of the words (or at least some of the words) used to formulate the doubt was known with certainty, and unless on the other hand the uses of terms such as 'true', 'false', 'deceive', and so on, were known with certainty (506, 507, 514). Fourthly, certain forms of arguments for doubt undermine themselves. Wittgenstein does not place particular stress on this fourth point, which is not altogether distinct from the third point about the meaningfulness of the formulations of doubts. But it is on the fourth point that I want to dwell.

What the third and fourth points have in common is that they raise doubts about the reasonableness of a given doubt (cf. 516)—and equally about the reasonableness of an invitation to doubt everything—and that these doubts about a doubt are not being raised by pointing to the opinions of reasonable people, nor by pointing to other *propositions* which support the proposition(s) which the doubter is questioning, but instead by suggesting that there is an incoherence in the given doubt itself or in the doubter's procedure or performance in raising it. Thus, for example, Wittgenstein imagines someone going to the doctor, showing him his hand, and saying 'This is a hand, not... I've injured it, etc., etc.' Except in very rare cases, the declaration 'This is a hand' is not only superfluous but also absurd, for if 'This is a hand' *were* a piece of information, 'how could one bank on his understanding this information? Indeed, if it is open to doubt "whether that is a hand", why isn't it also open to doubt whether I am a human being who is informing the doctor of this?' (460). Or again, 'if the shopkeeper wanted to investigate each of his apples without any reason, for the sake of being certain about everything, why doesn't he have to investigate the investigation?' (459). Finally, and most strikingly: 'The argument "I may be dreaming" is senseless for this reason: if I am dreaming, this remark is being dreamed as well—and indeed it is also being dreamed that these words have any meaning' (383).

Is Wittgenstein right here? The utterance 'I may be dreaming' does not seem senseless. But to offer as a good *argument* in a debate with oneself or an interlocutor the consideration 'I may be dreaming' *does* seem absurd. That is to say, the proposition (P) 'It can advance my hypothesis in this argument for me to suppose that I am dreaming in making this supposition and in conducting my side of the argument' is false. Such a supposition cannot advance an argument since dreaming is a state of experience in which what we could reasonably judge to be *rational* argument *via* reliably understood propositions towards acceptable conclusions does not occur. And since the falsity of the proposition (P) is self-evident to anyone who cares to distinguish dreaming from waking, it is absurd or, as Wittgenstein says, senseless to *act* as if it were not false, that is, to *argue* 'I may be dreaming'.

But Wittgenstein, in his notes *On Certainty*, did not capitalize on this method of excluding doubt and thereby establishing objective certainty (and knowledge: 308). And for this reason he wavers on one of the central matters in issue in his meditations. 'Since a language-game is something that consists in the recurrent procedures of the game in time, it seems impossible to say in any individual case that such and such [an empirical fact] must be beyond doubt if there is to be a language-game...' (519), and I think he here means the language-game of doubting and judging.

But this, as I interpret it, seems to me mistaken. There are propositions of empirical fact which are coherent and semantically definite in their reference, which are inevitably and indubitably false (and whose contradictions are inevitably and indubitably true), if there is any doubting or judging. That there is doubting and judging is one of the indubitable truths. For no one can consistently assert that there are no assertions or judgments; his statement is inevitably inconsistent with the facts that are given in and by his performance of stating the proposition assertively. And no one can consistently express a doubt about (the falsity of) the proposition that doubt is unintelligible or that doubting is not an available language-game or move in a language-game.

Now there are quite a number of other propositions which cannot be doubted because their contradictories are inevitably false by reason of their self-referential performative inconsistency. Obvious examples of this inevitable falsity are 'Nobody can make a move in a language-game' or 'Nobody can put words together to form sentences' or 'Nobody exists' or 'No one can remember anything' (for at least the meaning of those words is, so the person who utters them pragmatically implies, remembered by him).

It is important to see what sort of inconsistency is involved here. This is not an inconsistency or absurdity which flows simply from the meaning of the words used to form the sentences by which the propositions are formulated (articulated). Nor does it flow from the self-referential emptiness and consequent meaninglessness of statements such as 'This statement (or sentence) is false'. Nor is performative inconsistency strictly identical, I think, with the inevitable falsity which Aristotle remarks on in propositions such as 'All propositions are true' or 'All propositions are false'. For Aristotle's proof is: 'All statements cannot be false, nor all true— for this reason among others, that if all are false this statement itself is false, and if all are true it will be true that all are false' (*Meta.* IV.8: 1012b13;

XI.6). Whereas, in the cases I am thinking of, the inconsistency is, in the last analysis, not so much an inconsistency between propositions or statements or sentences as an inconsistency or discrepancy between a proposition and a state of affairs which falsifies it—in these cases, inevitably, in that the proposition *cannot* be stated or argued for without these discrepant facts being provided in and by the performance of so stating or arguing for it.

As Wittgenstein says of his meditations *On Certainty*, 'what interests us now is not being sure but knowledge. That is...the fact that about certain empirical propositions no doubt can exist if making judgments is to be possible at all' (308). And, at the same time, 'my mental state, the "knowing", gives me no guarantee of what will happen [if my statement is checked]. But it consists in this, that I should not understand where a doubt *could* get a foothold nor where a further test was possible'. And in the case of empirical propositions of the sort that Wittgenstein happened not to interest himself in in *On Certainty*, such as 'I exist' or 'I do understand some words', or 'making judgments is possible', I do have a guarantee (if there are guarantees for anything) in that I can see *why* doubt could not get a foothold. The great value of Wittgenstein's meditations is that they break fairly thoroughly with the notion that objectivity is established by taking a good look, either at what is out-there-now or at my mental state.

When I ask 'Do I know or do I only believe that I am called...?' it is no use to look within myself. But I could say: not only do I never have the slightest doubt that I am called that, but there is no judgment I could be certain of if I started doubting that (490; also 569).

Of course, as a matter of *fact*, one can always doubt anything, if by 'doubt' I may mean toy with questions, contemplate mere possibilities, and so on. But just as Wittgenstein's frequent references to reasonableness, the reasonable man, and so on, were not intended merely to point out a brute fact about the frequency of common opinions and a certain way of describing and appealing to those opinions *qua* frequent and common (for as he says 'this doubt isn't one of the doubts in our game. (But not as if we *chose* this game!)' [317], and again, more darkly but more significantly, 'To have doubts about [whether my friend has sawdust in his head] would seem to me *madness*—of course, this is also in agreement with other people; but *I* agree with them' [281]), so the peculiar strength and philosophical relevance of retorsive arguments from self-referential performative inconsistency is that they display, in closest possible conjunction, the three aspects or components of objectivity.

There is *first* the experiential objectivity (I use Lonergan's jargon) of what is simply given in experience independently of questions and answers.

And so Aquinas argues (like Descartes, as Hintikka contends; and more certainly, I incline to think, like Augustine, which Hintikka denies) that 'no-one can with assent consider himself not to exist, for in considering something, he *perceives* himself to exist'.[1]

Then, secondly, there is the absolute objectivity of the correct judgment, the proposition the affirmation of which is warranted because there is sufficient evidence or, as Wittgenstein puts it, compelling grounds (270), and no further questions arise or, as Wittgenstein puts it in relation to *certainly correct* judgments, one would not understand where a doubt *could* get a foothold nor where a further test is possible (356). Wittgenstein seems to recognize the distinction between experiential and absolute objectivity when he remarks: 'Whether I know something depends on whether evidence backs me up or contradicts me. For to say one knows one has a pain means nothing' (504).

Thirdly and finally, there is the normative objectivity which we strive for when we strive to be attentive, intelligent, reasonable in our doubting and judging and to exclude 'the subjectivity of wishful thinking' (Lonergan, *Insight*, 380)—of prejudice, presumption, *parti pris*, hope, fear, love, and detestation—from the unfolding of our straightforward desire to know. It is this normative objectivity of the pure desire to know that excludes mere toying with doubt. For though one can toy with the notion that it is possible that one does not exist or that one understands nothing, the retorsive argument cuts short such idle doubting by appealing simultaneously to (1) inescapable data of experience and (2) one's concern for consistency. For thereby the retorsive argument *shows* the irrationality of any further supposing that one's doubt *could* ever issue in a correct judgment that one does not exist.

Well, when I say that the retorsive argument cuts short idle doubting, I am speaking broadly, or rather, in the normative mode—*de jure*, as it were. For only doubters themselves can cut short their doubts. *De facto* one can shrug off the retorsive argument, and every other consideration of reason whatsoever. One's authenticity as a lover of truth is at stake in face of *all* evidence, *every* telling consideration or argument, not merely in face of the retorsive argument. The only special advantage of the retorsive argument is that the fact which it uses as a reminder and as a norm of judgment is a fact about the parties to the argument as such; the argument explicitly puts them in the presence of themselves as putative knowers, reasonable persons, objective judges, worthwhile disputants. But there is no denying that one can shut one's eyes both to argument and evidence and to an attractive object of

---

[1] Nullus potest cogitare se non esse cum assensu; in hoc enim quod cogitat aliquid, percipit se esse: *De Veritate* q.10 a.12 ad 7.

one's love: namely truth, the absolute objectivity of correct judgments, the reality that is what is known in such judgments. *De facto* anyone can buck the authority of rational argument, of questions that reveal the pointlessness of further questions, of normative objectivity, just as one can buck any other form of authority (without it ceasing thereby to be normative or authoritative).

Under what conditions can a retorsive argument get a grip on a disputant who argues for a self-referentially inconsistent proposition whose inconsistency that retorsive argument will display? First, the disputant must assert his proposition to be true (and must consider his assertion to be genuine and rational: this is what Aquinas meant by 'thinking [or speaking] with assent'). But, second, he must consider truth to be not merely a property of his asserted proposition but also an objective of the internal or intersubjective discussion in which he asserts it. And, thirdly, he must consider it to be an objective the realization of which may have instances which are genuine and worthwhile, precisely *qua* truth, notwithstanding that they are instances other than those which he had in mind or anticipated or concretely valued when he entered the discussion and put forward his proposition in pursuit of that objective. Otherwise he will never be willing to affirm as possessing the good of truth that proposition the contradictory of which he wrongly asserted. In short, he must value truth as an ideal, i.e. first, as something realized in but not exhausted by the particular instances in which it can be specifically embraced or repudiated, and secondly, as something authoritative over and against the self-love which is the root of prejudice, inattention, bias, and the other intellectual vices. (I shall say more in a moment about valuing truth as an ideal.)

Here we begin to see that Wittgenstein's references to the reasonable man have their value, in the search to distinguish subjective from objective certainties, not so much as flat reminders of the brute-fact universality of certain language-games, but rather as appeals to one's interlocutor (whether internal or intersubjective) to respect or be faithful to an authoritative ideal, a *good* (and indeed the only *worthy*) form of the *activity* of thinking. As he pertinently says, even 'the mathematical proposition has been obtained by a series of actions that are in no way different from the actions of the rest of our lives, and are in the same degree liable to forgetfulness, oversight and illusion' (651). So he goes out of his way to contrast the objective certainty, with which foundational propositions are held and 'stand fast', with a subjective certainty 'grounded in my stupidity or credulity' (235), 'hastiness or superficiality' (358; cf. 150), 'thoughtlessness' (657).

Perhaps we can inject another retorsive argument at this point. Wittgenstein evinces a preference for truth and clarity or lucidity about what can be known, as opposed to ignorance, error, misconception, pointless belief, muddle, illusion, and fantasy. The reasonableness of the preference and of the implied judgment of value cannot reasonably be challenged, disputed, or doubted. For to bother to question the preference and the implied judgment only makes sense if the questioner himself presupposes that this preference is sensible and that the implied judgment about value, worth, or desirability is warranted.

But notice that this retorsive argument makes its point only in as much as we distinguish between, *on the one hand*, the attaining of truth as the concrete objective of a particular inquiry or particular argument (e.g. the question and argument at stake in the last-mentioned retorsive argument), an objective that can be completely attained, achieved, executed by intelligent and artful disposition of effective means, a definite strategy, system, or technique (e.g. as here, of logical devices); and, *on the other hand*, the attaining of truth as what I have called (at some risk of being misunderstood) an ideal, viz. as a distinct but general possibility of human fulfilment, a human purpose, an aspect of human flourishing, a form of good-for-man, such that (i) the attaining of a particular truth, if the answer to a particular question by a particular person on a particular occasion, is but one embodiment of the purpose, one actualization of the possibility, one realization of that form of good-for-man, and (ii) the purpose, the form of good, in short the *value*, remains valuable, unexhausted, something fully capable of being further participated in and realized not only by other persons on other occasions but also by the same person in relation to other questions. Unless we understand 'preference for truth' as recognition of the value of truth in this latter sense the last retorsive argument fails to make any point and, more significantly, Wittgenstein's implicit appeal to reasonableness as against superficiality etc. has no significance.

Now the distinction between *'value'* in the just-stipulated sense of an aspect of human flourishing and self-determination, and 'good' in the sense of a definite goal or objective (however remote the goal and however complex the system of means for attaining it—for example the goal of victory in the war) is, I think, of importance in ethics. Aquinas's lack of systematic attention to it makes much of the groundwork of his exposition of ethics insecure. Lonergan has recently, it seems, become aware of it. In *Insight*, he defined value as 'the good as the possible object of rational choice'[2] but equally he made it clear that such possible objects of rational choice all are intelligible orders of objects of desire, that is, are instances of the good of order, of which paradigm cases are polity, economy, family, standing to objects of desire as system to systematized.[3] But in his Aquinas

---

[2] *Insight*, 601.   [3] *Ibid.*, 596.

Lecture 'The Subject' in 1968 he notes that by 'value' in that lecture (and thus presumably in ch. 2 of *Method in Theology*, likewise) he means neither the Aristotelian 'object of appetite' nor the intellectual and, he says, Thomist 'good of order' (that is, of objective arrangements that ensure the regular recurrence of things that satisfy appetite or desire), but rather he means something 'quite distinct', viz. 'what is worthwhile, what is right as opposed to wrong, what is good as opposed not to bad but to evil', such that the instances of value are the 'good choices and actions' whereby the good man freely and responsibly builds up his character, achieves his personality, and successfully makes himself what he is to be.[4]

Now, just as Lonergan's notion of value in *Insight* undershot the mark by running together operational systems-for-goals with aspects of human self-determination (that is, with values in my sense), so his notion of value in 'The Subject' and in *Method in Theology* overshoots the mark by running together these values (in my sense) with the morally good, the right.[†] The truth of the matter, I think, is that the morally good, the right, emerges only as that action, or that system of action, or that disposition to action, or that character or personality, which realizes or participates in the whole set of basic human values in a good, rational, right *way*. The elisions in Lonergan's discussions occur, I suppose, because neither he nor, so far as I know, any of his disciples has actually tried to work out an ethic, though Lonergan believes that an ethics worked out by a virtuous person who was explicitly aware of the structure of consciousness, being, and value identified by Lonergan would have 'a marked family resemblance to traditional views'.[5]

In *Method in Theology*, Lonergan evinces a high regard for the value-theory embodied in Dietrich von Hildebrand's *Christian Ethics*, with its apparatus of feelings (including 'moral feelings') which are 'apprehensions of values' (including, so it seems, moral values), and scales of such values (or of preferences of such values). Now as a way of describing the integration into the texture of personal life and action of an already settled (Christian) morality (and the causes of disintegration of moral life and judgment), von Hildebrand's analysis has much to commend it. But as an explanation or justification of the content of principles of that morality it has rather little to offer, for it relies completely if implicitly on supposed intuitions of fully moral principles and values, and portrays a practical intellect which bears an uncanny resemblance to the 'sausage machine turning out abstract concepts'[6] that Lonergan has so effectively discredited in epistemology

---

[4] See Lonergan, *A Second Collection*, 84, 79, 83.   [5] *Ibid.*, 40.
[6] *Ibid.*, 222; Lonergan, *Verbum*, 34.

and metaphysics. Indeed, it seems to rely on the common neo-Scholastic assumption that *synderesis* is an intuition of moral principles such as 'thou shalt not kill' and that the first principles of the natural law, which can never be expunged from the human heart, are likewise such moral principles—an assumption or set of assumptions which has made much Catholic ethical theorizing ridiculous. Perhaps it is permissible to remark that this assumption was not shared by Aquinas, who was quite clear that the first principles of *synderesis* and natural law, which people really *do not* radically lose sight of, are of the form 'life is a good to be sought after and realised and what threatens it is to be avoided' or 'knowledge of the truth is a good to be sought after and realised and what threatens it (viz. ignorance, etc.) is to be avoided'.[7] Now the term 'good' in these formulae corresponds in meaning to the term 'value' as I used it: a basic aspect of human well-being, capable of realization by the participation in it of indefinitely many persons in inexhaustibly many ways. To take the principle I mentioned last, it is the formulation of the attractiveness and practical relevance of the good of knowledge, which, Aquinas repeatedly says, is found attractive as a good of the thinking person (*bonum quoddam speculantis*), which good (that is, aspect of that person's well-being) is included in (*comprehenditur sub* or *continetur sub*) the knower's complete and perfect well-being (sc. happiness) as one particular kind of good (*ut quoddam bonum particulare*[8])—though, as I remarked before, Aquinas tends to spoil his expositions of the point by analogies which conflate the relationship between one's complete well-being and this aspect of one's well-being with the relationship between a concrete good and a specific method of attaining it, for example the good of good order in an army and the method of a chain of command.[9] Now Lonergan, too, considers that 'the pursuit of science is the pursuit of a value';[10] where he differs from Aquinas is, first, in offering and repeating a list of 'values' in which 'beauty, understanding and truth' are lumped together with 'virtuous acts, noble deeds, great achievements'; and, secondly, in proposing that 'vital, social, cultural, personal and religious values' be distinguished one from another '*in an ascending order*', that is, according to a 'scale of preference'.[11]

The philosopher who, so far as I know, has most energetically and competently carried out the rethinking of natural (and Christian) ethics with fully critical self-consciousness is Germain Grisez.[12] He identifies

---

[7] *ST* I–II q.94 a.2; q.10 a.1; I q.79 a.12c and ad 3; II–II q.47 a.6c and ad 3.
[8] *ST* I–II q.1 a.6 ad 2; q.9 a.1 ad 3; q.10 a.2c. [9] See e.g. *ST* I–II q.9 a.1c.
[10] Lonergan, *A Second Collection*, 143; cf. Lonergan, *Method in Theology*, 31, 38.
[11] *Method in Theology*, 31, 38.
[12] See Grisez, *Beyond the New Morality*; Grisez, *Contraception and the Natural Law*; Grisez, *Abortion*, ch. 6.

eight fundamental purposes, goods, or values in the sense which I have been defending, to which all other human purposes, all other ideals that people have actually had, can be reduced, as aspects or combinations of aspects of one or more of these eight. The eight are: life, play, aesthetic experience, speculative knowledge, friendship, inner integrity, authenticity (harmony between what one is and what one does), and religion (harmony with the gods). And he argues convincingly that 'there is no objective hierarchy of values among the eight fundamental purposes'; there is 'no common denominator, no yardstick or measure or criterion whereby one could be declared more important, more ultimate, more valuable, more intrinsic to human well-being than any other'; 'each of these eight fundamental purposes is—looked at from its own point of view—the most important'.[13]

Now the content of a sound ethics is going to be worked out by someone who is, yes, as Lonergan and Aristotle insist, a morally good person (or, at least, as Aristotle takes care to note, someone who recognizes moral good when he sees it); but even before this we can say that it is going to be done by someone who is objective, that is, one who is not deflected in the pursuit of a pure, unrestricted desire to know, in this case, to know what is the good for man. But this pursuit is, as we have been noticing, the pursuit of one value, and there is no reason to suppose that it (sc. knowledge) is the only value or the most important value. So, on the one hand, we have the fact that moral objectivity is not a matter of intuiting moral concepts and principles, fully fledged, and on the other hand we have the fact that there is a multiplicity of equally basic aspects of human good, with no single yardstick for ranking them in order of importance and no further concrete objective to which these particular goods could be disposed as efficacious means are disposed to determinate ends. How then is the trick done? I mean, of course, the trick of 'working out' (to use Lonergan's term) the good, right way of pursuing and realizing and participating in the basic human goods.

Alas, it is all too clear that I am not going to answer that question in a philosophical fashion in the time-on period (not to say, injury-time) which is left to me. So let me indicate in most summary fashion how Grisez offers to do it, adding a few twists of my own.

The criterion of moral responsibility, Grisez argues, is fullness of human being, of participation in human good which is nothing other than the full circle or sphere of human possibilities which is made up of the eight basic purposes, values, or aspects of human flourishing. If you prefer to say, as Grisez formerly preferred to say and in no way now denies, that the

[13] *Beyond the New Morality*, 71.

criterion of moral responsibility is being reasonable, then you can say that reasonableness involves allowing each of the eight basic and incommensurable principles or starting points of practical reason its place in one's deliberation, and avoiding any deafness to any one or other of them. In either case, any response to the values, or employment of the practical principles, is going to be adequate, or reasonable, to the extent that each of the eight values is taken and treated for what it is, that is, as a value, in the sense I have been stressing, and not as a concrete operational objective (though of course, realization of the value is only by particular actions and concrete operational objectives). And this general form of moral responsibility Grisez analyses into eight (no! not functional specialities! but) modes of responsibility. These he richly illustrates not only with practical situations but also with indications of the way in which well-known philosophical ethical systems emphasize one or other of these eight modes to the exclusion of others of the eight. So there is first the responsibility of making an intelligent and consistent commitment to a harmonious set of purposes or values, rather than following mere whim or inclination or living for specific future objectives. John Rawls makes much of this in the neglected third part of his *A Theory of Justice* (1972). Secondly, there is the responsibility of taking into account at all times all of the basic forms of good, and not merely *qua* realizable by oneself but also as realizable by everybody else—so that this second mode incorporates the principle of universalizability which grounds Kant's and R.M. Hare's ethics. Thirdly, there is the responsibility of being willing to serve the needs and development of others even where there is no structured relationship to that other. Fourthly, there is detachment, that is, unwillingness to regard or treat any specific operational objective as if it were the or a basic human value itself: Epictetus's *Discourses* can be said to be founded on this principle. Fifth, and balancing the fourth mode, there is fidelity to the commitments one has made, which requires not only stability but also resourcefulness and creativeness in finding newly appropriate ways of realizing the values one is particularly committed to through one's profession or marriage or whatever: Josiah Royce's *Philosophy of Loyalty* (1908) elaborates the fourth and fifth modes. Sixthly, there is the responsibility of efficiently pursuing specific operational objectives that will advance the broader, deeper values to which one has dedicated oneself, using the utilitarian calculus where it will work, which is (contrary to the irrational contention of utilitarian moralists) only where one is confronted with different ways of realizing one and the same basic value or form of good.‡ Seventhly, there is the moral responsibility of fulfilling not only one's contractual duties (which are sufficiently accounted for in general by the second mode of responsibility with its principle 'Do unto others what you would have them do unto you') but also one's duties as a member of one's various associations and communities, where community is characterized by shared commitment to realization of some fundamental human purpose or purposes and by structures, roles, and activities appropriate accordingly. Negatively, there is the responsibility of not being a 'free-rider', of not abandoning one's part in the common participation in the (common) value for the limited operational objective of getting what one can for oneself out of the situation. All this obviously has a vast range of applications.

Eighthly, there is the responsibility which, unlike the others, is essentially negative: never to act directly contrary to any of the eight basic values in any of its realizations. This is simply the general principle of morality as it operates in one's conscience when one purges one's thought of every trace of utilitarianism. And thought is to be purged of utilitarianism for very many reasons, of which the two most relevant ones are: because every form of utilitarianism confuses moral action (which is self-determination through participation in fundamental human purposes as values) with pursuit of concrete operational objectives (for only in terms of such an objective can the effectiveness and desirability of particular actions be *calculated*); and because every form of utilitarianism arbitrarily postulates some common denominator or yardstick as a basis for its calculations (whereas the basic values are incommensurable and each is from its own standpoint the most important).

This eighth point is one of several respects in which Grisez's ethics can be seen to be Christian in the 'humdrum' sense in which Lonergan speaks of a Christian philosophy which, he says, is one 'that is open to the acceptance of Christian doctrine, that stands in harmony with it, and that, if rejected, leads to a rejection of Christian doctrine'.[14] For I take it that one part or aspect of Christian *doctrina de moribus* [moral teaching] is that there are certain kinds of action which it is one's moral responsibility never to choose to engage in, whatever the foreseeable consequences: examples come to mind in relation to killing the innocent, sexual acts of a non-procreative, for example contracepted, type, and lying—and these are, not surprisingly, intelligible as actions which inescapably involve one in choosing, willy-nilly, directly against the basic values of life, including life-in-its transmission or procreation, and truth.

Let me, finally, illustrate this sort of elaboration of an ethic by returning to the normative objectivity which I think Wittgenstein was more or less explicitly aware of and certainly realized or actualized in his own person. 'The whole of philosophic investigation', says Lonergan, is 'guided and

---

[14] Lonergan in McShane (ed.), *Language, Truth and Meaning*, 309.

ruled by a deliberate and conscientious pursuit of truth'.[15] The pursuit of the value is grounded in desire or inclination, and very often indeed Lonergan characterizes the desire as 'the detailed, disinterested, unrestricted desire to know'.[16] The characterization is a good one. But the disinterest is not, in truth, a detachment from the one's desire, as (in some measure) a philosopher, for a many-sided fulfilment of oneself as a person. And if you feel that we are wandering into the morass in which Aristotle flounders when he asks whether the *eudaimonia* and *arēte* of the *spoudaios* are to be found in the philosophic life of contemplation or the active life in the *polis*, consider the word 'unrestricted'. The unrestricted desire does not demand for its conscientious fulfilment that one pursue truth without regard for life or health or for the well-being of others, or in any other respect with the fanaticism that would flow from allowing a specific operational objective such as finding the answer to a specific problem to usurp the role of one basic human value amongst others. In short, one is not falling short of normative objectivity when one suspends, even on many occasions or permanently, the pursuit of truth, to fulfil one's responsibilities as someone who also is a parent, friend, citizen, neighbour, worshipper. But one *does* fall short of objectivity, radically, and one does thereby by one's arbitrariness in a sense make nonsense of everything, in short one does act and live immorally, if and when one on even a single occasion directly chooses against truth, immediately by deliberately fudging or faking an answer to one's own questions or shutting one's eyes to a relevant question, or mediately by stating what one knows to be false in a context in which truth and its common pursuit are at stake, such as scientific or philosophical collaboration.

NOTES

The reading of *On Certainty* in the first part of this essay was in conscious opposition to that aspect of Anthony Kenny's 1973 reading which is summarized in almost the final statement in the chapter on Scepticism and Certainty in Kenny, *Wittgenstein*: 'Wittgenstein does not think the sceptic can be answered, only silenced.' The terms are ambiguous, but if they must be employed, it would be better to say that in Wittgenstein's view in *On Certainty* the sceptic cannot be silenced but can be answered.

† *Lonergan's theory of value*...(at nn. 4–5). For a more resolute and detailed critique of Lonergan on value and morality, see *FoE* 42–5, 54; and essay V.9 (1992d).

‡ *Utilitarian 'calculus' could work where the issue is which way to realize one and the same basic value or form of good*...(p. 141). This concession was badly mistaken. Incommensurabilities between morally significant options defeat utilitarian methods even when only one basic human good (e.g. life) is at stake: see e.g. essay 15, sec. II (and earlier, *FoE* 89; *NDMR* 251–67; essay IV.17 (1990d) at 357).

[15] *Ibid.*, 308. [16] *Insight*, e.g. 596.

9

IS AND *OUGHT* IN AQUINAS[*]

The title 'Natural Inclinations and Natural Rights: Deriving *Ought* from *Is* according to Aquinas' was proposed for me by the Secretariat, and I accepted it as a challenge. Natural inclinations are not, for Aquinas, the fundamental reality in relation to which propositions about what ought to be done have their truth. 'Natural rights' is a phrase he never uses, and 'rights' (*iura*) is never used by him *in the sense* which that term invariably and usefully has in modern usage.[†] And, according to Aquinas, moral 'ought-propositions', being propositions of practical reason, are not derived from the 'is-propositions' of theoretical reason in the logician's sense(s) of 'derived'.

Still, an analysis of the relation between natural inclinations and natural rights, an analysis showing the dependence of moral realities on human nature, can certainly be provided in full conformity with what Aquinas does say about natural law (or natural right), about the virtues which are shaped by man's grasp of natural law, and about the specific moral norms derivable from the first principles of natural law.

I

Aquinas's formal discussion of these themes, in *ST* I–II, q.94 a.2c, begins not with inclinations but with goods as grasped by human practical reason in *per se nota* propositional principles. For '*bonum* est primum quod cadit in apprehensione practicae rationis' [*good* is what first falls within practical reason's understanding], and so the *primum principium in ratione practica* and *primum praeceptum legis* is 'bonum est faciendum et prosequendum, et malum vitandum' [good is to be done and pursued, and bad is to be

---

[*] 1987a ('Natural Inclinations and Natural Rights: Deriving *Ought* from *Is* according to Aquinas'); for a conference on the philosophy of Aquinas at Rolduc Abbey, near Maastricht, organized by Leo J. Elders SVD ['the Secretariat'].

avoided]. But human good is a manifold, and so St Thomas immediately shifts to the plural: all the objects of 'ought' propositions, i.e. *omnia illa facienda vel vitanda* [*all* those things to be done or avoided], pertain to the precepts of natural law insofar as 'ratio practica naturaliter apprehendit [illa] esse bona humana' [practical reason naturally understands them to be human goods]. There is not just one *primum principium per se notum* [self-evident first principle], but many, each identifying one of the goods which reason grasps as pursuit-worthy. Q.94 a.2 will go on to identify some (and will expressly deny that it is identifying all) of these primary or *secundum se*[1] goods: human life, procreative union, knowledge of truth about God, sociability, *et alia huiusmodi* [and other things of this kind].

But, to prepare for this specification of the primary or basic human goods, St Thomas refers directly to the inclinations natural to man. 'Omnia illa ad quae homo habet naturalem inclinationem', he says, 'ratio naturaliter apprehendit ut bona, et per consequens ut opere prosequenda, et contraria eorum ut mala et vitanda' [Everything that man is naturally inclined to, reason naturally understands as good and so as to be pursued by action]. A little later, in the ad 2m, he will say that '*omnes* huiusmodi inclinationes quarumcumque partium naturae humanae, puta concupiscibilis et irascibilis, *secundum quod regulantur ratione*, pertinent ad legem naturalem' [*all* inclinations of this kind, whichever part of human nature they pertain to (for instance the desiring part or the resisting part), pertain to the natural law *insofar as they are ruled by reason*]. However, this statement seems by itself too weak to convey his full meaning; it can sound as if he were saying no more than that all human inclinations are relevant to moral law and moral life, insofar as they have to be integrated into that life by being mastered by reason. That, however, would be a serious misreading of the text, first because Aquinas is at this point not limiting his conception of practical reason and natural law to *moral* reasoning and *moral* criteria of choice and action; but secondly because the role of human natural inclinations in his account of practical reasonableness (*sapientia/prudentia*) is positive and constitutive, not merely the role of a rabble waiting for a leadership to be imposed upon them *ab extra*.

What then is this constitutive role of the natural inclinations in the explanation of reasoning to justify 'oughts' (specifically moral, or otherwise)?[2]

---

[1] See *ST* I q.60 a.2c.

[2] Often, of course, *naturalis appetitus* and *naturalis inclinatio* are used by Aquinas in contradistinction from *appetitus sensitivus* and *inclinatio intelligiblis* or *voluntas*: e.g. I q.19 a.1c; q.59 a.1c; q.87 a.4c. (Aquinas calls this sense of 'natural' precisive—as man is distinguished from *id quod est animal tantum* (*cum praecisione sumptum*) but not *absolute: De Veritate* q.22 a.5 ad 6.) But in e.g. I–II q.94 a.2 (cf. also *In Eth.* V, lect. 12, para. 1019), *naturalis inclinatio* includes (in relation to some at least of the

The explanation can start where St Thomas starts in the *Summa Theologiae*, in I q.19 a.1c, where *appetitus naturalis* is explained as a *habitudo ad bonum naturae*; for, more precisely: 'Quaelibet...res ad suam formam naturalem hanc habet habitudinem, ut quando non habet ipsam, tendit in eam, et quando habet ipsam quiescat in *ea*; et idem est *de qualibet perfectione naturali*, quod est *bonum naturae*' [every kind of thing has a disposition towards its natural form, a disposition such that when it lacks that form, it tends towards it, and when it has it, it rests in it; and the same is true of every kind of natural perfection, that it is a natural good]. Here is the clue we were seeking; to speak of natural inclination(s) is to speak of the perfection(s) of the being which has such inclination(s).

And even though the natural perfections, the irreducibly distinct and basic aspects of the flourishing of that being, are of most direct and proximate relevance to a consideration of the *content* of the choice-guiding propositional principles which we call natural law, it remains highly relevant to speak also of the inclinations—for at least two reasons.[3] First, without the inclinations of the will, the prospect of the goods or perfections identified in the *prima principia communia* of the *lex naturae*[4] would scarcely arouse anyone to deliberation, choice, or the effort of *action* (the very point of the practical thinking in which those *prima principia* are first grasped). Second, the inclinations are ontologically more proximate to the nature whose specific character makes what-is-good-for-a-specific-type-of-being indeed good for that being. Indeed, we come to know the essence or nature of such a being by knowing its potentialities and capacities: 'per obiecta cognosc[i]mus actus, et per actus potentias, *et per potentias essentiam* animae'.[5]

I have emphasized the last words of that leading principle of Aristotelian and Thomist methodology. But the principle must be taken as whole, and when it is so taken, it discloses both (A) the reason why 'ought' is *not* derived

---

inclinations specified) a reference to natural volition(s), intelligent desire (will) for an understood good, on the basis explained in e.g. I–II q.26 a.1 ad 3: 'amor naturalis non solum est in viribus vegetativae, sed in omnibus potentiis animae...cum unaquaeque res habeat connaturalitatem ad id quod est sibi conveniens secundum suam naturam'. 'Unde in natura intellectuali invenitur inclinatio naturalis [vel amor] secundum voluntatem...': I q.60 a.1c. On the relation between 'natural inclination' and 'natural volition', see Grisez, 'The Structures of Practical Reason', sec. III.

[3] On the relation between 'good' and 'perfection' or fullness of being (a relation which, as Aquinas himself says—*ST* I q.5 a.1c and ad 1—is even more fundamental to the understanding of good(s) than the appetibility on which I–II q.94 a.2c focuses), see I q.5 a.3c; q.6 a.3c; q.48 a.1c; I–II q.18 a.1c; *de Veritate* q.21 aa. 1–3. See also *NLNR* 78–9, stressing that, as object of intelligent inclination, each primary good is conceived precisely as perfective. (Thus Flippen, 'Natural Law and Natural Inclinations' at 308–14, is utterly mistaken in thinking that I treat 'good as object of inclination' as more basic and determinative than 'good as perfective', and the latter as a 'speculative afterthought'.) [On Flippen and the proper understanding of the role of natural inclinations in Aquinas's ethical theory, see also Grisez, 'Natural Law and Natural Inclinations'.]

[4] The phrasing used in I–II q.94 a.4c.

[5] *In II de Anima* lect. 6 no. 308. See also *Q.D. de Anima* q. 6 ad 8; *FoE* 21, 25.

I.9 IS AND OUGHT IN AQUINAS

from 'is' (according to Aquinas), and (B) the reason why 'ought' *is* derived from 'is' (according to Aquinas).

As to (A): Propositions about primary (*secundum se*) human goods are not derived from propositions about human nature or from any other propositions of speculative reason; as Aquinas says with maximum clarity, and never wavers from saying, they are *per se nota* and *indemonstrabilia* (I–II q.58 aa. 4c and 5c; q.91 a.3c; q.94 a.2c; *In Eth.* V, lect. 12 [para. 1018]). For we come to know human nature *by* knowing its potentialities, and these we come to know *by* knowing their actuations, which in turn we know by knowing their objects—and the objects of the characteristically human *inclinatio* and *actus*, the will, are precisely the primary human goods.[6] (So, if anything, an adequately full knowledge of human nature is derived from our practical[7] and underived (*per se notum*) knowledge of the human goods of which Aquinas speaks in I–II q.94 a.2.) In this sense, 'ought' is not derived, from 'is'.

But (B): if we shift from the epistemological to the ontological mode, the same methodological principle, in its application to human beings, presupposes and thus entails that the goodness of all human goods (and thus the appropriateness, the *convenientia*, of all human responsibilities) is derived from (i.e. depends upon) the nature which, by their goodness, those goods perfect. For those goods—which as ends are the *rationes* of practical norms or 'oughts'—would not perfect that nature were it other than it is. So, *ought* ontologically depends on—and in that sense certainly may be said to be derived from—*is*.[8]

---

[6] See *ST* I–II q.10 a.1c:

... principia intellectualis cognitionis sunt naturaliter nota. Similiter etiam principium motuum voluntariorum oportet esse aliquid naturaliter nota. Hoc autem est bonum in communi, in quod voluntas naturaliter tendit, sicut etiam quaelibet potentia in suum obiectum...et universaliter omnia illa quae conveniunt volenti secundum suam naturam. Non enim per voluntatem appetimus solum ea quae pertinent ad potentiam voluntatis sed etiam ea quae pertinent ad singulas potentias, et ad totum hominem. Unde naturaliter homo vult non solum obiectum voluntatis, sed etiam alia quae conveniunt aliis potentiis: ut *cognitionem veri*, quae convenit intellectui; et *esse et vivere* et alia huiusmodi, quae respiciunt consistentiam naturalem; quae omnia comprehenduntur sub obiecto voluntatis, sicut *quaedam particularia bona*.

[7] Obviously (but, alas, it needs saying), practical reason/knowledge must not be understood in any Kantian (or neo-Kantian, e.g. Gadamerian) sense. It is genuine, scientific, and true knowledge of truths (*ST* I q.79 a.11 ad 2) which, once attained and appropriated by practical understanding, become available to and, in some form, part of the patrimony of speculative knowledge, and so of metaphysics and theology. Thus, e.g., it is practical reason which has the role of 'considering' and 'determining' the ultimate end of human life and human affairs: *In Eth.* I, lect. 2 [n. 31]; II, lect. 2 [n. 256] and lect. 9 [n. 351]; VI, lect. 8 [n. 1233]; *In Pol.* proem [nn. 5–8]; *In Lib. Boet. de Trin.* q.5 a.1c and ad 4; essay 10 at 159–60, 168–70. To say this is not to dispute the supremacy of metaphysics (or of theology); see *In lib. Boet. de Trin.* q.5 a.1 ad 9 for a consideration of the way in which sciences can be interdependent without any vicious circle, because each science—even one subalternated to another—can call upon some principles which are *per se nota* and thus not derived from the other science.

[8] Moreover,

semper prius salvatur in posteriori. Natura autem prior est quam intellectus, quia natura cuiuscumque rei est essentia eius. Unde id quod est naturae, oportet salvari etiam in habentibus

II

Let us revert to the epistemological mode. The first principles of practical reason are *per se nota* and *indemonstrabilia*. They are, therefore, not deduced or inferred, by any propositional form of inference, from propositions of speculative reason. But this is not to say that there is a 'wall of separation'[9] between the 'is' of our speculative (including informal, common sense) knowledge of human nature, and the 'ought' of the practical norms. On the contrary, 'ad determinationem cognitionis [principiorum rationis practicae] sensu et memoria indige[]mus' [we need sense(s) and memory to settle knowledge of the principles of practical reason]: *Sent.* II d.24, q.2, a.3 sol.; and thus these first practical principles, like the first principles of speculative reason, can be said to be 'induced' from experiences,[10] an experience which will include not only the stirrings of desire and aversion, but also an awareness of possibilities, likelihoods, *ut in pluribus* [typical] outcomes, and so forth.[11] Despite phrases which invite misunderstanding,[12] Aquinas's theory of the first principles of practical reason and natural law is neither a theory of 'innate' knowledge, nor intuitionist in the usual modern sense of 'intuition'.

III

To understand Aquinas's conception of these *prima principia* of natural law or practical reason, let us revert to the question (not an unambiguous question) whether the principles are moral or, rather, somehow pre-moral in their sense and force.

The answer, I think, is that we must distinguish. They are moral principles in as much as they are understood, accepted, and developed and integrated

---

intellectum. Est autem hoc commune omni naturae, ut habeat aliquam inclinationem, quae est appetitus naturalis, vel amor.... Unde in natura intellectuali invenitur inclinatio naturalis secundum voluntatem. (*ST* I q.60 a.1c.)

Again: 'appetitus naturalis est inclinatio cuiuslibet rei in aliquid ex natura sua; unde naturali appetitu quaelibet potentia desiderat sibi conveniens': I q.78 a.1 ad 3.

[9] As some misread the distinction; see 1981e at 267–9.

[10] Cf. e.g. *In Post. Anal.* II lect. 20 [n. 14]; Veatch, *Two Logics*, 167–9; Veatch, *Aristotle*, 172–80. NB: at *ibid.*, 180, Veatch calls this form of induction an 'inference'; but I follow many philosophers in preferring to restrict the term 'inference' to reasoning which moves from one proposition or propositional principle to another proposition—a use which seems concordant with Aquinas's reference to principles which are *per se* (i.e. non-inferentially) *nota*.

[11] See *NLNR* 19, 65, 66, 71, 77, 85; *FoE* 22.

[12] e.g. *Sent.* II d.24 q.2 a.3 sol.:

Synderesis a ratione practica distinguitur non quidem per substantiam potentiae, sed per habitum, qui est *quodammodo innatus menti nostrae* ex ipso lumine intellectus agentis, sicut et habitus principiorum speculativorum...

For Aquinas's denial of innate knowledge, i.e. human knowledge acquired without experience, see *ST* I q.79 a.2c; *De Veritate* q.16 a.1c.

into a life which is shaped by *prudentia* and the other moral virtues because it is truly open to and in love with that *integral* human fulfilment which is the *bonum commune toti societati quod est bonum divinum prout est beatudinis obiectum* (i.e. the fulfilment of the citizens *illius beatae societatis quae vocatur coelestis Hierusalem*) of which St Thomas speaks in *De Caritate* a.2c.

But as grasped *naturaliter*, by each intelligent adult human being, the *prima principia* of practical reason are not moral principles, in as much as they retain a real intelligibility and practical relevance as they are understood, accepted, and applied (a) in the life of one who is radically alienated from *prudentia* and virtue, or (b) in the practical reasoning of those who prescind from virtue and vice for the purpose of purely technical reasoning (e.g. military tactics).

Everyone—at least everyone who has enough experience to grasp the significance of the words—understands and in some sense acknowledges these first practical principles, and has some inclination of the will towards the ends/goods/objects which they identify as choiceworthy. Even the damned.[13] Even people (like the Germans whom Caesar reported) 'apud [quos] olim latrocinium non reputabatur iniquum' [among whom, at one time, robbery was not thought wrong].[14]

For: these *prima principia communissima*, which 'nullo modo potest a cordibus hominum deleri in universali',[15] are not so much precepts as, rather, 'quasi fines praeceptorum'.[16] Equally, they are the *fines moralium virtutum*.[17] They are not yet moral principles or the actual *rationes virtutum*, but rather are *quaedam seminalia intellectualium virtutum et moralium*,[18] seeds which will not suffice to identify a moral virtue or its constitutive or dependent moral precepts without the supplementation which wisdom[19] and *prudentia*[20] afford to elementary practical understanding.

[13] *Sent.* II d.39 q.3 a.1 sol. and ad 5; *ST Supp.* q.98, a.2c.
[14] I–II q.94 aa. 4c and 6c. For the (imperfect) way in which immoral people respond to the *prima principia*, see 1982a at 27–8.
[15] ['in no way can be expunged entirely from human hearts'] I–II q.94 a.6c; also q.99 a.2 ad 2; q.100 a.5 ad 1; q.100 a.11c; q.58 a.5c; q.77 a.2c; q.79 a.12 ad 3; *De Veritate* q.16 a.3c.
[16] I–II q.100 a.11c; and see *ST* II–II q.56 a.1c ('fines humanae vitae se habent in agendis sicut principia naturaliter cognita in speculativis').
[17] 'necesse est quod fines moralium virtutum praeexistant in ratione...principia naturaliter nota...quia finis se habet in operabilibus sicut principium in speculativis... [V]irtutes morales...tendunt in finem a ratione naturali praestitutum. Unde relinquitur quod prudentia...moveat eas; sed synderesis movet prudentiam sicut intellectus principiorum scientiam': II–II q.47 a.6c and ad 3. See also I–II q.58 a.3 ad 2 and 4c; *Sent.* III d.36 d.1 ad 3.
[18] *ST* I–II q.63 a.1c and a.2 ad 3.
[19] I–II q.94 a.2: 'Quaedam vero propositiones sunt per se notae solis sapientibus'. Regrettably, Aquinas never clearly identifies which practical principles are *per se nota quoad solos sapientes*; cf. I–II q.100 aa. 3 and 11, which seem to treat the precepts which are known only to the wise as discovered by them by reasoning.
[20] *Prudentia* ('sapientia in rebus humanis': II–II q.47 a.2) includes everything reason must supply if the moral virtues are to attain the *medium rationis* which is essential to their goodness: see I–II

As the ends/goods identified in the *prima principia* of practical reason are, in this sense, pre-moral, so too they are, in a certain sense post-moral. For they are constituents (at least of the *bene esse*) of *beatitudo* (in which the moral virtues will need to subsist in only reduced mode). I will not here dwell on this complex and disputed issue, which I have recently analysed elsewhere.[21]

IV

The title I accepted requires that I follow the movement of thought from good as object of any natural inclination, all the way through to good as moral right. So it is time to observe that the *Summa Theologiae* is a work neither of *philosophia moralis* nor of the *prudentia* which Aquinas regarded[22] as essential to *philosophia moralis*. The *Secunda Pars* is structured on the great themes of beatitude as the consummation of the rational creature's *reditus* [return] to the Creator: and of the free and self-constituting human act as the means by which human persons both forward (or frustrate) that *reditus* and image (or contemn) the divine exemplar. St Thomas's decision to focus upon human *acts* is, of course, consistent with his attending, as he does, to the *principia* of human action, including the *principia* afforded by the moral norms, natural and revealed. But it is a decision whose immediate consequence was that the treatise's treatment of particular moral questions would be structured on the virtues (and vices), '*tota* materia morali ad considerationem *virtutum* reducta...'.[23]

And that decision, for all its instrinsic merit (which I do not question), had a regrettable side effect. The rational propositional principles which constitute and specify the *regula vel mensura rationis*, or *medium rationis*, which distinguishes virtue from vice[24] never became the central focus of Aquinas's attention. Later theologians and moral philosophers, until almost today, have not repaired the omission; many have seemed not to notice it; many have offered to fill the gap with principles more or less foreign to Aquinas and to reason.

---

q.63 a.1c; q.66 a.3 ad 3. On the 'naturalis inclinatio in...cuilibet homini ad hoc quod agat secundum rationem' ('hoc est agere secundum virtutem'), see I–II q.94 a.3c.

[21] Essay 10.

[22] Aquinas's lack of concern to distinguish *philosophia moralis* from *prudentia* is signalled by the opening words of his commentary on the *Ethics*: *sapientis est ordinare*. This *sapientia* is clearly the *sapientia in rebus humanis* which is *prudentia* and 'pertains solely to practical reason' (II–II q.47 a.2), as indeed does *philosophia moralis* (*In Pol.*, proem 5–8; *In Eth.* II, lect. 2 [n. 256]; lect. 9 [n. 351]).

[23] *ST* II–II, prologus. On the centrality of *actus*, see e.g. Lafont, *Structures et Méthode dans la Somme Théologique de Saint Thomas d'Aquin*, 111–32, 163 0, 210 00.

[24] I–II q.64 a.1c and ad 1.

Let me give two examples of what I have thus ventured to call an omission. In the *Summa Theologiae*, the morality of lying is discussed under the virtue of justice. But: that lying is unjust scarcely assists in the resolution of the cruxes of the morality of lying. Should we lie to save one person from being murdered by another? Perhaps the potential victim has the right, in justice, to be saved by a lie? Countless moral theologians today will say, 'Yes, for minus malum est eligendum ut vitetur maius malum; sicut medicus praescindit membrum ne corrumpatur totum corpus...Ergo licite potest homo mentiri ut unum praeservet ab homicidio et alium praeservet a morte.'[25]

Now Aquinas regards such theologians as in error; he simply rejects their claim, as he *everywhere* rejects every attempt to resolve moral problems by appeal to 'minus malum eligendum' [choose the lesser evil];[26] 'mendacium non solum habet rationem peccati ex damno quod infertur proximo, sed ex sua inordinatione...' [lying is sinful not only when it harms one's neighbour, but because of its disorder...].[27] But what is this *inordinatio* which entails that lying is 'secundum se malum ex genere' [evil in itself and of its kind] and so 'nullo modo potest bonum et licitum' [in no way can be good and permissible]?[28] There follows the famous explanation, stating that lying is an *actus cadens super indebitam materiam* [an act that has an inappropriate object] because 'cum voces naturaliter sint signa intellectuum, innaturale est et indebitum quod aliquis voce significet id quod non habet in mente'.[29] This explanation remains, however, simply obscure; Aquinas's own general theory has prepared us to treat the 'natural' or 'unnatural' as ethically relevant just insofar as those terms signify the 'reasonable' or 'unreasonable'.[30] But when that substitution is made, this explanation of the evil of lying seems question-begging.[31]

My other example is the treatment of sexual morality in *ST* II–II qq. 153 and 154. Here the virtues are, most generally, temperance, and specifically

---

[25] II–II q.110 a.3 obj. 4 ['for one should choose the lesser evil and avoid the greater, just as the doctor amputates the limb lest it rot the whole body...So it is permissible to lie to save one person from committing murder and the other from death'].

[26] II–II q.110 a.3 ad 4. Rejections of the tag: *Sent.* IV d.6 q.1 a.1 qa.1 obj. 4 and ad 4; d.9 q.1 a.5 qa.1 obj. 3 and ad 3; *ST* III q.68 a.11 obj. 3 and ad 3; q.80 a.6 obj. 2 and ad 2. Use of the tag, in analysis of inconstancy and rashness: *Sent.* IV d.29 q.1 a.2c. Generally, Lee, 'Permanence of the Ten Commandments: St Thomas and His Modern Commentators'; May, 'Aquinas and Janssens on the Moral Meaning of Human Acts'.

[27] II–II q.110 a.3 ad 4.   [28] *Ibid.*, a.3c.

[29] *Id.* ['since utterances are naturally to be signs conveying understandings, it is unnatural and inappropriate that someone's utterance signify what he does not have in his mind'.]

[30] e.g. I–II q.71 a.2c; q.18 a.5c; q.94 a.3 ad 3; q.100 a.1c; [and essay III.22 (1997d) at nn. 58–65, 72].

[31] Some progress can be made by referring back to II–II q.110 a.1 and q.109 a.2. But not enough. [*Aquinas* 154–63 subsequently expands greatly, and by reference to many more texts, on this suggested route to an explanation. The explanation still leaves something to be desired, I am inclined to think.]

temperance concerning the pleasures of sex, that is, chastity as opposed to *luxuria*. But the norm of *recta ratio*, by which chastity is distinguished from *luxuria* by reference to types of act such as fornication, is never clearly identified or stated. The premise of the arguments, it seems clear, is not any direct reference to the biological function or the teleology of the sex organs or of semen. Rather, there seems an effort to build up a notion of a general form of good (a *bonum commune* or *universale*)—specifically, the transmission or preserved continuity of human life—together with a form of human relationship (marriage),[32] a notion or pair of notions‡ to which various forms of sexual activity can then be said to be 'repugnant'. The *repugnantia* in question seems not to consist, essentially, in the creation of a likelihood or risk that those forms of sexual activity will consequently, empirically, break up or obstruct those human goods *as subsisting states of affairs* (whether present and enjoyed, or sought as operational objectives). Rather, it seems to consist in the elected failure of such activities to give such form or forms of good due expression in bodily fashion.[33] But any such interpretation of these texts must remain speculative and questionable, as do alternative explanations.

V

Now, to consider the morality of lying or fornication is, for Aquinas, a matter of considering moral norms of the form and content of the commands of the Decalogue[34]—not necessarily, of course, *qua* divinely commanded, but *qua* norms of natural law and knowable by reason.[35] And Aquinas states clearly enough that norms such as these are not *per se nota* but are conclusions—no doubt proximate and very easily reached, *statim*, but conclusions nevertheless. 'Derivantur quaedam a principiis communibus legis naturae per modum conclusionum: sicut hoc quod est *non esse occidendum* ut conclusio quaedam derivari potest ab eo quod est

---

[32] See I–II q.154 a.2c.

[33] See q.154 a.12c and ad 4. This line of thought is developed in 1985e at 49–55. But already in his *Contraception and the Natural Law*, 100–1, 106, Germain Grisez had noted that, if the distinction between human goods as operational objectives and human goods as 'ideals' (sc. as forms of good, each *commune* and a *universale*) is observed, Aquinas's argument against fornication and contraception, in *ScG* III, 122 'begins to make sense'. [And see essay III.22 (1997d) n. 116 and passim.]

[34] Indeed, 'legislator *per prohibitionem moechiae* prohibuit fornicationem simplicem, et *per falsum testimonium* prohibuit omne mendacium', in as much as the lesser moral evil is included in the greater, 'non...via syllogistica...tamen eo modo quo ea quae ex seminibus naturae progrediuntur, in rationibus seminalibus continentur': *Sent.* III d.37 q.2 a.3 qa.1 ad 2.

[35] 'Quaedam [praecepta moralia]...statim per se ratio naturalis cuiuslibet hominis diiudicat esse facienda vel non facienda: sicut... *Non occides*...Et huiusmodi sunt absolute de lege naturae': *ST* I–II q.100 a.1c. (As the end of the *responsio* makes clear, the *per se* here signifies, not a *per se notum principle*, but a principle knowable *per rationem* as opposed to *per instructionem divinam*).

nulli esse malum faciendum'.[36] Or again: 'illa [praecepta]...quae sunt prima et communia...sunt scripta in ratione naturali quasi per se nota, sicut quod nulli debet homo malefacere et alia huiusmodi...[et]...continentur [in praeceptis decalogi] sicut principia in conclusionibus proximis'.[37]

Now, if moral norms such as the norms prohibiting lying, fornication, or homicide are conclusions from premises, the premises must include one or more moral principles, too. What can be the content of such absolutely first *moral* principle or principles? And what can be the relation of such principle or principles to the principle expressly stated in *ST* I–II q.94 a.2—*bonum est faciendum et prosequendum et malum vitandum?* Or to the various particular *prima principia* implied by the argument of that article—for example 'human life is a good to be fostered and pursued, and what threatens it is to be avoided'; 'knowledge of God is a good to be pursued, and what prejudices it is to be avoided'? Aquinas neither poses these questions nor expressly tells us the answers to them.

He does say that the moral precepts of love of God and neighbour are more primary and more immediately knowable than the moral precepts of the Decalogue—at least to faith (since the existence and nature of God are not self-evident to reason)[38]—and that these radical moral precepts stand to the precepts of the Decalogue *quasi fines praeceptorum*.[39] This may be a helpful pointer to the identity of the truly first principle of morality.[40] But it is not a precise statement of such a principle, since (for one thing) there is, as he elsewhere says, a hierarchical relationship between love of God and love of neighbour: II–II q.26 a.2c. Moreover, these precepts do not themselves seem to constitute premises from which one can conclude to

---

[36] I–II q.95 a.2c ['some things are derived from the general principles of the law of nature by way of deduction [conclusion]: for example *killing is prohibited* can be derived as one conclusion from *no one is to be harmed*']. '... omne iudicium rationis practicae procedit ex quibusdam principiis naturaliter cognitis...Ex quibus diversimode procedi potest ad iudicandum de diversis. Quaedam enim sunt in humanis actibus adeo explicita quod statim, cum modica consideratione, possunt approbari vel reprobari per illa communia et prima principia': q.100 a.1c; an example from the Decalogue is then mentioned, in the passage quoted in the preceding footnote. See also q.100 a.5c. NB: there are passages in which Aquinas speaks of moral norms of the Decalogic type as if they were at the highest level and *naturaliter* or *per se nota*. But these must be understood as passages where the distinction between such norms and the norms from which they are derived is of no importance or of less importance than the distinction between all such norms and norms knowable only by the wise, or norms which have their force from their positive enactment.

[37] Q.100 a.3c ['those principles which are first and general...are inscribed in natural reason as if self-evident, as for example that one ought to harm no one, and so forth, and these are contained in the precepts of the Ten Commandments as principles are contained in proximate conclusions']; see also ad 1; a.6c; a.11c and ad 1; q.94 a.6c.

[38] I–II q.100 a.3 ad 1.

[39] I–II q.100 a.11c. See Boyle, 'Aquinas, Kant and Donagan on Moral Principles'.

[40] On the first principle of morality, see Grisez, *Christian Moral Principles*, 459–76, 807–30; *FoE* 72; *NDMR* ch. X, 4–5.

Aquinas's positions, that every lie, every intended or chosen killing of the innocent, or every adultery is morally wrong.

What Aquinas *does* seem to have thought is that such conclusions can be deduced from the moral principle already mentioned: one ought to do no harm to anyone. But to make it clear that the latter is a plausible candidate for inclusion amongst the first principles of morality, one needs *first* an explicit action theory which distinguishes between doing harm in the sense of intending it as an end or choosing it as a means, and doing harm only in the sense of accepting it as a side effect of an action, which involves neither the intention nor the choice of it. Main elements of such an action theory can be found in Aquinas,[41] but he does not propose and defend the account as such.

And one will need, *second*, a clearer answer than Aquinas offers to the question whether (and if so, why) one may intend or choose to harm those who are culpably causing harm or, perhaps, who are guilty of previously causing it.[42]

Moreover, behind the concept of 'harm' (*nocumentum, malefacere*) stands the more basic concept of human good. It is thus possible to surmise that Aquinas implicitly worked with a primary moral principle (one among others) of the form now clearly identified, proposed, and defended by Grisez, Boyle, May, Lee, myself, and others: 'Do not choose to destroy, damage or impede any instantiation of a basic human good' (i.e. any of the primary goods of the kind referred to in I–II q.94 a.2c).[43]

A principle such as this would explain and justify many of the claims Aquinas makes about types of act which are always wrong (*mala ex genere*) whatever the circumstances and the consequences of declining to choose and do them. It would, in the modern terminology of my title, explain and justify the claim that there are certain absolute human rights, such as the right of the innocent not to be directly killed, that is, killed as an end or as a means.

There is no reason to think that this (Do not directly attack any primary [basic] good) is the only moral principle needed to explain and justify the moral norms proposed or defended by Aquinas. Other 'intermediate principles' (mediating between the *prima principia communissima* of practical reason and moral norms as specific as the Decalogue's) are needed and can be identified. A principle of fairness, for example, is needed

---

[41] e.g. *ST* II–II q.64 a.7c.

[42] 'Nocumentum...inferre alicui non licet nisi per modum poenae propter iustitiam' [it is not permissible to inflict harm on anyone, except as punishment for the sake of justice]: II–II q.65 a.2c; cf. *FoE* 128–33.

[43] Lee proposes this as an interpretation of Aquinas, indeed as an interpretation of I–II q.91 a.2, in 'Permanence of the Ten Commandments' at 442–3.

to specify and explain the natural right to be respected in distributive justice. These intermediate primary principles have only recently, I think, become a prominent theme or topic in Thomistic reflection.[44] This essay has been able to do no more than sketch the Thomist framework in which the problematic of such principles emerges and calls, as it urgently does, for explanation and development.

NOTES

† *'iura' never used by Aquinas in modern sense of 'rights'*...(at 144). This is simply a mistake. See *Aquinas* 133–8; 2002c; summarized sufficiently in essay IV.5 (2002a), sec. VIII.

‡ *Transmission of life and relationship of marriage*...(at n. 32). The uncertainty about whether this is one good or two is resolved by understanding that the basic human good at stake here is the single good of marriage (with two aspects, procreation and friendship). Mistranscription of Aquinas's text at the crucial point in *ST* I–II q.94 a.2c helped obscure this: see *Aquinas* 82, 97–8.

[44] See, most recently, Grisez, *Christian Moral Principles*, chs 8 and 26; also *NLNR* ch. V.

Part Two

Building on the Foundations

10

ACTION'S MOST ULTIMATE END[*]

Our practical reasoning goes well and attains its truth when we identify ways of adequately getting or realizing really desirable objectives. And our objectives are really desirable (good) when they either are really desirable in themselves or are steps on the way to getting or realizing some such intrinsically desirable objective or objectives. If there is but one such intrinsically desirable objective, our practical reasoning cannot go well unless we know what it is. If, as seems much more plausible, there are a number of intrinsically desirable objectives, our practical reasoning cannot go well unless we know whether there is some further objective to be attained or realized by or in the pursuit of some or all of these intrinsically desirable objectives, that is, whether there is some *further* point to pursuing them; and if so, what that further point or objective ('last end') actually is.

Some say that the true last end is some one of the intrinsically desirable human goods, say, the highest instantiation of the highest good attainable in this life, thus *contemplation of God* to the extent that God is knowable through his creatures. Others agree that it is some one human good, but place it beyond this life, and beyond merely human capacities, in the *beatific vision* and contemplation of God. Others again deny that it is any *one* of the human goods, and say that it is *integral human fulfilment*, a manifold of goods; and that, given human capacities as we know them, such fulfilment can now be for practical reasoning no more than an inadequately attainable value, an ideal of practical reason, but could in a divinely completed realm and household of God be shared in and enjoyed, by each member of that realm and household, as an attained and realized goal.

This essay defends and elaborates the last-mentioned position.

A preliminary methodological note. As Thomas Aquinas very plainly says, the task of philosophically 'considering and determining the ultimate end of human life and human affairs' belongs to the principal *practical* science;[1] Aristotle called it ethics and Thomas moral philosophy,[2] but

---

[*] 1984a ('Practical Reasoning, Human Goods and the End of Man').
[1] *In. Eth.* I, lect. 2, (ed. Spiazzi) n. 31; see also III, lect. 8, n. 1233, with n. 3 below.
[2] See Gauthier and Jolif, *L'Ethique à Nicomaque*, ii, 1–2; *In Eth.* I, lect. 1, nn. 2, 3, 7.

both agreed that it is practical, from beginning to end.[3] This, then, is philosophizing to be done (if done intelligently) for the sake of realizing or getting intrinsically desirable human good(s).[4] Such philosophizing is thus (if one can only get one's act together) all of a piece with the rest of one's practical reasonings.

I

In *NE* I.2, Aristotle launches an argument that many have understood as the following mere fallacy: If any chain of choices must end somewhere, there must be a single place where all chains of choice stop. Aristotle's text,[5] however, is not so simple-minded:

If...

[1] we do not choose everything for some further thing (for that would be to begin an infinite regress, in which case desire would be empty and pointless),

and

[2] there is some one end of acts, which we want for its own sake while we want the others for it,

then it is clear that

[3] that one end will be the good and indeed the highest good.

Now this is no fallacy. Step (1) does not assert that there must, if choice is not to be vain, be one place in which all chains of choice end. It simply asserts that every chain of choice does have a point, its own point or end or final good (not necessarily the same point as other chains of choice). One chain of practical reasoning ends, Aristotle will suggest,[6] in a good such as honour, another in a good such as pleasure, another in the good of understanding, and others in one or other of the excellences or virtues.

---

[3] For Aristotle, see *NE* I.3: 1095a5–6; II.2: 1103b27–9; VI.8: 1141b23; and the arguments of Teichmuller amply summarized and defended in Ando, *Aristotle's Theory of Practical Cognition*, 121, 168–74. For St Thomas, see *In Pol.* proem. (ed. Spiazzi), nn. 5–8; *In Eth.* II, lect. 2, n. 256; lect. 9, n. 351; *In Lib. Boet. de Trin.* q.5 a.1c and ad. 4. It is clear that Aquinas has no interest in drawing a significant distinction between 'moral philosophy' and 'prudentia'; he will introduce the treatise on moral philosophy with the words 'sapientis est ordinare' (*In Eth.* I, lect. 1, n. 1), and the *sapientia* in question, as the development of the whole commentary makes clear, is that *sapientia in rebus humanis* [wisdom in human affairs] which is *prudentia* and 'pertains solely to practical reason' (*ST* II–II q 47 a,2).

[4] See *FoE* ch. 1.   [5] *NE* I.2: 1094a18–22, re-arranging the sentence order.
[6] *NE* I.7: 1097b2.

And now step (2) comes in to say that if even these 'other' final goods or ends-for-their-own-sake[7] are chosen not only for their own sake but also for the sake of some one end, then (3) that one end will be the highest good or, as Aristotle puts it (elliptically and at considerable risk of misleading), *the* good simpliciter.

In *NE* I.7 Aristotle is going to explain both this conclusion and his reason for affirming what is supposed in step (2), that is, for affirming that there is indeed 'some one end of acts, which we want for its own sake while we want the others for it'. Take the conclusion [step (3)] first.

To understand something possible or actual as good is to understand it as having or giving point, as a 'that for the sake of which...,' as end. And the good without qualification will be, he says, whatever is most an end. *The* good will be most final by making one's life (A) lacking in nothing, i.e. 'self-sufficient' (*autarchēs*) and (B) thoroughly desirable (choiceworthy, *airetos, eligibilis*).

Now self-sufficiency and unqualified desirability are both definitive of *eudaimonia*, a concept more ordinarily familiar to Aristotle's hearers than the technical concept of *the good*. So '*the* good' is *eudaimonia*, provided we understand by *eudaimonia* a state (whatever it may turn out to be) which (A) makes one's life self-sufficient, i.e. lacking in nothing, i.e. satisfying all desires,[8] and (B) is unrestrictedly final in that it is the point of all choices, even of choices for goods which are themselves final in that they are chosen for their own sake, as ends in themselves.

Troels Engberg-Pedersen has argued forcefully that in Book I of the *NE*, *eudaimonia* is, in fact, a purely formal concept, the concept of a satisfactory life: an indeterminate state which (A) involves the satisfaction of all desires and (B) is the point of all choice. Aristotle here makes no decision amongst the competing conceptions of this concept; the state is left wholly undetermined. Even when the argument leads Aristotle to affirm that the state is one of activity, 'it is left absolutely open whether just one thing or activity or more things or activities than one should in the end be said to fill in *eudaimonia*'.[9]

Now the formal property of *eudaimonia* in *NE* I.7 (1095b5) is this: When we stop our chains of choice (practical reasoning) at other ends or goods which *are* final, we do so not only because of the goodness of such

---

[7] For this interpretation of the term 'the others', see *In Eth.* I, lect. 2, n. 19. The recognition that basic goods can be desired and valued both for their own sake and as components in a completely final good (*eudaimonia*) is reached by Plato in his critique of Socrates: see Irwin, *Plato's Moral Theory*, 167.

[8] It goes without saying that 'desires', throughout, is to be taken in the Aristotelian, not the Humean sense: see *FoE* 44; also 30–7, 44–5; 1981e at 266–70.

[9] Engberg-Pedersen, *Aristotle's Theory of Moral Insight*, 31; see also 12, 17–18, 20, 31–2.

ends-for-their-own-sake but also because we believe that through these goods we will secure *eudaimonia*.

So here, at last, we find ground for asserting what was hypothesized in step (2). Precisely because the concept of *eudaimonia* simply is the concept of the fully satisfactory life—that is, a state (whatever it may be) which is the point of all choices and the satisfaction of all desires—it can be said that final goods such as (Aristotle supposes) honour, pleasure, understanding, and virtue are chosen not only for their own sakes but also for the sake of *eudaimonia*. Thus *eudaimonia* is the 'one end' Aristotle was envisaging.

But one may wish to test the matter. Are the various final goods *in fact* chosen for the sake of *eudaimonia*? Aristotle says so, but offers no argument to prove it. The missing argument must, I think, be that suggested by Aquinas.[10] For Aquinas, this fact is not a mere happenstance, which sometimes is the case and sometimes not; it is a necessity, a natural necessity and (since *will* simply is the power of intelligent and rational choosing) a rational necessity. Why? Surely because about every specific human good, however thoroughly and independently and non-derivatively good (and thus capable of terminating a chain of practical reasoning and rendering otiose the question 'What for?'), there can nonetheless be raised the further question: 'Is the state of affairs in which this good, or this set of goods, is realized by my choice a *fully satisfactory* state of affairs?'

The question is meaningful, and successful in relativizing even our most successful attainments of basic human goods; the question remains meaningful, and forceful, even though we remain quite unable to identify a practicable 'fully satisfactory life', or an attainable 'perfect good', a 'practicable state of affairs lacking nothing', *'perfectum et sufficiens'*.[11]

Specific basic goods, that is, goods which are underived and chain-of-choice-ending, have both a critique and a support in this category, this inescapable further question. They have a critique because no one of them can plausibly pose as itself the fully satisfactory object of choice. They have a support because each of them has its attraction not merely as 'a good in itself' but also as a component in, contribution to, *the fully satisfactory*, whatever that may be.

II

But how are the basic human goods in fact related to a 'fully satisfactory'? The 'fully satisfactory' that Aristotle and Aquinas have in mind is

---

[10] See *ST* I–II q.5 a.8c; see also q.5 a.8 ad 2 and a.4 ad 2; q.13 a.6c; I q.19 a.3c and a.10c; q.60 a.2c; q.82 a.1c and a.2c; q.94 a.1c; *de Malo* q.3 a.3c; *In Eth.* III, lect. 2, n. 103.

[11] *ST* I–II q.5 aa. 3c, 4c, quoting *NE* I.7: 1097b8.

'practicable'. But Aquinas quite reasonably points out that it is simply impossible to attain the fully satisfactory ('excluding all evil and fulfilling every desire') in this life.[12] Only an 'imperfect' beatitude, he says, is within our powers.[13]

But is 'imperfect beatitude' a coherent concept? After all, the 'perfect', the 'fully satisfactory', is what the concept of *eudaimonia/beatitudo* is about; an 'imperfect beatitude' is, by definition, a state that is *not* 'adequate to the aspirations of human nature'. The notion certainly seems paradoxical.

To see whether it is a worthwhile paradox, let us first inquire what Aquinas thought his *beatitudo imperfecta* consists in. I begin with the most illuminating of his various answers: 'beatitudo imperfecta consistit in operatione virtutis', imperfect beatitude consists in the workings of virtue (virtue in action).[14]

Now virtue is whatever renders *good* its possessor and his acts. Take the moral virtues, for example. They have, says Aquinas, a point: *bonum humanum*, human good;[15] and recognition and love of this good is necessary for virtue.[16]

And here we come to a matter decisive for my whole argument. This *bonum humanum*, the point or good of virtue, is a manifold; for there are, says St Thomas, a plurality of *fines moralium virtutum*, ends of the moral virtues.[17] These ends are identified by practical understanding working according to the natural disposition which he calls *synderesis*.[18] The understanding of these final or basic goods is formulated in the *prima principia* of practical reasoning, principles which Aquinas calls the *prima principia* of natural law or natural right.[19] The goods identified in these 'first principles' are naturally wanted; they are the appropriate objects of the inclinations which pertain to each of man's capacities and to his natural integrity.[20] As such they are included under the will's natural object, complete or universal good;[21] but each is final, good-for-its-own sake, as Aquinas most plainly affirms by describing the manifold of corresponding practical principles as *per se nota* and *prima*. Yet none of these basic goods is absolutely or simply or (as Aristotle would say) 'most' final.

Let me here interpose three summary remarks: (i) Aquinas has arrived at a rather better list of final or basic goods than that off-hand itemization in *NE* I.7 ('honour, pleasure, intelligence and the various virtues'),

---

[12] *ST* I–II q.5 a.3c; also *In Eth.* nn. 129, 202, 2103, 2136, 2110.
[13] I–II q.3 a.2 ad 4; a.5c and a.6c; q.5 a.3 ad 2; a.5c.   [14] I–II q.5 a.5c.
[15] *ST* II–II q.47 a.6c.   [16] *Q.D. de Caritate*, a.2c.   [17] *ST* II–II q.47 a.6c.
[18] II–II q.47 a.6 ad 1 ad 3; I–II q.58 a.4c; I q.79 a.12c.
[19] I–II q.94 aa. 2c, 4c; a.3c = q.63 a.1c = II–II q.47 a.6c = I–II q.58 a.4c; *de Malo* q.3 a.12 ad 13.
[20] *ST* I–II q.10 a.1; q.9 a.1; q.18 a.7c; q.94 a.2c.
[21] I–II q.8 a.2c and ad 1; q.9 a.1; q.19 a.1c and ad 3.

(ii) Aquinas's list includes knowing truth about God. But it is clear that no item in the list is highest in the sense that the others are merely means to it, or are more dispensable than it, or can rightly be directly attacked for the sake of securing it.[22] (iii) We began with a proposition about the moral virtues and looked for their point; but there are also the intellectual virtues or excellences, all of which (leaving aside *prudentia*) can exist without moral virtue.[23] St Thomas, intellectualist though he may be, will point out that one can make bad use of an intellectual, but not of a moral, virtue;[24] indeed, he will say that, if we are considering their relationship to human activity, the intellectual virtues are *less* noble than the moral.[25] There is, we may say, no single, privileged perspective from which such a human good as theoretical knowledge grasped and enjoyed contemplatively is simply and in all respects highest, particularly if by 'highest' we mean most choiceworthy.

To return now to Aquinas's 'imperfect beatitude'; we can now see why one might think it consists in the workings of virtue. For we can envisage a life in which each of the basic goods is somehow in place; none is suppressed; none is arbitrarily emphasized or contemned; reasonableness regulates their interrelations as it regulates the emotions and inclinations of the individual and the relations between individuals in friendship and other forms of community. These 'virtue-in-action' aspects of this person's flourishing do not add to the value of the basic components in that flourishing, the basic goods.[26] But they do constitute a further intelligible and worthwhile good which is simply an intelligible and worthwhile aspect of the realization of the other goods (derivative and non-final or underived and final/basic), a good in relation to which every other good takes its place, or under which each of them falls.

That is surely why Aquinas could helpfully speak of imperfect beatitude, even at the cost of some paradox: imperfect beatitude is worthy of the name just because, in some respect, it plays the same role in practical thinking and choosing as the natural and inescapable notion of (perfect) beatitude or *eudaimonia*, the notion of the *fully* (not imperfectly) satisfactory (whatever that may be).... Being imperfect, imperfect beatitude is neither the fully adequate point of all choices nor a state lacking nothing that we could desire. But specific goods-for-their-own-sake and ends-for-their-own-sake can and should be 'placed' (both critically and supportively) under

---

[22] I–II q.94 a.2c (the main list); II–II q.64 a.5 ad 3; a.6 ad 2; III q.68 a.11 ad 3.
[23] I–II q.58 a.5c.   [24] I–II q.57 a.1c.
[25] I–II q.66 a.3c. See also Buckley, *Man's Last End*, 208–10.
[26] See *NE* I.7: 1097b17–19.

some wider good, 'imperfect beatitude', a good somehow constituted by the realization, in some appropriate way, of basic human goods.[27]

III

But there is also a rather different story, perhaps more prominent in St Thomas's account, and certainly more well known. In its starkest form, this tells us that 'the imperfect human felicity which is attainable in this life consists in knowledge of the separated substances by the *habitus* of wisdom'.[28] With more formality:

> as is stated in [Aristotle's] *Ethics*, the imperfect beatitude which we can have in this life first and principally consists in contemplation, and secondarily in the activity of practical understanding governing our actions and emotions....[29]

The question, therefore, is this: Why does St Thomas say that in the imperfect beatitude available in this life, contemplation has 'first place'? (Whatever that may in practice amount to...) Various reasons are offered,[30] but the decisive one seems to be that in contemplation, and in the intellectual virtues, 'we have a kind of beginning of that [true] happiness which consists in the knowledge of truth'.[31]

To test the adequacy of this characterization of true beatitude and thus, by anticipation, of 'imperfect beatitude', we need to inquire whether our true and unrestricted fulfilment or flourishing would indeed consist *only* in contemplation, even contemplation of God's essence in the beatific vision.

Aquinas's statements to the effect that human beatitude is to be found '*only* in the vision of God'[32] are to be understood in the same sense as his statement that 'Deus est *totum* hominis bonum'.[33] Each is highly elliptical; they run the same risk of being taken literally (and thus being

---

[27] Notice that there is no reason at all to suppose that this as yet indeterminate 'aspect' of the realization of basic goods is instantiated by only one 'appropriate way' of so realizing them; there may be many such ways that have in some measure the relevant intelligibility and worth, and there is no reason to suppose that the measure must be capable of commensuration and measurement. See *NLNR* ch. 5.

[28] *In Lib. Boet. de Trin.* q.6 a.4 ad 3.   [29] *ST* I–II q.3 a.5c.

[30] St Thomas will appeal (II–II q.182 a.1c) to the seven reasons set forth by Aristotle in *NE* X.7: 1177a11–b13. The weakness of these reasons, and their incompatibility with so much of the *Ethics*, is well exposed by Moline, 'Contemplation and the Human Good' at 40–5 (though Moline's own thesis about Aristotle's ironical intent fails to convince).

[31] *ST* I–II q.66 a.4 ad 1; q.3 a.6c; q.57 a.1 ad 2.

[32] *Sola visio Dei*; cf. also 'in solo Deo beatitudo hominis consistit': I–II q.2 a.8c; q.3 a.8c.

[33] ['God is the whole good of man.'] II–II q.26 a.13 ad 3. Beatitude, the fully satisfactory, must surely include such a vision, since without it our concern to understand would be unsatisfied. Indeed, that vision could be said to be central to integral human fulfilment, because the goodness that would be revealed in it must be such that all other goods will then be understood ('seen') and appreciated as having their goodness as participations (likenesses and effects) of that primary and original goodness. See further sec. IV below.

misunderstood) as Aristotle ran when he said that *eudaimonia* is 'the good' (a statement conjoined by Aristotle, however, with the statement that there are many human ends-in-themselves). 'Deus est totum hominis bonum' is compatible with Aquinas's statement that to love God alone[34] is an 'inadequate and imperfect love of God', and actually inferior to love of neighbour for God's sake. God's goodness is our 'whole good' just in the sense that it is (a) the self-sufficiently adequate object of our love and (b) the cause of all other goods (including persons and including, too, the good constituted by our love of goods including persons). But God's goodness is also 'not our whole good', for God, by unnecessitated choice, has created a universe of other goods distinct from himself, including goods available to and worthy of our love-of-friendship (*amor amicitiae*) among human persons.

It is necessary, says St Thomas, that there be but one ultimate end of man insofar as he is man, because human nature is a unity.[35] Very well. But must we not acknowledge that the unity of human nature is a unity in complexity? For a start, 'Anima mea non est ego'.[36] For another thing, human nature is known through its capacities, and they are known through their acts, and these are known through their objects,[37] and those objects are, for the most part, precisely the basic goods identified in the *prima principia* of practical understanding.[38] As these are plural, so the human nature they disclose is complex. So: the last end, if it has the unity of human nature, must have the complexity which is unified in that nature.

Let me dwell on just one aspect of this complexity. Among the capacities (*potentiae animae*) intrinsic to human nature is our capacity for love-of-friendship,[39] the richest of the human objects of the basic inclination towards living *in societate*.[40] No one understands human nature who does not understand that a human being is deprived and stunted in his own being if he has no participation in the love-of-friendship. No one understands love-of-friendship who does not understand that it involves a mutual and reciprocal will that the other person flourish more fully, i.e. share more fully in goods, among which goods must therefore (precisely because the other has the same desire that one be more fully flourishing oneself) be, now for the sake of that other, the fuller flourishing of oneself. Self-love, in due measure, is intrinsic to the fullest, most generous love-of-friendship;

---

[34] II–II q.27 a.8c: 'dilectio Dei accip[i]tur secundum quod solus diligitur'.
[35] 'Propter unitatem humanae naturae': *In Eth.* I, lect. 9, n. 106.
[36] ['My soul is not me.'] Aquinas, *In I Cor.*, c. 15, lect. 2. [See *Aquinas* 318 n. 106; essay II. 2 at 40–2.]
[37] *ST* I q.26 a.2 ad 2; q.87 a.3c; etc.; see *FoE* 21–2, 25.
[38] See n. 19 above; for the order of thought in Aquinas on this key issue, read *ST* I–II q.94 a.2c with I q.80 a.1 ad 1; q.82 a.4c and I–II q.10 a.1c.
[39] I–II q.26 a.4; I–II q.25 a.2c.   [40] I–II q.94 a.2.

love-of-friendship, seeking true goods for another even at the hazard of one's own well-being, is intrinsic to one's own well-being. So: no one can understand the unity of human nature who does not understand this complexity of union-without-absorption, this irreducible duality (indeed, multiplicity) of the goods which must be realized if that nature is to be most fully actualized.

Hence we find Aquinas concluding that the *societas amicorum* [fellowship of friends] is of the '*bene esse* of [perfect] beatitude'.[41] But why 'of the *bene esse*'? Because, he says, it is not *absolutely* necessary to beatitude, since it is possible to envisage a universe in which there were but one soul in communion with God, and that one would have beatitude; but the actual universe is one in which we each have neighbours...

Still, we should press our question about Aquinas's references to the 'complete' perfection, or '*bene esse*' of perfect beatitude. For we find him using such expressions not only in relation to friendship but also in relation to bodily life: 'beatitude which is perfect *in all respects (beatitudo omnibus modis perfecta)* requires the well-being of one's own body'.[42] Such expressions are as paradoxical as 'imperfect beatitude' and are tantamount to conceding what in other places seemed to be denied: that the goods attained and realized in full beatitude are not one but *many*, in due order.[43] This requirement of loving the goods in beatitude in due measure does not differ in its intelligible structure from the measure of practical reasonableness that we discern and use in this life.

St Thomas himself draws the necessary conclusion: in the state of perfect beatitude, when faith and hope will have ceased to be virtues, practical reasonableness (*prudentia*) and justice will still, therefore, be needed virtues—along with that charity which includes with love of God a love of self (including one's body) and of neighbours *in patria*.[44]

At the outset of this essay, I said that man's true last end is *integral human fulfilment*.[45] In this life, that is not a practicable *goal* at all; its place in practical reasoning is rather as the ideal that provides the content of the first principle of morality.[46] It is faith, not philosophy, that proposes that

---

[41] I–II q.4 a.8c ad 3.   [42] I–II q.4 a.6c; also a.5c.

[43] II–II q.26 a.13. This concession appears in other ways, too. In the state of perfect beatitude, says Aquinas, the order of priorities in love, the *ordo caritatis*, will remain the same ranked order as it is in this life. And in that state of beatitude, *all* 'the proper grounds of love' (*honestae causae dilectionis*) will remain as in this life: a.13c. But what is a *causa dilectionis*, a ground of love? It is a good, which affords a *ratio diligendi*: II–II q.26 a.2 ad 1. So yet again we find Aquinas formally recognizing the multiplicity of goods involved in beatitude, and the necessity of loving and respecting each of those goods in due measure.

[44] I–II q.67; II–II q.26 a.13; q.52 a.3; *de Virt. Card.* 4; *de Car.* a.2c [*patria*: heavenly homeland]

[45] See also *FoE* 70–4, 120–1, 151–2.

[46] For the contrast between 'goal', as attainable objective, and 'ideal', see *NLNR* 61 and 75–6. On 'integral human fulfilment' as the first principle of morality, see n. 45 above.

that ideal may be realized, by divine power and grace. Its realization would be, I suggest, a state of affairs that would not be, formally, a human act, nor, formally, a human possession, though it would involve both activity and enjoyment. St Thomas himself from time to time overcomes the limitations of the Aristotelian categories in which he usually conceives the last end of human life: the categories of act and perfection, and the vocabulary which draws no distinction between ideal and goal, or between 'means' which are merely instrumental and means which are actually constitutive of a good. Often he says that the point (object) of our beatitude is divine good,[47] and sometimes he will add that that good, precisely as object of our beatitude, must be understood *not as something to be had or possessed* but rather as the *common good of a whole society*, that heavenly city whose citizens are the saints.[48]

To bring the whole matter to a head: we can now assess Aquinas's argument that 'imperfect beatitude' consists 'first and principally' in contemplation *because* perfect beatitude 'consists in' contemplation. Even on the rather relentlessly 'intellectualist' account in Aquinas's later writings, perfect beatitude consists not only in the contemplative vision which illuminates the being and worth of all else,[49] but also in an exercise of the virtues of practical understanding and reasonableness, and of justice; and in love-of-friendship; and in enjoyment of one's own bodily personal life in its fullness. Hence, even when one accepts the primacy within perfect beatitude of the vision of God, the argument from anticipation provides one with weak ground for according primacy to contemplation within imperfect beatitude; for the virtues of the active life, too, are, on St Thomas's own account, anticipations.

IV

Under the ever-present influence of empiricist images of knowing, we tend to think of the vision of God as if it were a gazing at a scene, a *much* more beautiful and satisfying scene than one we've ever seen.[50] And under the ever-present influence of empiricist models of experience, we tend to think of the satisfying of desires as the bringing about of effects in a subject which is passive but for the excitement of its own sensations under the influence of the cause.

---

[47] *ST* I–II q.2 aa. 7c, 8c; I q.65 a.2; I–II q.1 a.8.   [48] *de Car.*, a.2c.
[49] *ST* II–II q.25 a.1.
[50] Neo-Platonism such as Augustine's can be regarded as employing this inadequate model of knowing 'in its sublimest form': Lonergan, *Insight*, 412.

The critique of the empiricist model of experience is accomplished in ethics, which is the name given by Aristotle and St Thomas to the pursuit in which one comes more adequately to understand human nature by understanding the goods which are the objects of the acts which, one thus understands, realize the capacities which, one thus understands, constitute the human nature in question.[51] So one rejects the option of living as a contented cow (Aristotle's example) or as a brain plugged in to an experience machine (Grisez's and then Nozick's more vivid and adequate thought-experiment), and one rejects it precisely as unworthy, an inadequate and unsatisfactory (even though in itself wholly 'satisfying') form of life for oneself or any person.[52]

Similarly, the empiricist model of the *visio Dei* is overcome by a reflection on practical understanding. To see God in his essence would be to see him not merely as cause but also as Person(s), and not merely as Person(s) but as personally causing all the goods (including persons) of the universe. And, knowing our own action practically, we know that personal causing is not like the billiard-ball-colliding push-pull causing of empiricism. In personal causing, the achieved effect which comes last is the good envisaged from the first in the intelligent process of practical understanding and reasoning, choosing and acting. To see God would be to really understand, for the first time, the point (the good) of all created goods, including created persons and the love-of-friendship between them. To love oneself and others like one, in full measure, would thereby become not less possible, not less appropriate, but more possible and more appropriate than in this life.

And we can go further. Speculative questioning and understanding in contemplation disclose to us, already in this life, the existence of a God who is not Aristotle's purely contemplative *noēsis noēseos* [understanding of understanding] but rather the *dominus suorum actuum* [master of his own acts] and free creator and activator and governor of the universe. To attain the beatitude of a perfected human knowledge and love of God would be to attain the fullness of the image of God.[53] So the imaging of God in this life (a life in which a very imperfect but real knowledge and love of God is

---

[51] See at nn. 1, 3, and 37 above. Similar conclusions about the relative epistemological priority of ethics in our knowledge of human nature are reached by close students of St Thomas such as Belmans, *Le sens objectif de l'agir humain*, 142–3, 428; de Finance, 'Sur la notion de loi naturelle' at 209–10. For an important and neglected treatment of the way in which sciences can be interdependent without any vicious circle, precisely because each science (even one subalternated to another) can call upon principles which are *per se nota* and thus not derived from the other science, see St Thomas, *In Lib. Boet. de Trin.* q.5 a.1 ad 9.

[52] *Eud. Eth.* I.5: 1216a; Grisez, *Beyond the New Morality*, 26; Nozick, *Anarchy, State and Utopia*, 42–5; *FoE* 37–42, 46, 48, 89.

[53] *ST* I q.93 a.4c. [And see *Aquinas* 312–19.]

possible) would be an imitation not of the Aristotelian divine contemplative, but of the fully practical (as well as contemplative) intelligence and will of the true God, creator of irreducibly many forms of good.

One *understands* that truth is a good, and one's *intelligence* leads one on by questions that call for (and thus dimly envisage) answers but cannot be answered, and thus by the incomparably desirable prospect of a fuller truth that is no mirage but remains simply unattainable in this human life. To be aware of these questions, and of the unattained good of answering them, is to have a notion of transcendence and our openness to it.[54] But intelligence also grasps that friendship, or practical reasonableness, or human life itself, are goods, and this understanding lures us on to the intelligent realization of those goods as best we can, as well as to the incomparably desirable prospect and ambition of ever more fully understanding their goodness and its source and of ever more adequately realizing and enjoying them.

Empiricism tempts us to think of our inclinations as blind urges, pushing or pulling us from within. But, for us, things are in fact desired because they seem desirable, that is, because they appear and appeal to our intelligence as good.[55] The grasp of basic goods, and the intelligent assessment of their implications, and the immediate direction of their realization in choice and execution, are *all* the work of one's single intelligence. If one's intelligence opens one towards transcendence, it does so not just by the pursuit of speculative truth but also and equally by the pursuit of the truth of human goods and human actions (the truth which Thomas relentlessly calls practical). If our hearts are restless, it is not only for speculative truth but also for the practical truth that consists in (satisfaction of intelligent desire for) the realization, the making actual, of goods such as life, play, friendship.... It cannot be doubted that neither the full understanding of those goods nor their sufficiently satisfactory realization is possible otherwise than by a participation in God's creative understanding and personal life far fuller than any participation we can envisage or accomplish.

V

A simplistic catechesis taught (or was fragmentarily remembered as teaching) that man has one end, the vision of God, and treated that vision

---

[54] Here is St Thomas's principal argument for his famous assertion that every intelligent being 'naturally desires the vision of the divine substance': ScG III c. 57.

[55] See n. 8 above; *FoE* ch. 2.

simply as the reward for forms of virtue which have no apparent tendency to fit a person for a life of exclusive contemplation.[56]

Such a presentation has never been adequate to Christian faith. That faith is conveyed more amply by Vatican II, when it identifies the ultimate end of mankind, not simply as a vision of truth, nor even simply as a participation in holiness and grace, but as a participation by a plurality of persons in a plurality of goods, the goods of human dignity, brotherhood, and freedom and thus all the good fruits of our nature and our choices: 'a kingdom of truth and life, holiness and grace, justice, love and peace'.[57]

Thus the relationship between moral virtue in this life and the integral human fulfilment of beatitude is affirmed to be, not of instrumental means to extrinsic end, nor mere merit to sheer extrinsic reward, but rather a striking form of participation: the good works and virtues go to building up *here and now* the supernatural kingdom. And 'afterwards', in the fulfilled kingdom, those good works and virtues 'will be found again' as intrinsic to its heavenly life and constitution.[58] This underlines that the reward so insistently proposed by Scripture is *intrinsically* connected to the rightful pursuit of the goods: it is not like the prospect of a holiday in Miami rewarding long hours of work, but more like (*mutatis multis mutandis*) an orchestra's prospect of sublimely performing a symphony after years of self-discipline, study, work.[59]

VI

In the theory of practical reason advanced by Grisez and Boyle and myself and others, a number of goods are identified as basic. Against this, it has been objected that 'the pluralism implied in...eight basic goods...is diametrically opposed to St. Thomas's teaching that there is

---

[56] A deficient style of homily went further, reducing Christian moral life to a search for 'happiness'. Ethics books could be found to follow suit. E.g., Vernon Bourke's *Ethics* began:

[The] basic and natural urge for happiness is deep-rooted in the being of every man.... Each man's moral problem...is to select and do the kind of actions which are conducive to true happiness.... Ethics may be defined as the systematic study of human actions from the point of view of their rightness and wrongness as means for the achievement of ultimate happiness.... For the present, we can take right action to be that which should be done...in order to achieve happiness (3, 4).

And happiness was located in an 'intellectual contemplation of the perfect good' (*ibid.*, vi). A more adequate exposition of Christian faith sets aside these emaciated conceptions of the moral life. The search for one's own happiness is displaced as the moral norm; in its place we find, in the words of Vatican II:

the norm of human activity is this: that in accord with the divine mind [*consilium*] and will, human activity should harmonize with the genuine good of the human race, and allow men as individuals and members of society to pursue and fulfill their integral vocation (*Gaudium et spes*, 35).

[57] *Gaudium et Spes*, 39.   [58] Ibid.
[59] Cf. D'Arcy, 'The Withering Away of Disbelief' at 163.

but one ultimate good for all humans'.[60] But, as we have seen, one should be slow to speak of diametrical opposition to a theory which is as complex as Aquinas's on the one ultimate good for all human persons. St Thomas can be best understood as holding to a conclusion often obscured in his discourse. This conclusion, defended by Grisez and myself as valid apart from the authority of St Thomas, is: Any state which could count as the 'one ultimate good for all humans' must involve a plurality of goods, such is the irreducible complexity of integral human fulfilment.

Philosophical argument alone cannot conclude to the faith and hope re-expressed by the Council. But consider a philosophically elaborated treatment: (i) of the basic aspects of human flourishing, the basic human goods; (ii) of practical reasonableness as the architectonic good which, transparent for the master ideal and principle of integral fulfilment, provides the standards for good realization of those basic human goods; (iii) of human self-constitution by free choices which last indefinitely unless repented and which thus might conceivably go, intrinsically, to fit or unfit a person for full and eternal participation in the not merely contemplative life of God in the not merely speculative-truth-centred Kingdom; and (iv) of the possibility that practical reasonableness has a point beyond itself as a participation in God's free play, the play of creating and bringing-to-fulfilment, a fulfilment of Creation which would include the actual realization of integral human fulfilment. Can it reasonably be said, as some claim,[61] that all this amounts to 'a conscious rejection of the finality of man's nature'? To me it seems rather to be, from beginning to end, precisely an exploration and explication of that human finality (if you like, that metaphysical finality), in its irreducible complexity.

---

[60] Bourke, 'Justice as Equitable Reciprocity: Aquinas Updated' at 25.
[61] *Ibid.* at 24. Bourke added: 'Finnis does not tie in this list of proximate human goods with any consideration of an ultimate good'. But see *NLNR* 49, 405–10.

11

PRUDENCE ABOUT ENDS[*]

I

In a fine essay published in 1990, Terence Irwin argues that Aquinas so narrows the scope of deliberation that he is unable to give a consistent and realistic explanation of the difference between virtue and vice.[1] For since deliberation, according to Aquinas, is always about means not ends, deliberation and the intellectual virtue of deliberating well—prudence— cannot have a role in the virtuous person's identification and adoption of the right end or ends. Instead, Aquinas assigns that role to synderesis, the non-deliberative grasp of basic ends and first principles of practical reason. But synderesis is unfitted for that role, since the vicious and the virtuous alike share in synderesis. So, to explain the difference between virtue and vice (not least the fact that it is in our control to be virtuous or vicious), Aquinas is forced to ascribe a wider role to deliberation and prudence, in conflict with his own attempt to limit that intellectual operation and its virtue to means rather than ends.

Irwin adds that he is 'not sure that this is a genuine conflict in Aquinas...a better interpretation of his views might show that I [Irwin] have overlooked some distinctions that make them all consistent.' In this essay I suggest that Irwin has overlooked not so much some distinctions as some important (and very often overlooked) elements in Aquinas's understanding of practical reasoning, human ends, free choice, virtue, and natural law. Indeed, the interest of the textual and substantive issues

---

[*] Unpublished, 1997; written for a conference in the Philosophy Department at the University of North Carolina at Wake Forest in November 1997. There I learned from Terence Irwin that he had changed his views and that his current reading of Aquinas had been published the previous week as 'Practical Reason Divided: Aquinas and his Critics'. I comment briefly on the latter in sec. IV of essay 1, observing that there is a genuine interpretative problem about Aquinas's treatment of the issues and that Irwin's second thoughts, though on the right lines, leave something to be desired; hence the present essay remains pertinent. The endnotes touch on Irwin's more recent (2007) discussion of the matter.

[1] 'The Scope of Deliberation: A Conflict in Aquinas'. Parenthetical numbers in the text are to page numbers in this.

Irwin raises (not, as we shall see, for the first time in the tradition) is that they force us to come to terms with something about the sources of moral (and therefore legal) normativity which was, I believe, lost to sight in even the very moderated voluntarism of a Suarez and in Kant's well-meaning attempt to restore practical reasonableness to its proper dignity.

II

One can point out an apparent conflict in Aquinas even more straightforwardly than Irwin does. One need only juxtapose two passages from the *Summa Theologiae*. One is the passage on which Irwin principally relies: '...it does not belong to prudence to fix the end [or: fix ends][2] for the moral virtues, but only to arrange about the means to the end [or: to ends]'.[3] The other is a passage earlier in the *Summa*: 'prudence directs the moral virtues not only in the choosing of means but also in the fixing of end(s)'.[4] Irwin does eventually quote and consider this second, earlier passage, but he softens the evident conflict by adding, after 'but also...the "fixing"...of the end', the words 'in so far as prudence determines the mean that the virtue consists in' (35). The Latin scarcely supports this reading down, for its reference to the role of prudence in determining the mean is advanced neither as a ground for asserting that prudence fixes the end[5] nor as the sense or extension of that assertion, but merely as an exemplification of it. So the two texts, taken as they stand, seem pretty flatly contradictory: prudence does not, and does, fix the end(s) for or of the virtues. As Cajetan noted nearly five hundred years ago, the problem is a severe one {*arduum dubium*}, not least the '*ad hominem*' problem whether Aquinas is coherent.[6]

In the course of his essay, Irwin hardens Aquinas's negative thesis very considerably. For Irwin's Aquinas, prudence not only 'does not

[2] Here as so often, Aquinas's use of the singular without any hint of a Latin substitute for the English indefinite article means that an English translation that forces the noun into the singular-as-opposed-to plural is liable to be very misleading.

[3] *ST* II–II q.47 a.6c (Irwin's translation): 'ad prudentiam non pertinet praestituere finem virtutibus moralibus, sed solum disponere de his quae sunt ad finem'. [In his 1997 essay on broadly the same issues, 'Practical Reason Divided: Aquinas and his Critics', Irwin usually (but not always) translates *praestituere* by 'to present' rather than 'to fix' or 'determine'. But I think the latter words are closer to Aquinas's probable intent in the relevant uses of *praestituere*.]

[4] *ST* I–II q.66 a.3 ad 3: 'prudentia non solum dirigit virtutes morales in eligendo ea quae sunt ad finem, sed etiam in praestituendo finem'.

[5] Thus the sentence next following the quotation in the preceding footnote begins: 'est autem...', not 'est enim...'. In favour of his interpretation, however, Irwin might point to the passage from *Sent*. III d.33 q.2 a.3c paraphrased and quoted at nn. 8–9 below.

[6] Cajetan on *ST* I–II q.66 a.3 ad 3 (Aquinas, *Opera Omnia*, vol. VI (Leonine edn, Rome, 1891) 433).

itself prescribe the ends for moral virtue' (24), but indeed 'has *no* role in determining the right end' (25), and 'the inclination towards the right ends is *independent of prudence*' (32). Correspondingly (prudence being the virtue of deliberation), deliberation 'is not concerned with ends' at all (31), 'cannot alter one's views about ends'(33), and has *no* 'role in finding the right end' (40 n.); Aquinas 'assumes that deliberation is *confined* to the choice of "means to ends" in a sense that *excludes* the choice of ends of the sort that distinguish virtue from vice' (28). Of the six texts cited by Irwin in this connection (24 n.), only two express any sort of negative thesis: the passage from II–II q.47 a.6 which is one of our pair of apparently contradictory statements, and a brief text in II–II q.56 a.1, which refers back to that passage in asserting that 'prudence is not about end(s) but about means {circa ea quae sunt ad finem: about things which are to-an-end}'. None of the cited texts express or imply Irwin's various hardened versions of this thesis.

What, then, on Irwin's reading, does fix the end for the moral virtues? And what, indeed, is the (or an) 'end of the virtues', and what is at stake in 'fixing' (establishing) it? Irwin says a good deal about the former question, and little about the latter, preliminary issue.

Fixing the end of the virtues is, in Irwin's Aquinas, the role of synderesis, our intuitive grasp of first practical principles.[7] So: 'Virtue is focussed on the right end, not because of prudence, but because of a distinct nondeliberative intellectual state that grasps the right ends, and this is synderesis' (26). And again: 'Virtuous people differ from vicious in that they aim correctly at the end. Since this correct aim cannot be the product of prudence, it must be the product of synderesis' (27).

But this is an oversimplification. As Irwin notes, Aquinas's standard formula attributes 'the inclination towards the right ends to virtue' (29–30; also 24 citing *ST* I–II q.58 a.5). So though this inclination is doubtless guided by the practical principles grasped in synderesis (25), it cannot be right to say that 'the virtuous person's *acceptance* of these ends' is simply (in Aquinas's view) 'the product of synderesis' (31) or that synderesis alone 'explains' (cf. 38, 40) the difference between the virtuous and the vicious or alone explains how virtue makes the end right. As Aquinas makes clear in a passage not cited by Irwin,[8] the explanation of virtue involves three necessary factors {necessaria}: fixing of end(s), inclination towards the end(s) fixed, and choice of means. But the proximate end—he means the

---

[7] Irwin (25) calls this a 'special faculty' and interpolates into his translation of *ST* II–II q.47 a.6 ad 1 the words 'the natural virtue in [the natural reason]' where the Latin has simply *ratio naturalis*; but *ST* I q.79 a.12, which he cites, denies that synderesis is a power or capacity, and thus denies that it is a faculty in the usual sense of that word. It is a natural disposition of one's understanding (*habitus intellectus*). But nothing turns on this here. See further n. 14 below.

[8] *Sent.* III d.33 q.2 a.3.

proximate unifying or ultimate end—of human life is the good of practical reasonableness, *bonum rationis*, and in all moral virtues what is intended is practical reasonableness, *rectitudo rationis*. So the fixing of end(s) pertains in this way to natural reason (sc. synderesis) and precedes prudence. But the good of practical reasonableness is specified {determinatur} by prudence's settling the mean in actions and feelings. And 'thus in a way prudence fixes the end for the moral virtues, and its act is mixed into the acts of the moral virtues...'.[9] In this passage, Aquinas asserts in substance each of the two apparently contradictory statements with which we began this section, and indicates how they can cohere.

To understand this passage and its presuppositions, and to make progress in resolving the whole issue, it is time to be specific about the *content* of synderesis, that is about what the end or ends of human life and human virtue actually are. Specificity here will bring some clarity into the confusing melange of statements, and go far towards dissolving the apparent contradictions, conflicts, and paradoxes.

III

The ends of human life and of the virtues are the goods which Aquinas identifies (without pretending to be quite exhaustive) in his famous discussion of the first principles of natural law and practical reason,

---

[9] 'et sic quodammodo prudentia praestituit finem virtutibus moralibus, et ejus actus in earum actibus immiscetur'. Here is the context:

Respondeo dicendum, quod ad perfectionem virtutis moralis tria sunt necessaria. Primum est praestitutio finis; secundum autem est inclinatio ad finem praestitutum; tertium est electio eorum quae sunt ad finem. *Finis autem proximus humanae vitae est bonum rationis in communi*; unde dicit Dionysius, quod malum hominis est contra rationem esse: et ideo est intentum in omnibus virtutibus moralibus, ut passiones et operationes ad rectitudinem rationis reducantur. Rectitudo autem rationis naturalis est; unde *hoc modo praestitutio finis ad naturalem rationem pertinet, et praecedit prudentiam*, sicut intellectus principiorum scientiam; et ideo dicit Philosophus, 6 Ethic., quod prudentia habet principia fines virtutum. *Sed hoc bonum rationis determinatur secundum quod constituitur medium in actionibus et passionibus* per debitam commensurationem circumstantiarum, *quod facit prudentia*. Unde medium virtutis moralis, ut in 2 Ethic. dicitur, est secundum rationem rectam, quae est prudentia; *et sic quodammodo prudentia praestituit finem virtutibus moralibus, et ejus actus in earum actibus immiscetur*; sed inclinatio in finem illum pertinet ad virtutem moralem quae consentit in bonum rationis per modum naturae: et haec inclinatio in finem dicitur electio, inquantum finis proximus ad finem ultimum ordinatur. Et ideo dicit Philosophus, 2 Ethic., quod virtus moralis facit electionem rectam. Sed *discretio eorum quibus hoc bonum rationis consequi possumus et in operationibus et in passionibus, est actus prudentiae: unde praestitutio finis praecedit actum prudentiae et virtutis moralis*; sed inclinatio in finem, sive recta electio finis proximi, est actus moralis virtutis principaliter, sed prudentiae originaliter. Unde Philosophus dicit, quod rectitudo electionis est in aliis virtutibus a prudentia, sicut rectitudo in intentione naturae est ex sapientia divina ordinante naturam: et secundum hoc actus etiam prudentiae immixtus est actibus aliarum virtutum. Sicut enim inclinatio naturalis est a ratione, *ita inclinatio virtutis moralis a prudentia*; electio autem eorum quae sunt ad finem, secundum quod electio importat praeceptum rationis de his prosequendis. Sed actus prudentiae sibi proprius est, et distinctus ab actibus aliarum virtutum. (*Sent.* III d.33 q.2 a.3c (emphasis added, here as elsewhere).)

in *ST* I–II q.94 a.2, completed by a.3.[10] In a.2 he identifies the natural inclinations and corresponding basic goods of life and health, marriage, *societas*, and knowledge (particularly of the most important thing(s)); in a.3 he adds a further natural inclination: of acting according to reason, that is, according to virtue. Elsewhere, as in the passage from *Sent.* III d.33 q.2 a.3 considered at the end of the preceding section, the basic good corresponding to this inclination is called the *bonum rationis*: the good of practical reasonableness, that is, the good of being reasonable—for its own sake. So the first principles of practical reason, of the natural law which is normative for sound thinking about what to do, are principles of the form: human life is a good to be pursued and what threatens it is to be avoided; knowledge is a good to be pursued, and ignorance is to be avoided; reasonableness in acting is a good to be pursued and acted upon...; and so forth.[11]

Before proceeding with the main line of our inquiry by considering the content of these first principles, it may be helpful to say a word about two senses in which they are 'natural'. Irwin remarks that although the first principles, as Aquinas understands them, 'are a matter of knowledge and reason', that is 'not to say that they have any further rational justification; Aquinas seems to suggest that the ends are "built-in"; we just see that they are the correct ones, without any further argument or ground' (27). I would put the matter somewhat differently. The first practical principles

---

[10] Earlier sketches: *Sent.* I d.48 q.1 a.4c; *Sent.* IV d.33 q.1 a.1c; *ST* I–II q.10 a.1c.

[11] Though practical reason's absolutely first, formal principle, as articulated in *ST* I–II q.94 a.2, puts '*faciendum*' before '*prosequendum*', and is often mistakenly rendered by commentators in the form '*bonum est faciendum*' (or, even worse, as the imperative 'Do good and avoid evil!'), it is *prosequendum* ('is to be pursued') that gives the primary and essential sense of the principle. Aquinas makes this clear in the next sentence but one: 'everything to which people have a natural inclination reason naturally understands as good and consequently as to be pursued in action {opere prosequenda}...'. As he says in another mature text, *De Malo* q.10 a.1c:

all acts of an appetitive capacity [such as the will] come down to two common matters, pursuit {prosecutionem} and flight (as the acts of an intellectual capacity come down to affirmation and negation); so that pursuit {prosecutio} is in appetite [particularly, willing] what affirmation is in intellect...And good has the character 'attractive' {attractivi}, since 'good is what everything desires {appetunt}' (*NE* I.1: 1094a2–3)...

(In an effort to clarify the absolutely first principle of practical reason, *ST* I–II q.94 a.2c appeals to the same—ambiguous and so not too helpful—Aristotelian tag.) Texts treating '*prosequendum*' as the positive directiveness of practical reason (and '*vitandum*' as the negative counterpart) include I–II q.84 a.4c; II–II q.125 a.1c; q.147 a.1 ad 2; *ScG* I c. 90 n. 2 [750]; *Virt. Card.* q.1 a.1c; *In Meta.* V.1 n. 14 [762]; *In Eth.* VI.2 n. 5 [1128]. '*Bonum...faciendum*' is very much less frequent; indeed, outside I–II q.94 a.2c it is found only in relatively marginal texts, almost all concerned with moral or other laws: II–II q.79 a.3 ad 3 (praecept[a] affirmativ[a] pertinent ad faciendum bonum); *In Rom.* 7.4 ad v. 23 [586] (lex inducit ad bonum faciendum); 13.1 ad v.3 [1030]. The Suarezian tradition shows its mixture of voluntarism with intuitionistic and/or metaphysicizing ethical rationalism (i.e. its confusion of the third with the first of the four kinds of order and science identified by Aquinas in *In Eth.* prol.) by its simple elimination of *prosequendum* in favour of *faciendum* or *fac!* [the imperative: 'Do [such-and-such]!' or 'Act [thus-and-thus]!']

are not, properly speaking, innate;[12] babies do not know them at all, and young people come to know them more or less gradually.[13] One cannot, for example, understand that knowledge is a human good unless one has had both the experience of wondering whether... or why..., and of finding an answer to one's question, and has noticed that answers suggest more questions, and that the answers to questions tend to hang together as 'knowledge', and that other people share this ability and opportunity. Anyone who has this sort of ordinary experience can readily go beyond it by ordinary intellectual acts of the kind we simply call 'understanding' {intellectus}—the kind of simple insight which in every field of human knowledge is needed to provide the premises for all reasoning and every conclusion. These acts of insight yield new concepts, and propositions about universals that can be instantiated in inexhaustibly many particulars. Here the relevant new insight which is a *principium per se notum* in practical thinking is that knowledge is not simply a possibility but also an opportunity—that is to say, a good worth pursuing. And the insight is that knowledge (and not merely the answer to this question that grips me now) is a good for any being like me (and not merely for me). Similarly, *human life* (not just my survival in this present danger) is a good; and so forth.[14] To say that the understanding of such propositions is natural and 'innate' is just to say that anyone's experience (once it has been accumulated) and

---

[12] There are no concepts naturally given, *ab initio*, in the human mind: *Quaestio Disputata de Anima* a.8c. Aquinas often says that first principles are naturally 'given' {indita} to us; but he means that we are given an understanding, an intellectual 'light', whereby we can understand these principles as soon as we have the relevant experience of the world and of our sentient (emotional) appetites. It is this 'rational light' which is innate (*In Lib. Boet. de Trin.* II q.3 a.1 ad 4), and by transference Aquinas will sometimes say that the principles are innate and/or that the ends to which the principles direct us are innate (e.g. *Sent.* III d.33 q.2 a.4 sol. 4c). But all our knowledge begins with the senses: *In Eth.* II lect. 1 n. 2 [246], including our knowledge of first principles: *ex sensu acquiruntur* (*Sent.* III d.25 q.2 a.1 sol. 4 ad 1; *Sent.* IV d.9 q.1 a.4 sol. 1c; *ST* I–II q.94 a.1 ad sed contra). Shortly before discussing the *principia iuris communis*, Aquinas says that knowledge of principles comes to us from the senses {cognitio principiorum provenit nobis a sensu}: I–II q.51 a.1c. Our knowledge of such principles is 'natural' not because given at birth but because acquired spontaneously, without investigation (*De Veritate* q.16 a.1c; *De Virtutibus* q.1 a.8c), 'naturally, not from effort {studio} or from our willing' *ScG* III c. 43 n. 2 [[2203]]. Human intellect begins as a tabula on which 'nothing is written': *ST* I q.79 a.2c; *Sent.* I d.39 q.2 a.2 ad 4. Even when we know 'without investigation' we cannot come to know without getting something from the senses: *De Veritate* q.16 a.1c.

[13] *ST* I–II q.94 a.1 ad s. c.

[14] Aquinas has a name for the stock {habitus} (the acquired understanding and stable capacity to make use) of such practical, directive, universal propositions which anyone is likely to have acquired in childhood, by such entirely ordinary non-deductive insights: synderesis. See e.g. *ST* I–II q.94 a.1 ad 2; I q.79 a.12; II–II q.47 a.6c and ad 1 and ad 3; *Sent.* II d.24 q.2 a.3c; d.24 q.2 a.4c; *Sent.* III d.33 q.2 a.4 sol. 4c. But nothing whatever turns on that curious early mediaeval word; precisely for this stock of insights, Aquinas is often content to use the same name as he (like Aristotle) uses for the acquired grasp of first principles in non-practical matters: *intellectus* (*nous*): e.g. *ST* II–II q.49 a.2c; *De Veritate* q.5 a.1c. The practical principles, once understood, are etched {inscribuntur} on one's mind (even when one is not thinking of them) in the way that the principles of geometry are etched on the mind of someone who understands geometry: see *Sent.* II d.24 q.2 a.3 ad 3.

anyone's intelligence (unless impaired by disability) makes such undeduced (*per se nota* but not data-less) insights *obvious*.

There is another sense in which these first principles are 'natural'. One understands human nature by understanding human capacities, those capacities by understanding human acts, and those acts by understanding their objects. That is Aquinas's primary methodological or, if you like, epistemological principle for considering the nature of an active being.[15] But the objects of humanly chosen acts are precisely the basic purposes {fines}, that is, goods {bona} with which Aquinas is concerned, as we have seen, in his most elaborated account of first practical principles.[16] So the epistemic source of the first practical principles is not human nature or a prior, theoretical understanding of human nature (though a threshold level of theoretical knowledge of the efficacy, as means, of certain choosable conduct is relevant to our knowledge of first practical principles). Rather, the epistemic relationship is the reverse: any deep understanding of human nature, that is, of the capacities which will be fulfilled by action which participates in and realizes those goods, those *perfections*, is an understanding which has amongst its sources our primary, undemonstrated, but genuine practical knowledge of those goods and purposes. In short: it is not unfitting to use the word 'natural' to refer to the practical principles ('law', *qua* directive) which identify and direct towards those human goods and thus[17] that human nature. But if one does use the word 'natural' in this context, one must beware of sliding into any of the illegitimate senses or implications of that term. One must, for example, bear in mind statements like the following statement of Aquinas: 'There is in us a natural inclination towards what is appealing to bodily feelings *against* the good of practical reasonableness'.[18]

I return to the main thread. Our non-deliberative grasp of these intrinsically desirable ends, basic goods, first practical principles, equips us

---

[15] Aquinas finds this methodological principle in Aristotle's treatise on sensory and intellectual knowledge: *De Anima* II.4: 415a16–22; see Aquinas *In De An.* II.6 nn. 6–10 [304–8]; III.14 n. 9 [803]. See also *ST* I q.87 a.3c. But from the first few pages of his first major work (*Sent.* I d.1 q.1 a.1 ad 3), he puts the principle to work in every context where the nature of some active reality is in question.

[16] See *In De An.* II.6 n. 7 [305]; III.14 n. 9 [803]: '*Will* is the only appetite in *reason*. Now powers are differentiated by the character of their objects. But the object of an appetitive power is perceived good(s) {bonum apprehensum}', i.e., in the case of a rational as distinct from a sensitive power, understood good(s).

[17] 'Moral precepts are in accord with {consequuntur} human nature *because* they are the requirements/prescriptions of natural reason {*cum sint de dictamine rationis naturalis*}': *Sent.* IV 2 q.1 a.4 sol. 1 ad 2; likewise, repeatedly, *ST* I–II q.71 a.2c (e.g. 'virtues...are in accordance with human nature just insofar as they are in line with reason; vices are against human nature just insofar as they are against the order or reasonableness'); also q.94 a.3 ad 2; q.18 a.5c; q.78 a.3c; II–II q.158 a.2 ad 4 ('the activity [of the capacity for anger] is natural to human beings just insofar as it is in accordance with reason; insofar as it is outside the order of reasonableness it is contrary to human nature'); etc.

[18] *De Malo* q.16 a.2c.

with starting points for any and all deliberating about what to do. In this sense, natural reason, not deliberation, fixes/determines {praestituit} our ends, the ends of any decent person. That is the point that Aquinas insists upon in the passage (II–II q.47 a.6) on which Irwin's discussion primarily rests. But notice five features of what is thus fixed for us.

(1) There is not one basic, intrinsic end, but many, and no reason whatever to suppose that all can be pursued and realized at once, in the sense that one could be pursued and realized without cost to the pursuit of others. (2) Each basic end can itself be pursued and actualized in countless different ways, but again one way will be at the expense of others: my research into malaria will be at the expense so to speak of my research into Aquinas. (3) The basic principles do not come with proper names; what is good as actualized in my existence is also good as actualized in yours or in any Bangladeshi farmer's. (4) Moreover, one of the basic goods is *societas*, friendship, fellow-feeling, community as a state of relations between us, demanding an adjustment of the priorities I might have had as Robinson Crusoe alone on my island. (5) Another of the basic goods is practical reasonableness itself, the good of being fully reasonable, of being undeflected by emotions which are not fully in line with the directiveness of each of the first principles taken one by one and integrally together.

These five features of our ends demand, jointly and severally, that one deliberate about *how* to pursue, actualize, and do what is thus picked out by natural reason as good(s). In short: natural reason's fixing of ends and first principles—what Irwin (37) calls 'the elementary and schematic grasp of principles that [Aquinas] attributes to everyone'—creates for each and all of us a massive problem (or unending set of problems). Deliberation is the only rational response to that problem. Prudence is the name for responding to it successfully, fully reasonably.

And that response manifestly requires that one deliberate *about* those ends, that is, about how to order, prioritize, interrelate them, and their instantiations, as between each other and as between instantiation in my existence and the existence of other persons. All that deliberation could be called deliberating about 'means', that is, about *id quod ad finem est*, about *ea quae sunt ad finem*, about what realizes the ends, specifies them, constitutes them as actualized in the existence of a particular individual or group. Aquinas, as Irwin stresses, often speaks in this way. But the same deliberating, at least in one of its crucial phases or aspects, could equally be called deliberating about ends, and establishing more or less specific ends for oneself in preference to other ends one might have chosen (e.g. the end of becoming a tyrant/playboy).[19] And Aquinas (as Irwin indicates, but rather under-emphasizes) quite often speaks in the latter way, too. There is no conflict.

There is a structural, conceptual reason why there is no conflict between these two ways of speaking about deliberation and prudence. Every end, save the most ultimate, is also a means relative to more ultimate ends. Every means, save the closest-in (the very behaving, itself), is also an end relative to means more proximate to action.[20] So insisting that prudence is about means *as such* (and thus *not* about ends as such) is fully compatible with insisting that prudence extends to deliberating about ends and is essential to their reasonable identification-and-adoption (fixing).

IV

Let us look at some of the contexts in which Aquinas speaks of deliberating about ends.

In perhaps his earliest discussion of the basic goods, Aquinas speaks of these as the objects of 'a kind of interest {voluntas} which is natural to us' and which 'follows reason's understanding when it is considering things at large {sequitur apprehensionem rationis prout est aliquid absolute considerans}': thus 'one has this kind of interest in {vult} knowledge, virtue, health, and so forth'. 'And', Aquinas continues, 'there is in us also a kind of deliberated will which follows acts of reason deliberating *about ends and* circumstances {voluntas deliberata consequens actum rationis deliberantis de fine et diversis circumstantiis}.'[21] The passage does not explain itself further, but shows that long before he wrote *ST* I–II q.66 a.3 ad 3, Aquinas was happy—despite his already profound grasp of Aristotle's *Ethics*—to speak without inhibition about deliberation concerning ends. Further on in this early commentary on the Sentences, Aquinas will

---

[19] As Irwin (38) says, 'something more than merely instrumental reasoning is needed to see what kinds of actions and rules would properly embody or specify the very general principles grasped by synderesis'.

[20] 'It is not only the ultimate end, for the sake of which the agent acts, that is called *end* in relation to what precedes it: *each* of the intermediate means which are between the primary agent and the ultimate end is called an end in relation to what precedes it {omnia intermedia quae sunt inter primum agens et ultimum finem dicuntur finis respectu praecedentium}': *In Meta.* V.2 n. 9 [771]; also *In Phys.* II.5 n. 6 [181]; *ST* I–II q.1 a.3 ad 3; essay II.9 (1991a), sec. II; essay II.14 at 271 (2010a at 494–5). Reflection on this set of nested ends which are also means shows why 'means' has the meaning it has in this context and why it is a generally good translation of Aquinas's standard phrase *id quod ad finem est* ('that which is towards end'), provided one bears in mind (1) that 'means' here refers not to instruments {organa} nor even to techniques precisely as such, but to some action of the chooser (see *ST* I–II q.13 a.4c: 'choice is always of human acts'), and (2) that some 'means' are (as Irwin rightly emphasizes (22)) constituent parts or aspects of the relevant end.

[21] *Sent.* I d.48 q.1 a.4c.

note that when one is doing something, one cannot fix an end for oneself {finem sibi praestituere} unless one knows both the end's character {rationem finis cognoscat} *and* its relationship to the relevant means to it.[22] This relatively thoroughgoing 'knowing' of ends precisely as related or relatable to means can hardly be other than prudence. The fixing of ends is something which Aquinas speaks of, nearby, as if occurring not before but rather in the course of deliberation, as the first of three elements that make for deliberation's goodness as deliberation.[23] Soon afterwards, Aquinas, having noted that 'natural inclination presupposes a certain understanding'—doubtless synderesis—'which fixes the natural end and gives itself the inclination to the ultimate end', adds that 'so also *prudence precedes moral virtue's inclination to end*—precedes it by showing it, and directing it towards, the end'.[24]

I have paraphrased, in sec. II, the passage in III *Sent.* d.33 q.2 a.3c which explains how prudence, guided by the presupposed good of practical reasonableness itself, 'fixes the end for the moral virtues'. In a.5 of the same quaestio—having in the meantime made the remark which Irwin (26) quotes from a.4, that prudence concerns practical reason's dealings with means—Aquinas explains that the good judgment which is a matter of prudence {discretio quae ad prudentia pertinet} is the source, guardian, and governor of the virtues {genitrix et custos et moderator virtutum}. And this is so because virtue presupposes {praeexigit} 'a knowledge which fixes end(s) *and* inclines one to [such] end(s), *and* provides the means by which one attains the end(s)'. And, in this way, 'the reason *which prudence perfects and makes right* fixes the end for the other virtues—not just the overall {communis} end but also the proximate'.[25]

The general picture is clear. Prudence always presupposes some end the means to which is prudence's concern. But that presupposed end can be and indeed is an end no less ultimate, abstract, and formal/structural than 'being reasonable'—the *bonum rationis*—one amongst several such generic goods/ends each grasped as a primary principle of practical thought.[26]

---

[22] *Sent.* II d.25 q.1 a.1c. Years later, in *ST* I–II q.6 a.2c, and using virtually identical phrasing about 'knowing both the character of the end and its relation to the relevant means to it', Aquinas will say that

there is an imperfect knowledge of ends which consists simply in grasping {apprehensio} an end without knowing its character or how action bears upon it.... Willing in its more complete sense follows a relatively perfect knowledge of end, insofar as, having grasped the end {fine apprehenso}, one can, in *deliberating about the end* and about means to it, be either moved or not moved to [pursue] it.

[23] *Sent.* II d.40 q.1 a.2c: 'Ad bonitatem enim consilii... tria exiguntur. Unum scilicet, quod *consilians praestituat* sibi debitum finem...'.

[24] *Sent.* II d.41 q.1 a.1 ad 6. [25] *Sent.* III d.33 q.2 a.5c.

[26] 'The prudent person proceeds from one and the same starting-point {principio} in relation to everything with which the virtues are concerned; and that starting point is the intending of the

That leaves for prudence the whole domain of *how* to be reasonable, of the identification and effective adoption of specific ends—one might say, of a specific life-plan—which satisfies that criterion and enables one to participate in that supremely formal good.[27] This domain is from start almost to finish a matter of deliberating *about ends*—about the ends which are the means necessary or at least appropriate to one's actually being a reasonable person here and now and across a lifetime.

One has a natural interest in {inclinatio ad} the intelligible good of being reasonable. But this natural interest remains undeveloped {imperfecta} and 'insufficient for finding the reasonable mean'[28] unless and until it is integrated into a mature character and life of virtue, an integration which is the accomplishment of sound deliberation, choice, self-direction {imperium, praecipium}, and action—in short, of prudence.[29]

Aquinas interested himself in the initial moments of a fully moral life, when one comes to the 'age of reason' and can start making morally significant choices, right or wrong. Aquinas thinks that at that initial moment one confronts a momentous choice of one's overall end, by a voluntary, obligatory fixing {praestitutio} of an appropriate (or inappropriate) end for one's whole life (so far as one envisages it as a whole). He speaks of the appropriate end fixed-upon in various ways. Sometimes he will say that it is a matter of 'turning oneself to God and constituting one's end in him'.[30] Sometimes he will say that what is at stake is oneself, considered as an end in oneself to whom other things should be related as quasi-means {de seipso cogitet, ad quem alia ordinet sicut ad finem}, so that one does or fails to do what is in oneself {quod in se est}.[31] These are two ways of expressing the same thought: that one should, at this crucial

---

good of reason.' *Sent.* III d.36 q.1 a.1 ad 2. Likewise d.33 q.1 a.1 sol. 1c and sol. 2 ad 1; and see d.33 q.2 a.3c, at nn. 8–9 above.

[27] Thus the motivating *bonum rationis* is effectively the motivating *bonum prudentiae* of which Aquinas speaks in *ST* I–II q.57 a.5 ad 1, and II–II q.53 a.5 ad 1. As Irwin says (39):

if everything more specific than the general tendency to make desires conform with reason requires the deliberative operations of prudence, then deliberation must make the difference between the virtuous and the vicious person. Someone could begin with the schematic aim of acting in accordance with reason, and erroneously conclude from deliberation that this aim is achieved by injustice, cowardice, and so on. If he is to grasp the right end, his deliberation needs to be corrected.

He adds (41): 'But this is a different solution from the one that Aquinas offers.' The burden of my essay is to say: I think not.

[28] *ST* II–II q.47 a.7 ad 3.

[29] This development from imperfect/incomplete (the natural response to what is given in synderesis) to perfect/complete (the virtuous, integrated response to what is understood *about ends and means* in prudence) is the essence of Cajetan's characteristically energetic, thoughtful, and illuminating resolution of that 'serious problem' which Irwin later took up. See Aquinas, *Opera Omnia*, vol. VI, 433–4 (secs 12–14) ad I–II q.66 a.3 ad 3.

[30] *De Veritate* q.28 a.3 ad 4 (which speaks of this as a *praestitutio finis*).

[31] *ST* I–II q.89 a.6c and ad 3.

initial moment, be considering one's salvation {ut de salute sua cogitet},[32] oneself in relation to one's ultimate destiny (i.e. to one's source and the only satisfactory object of one's deepest hope). Be all that as it may, the point that concerns us here is that this thinking about oneself as an end, or in relation to God as one's end, this fixing of an appropriate end capable of organizing all one's subsequent choices, is called by Aquinas precisely a *deliberating* {deliberare de seipso}.[33]

V

Aquinas's insistence that prudence concerns means not ends certainly seems strange and unsettling to us. For to have *prudentia*, practical reasonableness or wisdom, is surely to have *all* that it takes to make morally sound judgment, and if prudence leaves out or merely takes uncritically for granted something as foundational as the very ends of human existence, or the very point of morality, it seems to be lacking in something both needed and decisive. For us, the decisive questions of ethics are whether there truly are worthwhile ends of human existence, and whether morality has a point which might be found by careful consideration and comparison of alternatives, rather than invented and adopted by sheer choice or blind following of example.

Those are not the concerns uppermost in Aquinas's mind when he discusses prudence. One might say that his primary concern, in these contexts, is to identify what is true and what misleading in the Socratic thought that virtue is a knowing and vice an ignorance. The thought cannot be conceded,[34] but the truth it half conveys and half hides is that vice's voluntary self-enslavement to passion always involves some failure of reason(ableness), some *imprudentia*.[35] For the role of prudence is to ensure that one's natural understanding of the basic human goods *is brought all the way down to action and a whole lifetime of actions*. Even making the right choice is not enough; prudence's essential domain is the *imperare* or *praecipere* by which, following one's conscientious judgment and (if one is virtuous) corresponding choice, one sets oneself to do, and directs oneself in doing, what one has chosen.[36]

In saying that prudence concerns means not ends, Aquinas expects us to remember that every means save the most ultimate is also an end, and conversely that no end, even the most ultimate, can be actually intended without being understood in its relationship to means,[37] that is, to whatever

---

[32] *Sent.* II d.42 q.1 a.5 ad 7.   [33] *ST* I–II q.89 a.6c.   [34] I–II q.58 a.2c.
[35] On *imprudentia*, see *ST* II–II q.53.   [36] II–II q.47 a.8.
[37] I–II q.12 a.4. And see essay II.9 (1991a).

might bring it to actuality in specific ways in particular lives. The ultimate end of human life, so far as philosophy can identify it, is the *beatitudo*, albeit *imperfecta*, of a life of effective virtue.[38] The whole intelligible content of this end, therefore, is the subject of deliberation, of the prudence which guides and directs the virtues. To say that prudence concerns means, not ends, amounts to saying no more than that this intellectual excellence has starting points, principles, which are accessible even to those who do not respond excellently to the attractive though demanding opportunity of being reasonable, of shaping up these initial givens into a reasonable individual and group life. My initial grasp of the first principles of natural law leaves me to deliberate and decide whether to be an egoist or to acknowledge the claims of general justice (virtue in general, as it bears in any way on my relation to other people). It leaves one to deliberate and decide whether to seek fulfilment in a life prioritized by love of neighbour as oneself, or in the gratification of passions. It leaves me to deliberate and decide—*de meipso*—whether to be a person of responsibility and self-possession or irresponsibility and dissipation. In these and other like ways, the domain of prudence extends to deliberating and deciding about all my ends.

There is, in short, no conflict among the propositions which—articulated by him in varying ways—constitute Aquinas's substantive account of natural law, virtue, and prudence.[39] The first principles of natural law, and the most basic and ultimate ends of human existence, are knowable by an understanding which is prior to reasoning and deliberating. But everything about the significance of those principles and ends—everything about their applicability, their interrelationships, and thus their *full meaning*—is a matter for the reasoning, deliberating, judging, and choosing which, when it is done well, we call prudence, *prudentia*, the practical reasonableness of individuals, families, and political and other communities.[40]

NOTE

FoE 67–8:

> [E]thics, I think, has made progress since Aristotle. His ethical treatises were decidely hazy about the starting points of practical reasoning. That is demonstrated by the great squabble, between nineteenth- and twentieth-century exegetes, about whether Aristotle envisaged that ends, as well as means, are the subject of deliberation or even of *intelligent* identification. Today

---

[38] I–II q.5 a.5c. And this means practical reason *in action*: I–II q.4 a.5c.

[39] This is in substance conceded in Irwin's 1997 treatment of the matter, which still lacks, however, a consideration of the fundamental question whether the ultimate point (end) of human existence is a single good or rather a complex good with multiple constituents each of which is a basic human good and underived principle or reason for action—and if so, what goods and reasons appear on a list of basic ends: see essay 1 at n. 21.

[40] The issues in this essay are considered further, and in a wider context, in *Aquinas*, esp. chs 3 and 4.

there are many (Allan, Gauthier, McDowell, Wiggins...) who rightly contend that Aristotle did envisage deliberation [about] and intelligent identification of ends, i.e. of the ends which somehow constitute *eudaimonia*, and meaningful or flourishing life. But no one has much to say about what those ends might be. That is an issue on which progress was made, I think, by Aquinas. But such progress as was made was lost to view, because Aquinas did not carry through and consolidate his own advance.

In his *The Development of Ethics* (2007), 175–6, Irwin says, economically:

> Prudence has a wide scope. It deliberates about what contributes to living well as a whole (1140a28).... Aristotle's view of deliberation explains why deliberation is the characteristic function of prudence, and is concerned with what contributes to the end, but nonetheless prudence is a correct grasp of the end (1142b32–3) (FN: A less probable translation makes prudence grasp the means to the end.) Aristotle does not imply that some non-deliberative aspect of prudence is needed to grasp the end, or that we cannot grasp the end through deliberation.

The earlier statements (*ibid.*, 162) about prudence and deliberation (as concerning only means, not ends) are thus to be read as elements in an understanding of Aristotle as an 'anti-rationalist', an understanding which Irwin will repudiate as based on a selective, incomplete survey of the textual evidence (167 et seq.).

But, *ibid.*, 575, Irwin says (with some shift of vocabulary):

> The only function that Aristotle explicitly attributes to practical reason is deliberation, but it has often been supposed that this cannot be the only function that he has in mind. Aquinas may be influenced by this argument: (1) Deliberation is about means to ends, and has to assume some initial grasp of ends. (2) This initial grasp of ends must be a function of practical reason. (3) Hence it must be intuitive rather than deliberative. (4) Hence it must consist in a grasp of self-evident principles.

Still, sec. 320, 'How Prudence Discovers Ends' (581–3), avoids—while not explicitly repudiating (cf. 585)—this unnecessary contrast between the 'intuitive' and the 'deliberative', and is broadly compatible with the position of this essay and essay 1 on these issues.

12

MORAL ABSOLUTES IN ARISTOTLE AND AQUINAS*

I

In the exact centre of his *Natural Right and History*, on pages 160 to 162 of that 323-page book, in the core of his discussion of the central type (the Aristotelian) among the 'three types of classic natural right teachings',[1] Leo Strauss proposed a teaching central to his own thought and influence.

Its articulation begins as if explaining Aristotle but manifestly goes beyond Aristotle into Strauss's own argumentation:

> All action is concerned with particular situations. Hence justice and natural right reside, as it were, in concrete decisions rather than in general rules.... In every human conflict there exists the possibility of a just decision based on full consideration of all the circumstances, a decision demanded by the situation. Natural right consists of such decisions. Natural right thus understood is obviously mutable. Yet one can hardly deny that in all concrete decisions general principles are implied and presupposed. Aristotle recognized the existence of such principles, e.g.... of 'commutative' and 'distributive' justice.... The common good consists normally in what is required by commutative and distributive justice or by other moral principles of this kind or in what is compatible with these requirements. But the common good comprises, of course, the mere existence, the mere survival, the mere independence, of the political community in question. Let us call an extreme situation a situation in which the very existence or independence of a society is at stake. In extreme situations there may be conflicts between what the self-preservation of society requires and the requirements of commutative and distributive justice. In such situations, and only in such situations, it can justly be said that the public safety is the highest law. A decent society will not go to war except for a just cause. But what it will do during a war will depend to a certain extent on what the enemy—possibly an absolutely unscrupulous and savage enemy—forces it to do. There are no

---

* 1990a.

[1] Strauss, *Natural Right and History* (an expanded version of the Charles R. Walgreen Lectures delivered in October 1949), 146. This, like the pages to be quoted, is from the book's central chapter, too, when we count the Introduction and the two demarcated halves of Chapters V and VI respectively.

limits which can be defined in advance, there are no assignable limits to what might become just reprisals. But war casts its shadow on peace.... [S]ocieties are threatened not only from without. Considerations which apply to foreign enemies may well apply to subversive elements within society. Let us leave these sad exigencies covered with the veil with which they are justly covered. It suffices to repeat that in extreme situations the normally valid rules of natural right are justly changed, or changed in accordance with natural right; the exceptions are as just as the rules.[2]

The conclusion: Plato and Aristotle succeed in avoiding 'the Scylla of "absolutism" and the Charybdis of "relativism"',[3] but St Thomas does not.

Strauss thus anticipated, remarkably, the main themes of the critique which, in the following forty years, was to be directed by certain Catholics against the Christian moral teachings which Aquinas helped transmit. These themes: Moral judgment has its truth only in and for 'particular situations'; in situations of 'conflict' one should decide by reference to a particular 'common good' which relativizes the principles of justice and suspends certain 'rules of natural right'; 'there is not a single [moral] rule... which is not subject to exception';[4] and what ultimately matters, in the exceptional situations, is not what one does but that one does it with an *attitude*, for example of 'reluctance'. Whatever Strauss's success in articulating the spirit of 'the classics', he certainly conveyed some characteristic elements of the spirit of the mid- and late twentieth century.

Moreover: this passage of Strauss's is to be taken as a studied defence of the 'total war' policy of the Allies in the war which ended only four years before Strauss's lectures—a policy extended into western post-war security policy. Nuclear deterrence treats the 'extreme situation' as, in a decisive aspect, the simply 'normal'.[5]

Strauss is teaching that a society whose 'mere independence' is threatened by an unjust enemy is justified in executing unlimited reprisals and other acts admittedly contrary to commutative justice. For Aquinas (who invented this use of 'commutative'), commutative justice is that justice whose very first component is the absolute exclusion of intentionally killing innocents.[6] But Strauss is simply representative of the moderns, who all *take for granted* that Caiaphas's principle is right: Better that one

---

[2] *Ibid.*, 159–60.   [3] *Ibid.*   [4] *Ibid.*, 161.

[5] Joseph Cropsey, co-editor with Strauss of *The History of Political Philosophy* and the disciple entrusted with editing the *Festschrift* for Strauss's sixty-fifth birthday, himself published in 1961 'The Moral Basis of International Action' (see esp. 184–5 in the 1977 version), a justification of nuclear deterrence on a basis which, in the entire scholarly literature, seems nearest to resting simply on 'Better dead than Red'—not forgetting the essence of the policy he defends: If we are to die at the hands of the Reds, it will *not be without unleashing an unlimited reprisal*.

[6] *ST* II–II q.64 a.2 ad 3; a.6. Q.64 is the first of the 15 questions and 65 articles devoted to commutative justice.

man—or quite a few—be unjustly killed than that the whole people perish. On this decisive moral-political question the differences between Strauss and Voegelin or Arendt or Rawls or Nagel or Dworkin or countless others simply disappear. Unanimously they all reject the moral absolutes to which our civilization until yesterday paid at least lip service.

II

Strauss claimed that this representative modern teaching is also Aristotle's view, and a safe middle road between the extremes of Averroist conventionalism and Thomist absolutism.[7]

What, in fact, did Aristotle think? Strauss relies on only one text, one or two rather conjectural lines from *NE* V.7: though the just by nature is 'that which everywhere has the same force', it is 'all changeable'.

Now one finds similar, apparently universal (all-embracing) statements in Aquinas. I shall refer to the two important instances. First: the primary, 'common' moral principles are true for everyone everywhere, but 'particular conclusions' are true only 'for the most part' (*ut in pluribus*), with exceptions (*ut in paucioribus*) ['in the minority of cases']; for the closer you get to the particulars with which all action is concerned, the more the general principles become inadequate.[8]

But this statement is, itself, only a generalization. It applies to most moral principles and norms, since most are affirmative directions specifying a responsibility *to do* something, such as to return what you have borrowed. But it does not apply to the few, but vital, negative moral norms which in every situation require one, for example, *not to* be choosing to kill the innocent, lying, or committing adultery or sodomy. Such precepts 'bind always and for every situation' (*semper et ad semper*). There is never a time to be stealing or committing adultery. But affirmative precepts, while always binding, do not bind in every situation, but only relatively to time and place (*semper, sed non ad semper, sed pro loco et tempore*),[9] (So one should not return what one has borrowed if it is a deadly weapon whose lender has now gone

---

[7] Careful readers will not take this talk of a *via media* too seriously, for Strauss's own view exactly coincides with that which he attributes to the Averroists (including the Islamic and Jewish Aristotelians): moral rules presented by society as universally valid are in truth only *generally* valid, so that as presented, without qualifications and exceptions, they are untrue, and thus not 'natural' but 'conventional'.†

[8] *ST* I–II q.94 a.4c; in the ad 2m, Aquinas adds that the statement in *Ethics* V.7 about natural right being 'all changeable' means just that.

[9] ['always, but not for every situation, but depending on place and time'] Aquinas, *in ad Rom*, c.13 lect. 2; also *Sent*. III d.25 q.2 a.1b ad 3; *Sent*. IV d.17 q.3 a.1d ad 3; *Q.D. de Virt*. III (*de Correct. Frat.*) a.1c and ad 4; *de Malo* q.7 a.1 ad 8; *ST* II–II q.33 a.2c.

mad or turned traitor.)[10] To repeat: 'Moral rules are generalizations, not universally true' is only a generalization, not universally true.

But there is a *second* set of statements in which Aquinas *seems* to treat all specific moral norms as subject to exceptions. For we find him saying that the commandments of the Second Table of the Decalogue (e.g. Do not kill, Do not commit adultery, Do not steal) are subject to divine dispensation in those exceptional cases where God miraculously communicates his will to allow killing, adultery, stealing, and so forth.[11]

Some theologians want to make these passages a basis for taking Strauss's 'middle road'. But Aquinas's teaching is different. Whenever he directly and formally considers whether God can dispense from the Decalogue, Aquinas's answer is clear: No, there can be no dispensation from any of the last seven Commandments.[12]

This is no contradiction. In the first-mentioned set of passages, where he incidentally mentions divine dispensation, Aquinas is considering the *physical behaviour* involved in human acts of killing, sexual intercourse, taking another's property; if the Commandments are considered as bearing simply on such behaviour, or on some *conventional* description of it, then behaviour which normally (or: under some conventional description) is forbidden can be, and exceptionally has been, divinely permitted. But morality, strictly speaking, deals not with physical behaviour as such (nor with its merely conventional descriptions) but with physical behaviour *as humanly chosen and intended*, that is, with *human acts*.[13] Considered as bearing on human acts, the Commandments in question are exceptionless and cannot be dispensed from, even by God (for God's goodness and holiness are incompatible with him willing any evil). Those occasions when—on the exegesis accepted by St Thomas—God seemed to make an exception to the Commandments are in truth, Aquinas teaches, situations in which God so changed the conditions or circumstances of the behaviour that what was humanly willed, chosen, intended was not an *act of* killing the innocent (but executing divine justice on the guilty), not an act of having intercourse with a woman not one's spouse (but intercourse with a woman divinely made one's spouse by God), and not an act of theft (but a taking possession of what God had already made one's own property).[14]

[10] I–II q.94 a.4c. *That* is the example given to illustrate the *ut in pluribus* character of (most!) moral norms.
[11] *Sent.* I d.47 q.1 a.4; *Sent.* IV d.33 q.1 a.2; *de Malo* q.3 a.1 ad 17.
[12] *Sent.* III d.37 q.un. a.4c and ad 1; *ST* I–II q.100 a.8.
[13] *Sent.* II d.36 q.un. a.5 ad 5; d.40 q.un. a.1 ad 4; a.2c and ad 3; *Sent.* IV d.16 q.3 a.1b ad 2; *de Malo* q.2 a.4c and ad 9; a.6 ad 9; *ST* I–II q.1 a.3 ad 3, q.20 a.2c.
[14] See Lee, 'Permanence of the Ten Commandments'.

Thus: 'There can be dispensations from the Decalogue', like 'Specific norms are not exceptionless', turns out to be asserted by Aquinas only with a tacit qualification. So perhaps Aristotle's 'Natural right is all mutable' is similarly intended to be taken with an unexpressed qualification?

In *NE* II.6, having defined right actions, passions, and dispositions as intermediate between excesses, Aristotle adds:

> But not every action nor every passion admits of a mean; for some have names that already imply badness, e.g. spite, shamelessness, envy, and in the case of actions adultery, theft, murder.... It is not possible, then, ever to be right with regard to them; one must always be wrong. Nor does goodness or badness with regard to such things depend on committing adultery with the right woman, at the right time, and in the right way, but simply to do any of them is to go wrong.[15]

W.F.R. Hardie's characteristic mid-twentieth century academic interpretation of this passage will assert that Aristotle is making

> a purely logical point which arises from the fact that certain words are used... with the implication, as part of the meaning of the word, that they are excessive or defective, and therefore wrong.... [I]t does not make sense to ask when murder is right because to call a killing 'murder' is to say that it is wrong... This, and no more than this, is what Aristotle means.[16]

It is as if Aristotle anticipated the theologians who say the Decalogue merely exhorts us, through 'formal', tautologous formulations, to abstain from whatever we know on other grounds to be wrong: Do no wrongful killing, Do not have intercourse with the wrong person or on the wrong occasion... For these theologians, St Paul's protest about doing evil for the sake of good (Rom. 3: 8) meant merely: 'Do not do moral wrong for the sake of non-moral good'—in their moral language: 'Do not, for the sake of overall greater good, choose overall lesser good!'

Hardie offers no argument, and is silent about the words 'Goodness or badness with regard to such things does not depend on committing adultery with the right woman, at the right time, and in the right way'. He leaves us to assume that Aristotle would agree that, of course, one can in the right circumstances (perhaps exceptional) have intercourse with someone not one's spouse. If so, Aristotle certainly chose a very misleading way of expressing himself. The parallel *Eudemian* passage, unmentioned by Hardie, seems even less 'purely logical': 'A man is not an adulterer through having intercourse with married women more than he ought (there is no such thing): that is already a vice'.[17]

---

[15] *NE* II.6: 1107a9–17. [16] Hardie, *Aristotle's Ethical Theory*, 137.
[17] *Eud. Eth.* II.3: 1221b20–2.

In the same *Eudemian* text, Aristotle notes that people accused of adultery will admit to having sex with a married woman but will deny that it was adultery, saying they were forced to—did it as a matter of necessity. And compulsion or necessity (Aristotle treats them as synonymous) is the theme of the other passage apparently touching moral absolutes (*NE* III.1). He is discussing 'involuntary' passions and actions, and asks whether there is involuntariness when one does 'something base' (*aischron*, in Latin *turpe*)

from fear of greater evils or for some noble object—e.g. if a tyrant were to order one to do something base, having one's parents and children in his power, and if one did the action they were to be saved, but otherwise would be put to death...(1110a4–7).

What are the 'base' acts which, Aristotle accepts, one can laudably choose for some great and noble object? Aristotle's early commentator, Aspasius (c. 200 BC), opens a line of interpretation adopted, independently, by Aquinas. What Aristotle had in mind, they say, was acts not morally bad but merely 'ignominious'.[18] So, says Aspasius, it would be praiseworthy to comply with a tyrant who threatens to destroy one's city and family unless one publicly wears clothes of the wrong sex.[19]

But the anonymous Old Scholiast (? c. 200 AD) offers an interpretation which, like nothing in Aristotle's text, forced the Christian mediaevals to make their own moral teaching clear—clear beyond even the late twentieth century revisionists' capacities for misunderstanding. For the Old Scholiast offered an example of the praiseworthy 'base acts': having intercourse with another's spouse in order to overthrow a tyrant. Moral wrong, he added, resides not in acts but in their *intentions*: as we might put his point, the end justifies the means.[20]

Robert Grosseteste, Bishop of Lincoln, transmitted the Old Scholiast to Latin Christianity. At this point in the commentary he interjected one of his own infrequent comments:

The Christian religion declares and holds that sin must not be committed, neither for the sake of pursuing any good (*utilitas*) nor for the sake of avoiding any loss. And so, since it is sin to lie and sin to have intercourse with another's wife (*alienae uxori misceri*), neither is in any way to be done. And so the teaching above is not doctrine but error, in the examples it proposes. For [and here Grosseteste echoes the Vulgate of St Paul in Romans 3: 8] the evils of sin are not to be done for the sake of goods. On the other hand, the evils of suffering or punishment (*poena*),

---

[18] *In Eth.* nn. 393–4.
[19] Aspasius in Heylbut (ed.), *Commentaria in Aristotelem Graeca*, vol. 10(1), 61.
[20] Heylbut (ed.), *Commentaria in Aristotelem Graeca*, vol. 20, 142.

even if they are truly shameful (*turpia*), but assuming that they are not sinful, are to be done and endured for the sake of goods.[21]

Thomas Aquinas, writing nearly thirty years later, was just as blunt, and rather terser. He postulates the following argument designed to show that sex outside marriage cannot be intrinsically wrong (*peccatum ex genere*, or *secundum se*):

> Whatever is intrinsically sinful may not be done for any purpose however good—as Paul says in *Romans* 3.8... But as the Commentator on the *Ethics* says, an upright man commits adultery with the tyrant's wife, so that the tyrant may be killed and the country liberated. Therefore adultery is not intrinsically wrong; still less any other act of fornication. (*de Malo* q.15 a.1 arg.4)

Aquinas's reply?

> The Commentator is not to be supported on this matter: for one may not commit adultery for any good (*pro nulla enim utilitate debet aliquis adulterium committere*), just as one may not tell a lie for the sake of any advantage (*propter utilitatem aliquem*), as Augustine says in *Contra Mendacium*.[22]

Thus, from Augustine in the fourth century (indeed, from before him, since in the midst of controversy Augustine treats this as uncontroverted) down to about 1964, terms such as 'adultery' were not *defined* by the great philosophers and theologians as wrongful sex. Rather, having been defined as, for example, sex involving a married person not married to the partner, they were *judged* always wrongful, whatever the circumstances—whatever, for example, the 'common good', the *salus populi* at stake.

And the same goes for murder. Aquinas defines it, in effect, as the intentional killing of the innocent. He argues that it is rightly excluded by the fifth commandment, and that it is an intrinsically wrongful act, *secundum se malum*. Such acts, he notes 'may not be done for whatever good end, as both Augustine and Aristotle make clear'.[23] For Aristotle's opinion he is relying on that passage, in *Ethics* II.6, which a modern interpretation reads as devoid of ethical content. To me, Aristotle's text seems not clear enough for any final adjudication between the mediaeval and the modern interpretations. But, by mentioning Aristotle alongside Augustine, Aquinas suggests that the exceptionlessness of absolute moral norms is something

---

[21] Mercken (ed.), *Corpus Latinum Commentarium in Aristotelem Graecorum*, VI,1, 239. See also *ibid.*, 57 for Grosseteste's similar *notula* on 1110a1.

[22] *de Malo* q.15 a.1 ad 4. The Commentator's (Old Scholiast's) opinion is rejected in very similar terms by St Albert, *Super Ethica Commentum et Quaestiones* [c.1250–2] 125 (ad 1107a8–32); 380 (ad 1136b15–1137a30) citing Romans 3: 8 and Augustine, *Contra Mendacium* c.9; and 142 (on *NE* III.1). Augustine's argument for moral absolutes in the *Contra Mendacium* became the standard witness by way of Peter Lombard's *Sentences* II d.40.

[23] *ST* II–II q.64 a.2 obj.3 and ad 3.

accessible to philosophical thought, to reflective practical reason unaided by divine revelation.

III

Is it? Though he never clearly denies, Aristotle never clearly affirms exceptionless moral norms. And this is not surprising. Unless certain clarifications have been made, to affirm them amounts to affirming that there are situations in which one faces a true 'conflict of duties', is strictly perplexed, and cannot fail to do wrong. The clarifications necessary to avoid this moral absurdity are these. (i) Within the complex of behaviour and results which one carries out and causes by one's choice, one must be able to distinguish what is *chosen*, that is, intended (whether as end or as means), and what is foreseen, caused, and accepted but *not* intended. (ii) One must notice that the *actions* excluded by absolute moral norms are described in terms of what is intended as end or means, not in terms of chunks of physical behaviour just as such, nor in terms of other foreseen (but unintended) results. (iii) One must be able to say why the exclusion of certain intentions of ends and means, and of the physical actions which execute those intentions, is morally important. To do this, one will need both (iv) an account of basic human goods which provide the ultimate reasons for choices, and (v) a conception of free choice as the commitment of oneself to ends and means as identified in a proposal which one adopts for oneself without being determined thereto by any factor whatsoever (whether reasoning or desire).

Though none of these desiderata is denied by Aristotle, and elements of each are scattered about in his works, none is affirmed. In Aquinas, each is affirmed and to some extent explained and justified. But they are not brought together into an orderly, accessible account of the rational sense and force of moral absolutes. Nor did Aquinas's followers supply the missing account. It became standard to claim that the moral absolutes excluding murder, adultery, theft, etc. are intuited as absolutely basic and primary, underived principles, in that 'habit of first principles' which Aquinas named *synderesis*. No one should fiercely blame Strauss for ascribing this view to Aquinas. But it is certainly not Aquinas's view.

For Aquinas states very clearly that moral norms of the form and content of the Decalogue are not primary, *per se nota*, underived principles, but rather are conclusions from prior, underived, truly *per se nota* principles.[24]

---

[24] e.g. *ST* I–II q.99 a.2c; q.100 aa. 1c, 3c and ad 1, 6c, 11c and ad 1; also q.94 a.6c. See essay 9, sec. V.

But we need an account of the moral first principle(s) from which these conclusions are derived.

Offering such an account, as a free-standing philosophical effort to be judged in its own right, has been the focus of the work in ethical theory undertaken these last twenty-five years by Germain Grisez, Joseph Boyle, myself, and others. Our theory, as it stood in 1986, is summarized in Chapters 10 and 11 of our *Nuclear Deterrence, Morality and Realism*. Here I mention only a few key fragments.

Action is immoral when against reason. Now, a choice of action will be against reason if there is *a* reason against doing the action and no *rationally preferable* reason to do it. Amongst the various possible reasons against choosing an option is this: that the option embodies a proposal to damage or impede some instantiation of a basic (i.e. non-instrumental, intrinsic) human good—some irreducible aspect of a human person's well-being such as bodily life, knowledge of truth, harmony with other persons, and such like. But in any situation where such an action could be chosen, no reason *for* choosing it could rationally be preferable to the reason *against* choosing it.

For if there were a reason (for doing X) which some rational method of comparison identified (prior to moral judgment) as preferable, the alternative reason (against doing X) thus identified as rationally inferior would cease to be rationally appealing in respect of that situation of choice. The reason thus identified as preferable, and the option favoured by that reason, would be rationally unopposed. There would remain no possibility of a rationally motivated, morally significant *choice* between the alternative options. For choice is morally significant when *free*, no factor but the choosing itself *settling* which alternative is chosen; and one makes a rationally motivated choice just where one really does have reasons for alternative options.

So the reason why there are morally significant choices is precisely that, *prior to moral judgment*, there is no rational method of identifying the reasons for alternative options as rationally superior and inferior. For the instantiations of basic human goods, instantiations considered precisely as reasons for moral judgment and for action, are incommensurable with one another. And this is not surprising, for these instantiations are nothing other than aspects of human persons, present and future, and human persons cannot be weighed and balanced.

Among the factors giving rise to this pre-moral rational incommensurability of morally significant options is the *reflexivity* of free choice itself. Choices, being determined by nothing save the chooser's act of choosing, reflexively shape the chooser's character, personality, soul.

Choices, in fact, *last*; they persist in the chooser until, if ever, they are reversed by an inconsistent choice. How could one conceivably assess the overall net pre-moral value and disvalue of that change, and of the changes of attitude, ethos, and practice which so often result from a single choice? This sort of consequence simply cannot be commensurated with a choice's other consequences.

Aquinas never once seeks to resolve a moral question by identifying one option as the lesser evil. He everywhere rejects the attempt to resolve moral problems by that principle which the late-twentieth century, including its theological epigones, treats as self-evidently *the* master principle of morality (or at least the moral master principle in 'conflict situations'): 'choose the lesser evil!'.[25] Though he never argues the matter out, Aquinas seems clear that, in a situation of morally significant choice, it is impossible—not merely immoral, but impossible—to obtain guidance for one's moral judgment by identifying one option as involving overall greater good or less harm than alternative options.

Many uses of 'greater good' and 'lesser evil' are legitimate and do not presume that one can do the impossible: (i) in technical reasoning, in which one ranks reasons for their instrumentality, their utility relative to some single definite goal; (ii) in contemplatively ranking aspects of the universe on some hierarchy of dignity or worth; (iii) in expressing moral judgments already made; or (iv) in expressing some ranking one has not found by reason but *made* to correspond with one's feelings and emotions.[26] None of common speech's legitimate hierarchizations gives the sense of 'greater good' or 'lesser evil' needed by those who, since the Enlightenment,[27] have sought to assume the role of divine providence by rational assessments of all the pre-moral goods and bads involved in options and consequences.

A substantive (not merely formal) moral absolute is a norm in which a human act is described in terms which, though themselves non-moral, enable us to tell that no act of that precise description can be chosen without preferring emotion to reason, that is, without following some emotional

---

[25] Aquinas rejects it in *Sent.* IV d.6 q.1 a.1 qa.1 ad 4; d.9 q.1 a.5 qa.1 ad 3; *ST* II–II q.110 a.3 ad 4; III q.68 a.11 ad 3; q.80 a.6 ad 2. His only appeal is in an analysis of inconstancy and rashness, where no moral question stands to be resolved.

[26] All moral action is made possible by feelings and emotions; preferences and prioritizations shaped by feeling are very common, take many legal, political, and other cultural forms, and are often 'reasonable' just in the sense that they are not against any reason: they involve no choice to destroy or damage a basic human good, no unreasonable partiality as between persons, and, in short, do not express a will deflected from openness to integral human fulfilment—the good of all persons and communities—by merely emotional desire, aversion, hostility, or inertia. Yet, being preferences based on feeling, they do not disclose a rational preferability such as could give reason to choose what there is also reason not to choose—a reason not based on feeling but constituted by (the immediacy to one's will of) some instantiation of a basic human good.

[27] Which professing Catholic theologians publicly began buying into in about 1964–66.

preference at the expense of the sort of reason that is constituted by an instantiation of a basic human good: for example *human life* (in the case of direct killing), truth in communication (as in the case of lying, properly defined), *interpersonal harmony* (as in the case of chattel slavery, understood more precisely than Aristotle or even Aquinas did; or of manufacturing human beings), or the complex of basic goods of life and interpersonal harmony involved in the sexually expressed conjugal relationship of procreative friendship (as in the case of adultery).

Absolute moral norms of this sort are only a fragment of morality's basic principles. One should always choose and otherwise will those and only those possibilities whose willing is compatible with integral human fulfilment—the good of all persons and communities understood not as the definite goal of some million-year plan but as a guiding, critical ideal. This principle is nothing other than an expression of one's intelligent practical grasp of the integral directiveness of the basic human goods as open-ended reasons for action—as all the *reasons* for action there can be.

Life, truth, and interpersonal harmony as such are all basic human goods which give reasons for fostering and respecting community not only at the level of the polity, the state. A most common and plausibly disguised emotion, then, is that which invites one to absolutize one's own concrete polity by making its fate, rather than integral human fulfilment as such, the horizon of one's deliberation and choice. Perhaps only the horizon of Christian faith and eschatology, unavailable to Aristotle, reliably allows one to overcome that absolutization of emotionally determined horizons.

Some such emotion grounds the policy implicitly defended by Strauss and virtually every political philosopher of our generation: the policy which seeks to secure the future of our polity (with all its undoubted and real goods, including its justice) by forming and publicizing the intention, conditional but real, of imposing directly upon the innocents of an aggressor state, and indirectly upon the innocents of many or all other states, bodily destruction and death along with the ruin of every other human good which they value for its own sake.

All arguments that this policy is a rational preference of 'the common good' are demonstrably fallacious, as we contended in Chapters 7 and 9 of *Nuclear Deterrence*. Equally fallacious, as we contended in Chapters 8 and 9, are arguments that the policy involves 'greater (pre-moral) evil'. The inevitable failure of all such consequentialist arguments opens the way for a more adequate method of guiding morally significant choice.

It also opens the way for a conception of politics in which securing and respecting the common good includes neither the *injustice* of getting ready to carry out, 'if need be', vast massacres of innocents as reprisals, nor the *absurdity* of being ready and willing to carry out such reprisals 'if need be', after the entire destruction of our own community with its all too narrowly conceived and too 'technically' pursued 'common good'.

NOTES

The issues in this essay are revisited in *MA* ch. II.

† *Averroism of the Islamic and Jewish Aristotelian falāsifa (and Strauss)*...(n. 7). This view, as described with approval by Strauss, is analogous to the esoteric/exoteric, two-level, or 'archangels and proles' utilitarianisms espoused cautiously by Henry Sidgwick at the end of his *The Methods of Ethics* (1874) and incautiously by R.M. Hare throughout his *Moral Thinking: Its Levels, Method, and Point* (1981).

13
'NATURAL LAW'*

I. WHY CALLED 'NATURAL'? WHY CALLED 'LAW'?

In the discourse of ethics, political theory, or *philosophie de droit* (philosophy of law), the claim that there is a natural law is an offer to explain and defend the substance of certain assertions often made in different terms in pre-theoretical discourse (moral argument, politics, and/or law). Pretheoretically (so to speak), choices, actions, and/or dispositions may be said to be 'inhuman', 'unnaturally cruel', 'perverse', or 'morally unreasonable'; proposals, policies, or conduct may be described as violations of 'human rights'; actions of states, groups, or individuals may be described as 'crimes against humanity' and citizens may claim immunity from legal liability or obligations by appealing to a 'higher law'. A natural law theory offers to explain why such assertions can be rationally warranted and true. It offers to do so by locating these assertions in the context of a general theory of good and evil in human life so far as human life is shaped by deliberation and choice.

Such a theory of good and evil can also be called a general theory of right and wrong in human choices and actions. It will contain both (i) normative propositions identifying types of choice, action, or disposition as right or wrong, permissible, obligatory, etc., and (ii) non-normative propositions about the objectivity and epistemological warrant of the normative propositions.

Theorists who describe their account of good and evil, right and wrong, as a 'natural law theory' are not committed to asserting that the normative propositions they defend are 'derived from Nature' or 'read off' or 'inspected in' 'the nature of things'. Indeed, it is rare for a natural law theory to make such assertions, for their sense is deeply obscure; it is difficult, if not

---

* [1996e] ('Loi naturelle' in Canto-Sperber ed., *Dictionnaire de Philosophie Morale*); an earlier version is 1986a.

impossible, to understand what epistemic or rational processes would be involved in such 'derivation' or 'reading off' or 'inspection in'.

Still less are natural law theorists committed to claiming that the normative propositions they defend stand in some definite relationship to, or are warranted by, the 'laws of nature' in the sense of the regularities observed, and explanatory factors adduced, by the 'natural sciences' (physics, biology, 'experimental psychology', ecology, etc.). Thomas Aquinas, a leading natural law theorist, sharply differentiates the propositions of moral and political philosophy (in which the principles and norms of natural law are identified and elaborated) from (1) the propositions which constitute the natural sciences, (2) the principles and norms of logic, and what others have called the 'laws of thought', and (3) the principles and norms of any and every human technique of manipulating matter which is subject to our will.[1]

Nor is the typical natural law theory (classical, mediaeval, or contemporary) concerned with any alleged 'state of nature', in the sense of some golden age or state of affairs prior to human wrongdoing or to the formation of human societies or of states or political communities.

As for the term 'law', as understood in the phrase 'natural law', it does not connote that the relevant principles and norms have their directive force precisely as the commands, imperatives, or dictates of a superior will. Even those natural law theorists who argue (as most do) that the most ultimate explanation of those principles and norms (as of all other realities) is a transcendent, creative, divine source of existence, meaning, and value, will also argue that the principles and norms are inherently fitting and obligatory (not fitting or obligatory because commanded), or that the source of their obligation is rather divine wisdom than divine will.

Instead, the term 'law' in the phrase 'natural law' refers to standards of right choosing, standards which are normative (that is, rationally directive and 'obligatory') because they are true and choosing otherwise than in accordance with them is unreasonable.

And the term 'natural' (and related uses of 'by nature', 'in accordance with nature', and 'of nature') in this context signifies any one or more of the following: (a) that the relevant standards (principles and norms) are not 'positive', that is, are directive prior to any positing by individual decision or group choice or convention; (b) that the relevant standards are 'higher' than positive laws, conventions, and practices, that is, provide the premises for critical evaluation and endorsement or justified rejection of or disobedience to such laws, conventions, or practices; (c) that the relevant standards

[1] *In Eth.*, prol.

conform to the most demanding requirements of critical reason and are objective, in the sense that a person who fails to accept them as standards for judgment is in error; (d) that adherence to the relevant standards tends systematically to promote human flourishing, the fulfilment of human individuals and communities.

II. CRITIQUE OF SCEPTICISM AND DOGMATISM

Historically, natural law theories have been articulated as part or product of a philosophical critique of ethical scepticisms (whether nihilism, relativism, subjectivism, or hedonism). Since the sceptical views thus criticized and rejected by theorists of natural law (e.g. Plato) or natural right/justice (e.g. Aristotle) were themselves articulated in reaction to uncritically accepted conventions or religiously promoted norms, the philosophical critique of scepticism included a differentiation of the rationally grounded norms of natural law (or natural right) from moral dogmatism or conventionalism.

In contemporary thought, scepticism about natural law (and about other moral theories claiming to be objective or true) is very often based upon a logically illicit and rationally unwarranted inference from certain propositions about what 'is' the case to certain propositions about what is good or obligatory. This particular form of invalid reasoning was assiduously employed in the ancient manuals of scepticism, reintroduced into European discourse in the sixteenth century (see e.g. Sextus Empiricus, *Pyrrhonean Hypotyposes* III, xxiv, 198–238; Sextus Empiricus uses the term 'dogmatism' to insinuate that all non-sceptical ethical theories, such as natural law theory, are uncritical; but this charge is not well grounded, and the term is used in this essay to refer to moral positions held without openness to critical questions).

Examples of the invalid reasoning commonly encountered today include the following:

— X is not universally regarded as good/obligatory; therefore X is not good/obligatory.

— In modern thought ('modernity') X is widely regarded as not good/obligatory; therefore X is not good/obligatory.

— In contemporary society X is widely regarded as good/obligatory; therefore X is good/obligatory.

— I have a sentiment of approval of X; therefore X is good (or worthwhile... or obligatory...), at least for me.

— I have opted for or decided upon or am committed to the practical principle that X ought to be done; therefore X ought to be done, at least by me.

As this list of *non sequiturs* suggests, there is a link between ethical scepticism (at least in its popular forms) and ethical conventionalism. There are many natural law theories, on the other hand, which are not guilty of these or other fallacies, fallacies which consist in concluding to a normative judgment from premises which include no normative proposition.

David Hume suggests that 'every system of morality' prior to his critique illogically purports to infer *ought* or *ought not* from *is* or *is not*.[2] The suggestion is ungrounded, though the illicit inference may perhaps be detected in certain eighteenth-century rationalists (especially Samuel Clarke) whom Hume seems to have had prominently in mind when writing this part of his *Treatise*. Insofar as Hume's predominant view (among four or five inconsistent views which he seems to have entertained) concerning the nature and basis of moral judgments was that they are judgments about what characteristics and actions arouse approval or disapproval, Hume was himself plainly guilty of this kind of illegitimate inference. The same cannot be said of Plato, Aristotle, and Aquinas, for example.

The modern form of 'fact-value distinction' and denial of the 'objectivity of value judgments' may be found clearly articulated in Max Weber's methodological writings, which conclude that any meaning or value must be imposed upon the world by an act of will. (The question how an act of will could create or impose value remains unanswered.) Weber's primary argument for his denial of ethical objectivity seems to have been simply that people, or educated people, in fact disagree with each other about values. But this has no more validity than the popular arguments listed above; the fact of disagreement no more disproves a proposition than the fact of agreement proves it. Weber had three other lines of argument. The first was a neo-Kantian argument that all judgments must rest upon pre-suppositions, and that selection among competing pre-suppositions must be non-rational. This argument is self-refuting in its general form, and there is no way to limit it (as Weber sought to do) to judgments of value. Weber's next argument pointed, like Sartre after him, to certain supposed political and/or ethical dilemmas before which reason is supposed to fall silent. Such 'dilemmas', however, seem in truth to be no more than a stimulus to a more nuanced and resourceful practical reasoning, in which

---

[2] Hume, *A Treatise of Human Nature*, III, i, 1.

one may identify good reasons for preferring one horn of the dilemma, or for settling upon some third course of action, or for narrowing the choice to a small range of reasonable and choiceworthy options (any of which could reasonably be adopted in preference to the indefinitely vast range of irrational or at least unreasonable alternatives). Weber's final argument alleged that there are distinct and incommensurable 'spheres' of practical judgment, such as the political, the erotic, and the ethical, each with its own ultimate values between which reason cannot adjudicate because reason operates only within spheres. This final claim, not defended by Weber, is contradicted by his own acknowledgement that the spheres interpenetrate one another.[3]

As for Weber's direct confrontation with natural law theory, it is abortive. For he asserts that in such theory 'general propositions about regularities of factual occurrences and general norms of conduct are held to coincide... The ought is identical with the "is", i.e. that which exists in the universal average'.[4] In truth, however, Aristotle explicitly contrasts the natural with the average (*Pol.* IV.1: 1288b10–40 and *NE* V.7: 1135a5), and Aquinas frequently stresses that most people and their actions are foolish and corrupt (*ST* I q.113 a.1; I–II q.9 a.5 ad 3; q.94 a.4; etc.).

Perhaps the most fruitful critique of ethical scepticism is one which takes its cue from Aristotle's critique of general scepticism (*Metaphysics* IV.4: 1005b35–1006a28; IV.8: 1012a29–b18; XI.5: 1062b1–11; XI.6: 1063b30–5). If sceptics are willing to affirm their position as rationally warranted they can be shown to be denying (i) something given, instantiated, in the activity of rationally considering and proposing their or any other position, and/or (ii) some proposition to which their assertion of their position rationally commits them. In the case in hand, the relevant givens include the rationality norms which guide the rational inquiries of those who choose to follow them and to resist temptations to reach conclusions by sub-rational processes; and the propositions to which an argued assertion commits the person asserting it include the proposition that knowledge of truth (at least the truth of such propositions as the one asserted) is a good worth pursuing and instantiating in that argument and assertion, a good worthwhile for its own sake as well as for any instrumental advantage it might yield. An analysis of the activity of inquiring, arguing, and judging can show that it is self-refuting to deny that there are ever free choices,[5] and self-refuting to deny that there are any intrinsic, non-instrumental

---

[3] See Turner and Factor, *Max Weber and the Dispute over Reason and Value*, 31–46.
[4] Weber, *Economy and Society*, 869. [See essay IV.9 (1985b), sec. III.]
[5] See Boyle, Grisez, and Tollefsen, *Free Choice: A Self-Referential Argument*. [And essays 3–4.]

goods.[6] The proposition, 'Knowledge of truth is a good to be pursued, and ignorance, self-deception, and confusion are to be avoided', is a practical principle which is not grounded on, but is defensible by way of, the analysis of self-referentially inconsistent denials of it.

III. COGNITIVISM AND NATURAL LAW

Not every non-sceptical ethics is appropriately called a natural law theory. Natural law theories are distinguished from the broader set of cognitivist or objectivist ethical theories in four main ways.

First, they are differentiated from any ethics in a Kantian mould by their willingness to identify certain basic human goods, such as knowledge, life and health, and friendship, as the core of substantive first principles of practical reasoning. Taken together, these basic human goods give shape and content to a conception of human flourishing and thus, too, to a conception of human nature. For: an axiom of Aristotle's method (*De Anima* II.4: 415a16–21), deployed more generally by Aquinas, shows that while nature is metaphysically (ontologically) fundamental, knowledge of a thing's nature is epistemically derivative: an animate thing's nature is understood by understanding its capacities, its capacities by understanding its activities, and its activities by understanding the objects of those activities. In the case of the human being the 'objects' which must be understood before one can understand and know human nature are the basic goods which are the objects of one's will, i.e. are one's basic reasons for acting and give reason for everything which one can intelligently take an interest in choosing.

Secondly, natural law theories are distinguished from any theory which asserts that moral truths are known essentially by discrete 'intuitions'. Rather, natural law theories contend that specific moral judgments concerning obligation or right are applications or specifications of higher principles. The first principles of the 'system' are known by insight (*nous*: cf. *NE* VI.6: 1141a8 with 5: 1140b17 and 6: 1142a26), without deduction via any middle term (they are *per se nota*: *ST* I–II q.94 a.2). But the insights whose content is the self-evident principles of practical knowledge are not intuitions—'insights' without data. Rather they are insights whose data are, in the first place, natural and sensory appetites and emotional responses. These data are subsequently enriched by theoretical knowledge or true opinion about possibilities (e.g. about what threatens and enhances health, or about what knowledge is available), and by experience of disharmony

---

[6] See *NLNR* 73–5.

(frustrated intentions). It should be added that the classical natural law theorists would reject Maritain's theory that the knowledge of first practical principles is 'connatural' or 'by affinity or congeniality' or 'through inclination' *rather than conceptual*.[7] As Maritain conceded in relation to the expression 'knowledge through inclination', such terms are never used by Aquinas in discussions of the principles of natural law.[8] Nor does Aquinas resort to any sort of non-conceptual knowledge as an intuitionistic source of confessedly inexplicable exceptions to moral norms, as Maritain does.[9] And there seems compelling reason not to accept Maritain's claim that Aquinas must have been referring to such 'knowledge' when saying (in *ST* I–II q.94 a.2) that 'reason naturally understands as good all the objects of man's inclinations'. For Aquinas all knowledge is conceptual (*De Veritate* q.4 a.2 ad 5), and the understanding of basic human goods is quite ordinary, unmysterious, *conceptual* understanding,[10] albeit practical, that is, directive or prescriptive ('is-to-be-done-and-pursued'), rather than purely 'theoretical' or descriptive ('is'). The first principles of natural law are not inclinations, but fundamental human goods understood as reasons for action.

Thirdly, natural law theories are distinguished from any fundamentally aggregative conception of the right and the just. For: viable natural law theories postulate no one end to which all human actions might be effective means, no one value in terms of which one might commensurate alternative options as simply better or worse, and no one principle which, without further specification in other principles and norms, should guide deliberation and choice. Rather they claim to identify a number of basic human goods, none of which is simply a means to or simply a part of any other such basic good; they further identify also a number of principles to guide ('morally') the choices necessitated by (i) the variety of basic goods and reasons for action and (ii) the multiple ways of instantiating these goods and acting on these reasons for action by intelligent and creative choice (or indeed by misguided choices whose primary motivation is not reasons but emotion).

Fourthly, natural law theories typically differ from other ethical theories by offering to clarify not only the normative disciplines and bodies of discourse, but also the methods of the descriptive and explanatory social theories (political theory or political science, economics, legal theory...). How best can human societies and their formative concepts be understood, without illusions, but in a general way (as in a project such as Aristotle's *Politics* or Max Weber's *Wirtschaft und Gesellschaft*)? Could such projects

---

[7] Maritain, *Man and the State*, 91–4; *La loi naturelle ou loi non écrite*, 30.
[8] *Man and the State*, 91.   [9] *La loi naturelle*, 155–6.
[10] Grisez, 'The First Principle of Practical Reason' at 172, 196–7.

be 'value-free'? Or must even descriptive-explanatory theorists, in selecting their concepts, rely upon some definite conceptions of what is important in human existence? Must they not use such conceptions as criteria for selecting topics for study and concepts for describing those topics? Must they not also employ such criteria in judging some types and instantiations of human institutions or practices to be the 'central cases' of such institutions or practices, and also in judging some uses of terms such as 'law' or 'constitution' or 'authority' to be, for critical descriptive theory, the 'focal' uses and senses of those terms? And must not such conceptions and criteria of importance be the subject, not of selection by 'demonic' personal preference (Weber) or silent conformism to academic fashion or political *parti pris*, but rather of an open, public, critical justification? Natural law theories of the classical type, as Aristotle and Aquinas, claim to offer such a justification.[11]

IV. *LOI NATURELLE, DROIT NATUREL, DROITS NATURELS*

Reflection on natural law has in recent time been complicated by the claim of some authors (notably Michel Villey) that there is, in Aquinas and in truth, 'une opposition capitale entre *droit* et *loi*'. Though much insisted upon, it is not easy to understand the alleged 'opposition' or 'radical distinction'. Villey understood *droit* as, centrally, the 'that which is just', the ensemble of right relations between persons and 'things' (in a very broad sense of 'things' which includes freely chosen human actions, e.g. paying compensation); this understanding corresponds to Aquinas's primary definition of *ius* as *id quod iustum est* (that which is just). But Villey insisted that knowledge of this *droit*, even of *droit naturel* as distinct from *droit positif*, comes not from the specification of the higher principles of practical reason which Aquinas called (interchangeably!) *lex naturalis* and *ius naturale*, but from 'l'observation de la nature' (including, of course, 'la nature des hommes' and of 'les sociétés elles-mêmes, données présentes dans la nature'). He drew a sharp distinction between 'la morale individuelle', which he considered could properly be guided by the principles and precepts of natural law, and 'le droit' (juridique), which is guided by the aforesaid 'observation'.[12] No such epistemic distinction can be found in Aquinas, however. More important, the claim that juridical science, law-making, or legal interpretation can be grounded on *observation of facts* must be judged a flight from the rational requirement of pointing to reasons—which in the

---

[11] On this issue see *NLNR* 3–22.   [12] Villey, 'Abrégé du droit naturel classique'.

field of *praxis*, whether individual or social, must be reasons (principles and specifications of principles) that are normative (directive) because pointing to aspects of human fulfilment (individual and social).

There is, of course, a distinction to be made between *loi naturelle* and *droit naturel*, if the latter is understood (as it is sometimes, but not always, in Aquinas) as referring to the Roman law concept of *ius* as the ensemble of morally (or juridically) cognizable relations between say two persons and a subject-matter (e.g. some action of one of them). The distinction is simply that the *loi naturelle* is as such the set of reasons (principles) which justify the assertion of the *droit naturel* in question. The latter is the former in its application to a specified class of persons and subject-matter. There is distinction but no question of opposition, still less '*opposition capitale*'.

Villey and many others have also underlined the importance of the shift from the Roman law sense of *ius*, mentioned above, to the modern sense (perhaps beginning to emerge c. 1325 in Ockham's polemics against the Thomist Pope John XXII) of 'my right', '*droits naturels*', subjective right. But while it is clear that this shift is correlated with the emergence of contractualist and voluntarist conceptions of society, authority, law, and obligation, and with modern conceptions or attitudes which can be vaguely called 'individualist', it seems unlikely that the differing semantics and logic of *droit* and *droits* has any truly fundamental importance.† Villey was right to call attention to the danger that unilateral claims of right (that is, of rights) would mask sheer unconcern with the interests of others and with the 'whole' which is available for just distribution. But this danger must be confronted not by insisting on semantic distinctions superseded in living usage, but by identifying and insisting upon the rational principles which are available to guide both individual and social judgment and choice and to criticize the unfair (unilateral) demands of individuals or groups and the claims of right which neglect the comparable rights of others. The issue is one of adequately specifying rights, not of seeking to banish talk of them. It is a logical truth that one and the same moral or juridical relationship between, say, two persons and one subject-matter can be spoken of either as an ensemble (a single *ius*) or by articulating its content in terms of the respective benefits which the relationship involves for one or both of the parties to it, benefits which are articulated by statements about the 'subjective' right(s) involved in the relationship.

V. DERIVATION OF POSITIVE LAW

The history of moral and political philosophy, and of natural law theory, is much affected by certain *lacunae* in Aquinas's work. He was the thinker who most clearly articulated and developed the elements of practical philosophy in Aristotle (and thus, in a sense, in Plato), so as to represent them as propositions of or about natural law. Yet he failed to give a clear, full, careful, and consistent statement of the first principles of practical reason, and a satisfying set of illustrations of the way in which first practical principles (such as 'human life is a good to be advanced and respected'), or first moral principles (such as the Golden Rule) are given specificity in less fundamental principles and norms. This failure contributed significantly to the spread of voluntarist and fideistic currents which virtually overwhelmed the tradition of natural law theory, as a living school of thought. It later resulted in neo-Thomistic claims (e.g. those of Maritain and Villey noted above) which are scarcely defensible either as interpretations or as philosophical theses.

Aquinas was the first philosophical thinker to exploit the concept of 'positive law' which emerges in mid-twelfth century theological and juristic speculation. He gave an original and helpful sketch, scarcely surpassed even today, of the differing types of relationship between the high-level principles of natural law and (1) the more specified principles which can be attained by practical reasoning about the implications of those principles in recurrent types of human predicament and opportunity, and (2) norms, rules, precepts, and juridical institutions which cannot be said to be required as the conclusion of any course of practical reasoning, yet which are in some other way rationally connected to, or derived from, principles of the first two sorts, and which are authoritative for upright judges and good citizens if and when chosen and promulgated ('posited') by an appropriate authority. Laws, rights, and institutions derived in the second way are 'positive', yet have moral force in conscience similar to the moral force of the higher level principles of natural law, provided that their positing was by a person or body constitutionally authorized to make such decisions and they were made without serious disregard either for other relevant moral principles and rights or for the 'common' (as opposed to partisan) good of all the members of the community subject to their authority.

This second mode of derivation was called by Aquinas *determinatio*, which might be translated 'concretization'. It is best understood by a comparison such as he offered by way of explanation. From his commission ('build a maternity hospital for our town') an architect can deduce various specifications (the building must be more than one metre in height, and must include doors, means of warming the spaces in winter, etc.). But no amount of attention to the commission (the 'principle' of his work) and to the circumstances (including the 'nature of things') will yield a single, rationally required answer to the unavoidable questions. Should the doors be 2.1 or 2.2 metres high? Of this metal or that? Questions of the latter kind must be answered by decisions (*determinationes*) which are rationally under-determined, yet intelligibly related to (and in this weak sense 'derived from') the master principle (the commission taken with its more or less necessary implications).

In this account the sheer positivity of much of a country's legal system is fully acknowledged. But at the same time the moral significance of the law's directives and institutions is affirmed and explained. The affirmation is conditional. If the relationship of 'derivation', albeit non-deductive and 'free', is broken by *ultra vires* (lack of legal authority) or unjust discrimination or violation of inviolable rights, the positive's law's proper moral authority is eliminated. From the point of view of the conscientious judge, citizen, or indeed legislator, this lack of the proper ('normal') moral authority was marked by the sayings found in Plato, Cicero, Aquinas, and most of the philosophical, theological, and juridical tradition down to the nineteenth century: an unjust law, albeit valid by the legal system's own criteria of validity (and in this sense properly described as a law), is not really a law, or is not a law *simpliciter*, that is, sans phrase. It can have some collateral obligatoriness, in that it may be unfair to others to disobey it publicly (e.g. because doing so would encourage others to disobey other laws without good reason). This classical thesis, *lex iniusta non est lex* properly interpreted, is fully compatible with the jurist's or historian's wish to employ an amoral criterion of 'legal validity' or historical cognizability.

VI. INVIOLABLE HUMAN RIGHTS

The collapse of Christianity and other religious cultures, as the matrix for contemporary legal and political orders, has posed a challenge to those who wish to affirm that there is a natural law: to show that, even without the support of a religiously warranted ethic (revealed divine law) having an identical or overlapping content, there are philosophically sound reasons to affirm the truth of non-posited principles or norms which, although not claiming to be authoritative because posited, are sufficiently definite to exclude gross 'crimes against humanity' (Nuremberg, 1945; chattel slavery; abortions of convenience; non-voluntary euthanasia) and to underpin the main institutions of civilized societies (family, property, religious liberty, and so forth). In particular, the challenge is to show that aggregative conceptions of moral and political reasoning, such as classical or contemporary utilitarianism or consequentialism or 'economic analysis of law', are unsound.

Contemporary work in natural law theory therefore includes extensive attempts to criticize aggregative ethics, by showing that their conceptions of value overlook some or all of the basic human goods, and/or that their master principle of maximizing value overlooks the incommensurability not only of one basic human good relative to other such goods, but also of particular instantiations of even one and the same good in alternative options for morally significant choice. The supposition of those undertaking such a critique is that, if the critique is successful, the way will be open to identifying a richer set of moral principles guiding choice. A working postulate has been that any principle which has been the organizing or dominant principle of an entire philosophical ethic (e.g. Kantian universalizability, Epictetan detachment, the principle of commitment expounded by Royce and Marcel) has some place in a developed natural law theory.

But theoretical reflection has yielded a more systematic and unifying 'master principle of morality'. This principle is reached by way of the consideration that, so far as it is in one's power, one should allow nothing but the principles corresponding to the basic human goods to shape one's practical thinking. Aquinas's first principle, 'Good is to be done and pursued and evil avoided', taken as it stands, is not yet moral; it requires only that one not act pointlessly, that is, without reason; it requires only that one take at least one of the principles corresponding to a basic human good and follow through to the point at which one somehow instantiates that good through action. The first *moral* principle makes the stronger demand, not merely that one be reasonable enough to avoid pointlessness, but that one be entirely reasonable in one's practical thinking, choice, and action. It can be formulated: in voluntarily acting for human goods and avoiding what is opposed to them, one ought to choose and otherwise will those and only those possibilities whose willing is compatible with a will toward integral human fulfilment (i.e. the fulfilment of all human persons and communities).

Integral human fulfilment, so defined, is not a goal towards which actions could be organized as means. But it is not empty of critical force, in identifying choices motivated by emotion fettering and deflecting reason. Unfairness, being contrary to the Golden Rule (a principle superior in determinacy to Kant's substitute, universalizability), is one sort of willing that is incompatible with openness to integral human fulfilment. A choice to destroy some instantiation of a basic human good out of hatred is another. A choice precisely to destroy or damage some instantiation of a basic human good as a means to some other end is a third; the exclusion of such choosing is shown to be a demand of reason once the critique of aggregative theories has demonstrated the rational incommensurabilities overlooked by those who think that the goods promised by some envisaged end 'outweigh' the destruction or damage to human personal goods which is intended in a choice of this type.

This third moral principle corresponds not only to the traditional thought, 'the end does not justify these means', but also to the Kantian imperative, 'treat humanity always as an end and never as a means only'—though in recent natural law theory 'humanity' is understood without Kant's dualistic restriction of it to the rational faculties as such. It is a principle specified (made more specific) in the form of the traditional moral norms against murder and fraud. As such it is the backbone, so to speak, of traditional and modern legal systems. Articulated from the viewpoint of the beneficiaries of its moral protection, it is specified in those human rights which are not only inalienable but also, properly speaking, inviolable and absolute. It is the resultant of the classical principle that reason neither need nor should be the slave of the passions, together with (i) a precise understanding of free choice (enabling a firm and definite distinction between what is chosen and what is only accepted as a side effect), and (ii) an understanding, developed in dialectic with Enlightenment and post-Enlightenment aggregative ethics, of the incommensurabilities of the goods, persons, and probabilities at stake in alternative options for choice. In these and related ways, one can think that natural law theory of the classic type is capable of philosophically warranted development.

NOTE

† *Rights in the subjective sense*...(at 207). The 'shift' in vocabulary may well be of even less importance than this essay suggests: see *Aquinas* 133–8; 2002c; and essay IV.5 (2002a), sec. VIII, at 116; and 2002c.

14

LEGAL REASONING AS PRACTICAL REASON[*]

Moral reasoning, legal reasoning, and their interrelationships can scarcely be understood reflectively without attention to two different sources of ambiguity. The source is, in each case, well known: the distinction between reasons and feelings; and the distinction between doing (the shaping of one's own 'existence' by one's choices) and making (the exercise of technique by activity on some form of 'cultural' object or method). But the distinctions are commonly not well understood, and the traps they lay for the analysis of morality and adjudication are usually neglected.

I

We are animals, but intelligent. Our actions all have an emotional motivation, involve our feelings and imagination and other aspects of our bodiliness, and can all be observed (if only, in some cases, by introspection) as pieces of behaviour. But rationally motivated actions also have an intelligent motivation—seek to realize (protect, promote) an intelligible good.

So our purposes, the states of affairs we seek to bring about, typically have a double aspect: the goal which we imagine and which engages our feelings; and the intelligible benefit which appeals to our rationality by promising to instantiate, either immediately or instrumentally, some basic human good. While some of the purposes we employ intelligence to pursue *may* be motivated ultimately by nothing more than feeling, others are motivated ultimately by (an understanding of) a basic human good.

The idiom in which 'reason' refers to purposes—'the reason he did that', equivalent to 'his purpose in doing that'—fails to mark this distinction. But none of common speech's related terms—'purpose', 'goal', 'intention'—is free from the same ambiguity. So I stipulate that when I speak of 'reasons'

---

[*] 1992a. An earlier version is 1990c, on which see essay IV.17 at 357 n. 11.

in this essay, I refer (except when discussing technical reasons) to reason(s) as giving ground for intelligent action motivated ultimately by a basic human good (more precisely, by the intelligible benefit promised by the instantiation of a basic good).[1]

An account of basic reasons for action should not be rationalistic. Human flourishing is not to be portrayed in terms only of exercising capacities to reason. As animals, we are organic substances part of whose well-being is *bodily life*, maintained in health, vigour, and safety, and transmitted to new human beings. To regard human life as a basic reason for action is to understand it as a good in which indefinitely many beings can participate in indefinitely many ways, going far beyond any goal or purpose which anyone could envisage and pursue, but making sense of indefinitely many purposes, and giving rational support to indefinitely many goals.[2]

This sense of '(basic) reason for action' holds for all the other basic human goods: *knowledge* of reality (including aesthetic appreciation of it); *excellence in work and play* whereby one transforms natural realities to express meanings and serve purposes; *harmony between individuals and groups* of persons (peace, neighbourliness, and friendship); *harmony between one's feelings and one's judgements and choices* (inner peace); *harmony between one's choices and judgments and one's behaviour* (peace of conscience and authenticity in the sense of consistency between one's self and its expression); and *harmony between oneself and the wider reaches of reality* including the reality constituted by the world's dependence on *a more-than-human source of meaning and value.*

Such a statement of the basic human goods entails an account of human nature.[3] But it does not presuppose such an account. It is not an attempt to deduce reasons for action from some pre-existing theoretical conception of human nature. Such an attempt would vainly defy the logical truth (well respected by the ancients)[4] that 'ought' cannot be deduced from 'is'—a syllogism's conclusion cannot contain what is not in its premises. Rather, a full account of human nature can only be given by one who understands the human goods practically, that is, as reasons for choice and action, reasons which make full sense of supporting feelings and spontaneities.

---

[1] For my use here of 'purpose', 'goal', 'feeling', 'benefit', 'motivated', and 'basic human good', see 1987f at 99–110.

[2] See *NDMR* 277–8; *NLNR* 84–5, 100.

[3] See *FoE* 20–2; essay 9, at 146–7. [For a more adequate 'statement of the basic human goods', see essay 15 at 244 n. 25 below, or essay III.5 at 88 (1996a, sec. III).]

[4] So Aristotle's principal treatise on human nature is his *Ethics*, which is an attempt to identify the human good, and is, according to its author, from beginning to end an effort of practical, as opposed to theoretical, understanding (see e.g. *NE* I.1: 1094a26–b12 with Aquinas's commentary); *FoE* 24. Aristotle's *Ethics* is not derivative from some prior treatise on human nature, not even his *De Anima*.

An account of practical reasonableness can be called a theory of 'natural law' because practical reasoning's very first principles are those basic reasons which identify the basic human goods as ultimate reasons for choice and action—reasons for actions which will instantiate and express human nature precisely because participating in those goods, i.e. instantiating (actualizing, realizing) those ultimate aspects of human flourishing.[5]

II

To the extent that legal reasoning derives from and participates in practical reasonableness, a sound theory of legal reasoning must differ from some theories now current. At the heart of 'Critical Legal Studies', for example, is a denial that there are any objective human goods. Of the four reasons (all bad) which Roberto Unger offers for denying that there are objective human goods, the argument closest to his heart, I think, is that by affirming that there are such goods one

> denies any significance to choice other than the passive acceptance or rejection of independent truths... [and] disregards the significance of choice as an expression of personality.[6]

But, in reality, it is the diversity of *rationally* appealing human goods which makes free choice both possible and frequently necessary. Like every other term concerning human activity, 'choice' is afflicted, in common idiom, by ambiguities originating particularly[7] in the distinction between reason and feeling. In its strong, central sense, free choice is the adoption of one amongst two or more rationally appealing and incompatible, alternative options, such that nothing but the choosing itself settles which option is chosen and pursued.[8] Many aspects of individual and social life, and many individual and social obligations, are structured by choice between rationally appealing options whose rational appeal can be explained only in terms, ultimately, of basic human opportunities understood to be objectively good (though variously realizable). No sound sense can be made of 'objectivity' and 'truth', here or elsewhere, otherwise than in terms of rational judgment, open to all relevant questions.

---

[5] In Aristotle, 'natural' (as in 'natural right' or 'right by nature') also connotes objectivity or truth: see *FoE* 24.

[6] Unger, *Knowledge and Politics*, 77. On this, and the other arguments, see essay IV.13 (1985c), sec. VI.

[7] But not exclusively; ambiguities arise here also from various phenomenal and cultural sources; so movements can be said to be 'chosen' and 'free' just insofar as they are not subject to physical constraints, or external constraint, or social constraints; and so on.

[8] On free choice and its conditions, see e.g. *NDMR* 256–60; Boyle, Grisez, and Tollefsen, *Free Choice: A Self-Referential Argument*; Aquinas, *De Malo* q.6 a.un.

But if the basic human goods, for all their objectivity and truth, open up so much to free choice, what can be the basis for identifying choices which, though rational, ought to be rejected because unreasonable, wrong, immoral?

Moral thought is simply rational thought at full stretch, integrating emotions and feelings but *undeflected* by them. Practical rationality's fundamental principle is: take as a premise at least one of the basic reasons for action, and follow through to the point at which you somehow bring about the instantiation of that good in action. Do not act pointlessly. The fundamental principle of moral thought is simply the demand to be fully rational: insofar as it is in your power, allow nothing but the basic reasons for action to shape your practical thinking as you find, develop, and use your opportunities to pursue human flourishing through your chosen actions. Be entirely reasonable.[9] Aristotle's phrase *orthos logos*, and his later followers' *recta ratio*, right reason, should simply be understood as 'unfettered reason', reason undeflected by emotions and feelings. And so undeflected reason, and the morally good will, are guided by the first moral principle: that one ought to choose (and otherwise will) those and only those possibilities whose willing is compatible with a will towards the fulfilment of all human persons in all the basic goods, towards the ideal of integral human fulfilment.

Take a simple, paradigmatic form of immorality. Emotion may make one wish to destroy or damage the good of life in someone one hates, or the good of knowledge; so one kills or injures, or deceives, that person just out of feelings of aversion. It is immoral, because hereabouts there is a general, so to speak methodological, moral principle intermediate between the most basic principles of practical reason (the basic goods or reasons for action, and the first moral principle) and particular moral norms against killing or lying. This intermediate moral principle, which some call a mode of responsibility,[10] will exclude meeting injury with injury, or responding to one's own weakness or setbacks with self-destructiveness.

Perhaps more immediately relevant to political and legal theory is the intermediate moral principle requiring that one act fairly: that one not limit one's concern for basic human goods simply by one's feelings of self-preference or preference for those who are near and dear. Fairness (and its paradigmatic formulation in the Golden Rule) does not exclude treating different persons differently; it requires only that the differential treatment be justified either by inevitable limits on one's action or by intelligible

---

[9] See *NDMR* 119–25.
[10] Thus *NDMR* 284–7. In *NLNR* 100–13, I call them 'basic requirements of practical reasonableness', and in *FoE* 69–70, 74–6, I call them 'intermediate moral principles'.

requirements of the basic goods themselves. I shall say more (sec. VII below) about the legitimate role of feelings in making fair choices in which one prioritizes goods (or instantiations of basic goods) by one's feelings without prioritizing persons simply by feelings.

There are other intermediate moral principles. Very important to the structuring of legal thought is the principle which excludes acting against a basic reason by choosing to destroy or damage any basic good in any of its instantiations in any human person (sec. VI below). A basic human good always is a reason for action and always gives a reason *not* to choose to destroy, damage, or impede some instantiation of that good; but since the instantiations of human good at stake in any morally significant choice are not commensurable by *reason* prior to choice, there can never be a sufficient reason not to take that reason-not-to as decisive for choice. Only emotional factors such as desire or aversion could motivate a choice rejecting it.

Of course, the basic reasons for action, as the phrase suggests, present one with many reasons for choice and action, many reasons to...And since one is finite, one's choice of any purpose, however far reaching, will inevitably have as a side effect some negative impact on (minimally, the non-realization of) other possible instantiations of this and other basic goods. In that sense, every choice is 'against some basic reason'. But only as a side effect. In the choices which are excluded by the intermediate moral principle now in question, the damaging or destruction or impeding of an instantiation of a basic good—the harming of some basic aspect of someone's existence and well-being—is chosen, as a means, that is, *as part* of the description of the option adopted by choice. Whereas the first intermediate principle excludes making such damage or destruction one's end, the present principle excludes making it one's means. The concepts of (the) end and means (defining an option) come together in the conception so fundamental to our law: intention.[11]

III

Even so rapid a sketch begins to make clear that a theory of natural law, while primarily a theory of human goods as principles of practical reasoning, must accommodate within its account—as practical reasoning itself must take into account—certain features of our world.

Among these features are the reality of free choice, and the significance of choices as lasting in the character of the chooser beyond the time of the

---

[11] On intention, see essay II.10 (1991b); for the relation between the analysis of action here sketched and the mode of responsibility which excludes choosing to destroy, damage, or impede any instantiation of any basic human good, see *NDMR* 286–90.

behaviour which executes them; and the distinction between what is chosen as end or means (i.e. as intended) and what is foreseen and accepted as a side effect (i.e. an unintended effect). Again, there are such basic facts as that which Robert Nozick overlooked in declaring that (virtually) everything comes into the world already attached to someone having an entitlement over it—the reality being, on the contrary, that the natural resources from which everything made has been made pre-exist all entitlements and 'came into the world' attached to nobody in particular; the world's resources are fundamentally common and no theory of entitlements can rightly appropriate any resource to one person so absolutely as to negate that original communality of the world's stock.[12]

A further feature of the world to be accommodated by a sound natural law theory is the distinction between the orders of reality with which human reason is concerned. In attending to this set of distinctions, we shall be noticing the second of the two sources of ambiguity I mentioned at the outset.

Almost any interesting human state of affairs instantiates the four orders of reality with which human reason is concerned. Consider, for example, a lecture. (1) One hears the *sounds* produced by the speaker's vocal chords: there is an order of nature which we in no way establish by our understanding but which we can investigate by our understanding, as in the natural sciences or (as right now) in metaphysics. (2) One hears the speaker's *expositions, arguments, and explanations* and brings one's understanding into line with them (if only to the extent necessary to reject them as mistaken): there is an order which one can bring into one's own inquiries, understanding, and reasoning, the order studied by logic, methodology, and epistemology. (3) One hears *the lecturer,* who (like the audience) is freely engaging in an activity and thereby participating in a human relationship: there is an order—which one can bring into one's own dispositions, choices, and actions—one's *praxis*, one's doing, one's *Existenz*—the 'existential' order studied by some parts of psychology, by biography and the history of human affairs, and by moral and political philosophy. (4) One hears the *English language* and statements ordered by an expository or rhetorical technique, making and decoding the formalized symbols of a language and the less formalized

---

[12] Nozick, *Anarchy, State and Utopia*, 160; *NLNR* 187. Cf. the principle of eminent domain, or the way in which laws of insolvency, while quite reasonably varying from country to country, are all structured around some principle of equality amongst creditors or within ranks of creditors. But the most obvious implication is the principle that in conditions of great scarcity and deprivation, goods become once again common just to the extent necessary to allow those in danger to appropriate what they need to avert, e.g. starvation; this moral principle can qualify even the legal definition of theft, whether directly or via the concept of (dis)honesty: Smith, *Justification and Excuse in the Criminal Law*, 50–2.

but still conventional symbols and expressive routines of a cultural form and technique: the order one can intelligently bring into matter which is subject to our power, so as to make objects such as phonemes, words, poems, boats, software, ballistic missiles and their inbuilt trajectories—the order of *poiēsis*, of making, of culture—studied in the arts and technologies, and in linguistics and rhetoric.[13] (Corresponding to these four orders are four irreducibly distinct senses of 'hearing'.)

Almost every form of reductionist deformation in social (say, political) theory, and many destructive misunderstandings in almost every aspect of, say, legal theory, can be traced to oversight of the complexities and ambiguities created by the irreducible distinctions between these four orders—whose irreducibility to one another is disguised by the fact that each includes at least aspects of all the others.

The distinction particularly relevant to legal theory is that between the third (existential, moral) order and the fourth (cultural, technical) order. Few morally significant choices can be carried out without employing some culturally formed technique; and no technique can be put to human use without some morally significant choice. But every technique has an integral, fourth-order intelligibility which can be explicated without referring to the morally significant choices by which it might be put to use and the moral principles of practical reasonableness pertinent to such choices.

Amongst the ambiguities created by the distinctions between the third and fourth orders is the ambiguity of the term 'rational choice'. It has (at least) three important, distinct senses:

(1) choice which is fully reasonable, complies with all the requirements of practical reasonableness, and is thus morally upright;

(2) choice which is rationally motivated in the sense that its object has been shaped by practical intelligence and has rational appeal, even if it is in some respect(s) motivated ultimately by feeling rather than reason, feelings which have to some extent fettered and instrumentalized reason, and is therefore unreasonable and immoral, though rational;

(3) decision and action which is technically (technologically) right, that is, is identifiable according to some art or technique as the most effective for attaining the relevant technical objective—typically, the decision for which there is, within this technique (e.g. this game),

---

[13] For an elementary account (differently enumerated), see *NLNR* 136–8, 157; for profound exposition, explanation, and reflection concerning the four orders, see Grisez, *Beyond the New Theism*, 230–40; [and now essay II.2 (2005c), secs II and IX].

a dominant reason which can be commensurated with the reasons for alternative options and which includes all that these offer and some more.

Sense 3 is the only sense in which economists and exponents of 'game' or 'decision' theory commonly use the phrase 'rational choice'. I have used the terms 'rational' (and its cognates) and 'choice', in sec. II above, in sense 2 (or senses 1 and 2) but never in sense 3. Here is rich opportunity for misunderstanding.[14] In senses 1 and 2, what makes rational choice necessary is the incommensurability of the intelligible goods and bads involved in alternative options; if options were fully commensurable, alternatives could be identified as unqualifiedly superior and inferior, and the unqualifiedly inferior would lose its rational appeal, fall out of rational deliberation; rational choice would be unnecessary and, in a significant sense, impossible (sec. VI below). But in sense 3, rational choice is possible *only* when one option can be identified as unqualifiedly superior.

IV

Legal reasoning and rationality has, I suggest, its distinctiveness and its peculiar elusiveness because, in the service of a third-order, existential, moral, and chosen purpose—of living together in a just order of fair and right relationships—there has been and is being constructed a fourth-order object, 'the law' (as in 'the law of England'). This is a vastly complex cultural object, comprising a vocabulary with many artfully assigned meanings, rules identifying permitted and excluded arguments and decision, and correspondingly very many technical routines or processes (such as pleading, trial, conveyancing, etc.) constituted and regulated according to those formulae, their assigned meanings, and the rules of argument and decision.

This cultural object, constructed or (as we say) posited by creative human choices, is an instrument, a technique adopted for a moral purpose, and adopted because there is no other available way of agreeing over significant spans of time about precisely how to pursue the moral project well. Political authority in all its manifestations, including legal institutions, is a technique for doing without unanimity in making social choices—where unanimity would almost always be unattainable or temporary—in order to secure practical (near-)unanimity about how to coordinate the actions (including forbearances) of members of the society.[15]

---

[14] See essay IV.17 (1990d), sec. II, at 358.
[15] See further *NLNR* 231–7; essay IV.2 (1984b); essay IV.3 (1989b).

Legal reasoning, then, is (at least in large part) technical reasoning—not moral reasoning. Like all technical reasoning, it is concerned to achieve a particular purpose, a definite state of affairs attainable by efficient dispositions of means to end. The particular end here is the resolution of disputes (and other allegations of misconduct) by the provision of a directive sufficiently definite and specific to identify one party as right (in-the-right) and the other as wrong (not-in-the-right).

Hence the law's distinctive devices: defining terms, and specifying rules, with sufficient and necessarily artificial clarity and definiteness to establish the 'bright lines' which make so many real-life legal questions *easy questions*. Legal definitions and rules are to provide the citizen, the legal adviser, and the judge with an algorithm for deciding as many questions as possible—in principle every question—yes (or no), this course of action would (or would not) be lawful; this arrangement is valid; this contract is at an end; these losses are compensable in damages and those are not; and so forth. As far as it can, the law is to provide sources of reasoning—statutes and statute-based rules, common law rules, and customs—capable of ranking (commensurating) alternative dispute resolutions as right or wrong, and thus better and worse.

Lawyers' tools of trade—their ability to find and use the authoritative sources—are means in the service of a purpose sufficiently definite to constitute a technique, a mode of technical reasoning. The purpose, again, is the unequivocal resolution of every dispute (and other questions for just decision) which can be in some way foreseen and provided for. Still, this quest for certainty, for a complete set of uniquely correct answers, is itself in the service of a wider good which, like all basic human goods, is not reducible to a definite goal but is rather an open-ended good which persons and their communities can participate in without ever capturing or exhausting: the good of just harmony. This good is a moral good just insofar as it is itself promoted and respected as one aspect of the ideal of integral human fulfilment. As a moral good its implications are specified by all the moral principles which could bear upon it.

Thus there emerges the tension around which Ronald Dworkin's work on legal reasoning revolves.

V

Dworkin seeks to resolve the tension between law's and legal reasoning's character as a culturally specified technique of attaining predictable answers to problems of social coordination and its character as, in each of its decisive legislative, executive, and judicial moments, a moral act participating in justice (or injustice). His attempted resolution fails, I think, to grasp the real nature and implications of that tension.

In judicial reasoning as portrayed by Dworkin, two criteria of judgment are in use; as we shall see, there is between these two criteria a kind of incommensurability analogous to the incommensurability between the human goods involved in morally significant, rationally motivated choices. One of these criteria or dimensions belongs to what I have called the third (moral) order or rationality, and the other to the fourth (technical) order. The first dimension Dworkin calls 'fit': coherence with the existing legal 'materials' created by past political decisions, that is, by legislation and authoritative judicial decision (precedent). The second dimension he now calls 'justification'.[16] And he tries to show that a *uniquely* correct ('the right') answer is available in 'most' hard cases.

One can deny this last thesis without committing oneself to any scepticism about the objectivity of human good(s) or of correct judgments about right and wrong. Nor need one's denial be predicated on the popular argument which Dworkin is rightly concerned to scorn and demolish—the argument that disagreement is endemic and ineradicable. (For disagreement is a mere fact about people, and is logically irrelevant to the merits of any practical or other interpretative claim.) Nor need a denial of Dworkin's one-right-answer thesis rest on the fact that no one has the 'superhuman' powers of Dworkin's imaginary judge.

Even an ideal human judge, with superhuman powers, could not sensibly search for a uniquely correct answer to a hard case (as lawyers in sophisticated legal systems use the term 'hard case'). For in such a case, the search for the one right answer is practically incoherent and senseless, in much the same way as a search for the English novel which is 'most romantic and shortest' (or 'funniest and best', or 'most English and most profound').

Assuming with Dworkin that there are two 'dimensions' or criteria of judicial assessment, we can say that a case for judicial decision is hard (not merely novel) when not only is there more than one answer which is not in evident violation of an applicable rule, but also the answers which are in that sense available can be ranked in different orders along each

---

[16] See Dworkin, *Law's Empire*, 255. This term seems confusing, since both dimensions are, on his account, necessary to justify a judicial decision. His previous name for the second dimension, (inherent, substantive, moral) 'soundness', was better: see *TRS* 340–1. Still, the labels adopted by Dworkin have the merit of making it clear that fit, although relevant precisely because a necessary condition for securing certain moral and political goods and requirements such as community and integrity, is itself a matter of historical fact, namely, the facts about what judgments and decisions have been made by the relevant institutions in a given society over a given span of time, and the extent to which some actual or hypothetical judgment or decision corresponds in content to earlier judgments and decisions.

of the relevant criteria of evaluation: for novels, their brevity and their Englishness (or humour, or profundity, or...); for judicial judgments their fit with previous legislation and precedent, and—let us grant (not concede) to Dworkin—their *inherent* moral soundness.[17] In such a case there is found what theorists of 'rational choice' (in sense 3) call 'intransitivity', a phenomenon which such theories confessedly cannot really handle:[18] solution A is better than solution B on the scale of legal fit, and B than C, but C is better than A on the scale of 'moral soundness'; so there is no sufficient reason to declare A, or B, or C the overall 'best judicial decision'. If the rank order was the same on both dimensions, of course, the case was not a hard one at all, and the legal system already had what one always desires of it: a uniquely correct answer.

In his works before *Law's Empire*, Dworkin tried to overcome this incommensurability of the dimensions or criteria of assessment by proposing a kind of lexicographical (in Rawls's terminology 'lexical') ordering. Candidates for the 'best account' of the law of England in 1980 must fit the then existing English legal materials adequately, and of those which satisfy this threshold criterion, that which ranks highest on the other criterion (moral soundness) is overall, absolutely, 'the best', even though it fits less well than (an)other(s).[19] But this solution was empty, since he identified no criteria, however sketchy or 'in principle', for specifying when fit is 'adequate', that is, for locating the threshold (of fit) beyond which the criterion of soundness would prevail. (It was like being told to search

---

[17] Throughout this discussion of Dworkin's dimensions of assessment, I shall take for granted his assumption that 'morality' and 'moral soundness' refer to a 'dimension of assessment' which can sometimes be rightly (in some sense of 'right' relevant to judicial duty) subordinated to some other criterion or criteria (such as 'fit'). But the truth here is different, though not simple: morality always trumps every other criterion of choice, though not in such a way as to make immoral choice irrational; but the truth conditions of any moral truth(s) relevant to a judge include facts about fit; if the facts about fit cannot (on moral standards of judgment) be reconciled with morality, one is in a *lex injusta* situation, as to which see *NLNR* ch. 12. [See also essay 15 at 251–3 below.]

[18] In 'game theory'—a vast and sophisticated body of reasoning about situations of ordinary life (e.g. 'bargaining') conceived *as if* they had the simple, unitary-goal, self-interested structure of a competitive game—the first axiom is that of transitivity: if *a* is better than *b* and *b* is better than *c*, then *a* must be better than *c*; if *x* is worse than *y* and *y* than *z*, then *x* is worse than *z*; etc., and similarly for comparative predicates other than 'is better than' or 'is worse than', e.g. 'is preferable to'. See Luce and Raiffa, *Games and Decisions*, ch. 1. Clear-headed masters of game theory acknowledge that in real life intransitivities abound: *a* is better than *b* in one respect (e.g. proximity to school), and *b* is better than *c* in another respect (e.g. physical amenities), but since the two bases of comparison (proximity and amenities) are not commensurable with each other, it does not follow that *a* is better than *c* in any respect, let alone unqualifiedly better. So Luce and Raiffa are reduced to saying: 'We may say that we are only concerned with behavior which is transitive, adding hopefully that we believe this need not always be a vacuous study' (*ibid.*, 25). On the same page they acknowledge the typical cause and effect of intransitivities: a topic or situation forces 'choices between inherently incomparable alternatives. The idea is that each alternative invokes "responses" on several different "attribute" scales and that, although each scale may itself be transitive, their amalgamation need not be.'

[19] See e.g. *TRS* 340–2.

for the funniest novel among those that are 'short enough'.) Presumably, candidates for the one right answer to the question 'When is fit adequate?' would themselves be ranked in terms both of fit and of soundness. An infinite regress, of the vicious sort which nullifies purported rational explanations, was well under way.

In *Law's Empire*, Dworkin abandons the simple picture of a lexical ordering between these two criteria. We are left with little more than a metaphor: 'balance'—as in 'the general balance of political virtues' embodied in competing interpretations or accounts of the law (of England (in 1990)). But in the absence of any metric which could commensurate the different criteria, the instruction to balance (or, earlier, to weigh) can legitimately mean no more than 'Bear in mind, conscientiously, all the relevant factors, and *choose*'. Or, in the legal sphere, 'Hear the arguments, sitting in the highest court, and then *vote*'.

In understanding practical rationality in all its forms, one should notice a feature of the experience of choice. *After* one has chosen, the factors favouring the chosen option will usually seem to outweigh, overbalance, those favouring the rejected alternative options. The option chosen—to do x, to adopt rule or interpretation y—will commonly seem (to the person who chose, if not to onlookers) to have a supremacy, a unique rightness. But this sense of the supremacy, the rightness of one (the chosen) option will not alter the truth that the choice was not rationally determined, that is, was not guided by an identification of one option or answer as 'the right one'. (And this does not mean that it was irrational; it was between rationally appealing options.) Rather, the choice established the 'right' answer—that is, established it in, and by reference ultimately to, the dispositions and sentiments of the chooser.[20] When the choice in a hard case is made by (the majority in the) highest appeal court (a mere brute fact), the unique rightness of the answer is established not only by and for the attitude of those who have chosen it, but also for the legal system or community for which it has thus been authoritatively decided upon, and laid down as or in a *rule*.

VI

The incommensurability of Dworkin's two dimensions or criteria for judicial judgment has significant similarities to the incommensurability of the goods (and reasons) at stake in alternative options available for morally significant choice in any context. The moral and political rationality which

---

[20] See Grisez, 'Against Consequentialism' at 46–7.

underpins (though does not exhaust) legal rationality cannot be understood without an understanding of incommensurability.

Incommensurability, the absence of any *rationally* identified metric for measuring, or scale for 'weighing', the goods and bads in issue, is much more pervasive and intense than one would imagine from the simple Dworkinian picture of legal reasoning along the two dimensions of legal fit and moral soundness. One meets incommensurability in humble contexts, such as having to choose between going to a lecture, reading a good book, going to the cinema, and talking to friends. One meets it in relation to grand social choices, such as whether to reject or renounce a nuclear deterrent:[21] exploring such a choice will amply illustrate the impotence of all forms of aggregative reasoning towards morally significant choice—choice outside the purely technical or technological task of identifying the most cost-efficient means to a single limited goal.

The reasoning most characteristic of technical rationality is 'cost-benefit analysis', comparing the costs of alternative options with the probable benefits.[22] This can be carried through with full rationality only when (a) goals are well defined, (b) costs can be compared with some definite unit (e.g. money), (c) benefits can also be quantified in a way that renders them commensurable with one another, and (d) differences among means, other than their efficiency, measurable costs, and measurable benefits, are not counted as significant. None of these conditions is fulfilled in moral reasoning.

Indeed, morally significant choice would be unnecessary and, with one qualification,[23] impossible if one option could be shown to be *the best*

---

[21] See *NDMR* 207–72. Raz, *The Morality of Freedom*, 321–66, explores incommensurability with some similar conclusions.

[22] There are other forms of reasoning in the fourth, cultural order, e.g. aesthetic. Here, makers are not guided by any goal adequately identifiable independently of the efficacious means which they might calculate and adopt for achieving it; artistic creation thus outruns technique. Instead, such makers, responding to the sensible particularity of the matter on or with which they work, are each guided by a 'sense' of the object, a sense which cannot be articulated otherwise than by producing the object, yet which somehow serves to measure the adequacy of any particular attempt. There is interaction between the process of creation and this imaginative 'conception' or 'intuition' or 'anticipation' of the object; the anticipation may be refined and altered, even radically, without however disappearing, during the process. To assess the artistic, aesthetic worth (goodness or badness) of the final product involves an aesthetic appreciation of the unity between 'what the work is trying to say' and 'how the work is saying it'; the aesthetic understanding does not come to rest at either pole; nor does it use criteria wholly prior and external to the composition itself. Provided that a composition has a kind of inner unity, clarity, integrity, it can have an aesthetic worth which can govern and reshape, rather than be governed by, pre-existing standards generalizing the features of previous aesthetic objects which by their own inner unity, clarity, integrity established *for themselves* their artistic worth.

[23] The qualification: there may be choice between, say, two options, one of which is rationally motivated, but the other of which, though shaped in its structure of means by intelligence, is ultimately motivated *only* by feeling. But this is not the sort of choice with which moral reasoning is concerned, although the struggle against temptations arising from emotional motivations is undeniably of moral significance.

on a single scale which, as all aggregative reasoning does, ranks options in a single, transitive order. If there were a reason (for doing x) which some rational method of comparison (e.g. aggregation of goods and bads in a complete cost-benefit analysis) identified as rationally preferable, the alternative reason (against doing x), being thus identified as rationally inferior, would cease to be rationally appealing in that situation of choice. The reason thus identified as dominant, as unqualifiedly preferable, and the option favoured by that reason, would be rationally unopposed. There would remain *no choice* of the sort that moral theories seek to guide. For, the morally significant choices which moral theories seek to guide are between alternative options which have rational appeal.

To identify options as morally wrong does not entail identifying one option as (morally) uniquely right. Indeed, even when one option can be judged the only (morally) right option for a given person (a moral judgment which only that person's prior commitments and dispositions will make possible), this entails only that the alternative, immoral options are not fully reasonable. It in no way entails that these alternative options are irrational, that is, lack rational appeal in terms of genuine, intelligible human goods which would be secured by the immoral options and sacrificed by the morally upright option. Thus rationally motivated, morally significant choice remains possible—indeed characteristic of the human situation—even in the perhaps relatively uncommon case of the moral 'one right answer (option)'.

But when technical reasonings identify one option as uniquely correct, that is, as dominant, they do so by demonstrating that it offers *all that the other options offer and some more*; it is unqualifiedly better. The other options then lack *rational* appeal. Such deliberation ends not in choice—in the rich, central sense of that ambiguous term—but rather in insight, 'decision' (not choice, but rationally compelled judgment), and action.

One of morality's principles, I have said (sec. II above), excludes acting against a basic reason by choosing to destroy or damage any basic human good in any of its instantiations in any human person. For these instantiations are nothing other than aspects of human persons, present and future, and human persons cannot rationally be reduced to the commensurable factors captured by technical reasoning. These instantiations of human good constitute *reasons against* any option which involves choosing (intending) to destroy or damage any of them. The significance of the incommensurability of goods involved in such morally significant options is this: no reason *for* such an option can be rationally preferable to such a reason against. And the same is true of the *reason against* an option which is constituted by that option's unfairness.

What, it may be asked, are the grounds for regulating one's choice according to the reason-*against* rather than by any reason-*for*? Once again, they cannot be stated without reference to some features for our world, the fundamental context of all human choosing. Options which there are reasons *for* my choosing are infinite in number. Being finite, I simply cannot do everything, cannot choose every option for which there are reasons. But I can refrain from doing anything; I can respect every serious reason-against. So, an unconditional or absolute affirmative duty (duty *to*...) would impose an impossible burden and be irrational; but negative moral absolutes (duties *not* to...), if correctly stated with attention to the distinction between intention and side effect, can all be adhered to in any and every circumstance.

Moreover, many human goods (e.g. the lives of others) are gifts, givens, which we can destroy or damage, but cannot create. Here, too, is a ground of the intelligible asymmetry between reasons-for and reasons-against. Nor does the priority, within their ambit, of reasons-against give morality as a whole a negative cast, or elevate 'moral purity' to the rank of a supreme goal. The first limb of practical reason's first principle remains that human good is to be done and pursued. Its second limb is that evil is to be avoided. But a full respect for and adherence to the absolute duties to forbear from evil leaves open a wide field of (more numerous) individual and social positive responsibilities.

VII

The moral absolutes give legal reasoning its backbone: the exclusion of intentional killing, of intentional injury to the person and even the economic interests of the person,[24] of deliberate deception for the sake of securing

---

[24] English law claims not to recognize the principle that an intent to injure is sufficient to make unlawful an otherwise lawful action: *Bradford Corporation v Pickles* [1895] AC 587; *Allen v Flood* [1898] AC 1. But the significance of this claim is greatly reduced by (i) the doctrine, established in *Quinn v Leathem* [1901] AC 495 and *Crofter Hand Woven Harris Tweed v Veitch* [1942] AC 435, that an agreement to do acts which harm the plaintiff with the predominant intention of harming him is a tort even if the acts themselves are otherwise lawful, and by (ii) the further doctrines which give actions in tort to those who are harmed by a wrongful act, e.g. of fraud, inducing or threatening breach of contract or interference with contract, etc., when that act is intended to harm them, even when they would otherwise have no action in respect of the fraud, intimidation, or breach of or interference with contract; see e.g. *Lonrho plc v Fayed* [1992] 1 AC 448 (HL). Moreover, the foundational character of the doctrine in *Bradford Corporation v Pickles* and *Allen v Flood* is put in question by the fact that in American common law it has been rejected: see Ames, 'How Far an Act May Be a Tort Because of the Wrongful Motive of the Actor'; and *Prosser on Torts*, sec. 130. Moreover, the House of Lords' adoption, in the 1890s, of the principle that motive alone cannot make an individual's act unlawful was deeply confused by a flawed analysis of action and intention. (1) There was a fundamental failure to distinguish feelings from reasons for acting; e.g. Lord Watson expressed the principle as: 'when the act done is, apart from the feelings which prompted it, legal, the civil law ought to take no cognizance of its motive' ([1898] AC at 94). (2) Correspondingly there was a failure to see that acts

desired results, of enslavement which treats a human person as an object of a lower rank of being than the autonomous human subject. These moral absolutes, which *are* rationally determined and essentially determinate, constitute the most basic human rights, and the foundations of the criminal law and the law of intentional torts or delicts, not to mention all the rules, principles, and doctrines which penalize intentional deception, withdraw from it all direct legal support, and exclude it from the legal process.

The rationality of all these moral and legal norms depends upon the incommensurability of the human goods and bads at stake in morally significant options for choice. This incommensurability has further implications of importance to legal reasoning.

The core of the moral norm of fairness is the Golden Rule: 'Do to others as you would have them do to you; do not impose on others what you would not want to be obliged by them to accept.' This has two aspects. First: practical rationality, outside the limited technical context of competitive games, includes a rational norm of impartiality. This norm excludes not all forms and corresponding feelings of preference for oneself and those who are near and dear, but rather all those forms of preference which are motivated only by desires, aversions, or hostilities which do not correspond to intelligible aspects of the real *reasons* for action, the basic human goods realizable in the lives of other human beings as in the lives of oneself or those close to one's heart.

The Golden Rule's second aspect is this. Although fairness is thus a rational norm requiring one to transcend all rationally unintegrated feelings, its concrete application in personal life presupposes a ranking of benefits and burdens which reason is impotent to commensurate. To apply the Golden Rule, one must know what burdens one considers too great to accept. And this knowledge, constituting a pre-moral commensuration, cannot be by rational commensuration. Therefore, it can only be one's intuitive awareness, one's discernment, of one's own differentiated *feelings* towards various goods and bads as concretely remembered, experienced, or imagined. This, I repeat, is not a rational and objective commensuration of goods and bads; but once established in one's feelings and identified in one's self-awareness, this commensuration by feelings enables one to

---

should be described, identified, in terms of the ends and means identified in the deliberations which shaped the options amongst which the actor chose, and so must distinguish clearly between ends or means and side effects; the argument which the Lords rejected in 1898 included within 'malice' a purpose to 'benefit oneself at the expense of one's neighbour'—which confuses the case where loss to the neighbour is the object (and financial benefit to self no more than a welcome side effect) with the case where financial benefit to self is the object (and loss to the neighbour no more than a foreseen, perhaps even a welcome side effect); the Lords rejected the argument without identifying the radical ambiguity. [See essay II.11 (1995a) esp. endnote at 215–17.]

rank one's options by a rational and objective standard of interpersonal impartiality.

Analogously, in the life of a community, the preliminary commensuration of rationally incommensurable factors is accomplished not by rationally determined judgments, but by *decisions* (choices). Is it fair to impose on others the risks inherent in driving at more than 10 mph? Yes, in our community, since our community has by custom and law *decided to* treat those risks and harms as *not too great*. Have we a rational critique of a community which decided to limit road traffic to 10 mph and to accept all the economic and other costs of that decision? Or not to have the institution of trusts, or constructive trusts? No, we have no rational critique of such a community. But we do have a rational critique of someone who drives at 60 mph but who, when struck by another, complains and alleges that the mere fact that the other's speed exceeded 10 mph established that other's negligence. Or of someone willing to receive the benefits (e.g. the tax benefits) of trusts but not willing to accept the law's distinction between trust and contract in his bankruptcy.

And, in general, we have a rational critique of one who accepts the benefits of this and other communal decisions but rejects the burdens as they bear on him and those in whom he feels interested. In short, the decision to permit road traffic to proceed faster than 10 mph, or to define trusts just as English law does, was rationally underdetermined.[25] (That is not to say that it was or is wholly unguided by reason; the good of human bodily life and integrity is a genuine reason always practically relevant, and the rational demand for consistency with our individual and communal tolerance or intolerance of other—non-traffic—threats to that good provides some rational criteria for decision. And similarly with the trust, whose rationality defied many legislative attempts, for centuries, to suppress this peculiar double ownership.) Still, though rationally underdetermined, the decision to permit fast-moving traffic, once made, provides an often fully determinate rational standard for treating those accused of wrongful conduct or wrongfully inflicting injury. Likewise with trusts, in bankruptcy.

In the working of the legal process, much turns on the principle—a principle of fairness—that litigants (and others involved in the process)

---

[25] Of course, this does not mean that it was 'indeterminate' in the strong sense of the word which the Critical Legal Studies Movement uses so vaguely and uncritically, i.e. indeterminate in the sense of being wholly unguided by reason. (See essay IV.13 (1985c), sec. II.) For the good of bodily life and integrity is a genuine reason always practically relevant; and some further rational criteria for decision are provided by facts about human reaction times and susceptibility to impact, and by the rational demand for consistency with our individual and communal tolerance or intolerance of other—non-traffic—threats to that good.

should be treated by judges (and others with power to decide) *impartially*, in the sense that they are as nearly as possible to be treated by each judge as they would be treated by every other judge. It is this above all, I believe, that drives the law towards the artificial, the *technē* rationality of laying down and following a set of positive norms identifiable as far as possible simply by their 'sources' (i.e by the fact of their enactment or other constitutive event) and applied so far as possible according to their publicly stipulated meaning, itself elucidated with as little as possible appeal to considerations which, because not controlled by facts about sources (constitutive events), are inherently likely to be appealed to differently by different judges. This drive to insulate legal from moral reasoning can never, however, be complete.

Incommensurability has further, related implications for legal reasoning. It rules out the proposed technique of legal reasoning known as Economic Analysis of Law. For it is central to that technique that every serious question of social order can be resolved by aggregating the overall net good promised by alternative options, in terms of a simple commensurating factor (or maximand), namely wealth measured in terms of the money which relevant social actors would be willing and able to pay to secure their preferred option. Equally central to Economic Analysis is the assumption, or thesis, that there is no difference of principle between buying the right to inflict injury intentionally and buying the right not to take precautions which would eliminate an equivalent number of injuries caused accidentally.[26] A root-and-branch critique of Economic Analysis of Law will focus on these two features of it.

Less fundamental critiques, such as Dworkin's (helpful and worthwhile though it is),[27] leave those features untouched. Indeed, Dworkin's own distinction between rights and collective goals (the latter being proposed by Dworkin as the legitimate province of legislatures) is a distinction which uncritically assumes that collective goals can rationally be identified and preferred to alternatives by aggregation of value, without regard to principles of distributive fairness and other aspects of justice—principles which themselves constitute rights, and which cannot be traded off, according to some rational methodology, against measurable quantities of value.[28]

VIII

In sum: much academic theory about legal reasoning greatly exaggerates the extent to which reason can settle what is greater good and lesser

---

[26] See essay IV.16 (1990b), sec. IV.   [27] Dworkin, *A Matter of Principle*, Pt. IV.
[28] See essay III.1 (1985a), secs IV and V.

evil. At the same time, such theory minimizes the need for authoritative sources. Such sources, so far as they are clear, and respect the few absolute moral rights and duties, are to be respected as the only reasonable basis for judicial reasoning and decision, in relation to those countless issues which do not directly involve those absolute rights and duties. A natural law theory in the classical tradition makes no pretence that natural reason can identify the one right answer to those countless questions which arise for the judge who finds the sources unclear.

In the classical view, expressed by Aquinas with a clear debt to Aristotle,[29] there are many ways of going wrong and doing wrong; but in very many, perhaps most situations of personal and social life there are a number of incompatible *right* (that is, not-wrong) options. Prior personal choice(s) or authoritative social decision-making can greatly reduce this variety of options for the person who has made that commitment or the community which accepts that authority. Still, those choices and decisions, while rational and reasonable, were in most cases not required by reason. They were not preceded by any rational judgment that *this* option is *the* right answer, or the best solution.

---

[29] See *ST* I–II q.95 a.2; *NE* V.10: 1134b19–1135a6; *NLNR* 281–90, 294–5.

Part Three
Public Reason and Unreason

15

COMMENSURATION AND PUBLIC REASON*

A classic explanation of law calls it a measure: *quaedam regula et mensura actuum*, a kind of rule and measure of actions.[1] The law's own terms, like its makers and officers, hold out its principles and rules as a (non-optional) standard for comparing options and ranking them as obligatory, permissible, or impermissible, or as legally valid and enforceable or unenforceable, voidable or void, and so forth. The law is indeed a set of publicly adopted reasons for adopting or rejecting proposals for action, public or private. In this essay I consider law as a paradigm of public reason and choice, and use this paradigm to illustrate the bearing of (in)commensurability on decision-making in the public sphere.

Obviously, law does not deserve the place it claims in our deliberations unless it, too, meets some standards. Though we need law, and though anarchy as a form of life has little intelligible appeal, the Hobbesian redefinition of 'justice' as conformity to the law strikes everyone as impoverishing our lexicon profitlessly. For what are requirements of justice if not the standards of reasonableness in dealing with others? And must not law measure up as reasonable, if it is to earn the respect of its subjects as providing standards for action which are rightly directive in their deliberations?

Before a law is taken up in its subjects' deliberations, it has itself been deliberated on by those who made it. (Among *law-makers* are also those who can and do decide, with some authority, that the legal materials relevant to some issue shall be taken to mean this rather than that.) The law-maker's

---

* 1997b.
[1] *ST* I–II q.90 a.1c (the account concludes, in a.4c, in the definition: 'a kind of ordination of reason, directed to the common good, promulgated by the person or body that has responsibility for the community'). The phrase *regula et mensura* translates the phrase *kanōn kai metron* used by Aristotle in *NE* III.4: 1114a33, where, however, Aristotle is giving expression to his pervasive thesis that the standard and measure of what is truly noble and pleasant is not so much a proposition (rule) or set of propositions as a person, the good person (the *spoudaios*, the man of maturity and substance), as distinct from the mass of humankind. And see text at n. 32 below.

deliberations ended in choice; alternative practical possibilities—including, perhaps, just leaving things be—will have had some attraction, been options. Those deliberations will have sought, at least purportedly, to *compare* and *rank* the options as better and worse, as involving respectively greater and lesser good (or perhaps lesser or greater evil). In turn, the law-maker's assessments, comparisons, and rankings, whether adequate or not, can and will be tracked and reassessed by critics, reformers, supporters, and everyone wondering whether the law is justified and, more radically, whether it is reasonable to take the law, and/or this particular rule of law, as the normal measure, the standard for evaluating in conscience one's own day-to-day options.

I

It was law reformers—notably, Beccaria and Bentham—who proposed that the legislator's assessing of options as better and worse can and should be by commensuration in a stricter sense. As one might put the principle they offered: aggregate the pluses, subtract the minuses, and pursue the option with the highest balance. For the founders of the aggregative tradition in individual and political ethics, the unit was pleasures (pains being presumed, too casually, to be a negative quantity on the single scale supposed to run from exquisite pleasures down to atrocious pains).[2] And desire for pleasure, as Bentham learned from Hume, is not a *reason*. Still, the principle that good (pleasure) is to be maximized and bad (pains) minimized was conceived and offered as a principle of reason.

Utilitarianism was addressed not to those whose only concern is to get what they happen to want, here and now or in any other horizon they fancy, but to those interested in being guided by reason, that is, by reasons.[3] So too is utilitarianism's self-appointed successor in legal theory, the normative Economic Analysis of Law. In its uncompromised forms,[4] this takes as the supreme, and indeed exclusive, measure of law's rationality the goal of 'efficiency', that is, of efficiency in maximizing social wealth or

---

[2] Bentham did envisage that the unit for utilitarian commensurating might have to be money. See the quotations and citations (and helpful discussion of commensuration and incommensurability in general) in Grisez, 'Against Consequentialism' at 35–6; see also *ibid.* at 30 for Bentham's confession that 'the addibility of happiness of different subjects' is a fiction.

[3] See 1990f. In their surrejoinder, Simpson and McKim, 'On the Alleged Incoherence of Consequentialism' continue to beg the question by assuming that someone following a merely emotional motive such as selfishness acts for a 'rational motive' even though not acting for a good such as might be included in the 'calculation of the goods offered by the several alternatives'.

[4] Posner, *The Problems of Jurisprudence*, 373, 377, finally compromises by arbitrary deference to moral standards that 'we', on unexplained grounds, happen to hold.

value, as measured by what those concerned would be willing and able to pay for in money.

Like other theories of justice, all such notions of guiding social choice by measuring and comparing the expected net value of alternative foreseeable outcomes are the target of a popular objection. Options (and their outcomes), it is said, are incommensurable because evaluative perspectives are irreducibly plural. The ideals, ideologies, and interpretations and forms of life to be found in a modern society are radically and insurmountably diverse. The 'interpretive incommensurability of values',[5] in excluding any significant collective ranking of options, precludes also the utilitarian or economistic proposals for ranking.

But this denial of commensurability fails. It fallaciously deduces a conclusion about what are or are not good reasons for action from premises which refer only to facts—facts about public opinion, the sheer plurality of views, and the like. Or else it simply misses the question of good reasons for action, as that question is raised in or with a view to deliberation and choice, and instead discourses about another matter (the existing and foreseeable diversity of opinion about them). Or, if it does attend to reasons for action 'from the internal point of view' (practically) and commends a political option (say, neutrality among the 'incommensurable' conceptions of the good life), it fails to show that, say, utilitarianism errs in envisaging a social conversion, critical education, and reform by which the truth about individual and social good could overcome the supposedly 'ineradicable' pluralism of uncritically accepted worldviews.

The assertion that worldviews are incommensurably plural because opinions seem ineradicably diverse overlooks the commensurability of truth with untruth, of attention to evidence with inattention, of insight with stupidity and oversight, of sound with unsound reasoning—in short, the commensurability of reasonable with more or less unreasonable grounds for making the judgments involved in a worldview or a conception of human goods and human fulfilment. And the implications of asserting this sort of incommensurability of opinions are typically glossed over. Where there are no reasonable grounds for disagreeing, agreeing, and resolving disagreement, the only bases for social cooperation are sub-rational motivations such as lust or terror, self-preference or inertia. If worldviews are incommensurable, we have no *reason* to accept a scheme of social decision-making, a constitution, a Rule of Law. For each person, then, the challenge is simply to become and remain one of those who are

---

[5] Pildes, 'Conceptions of Value in Legal Thought' at 1529; see also Pildes and Anderson, 'Slinging Arrows at Democracy' at 2162–5.

in charge. Domination will be bereft of justification, for no combination of wants and preferences, even when considered from the internal point of view ('I want...', 'I prefer...'), can constitute or entail an *ought*, a *reason* justifying or *demanding* a course of conduct.

In a Kantian critique, on the other hand, the utilitarian aspiration to guide individual and social choices by commensurating the goods and bads in alternative options is censured precisely for conceding too much to the non-cognitivists and relativists. Morality and right are matters of practical reason. But what the utilitarian proposes to maximize is not any sort of reason, but rather something sub-rational—desire, sensible impulse, 'sensuous motives',[6] 'happiness',[7] in short merely 'empirical grounds' from which one can derive no 'ought'.[8] So utilitarian conclusions offer deliberating subjects no rational norms by which to measure as right or wrong their acts of free choice (the supreme concept of the metaphysics of morals),[9] or by which their wills could be given any sort of direction capable of being called 'categorical', that is, unconditional, 'binding', or 'obligatory'.[10]

So far, so good. But the criteria proposed by Kant to replace utilitarian maximization of satisfaction fail to supply the rational measure of right and wrong in choosing. Most well known is the criterion of universalizability of the maxim of one's chosen action (i.e. the universalizability of the intelligible content of the proposal which one adopts by choice). But what does it mean to say that a maxim *cannot* be universalized? What sort of modal is this? Kant's way of dealing with ethical issues makes it clear that the (im)possibility he has in mind is essentially logical: a choice is wrong if its universalized maxim contains a *contradiction*. This attempt to explain immorality as a form of illogicality yields no fruit. Whether in the *Grundlegung*'s well-known examples (suicide, borrowing on false promises, neglect of talents, and indifference to others' interests)[11] or in the *Rechtslehre*'s (courts of equity, the deduction of rightful possession, swearing to beliefs, coercion of rulers, punitive war, and prescriptive acquisition on the basis of abandonment or long use),[12] no contradiction is found without premising principles of the very kind the arguments were meant to validate.

Its official master principles being empty of rational guidance, Kantian ethics (and his theory of justice) measures deliberation only with makeshift

---

[6] See Kant, *Grundlegung zur Metaphysik der Sitten*, 442.
[7] See Kant, *Die Metaphysik der Sitten: Tugendlehre*, 377, 382.   [8] *Ibid.*, 377.
[9] See the footnote to the title of sec. III of the general introduction to the metaphysics of morals in *Die Metaphysik der Sitten: Rechtslehre*, 218 n.   [10] *Ibid.*, 215–16; *Grundlegung*, 441–4.
[11] *Grundlegung*, 421–3.   [12] *Rechtslehre*, 234–5, 245–6, 250, 317, 348, 365.

'principles' such as that 'nature's end' should be respected.[13] (Here Kant, foiled in his attempt to find principles for the moral order in the logical order, illogically uses as premise for a moral conclusion a proposition pertaining to another non-moral order, the natural in the sense of 'natural' that we use in speaking of the natural sciences.) Moreover, in the 'casuistical questions' which he quietly puts to himself at the end of his famously rigorous reaffirmations of the western moral tradition on killing the innocent, sex, lying, intoxication, and so forth, Kant employs a mix of intuitionistic and consequentialist considerations[14] like nothing so much as late twentieth-century academic ethics.

For intuitionism, though officially dead and buried with Prichard, Ross, and their generation of philosophers, is in fact very much alive. The ethical ('metaethical') scepticism of the 1950s having officially perished (in the Vietnam War?), the staple of academic discussion of individual and political morality is now the appeal to 'my' or 'our' *intuitions* about specific types of conduct. The term 'intuition' claims respectability for positions which are defended not by *reasons* but by the more or less tacit appeal to consensus. But as a response to questions and objections, appeal to consensus is fallacious and rationally futile. Against objectors it merely insinuates that *we*, not they, are in charge around here.

Setting relativist, Kantian, and intuitionist objections aside, therefore, there remains a sound response to notions that social choice can and should be guided by measuring the expected value of alternative foreseeable outcomes. The response has several elements.

II

The first element is this. Commensuration of the goods and bads in alternative available courses of action is possible insofar as the deliberation about alternatives remains in the technical domain. This is the domain proper to cost-benefit analysis. Here, (1) goals are well defined, (2) costs can be compared by references to some definite unit of value (e.g. money), (3) benefits too can be quantified in a way that renders them commensurable with one another, and (4) differences among the means, other than their

---

[13] *Tugendlehre*, 424, 426, where Kant opines that in human sexual activity, nature's end is procreation.

[14] e.g. having suggested (against the mainstream of western philosophical and theological ethics) that sexual intercourse between a sterile wife and husband is contrary to reason ('nature's end'), Kant envisages a countervailing

permissive law of morally practical reason, which in the collision of its determining grounds makes permitted something that is in itself not permitted (indulgently, as it were), in order to prevent a still greater violation. (*Tugendlehre*, 426 (in Kant, *The Metaphysics of Morals*, 221–2).)

measurable costs, measurable benefits, and other aspects of their respective efficiency as means, are not counted as significant.

The response's second element is this. Because none of those four features obtains in the case of morally significant choice as such, it is not possible to commensurate—though it is possible to compare in some other important ways—the goods and bads in alternative available courses of action considered as options between which an individual or group has occasion to make a morally significant choice. In particular, it is not possible to make the type of commensuration required by utilitarianism in any of its forms, or by its consequentialist or proportionalist or economistic successors. (When I refer hereafter to commensuration and incommensurability, it is this type I have in mind, unless the context shows otherwise.) So since the making of a law is always a morally significant social act, engaging the moral responsibility both of the individuals who participate in it and of the group for whom they act, and self-determining both for these individuals and for the group, the incommensurability of the goodness of alternative options is of great importance for legal thought and practice. Indeed, as we shall see, it is an essential element in the grounding of the inviolable human rights which are properly the law's backbone.

The response has two elements because the technical and the moral are irreducibly distinct domains. That distinction is not grounded on some moral principle or norm. (If it were, the defence of that principle or norm against objections and 'exceptions' by utilitarian, consequentialist, proportionalist, or other commensuration-presupposing moral theories would be question-begging, as would appeal to the principle or norm in critiques of such theories.) Rather, it is grounded in the realities involved in freely chosen human action. Any philosophical reflection on morality and law must give careful attention to those realities. Still more so must a reflection on incommensurability in morality, public reason, and law. No one should assume that there is a general theory of incommensurability, or indeed of incomparability, such that what is true of commensuration or comparison in the domains of nature, logic, or technique is also true in the domain of deliberation about *options*. The question whether or in what ways X and Y are (in)commensurable and/or (in)comparable must always turn on *what X and Y are*.

In morality and law, X and Y are, generically, options: proposals for action which could be adopted by choice. Throughout this essay I mean by 'option' just such a proposal: one that comes up for deliberation and adoption or non-adoption, not as a possible move within the confines of a game or other technique as such, but as an apparently eligible answer to the unspoken question, What shall I, or we, *do* with this part of our one and only life? That being so, and the making and following of law being always a matter of such real-life options, the question of incommensurability in law turns on the prior question: What are the realities involved in any and every choice—in any and every adopting of one proposal (option) for action in preference to another or others?

Whether it be large scale (such as the choice to marry, or to become a lawyer rather than a philosopher) or small scale (such as the choice to write a friendly letter to an opponent, or to spend a week of one's life reflecting and communicating one's reflections on commensurability), every human choice is a step into a new world. To be sure, the proposal adopted by one's choosing will involve more or less definite goals. But the content and the significance of the choice are not exhausted by these goals. For the choice anticipates benefits (the very reasons for the choice and action) that are open-ended—capable of being instantiated not only in the envisaged and intended goals but also in further developments, opportunities, payoffs, many of them as yet envisaged only dimly, if at all. And the choosing itself has a further significance.

Determinisms hard and soft to the contrary notwithstanding, choices can be free.[15] In free choice, one has reasons for each of the alternative options, but these reasons are not causally determinative. One's having these reasons is a necessary but (even when morally sound and obligatory) not a sufficient condition for making one or the other choice. No factor but the choosing itself *settles* which alternative is chosen. So there is real creativity in free choice.

And this creativity is also self-creative, self-determining, more or less self-constitutive. One more or less transforms oneself by making the choice, and by carrying it out, and by following it up with other free choices in line with it. One's choice in fact *lasts* in, and as part of, one's character. In this respect, it is analogous to the insights which last as one's habitual knowledge (e.g. of arithmetic, logic, or history) and are part of that knowledge (and effective in guiding one's further inquiries) even when rarely or perhaps never consciously recalled and put to use. But choices differ from habitual knowledge in that they can be reversed by subsequent, inconsistent choices, especially choices to repudiate or repent of the former choice. Still, until such reversal, they last. That lasting of choices, which shapes character (and further choices) around those persisting adoptions of proposals, is a real effect of the choice—classically called an 'intransitive' effect, to mark its radical difference from every effect which transits beyond the chooser's will. To choose is not only to set out into a new world;

---

[15] Boyle, Grisez, and Tollefsen, *Free Choice*; and *NDMR* 256–7.

it is already to become a person (or society) more or less different from the person (or society) that deliberated about the goods and bads in the alternative available options.

Such, in bare outline, are the realities which Aristotle, notwithstanding his obscurities about the freedom possible in choosing, discerned clearly enough (on the whole) for him to insist on the basic distinction between *praxis* and *poiēsis*, between doing and making, and correspondingly between the ethical and the technical as irreducibly[16] distinct domains.[17] Life—the life one lives through one's chosen activities and lives well by (in large measure) one's acting well—neither is nor has a goal that one might sometime *have accomplished* by one's acts as one can accomplish one's technical objectives through skilful and unimpeded deployment of one's art/technique.[18] If you are tempted here to reply (as Aristotle perhaps was) that the goal is 'obtaining or realizing human goods or human fulfilment', think again about the aspects of human fulfilment that prevent obtaining it being the description of such a goal—the aspects sketched in this section.

And the same is true, even more evidently, of the life of groups such as politically and legally ordered societies. Every student and practitioner of law becomes aware of its open-endedness—of the ceaseless change in rules and institutions, changes which are guided by more or less stable principles and policies and in many cases have a specific goal, but which are not measured by their efficiency in moving society toward an overarching goal which might, even in principle, be attained by 'one more change'. The intransitive effect of choice on individual character has its clear analogue in the effect that every change in the rules on one subject-matter is liable to have—by way of arguments about coherence and integrity—on the rules and argumentation on other subject-matters.

In many respects the law (the legal ordering of a political society) is a technique, and many aspects of legal reasoning are, for good reason, technical—a manipulation of cultural artefacts for specific goals (such as effecting a transfer of property or change of status) which can be successfully accomplished and finished off. But as the debates around legal positivism and interpretation have made amply clear, the law is also a moral

---

[16] See *NE* VI.4: 1140a7.
[17] See e.g. *NE* VI.4: 1140a2–23, which also (like I.1: 1094a4–6) assimilates *poiēsis* with *technē*; VI.5: 1140b3–4; also see *Pol.* I.4: 1254a8 (*bios praxis, ou poiēsis*: life is doing things, not making things, action not production).
[18] In *Metaphysics* IX.6: 1048b18–34, Aristotle perhaps gives some clues to the rationale of his famous but difficult teaching (e.g. *NE* VI.2: 1139b4) that *praxis* (quite unlike *poiēsis*) is its own end; the point he there makes is that in actions (*praxis*) properly speaking there is no inherent limit, since they have no end beyond themselves the attainment of which would provide for them their terminus. In other words it is the *open-endedness* of action (and thus of life, and of *euzen* [living uprightly and well], and of flourishing) that Aristotle counts as its most decisively characteristic feature.

undertaking by society and by each of those individuals and groups whose acts go to constitute, maintain, put into effect, and develop the law, guided by many reasons of principle and/or policy but by no specifiable goal.

It is, above all, this open-endedness of individual and social life that makes impossible (not merely impracticable) the commensuration of the goods and bads in alternative available courses of action considered as options between which an individual or group must make a morally significant choice. When Socrates and four other Athenians were ordered by their government to help liquidate a political opponent, the four went off to do the job but Socrates simply 'went home'.[19] A game theorist, a utilitarian, or a proportionalist would try to commensurate the goods and bads in 'states of affairs'—presumably the states of affairs most obviously likely to eventuate from the two most obvious alternative choices for Socrates: go on the liquidation mission versus go home and therefore quite probably be liquidated oneself (two lives lost instead of one).[20]

But either choice was a step into a new world: either the world in which Socrates was a participant in what he judged to be murder (choosing to help kill the innocent) or the world in which Socrates put into practice his own teaching[21] that it is better to suffer wrong than to do it. Our world today is (and tomorrow, though changed, will still be) a world which Socrates shaped by choosing to go home. The proposal to evaluate the alternative choices facing Socrates by commensurating the goods net of bads in *our* world with the goods net of bads in the hypothetical world(s) into which Socrates chose *not* to step would be senseless even if our world were not itself being changed by the choices we are making. Why pick our world as one term of the comparison, given that (1) our world has been shaped by many free choices and events besides Socrates' acts, (2) the state of affairs which we call our world has no special priority of rational significance over the various states of affairs which lie between Socrates and us and the indefinitely many states of affairs which lie in the future though still somehow affected for good and ill by Socrates' choice, and (3) there is no theory of probability, subjective or objective, which could even in principle have identified for Socrates the relevant consequences of his choice, let alone assigned to our world some priority in his assessment of risk, still less settled the comparative weight of probabilities and values or disvalues?[22] Nor would the proposal be saved by stipulating that as a proportionalist

---

[19] Plato, *Apology*, 32c–d; see *FoE* 112–20 [and essay 1 at 50–2 above].

[20] *Apology*, 32d. In fact the government of the Thirty was overthrown shortly afterwards, and so Socrates was, on that occasion, spared.

[21] e.g. Plato, *Crito*, 49c–d.

[22] On the 'ripples in the pond' problem, and the want of any objective theory of probability, see *FoE* 88–9; on the incommensurability of risk with gravity, see *NDMR* 243–4.

Socrates himself need be concerned only with 'foreseeable effects'. For Socrates could foresee as well as anyone that choice will necessarily (and therefore, in principle, foreseeably) have self-constitutive intransitive effects on the chooser, and on all who condone or admire the choice and accordingly employ in their own deliberations what they take to be its rational principle(s). And he could equally well foresee that the irreducibly different kinds of effects of his choice would ripple out through history, in ways affected by many other free and self-constitutive choices, some affected and others unaffected by knowledge of his own choice. He had no reason whatever to think that the accounts, however rigged or simplified to produce a bottom line, should be drawn up in, or by reference particularly to, the state of affairs in 1997. And nor do we. None of this open-endedness of Socrates' choice, of course, prevented him from choosing, and choosing (as we shall see) quite rationally!

Why did no substantial philosopher before the Enlightenment entertain the notion that moral or legal reasoning can and should be guided by some principle of commensurating and maximizing the net overall goods promised by alternative options? The answer must, I think, have much to do with an insight more or less lost in the Enlightenment's adoption of more or less scientific models of human nature, individual and social action, and historical development—the insight that the subject-matter of deliberation toward free choice (moral reasoning) differs from that of technical reasoning in the ways which I have summarized as 'open-endedness'.

Hume treated as an admirable novelty his insight that 'ought' cannot be derived from 'is'. (He ignored or flouted it in his own affirmative work in ethics and metaethics.)[23] But there were earlier philosophers who had better understood that the moral *ought*, the directiveness of reason in deliberation toward choice and action, cannot be derived from (or reduced to) the *is* of nature, or the logic of non-contradiction, or the how-to (including the how-to-measure) of any technique. Aquinas thought this so important that he began his commentary on Aristotle's *Ethics* (and thus also his *Politics*) by pointing out the four irreducibly distinct types of order with which our reasoning is concerned: the 'natural' (for example, natural scientific), the logical, the moral, and the technical.[24] Where Kant confused the moral with the logical (eked out with the natural), utilitarian and other aggregative theories for guiding morally significant choice confuse the moral with the technical. The confusion lends its spurious support to (and is supported by) the mistaken notion that, prior to moral judgment, the goodness in a

---

[23] See *NLNR* 36–42.   [24] See *In Eth.* proem.; essay 14, sec. III.

morally significant option and the goodness in any alternative available option must be commensurable by reason as, all things considered, greater and lesser (or, perhaps, equal or approximately equal).

III

Of course, technical reasoning and technical commensurability are often of great importance to moral deliberation. Whenever technical reasoning can show that proposal X has all the beneficial features of proposal Y *and some more*, the latter proposal ceases to be a live *option*.

Technical commensurability of this kind is not restricted to the obvious instances of economics or engineering (where Y costs more, delivers less, and is less safe). It includes also legal considerations, as where argument Y relies on a statute that can be shown to have been repealed or a holding that has been overruled.

In all such cases, proposal X can be preferred, adopted, and carried out without the need for any *choice* (in the strong, morally relevant sense of 'choice') between X and Y, and without the need to appeal to the sorts of *justifying reason* we call moral (including legal principles and rules insofar as they address the deliberations, the consciences, of judges, officials, and citizens).

IV

What, then, is the source and character of the justifying (and the critically demanding and excluding) reasons which do give us standards for comparing *options*, 'weighing' those options (as the loose phrase goes), and finding reason to prefer one to another—reasons that direct but do not determine choice? If law-makers, as I said at the outset, must evaluate and rank options as better and worse, how can they do so?.

The reasonable standards for comparing and, so far as possible, ranking options are moral standards. Each of them is itself a specification, a making specific, of the following idea: everybody, all human persons and their communities, being fulfilled in all the basic human goods—integral human fulfilment. Integral human fulfilment is not some gigantic synthesis of all the instantiations of human goods in a vast state of affairs such as might be projected as the goal of a worldwide billion-year plan. Human goods and their instantiation through creative free choices are open-ended. Yet wishing for everybody, present and future, to flourish in all the goods intrinsic to human persons, while it does not amount to forming an intention, is not empty.

On the contrary, that wish is the only rational response to the directiveness of the reasons for action, the practical reasons, which each of the basic human goods provides. What gives reason for action is always some intelligible benefit which could be instantiated by successful action, benefits such as the basic forms of human opportunity and need. Each of these basic goods (basic reasons for action) is desirable for its own sake as a constitutive aspect of the well-being and flourishing of human persons in community (and none is unqualifiedly commensurable as more or less valuable than the others).[25] (Kant's ethics and doctrine of right remain empty precisely because, failing to break with empiricist assumptions, he did not differentiate the basic goods, the basic reasons for action and principles of practical reason, from the sub-rational inclinations and desires which are, in truth, data for practical understanding's original, underived insights into these intelligible goods and reasons, insights articulated as principles of reason.)

The combined or integral directiveness of all these basic practical reasons, these first principles of reasonable deliberation and practical reasonableness in choice and action, is not another good or additional reason for action to add to the list. (In that sense of the elusive term, it is not a 'covering value'.) Rather, that integral directiveness of all these reasons for action is articulated in—their interplay, unfettered and undeflected by emotions is, so to speak, moderated by—the rational principle which is the conceptual content of a sufficiently reflective wish for integral human fulfilment. The principle can be formulated thus: in all one's deliberating and acting, one *ought* to choose and in other ways will—and other persons, so far as satisfying their needs is dependent on one's choosing and willing, have a *right* that one choose and will—those and only those possibilities the willing of which is compatible with integral human fulfilment.[26]

That principle is the first, master principle of morality, in its most abstract formulation. All other moral standards are specifications of it.

---

[25] See *NLNR* chs 3–4; 1987f at 104–15. A list: (1) *knowledge* (including aesthetic appreciation) of reality; (2) *skilful performance*, in work and play, for its own sake; (3) *bodily life* and the components of its fullness, viz. health, vigour, and safety; (4) *friendship* or harmony and association between persons in its various forms and strengths; (5) the sexual association of a man and a woman which, though it essentially involves both friendship between the partners and the procreation and education of children by them, seems to have a point and shared benefit that is not reducible either to friendship or to life-in-its-transmission and therefore (as comparative anthropology confirms and Aristotle came particularly close to articulating [e.g. *NE* VIII.12: 1162a15–29] not to mention the 'third founder' of Stoicism, Musonius Rufus) should be acknowledged to be a distinct basic human good, call it *marriage*; (6) the good of harmony between one's feelings and one's judgments (inner integrity), and between one's judgments and one's behaviour (authenticity), which we can call *practical reasonableness*; (7) *harmony with* the widest reaches and most *ultimate source* of all reality, including meaning and value. [And see second endnote to essay 3, at 80 above.]

[26] See also *NDMR* 281–4; 1987f at 121–9.

The Kantian imperative that in every act one regard oneself as legislating for 'a kingdom of ends' (a 'whole of all ends in systematic conjunction')[27] is an intimation of that first principle; Christianity's love of neighbour as oneself for the sake of the Kingdom is another; the utilitarian injunction to seek 'the greatest good/happiness of the greatest number' is another attempt, unhappy precisely because of its several confusions about commensurability.[28]

How, then, is the first principle and measure of morality specified into less abstract moral principles and norms? How is its rational prescription shaped into definite responsibilities? Well, what that master principle itself prescribes is that one not narrow voluntarily the range of people and goods one cares about, by following non-rational motives, that is, motives not grounded in intelligible requirements of the basic *reasons* for action, the basic human goods. Now, one type of non-rational motive is hostile feelings such as anger and hatred toward oneself or others. A person or group motivated by feelings of, for example, revenge does not have a will open to integral human fulfilment. So a first specification of the master principle is: do not answer injury with injury. This principle is treated as foundational in all decent legal systems and is quite compatible with principles of just compensation (even by self-help) and of retributive punishment to restore the balance of fairness between wrongdoers and the law-abiding.

Another specification of the master principle is the principle which every form of consequentialist, proportionalist, or other purportedly aggregative moral theory is tailor-made to reject: do not do evil—choose to destroy, damage, or impede some instance or a basic good—that good may come. The previous principle excludes making harm to another one's end; the present principle excludes making it precisely one's means (as distinct from causing it as a side effect of what one intends and does). In such a case, one unreasonably treats a good end as justifying the bad means. For: the instantiation of good which one treats as end (call it E), and for the sake of which one acts *against* the reason constituted by that instantiation of

---

[27] Kant, *Grundlegung*, 433–4.
[28] On the incoherence involved in attempting to maximize, simultaneously, two non-independent variables, see Griffin, *Well-Being*, 151–4. Griffin (151) thinks the formula is 'typically' used by utilitarianism's enemies, but the sources he cites (357–8) scarcely support this, and his own commentary belies it by his final reflection (359) that 'many persons...will still think that the formula is all right and that our job is to find words to express what we have always really had in mind in using it'—these 'many persons' are not enemies of utilitarianism. Griffin's own theory of morality (see e.g. 155–62, 201–6, 251), though purportedly in the utilitarian tradition, moves a long way toward the open-endedness of integral human fulfilment and the first principle of morality, which I defend. But he sees rational commensurability between forms of good where I would deny it, because the *decisions* whereby we 'form' the 'basic preferences' with which we '*construct*' a 'scale of measurement of well-being' are treated by him (103) as if those decisions were rational *judgments*. I would say: creating a measure is not to be equated with identifying a measure.

a basic good which one is choosing to harm (call this reason *M*), could not constitute a *reason* thus to act against *M* unless *E* could be weighed and balanced against, commensurated with, *M* and—prior to moral judgment—*rationally* judged to be greater, more weighty, the greater good (or, where both reasons concern avoiding evil, the lesser evil). But by virtue of, inter alia, the considerations set out in sec. II, *that* sort of rationally commensurating *judgment* is not possible. So one's preference for *E* over *M* is motivated not by reason but by differential *feelings* as between *E* and *M*, and choosing to act on it violates the master principle of morality. The feelings which thus motivate the judgment that *E* is the greater good or lesser evil may well, of course, be veiled (more or less in good faith) by rationalizations or by conventional 'wisdom', which prescribes or licenses some narrowing of horizons or ranking of persons or other way of making the incommensurable seem rationally commensurable.

The principle that evil may not be done for the sake of good, interpreted in this way, is the foundation of truly inviolable (absolute) human rights and is the backbone of decent legal systems. For a decent legal system excludes unconditionally the killing or harming of innocent[29] persons as a means to any end, whether public or private. On the basis of other specifications of morality's master principle, it also excludes the use of perjured testimony, the choice to render false judgment, judicial or other official support of fraud, resort to sexual seduction as an instrument of public policy, and chattel slavery. These unconditional norms, and the associated absolute or truly inviolable human rights not to be mistreated by the violation of any of those norms, give the legal system its shape, its boundaries, the indispensable humanistic basis (at least some necessary conditions) for its strong claim on our allegiance. Without these norms, and respect for the underlying principle, the legal system becomes an organization of powerful people willing to treat others as mere means.[30]

This principle excluding all *intentional* harm to persons (in any basic aspect of their well-being) also rules out the economistic ambition to explain and justify the main institutions of our law as devices for maximizing economically assessable (commensurable) value. For central to Economic Analysis of Law is the assumption, or thesis, that (though there might be a difference in the purchase price) there is no difference of principle

---

[29] Why only of *innocent* persons? On the relevance of innocence and the question whether this restriction is justified, see *NDMR* 309–19.

[30] Kant's second/third formulation of his categorical imperative ('treat humanity in oneself and others always as an end and never as a means only'; *Grundlegung*, 429) is another formulation of this specification of morality's master principle. Kant's own interpretation of it is unsatisfactory because his conception of 'humanity' is too thin, and this because he fails to acknowledge the basic human goods and reasons for action. See *FoE* 120–4.

between buying the right to inflict intentional personal injury even on non-consenting persons and buying the right not to take precautions which would (supposedly) eliminate an equivalent number of injuries caused accidentally.[31] But in every decent legal system, the former right is not available, whether by purchase or otherwise. For a decent legal system is in the service of human persons, and its first and most fundamental service is in protecting and vindicating their right not to be made the object (end or means) of someone's will to harm them.

A third principle giving relative specificity to the master principle of openness to integral fulfilment is the Golden Rule, the core principle of fairness: 'Do to others as you would have them do to you; do not impose on others what you would not want to be obliged by them to accept'. For a will marked by egoism or partiality cannot be open to integral human fulfilment. This rational principle of impartiality by no means excludes all forms and corresponding feelings of preference for oneself and those who are near and dear (e.g. parental responsibility for, and consequent prioritizing of, their own children). It excludes, rather, all those forms of preference which are motivated only by desires, aversions, or hostilities that do not correspond to intelligible aspects of the real *reasons for* action, the basic human goods instantiated in the lives of other human beings as in the lives of oneself or those close to one's heart.

Although fairness is thus a rational norm requiring one to transcend all rationally unintegrated feelings, its concrete application in personal life presupposes a kind of commensurating of benefits and burdens which reason is impotent to commensurate. For, to apply the Golden Rule, one must know what burdens one considers *too great* to accept. And this knowledge, constituting a pre-moral commensuration, cannot be a commensurating by reason (see sec. II). Therefore, it can only be by one's intuitive awareness, one's discernment, of one's own differentiated *feelings* toward various goods and bads as concretely remembered, experienced, or imagined. To repeat: this is not a rational and objective commensuration of goods and bads. But once established in one's feelings and identified in one's self-awareness, this commensuration by feelings enables one to measure one's options by a rational and objective standard of interpersonal impartiality.

Of course, it is implicit in what I have said that the feelings by which someone makes the commensuration identifying what it is fair for that person to choose or otherwise will (e.g. to accept as a side effect) had better be the feelings of someone whose deliberation and action is open

---

[31] See e.g. Calabresi and Melamed, 'Property Rules, Liability Rules, and Inalienability' at 1126 n. 71; and essay IV.16 (1990b), secs V–VI.

to and in line with integral human fulfilment and each of that master principle's specifications. That is what is sound in Aristotle's pervasive methodological principle of ethical and political theory: it is the mature person of fully reasonable character who is the standard and measure, *kanōn kai metron*, of what is and is not truly worthy, worthwhile, and enjoyable.[32]

Analogously, in the life of a community, the preliminary commensuration of rationally incommensurable factors is accomplished not by rationally determined judgments but by *decisions* (themselves presumably based ultimately on commensuration of alternative options by feelings). And these too had better be made within the framework established by complete consistency with the other specifications of morality's master principle. Is it fair to impose on others the risks inherent in driving at more than 10 mph or in planting trees near the roadside? Yes, in our community, since our community has by custom and law *decided* to treat those risks and harms as *not too great*. Have we a rational critique of a community which decided to limit road traffic to 10 mph and to accept all the economic and other costs of that decision? Or to have no trees along the road? Or not to have the institution of trusts, or constructive trusts? No, we have no rational critique of such a community. In short, the decision to permit road traffic to proceed faster than 10 mph, or to plant trees along the verge, or to define trusts just as English law does was rationally underdetermined.[33]

But we do have a rational critique of someone who drives at 60 mph but who, when struck by someone driving at 45 mph, complains that the other's driving so fast is negligent. Or of someone willing to receive the benefits (e.g. the tax breaks) of trusts but not willing to accept the law's distinction between trust and contract in bankruptcy. And, in general, we have a rational critique of those who accept the benefits of this and other communal decisions but reject the correlative burdens as they bear on them and those in whom they feel interested.

---

[32] *NE* III.4: 1114a33 (see n. 1 above); *NLNR* 102, 129.

[33] Of course, this does not mean that it was 'indeterminate' in the strong sense of the word which the Critical Legal Studies Movement uses so vaguely and uncritically, i.e., indeterminate in the sense of being wholly unguided by reason. See essay IV.13 (1985c), sec. II. The good of bodily life and integrity is a genuine reason always practically relevant; and some further rational criteria for decision are provided by facts about human reaction times and susceptibility to impact, and by the rational demand for consistency with our individual and communal tolerance or intolerance of *other*—non-traffic—threats to that good. And though rationally underdetermined, the decision to permit fast-moving traffic, *once made*, provides an often fully determinate rational standard for treating those accused of wrongful conduct or wrongfully inflicting injury. Likewise with trusts, bankruptcy, and so forth.

Fundamental to the working out of the Golden Rule across time are expectations such as that those who have received the benefit of a scheme of cooperation involving onerous burdens will shoulder the burdens when it is their turn to do so; or that we who have shouldered the burdens will in due course receive, and not be deprived of, the reasonably expected benefits. Claims based on appeals to fairness in view of such expectations vary in rational force, according as, for example, the collaborative enterprise is subject to chances of success, and risks of failure, arising from factors external to it and independent of the intentions (i.e. outside the control) of its participants. Where the non-accrual, or the confiscation, of expected benefits arises because one of the parties to the collaboration intends to deny or confiscate the benefit, it cannot fairly be treated as merely the crystallizing of a risk which, just like risks of the kind referred to in the previous sentence, could (and should!) have been discounted by putative beneficiaries when considering their 'investment in' (assumption of the burdens of) the collaborative enterprise. Economic Analysis of Law errs again here in equating confiscation with other forms of loss of expected benefit, commensurating all these forms of loss by reference to one factor assumed to be quantifiable: probability or degree of foreseeable risk of loss.[34]

In this section, I have identified three of the measures or standards of reasonableness that are intermediate between the supreme moral measure of choice and action and the specific moral norms which give more determinate guidance and which in some but not all cases, are taken over and applied more or less directly by the law of any decent community. There are other such intermediate, high-level principles, but they are not so directly constitutive of justice between persons and thus not so central to the understanding of legal systems, rules, institutions, and practices. What I have said is sufficient to establish that the failure of utilitarian and other consequentialist or proportionalist attempts to guide moral judgment by commensurating the goods and bads in options does not leave reason impotent to evaluate options and rank them as, if you will, better and worse, or as involving respectively greater or lesser evil. Because morality is nothing other than integral, unfettered reasonableness, an option which violates one or more of the principles I have mentioned and so is morally wrong can always be described as 'worse' compared to options which are not morally wrong. Because even morally upright choice, fully in line with integral human fulfilment, can never definitively avoid side

---

[34] This commensurability is asserted, in effect, in writings such as Kaplow, 'An Economic Analysis of Legal Transitions'; see the discussion in Pildes, 'Conceptions of Value in Legal Thought' at 1534–7.

effects more or less harmful to the goods constitutive of human fulfilment, a morally upright action which involves no *choice* of evil (no intent to do harm as an end or a means) can be described (though not without risk of being misunderstood as supposing an impossible consequentialist commensuration) as choosing the lesser evil.

Indeed, since the consequentialist project of commensurating is impossible, but rational deliberation must go forward and be articulated, we often find such a non-consequentialist usage on the lips of avowed consequentialists. Thus Justice Oliver Wendell Holmes in the US Supreme Court:

> We must consider the two objects of desire, both of which we cannot have, and make up our minds which to choose. It is desirable that criminals should be detected, and to that end that all available evidence should be used. It is also desirable that the Government should not itself foster and pay for other crimes, when they are the means by which the evidence is to be obtained.... We have to choose, and for my part I think it *a lesser evil* that some criminals should escape than that the Government should play an *ignoble* part.[35]

'Lesser evil' here either (1) merely expresses an opinion *consequent* on choice, rather than a moral judgment antecedent to and suited to guide choice, or (2) implies an appeal to a prior, non-consequentialist moral standard according to which covert manipulation of legal rules by officers of the law violates the Golden Rule and perhaps even the principle that evil may not be done for the sake of good, and for either reason, or both, is something 'ignoble', especially for professional guardians of the law (whose appeal is to reason and whose authority is thus from morality).

Law can effectively provide a community with a common 'rule and measure' for guiding and evaluating the actions of its members (including lower-level communities within it)—and thus for attaining the benefits of cooperation—only if it provides those members with a standard which each can adopt and use just as if it were his or her own scheme of action autonomously excogitated and adopted. It can provide this standard only by establishing more or less content-independent criteria for assessing the validity of rules and thus the validity and/or legality of the acts those rules regulate. These criteria refer us to past acts and other facts (of types picked out in other rules), which often are exercises of the *technē* of rule-making (by any of the three constitutional branches) but need not be (as in the case of the emergence of customary rules) and in any case are evaluated by the *technē* (*not* exclusively a lawyers' craft) of rule-finding. In an important

---

[35] *Olmstead v United States* 277 US 438 (1928) at 470, per Holmes J. (dissenting), emphases added.

sense, a legal rule just *is* the relation between such a past act or fact and my present deliberation, choice, and action as a member, official or otherwise, of the community that measures its conduct by looking back to such past acts and facts. But in another important sense, a legal rule just *is* the relation between the master principle of morality (and the ideal of integral human fulfilment) and that same deliberation, choice, and action of mine, insofar as that master principle has been given specificity not merely in the intermediate principles and other norms of morality but in the particular choices of the rule-makers acting as rule-makers, *including* the choices of those who settled the constitutional criteria of validity of other legal rules.

Judges in superior courts in the common law world have (relatively determinate) authority not only to find, declare, and enforce the existing 'common law' rules but also (relatively indeterminate) authority to reshape them and/or make new ones. Moreover, the complexity of the judicial system, and of the cultural materials relevant to judicial rule finding, makes it necessary (and therefore morally and institutionally possible) for rule finders to treat some of the relevant materials as lacking the authority which would otherwise be attributed to the past acts (say, of rule-finding and declaring) of the author(s) of such material. So there emerge the two dimensions on which to compare and evaluate the rival interpretations of a particular part of the law in dispute between the parties before a court: the dimension of fit with the legal materials and the dimension of moral soundness.

One could say that a *hard* case is one in which one interpretation of the law is the best of all rival interpretations on the dimension of fit, while another is best on the dimension of soundness. I have argued in the past that fit and soundness are incommensurable, so that there cannot be a *uniquely* right interpretation in a hard case so understood (though countless interpretations can be identified as wrong because inferior to the right, that is not-wrong, interpretations on both dimensions).[36] To the extent that fit is simply a matter of understanding and applying the technical criteria of validity of rule-making or other ways of generating legal rules, it is indeed incommensurable with the moral considerations relevant to soundness. The cultural-technical order as such shares no common measure with the moral as such.

But fit, and indeed the whole technique of rule-making and rule-finding to which 'fit' synoptically refers, is in the service of the community's common good. Indeed, the technique was instituted and is maintained for

---

[36] Essay IV.12 at 292–5 (1987e at 372–5); and essay 14, sec. V, above.

the sake of a morally required (and therefore sound) end, the common good attainable by a fair and peaceful cooperation which fully respects the rights of every member of the community (including the rights which properly must be respected and prevail whatever the circumstances). Ultimately, rule-finding is no mere game or technique, but a morally significant act which, like all other choices to act, will be fully reasonable only if in line with integral human fulfilment. So there is a measure common to the two dimensions: moral soundness.

It was not a mere mistake to speak of two dimensions, the one being concerned with such morally significant considerations as the disappointing of expectations, the overriding of acquired legal rights, and the desirability of like cases getting like treatment by the various tribunals disposing of them; the other being concerned with the merits of the alternative ways of dealing with these parties (and future parties in like case) and of guiding the conduct of citizens and officials generally. These 'substantive merits' can never reasonably be considered entirely in abstraction from the network of other substantive principles and rules legally adopted in that community.[37] But they can be considered in abstraction from the technical authoritativeness of the alternative solutions, respectively. The possibility of doing so is the possibility of there being two distinguishable dimensions or moments of the one, ultimately moral assessment.

Does it follow that, morality being a matter of unfettered reasonableness, there is in truth a uniquely right answer even in hard cases at law? No. Although I was mistaken, I now think, in contending that the two dimensions are simply incommensurable, it remains that assessing the moral significance of differing degrees of fit and soundness will usually be a matter of fairness. And fairness, though a rational requirement, is one whose content in any given circumstances is determined, as I have argued above, in part by *feelings* ('How would I like it if…?', and so forth). The commensurating here must be done by discernment of one's feelings. It is not reason, whether moral or technical, that settles for each judge the stance he or she will adopt on the great strategic questions whose answers do dispose of hard cases: whether to uphold national/federal power or constitutionally legitimate state/provincial interests, whether to countenance judicial reform or defer to the legislature, whether and when to swim with and when to breast a tide of judicial opinion one thinks technically inferior or based partly on morally unsound arguments, and so forth. In such cases, reason does no more (and no less) than hold the ring,

[37] See Dworkin, *Law's Empire*, 404–7.

disqualifying countless 'solutions' as contrary to reason and wrong, but identifying none as *uniquely* right.

Many cases at law are not hard but are settled easily by reason. Of these, many are settled by technical considerations of validity and authoritativeness, and the rest by moral considerations, for example, of inviolable rights. Where a moral right is entailed by 'Do not return harm for harm' or 'Do not do evil (choose precisely to inflict harm) for the sake of good', it is truly inviolable and itself entails what some have called a 'hierarchical incommensurability'[38] or 'lexical priority' or genuinely[39] 'trumping' status, in relation to all other technical and/or otherwise morally relevant considerations. Where a moral right results from the Golden Rule of fairness, it trumps all considerations of technique or interest except where those considerations themselves create, in the relevant circumstances, a moral responsibility and/or countervailing fairness-based right. This priority of moral considerations over all, but only, *non-moral* considerations in deliberation is the source and content of the 'constitutive incommensurabilities' which Joseph Raz's work has highlighted. One does not rightly exchange one's friend for cash, however much cash (where 'cash' stands for interest and advantage); that moral truth is a constitutive element of the relationship of friendship. But there can be a moral responsibility to take and use cash for good purposes even though, in the circumstances, this may defeat a friend's expectations and end the friendship.[40] So that sort of 'constitutive incommensurability' is bounded by the commensurability of each moral consideration with all others.

The same boundedness obtains in somewhat analogous relationships such as patriotic allegiance. One does not rightly give up one's allegiance for cash. But the moral obligation to obey one's country's laws—an obligation derived from multiple considerations of fairness,[41] and constitutive of a decent relationship of allegiance and citizenship—is measured by moral principle, and so is defeasible by other serious moral responsibilities.

---

[38] Pildes and Anderson, 'Slinging Arrows at Democracy' at 2147–58.
[39] Unlike Dworkin's trumping rights, which are not inviolable but can be overridden in 'emergency': *TRS* 354.
[40] The obligations of friendship, speaking generally, are not very strong; the relation one has with friends is really a kind of instance of the relations one ought to have with every 'neighbour' and is subject to virtually all one's other responsibilities. It is different if the friendship is specified to *marriage*; here there are unconditional rights and obligation.
[41] See essays IV.2 (1984b) and IV.3 (1989b).

V

In sum, talk of incommensurability takes its measure from a presupposed concept of *measure*, and talk of measure is not univocal but highly analogous. Law is a measured measure; its immediate rational measure is the common good of the community whose law it is. That common good is a kind of specification (relative to a particular group) of integral human fulfilment, the primary rational measure of all human action. The ideal of integral human fulfilment does not measure our deliberations in the way that goals enable us to measure the efficiency of means, nor does it provide a unit of aggregation. It measures rather by another kind of specification (relative to the ways in which emotion can subordinate rather than support reasons), a specification in and of the standards of fully reasonable conduct, including the conduct of law-makers. Within the rational/moral limits fixed by those standards, much remains to be settled by individual and group commitment in accordance with discernment of feelings and fair procedures of collective or representative decision-making. The essential role of feelings and emotions in individual life and action is closely paralleled by the essential role of procedures for decision-making in the life and action of communities; in each case, that role is beneficial so long as subordinated to the fundamental reasons for action (basic human goods) and to the standards of unfettered practical reasoning (moral principles and norms). Feelings and commitments (including such collective or community commitments as constitutions) enable individuals and groups reasonably to compare and rank, and in that sense commensurate, many options which by reason's own standards are incommensurable. So the incommensurabilities with which deliberation must contend, and which necessitate morally significant *choice*, do not prevent our choices being in a genuine (though not game-theoretical) sense instances of *rational choice*.[42] Choice between options neither (or none) of which is required by reason's principles and norms should nonetheless respect all of those requirements and be made, so far as possible, for relevant reasons.

A sound understanding of practical reason, then, denies many of the types of incommensurability implicit in unsound conceptions. These include the incommensurabilities that result from a pure 'will' theory of law which, as in Kelsen's final works, denies that legal directives need be coherent (non-contradictory); the incommensurabilities implicitly embraced by value-relativist and ethical-intuitionist rejections of the possibility of rational

---

[42] For the spectacular misunderstandings that occur when game theory's 'rational choice' jargon is transferred to ethical or other third-order discussions, see essay IV.17 at 358–60 (1990d at 235–7).

unity of principle; and the incommensurabilities implicit in every method of practical reasoning which proposes, with whatever subtlety, to guide deliberation by aggregating value, and so for want of a rationally defensible understanding of *value* remains at the mercy of its exponents' diverse and shifting preferences, conventional opinions, and non-rationally determined horizons of concern.

16

'PUBLIC REASON' AND MORAL DEBATE*

I. PUBLIC REASON AND THE 'RIGHT TO KILL THE UNBORN'

Every society, liberal or illiberal, takes a public stand on the question whether abortion is or is not a form of criminal activity. If that question were left to private judgment, people who judge it homicide would be entitled to use force to prevent their fellow citizens engaging in it (just as they are entitled to use force to prevent infanticide, or sexual intercourse between adults and 8-year-old children).

The need for the law and public policy to take a stand has become more and more obvious for two reasons. The first has to do with the standard purpose of abortion, as that term is commonly used: to end the life of a fetus/unborn child. As Jeffrey Reiman argues in his 1997 book, *Critical Moral Liberalism*, the right to abortion which he is interested in defending, and which many others are interested in having, is a right which would be *negated* if it were reduced to '[a woman's] right to expel an unwelcome fetus from her body, and only to end its life if necessary for the expulsion'.[1] The right which Reiman and so many others defend is the right precisely to kill the unwelcome fetus. The significance of this is made clear by the second reason: unborn children who are welcome, and who are thought to be in danger, can nowadays be the beneficiaries of elaborate therapeutic attentions. From a month or so after conception, their condition, their

---

* 1998a; the section headings, some endnotes, and supplementary footnotes draw on a later version (2000c) written for debate directly with Jeffrey Reiman. The final section of 1998a, on cloning, is omitted here; its substance can be found in essay II.17 (2000b); see also essay III.17, and 1983e and 1984c.

[1] Reiman, *Critical Moral Liberalism*, 190, which goes on to say (*ibid.*) that unless the right to abortion includes the right to get the fetus dead—

> As early as a living fetus can be safely and easily removed from a pregnant woman, her right to abortion might be transformed into a duty to provide extrauterine care for her expelled fetus. If (when!) medical technology pushes this point back towards the earliest moments of pregnancy, *the right to abortion will disappear entirely.* (Emphasis added, as elsewhere in this essay.)

individual appearance and characteristics, their every movement, can be clearly seen and followed on the ultrasound screen; their medical problems can be and very frequently are attended to in much the same way as after their birth. Medical practitioners engaged in such activities routinely say and think that they have two patients. And it is obvious to everyone that any medical practitioners who took advantage of this sort of opportunity to kill an unborn child (without the request of the mother), pursuant to some private policy of, say, killing Jews or the children of atheists, would be ethically and should be legally liable to some plausible charge of homicide or something savouring of homicide[2] (say, the 'great misprision' of abortion—as the seventeenth- and eighteenth-century textbooks of English and therefore American criminal law put it).[3] Minimally, any society, liberal or not, in which the difference between the unborn, the partially born, and the newborn is, for practical purposes, no more (and no less!) than the difference between being (wholly or partly) inside or outside the mother's body must, and will, publicly regulate the ways in which medical practitioners and others deal with the unborn (or partially born), and particularly those dealings which by intention or negligence result in the death of the unborn (or partially unborn).

II. 'PUBLIC REASON' AND POLITICAL THEORY'S CENTRAL TRADITION

The term 'public reason' was introduced into recent[†] political theoretical discourse by John Rawls, and he chose to illustrate his use of the term by reference to the issue of the regulation of abortion. Rawls's remarks about abortion do not, perhaps, show his work to best advantage. But it will be worth making our own exploration of the question of whether 'public reason' is a concept or nest of concepts worth adopting into legal

---

[2] As Reiman says (195), 'it is so natural to us to think this way', namely, of the fetus 'as a person-like victim—which is a moral status that a not-yet-existing fetus lacks'. This in turn is tightly linked to the assumption, which Reiman grants and perhaps even concedes, that (194)

the being that traverses the span from conception to death is a self-identical individual. That is a more or less natural extension of the common belief that a human being from birth to death is a self-identical individual—the one named by its proper name.

[3] [Since the debacle of *Roe v Wade* 410 US 113 (1973), a majority of states in the United States have enacted laws making killing an unborn human being at some stage of gestation a form of homicide (in some states called feticide, in some homicide, in some murder). In some states it is a homicide whatever the stage of gestation, and in a few it is murder at any stage. The validity of such laws has been upheld in the highest courts of Illinois, Minnesota, and California: the state of doctrine was reviewed and summarized in *People v Davis* 872 P2d 591, 599 (California Supreme Court en banc, 1994): '[W]hen the mother's privacy interests are not at stake, the Legislature may determine whether, and at what point, it should protect life inside a mother's womb from homicide'. For the state of the law, see Forsythe, 'Human Cloning and the Constitution'.]

and political theory, using abortion and cloning as test cases whenever our exploration would be advanced by carrying out a test.

I should say at the outset that the attractions of the term 'public reason' have not been much diminished for me by the discovery that Rawls's own usage (as almost everyone agrees) is confused and arbitrary. 'Public reason' seems to me quite a good phrase for summarily conveying the gist of at least four features of classical political thought as expounded by, say, Thomas Aquinas:[4]

(1) The proper function of the state's law and government is limited. In particular, its role is not (as Aristotle had supposed) to make people integrally good but only to maintain peace and justice in interpersonal relationships.[5] In this respect, the public realm, the *res publica*, is different from certain other associations such as family and church, associations which, albeit with limited means, can properly aspire to bring it about that their members become integrally good people. As Rawls says, 'public reason' is contrasted not with 'private reason'—'there is no such thing as private reason'[6]—but with the ways of deliberating appropriate to all non-public associations, that is, all associations other than the political community.[7] The deliberations of the political community as such—that is, of its rulers, including voters, as such—proceed in the appropriate way only if they are concerned to determine those requirements of justice and peace which Aquinas regularly names 'public good'.[8]

(2) In determining and enforcing the requirements of public good, the state's law-makers and other rulers (including voters) are entitled to impose as requirements only those practical principles which are accessible to all people whatever their present religious beliefs or cultural practices. These are the principles (*communia principia rationis practicae*)[9] called in the tradition 'natural law', on the

---

[4] See *Aquinas*, esp. ch. VII.

[5] Aquinas argued:

[K]ings are constituted to preserve inter-personal social life (*ad socialem vitam inter homines conservandam*); that is why they are called 'public persons', as if to say promoters or guardians of public good. And for that reason, the laws they make direct people in their relationships with other people (*secundum quod ad alios ordinantur*). Those things, therefore, which neither advance nor damage the common good are neither prohibited nor commanded by human laws.

Aquinas, *Opera Omnia*, vol. 14 (Rome, 1926), p. 46* col. 1; see also *ST* I–II q.96 a.3c; q.98 a.1c; q.100 a.2c.

[6] This needs qualification if and only to the extent that there are private revelations from God. So the Catholic faith claims that its own teaching is a matter of public reason, in as much as it is a matter of public, not private revelation. See the claim made in Peter's preaching in Jerusalem (Acts 2: 22), in Paul's in Athens (Acts 17: 31), and Second Vatican Council, *Lumen Gentium* §25 (1964).

[7] Rawls, *Political Liberalism*, 220.   [8] *Aquinas* 226.   [9] *ST* I–II q.94 a.4c.

understanding that they are 'natural' because, *and only because*, they are rational—requirements of being practically reasonable—and thus accessible to beings whose nature includes rational capacities.

(3) The central case of government is the rule of a free people, and the central case of law is coordination of willing subjects by law which, by its fully public character (promulgation),[10] clarity,[11] generality,[12] stability,[13] and practicability,[14] treats them as partners in public reason.[15]

(4) 'Any activity is to be pursued in a way appropriate to its purpose.... One sort of academic disputation is designed to remove doubts about *whether* such-and-such is so. In disputations of this sort you should above all use authorities acceptable to those with whom you are disputing.... *And if you are disputing with people who accept no authority, you must resort to natural reasons*'.[16]

III. 'PUBLIC REASON' AND RAWLS

The central tenet of Rawls's construct 'Political Liberalism', in his 1993 book *Political Liberalism*, is 'the liberal principle of legitimacy':[17] political questions which concern or border on constitutional essentials or basic questions of justice will be settled fully and properly only if settled by principles and ideals that *all* citizens '*may reasonably be expected to endorse*'. Rawls terms *such* principles and ideals 'public reason(s) and [public] justification'.[18] The whole point of the principle of legitimacy is to rule out as illegitimate, in a certain context, certain principles and ideals and in general *theses*, even though they are or may well be true—that is, to rule them out on grounds completely distinct from their falsity[19] or their unreasonableness judged 'comprehensively'.[20]

---

[10] I–II q.90 a.4c.
[11] I–II q.95 a.3c (laws lacking clarity in expression [*manifestatio*] are harmful).
[12] I–II q.96 a.1.   [13] I–II q.97 a.2c.
[14] I–II q.95 a.3c (*disciplina conveniens unicuique secundum suam possibilitatem*).
[15] Aquinas thus pointed to all the main features of the Rule of Law, as was acknowledged by Fuller, *The Morality of Law*, 242.
[16] Aquinas, *Quodlibetal Questions* IV q.9 a.3c (emphasis added).
[17] Rawls, *Political Liberalism*, 137.   [18] *Ibid.*, 137 (emphasis added); see also *ibid.*, 217.
[19] Similarly, Nagel, 'Moral Conflict and Political Legitimacy' at 229: 'The defense of liberalism requires that a limit somehow be drawn to appeals to the truth of political argument'. For Raz's decisive critique of both Rawls and Nagel in this regard, see *Ethics in the Public Domain*, 60–96.
[20] Very often Rawls states the principle of legitimacy expansively, so that it outlaws not only using public coercive power on certain (i.e., non-public) grounds, but also outlaws the appeal to such grounds in all political discussion (at least of constitutional essentials and matters of basic justice) even on the part of those who wish to resist that sort of use of public power. *Ibid.* at 138, 153, 214–15. This expansion seems to me inevitable, for if the legitimacy principle sieved out political theses only when and because they demand the use of public power (as Rawls often suggests when setting up

Rawls's formulations of the legitimacy principle are remarkably ambiguous. When one says of a thesis, 'all may reasonably be expected to endorse it', is one predicting the behaviour of people or assessing the rational strength of the thesis? Does one mean that reasonable observers will agree that practically all citizens *will* (or at least *are likely to*) endorse it? Or does one make a judgment about the grounds, evidence, or reasons for and against the thesis and thus about the (un)reasonableness of any refusal to endorse it?

There is evidence in favour of the predictive, external-viewpoint reading. For example, Rawls says of a particular thesis that, even though it may be true, 'reasonable persons *are bound to* differ uncompromisingly' about it.[21] The phrase 'are bound to' seems fairly clearly (though it too is elusive!) to be in the predictive mode, not the mode of speech of someone assessing the thesis itself as reasonable or unreasonable.[22]

But the external-viewpoint interpretation obviously entails a particularly gross form of veto, by majorities or indeed by minorities. So it is not too surprising that there is also plenty of textual evidence in favour of a normative, internal-viewpoint of Rawls's own legitimacy principle, such that 'can reasonably be expected to endorse' thesis X is to be read as signifying a *judgment on* the sorts of *grounds* there are for endorsing

---

his legitimacy principle and trying to make it palatable), it would in many cases result only in a grotesque free-for-all of private power. Take abortion: one thesis says that public power should be used to prevent the aborting of, say, healthy children in healthy mothers; if we reject that as illegitimate just because it seeks the use of public power, we still confront the thesis of those who say that public power should be used to prevent abortion rescuers who seek to use their private power to stop the killing of fetuses just as they would try to stop the killing of infants; if we rule out this thesis because it too seeks to harness public power, we are left with a sheer power struggle between the abortionists and the rescuers. And as a matter of fact, quite appropriately Rawls's own discussion of what theses are legitimate in relation to abortion makes no reference to the use of public power, but only to the substantive facts and political values (life, equality, nature of early as opposed to late pregnancy, and so forth: *ibid.* at 243).

[21] *Ibid.* at 138 (emphasis added). Note, incidentally, the tension between Rawls's approval of 'uncompromising' refusal to endorse certain religious opinions, here, and his statement earlier that '[p]olitical liberalism starts by taking to heart the absolute depth of th[e] irreconcilable latent conflict' which is introduced when a 'salvationist, creedal, and expansionist religion' 'introduces into people's conceptions of their good a transcendent element not admitting of compromise'. *Ibid.* at xxviii. In reality, a 'transcendent element not admitting of compromise' is in no way peculiar to such religions.

[22] Notice: if reasonable persons are differing about this thesis *uncompromisingly*, they must think that their own position endorsing or withholding their endorsement from it is correct. If they are modest objectivists, they will each hold that under ideal epistemic conditions—'favourable conditions of investigation' and reflection (*FoE* 64, citing Wiggins, 'Truth, Invention and the Meaning of Life')—reasonable people would agree with their affirmation (or denial); for (i) that is entailed by the ordinary concept of truth which modest objectivists simply unpack, and (ii) that is also the presupposition on which people engage in reasonable debate with each other (assuming that they are not mere propagandists willing to use any and every rhetorical device to win non-rational endorsements of the theses for which they are 'arguing'). (So this quasi-prediction (for the effectively unattainable ideal case), unlike Rawls's apparent prediction of disagreement, is really based upon a normative, internal assessment of the rational grounds for endorsing (affirming) or denying the thesis.)

or denying X.[23] Particularly interesting is the passage where Rawls finally faces up to 'rationalist believers' in a 'comprehensive religious or philosophical doctrine' who 'contend that their beliefs are open to and can be fully established by reason' and are 'so fundamental that to insure their being rightly settled justifies civil strife'.[24] Having curiously suggested that this view is uncommon—when actually it is (in some form) the claim of the entire central tradition of natural law theory in philosophy and theology—Rawls interprets the rationalist believers' claim as a denial of 'what we have called "the fact of reasonable pluralism"'.[25] But their claim could not be a *denial* of that 'fact' unless the so-called fact of reasonable pluralism is in the same logical field as the rationalist believers' claim that their beliefs can be fully established by reason. And Rawls's recipe for dealing with the rationalist believers is to claim, not that others do not in fact agree with them, but rather that they are 'mistaken' in thinking that their beliefs can be 'publicly and fully established by reason'[26]—a claim that cannot reasonably be made by Rawls without looking, in what I call an internal, normative way, at the merits of the rationalist believers' arguments as arguments.

So much then for the radical ambiguity of Rawls's principle of legitimacy, and thesis about public reason.[27] What are Rawls's grounds for putting it forward in any of its possible senses?

The principle of legitimacy and the limits or guidelines of public reason 'have the same basis as the substantive principles of justice'.[28] That is, they would be adopted by the parties in the Original Position, because those parties would be failing in their responsibility as trustees for everyone who has to live under the principles they adopt in the Original Position,

---

[23] Consider the following passages from *Political Liberalism*:

(i) [I]n discussing constitutional essentials and matters of basic justice, we are not to appeal to comprehensive religious and philosophical doctrines—to what we as individuals or members of associations see as the whole truth—... [but to] the plain truths now widely accepted, *or available*, to citizens generally (224–5; emphasis added);

(ii) [E]ach of us must have, and be ready to explain, a criterion of what principles and guidelines we think other citizens... may reasonably be expected to endorse along with us.... Of course, we may find that actually others fail to endorse the principles and guidelines our criterion selects. That is to be expected [!] (*ibid.* at 226–7).

[24] *Ibid.* at 152–3.   [25] *Ibid.* at 153.   [26] *Ibid.*

[27] [Reiman, in his article in response, 'Abortion, Natural Law and Liberal Discourse' at 110, said that I am overlooking the fact that 'Rawls's notion of the burdens of judgment is an empirical claim'. Not so. That phrase, as used by Rawls, is infected with precisely the same ambiguity (between normative and empirical) that infects his phrases 'public reason' and 'political conception'. Nor does it restrain Rawls for a moment from passing adverse judgment on those who reject his claim that abortions of convenience during the first three months of gestation are obviously acceptable. Reiman, too, freely pronounces many unburdened but eminently controvertible, judgments in his book and his response essay. As actually deployed by Rawls and Reiman, the claim about the political implications of 'the burdens of judgment' is self-refuting.]   [28] *Political Liberalism* at 225.

unless they adopted the principle that the application of the substantive principles be 'guided by judgment and inference, reasons and evidence that [everyone] can reasonably be expected to endorse'.[29]

So the legitimacy thesis stands and falls with the 'political constructivism' employed in Rawls's famous 1971 book, *A Theory of Justice*. So it falls. That book rests on a fallacious or undefended claim. It proposes that we recognize as principles of justice those, and only those, principles which would be adopted in a hypothetical Original Position, behind a 'veil of ignorance', an artificial ignorance and risk-aversion supposed to be characteristic of the hypothetical parties who are to choose those principles of justice which will apply, outside the Original Position, in the real world. We can accept that principles which *would* be chosen in the Original Position would be free from self-interested bias. But we cannot assume, as Rawls simply does assume, that principles which would *not* be chosen in the Original Position are therefore not principles of justice in the real world in which we may judge them without being hampered either by the Original Position's veil of ignorance about theoretical and practical truths, or by a degree of risk aversion which, if not unreasonable, is at best only one reasonable attitude among other, often less-risk-averse, attitudes.[30]

Political Liberalism is a vast elaboration—and perhaps to some extent is intended as a defence—of *A Theory of Justice*'s basic strategy and postulate of ignorance of value (i.e. thin theory of the good and 'thick veil of ignorance'[31]), a device whose entire motivation is to ensure: (i) that the Original Position construct will yield principles in line with Rawls's settled political opinions (what he calls the 'acceptable conclusions' which a 'model of practical reason' such as the Original Position must fit on pain of being revised or even abandoned altogether[32]); and (ii) that Rawls will not have to offer a defence of those opinions against the criticism that they ignore or contradict certain truths about human good.

Does *Political Liberalism* offer any further and more satisfactory defence of the legitimacy principle's exclusion of 'non-public' truths and reasons from one's public discussion and one's individual act of 'voting on the most fundamental political questions'?[33] It seems not. No doubt Rawls intends a defence in his remarks about 'reasonable pluralism', the 'ideal of democratic citizenship', and 'civility'. However, all these simply assume what needs to be shown: that it is uncivil and undemocratic to propose to one's fellow citizens theses (on matters of fundamental justice) which one regards as true and established by evidences or reasons *available* to any reasonable

[29] Ibid.; see also ibid. at 62.
[30] See e.g. *NLNR* 108–9; essay III.3 (1973a) and essay III.2 (1987c), sec. II.
[31] See *Political Liberalism*, 24 n. 27.   [32] Ibid. at 96 and n. 8.   [33] Ibid. at 216.

person *willing to consider them* in an open-minded way—notwithstanding that, de facto, very many people do reject them.

Moreover, the legitimacy principle, as stated and understood by Rawls, is itself (I shall argue) illegitimate, uncivil, and unreasonable. It is illegitimate because it censors truthful and reasonable public discourse and—worse—prohibits individual resort to correct principles and criteria of practical judgment, in relation to fundamental political questions, without any coherent, principled reason for the prohibition. It is unreasonable because it restricts public deliberation and individual public action precisely on those matters where it is most important to be correct, that is, where people's fundamental human rights are at stake.

Consider the example which Rawls himself brings forward to illustrate how his legitimacy principle works out in practice—in his remarks about one of the most important of the 'fundamental political questions' currently debated: abortion.[34] Here his legitimacy thesis makes him claim (in effect) that one not only will be mistaken but will moreover be violating one's duties of democratic citizenship if one reasons, for example, in the following way:

> Every human being is entitled to an equal right to life;[35] unborn children, even in the first three months of their life, are human beings (as any medical textbook shows); therefore unborn children are entitled to the protection of the law against being deliberately killed even in the first three months of their life; and so I should vote for a law or constitutional amendment which recognizes that right.

Having asserted (by implication) that anyone who argues in such a way is not only mistaken but also anti-democratic (and having explicitly claimed that such a person subscribes to a doctrine which would be cruel and oppressive even if it allowed exceptions for rape and incest), Rawls adds that any comprehensive doctrine which supports that reasoning 'is to that extent unreasonable'.[36] So he asserts not merely that pro-life arguments on the abortion question are mistaken, but that they could not possibly be grounds for political action such as voting. And he claims to be able to say all this without publicly discussing the comprehensive doctrine(s) he condemns, and without shouldering the responsibility of saying where the error in the reasoning about abortion lies. Instead of joining in the rational debate about abortion, he sidetracks and short-circuits it by simply *declaring* that 'all reasonable people can be expected to agree' that healthy, mature

---

[34] *Ibid.* at 243 n. 32.
[35] Bizarrely, this right is not one of Rawls's 'principles of justice', and so anyone who asserts it (as in numerous Bills of Rights, though not *directly* in the antique United States one) is asserting a comprehensive, not a political, doctrine!
[36] *Ibid.* at 243.

women have the right to kill their child during the first three months of his or her unborn life and probably for longer.[37] So the legitimacy principle has an effect exactly the opposite of what Rawls clearly intended: it generates a kind of incivility of its own—heat instead of light.

Rawls's legitimacy principle is a distorted and unwarranted analogue of a genuine principle of public reason, namely: fundamental political, constitutional, legal questions ought to be settled according to *natural right*, i.e. to principles and norms which are reasonable, using criteria of evidence and judgment that are available to all. One reason why he overlooks this alternative is that in thinking of the tradition, he clearly supposes that liberalism—in the first instance, the comprehensive liberalism of Hume and Kant, and then his own 'political' liberalism—differentiated itself from the tradition by adopting two views: (i) that knowledge of how we are to act is accessible to every person who is 'ordinar[il]y [or: normally] reasonable and conscientious' *rather than* 'only to some, or to a few (the clergy, say)'; and (ii) that the moral order required of us arises 'in some way from human nature itself', say by reason, together with the requirements of our living together in society, *rather than* 'from an external source, say from an order of values in God's intellect'.[38] He seems completely unaware that what I shall call *the tradition* in fact rejected these as false contrasts and so embraced precisely the positions he thinks characteristic of liberalism: moral knowledge is available or accessible to all and arises in some way from human nature and reason and the requirements of social living.

Where the tradition parts company with Rawls is in relation to his 'fact of reasonable pluralism/disagreement'. When Rawls says, 'It is unrealistic—or worse, it arouses mutual suspicion and hostility—to suppose that all our differences are rooted solely in ignorance and perversity, or else in the rivalries for power, status, or economic gain',[39] the tradition of natural law theorizing says, 'Let's distinguish'. There are many reasonable differences which arise from differences of sentiment, of prior commitment, and of

---

[37] *Ibid.*

[38] See *ibid.* at xxvi–xxviii. [Rawls says, xxvii n. 13, that he is here following Schneewind, particularly his 'Natural Law, Skepticism, and the Method of Ethics'; but the remarkable opacity of that article's discussion of the *accessibility* of moral knowledge may be gauged from, e.g., its remarks about Barbeyrac. Having declared (at 290) that Hobbes's appeal to the maxim 'Do not that to others, you would not have done to yourself' is 'opaque' because it 'does not even try to explain why the act is right', and departs little 'from the usual cavalier attitude of natural law theory toward ordinary people', Schneewind says (*ibid.*) that 'Barbeyrac [in 1706] gives us a reason for supposing that God must have made moral knowledge accessible to everyone', namely that 'God has given us the ability to grasp "a vast number of mathematical truths," so he must have made us capable of "knowing, and establishing with the same evidence, the Maxims of Morality...".' But Schneewind does not pause, here or later, to consider whether 'ordinary people', even when reasonably conscientious, are de facto in a position to grasp a vast number of demonstrable—and thus fully *accessible*—mathematical truths.]

[39] *Ibid.* at 58.

belief about likely future outcomes. In such cases, there is no uniquely correct opinion, though there are many incorrect opinions. But in relation to some matters, including at least some matters of basic rights, there are correct moral beliefs, accessible to all (even to those who *in fact* reject them). In relation to such matters, differing opinions can only be rooted in ignorance or some sub-rational influence, and it is mistaken—though this of course needs to be shown, by rational argument—to say that there is more than one 'fully reasonable'[40] or 'perfectly reasonable'[41] belief. If by *'perfectly reasonable' though erroneous belief* Rawls means a belief which is held without subjective moral fault in respect of the forming of it, I would say that that is an important category of de facto beliefs but one which would better be called, not 'perfectly reasonable'—which it quite clearly is not!—but 'inculpably erroneous', blamelessly mistaken, or, in one traditional idiom, 'invincibly ignorant'. Public reasoning should be directed to overcoming the relevant mistakes, and public deliberations should be directed to avoiding them in practice—not pre-emptively surrendering to them.[42]

Of course, a 'liberalism of fear'[43] is sometimes or even quite often warranted. It can often be morally reasonable to refrain from enforcing basic human rights, for fear of provoking a war which one cannot win or which will impact unfairly, as most wars do, on the weakest.

The Rawlsian version of public reason is, as I said, particularly unreasonable because its demand—that moral truths and complicated ('elaborate') factual questions[44] be excluded from public discourse and deliberation—is made *only* in relation to the most important questions of justice, such as whether it is acceptable to kill your unborn child at your choice, or acceptable to base our nation's defence policy on a plan to, under certain conditions, incinerate an enemy's civilian population with the side effect of poisoning half or more of the people of bystander nations. Such matters are apparently to be remitted to hunches or 'judgments' untested

---

[40] *Ibid.*   [41] *Ibid.* at 24 n. 27.

[42] [Again confusing the normative with the empirical (an argument with a prediction), Reiman, 'Abortion, Natural Law, and Liberal Discourse' at 110, says that 'Finnis is sure' that 'some very good arguments will succeed in getting themselves publicly and fully established', and (at 119) that 'Finnis cannot understand why' philosophical disputes such as those about abortion are intractable. These remarks also exemplify, in relation to public reason and natural law, precisely that inattention to opposing arguments that I say is characteristic of defenders of abortion. Like the main theorists of the tradition from Plato through Aristotle and Aquinas to today, I have often explained why, in the non-ideal conditions of human life and character which we should expect to prevail until the end of history, *no one* should anticipate, let alone 'be sure', that good arguments *will* succeed in getting themselves generally—let alone fully—accepted. 'Accessible to all' is in no way a prediction (except, formally, in relation to ideal epistemic conditions), but is an implication of 'can be shown by rational argument': see n. 22 above. Epistemic conditions are not ideal while 'perversity' or 'ignorance' (to use Rawls's terms) remain to any degree at large.]

[43] See *Political Liberalism* at xxvi n. 10.   [44] *Ibid.* at 225.

by public political discourse about matters of principle or fact. That means they are remitted to the status quo established by sheer power of numbers or influence, a status quo—underpinned by abortion on demand and anti-civilian nuclear deterrence—with which Rawls happens, it seems, to be well satisfied 'on balance'.

IV. LEGITIMACY, BIAS, AND THE RIGHTS OF CHILDREN

Still, much remains to be said in favour of the underlying concern which gives both *A Theory of Justice* and *Political Liberalism* an initial plausibility and an appeal which survives the recognition that their central arguments are fallacious. That concern is the concern to avoid *bias*, unfairness between persons, violations of the Golden Rule. In the introduction to the paperback edition of *Political Liberalism*, and his more or less contemporaneous article 'The Idea of Public Reason Revisited', Rawls gives a new prominence and a new formulation to a principle intended to make full sense of the demand that voting and other political determinations be made only by or on the basis of 'public reasons'. This principle is the

> criterion of reciprocity: our exercise of political power is proper only when we sincerely believe that the reasons we offer for our political action may reasonably be accepted by other citizens as a justification of those actions.[45]

It is indeed the *source* of the liberal principle of legitimacy,[46] and thus of the conception of public reason defended by Rawls. The reciprocity criterion's role 'is to specify the nature of the political relation in a constitutional democratic regime as one of civic friendship'.[47] And it is itself the expression, or an immediate entailment, of the 'intrinsic normative and moral ideal' without which 'political liberalism' and Rawls's 'political conception of justice' would fail to count as a moral conception at all (and thus would fail to be available to guide anyone's conscientious deliberations as a voter or other participant in governing). This ideal, Rawls says,

> can be set out in this way. Citizens are reasonable when, viewing one another as free and equal in a system of social cooperation *over generations*, they are prepared to offer one another fair terms of social cooperation (defined by principles and ideals) and they agree to act on those terms, *even at the cost of their own interests in particular situations*, provided that others accept those terms. For these terms to be fair terms, citizens offering them must reasonably think that those citizens to whom such terms are offered might also reasonably accept them.[48]

---

[45] *Ibid.*, xlvi.   [46] *Ibid.*   [47] *Ibid.* at li.   [48] *Ibid.* at xliv (emphases added).

This ideal, with its corresponding normative requirement, seems broadly reasonable. So we can ask how it bears on the situation of children.

Would it be consistent with justice, with civic friendship, with fairness and the criterion of reciprocity to adopt a scheme in which infants and children unwanted by their parents could be reared for the purposes of satisfying the desires of paedophiles by being fed up to the age of sexual desirability in circumstances (including euphoric drugs) such that their eventual fate was entirely concealed from them, and on condition that after a sufficient period of use for sexual services they would be killed painlessly, without warning, while they slept? This is not a question of exegesis of Rawls's or anyone else's texts ('Does "citizen" mean adult citizen?', 'What does "across generations" really mean?', 'Are the parties to the criterion of reciprocity more narrowly defined than the parties to the Original Position?'). The question is one of substance, and the answer to it is clear enough.

Rawls himself seems plainly to accept that infants and children get the benefit of the criterion of reciprocity: 'The fundamental political relation of citizenship... is a relation of citizens within the basic structure of society, *a structure we enter* only *by birth* and exit only by death...'[49] The dealings of adults with infants and children must satisfy the criterion of reciprocity,[50] even when doing so is 'at the cost of their [the adults'] own interests in particular situations'; such dealings cannot be justified by the plea that children are not the equals of adults and *these* children will never enter the circle of free and equal citizens because we will kill them before they do and before they realize what we have done, or will do, to them.

This being so, the question arises why Rawls draws the boundary of justice, fairness, and reciprocity at *birth*. This question does not seek to settle the rights of the mother over and against the unborn child. It is just the question of how it could be rational to think that the child just before birth has no rights (no status in justice, fairness, reciprocity) while

---

[49] *Ibid.* at xlv (emphasis added).
[50] See also, very clearly, *A Theory of Justice*, 509:

[T]he minimal requirements defining moral personality refer to a capacity and not to the realization of it. *A being that has this capacity, whether or not it is yet developed, is to receive the full protection of the principles of justice.* Since *infants and* children are thought to have basic rights (normally exercised on their behalf by parents and guardians), this interpretation... seems necessary to match our considered judgments. Moreover, regarding the potentiality as sufficient accords with the hypothetical nature of the original position, and with the idea that as far as possible the choice of principles should not be influenced by arbitrary contingencies. Therefore it is reasonable to say that those who could take part in the initial agreement, were it not for fortuitous circumstances, are assured equal justice (emphasis added).

Well said.

the child just after birth has the rights of a citizen free and equal to other citizens.⁵¹ Why should the child a week before birth be subject to the uttermost *coercion*⁵² of being destroyed at someone else's 'balancing of values' or 'ordering of values' (if not sheer whim)?

The public reason of the United States, as manifested in the loquacious judgments of its Supreme Court, has after a quarter of a century uttered not a sentence that even appears intended to offer a rational response to that question. The response, rather, is of the form: 'We are in charge; *these* are the human beings (and other entities, such as corporations) we—by our Constitution—have chosen, or now choose, to protect and *those* are not.'‡ Save in its phrasing, the US Supreme Court's neglect of its responsibility to offer public *reasons* is as truculent as that.⁵³ (This refusal has been made possible partly by the position of minority Justices such as Justice Scalia, who for clearly inadequate reasons would leave to the states the fundamental question of who is and who is not entitled to the protection of the US Constitution's guarantees against deprivation of life without due process of law.) The failure of public reason in action is made all the more obvious by the position of the German Constitutional Court, which has repeatedly held—albeit without following through consistently—that the constitutional right to protection of life is enjoyed by the unborn human being from the time of conception.

Rawls says that the outcome of the vote on the abortion question 'is to be seen as reasonable provided all citizens of a reasonably just constitutional regime sincerely vote in accordance with the idea of public reason'.⁵⁴ The decisive votes on this question have been conducted among the fifteen or so Justices involved in *Roe*, *Webster*,⁵⁵ and *Casey*.⁵⁶ Do the pro-abortion votes of these citizens satisfy the requirement of being cast 'sincerely...in

---

⁵¹ As Reiman says (though with his own intent), a decent moral-political theory 'must remain open to the possibility that as-yet-unrecognized forms of unjustified coercion may be discovered and that new rights'—he means legal, recognized rights—'may be needed to defend freedom against them': *Critical Moral Liberalism*, 1.

⁵² [This must be remembered when reading Reiman's response to this essay, when he says 'public reason is...talk *aimed at determining what may or may not be coerced*' and refers to the liberal's 'special allergy to coercion': 'Abortion, Natural Law, and Liberal Discourse' at 110.]

⁵³ The open unreasonableness is encapsulated in the statement by the Court in *Roe v Wade* that 'We need not resolve the difficult question of when life begins', followed by statements and rulings which presuppose and indeed assert that before birth the child's life is merely 'the potentiality of human life': 410 US 113, 159–62 (1973). The same pretence of agnosticism is maintained in *Planned Parenthood v Casey*:

> [Abortion] is an act fraught with consequences for others: for the woman...; for the persons who perform...; for the spouse, family and society which must confront the knowledge that these procedures exist[!], procedures which some deem [!] nothing short of an act of violence against innocent human life; and, depending on one's beliefs, for the life or potential life that is aborted. (505 US 833, 852 (1992).)

⁵⁴ *Political Liberalism*, lvi. ⁵⁵ *Webster v Reproductive Health Services* 492 US 490 (1989).
⁵⁶ *Planned Parenthood v Casey* 505 US 833 (1992).

accordance with the idea of public reason', in Rawls's restrictive sense of that term? I cannot think of any evidence that they were.[57] The anti-abortion arguments they faced were founded squarely on claims about the human and personal nature and status of the unborn, that is, about the absence of any significant difference between unborn and newborn. Those claims, none of them more controversial than the rival claims about the moral rights of privacy or liberty, are not substantially addressed, even for a sentence or two, in any of the pro-abortion judgments in those cases. Addressing them would not have involved moving from public to non-public reason. A doctrine which says (as Rawls and the pro-abortion Justices say) 'children must be treated as equal to adults in basic constitutional rights applicable to their situation from the day of their birth' is no less 'comprehensive' and no more 'public' than one that says 'children must be treated as equal to adults in basic constitutional rights applicable to their situation even before birth'.

By pointing to an argument made by Judith Jarvis Thomson in 1995, Rawls in his recent work[58] tries to give the status 'reasonable' to pro-abortion views which are in fact unreasonable. Thomson's Rawlsian argument runs:

First, restrictive regulation [of abortion] severely constrains women's liberty. Second, severe constraints on liberty may not be imposed in the name of considerations that the constrained are not unreasonable in rejecting. And third, the many women who reject the claim that the fetus has a right to life from the moment of conception are not unreasonable in doing so.[59]

The whole point of this argument, as Thomson makes clear, is to gain its conclusion *without contesting* the central anti-abortion claims that unborn children have a right not to be intentionally or unjustly killed and a right

---

[57] And I heard on the radio a set of remarks in which the speaker, said by the BBC to be Justice Powell, explained that his vote in *Roe v Wade* was cast on the basis of what he felt he would want for his daughter if she were pregnant. This is in line with remarks made by Justice Powell in 1979 in an interview with Harry M. Clor (quoted in Garrow, *Liberty and Sexuality: The Right to Privacy and the Making of* Roe v Wade, 576) which seem utterly indifferent to the demands of the 'criterion' of reciprocity:

The concept of liberty was the underlying principle of the abortion case—the liberty to make certain highly personal decisions that are terribly important to people.... It is difficult to think of a decision that's more personal or more important to a pregnant woman than whether or not she will bear a child.

Like the Court's opinion in *Casey*, which on the point in issue says little more but in many more words, this is simply a diaphanously veiled appeal to power regardless of questions of justice. It is difficult to think of a decision that is less personal, and more important to another person, than the decision to kill that person.

[58] *Political Liberalism*, lvi n. 31; also 'The Idea of Public Reason Revisited' at 798 n. 80.

[59] Thomson, 'Abortion' at 15.

to the equal protection of the laws against homicide.[60] The argument fails to meet its objective. *In the admitted absence of an argument to show that in these precise respects the unborn are in different case from, say, the newly born, the position of the many women who reject the claim that the fetus has a right to life is indeed unreasonable.* The fact that these many women, or some of them, are otherwise reasonable in no way establishes that this position of theirs is reasonable or in accordance with public reason. As Rawls says, 'a comprehensive doctrine is not as such unreasonable because it leads to an unreasonable conclusion in one or even in several cases';[61] so too a person is not disentitled to the description 'a reasonable person' just because she adopts an unreasonable position in one or even several cases (especially cases which so obviously engage her self-interest or other special emotional sources of bias).[62]

Having claimed that a majority decision which authorizes the free killing of the unborn 'is to be seen as reasonable' and 'binding on citizens by the majority principle', even if it is fallacious and erroneous and is thus a denial of basic justice, Rawls goes on to make several claims about anti-abortion citizens (prejudicially called by him 'Catholics'):

[1] [T]hey need not exercise the right of abortion in their own case. [2] They can recognize the right as belonging to legitimate law and therefore [3] do not resist it with force. [4] To do that would be unreasonable: it would mean their attempting to impose their own comprehensive doctrine, which a majority of other citizens who follow public reason do not accept.[63]

None of these four claims is reasonable. Claim [1] reveals the negligence which passes itself off as public reason on Rawls's side of the debate. The anti-abortion citizens are claiming, with some good arguments, that abortion is rather like slave-owning: a radical, basic injustice imposed on people deprived of the protections of citizenship. The response, '*You* free citizens need not exercise the right to [own slaves] [abort your children] in your own case, so you can and must recognize our law as legitimate as it applies to the rest of us', is mere impudence or thoughtlessness.

Claim [2] assumes that 'the majority principle' is binding even when the majority authorize gross injustice, and even when they do so without attempting to show that it is consistent with the principle or criterion of

---

[60] *Ibid.* at 14–15.   [61] *Political Liberalism*, 244 n. 32.

[62] Moreover, the fact that the three-step Thomson–Rawls argument is 'clearly cast in the form of public reason' does not entail that it is reasonable: '[W]hether it is itself reasonable or not...is another matter. As with any form of reasoning in public reason, the reasoning may be fallacious or mistaken', *ibid.* at liv n. 32, in relation to an argument attributed to Cardinal Bernardin. Step (3) of the Thomson argument equivocates on 'are unreasonable'.

[63] *Ibid.* at lvi–lvii; see also Rawls, 'The Idea of Public Reason Revisited' at 787 n. 57, 798–9.

reciprocity. Does anyone believe that Rawls himself accepts this assumption in relation to injustices which engage his sympathies?

Claim [3] switches without warning into the descriptive mode. The interesting question, however, is whether there is *good reason* not to defy the law which penalizes the use of reasonable force to rescue the unborn from their killers. I can think of only one plausible reason to exclude such defiance as a conscientious option for those whose vocations are consistent with such an undertaking: that to attempt forcible rescue would generally, in present conditions, be to launch a civil war. That resultant in itself does not settle the argument. But (as I indicated above, in my remarks about the liberalism of fear) a condition for justly launching war is that one have some prospect of winning it, and that condition is not, in present circumstances, satisfied.

Claim [4] again depends on an arbitrary and unwarranted premise: that those who enforce their view that a *newborn baby* must be treated as equal to adults in basic rights—or those who imprison paedophiles—*are not* imposing their own 'comprehensive doctrine', whereas those who insist that the baby a day before birth is entitled to the same forcible protection *are*. Of course, this sort of selective inattention to the strongly substantive and controversial character of self-styled liberal theories is very characteristic of such theories; we see it, for example, in the claim that 'the right of a woman to control her body' is 'undisputed' (and therefore trumps the disputed right of the unborn child to live) when in reality the alleged right of the woman is manifestly disputed and was never accepted by any state until the Supreme Court overthrew the abortion laws of every state (and indeed it is not a right accepted even by the Supreme Court to this day). This sort of inattention often leads to outright self-contradiction, as when people say that arguments about the use of public force must never appeal to what has intrinsic value, but only to what people subjectively prefer, and then offer to justify this 'principle of subjective preference' by arguing that self-governance is intrinsically valuable and/or is a necessary condition of a good—that is, an intrinsically valuable—life!

V. PRIVATE POWER VERSUS PUBLIC REASON

The public 'public reason' of the United States (and other such nations) presents, as I have said, an extraordinary spectacle: blank refusal to state any reason justifying the dramatic, radical, total difference in the moral and legal status of the baby inside and the baby outside the womb—the same baby on perhaps the same day. The wider 'public reason' which includes the philosophers and others who offer to guide public deliberation on the abortion question presents a different but analogous spectacle. There is an immense literature claiming to justify the right to abortion, that is (we recall), the right to expel the fetus with intent to kill it. But this has two striking features. First, there is in this pro-abortion literature no consensus on the nature of the unborn child, nor on the question of when the conceptus becomes human or a person or otherwise entitled to a right to life, nor on any other major metaphysical or moral question involved. There is no 'overlapping consensus' except in the result: women are to have some opportunity to destroy their unborn children. And second, there is almost complete inattention to the substantial scholarly literature presenting the opposing position,[64] a consensus which denies the abortion right on the basis that the conceptus has the nature and rights of a human person from conception.[65]

The silence of public 'public reason' about the justification for denying to the unborn the basic equality rights acknowledged in the newly born is easy to explain. The prospects for producing such a justification are faint indeed. For any such justification will have to have abandoned the one real basis of human equality and equality rights: namely, the fact that each living human being possesses, *actually and not merely potentially*, the *radical capacity*[66] to reason, laugh, love, repent, and choose *as this unique, personal individual*, a capacity which is not some abstract characteristic of a species, but rather consists in the unique, individual, organic functioning of the organism which comes into existence as a new substance at the conception of that human being and subsists until his or her death whether ninety minutes, ninety days, or ninety years later—a capacity, individuality, and personhood which subsists as real and precious even while its operations come and go with many changing

---

[64] Two good examples: Grisez, *Abortion: The Myths, the Realities, and the Arguments*; Lee, *Abortion and Unborn Human Life*. See also George, 'Public Reason and Political Conflict'.

[65] The asymmetry is far reaching. There are a good many scholars opposing the abortion right who labour through the myriad confused and diverse arguments for abortion (or abortion and infanticide) rights, and publish careful, well-documented critiques. Scholars favouring abortion (or abortion and a right to infanticide) seem for the most part to invent the positions they offer to refute, and to display little or no awareness of the arguments actually advanced by defenders of the unborn.

[66] [Reiman, 'Abortion, Natural Law, and Liberal Discourse' quotes this sentence and then, in making the assertion that my proposition 'is simply false' (115), repeats the statement but omits the key word 'radical'. For the idea of *radical capacity* (with its reference to *radix*, root), see essay III.14 (1995b), secs IV and XI. One can easily begin to understand the notion by reflecting on the coherence of the statement 'I have the capacity to speak Icelandic though I cannot speak it at all'. Here the reference to 'capacity' is to a capacity more basic (radical) than the developed capacity (non-existent in my case) to speak the language here and now. A human zygote which has the necessary genetic primordia for development already has the capacity—radical capacity—not only to develop legs but also to use them for walking. A salmon zygote does not have this radical capacity to walk. In short, an organism's capacity to develop, by autonomous natural growth, a capacity to X is an already actual radical capacity to X. It is not 'distant from' capacity X, let alone too distant; it is precisely capacity X in its earliest form.]

factors such as immaturity, injury, sleep, and senility. Human beings are not just 'values', as Reiman imagines when asking why we do not think the number of people should be maximized; rather, they are persons, each incommunicably, non-fungibly individual in this peculiar, *deep* way, and so entitled, one by one, to be respected.

(Is belief in the reality and value of personhood, understood in the way that I have just summarized, to be called 'religious'? It is rather a belief that results from a close attention to the solidity and depth of this universe and its various constituents, the kind of close attention which is the *cause* of religious beliefs—and also of good science—rather than a mere resultant of them.)

Once one has decided not to base equality rights on the real personhood which is instantiated in the unborn as well as the born, one will be reduced to grounding them on some factor which is not coextensive with membership of the human race and which is lacked by newborns, infants, and some mentally handicapped persons. But drawing the circle around, say, sane adults and non-infant children, on the basis that they have self-awareness and concern for self, will then prove as groundless as drawing it around all and only the born. Reiman's efforts to work with self-awareness and self-concern as the basis for a right to life make this fragility manifest. (I leave to one side his half-hearted effort to show that there is some reason for 'protecting infants' lives' even though no infant—on Reiman's account—has any right to life, deserves to live, or is worthy of our respect.[67]) For if my right to be respected (i.e. to be counted in the reciprocity criterion; not killed; etc.) depends upon my being aware of and concerned to continue my existence, why should I not be killed suddenly and without warning? Reiman responds that 'the loss to an aware individual of the life whose continuation she is counting on, is a loss...that remains a loss, a frustration of an individual's expectations...'.[68] But this will not do. If a sleeping individual is killed without warning, there is at no time any *individual with frustrated expectations*, and at no time any *individual suffering from a loss*. Searching around for an entity which undergoes this loss and frustration, Reiman doubles up the entities in play:

Once a human being has begun to be aware of her life, that life unfolds before a kind of inner audience that has an expectation of its continuation, an affective stake in living on. This expectation persists until the audience shuts down for

[67] Reiman offers to explain why 'we' think it is wrong to kill infants, but has nothing to say which could show the immorality of the attitudes of someone who does not 'love infants' (but only perhaps two or three infants) and thinks it is not wrong to kill infants (at least infants not loved in particular by anybody particular): *Critical Moral Liberalism*, 202–3.

[68] *Ibid.* at 197.

good—even if, before that, the audience dozes off from time to time. We defeat this expectation even if we kill a temporarily sleeping or comatose individual who has begun to be aware of her life.[69]

But this doubling up gets Reiman nowhere. When the sleeping individual is killed without warning, the alleged audience, too, is simultaneously 'shut down for good'. So the plain fact remains that there is never anyone (actor or audience) of whom we can rightly say 'this individual has some defeated expectations'. Reiman is just equivocating[70] on 'defeated expectations'; *when someone has them*, they are a cause or kind of misery and often the resultant subject-matter of injustice. Looking at the expectations, as Reiman invites us to do, we can see that, in the case I am considering, there never are any defeated expectations. First, there are X's *undefeated* expectations, and then, a moment later and forever after, *nothing* in the way of expectations, defeated or undefeated. There is no change *in* X's subjective awareness; as happens with modern anaesthesia, that awareness simply ceases, without any awareness *of* its cessation.[71]

Reiman's entire discussion of the unborn and the early infant is, then, a timely warning that the right to life, respect, justice, and equality loses its intelligibility, and its rational claim on conscientious deliberations and choices, once it is uprooted from the foundations which were everywhere acknowledged as a matter of public reason until the unprincipled will to private power ('subjective preference', 'choice') closed down public reason on the abortion question.

NOTES

† *'Public reason'* in political discourse…(sec. II, beginning). As essay 2 at 58 puts it, 'A sound "natural law" theory has never been other than an appeal to public reasons…'. But the actual phrase 'public reason' has a curious history, which (like Rawls's eccentric usage) might obscure its appropriateness for political philosophy and civil discourse. In 2005e some elements of this history are summarized:

> The term 'public reason' enters English discourse, so far as we can see, on the lips of Satan, at one of the pivotal moments in England's greatest epic poem, *Paradise Lost*. The poet John Milton wrote it, for the most part, while a leading public servant of the 11-year Commonwealth, the regime of the godly, the Puritan and Republican victors in our civil war of 1642–49. Satan, under the black form of a cormorant high in a tree, surveys the harmonious paradise soon to be lost to human beings by his stratagems. His heart, he professes in his soliloquy, 'melts' when he contemplates the endlessly cruel revenge he is about to take on the 'harmless innocence' of our first parents. But he is compelled, he says, to this revenge—a deed that otherwise even he would 'abhor'. Compelled by what? *'Public reason just'*, that is, 'Honour and empire [rulership] with revenge enlarg'd / By conquering this new world'—the human world from 'now' down to

[69] *Ibid.* at 198.
[70] This is not the occasion to deal with the other arguments in his chapter, but I should say that many of them too seem to me to fail by equivocation.
[71] [For Reiman's reply to this paragraph, and my response, see 2000c at 104 J, the paragraph as it stands suffices.]

the world's end. And there his soliloquy ends. The poet's immediate comment is more famous with us: 'So spake the Fiend, and with necessity, / The tyrant's plea, excus'd his devilish deeds.' (Book iv, ll. 380–94)[72]

Public reason thus makes its bow (among us in England) as a primary component in a sophistical mask for motivations one could accurately call private, however widely they may be shared: motives of revenge, will to power, and personal 'honour', all of them passion(s) yoking reason to their service, and by reason masked and glamourized ('rationalized') as reasons. This particular mask, 'public reason', belongs in the same semantic and associational zones as *'raison d'état'*, or (analogously, not identically) as 'People's Democracy' in the usage of the mid- to late twentieth century.

Postscript: Looking harder, we can see that it had entered English public discourse a few years earlier, in Chapter 37 of Hobbes, *Leviathan* (1651), where Hobbes asserts that the question whether it may be taught that miracles occur, e.g. that transubstantiation occurs in the Mass, is one

> [i]n which... *we are not every one to make our own private reason or conscience, but the public reason*, that is the reason of God's supreme lieutenant, *judge*; and indeed we have made him judge already, if we have given him a sovereign power to do all that is necessary for our peace and defence. A private man has always the liberty, because thought is free, to believe or not believe in his heart those acts that have been given out for miracles.... But when it comes to confession of that faith, the private reason must submit to the public; that is to say, to God's lieutenant [that is, Hobbes holds, to the secular sovereign] (emphasis added).

The phrase can also be found, signifying the law of the state, in the sixth paragraph of Rousseau's *Discourse of Political Economy* (1755); and in Thomas Jefferson's First Inaugural Address as President of the United States on 4 March 1801, where 'the diffusion of information and arraignment of all abuses at the bar of the public reason' is the tenth in a list of twelve 'essential principles of our Government'.

‡ *Abortion judgments of the US Supreme Court are failures of public reason*...(text at nn. 52–7). Reiman, 'Abortion, Natural Law, and Liberal Discourse' at 119, says that *Roe v Wade* did not ignore or skirt the issue of why the unborn child does not have rights:

> On the contrary, the Court addressed it directly—*as a question of legal precedent* [his emphasis]— and reviewed the history of the notion of legal personhood in Anglo-American law (and in particular in the Fourteenth Amendment to the US Constitution), and concluded that 'the unborn have never been recognized in the law as persons in the whole sense'.

Reiman's claim is indefensible. There is in *Roe v Wade* no review whatever of the 'history of the notion of legal personhood in Anglo-American law' and no mention even of the Court's own earlier holdings about the meaning of 'person' in the Fourteenth Amendment. There is thus, for example, no mention of the Court's ruling in *Santa Clara County v Southern Pacific Railroad* 118 US 394 (1886), overruling precedent and holding that corporations are persons for the purposes of the Fourteenth Amendment's enshrining of the equal protection of the law, a ruling maintained (over reasoned dissents, never responded to) ever since. Justice Blackmun's judgment in *Roe* offers nothing of what

---

[72]
'...Hell shall unfold,
To entertain you two, her widest gates,
And send forth all her kings; there will be room,
Not like these narrow limits, to receive
Your numerous offspring; if no better place,
Thank him who puts me, loath, to this revenge
On you, who wrong me not, for him who wrong'd.
And, should I at your harmless innocence
Melt, as I do, yet public reason just—
Honour and empire with revenge enlarg'd
By conquering this new world—compels me now
To do what else, though damn'd, I should abhor.'
So spake the Fiend, and with necessity,
The tyrant's plea, excus'd his devilish deeds.

(*Paradise Lost*, iv, 380–94)

Reiman has imagined, save a four-sentence summary of the instances in which the word 'person' is used in the Constitution, followed by only two sentences:

> but in *nearly* [!] all these instances, the use of the word is such that it has application only postnatally. None indicates, *with any assurance*, that it has any possible pre-natal application. (410 US 113, 157 (1973))

(The same can certainly be said of the application of the Constitution's use of 'person'—e.g. in connection with voting, membership of Congress, eligibility to be President, etc.—to corporations.) The 'conclusion' quoted by Reiman is not a rational response to the argument of the state of Texas that the unborn have been recognized in Anglo-American law—and by the constitution of Texas as interpreted by its own courts—as persons for the purposes of *relevant* legal protection, and in any event *should now* be so recognized. Nor is it a response to the question I have posed in the text. Reiman would like us to forget that the most famous American appeal to 'legal precedent' to settle who is and who is not a legal person for the purposes of US law is *Dred Scott v Sandford* 60 US 393 (1857), in which the Court had little difficulty in proving from precedent, to its own satisfaction, that Negroes, even after emancipation, and even if born free, were not citizens of the United States *and could not be made citizens either by a state or by Congress*. So much for the determination of great questions of right and principle and personal status by a review restricted to precedent and uninformed by concern for persons in their pre-legal reality and worth. On the grotesque inaccuracy of the references to the common law, nineteenth-century abortion law, and modern tort and criminal law in the Court's judgment, see (among many others to like effect) Byrne, 'An American Tragedy'; Destro, 'Abortion and the Constitution'; Witherspoon, 'Re-examining *Roe*'; Kader, 'The Law of Tortious Prenatal Death since *Roe v Wade*'; Forsythe, 'Human Cloning and the Constitution'; and 1994d. On the legal precedent, then, the Court's argument in *Roe* is shamefully weak; on the level of *reasons* for discriminating between the born and the unborn it has precisely nothing to say.

17

REASON, PASSIONS, AND FREE SPEECH[*]

In recent obscenity cases, the US Supreme Court has been attempting to define the constitutional meaning of 'speech'.[1] This is not as banal a statement as it may seem, for there are critics, both on and off the Court, who think that the Court's task is to define 'freedom'.

Some advocate boundless freedom in this area. For them, obscenity raises no special problems of definition, and is simply an exercise of speech or press presenting dangers which are remote and disputable, rather than clear and present. From this point of view, exemplified by Justices Black[2] and Douglas,[3] the only relevant distinction is that between 'speech' and 'conduct'. Obscenity is self-evidently a matter of 'expression of ideas' as opposed to 'conduct', and so the only remaining question is rhetorical: Does the Constitution permit a line to be drawn between good ideas and bad?

Other critics, however, have refused to be bluffed by rhetorical questions. They would limit freedom of speech only to the extent required by a careful balancing with other values. This tradition, exemplified by Justices Frankfurter[4] and Harlan,[5] demands a strenuous examination of the concept of obscenity in order to reveal the vice it may connote and the values it may threaten.[6] In each individual case, the courts must balance

---

[*] 1967a.

[1] There is a distinction between 'speech' and 'press', but generally 'expression' encompasses both. Cf. Lockhart and McClure, 'Literature, the Law of Obscenity and the Constitution' at 299 n. 31.

[2] See e.g. *Ginzburg v US* 383 US 463, 476 (1966) (Black J dissenting); *Mishkin v New York* 383 US 502, 517–18 (1966) (Black J dissenting).

[3] See e.g. *Ginzburg* at 491–2 (1966) (Douglas J dissenting); *A Book Named 'John Cleland's Memoirs of a Woman of Pleasure' v Attorney General* 383 US 413, 433 (1966) (Douglas J concurring) [hereinafter cited as *Memoirs v Massachusetts*].

[4] See e.g. *Kingsley Int'l Pictures Corp. v Regents of Univ. of NY* 360 US 684, 691 (1959) (Frankfurter J concurring).

[5] See e.g. *Memoirs v Massachusetts* 383 US 413, 455 (1966) (Harlan J dissenting); *Roth v US* 354 US 476, 496 (1957) (Harlan J concurring).

[6] Cf. Kauper, *Civil Liberties and the Constitution*, 58–60, 111–26; Lockhart and McClure, 'Censorship of Obscenity', 5; Lockhart and McClure, 'Literature, the Law of Obscenity and the Constitution' at 373–87.

the requirements of free speech against the evils which American society believes will flow from certain expressions of ideas.[7]

Both these schools have tended unreflectingly to tie the problem of obscenity to traditional doctrines developed in the more general context of free speech, for both fallaciously assume that obscenity involves the expression of ideas. Both schools thus fail to discern the core problem of defining 'speech', or to appreciate the bedrock concept which underlies the prevailing attempts by the Court to solve this problem.[8] This concept, which stands in sharp contrast to the two traditional perspectives just outlined, is that *obscene utterances 'are no essential part of any exposition of ideas'*.[9]

The aim of this essay is to sketch the intellectual basis of this newer perspective, to amplify its background, and to indicate the way in which it has shaped the substantive constitutional law on obscenity.

I

Obscenity involves the expression of 'ideas', as that term is commonly used and understood. However, for Brennan J, there are some communications which have 'saving intellectual content'[10] and others, including obscenity, which involve neither the exposition nor advocacy of ideas.[11] Thus, he describes the reader of obscenity as looking 'for titillation, not for saving intellectual content'.[12] This contrast, much relied upon by Brennan J in the obscenity cases, corresponds to a distinction between two often competing aspects of the human mind: the intellect or reason and the emotions or passions. Since Brennan J would agree with a characterization of protected first amendment 'speech' as 'the communication of information or opinion',[13] 'the exposition of ideas'[14] or, in general, the intellectual component in the psychology of communication, and since he characterizes obscenity as pertaining to the realm of emotion and passion, it follows that for him

---

[7] See e.g. *Kingsley v Regents* at 708 (1959) (Harlan J concurring); *ibid.* at 694–7 (Frankfurter J concurring).

[8] The problem of defining 'speech' to exclude obscenity is briefly noted in Cairns, Paul, and Wishner, 'Sex Censorship' at 1012–13. Cf. Murphy, *Censorship: Government and Obscenity*, 120–9. In both sources, however, the constitutional problem is muddled with the problem of why obscenity should or should not be proscribed. See also Slough and McAnany, 'Obscenity and Constitutional Freedom' at 347–8, 455–6, 476; Note, 'Obscenity Prosecution' at 1084–6.

[9] *Chaplinsky v New Hampshire* 315 US 568, 572 (1942), quoted with emphasis in *Roth v US* 354 US 476, 485 (1957).

[10] *Ginzburg v US* 383 US 463, 470 (1966). See also n. 37 below.

[11] *Roth* at 484–5 (1957); cf. *Jacobellis v Ohio* 378 US 184, 191 (1964).

[12] *Ginzburg* at 479 (1966).   [13] *Cantwell v Connecticut* 310 US 296, 310 (1940) (Roberts J).

[14] *Beauharnais v Illinois* 343 US 250, 257 (1952) (Frankfurter J).

obscenity is outside the protection of that amendment.[15] This contrast between reason and the passions is the distinctively formative concept in the emerging constitutional law of obscenity. What is notable and frequently overlooked about *Roth*[16] is its abandonment[17] of the notion, formulated in English and earlier American law, that obscenity should be constitutionally defined in terms of the tendency to 'deprave and corrupt'.[18] Although a shift away from the 'deprave and corrupt' formula had been evident in earlier decisions of federal courts,[19] *Roth* completed the replacement of the ambiguous notion of tendency to sexual corruption (which had been accepted even by the Supreme Court[20]) with the relatively less ambiguous notion of 'appealing to prurient interest'.[21] 'Corruption' provided an ambiguous standard because it straddled the realms of ideas and passions. Hence, if the first amendment was to protect all expositions of ideas, 'corruption' had to be replaced by a formula which unambiguously excluded passions, emotions, and desires. Such was the task and achievement of *Roth*.

Some modern commentators have noted that obscenity may connote not only offensiveness and stimulation, but also an ideological element—that is, ideas capable of undermining the community's sexual philosophy and values.[22] Commentators rarely recognize, however, that this potentially confusing duality is linked to the ambiguity of the 'deprave and corrupt' formula as formerly used by English and American courts.[23] The trial in London, in 1877, of Charles Bradlaugh and Annie Besant for obscene libel illustrates that ambiguity.[24] The trial was conducted by Lord Chief Justice Cockburn, the author of the so-called *Hicklin* test. In his remarks to the jury, the judge offered four alternative theories on which the defendants, who had distributed a book about contraception, could be found guilty of

---

[15] A genealogy of this syllogism would include *Cantwell* (1940); *Chaplinsky* (1942); *Dennis v US* 341 US 494 (1951); *Beauharnais* (1952); *Joseph Burstyn, Inc. v Wilson* 343 US 495 (1952).
[16] 354 US 476 (1957).   [17] *Ibid.* at 489.
[18] The 'deprave and corrupt' test stems from *R v Hicklin* (1868) LR 3 QB 360, 371. For the reception of *Hicklin* into American law, see *US v Bennett* 24 F Cas 1093, 1104 (No. 14,571) (CCSDNY 1879); *US v Kennerley* 209 F 119, 120 (SDNY 1913) (Learned Hand J); Slough and McAnany, 'Obscenity and Constitutional Freedom' at 285–92.
[19] See e.g. *US v Dennett* 39 F 2d 564, 569 (2d Cir. 1930); *US v One Book Called 'Ulysses'* 5 F Supp 182 (SDNY 1933), aff'd, 72 F 2d 705 (2d Cir. 1934); Lockhart and McClure, 'Literature, the Law of Obscenity and the Constitution' at 327–33.
[20] See e.g. *Rosen v US* 161 US 29, 43 (1896). But cf. *Dunlop v US* 165 US 486, 500 (1896).
[21] *Roth v US* 354 US 476, 487 (1957).
[22] Chafee, *Government and Mass Communication*, 210–12; St John-Stevas, *Obscenity and the Law*, 126. Also see the discussions of 'thematic' or 'ideological' obscenity in Kalven, 'The Metaphysics of the Law of Obscenity' at 3–4, 28–34; Lockhart and McClure, 'Literature, the Law of Obscenity and the Constitution' at 99.
[23] The ambiguity here discussed is not the ambiguity (as between thought and action) detected in the *Hicklin* test by Lockhart and McClure, *ibid.* at 332–3.
[24] Bradlaugh and Besant, *The Queen v Charles Bradlaugh and Annie Besant* (a verbatim report). This case is discussed in St John-Stevas, *Obscenity and the Law*, 70–4.

depraving and corrupting: (i) if the defendants had a purpose of exciting libidinous thoughts, intending 'to give to persons who take pleasure in that sort of thing the impure gratification which the contemplation of such thoughts is calculated to give';[25] (ii) if the book in fact contained details inconsistent with decency and calculated to enkindle the passions and desires of lust and excite libidinous thoughts;[26] (iii) if the book had the effect, even if unintended, of corrupting the morals of the unmarried, by suggesting means of escaping a salutary restraint on their sexual conduct;[27] or (iv) if the book recommended practices of contraception that were contrary to the sound morals that ought to prevail within marriage.[28] On the fourth theory, the jury was instructed that a man who recommends an immoral course of proceeding in an open publication is guilty, and was warned:

You must decide... with a due regard and reference to the law, and with an honest and determined desire to maintain the morals of mankind. But, on the other hand, you must carefully consider what is due to public discussion, and with an anxious desire not, from any prejudiced view of this subject, to stifle what may be a subject of legitimate inquiry.[29]

The third and fourth theories of guilt bestow on the English jury a controlling jurisdiction over the marketplace of ideas, limited only by the jury's self-restraint. It is quite clear that, questions of incitement and imminency of illegal action aside, the analysis just quoted cannot be applied in the United States once the implications of the first amendment are firmly grasped. For in America 'even ideas hateful to the prevailing climate of opinion'[30] are constitutionally protected.

So the concept of corruption, tainted as it is with a political theory which America has abandoned, has had to be replaced by a concept embodying only the first and second of Lord Chief Justice Cockburn's theories; the result is to preserve the historical notion of obscenity,[31] while narrowing the definition of obscenity to constitutionally acceptable limits.[32] The test

[25] Bradlaugh and Besant, *The Queen v Bradlaugh*, 261.   [26] *Ibid*. at 258.
[27] *Ibid*. at 266.   [28] *Ibid*. at 263.   [29] *Ibid*. at 265.
[30] *Roth v US* 354 US 476, 484 (1957).
[31] The idea of 'prurient desires' makes its first appearance in *The Queen v Bradlaugh* at 270, 'prurient' being used also at 15, 29, 73, 145, 230, 247, 252, 259, and 262.
[32] Of course, it is true that directions on obscenity have almost always included the notion of suggesting impure and libidinous thoughts or something similar. But, as in *Bradlaugh*, this notion was always linked with, and liable to be affected by, the intrinsic ambiguity of the concept of depraving and corrupting. It was often believed that to preach against accepted moral and sexual ideas might *ipso facto* arouse lewd thoughts. Cf. *Burton v US* 142 F 57, 63 (8th Cir. 1906). That is why, in *Bradlaugh*, Cockburn LCJ, without concern, could slip from the test of 'tending to suggest unchaste and unclean thoughts, and therefore calculated to lead to immorality', to the test of 'tending to influence the passions, *or* recommending some course of conduct inconsistent with public morals'. *The Queen v Bradlaugh*, 15, 17 (emphasis added). Cf. *US v Harmon* 45 F 414 (CCD Kan. 1891); *US v Clarke*

currently adhered to is Judge Woolsey's test of tendency 'to stir the sex impulses or to lead to sexually impure and lustful thoughts',[33] reworked into the *Roth* test of 'appealing to prurient interest'.[34]

Thus, when Brennan J talks of 'expression of ideas', it is in a far more limited sense than that conveyed by ordinary usage. The Brennan theory of free speech is, indeed, as Professor Kalven said,[35] a two-level theory; one of these levels, moreover, is held to have social utility, and the other not.[36] But, obscenity is regarded by Brennan J as devoid of relevant or 'redeeming'[37] social utility precisely because it pertains, not to the realm of ideas, reason, intellectual content, and truth-seeking, but to the realm of passion, desires, cravings, and titillation. As such, obscenity belongs

---

38 F 732, 733–4 (CCED Mo. 1889); *People v Wendling* 258 NY 451, 180 NE 169 (1932). Sometimes the reference to lustful desires drops out altogether: *People v Dial Press, Inc.* 182 Misc 416, 417, 48 NYS 2d 480, 481 (Magis. Ct. 1944). Also see the cases cited by Lockhart and McClure, 'Literature, the Law of Obscenity and the Constitution' at 334 n. 68. As the authors there remark, 'even though courts have not often mentioned ideological obscenity as a basis of their decisions, there can be no doubt that it has exerted a powerful influence on the law of obscene literature': *ibid.* at 334. *Commonwealth v Allison* 227 Mass 57, 116 NE 265 (1917), is similar to *Bradlaugh*, not only in its facts and result, but also in its logic and conceptual structure.

[33] *US v One Book Called 'Ulysses'* 5 F Supp 182, 184 (SDNY 1933).

[34] 354 US at 487. Compare the reasons advanced in *Roth* for excluding obscenity from the first amendment, at 484–5, with those advanced in *Ex parte Jackson* 96 US (6 Otto) 727 (1878):

> In excluding various articles from the mail, the object of Congress has not been to interfere with freedom of the press,... but to refuse its facilities for the distribution of matter deemed *injurious to the public morals*. (*Ibid.* at 736 (emphasis added).)

This necessary evolution in legal analysis is obscured, if not denied, by Lockhart and McClure, when they imply that the *Roth* test includes the 'deprave and corrupt' test, Lockhart and McClure, 'Censorship of Obscenity' at 58, and by Harlan J in *Manual Enterprises, Inc. v Day* 370 US 478, 482–5 (1962). Harlan J's purpose in equating 'tendency to deprave' with 'prurient appeal', as equally an '"effect" element' in obscenity, *ibid.* at 484, was simply to facilitate the *tour de force* by which he derived from *Roth* both that 'effect element' and the 'concept of patent offensiveness'. Thus, Harlan J states that:

> The Court there [in *Roth*] both rejected the 'isolated excerpt' and 'particularly susceptible persons' tests of the *Hicklin* case, 354 U.S., at 488–489, and was at pains to point out that not all portrayals of sex could be reached by obscenity laws but only those treating that subject 'in a manner appealing to prurient interest' 354 U.S., at 487. That, of course, was but a compendious way of embracing in the obscenity standard *both* the concept of patent offensiveness...and the element of the likely corruptive effect....

Ibid. at 487. This analysis in terms of 'effects', which obscures the differences of remoteness and causality among arousing lustful thoughts, changing moral ideas, and evoking action, probably derives from Lockhart and McClure, 'Literature, the Law of Obscenity and the Constitution' at 329.

[35] Kalven, 'Metaphysics of the Law of Obscenity' at 10–16.

[36] *Ibid.* Kalven's emphasis can be misleading. This is true despite the emphasis on 'social utility' in Brennan, 'The Supreme Court and the Meiklejohn Interpretation of the First Amendment'. The question that must always be pressed is *why* obscenity is held by the Court to be without *redeeming* social merit or value, bearing in mind that the Court is not considering whether or why obscenity should be legislatively proscribed. Failure to put this question apparently derails the argument in Kalven, 'The New York Times Case: A Note on "The Central Meaning of the First Amendment"'. See n. 101 below.

[37] *Roth v US* 354 US 476, 484 (1957). Notice how the *Roth* phrase, 'redeeming social importance' becomes 'saving intellectual content' in *Ginzburg v US* 383 US 463, 470 (1966).

to a realm outside first amendment protection.[38] The two constitutional levels of speech, in effect, are defined in terms of two realms of the human mind.

II

It might be said, quite truthfully, that the Supreme Court is not bound to subscribe to any particular theory of psychology; one might go on to assert that the alleged two realms or aspects of the human mind are cognizable only within the confines of an outmoded faculty psychology. It is not our present purpose to defend the Court's stance, nor to establish that it is constitutionally or philosophically necessary, nor even to show that it would be viable in the light of a full understanding of personality. Our aim is simply to emphasize the vital cultural sources of the prevailing view, and to suggest that its foundations are not to be overturned lightly.

Empirical psychology could abandon the distinction between intellect and emotions without the distinction being thereby invalidated either for common sense or for the philosophy of human nature. The empirical psychologist, by the procedures of experimental science, explores various laws and recurring operations of the human psyche; and the formulation of these laws and schemes of recurrence may not require use of terms such as 'intelligence', 'reason', 'emotion', or 'passions'. Both common sense and philosophy, however, are likely to insist that, if the psychologist's own statement of his results is intelligent and reasonable, it is not merely a product of psychic laws and operations, and still less a product of his emotions. By this insistence, common sense and philosophy promote a more comprehensive analysis of human nature, such as Freud proposed when he stated that, although 'purely reasonable motives can effect little against passionate impulses' and 'emotional forces', nevertheless 'we have no other means of controlling our instinctual nature but our intelligence'.[39]

The distinction was emphasized by Plato, who likened man's mind to a charioteer (reason) controlling the horses of passions and desires, to a world at war with itself, and to a puppet drawn by the strings of reason and passion.[40] Aristotle reported that it was the 'reputable common opinion' of his own time that weak-willed men act as a result of passion,

---

[38] It is ironic that the theory that 'such utterances are no essential part of any expression of ideas' originated in Chafee, *Free Speech in the US*, 150 (1941), and was repeated by Frankfurter J in *Beauharnais v Illinois* 343 US 250, 257 (1952), for both Professor Chafee and Frankfurter J were radically opposed to absolutism in this area, and both espoused a balancing-of-interests doctrine. See e.g. Chafee, 'Meiklejohn's *Free Speech*' at 894 (1949); *Dennis v US* 341 US 494, 524–5 (1951) (Frankfurter J concurring).

[39] Freud, *The Future of an Illusion*, 42, 47, 52.   [40] *Phaedrus* 246a; *Laws* I 644d–45c.

whereas continent and virtuous men follow their reason, rather than their appetites.[41] No doubt this remains a general opinion; our culture has been formed not only by the Greeks but also by the Christian awareness that 'flesh lusteth against the spirit',[42] and that 'the spirit indeed is willing but the flesh is weak'.[43]

Still, an appeal to such a philosophy is likely to occasion the remark that the alleged distinction between reason and emotion is nothing but a naïve and incoherent dualism, quite unfitted to support reasoned legal distinctions. This criticism, however, is too facile. Philosophy has seen many attempts to explicate the perceived distinction between aspects of the mind, and no doubt some can be convicted of dualist incoherence. But in relying on the distinction, the Justices of the Court would not commit themselves to any particular philosophical explication of it.

Now there is another reputable philosophical tradition which believes that: 'Reason is, and ought only to be, the slave of the passions, and can never pretend to any other office than to serve and obey them.'[44] This formulation is extreme, but David Hume's radical softening of the contrast between intellect and emotion has profoundly influenced modern thought. Yet even Hume retains the contrasted notions of reason and passion, though his explanation of the terms and their interrelations might, if adopted, make the two-level theory of speech less attractive (although a Justice, as a private philosopher, might be inclined to ask how Hume's own cool and penetrating intelligence can be reconciled with an account of human nature in which there is such scant place for intelligence and pure reasonableness).

James Madison, who wrote his *Federalist* papers with Hume's political writings beside him,[45] shared with Hume that wholly typical eighteenth-century outlook which saw human life in terms of a struggle between reason and the passions. But, unlike Hume, Madison stood in the classical tradition, which expressly exalted reason above the passions. Every reader of *The Federalist* will recall the central importance, in Madison's theory of republicanism, of control of the passions by reason: '[I]t is the reason, alone,

---

[41] *NE* VII.1: 1145b1–20. Aristotle elaborated a complete philosophical psychology of the intellect in his *De Anima*, and of the passions in his *Rhetoric*. The Aristotelian theory of virtues is essentially a theory of the harmonious interaction of the rational and sensitively appetitive principles in a human person's make-up. It is worth noting, incidentally, that Aristotle and his followers consider that defects in reasonableness, such as imprudence, precipitateness, thoughtlessness, and inconstancy, derive from the sensitive appetite for pleasure, and (some add) 'above all for sexual pleasure, which quite absorbs the mind and entices it to sensible delights': *ST* II–II q.53 a.6; cf. *NE* VII.10: 1152b17.

[42] Galatians 5: 17. See also Romans 7.   [43] Matthew 26: 41.

[44] Hume, *Treatise of Human Nature*, vol. 2, pt. 3, §2.

[45] See Adair, 'That Politics May be Reduced to a Science' at 358 n. 17.

of the public, that ought to control and regulate the government. The passions ought to be controlled and regulated by the government.'[46]

Madison realized, moreover, that the evils of faction derive from passion; faction, by definition, arises from 'some common impulse of passion'.[47] Yet, although '[l]iberty is to faction, what air is to fire, an aliment, without which it instantly expires',[48] liberty in Madison's view 'is essential to political life'.[49] Clearly, liberty cannot be essential for the sake of allowing passions and faction their sway. Rather, that liberty which is so essential is liberty of *opinion*, not *passions*, even if regrettably, 'the former will be objects to which the latter will attach themselves'.[50]

When men exercise their reason coolly and freely on a variety of distinct questions, they inevitably fall into different opinions on some of them. When they are governed by a common passion, their opinions, if they are so to be called, will be the same.[51]

Hence, Madison valued freedom of speech because it supplied the community with independent (rational) critics of the government.[52]

It is thus possible to draw a constitutional theorem from the basic thought of *The Federalist*: to the extent that expressions derive from the passion end of the reason-passion continuum, the rationale for their freedom disappears. Translated into a twentieth-century context, this is the basis of the two-level theory in *Chaplinsky v New Hampshire*[53] and *Roth*.

Although the eighteenth-century distinction between reason and passion has overtones to which we are now more or less deaf, a similar distinction has preserved a central place in our thought. For example, standard modern textbooks of philosophy contain discussions of the emotive as opposed to the cognitive meaning or force of words, or of cognitivist as opposed to emotivist theories of ethics. The average modern critic of censorship is apt to remark that its supporters are guided by feeling, not reason. There is no point in multiplying examples, for they lie to hand in every field of modern thought.

In short, the two-level theory of speech and of the mind cannot be convicted of provincialism. While it is not the place of a judge to espouse controversial philosophical theories as such, he is entitled, and indeed required, to adopt some viewpoint on human nature by which to orientate

---

[46] *The Federalist*, No. 49 at 351 (Wright ed.) (Madison).
[47] *The Federalist*, No. 10 at 130 (Madison).   [48] *Ibid*.   [49] *Ibid*.   [50] *Ibid*.
[51] *The Federalist*, No. 50 at 353 (Madison).
[52] Cahn, 'The Firstness of the First Amendment' at 476. See also *Roth v US* 354 US 476, 484 (1957). 'The protection given speech and press was fashioned to assure unfettered interchange of ideas for the bringing about of political and social changes desired by the people.
[53] 315 US 568 (1942).

his reasoning. He is not obliged to desist on the plea that his viewpoint may include controverted questions.

III

The Supreme Court's opinion in *Joseph Burstyn v Wilson*,[54] although it deals directly with problems of sacrilege rather than obscenity, and Stewart J's opinion in *Kingsley International Pictures v Regents*[55] share with *Roth* a foundation in the two-level conceptual structure.

Burstyn offered to answer the question 'whether motion pictures are within the ambit of protection which the First Amendment... secures to any form of "speech" or the "the press"'.[56] The major premise of the answer to this significantly worded question was

that motion pictures are a significant medium for the communication of ideas. They may affect public attitudes and behavior in a variety of ways, ranging from direct espousal of a political or social doctrine to the subtle shaping of thought which characterizes all artistic expression.[57]

In *Kingsley* the Court conceded that the film in question presented adultery as a desirable or proper pattern of behaviour, and also accepted that the film did not constitute an incitement to illegal action. The Court then determined that:

[w]hat New York has done, therefore, is to prevent the exhibition of a motion picture because that picture advocates an idea—that adultery under certain circumstances may be proper behavior. Yet the First Amendment's basic guarantee is of freedom to advocate ideas.... Its guarantee is not confined to the expression of ideas that are conventional or shared by a majority. It protects advocacy of the opinion that adultery may sometimes be proper...And in the realm of ideas it protects expression which is eloquent no less than that which is unconvincing.[58]

But this exposition of the two-level theory of speech raises further questions: Is art constitutionally protected *only* because it advocates ideas?[59] Would not such a theory be radically untrue to the nature of art? Would it not make nonsense of the Court's recognition of the redeeming value of art?

---

[54] 343 US 495 (1952).   [55] 360 US 684 (1959).   [56] 343 US at 501.   [57] *Ibid.*

[58] 360 US at 688–9. At a later date, Stewart J attempted to amplify his special notion of 'hardcore pornography', as including material which 'cannot conceivably be characterized as embodying communication of ideas or artistic values inviolate under the First Amendment': *Ginzburg v US* 383 US 463, 499 n. 3 (1966) (quoting from Brief of Solicitor General).

[59] See at nn. 104–8 below. The question is fairly raised in Kalven, 'The Metaphysics of the Law of Obscenity' at 15–16, and given a simplistic solution in Note, 39 NYUL Rev 1063, 1084–5 (1964), and in Note, 34 U Chi L Rev 367, 383 (1967). Semonche, 'Definitional and Contextual Obscenity' at 1186–7 asks: 'Is the Court saying that the life of the intellect is more worthy of protection than the life of the imagination?'.

Indeed, would it not amount to the constitutional canonization of sheer philistinism?

Aesthetics contains a welter of conflicting doctrines, but there is universal agreement that artistic work does not derive its *artistic* value from any 'message' which it may happen to convey and which could be presented in the form of ordinary discursive thinking. Aesthetic attention is not looking at something in order to *find out about* something. There is universal agreement, too, that art in all its forms neither derives from, nor appeals to, pure reason alone or even primarily. The stock-in-trade of reason is conceptions, definitions, reasons, judgments, doctrines, formulae, arguments, discourse. But none of these constitute the substance of artistic work or aesthetic experience as such; hence, none of them can constitute the redeeming value of art as art (though it would be absurd to say that they have no place in artistic production or appreciation; literature is art, and criticism thrives). In the foregoing sections of this essay, we spoke of another realm, that of emotions and passions. We did not distinguish, within this realm, between sensation, feelings, experience, imagination, emotion. Be that as it may, there is universal agreement that this other realm, however it is to be characterized, is vitally engaged in all artistic work and appreciation. If this is true, what becomes of the constitutional theorem adduced to outlaw obscenity from the protection of the first amendment?

It is to that question that the present section is addressed. The answer proposed is not, perhaps, one that would gain the sort of universal assent mentioned in the foregoing paragraph. But it occupies a central place in the varied doctrines of aesthetics, and commands support, in the main, from widely ranging philosophical traditions. It does not diverge from the commonsense view of the matter, and it is capable of explaining the status accorded to art in our culture and in the theory of the Supreme Court.

By 'art', in this account,[60] is meant the 'creation of forms symbolic of human feeling'.[61] A symbol is a sensuous object which by virtue of its highly articulated structure can express the forms of vital experience— feeling, life, motion, and emotion—which purely intellectual discourse cannot convey. The contrast, noted above, between rational discourse and art is so marked that superficial thinkers are tempted to suppose that the function of art is to stimulate feelings.[62] But an artist is not a manipulator who, having studied the psychology of his audience, allows his findings to

---

[60] This account is primarily based on the ideas and terminology of Langer, *Feeling and Form*. It also draws on other traditions, such as the 'Oxford' linguistic-philosophy school and neo-Thomism, as indicated in following notes.
[61] *Ibid.*, 40.   [62] *Ibid.*, 18.

guide his work; he is not a cook selecting the recipes that will appeal to the palate.[63] Aesthetic attention is not to be equated with the exploitation of gratifying sensory stimulants. What makes art art is not that it stimulates feelings, which any family picture album can do,[64] but that it expresses them symbolically. To be more precise, art expresses *ideas* of feeling,[65] and it does this by embodying these ideas in the more or less conventional symbolic forms[66] of music, painting, sculpture, architecture, poetry, drama, and prose.

Just as an actor does not vent his own emotions, but conceives and enacts the emotions of the character being played,[67] so the creative artist is not so much venting his own emotions, as imagining and conceiving emotions and feelings in such fashion that his understanding of them can be communicated through the symbolic form of his chosen art.[68] Art, then, gives to those who attend to it aesthetically, an insight into the life of feeling, vitality, and emotion.[69] But it communicates the insight not by discourse, reasoning, or judgments, not by saying anything about the nature of feeling, but by showing it in symbolic form.[70] This is true even of the symbolic forms of the literary arts that use propositional discourse as their material.[71] '[T]he emotion in the work is the thought in the work';[72] 'the sensuous quality is in the service of its vital import'.[73]

---

[63] Ibid., 107. See also Strawson, 'Aesthetic Appraisal and Works of Art' at 12:

...an aesthetic interest in an individual is not any kind of practical interest, not an interest in anything it can or should do, or that we can do with it, not even an interest in specific responses (say, excitement or stupefaction) which it will produce in us. (If it were this sort of interest, there could indeed be general rules and recipes.)

[64] See Berger, *The Language of Art*, 32.

[65] Langer, *Feeling and Form*, 59. See also Berger, *The Language of Art*, 54: 'Instead of trying to define *the* truth as an idea does, form seeks to convey the feeling, the *sensation* of truth. By its means truth ceases to be an abstract notion and becomes an experience.' Berger's terminology differs from Langer's, but the thought is the same.

[66] See Langer, *Feeling and Form*, 280.   [67] Ibid., 323.   [68] Ibid., 28.

[69] Ibid., 129. See also Maritain, *Art and Scholasticism*, 163: '[i]n the perception of the beautiful the intellect is, *through the means of the sensible intuition itself*, placed in the presence of a radiant intelligibility...'.

[70] Langer, 227, 393. Consider Maritain, *Art and Scholasticism*, 164:

If it [the intellect] turns away from sense to abstract and reason, it turns away from its joy and loses contact with this radiance.

To understand this, let us recall that it is intellect and sense as forming but one, or, if one may so speak, the *intellegentiated sense*, which gives rise in the heart to aesthetic joy.

See also Kant, *Analytic of the Beautiful*, §15.

[71] Cf. Miller, 'Obscenity and the Law of Reflection' at 582:

...painters, however unapproachable their work may be, are seldom subject to the same meddling interference as writers. Language, because it also serves as a means of communication, tends to bring about weird obfuscations.

[72] Langer, 82

[73] Ibid., 59. See also Kaplan, 'Obscenity as an Aesthetic Category' at 548.

Artistic creation and appreciation, then, operate between the two main levels of the mind. Art forces a modification of the two-aspects theory of the mind,[74] since the peculiar triumph of art is to weld these levels of experience in a unique way that gives deep emotional and intellectual satisfaction.[75] In artistic experience, sentience is liberated from the drag of biological relevance, while intelligence is liberated from the constraints of discursive reasoning.[76]

This is why aestheticians of every school have insisted on the requirement of detachment, 'contemplation', 'aesthetic' attitude or attention, or objectivity.[77] It is the basis for the aesthetic psychologist Edward Bullough's famous theory of the need for 'psychical distance' between the work and its public (including the artist).[78]

Professor Bullough believed this distance is obtained by 'separating the object and its appeal from one's self, by putting it out of gear with practical needs and ends'.[79] It does not imply a purely intellectual or impersonal relation between man and work, but a peculiar relation 'filtered' of the 'practical, concrete nature of its appeal'.[80] The ideal in both creation and appreciation is the *'utmost decrease of Distance without its disappearance.'*[81]

The ability to maintain this distance varies.[82] Artists can distance even the most personal affections sufficiently to make them aesthetically appreciable, at least to themselves. For the average person, however,

---

[74] Such a modification is attempted in Jenkins, 'The Human Function of Art'. He argues that the three relevant aspects of the psyche are the 'affective', 'aesthetic', and 'cognitive'.

[75] Langer, 397.   [76] See Lonergan, *Insight*, 185.

[77] Langer, 166–7:

> Of course, artistic works affect people otherwise than as art, just as pictures activate almost every one's imagination, but only clear and intuitive minds really understand the vital import, while the average person reacts to the things depicted, and turns away if he can find nothing to promote his discursive thoughts or stimulate his actual emotions.

[78] *Ibid.*, 318; Bullough, *Aesthetics*, 93–130. On the vital relevance of 'distance' to aesthetic experience, and its incompatibility with obscenity or pornography, see Kaplan, 'Obscenity as an Aesthetic Category' at 548:

> Only when we hold the work of art at arm's length is it artistic at all. The work brings emotions to mind or presents them for contemplation. When they are actually felt, we have overstepped the bounds of art.

See also Gardiner, 'Moral Principles Towards a Definition of the Obscene' at 563. The concept of distance makes a Supreme Court appearance in Brennan J's footnote quotation from a dissenting opinion in the lower court, in *Memoirs v Massachusetts* 383 US 413, 415 n. 2 (1966).

[79] Bullough, *Aesthetics*, 96.

[80] *Ibid.*, 97. See also Langer, 49:

> Schiller was the first thinker who saw what really makes 'Schein,' or semblance, important for art: the fact that it liberates perception—and with it, the power of conception—from all practical purposes, and lets the mind dwell on the sheer appearance of things.

[81] Bullough, *Aesthetics*, 100.

[82] This, and what follows, is the most solid basis for the concept of 'variable obscenity'. Arguments for the concept more usually have been based on a balancing-of-interests analysis which, as we have argued, is not the bedrock of the present law. See Gerber, 'A Suggested Solution to the Riddle of Obscenity' at 847–56; Lockhart and McClure, 'Censorship of Obscenity' at 68–88 (1960).

'a limit does exist which marks the minimum at which his appreciation can maintain itself in the aesthetic field',[83] and as this limit varies from person to person, so it varies from time to time, from subject-matter to subject-matter and from culture to culture.[84] In general,

> explicit references to organic affections, to the material existence of the body, especially to sexual matters, lie normally below the Distance-limit, and can be touched upon by Art only with special precautions.[85]

Professor Bullough and his adherents were not concerned with discussing obscenity and pornography, and still less with condemning them. But within their conceptual scheme it is easy to characterize the pornographer as one calculating to avoid all the 'special precautions' with which art must handle certain topics, if the psychical distance necessary for aesthetic appreciation is to be maintained. Some ages and cultures require fewer precautions than others; but whichever are required at any given time and place, the pornographer is the man who sets out to defy them.[86]

The techniques by which the pornographer deliberately destroys the aesthetic attitude include the attribution of male psychology to the female, the arousing of identification with, and the compelling of envy for, the fictional characters in their sexual opportunities and exploits,[87] and many other narrative and descriptive devices which may profitably be analysed.[88] The designed effect of these techniques is always the same—the replacement of aesthetic attention to the material with an attitude in which the practical concerns of the reader or viewer (in this case, a concern to achieve the emotionally aroused states which he desires for himself) intrude upon and suppress an understanding contemplation of the created symbol.[89]

---

[83] Bullough, *Aesthetics*, 101; cf. *Commonwealth v Buckley* 200 Mass 346, 86 NE 910 (1909).

[84] Langer, 319. Distance also varies from context to context. Hence, the concept of variable obscenity, which seems to have been adopted in *Ginzburg v US* 383 US 463 (1966).

[85] Bullough, 101.

[86] See Kaplan, 'Obscenity as an Aesthetic Category' at 548:

> Now *pornography* is promotional: it is the obscene responded to with minimal psychic distance... [A]s to esthetic intent, this is lacking altogether in so far as the object is being read as pornographic.

As the psychologist van den Haag remarks, aesthetic merit is likely to reduce, if not to eliminate, rather than augment the obscene effect. 'The pinup has it all over art, if it comes to sheer erotic stimulation': Haag, *'Quia Ineptum'* in Chandos, *'To Deprave and Corrupt'* at 118. Thus, also, Santayana's famous theorem, that beauty tends to cancel lust: Santayana, *Reason in Art*, 171.

[87] Cf. Sylvester, 'Tassels, and Other Gadgets' at 36, 38.

[88] See the attempts set out in Lockhart and McClure, 'Censorship of Obscenity' at 58–68.

[89] See Henry Miller's remark:

> When obscenity crops out in art, in literature more particularly, it usually functions as a technical device; the element of the deliberate which is there has nothing to do with sexual excitation, as in pornography.... Its purpose is to awaken, to usher in a sense of reality. (Miller, 'Obscenity and the Law of Reflection' at 587.)

Obviously, what Miller (like Kaplan) calls 'obscenity' would in principle, on our analysis, be constitutionally protected art, and not obscene.

This is not to argue that obscenity should be proscribed because it destroys aesthetic appreciation or threatens art, nor, indeed, that it should be proscribed for any other reason. The concern of this essay is not with the rights and wrongs of obscenity, but with the purely constitutional question of whether obscenity is within the first amendment's protected area of 'speech'. Under the present constitutional dispensation, expression is protected 'speech' precisely to the extent that it derives from and appeals to the intellectual end of the intellect-emotion continuum. The relevant implication of our discussion of psychical distance and its destruction by obscene expression is this: expression that threatens psychical distance does so by shifting its appeal towards the emotion end of the intellect-emotion continuum, and by suppressing the intellectual component in the aesthetic attitude.

The aesthetic attitude is constituted by a unique balance of intellect and feeling in the contemplation and grasp of a symbol that expresses the idea of emotion or feeling. In Langer's words, psychical distance is simply 'our natural relation to a symbol that embodies an idea and presents it for our contemplation..."cleared of the practical nature of its appeal"'.[90] It is intelligence that contemplates and grasps ideas, in whatever form they are embodied; the ideas in art are embodied in a sensuous symbol. Hence, whatever attacks contemplation and aesthetic understanding must, by the same token, obscure the expressive and intelligible form of the work as symbol, leaving only its potentiality for being *used* to stimulate feelings.

Burstyn[91] and *Kingsley Pictures*[92] imply that art by definition must fall within the area of what is constitutionally protected 'speech'. It would be a mistake, however, to adopt a simplistic notion[93] of the sort of *idea* that art expresses. That idea is not a 'message' or doctrine that ratiocination can conceive or discourse communicate. It is the symbol of feeling, whose sensuous quality is in the service of its vital import and whose unique power 'lies in the fact that it is an abstraction, a symbol, the bearer of an idea'.[94] Art 'gives us *forms of imagination* and *forms of feeling*'.[95] Usually, 'when one speaks of "reason" at all, one tacitly assumes its discursive pattern'.[96] Such an assumption might be thought to lie behind the *Kingsley Pictures* explanation of art's status within the protected realm of ideas, intellect, and reason. 'But in a broader sense any appreciation of *form*...is "reason"; and discourse with all its refinements...is only one possible pattern'.[97]

---

[90] Langer, 319.   [91] *Joseph Burstyn v Wilson* 343 US 495 (1952).
[92] *Kingsley Int'l Pictures v Regents of Univ. of NY* 360 US 684 (1959).
[93] See e.g. Note, 39 NYUL Rev 1063, 1084–5 (1964).   [94] Langer, 41.
[95] *Ibid.*, 397 (emphasis in original).   [96] *Ibid.*, 29   [97] *Ibid.* (emphasis added).

In sum, artistic creation and appreciation, though they do not belong to the realm of ideas rather than to the realm of emotions, are, in a special way, at least as irreducibly bound up with intelligence as with feeling.[98] It remains only to point out that, though practical difficulties of characterization are undeniable, obscene expressions as constitutionally defined cannot claim the protection due to art; to the extent that an appeal is made to prurient interest, the psychical distance essential to an aesthetic attitude is liable to be destroyed. Such destruction is achieved, moreover, in a precisely relevant fashion; it disrupts the contemplative and intellectual component of the aesthetic attitude and, through direct emotional stimulation, obscures the *idea* which the work, as art, symbolically expresses and communicates to those willing to give it the aesthetic attention required to understand it.

IV

It remains only to show in more detail how the dialectic of 'reason' and 'passion' has shaped the constitutional law of obscene expression. We have already argued that the two-level or reason-passion theory provides a working rationale for the application or refusal of constitutional protection to expressions alleged to be obscene. In fact, it is clear that whenever the type of speech, as distinct from the time, place, and manner of expression, is in issue the majority on the Court will respond to the seminal passage in *Chaplinsky*:

Such utterances are no essential part of any exposition of ideas, and are of such slight social value as a step to truth that any benefit that may be derived from them is clearly outweighed by the social interest in order and morality.[99]

The constitutional premise of this passage is clarified by *New York Times Co. v Sullivan*:

The constitutional safeguard, we have said, 'was fashioned to assure unfettered interchange of ideas for the bringing about of political and social changes desired by the people.'[100]

---

[98] See Berger, *The Language of Art*, 80: '... aesthetic awareness is *at one and the same time* an experience and a judgment....' As the critic Clive Bell has said:

> Before we feel an aesthetic emotion for a combination of forms, do we not perceive intellectually the rightness and necessity of the combination? If we do, it would explain the fact that passing rapidly through a room we recognize a picture to be good, although we cannot say that it has provoked much emotion. (Bell, *Art*, 26.)

[99] 315 US 568, 572 (1942). This passage has been quoted many times. See e.g. *Garrison v Louisiana* 379 US 64, 75 (1964) (libel case); *Roth v US* 354 US 476, 485; *Beauharnais v Illinois* 343 US 250, 256–7 (1952). See also the reference to 'the dissemination of information' in *US v Carolene Products* 304 US 144, 152 n. 4 (1938).

[100] 376 US 254, 269 (1964) (quoting *Roth*).

The constitutional protection does not turn upon 'the truth, popularity, or social utility of the ideas and beliefs which are offered.'[101]

Even Justices Black and Douglas pay an oblique tribute to this implicit constitutional reliance on the contrast between reason and passion, by their repeated allegations that the Court has refused to protect 'discussion or opinions'[102] in the obscenity cases. Thus sadomasochistic fiction sold at a profit of several thousand per cent is euphemistically referred to by Black J as 'views about sex' and 'subjects discussed'.[103]

Only the dictum in *Winters v New York*[104] that 'we do not accede to appellee's suggestion that the constitutional protection for a free press applies only to the exposition of ideas',[105] seems to stand in the way of this kind of analysis. But the meaning of this passage is clarified by what immediately follows:

The line between the informing and the entertaining is too elusive for the protection of that basic right. Everyone is familiar with instances of propaganda through fiction. What is one man's amusement, teaches another's doctrine.[106]

Hence, the foregoing dictum in *Winters* is capable of being explicitly absorbed into the two-level reasoning of *Burstyn* that 'motion pictures are a significant medium for the *communication of ideas*'.[107] Despite its protestations, the Court in *Winters* was protecting entertainment, at least in part, because of its significance in the exposition of ideas as 'propaganda' and 'doctrine'. An answer to the dilemma with which the Court was struggling in *Winters*, *Burstyn*, and *Kingsley Pictures*[108] lies in the recognition that, quite apart from propagation of doctrine, some 'entertainments' have artistic value, meaning, and symbolic significance and appeal to contemplation and understanding, while others appeal to the sensual emotions in order to achieve a calculated effect of obfuscating understanding with titillation, stimulation, and gratification.

---

[101] *Ibid.* at 271 (quoting *NAACP v Button* 371 US 415, 445 (1963)). This passage shows how wide of the mark Kalven was ('The New York Times Case' at 217–18) in announcing that the *Times* case disposed of the two-level theory. As did other commentators, Kalven leapt from the premise that '"mere labels" of state law' cannot control constitutional judgment, to the conclusion that no category of speech is any longer beneath the protection of the first amendment. The mistake lies in forgetting that the obscenity which is beneath first amendment protection, on the two-level theory, is not a 'mere label of state law' claiming 'talismanic protection' but a category which has *ex hypothesi* been 'measured by standards that satisfy the first amendment' before being declared outside the protection of that amendment. See also *New York Times v Sullivan* 376 US 254, 265–6, 270.

[102] See e.g. *Mishkin v New York* 383 US 502, 517 (1966) (Black J dissenting).
[103] *Ibid.* at 516–17.   [104] 333 US 507 (1948).   [105] *Ibid.* at 510.   [106] *Ibid.*
[107] 343 US at 501 (emphasis added).
[108] *Kingsley Int'l Pictures Corp. v Regents of Univ. of NY* 360 US 684 (1959). See at nn. 54–66 above.

A further question now arises, however, for if there is a simple bedrock rationale for the exclusion of obscenity from constitutional protection, that rationale can be expected to manifest itself in some, if not all,[109] of the tests used in defining 'obscenity'. Such indeed is the case. We argued in the first section that the adoption of the 'prurient interest' test and the abandonment of the 'deprave and corrupt' test are ascribable to the two-level theory that obscenity pertains to passion rather than reason. Appeals to passion are not the concern of the first amendment; hence the priority of the prurient interest test ever since the constitutional issue was squarely faced. The cases since *Roth* confirm that the phrase 'prurient interest' was not intended by the Court to have the limited meaning attached to it by the Model Penal Code:

an exacerbated, morbid, or perverted interest growing out of the conflict between the universal sexual drive of the individual and equally universal social controls of sexual activity.[110]

It has been argued that, under such a formulation, 'totally erotic' material might escape sanctions because it does not produce a sense of guilt and shame in the average man.[111] But a Court which considers as synonyms for 'prurient interest', phrases such as 'lustful thoughts', 'lascivious longings',[112] 'erotic interest',[113] 'titillation',[114] and 'erotically arousing' material providing 'sexual stimulation'[115] to the 'salaciously disposed',[116] would hardly accede to such an argument. 'Passions', in the two-level theory, are not tricked out with psychological theories of 'psycho-social tension'.[117] The fundamental question is simple: does the reader look for 'titillation' or for '*intellectual content*'?[118]

The second of the three definitive elements of obscenity, as crystallized in *Memoirs v Massachusetts*, requires that 'the material is utterly without redeeming social value'.[119] The link between this test and the underlying reason-passion rationale, though not self-evident, is revealed by the Court's

---

[109] Even a bedrock rationale need not be pushed to the full limits of its logic; it may be qualified by competing rationales or considerations: see Hart, 'Prolegomenon to the Principles of Punishment', in his *Punishment and Responsibility* at 3.

[110] Model Penal Code §207.10, Comment 6(c) (Tent. Draft No. 6, 1957).

[111] Note, 51 Cornell LQ 785, 789 (1966).   [112] *Roth v US* 354 US 476, 487 n. 20 (1957).

[113] *Ibid.* at 496 (Warren CJ concurring).   [114] *Ginzburg v US* 383 US 463, 470 (1966).

[115] *Ibid.* at 471.   [116] *Ibid.* (quoting *US v Redbuhn* 109 F 2d 512 (2d Cir. 1940) (Hand J)).

[117] See Model Penal Code §207.10, Comment 6(c) (Tent. Draft No. 6, 1957).

[118] *Ginzburg v US* 383 US 463, 470 (1966). The fact that the notion of 'arousing lustful thoughts' is central to the constitutional rationale for excluding obscenity from the first amendment does not imply that the same notion need be central to the legislative rationale for proscribing obscenity. See sec. V of text below.

[119] 383 US at 418.

incorporation in *Memoirs v Massachusetts*[120] of Brennan J's comment in *Jacobellis v Ohio* that

> material dealing with sex in a manner that advocates ideas...or that has literary or scientific or artistic value or any other form of social importance, may not be branded as obscenity...[121]

This list of species of socially valuable material indicates the intended character of the whole genus; it suggests that relevant social importance derives from connection, direct or indirect, with the intellectual realm. At the same time, assuming some consensus in the relevant levels of American culture, this second defining element provides the courts with a broad commonsense criterion ('social importance') in place of the intricate and controversial philosophical categories which underpin that criterion, and which we have illustrated in the preceding sections.

The third defining element of obscenity named in *Memoirs v Massachusetts* is that of patent offensiveness and affront to contemporary community standards relating to the description or representation of sexual matters. Offensiveness correlates with that which destroys psychical distance for a given culture, person, and context. There are people, of course, who often like to eliminate distance, but others feel threatened and shocked when confronted with objects that might overcome their ability to distance and their rational control. Moreover, ability to maintain distance varies widely. The test of patent offensiveness as judged by current community standards seeks to ensure that the law is geared to an average standard of robustness in these matters. The test tends to protect at least the 'classics', since current community standards can be taken to recognize implicitly that the classics are part of, rather than offenders against, those standards and that the classics discipline, rather than disturb, people's ability to maintain psychical distance. The use of the test in *Ginzburg* is evidence of its connection with the reason-passion rationale, for Brennan J says that to represent one's publications as erotically arousing not only stimulates the reader to look for titillation rather than intellectual content, but also 'would tend to force public confrontation with the potentially offensive aspects of the work' and 'heightens the offensiveness of the publications to those who are offended by such material'.[122]

Finally, the reason-passion theory of the first amendment fits closely the Court's increasing concern with commerciality. As *Ginzburg* indicates, the Court will judge the obscenity of publications

> ...against a background of commercial exploitation of erotica solely for the sake of their prurient appeal.[123]

[120] *Ibid.* at 419 n. 7. [121] 378 US 184, 191 (1964). [122] 383 US at 470.
[123] *Ibid.* at 466.

'[I]f the object [of a work] is material gain for the creator through an appeal to the sexual curiosity and appetite,' the work is pornographic.[124]

The relevance of commerciality is not that the seller profits from his activity;[125] rather, the fact that he is a *mere* seller might indicate that he is not trying to engage in activity protected by the first amendment, that is, the communication of ideas in whatever form.

The panderer is participating in the marketplace of prurient interest, not in the marketplace of ideas. His participation, therefore, will be taken at face value, even if the material is not devoid of value.[126] This emphasis on commercial exploitation is wholly consistent with the two-level theory. The two levels of the marketplace correlate with the two functional levels of the mind; to 'peddle' material to the public on the strength of its appeal to the passions tends to negate any intrinsic social value the material may have and to remove it from the level of constitutionally protected speech.

The foregoing discussion of the current tests for defining obscenity attempts merely to indicate the conceptual link between these tests and the fundamental two-level rationale; it is not intended as a full exposition of the tests, still less as an exploration of the many practical legal problems that they raise. Nor does it attempt to show that these tests are preferable to others which might be derived from the same rationale. For example, the test championed by Justices Clark and White in *Memoirs v Massachusetts*[127] is just as derivable from the reason-passion rationale as is the test of redeeming social value; the selection of one in preference to the other will depend on other factors. A rationale may be recognized as fundamental, without being adopted as exhaustive and exclusive of all other constitutional or legal considerations.

V

We have been discussing why obscene expression is outside the first amendment. Nothing we have said has been directed to the questions of whether and why obscenity should be regulated. A discussion of these questions would take us far afield, not only into empirical inquiries but also into the fundamental question of whether our criminal law is, and ought to be, designed to eliminate 'harms' or whether it also seeks, and should seek, to express, vindicate, and uphold wider values. Moreover, there is

---

[124] *Ibid.* at 471.
[125] *Ibid.* at 474–5 (1966); *Joseph Burstyn, Inc. v Wilson* 343 US 495, 501 (1952).
[126] 383 US at 470. It is the participation in the marketplace, not the work as such, that is suppressed in this case.
[127] 383 US at 441–2 (Clark J dissenting); *ibid.* at 461–2 (White J dissenting).

no reason why any rationale for excluding obscenity from constitutional protection must coincide with a rationale for proscribing obscenity by criminal or administrative measures.

Still, the approach we have described has three advantages over alternative approaches. First, the prurient interest test does have an explicit and intelligible connection with the rationale for excluding obscenity from constitutional protection. That rationale is the two-level theory. On the other hand, the 'hard-core pornography' test[128] has no intelligible connection with any constitutional rationale for denial of first amendment protection, except perhaps in Stewart J's suggestion that hardcore pornography 'cannot conceivably be characterized as embodying communication of ideas'[129]—in which case the rationale is the same as that adopted by Brennan J. The question then must be why the modified prurient interest test should not be adopted in place of the uninformative notion of 'hardcore pornography'.[130]

Second, the reason-passion theory of speech has the merit of emphasizing the serious unreality of Justices Black and Douglas's notion that men like Roth, Alberts, and Mishkin are somehow engaged in the same activity— 'expression of views and opinion'—as are the bona fide participants in the marketplace of ideas, who advance the contest of reason visualized in the *Federalist*.

Third, the theory that obscenity is not protected speech has the advantage of not involving the Court in a 'balancing-of-interests' test. For in such a speculative and controversial area, any attempt to balance interests or even to articulate the rationale for proscribing obscenity, would be beyond judicial competence. It is better left to the experiments of legislatures and the changing worldly wisdom of juries, working within the relatively narrow area now left them by the Court.

---

[128] The test is employed differently by Harlan J in relation to federal censorship, e.g. *Ginzburg v US* 383 US 463, 493 (1966) (Harlan J dissenting), and by Stewart J generally. E.g. *ibid.* at 499 (Stewart J dissenting); *Jacobellis v Ohio* 378 US 184, 197 (1964) (Stewart J concurring).

[129] *Ginzburg v US* 383 US 463, 499 n. 3 (1966).

[130] It is interesting that in Magrath, 'The Obscenity Cases: Grapes of *Roth*' at 72, the attempt to explain 'hard-core pornography' falls back on 'patent offensiveness' plus a 'self-defining' element found in 'writings designed to act as psychological aphrodisiacs or stimulants' where

[t]he reader is meant to identify either with the narrator...or with the general situation to a sufficient extent to produce at least the physical concomitants of sexual excitement...that he would have were he taking part in the activities described. (Quoting the sociologist Geoffrey Gorer in Rolph (ed.), *Does Pornography Matter?*, 32.)

This amounts to little more (or less) than a deliberate 'appeal to prurient interest', accomplished by the destruction of aesthetic distance. Magrath's suggestion (at 74) that discovery of this second 'element' involves 'attention solely to the material per se' cannot be admitted; to discover whether material is 'too sexually arousing' (at 75), one has to look beyond 'the material alone' to its 'prurient interest to some hypothetical average person'. In any event, Magrath's test, if adopted, would rest on the same bedrock rationale as the current test.

NOTE

The essay was cited and relied upon in the judgment of the court in *Paris Adult Theatre I v Slaton* 413 US 49, 67 (1973). It is criticized, along with some similar theorizing by Frederick Schauer, in Koppelman, 'Is Pornography "Speech"?', which in n. 48 effectively refutes the essay's 'most prominent critic', Stephen Gey. But Koppelman too misunderstands the argument; at p. 84 he paraphrases and quotes the essay's thesis that the aim of the pornographer's techniques is

> the replacement of aesthetic attention to the material with an attitude in which the practical concerns of the reader or viewer (in this case, a concern to achieve the emotionally aroused states which he desires for himself) intrude upon and suppress an understanding contemplation of the created symbol

(n. 89 above), and then immediately adds:

> Let us call the viewer Finnis hypothesizes the Grimly Purposive Masturbator, or GPM for short... He wants his orgasm and does not care how he gets it.

This misstates, rather grossly, the essay's characterization of the pornographer's aim, an aim well described by Clark J, dissenting in *Memoirs v Massachusetts* (n. 127 above) at 447, in relation to the book in question, *Fanny Hill*: 'to arouse prurient interest and produce *sustained erotic tension*'. That aim looks, answers, and corresponds precisely to the 'practical concerns' that I had in mind and characterized in terms similar to Clark J's.

What the essay fails to address (as it itself indicates more than once) is why it is desirable, and is or should be constitutionally permissible, to prohibit publications which appeal (as judged by the aims of author or publisher) predominantly to prurient interest, even when the means chosen have artistic merit. Clark and White JJ and to some extent Harlan J, all dissenting in *Memoirs v Massachusetts*, held that it is. They could see, more clearly than I think I did when writing the essay, that what Brennan J was doing in that case was transforming *Roth*, and in a sense standing it on its head. In *Roth* the satisfaction of two preconditions—primary appeal to prurient interest, and (patent) offensiveness— authorized the *conclusion* that pornography is of no redeeming social value (and is not so *relevantly* involved with ideas as to be entitled to first amendment protection). In *Memoirs v Massachusetts*, Brennan J and the majority transformed the conclusion into a third precondition for constitutionally permissible prohibition: to be pornographic, a publication must appeal primarily to prurient interest and be offensive *and* have no redeeming social value such as artistic merit. That move, ratified in *Paris Adult Theatre I v Slaton* and its companion and successor cases, puts almost insurmountable obstacles in the way of restriction—an effect doubtless intended by Brennan J, whose favour for a radically new form of social life had by 1967 not yet become really manifest, as it later did. The essay's being cited in *Paris Adult Theatre I v Slaton* was an empty success.

18

FREEDOM OF SPEECH[*]

I

Like Milton, Locke, and Mill, I think the claim that there is a strict human right to freedom of speech is too implausible to be worth much discussion. So at best I have only marginal remarks to offer.

If you find that I seem to have gone rather far afield, it is because I am impressed by the page of Mill *On Liberty*, in which he spoke of that climate of opinion that 'kills no-one, roots out no opinions, but induces men to disguise them, or to abstain from any active effort in their diffusion'—a state of things in which

> a large portion of the most active, and inquiring intellects find it advisable to keep the general principles and grounds of their convictions within their own breasts, and attempt, in what they address to the public, to fit as much as they can of their own conclusions to premises which they have internally renounced: their arguments on all great subjects are meant for their hearers and are not those which have convinced themselves. Those who avoid this alternative, do so by narrowing their thoughts and interest to things which can be spoken of, *without venturing within the region of principles*...[1]

So I have ventured a few remarks on principles. Everybody who has spent a few years in modern universities knows well which matters are meant to be 'kept within one's own breast', and knows that these matters have nothing to do with sex or decency or slander or any of the other objects of legal prohibition.

I think we can best penetrate to 'the region of principles' by first reminding ourselves of the phenomena of the problem. This reminder would best be a historical survey; but that I can't manage, so I content myself with the present state of English law, from which American law

---

[*] Unpublished: read at Professor R.M. Dworkin's seminar on Rights, Oxford, 8 March 1979.
[1] Mill, *On Liberty*, ch. II (emphasis added).

differs so far as I can see, only in matters of emphasis (though emphasis is important, as we shall see).

In law, speech and expressions of many types are directly prohibited. It is an offence to perjure oneself; to libel a fellow citizen; to commit seditious libel; to conspire to commit a crime or any unlawful or indecent act; to use threatening, abusive, or insulting language whereby a breach of the peace is likely to be occasioned, or to incite racial hatred; to obtain property or credit or pecuniary advantage by deception; to make false declarations of many sorts; to induce breaches of contract; to shock public decency; to use obscene language; to glorify the use of drugs; to deprave and corrupt, or to use words tending to deprave and corrupt people likely to hear or read one; to make false reports tending to show that a crime has been committed; to cause panic by shouting 'fire' in a theatre—though I don't know that the law takes so strict a view as Mill's view that, as he says in Chapter III of *On Liberty*:

> An opinion that corn-dealers are starvers of the poor, or that private property is robbery... may justly incur punishment when delivered orally to an excited mob assembled before the house of a corn-dealer, or when handed about among the same mob in the form of a placard...

—to communicate official secrets; to interrupt public meetings with intent to prevent business; to commit contempt in face of a court; to cheat the revenue; to advertise rewards for return of stolen goods on a no-questions-asked basis; to incite disaffection amongst the police and armed forces; and so on and so on. Some people would like to see the list extended—for example, so as to make it at least a public duty not to record or communicate certain types of objective information.[2]

After reminding ourselves of the source of the phenomenon in the background, we ought perhaps to try some clarification of the terms. What is being asserted when it is said that there is a right to freedom of speech?

Let us suppose that there are three citizens, A, B, and C, and state officials S, S1, S2, Sn...

What can it mean to say that 'A has a right to say X to B'? Let us suppose first that B is merely a potential listener, not under a duty to listen to A.

Then we might be asserting (1) that C has (or ought to have) no right of action in tort or contract against A for saying X to B; and/or we might be asserting (2) that A will not be criminally liable for saying X to B. There are many situations where assertion (1) is true while (2) is false, and vice versa, and many where both are true.

---

[2] [This was an allusion to the proposals which eventually resulted in the Rehabilitation of Offenders Act 1974.]

Alternatively, or additionally, we might be asserting that C has a duty not to interfere with A's communicating X to B; and to say *this* may mean that if C does interfere he will be penalized by S, and/or it may mean that A can get damages against C for C's interference, and/or that A can get an injunction against C's interfering, and/or that A can resort to self-help against C's interferences without incurring thereby criminal liability or liability in damages to C or to an injunction by C or to counter-self-help by C—or any combination of any of these combinations of combinations...

Alternatively, or additionally, we might be asserting that A has the right to communicate X to B without being snooped on by C (an informer, or a student) or by S, S1, etc. And this may mean that snooping by C is an offence penalized by S, and/or actionable in damages and/or by way of injunction by C, and/or a trespass against C giving a right to self-help... and so on as before.

Alternatively, we might mean that A's communicating X to B is or should be free from prior censorship by S, but not from *ex post facto* suit by C or prosecution by S. As Milton says in the *Areopagitica* (after condemning prior censorship),

> it is of greatest concernment in the... Commonwealth, to have a vigilant eye how books demean themselves as well as men; and thereafter to confine, imprison and do sharpest justice on them as malefactors.[3]

Alternatively, or additionally, we might be asserting that C and S are under a duty to A not to deny him access to B and/or the means of communicating with B; and/or that C and/or S are under a duty to allow access to him and the means of communicating with him—and again, what it is to assert that C and S have a duty and A or B a corresponding claim-right varies along the range of types of enforcement action, self-help, non-interference, etc.

So, long before we examine the content (X) of the act of communication, it is evident that the assertion: 'A has a right to say X to B' has hundreds or thousands of possible legal meanings. Correspondingly, it has hundreds or thousands of possible *moral* meanings within the moral discourse on what the morally just legal system should stipulate concerning acts of communicating X. In particular, there is no reason to suppose, as Prof. Dworkin supposed last week, that our *principal* moral concern should be to secure a legal system in which A's act of communication is free from interference by S, S1, S2. Why should we not be equally if not more concerned to secure a legal system in which A's act is free from interference by C? And by 'free from' one might mean that A should be protected by

---

[3] Milton, *Areopagitica*, 4.

S from interference by C. After all, to Kant it seemed that the particular concern of law ought to be hindering hindrances to freedom; if so, the very point of having S is to hinder C's hindrances to A's freedom. Could there then be sufficient reason to concentrate exclusively on the danger that S might hinder A's freedom?

In other words, to say that we ought to devise a legal system in which S is obliged to bend over backwards not to interfere with *freedom of action by citizens* is empty, even on Kant's freedom-obsessed ethics of law. For the point of having S is to interfere with actions which interfere with other people's actions, activities, enterprises, way of life, or freely chosen and cultivated milieu. The actions of C with which S ought to interfere will often be done by C in pursuance of claims of right, just as much as the actions of A with which the actions of C interfere. There is no easy method of determining whose action S should protect; this is the whole problem of ethical politics. A's claim to *protection* by S is as important to A, to his 'dignity, autonomy, and equality', as his claim to *immunity from* S. Professor Dworkin's analysis, concentrating on man versus the State, *Abbie Hoffman v Judge Julius Hoffman*,[4] gave scant attention to the interests of all the citizens (in principle identifiable) who were claiming from Julius and the Chicago police some protection to secure this immunity from Abbie, whose riot-fomenting action, they could plausibly claim, tended to interfere with their actions, activities, businesses, etc. In assessing the plausibility of the claims and counterclaims no presumption or predetermined onus of proof can be derived by analysis of the notion of *rights* and claims of right. Nor could such a presumption or onus be inferred by appeal to the presumption of fallibility: for if S might be wrong about A's claims, he/it might equally be wrong about C's claims that A's action is an unjustified hindrance of his (C's) action and freedom.

That was a digression; I wanted to stress the ambiguity inherent in claims that there is, or morally ought to be, a *right* to speak. The only way to avoid this ambiguity in the notion of 'a right' is to claim that everyone has a right to do and say whatever he likes—a heroic, absurd, and corrupt claim which evacuates the notion of 'right' by eliminating from discourse its negations and correlatives; indeed eliminating moral discourse. But if this move is not made, one confronts the fact that no one of the thousands of possible meanings is self-evident. So the only way to specify the meaning of 'right' in some claim of right, and then to justify the restriction of the

---

[4] [An allusion to the 1969–70 trial of eight (later seven) defendants, including 'Abbie' Hoffman, by a Chicago court presided over by Judge Julius J. Hoffman for offences connected with the 'antiwar' riots on the occasion of the Democratic Party Convention in Chicago in August 1968; and to the discussion of the case by Dworkin in 'Taking Rights Seriously' [now in *TRS* at 197, 201–2].]

claim to *this* specified sense of 'right', will be to appeal to some principles which are pertinent in moral discourse and which are *not* expressed in terms of rights at all.

To this ambiguity and the problem of its resolution must be added the ambiguity which I veiled by speaking of A saying X to B. Unless one takes the heroic and corrupt view that A has the right to say *anything* to B, however treasonable, damaging, or vile it may be when uttered to B, one is faced with the problem of specifying X, and here again the postulate that human beings have rights is of no help. Far from it being self-evident that A has or should have the right to say anything to B, it is self-evident that he does not. But it is *not* self-evident what utterances A has or should have the right (in any sense of right) to make to B. And this lack of self-evident solutions has two types of cause: it results not only because the morally justifiable specification of X will vary with the breadth or narrowness of the specification of 'right', but also because the justifiable specification of X will vary according to time, place, circumstances, and everything else that affects the good of B, of C, and of the whole community for which S is immediately responsible and for which we, as imagined architectonic legislators and/or as good citizens, are ultimately responsible.

II

With the notion of the good, my good, your good, we enter 'the region of principles'. Some people would say that we enter the realm of ideology. They distinguish between (a) *political and legal science*, which offers factual or descriptive accounts of political institutions and legal systems; (b) *ideology*, which offers recommendations about the ideal ends that political activity and legal organization should pursue; and (c) *political and legal philosophy* which offers classifications and analyses of the terms, statements, and arguments of scientists and ideologists. But this orthodox piece of intellectual botany (which I have transcribed from A.M. Quinton's introduction to *Oxford Readings in Political Philosophy* (1967)) is superficial and misleading. Prior to the so-called factual and descriptive accounts and the so-called recommendations of ideal ends there is simply the activity of raising questions about man's life in political society. Questions presuppose nothing but a desire for correct rather than mistaken accounts of facts and for clear-headed rather than muddled schemes of action. But the satisfaction of this desire depends on more than the mere wish. The attainment of truth and reasonable opinion has conditions. One is not likely to attain truth and reasonable beliefs unless one understands something of one's psychical make-up and the snares it lays for fully rational thinking; unless one is willing to impose on oneself the necessary disciplines of learning, reflecting, testing, and rejecting *parti pris* and *amour propre*; unless one can engage in rational discussion with one's fellows, or has experienced the exigencies of oral discussion and can reproduce them in one's private debate; unless the economic, social, and political conditions in which one works permit one leisure and rest from hard physical labour, and the information necessary for sound judgment about human nature and society; and (but this list will scarcely have exhausted the preconditions) unless one is equipped with the linguistic (conceptual) skills necessary to conceive, let alone complete, the project of reaching truth and reasonable opinion about human life in political society.

So, however political and legal philosophy is defined, the activity of carrying on political philosophy as a process of rational questioning will be dependent on factual conditions of social context, language, education, economic attainment, and a measure of social stability and political freedom. Now the proposition I have just uttered is not a proposition within political science's factual or descriptive accounts of political institutions and activities; it goes beyond accounts of the institutions which may happen to exist and, drawing on the empirical findings of political theory, states some principles of politics necessary, in view of the empirical characteristics of human nature, to encourage the realization of at least one important good. Moreover, the proposition that it is so importantly worthwhile to attain truth-rather-than-error and clarity-rather-than-muddle is not an ideological recommendation of some fancied 'ideal end'. Implicit in all rational questioning and discussion is an affirmation of the value or worth or good of truth and clarity; this affirmation is not of 'an essentially contested concept'. For to bother to question or rationally contest the affirmation would be implicitly to affirm it by one's performance if not one's utterances.

This is not to say that attaining truth and clarity about law or politics (or about shellfish for that matter) is the best good one can pursue, or that society had best be organized to support a contemplative elite—though that is the conclusion that Aristotle drew. After all, even within the sphere of strictly intellectual activity, just as self-evidently worthwhile as my attaining truth and clarity is my sharing it with my friends. And of course, the worthwhile range of friendship and of goods that one would wish for one's friends is wider than the sharing of intellectual pursuits and attainments: there is no need to elaborate on this here.

But the phenomenon of friendship will remind us of the great problem that underlies all discussions of human rights. Why do we have *duties* to our fellows? (For if *we* have no duties in justice they have no rights in any interesting sense.) Granted: to be a real friend, one must love one's friends' good, their flourishing and attainment, as if it were one's own. Still: why have I a *duty* to my friends in cases where helping them puts at risk my own good? *A fortiori*, why have I duties to those whom I would *not* be willing to call my friends? The question is particularly acute of course, for someone like Aristotle, for whom the highest good is rational contemplation and discussion, of which only the philosopher and his philosopher friends are capable: it is not clear that the good of those not intellectually capable of participating in this activity should count against the good of those who can.

To the question 'Why should I be just and respect my fellow's good?' three lines of answer have been developed recently. The first is the utilitarian, which claims that it is self-evident that one ought to pursue utility, the greatest happiness of the greatest number. But, as Mill says at the end of his *Utilitarianism*:

the Utility or Greatest Happiness Principle…is a mere form of words without rational signification unless one person's happiness, supposed equal in degree…is counted for exactly as much as another's.

The problem that he is tackling, signified by 'is…without rational signification', is the indeterminacy created, with logical necessity, by conjoined independent superlatives—such as 'the greatest happiness of the greatest number'—unbounded by a measure such as *rate*. Who wins the prize offered 'for writing the greatest number of poems in the shortest time/at the greatest speed'? A, who after an hour presents three sonnets, or B, who after an hour has nothing but after three hours presents ten limericks…? The solution that Mill offers is an injunction addressed to each of us as someone deliberating about what to choose: 'count each person's happiness as equal to each other person's'. But the question we were asking Mill was '*Why* should my happiness not count, for me, more than yours or any other person's?'. Well, Mill does face up to this question, in his footnote to the sentence after the one I quoted. His answer is a kind of pun, an equivocation or series of equivocations: 'equal amounts of happiness are equally desirable, whether *felt* by the same or by different persons'—to explain which Mill offers: '[F]or "happiness" and "desirable" are synonymous terms'. But again: *for whom* are 'equal amounts' 'equally desirable'? And are ten units 'felt' by one person 'equal in amount' to, and as 'desirable' as, ten units felt by ten people at the rate of one *per* person? No one is deceived by Mill's attempt to break, by sleight of hand, the circle of our self-love, one's desire—each of us—for one's own happiness.[5]

So a second line of answer to the question 'Why should I respect the good of others?' has more recently been developed by appealing directly to our self-love. Philippa Foot argues that no reason can be given to a man to show him that he should be just, other than that it will be to his benefit, that it will be profitable to him.[6] But can't I envisage that my injustice, if performed with sufficient cunning and camouflage, may well pay handsomely, and that my respect for justice can lead me to irrevocable disaster—death and an end to all profits? In any case, Foot's *type* of answer does not respond to the sense of the original question, which asked precisely what rational grounds there are for acting contrary to one's expectation of personal advantage. The questioner must be taken to be aware of, and puzzled about, that range of human experience in which the profit motive is in competition with other claims on one's action: to be aware, and puzzled, that for example it is *necessary* to one's well-being that one should have real friendships, but acquaintances cultivated for the sake of one's own well-being are not real friendships.

Back, then, from self-love to disinterestedness, which has been made the basis of the third line of answer recently developed without benefit of Mill's luxurious *petitio principii* and equivocation on 'desired', 'desirable', and 'equal', in response to the question 'Why should I, in justice, respect other people's good?'. It is said that I have no rational ground to prefer my good to that of anybody else: the only difference between my good and your good granted our equal humanity is my mere identity and yours, and *that* doesn't provide any reason for me to pursue my good at your expense, or vice versa. But this argument proves too much; for if it proves that I ought to respect your rights, it also proves that I ought not to compete against you for any prize or scarce resource, nor you against me; and

---

[5] [My doctoral thesis in 1965 described Bentham's awareness that the problem required more than equivocal words:
Bentham [in drafting his 600-page *Constitutional Code* (c. 1820–32)] professes two substantive principles...: first that the object of every branch of the law ought to be the greatest happiness of the greatest number ('greatest happiness principle'); and second, that the actual and inevitable object of government is the greatest happiness of the governors ('self-preference principle'). [*Works* IX, 5–8.] The aim of Bentham's code is to reconcile these two principles by providing that the powers of government be shared by the largest possible number of people. His procedure in this project, elsewhere announced [e.g. *Works* VIII, 380, 385, 424] as the 'Duty and Interest junction principle', is grounded on the assumption that the greater the number who are empowered to act politically for their own happiness, the greater the number made happy by such activity. In formulating this assumption or principle thus, one must not be misled by the ambiguous distribution of the words 'their own': if one were to say, 'where every citizen has the power to act, and acts in his own interests, the interests of everyone will be maximised', the dubious character of Bentham's assumption would be plainer.]

[6] [See essay 6 at 120 n. 4 and endnote.]

that I am no more responsible for my aged father or my children than for anybody and everybody else in the world—which is absurd. Some forms of self-preference are just, even though others are not. But how do we know which? And why should we care?

It seems to me that the answer to the question 'Which forms of self-preference are just?' can only be found by adopting the viewpoint of somebody who is outside the arena in which you and I are involved in mutual actions, reactions, and passions; someone who is supposed to have *equally* in mind the good of each person within the arena. To use Mill's crude psychological hedonist terminology: such an observer can be supposed to desire that each man within the arena 'feel' the 'same amount of happiness'. From such a viewpoint, some forms of competition between us within the arena may be the best way to benefit each of us—although some will win and some will lose in the race for the prize as such—for all may be strengthened and invigorated by the race. So such an observer could consider fair at least those forms of self-preference, of effort to win, which did not leave the unsuccessful competitors worse off than if there had been no competition. Such an observer could also perceive the areas of responsibility which each person in the arena should take if everybody is to profit—for if each person takes the wide world as his parish, the effort of each will be spread so thin that no one will profit.

But you and I are in the arena. Why should we care to adopt the observer's viewpoint, especially if we are fit and strong and can win competitions by fair means or foul and get away with it? To this question two answers might in principle be available. The first is that perhaps the observer would not think it fair that, in the long run, we *should* get away with it, and would take steps to exact recompense for our ill-gotten gains. The second answer is closer to the range of experience which I said that Philippa Foot had not taken sufficiently into account—the experience of friendship which Aristotle has marvellously analysed in the VIIIth and IXth books of the *Ethics*. To love a friend is to wish him well and value his well-being and whatever he has set his heart on. But if he is your friend, he will have set his heart on you, and so you must value yourself for his sake. And if he is the friend of P, he will have P's good at heart, so that you will not be a *real* friend of your friend unless *you too* value P's good, for your friend's sake. Of course, the ramifications of this may extend no further than a closed circle of friends. Moreover, there remains no reason, certainly no reason in justice, why I should *prefer* my friend's good to my good, let alone prefer the good of my friend's friend to my good.

But now suppose that I am the friend, if that were possible, of the observer of the arena, and have reason to value his friendship above everything else, and have reason to believe that he has the well-being of everybody in the arena equally at heart. Then I have sufficient reason to adopt his viewpoint and to consider it *necessary*, on pain of losing his friendship which is my highest good, to respect the good of everybody in the arena to the extent and in the ways that (so far as I can see) he, the observer who also has my good in mind, would wish.

To recapitulate: to the question 'How do I know what my duties are in justice?' there is available the answer in which Plato has concentrated the whole of his political philosophy (though I have only tried to unravel a single thread): God is the measure. And to the question 'Why should I care for this measure, what makes it obligatory?' there is available, now, the answer which Aristotle's analysis of friendship and contemplation head towards but do not reach (since for Aristotle, as he says with great simplicity, God is too remote to be my friend or to be the object of my contemplation)—the answer that God is my highest good, and highest good of everyone whether capable of philosophy or not; and has the good of every man equally at heart.

III

Such, I think, are the ultimate principles of political and legal philosophy; they are the classical principles and I know of no other principles which could explain or justify that measure of respect we owe, as a duty to others and *which specifies their correlative rights*.

Hence you will see why I agree with Mill that one cannot profitably found arguments for freedom of expression on 'the idea of abstract right, as a thing independent of utility'.[7] Utility, says Mill in his introduction to *On Liberty*, is 'the ultimate appeal on all ethical questions; but it must be utility in the largest sense, grounded on the permanent interests of a man as a progressive being'.[8] This account of the common good that each man ought to pursue is obviously equivocal and unsatisfactory, even without its psychological hedonist backdrop. But let that pass. Mill is right, it seems to me, in basing his whole argument for liberty on what he calls 'the end of man'.[9] The whole point of social and legal organization is to provide an encouraging milieu for this:

for what more or better can be said of any condition of human affairs, than that it brings human beings themselves nearer to the best thing they can be? or what worse can be said of any obstruction to good, than that it prevents this?[10]

---

[7] *On Liberty* ch. 1 para. 11. [8] *Ibid.* [9] *Ibid.*, ch. 3 para. 2.
[10] *Ibid.*, ch. 3 para. 10.

And again: 'Human beings owe to each other help to distinguish the better from the worse and encouragement to choose the former and avoid the latter'.[11]

So, as he says in the Introduction and again in Chapter V, children and savages and people of no more education than savages should be placed under 'an education of restraint, to fit them for future admission to the privileges of freedom'.[12] And, as he says in the Introduction, 'in small republics surrounded by powerful enemies in constant peril of being subverted by foreign attack or internal commotion, and to which even a short interval of relaxed energy and self-command might so easily be fatal that they could not afford to wait for the salutary permanent effects of freedom', it 'may have been admissible' for 'the state to take a deep interest in the whole bodily and mental discipline of every one of its citizens'[13].

But why was that sentence framed in the perfect tense: 'it may have been'? Might not there be dangers today analogous to those threatening 'a small republic'? Mill appealed to 'the greater size of political communities' in the modern world—but he spoke before communications had made communities 'small' again. Does he have more to say on this? He does, and here we penetrate to the core of his treatise, which is also the core of modern liberalism and totalitarianism—his pretended knowledge (we might say his irrational *gnosis*) of 'the stage of progress into which the more civilized portions of the species have now entered'. (I quote the expression of faith or *gnosis*—esoteric 'knowledge'—which he puts in the first paragraph of the treatise.) The doctrine that a man has a strict right to freedom of expression of opinion is, he says,

meant to apply only to human beings in the maturity of their faculties. We are not speaking of children, or of young persons below the age which the law may fix as that of manhood or womanhood.[14]

---

[11] *Ibid.*, ch. 4 para. 4.   [12] *Ibid.*, ch. 5 para. 10.   [13] *Ibid.*, ch. 1 para. 14.

[14] *Ibid.*, ch. 1 para. 16. [The explicit subject of the sentence, in Mill's book, is not 'freedom of expression of opinion' but 'this doctrine', referring back to the preceding paragraph, which begins with the famous 'one very simple principle' and ending 'Over himself, over his own body and mind, the individual is sovereign'. Yet the essay's procedure here was justified. For only two paragraphs later, Mill states:

the appropriate region of human liberty...comprises, first, the inward domain of consciousness; demanding liberty of conscience, in the most comprehensive sense; liberty of thought and feeling; absolute freedom of opinion and sentiment on all subjects, practical or speculative, scientific, moral, or theological. The liberty of expressing and publishing opinions may seem to fall under a different principle, since it belongs to that part of the conduct of an individual which concerns other people; but, being almost of as much importance as the liberty of thought itself, and resting in great part on the same reasons, is practically inseparable from it.

And a couple of paragraphs later, the second chapter, 'Of the Liberty of Thought and Discussion', begins with the flat denial that there is any legitimate governmental power to coerce either thought or discussion.]

—as if the law could affect the nature of the problem, the problem which Aristotle has rightly characterized as the permanent problem of politics: Who and how many are, by reason of the facts concerning their emotional and intellectual and moral development, the 'natural slaves'? For, as Mill goes on:

> Those who are still in a state to require being taken care of by others, must be protected against their own actions as well as against external injury. For the same reason, we may leave out of consideration those backward states of society in which the race itself may be considered as in its nonage. The early difficulties in the way of spontaneous progress are so great that there is seldom any choice of means for overcoming them; and a ruler of the spirit of improvement is warranted in the use of any expedients that will attain an end perhaps otherwise unattainable. Despotism is a legitimate mode of government dealing with barbarians, provided the end be their improvement, and the means justified by actually effecting that end. Liberty, as a principle, has no application to any state of things anterior to the time when mankind have become capable of being improved by free and equal discussion.[15]

The basic flaw in Mill's *On Liberty* and in later less subtle liberal contributions to the debate on law, liberty, and morality is the claim to reveal a now *timelessly* valid casuistry or mapping of freedom and restriction on the basis of a revelation to Mill that 'the time' had come, a 'stage of progress' had been reached and would be maintained, that 'man', 'the race', 'the nation', or some other imagined totality had literally *come of age*; that *never again* need we raise the impertinent (but most pertinent) question, 'How much freedom can the members of this society here and now stand without lapsing into a state of decadence or disorder in which there will flourish those who have bigger fish to fry than freedom and who may, perhaps, when they seize power be only too devoted to a "spirit of improvement" in which rather little attention is paid to the worth of the free search for and personal attainment of truth?'

This question is, I repeat, the permanent question of politics, and it cannot be rationally answered by pretending to know the direction and meaning of history, or by romantically identifying one's own society as an elect. The argument of Milton's *Areopagitica*, incidentally, pivots like Mill's on an analogous claim to knowledge of the elect status of England:

> Lords and Commons of England, consider what Nation it is whereof ye are, and whereof ye are the governors: a Nation not slow and dull, but of quick, ingenious and piercing spirit, acute to invent, subtle and sinewy to discourse, not beneath the reach of any point, the highest that human capacity can soar to.... Yet that which

---

[15] *Ibid.*, ch. 1 para. 16.

is above all this, the favour and love of Heaven, we have great argument to think in a peculiar manner propitious and perpending towards us.... Behold... this vast City: a city of refuge, the mansion house of liberty, encompassed and surrounded by *His* protection.... What could a man require more from a Nation so pliant and so prone to seek after knowledge? What wants there to such a towardly and pregnant soil, but wise and faithful labourers, to make a knowing people, a Nation of Prophets, of Sages and of Worthies?... A little generous prudence, a little forbearance of one another, and some grain of charity might win all these diligences to join and unite in one general and brotherly search after Truth: could we but forgo this prelatical tradition of crowding free consciences and Christian liberties into canons and precepts of men.

Of course, English intellectuals are not the only ones to have had this revelation of a manifest destiny and a New World that will be attained only if a few more restrictions on freedom are set aside. David Hume has some pages of praise for the liberty of the press, 'this peculiar privilege of Britain', 'attended with so few inconveniences that it may be claimed as the common right of mankind'. Just as Milton later in his life came to see more clearly, and to say with bitterness, what manner of Nation it in fact was whereof he had been a governor, how unfit for freedom, so Hume struck out in later editions his confident pages on the harmlessness of a free press, and replaced them with one sentence: 'The unbounded liberty of the press, though it be difficult, perhaps impossible to propose a suitable remedy for it, is one of the evils attending... mixed forms of government'—and there ended his essay.

Well, earlier in this essay I sang the praises of the free search for truth and the worth of attaining it by free questioning and of sharing it by free discussion. I do not need to repeat that it has a claim to be the highest human good, and thus is something that a legal system should strive at some cost to foster and protect, something to which everybody has rights to the extent (which shifts with time, place, and circumstance) that his exercise of those rights is not likely to seriously prejudice the other components of that common good of individuals which the legal order ought to protect. In the same derivative sense of 'right' and for *just the same reason*, namely that free rational discussion is a true good, parents have a right to bring up their children in a milieu which to the greatest extent consistent with the wholly common good of individuals (an extent which will vary with time, place, circumstance) will encourage in children of all ages those habits of self-respect, of love of truth, of love of other people, and of self-discipline which are necessary if those children are to participate in free questioning and discussion and sharing of truth and friendship. Such a milieu that will encourage children of all ages to realize that free discussion and friendship are better than self-gratification, than the drugged solitariness of 'inner space', and than that attitude to other people which pornography openly inculcates: that others are so much flesh to be possessed, that they are not free persons but the objects of a *libido dominandi*, a lust for domination, which runs underground from sex to politics. What such a milieu is is a matter for rational discussion without benefit of appeals to a doubly unspecified 'right' to freedom of 'speech' which, for want of specificity, is nowadays given content and rhetorical weight by the ideological, openly irrational faith that 'man has come of age'.

NOTE

The discussion of Mill here draws to some extent on Voegelin, 'Readiness to Rational Discussion'. The use of the Aristotelian category 'natural slaves', at 309, is also shaped by Voegelin's discussion of it in his *Plato and Aristotle*, 329–30; but Voegelin's defence of it, as relevant to a society of free citizens and compatible with recognition of 'our common and equal nature' (*ibid.*, 330), is unsatisfactory. For recognition of the permanent and pervasive political problem of moral immaturity among adult citizens does not warrant the adoption of a category ('slave') whose content ineluctably connotes that the necessary governance of such persons need not count their interests (as distinct from their immoral desires) as intrinsic to the common good. So the essay should not have said that Aristotle 'rightly characterized' the problem of intellectual, emotional, and moral immaturity; nor should it have accepted that this is 'the' permanent problem of politics.

19

PORNOGRAPHY*

I should like to say, first, how much I regret that I have not been able to come to the other seminars this term. There are two reasons for this regret: that I shall probably say much that is offbeat or repetitious, given what you and your other speakers have already said and talked over; and because no one likes to break into a conversation, to break into that *space of meaning*, of shared experience and understanding which is established between interlocutors even when they deeply disagree with one another, and which enables them to take for granted, as a kind of common possession, what to outsiders is still unknown, or uncertainly grasped—all of which shows itself in the touch of impatience, or of condescending tolerance, with which the interlocutors will put the new boy in the picture. I have no doubt that by now, by the beginning of this seventh of your seminars, some such common space of meaning and indeed of sentiment will have been established among you, and I hope (without confidence) that I'll not stray too irritatingly along its boundaries, sometimes inside and sometimes outside them.

I intend my discussion of pornography to be a part of the discourse of political philosophy, that is of the *philosophia* concerning human affairs[1] which Aristotle called political science.[2] I do, of course, feel uneasy about the term 'political', since Aristotle's selection of the *polis*, and even of the whole cycle of forms of the *polis*, as the relevant unit for empirical inquiry was obviously (to us) a premature generalization, and his assumption that human nature finds its fullest and finest representations in that public space of meaningful words and deeds which he labelled the *polis* is an assumption that cannot, in my view, withstand the critique which Christian culture levelled against it both in word and in deed: Augustine's two cities; Gelasius's two swords; St Paul's *koinōnia* in which there is neither Jew nor

---

* Unpublished: read on 7 March 1973, at the seventh of eight seminars on Freedom of Speech held in Oxford that term by Professors R.M. Hare and R.M. Dworkin.
[1] *NE* X.9: 1181b15.   [2] *NE* I.2: 1094a24–b16.

Greek, male nor female, freeman nor slave...[3] And I mention this not as an idle methodological remark, but as a gesture towards an explanation of the fact that even a political science which undertakes to consider human affairs according to Aristotle's empirical but critical method cannot expect to arrive at Aristotle's or Plato's results. Our sense of personality, of privacy, of what Pascal called the heart, and of conscience, is such that even when we are responding to the charm of Plato's play of character or to Aristotle's *pièce de résistance* on friendship,[4] still we cannot but feel that the Greeks were not humanists; their understanding of themselves and their response to each other had not been *formed* by, for example, the parable of the Prodigal Son.

Still, no one was more aware than Plato or Aristotle that human self-understanding and responses *are formed* by symbols, such as myth and music—by the participation of the young in the educative play that will discipline and shape their tastes and dispose them for the serious lifelong play of participation in the politics of the *polis*. So the single topic treated at greatest length in Aristotle's esoteric *Politics* is the role of music in the education of the young.[5] But more important than the discourses *about* education in the works of Plato and Aristotle is the formative education of taste and disposition which is accomplished *in and by* those works themselves—so much so that their world-historical influence far exceeds that of any ruler of their or perhaps of any time. That their works create a shelter of meaning within which the questioning, hypotheses, and judgments of generation after generation are located—all this is obvious when one reflects on one's own vocabulary and its sources. What may not be quite so obvious, though it becomes equally clear on further reflection (particularly in reflecting on western culture and politics compared with the culture and politics of other civilizations), is the success of Plato and Aristotle in forming a sensibility corresponding to the human work and play of maintaining and inhabiting that space of meaning. It is a complex sensibility, formed by respect for the sinewy rigour of an esoteric Aristotelian lecture; by sharing Socrates' disgust at the speech-making of the sophist; by admiration for Socrates-Plato's willingness to return again and again to problems rather than rest in smooth solutions; by fear of being as complacent as old Cephalus; by shame at the thought of being less honest than Glaucon and Adeimantus or, rather, than the Plato who created them to press the question of moral nihilism to its end...Or

---

[3] Galatians 3: 28.   [4] *NE* VIII and IX.
[5] *Pol.* VIII.3–7: 1337b23–1342b34; likewise Plato, *Laws* II 653d–673d; III 700a–701a; VII 812b–816d.

consider the profound formation of sensibility accomplished, at a stroke, by the portraits of the philosopher:

> One who has joined this small company and tasted the happiness that is their portion; who has watched the frenzy of the multitude and seen that there is no soundness in the conduct of public life, nowhere an ally at whose side a champion of justice could hope to escape destruction; but that, like a man fallen among wild beasts, if he should refuse to take part in their misdeeds and could not hold out alone against the fury of all, he would be destined, before he could be of any service to his country or his friends, to perish having done no good to himself or to anyone else—one who has weighed all this keeps quiet and goes his own way, like a traveller who takes shelter under a wall from a driving storm of dust and hail; and seeing lawlessness spreading from all sides, is content if he can keep himself free from all iniquity while this life lasts, and take his departure with good hopes, in serenity and peace when the end comes.
>
> Surely, said Adeimantus, that would be no small achievement.
>
> Yes, but far less than he might achieve if his lot were cast in a society congenial to his nature, where he could grow to his full stature and save his community as well as himself.[6]

The temptation is to go on and on with this great celebration by Plato of the *erōs* of philosophic life in the *polis*. But I see no reason to doubt the explicit conclusion of classical political science—a conclusion on which the classical philosophers, moreover, *acted*, by devoting themselves to the educative effort of lifetimes—that the exercise of the mind and the experience of the play of intelligible symbolic forms not only are supremely worthwhile and in need of no further justification but also are indispensable and efficacious determinants of dispositions for political action.

Indeed, it is absurd to have to labour the point. Everyone here has experience of the intellectual life. Everyone knows how it is maintained by the powerful inclination of curiosity, of desire to know, to be aware of realities and not deceived by appearances, clear-headed and not muddled...Everyone knows how it is formed not only by straightforward learning and inquiry, but also by emulation, by respect for admired models, by attention to and imitation of *paradigms* of reason. And one knows, each of us from our own experience, how one's intellectual life is threatened with deformation by other powerful inclinations: to shirk, to fake, to conform, to

---

[6] *Republic* VI 496 (trans. F.M. Cornford). [In a footnote to the first and longer Socratic speech, Morrison, 'The Origins of Plato's Philosopher-Statesman' at 212, which reproduces the whole passage as I quote it, persuasively says:

> Cornford notes (in his translation): 'this last sentence alludes to the position of Plato himself, after he had renounced his early hopes of a political career and withdrawn to his task of training philosopher-statesmen in the Academy.' I do not agree. The position described is that of Plato before he was brought to feel that he could realize his political ambitions through the Academy.]

dogmatize, to bluster, to imitate not the philosopher but the sophist or the preacher or the journalist or the politician, with whose realms of discourse we cannot but be familiar. Everyone here knows what a delicate matter it is, being authentic in these matters. It would be difficult to have much experience of the joy of the serious play of intelligence without having experience of disgust at the shoddiness of what is offered as reasoning, and of shame at one's own shortcuts and evasions.

Well, there is much more to humanity than what I lamely called, just now, the 'intellectual life'; indeed, as I have already remarked, there is more to humanity than is clearly recognized even by Plato. In particular, the relationship between man and woman is quite imperfectly integrated into the Greek sensibility and into its images of the full stature of humanity. If the role of music in education gets the longest treatment in the *Politics*, friendship gets the longest (and much longer) treatment in Aristotle's *Ethics*, and his discussion of the forms and conditions of friendship is unsurpassed in perceptiveness. But he bluntly declares that there can be no full friendship between man and women, and sexual attraction and consummation plays little part in his account. If one wants an imaging of the sexual intercourse of man and woman as expression of a personal relationship, one will turn elsewhere. At the roots of our culture one will find, for instance, the *Song of Songs*, of which the first words are the Bride's: 'Let him kiss me with the kisses of his mouth':[7]

> I hear my Beloved.
> See how he comes
> leaping on the mountains,
> bounding over the hills...
>
> See where he stands
> behind our wall.
> He looks in at the window,
> he peers through the lattice.
>
> He lifts up his voice,
> My Beloved says to me
> 'Come then, my love,
> my lovely one, come.
> For see, winter is past, the rains are over and gone...'
> My beloved is mine and I am his....

---

[7] Song of Songs 1: 2; the quotations that follow are from 2: 8–11, 16–17, 3: 1–4, 4: 12, 16, 5: 1–6, 6: 2–3, 7: 12–13, 8: 5–7; the translation is, with minor alterations, from Jones, *The Jerusalem Bible*, where the footnotes supply one of the traditional versions of the allegorical interpretation of this part of the Bible; the footnotes to the Douai-Rheims translation give another; and there are other traditions, also reasonable.

> Before the dawn wind rises, before the shadows flee,
> return! Be, my Beloved, like a gazelle,
> a young stag on the mountain of the covenant.
>
> On my bed, at night, I sought him whom my heart loves.
> I sought but did not find him.
> So I will rise and go through the City;
> in the streets and the squares I will seek him
> whom my heart loves...
>
> The watchmen came upon me on their rounds in the City:
> 'Have you seen him whom my heart loves?'
>
> Scarcely had I passed them when I found him
> Whom my heart loves.
> I held him fast, nor would I let him go till
> I had brought him into my mother's house,
> Into the room of her who conceived me.

Later the Bridegroom sings:

> She is a garden enclosed, my sister, my promised bride;
> A garden enclosed,
> A sealed fountain...

And she replies:

> Awake, north wind, come, wind of the south,
> Breathe over my garden, to spread its sweet smell around.
> Let my Beloved come into his garden,
> Let him taste its rarest fruits.

He:

> I come into my garden,
> my sister, my promised bride,
> I gather my myrrh and balsam, I eat my honey and my honeycomb,
> I drink my wine and my milk.

Again, she sings:

> I sleep, but my heart is awake.
> I hear my Beloved knocking.
> 'Open to me, my sister, my love, my dove, my perfect one,
> for my head is covered with dew,
> my locks with the drops of night.'
> —'I have taken off my tunic; am I to put it on again?
> I have washed my feet, am I to dirty them again?'
> My Beloved thrust his hand through the hole in the door;
> I trembled to the core of my being.

> Then I rose to open to my Beloved,
> myrrh ran off my fingers
> pure myrrh off my fingers,
> onto the handle of the bolt.
>
> I opened to my Beloved, but he had turned his back and gone!
> My soul failed at his flight.
> I sought him but I did not find him....

But he turns up again, at the end of the *Song* (the set of songs):

> My Beloved went down to his garden,
> to the beds of spices,
> to pasture his flock in the gardens
> and gather lilies.
> I am my Beloved's, and my Beloved is mine.
> He pastures his flock among the lilies.
>
> Come my Beloved,
> let us go to the fields.
> We will spend the night in the villages,
> and in the morning we will go to the vineyards.
> We will see if the vines are budding,
> if their blossoms are opening, if the pomegranate trees are in flower;
> There I shall give you the gift of my love.

And as the first words were the Bride's, who compared the Bridegroom to an apple tree among the trees of the orchard (2: 3), so the last are the Bridegroom's:

> I awakened you under the apple tree,
> there where your mother conceived you,
> there where she who gave birth to you conceived you.
>
> Set me like a seal on your heart, like a seal on your arm.
> For love is strong as Death, jealousy as unyielding as the place of Death.
> The flash of it is a flash of fire, a flame of the Lord himself.
> Love no flood can quench, no torrents drown.

Such an imaging of the aspiration to marry such ardour and fidelity to the procreative capacities of men and women has powerfully shaped our sensibilities and thus our relations to each other as persons. It reveals, displays, and makes attractive the possibility of integrating powerful inclinations (which would and do otherwise issue in egocentric lust or casual procreation) into a new space of meaning and sentiment in which one's whole intentionality, plan of life, or sense of the point of living is redirected and reformed around a cooperation in friendship with an equal partner in sensuous, serious, ardent, and faithful marriage.

Everybody who has been disgusted at the rubbish in certain, say, Catholic or Communist pseudo-academic journals knows how bad models corrupt intellectual taste and standards of individual performance. The efficacy of bad models in that sphere of meaning in which our sexual interaction or activity takes place is, I think, no more doubtful.

English law indentifies a criminally obscene article as one whose 'effect is, if taken as a whole, such as to tend to deprave and corrupt persons who are likely...to read, see or hear the matter contained or embodied in it', although publication of such an article may now be 'justified as being for the public good on the ground that it is in the interests of science, literature, art or learning, or of other objects of general concern'.[8] Though there are practical difficulties associated with the application of this description of obscenity, I think it has the merit of correctly identifying the reason for proscribing obscene publications, namely, not that they shock or offend, but that they tend to deprave and corrupt. As the Appellate Committee of the House of Lords stressed with great force,

the words 'deprave and corrupt' in the statutory definition refer to the effect of an article on the minds (including the emotions) of the persons who read or see it. Of course, bad conduct may follow from the corruption of the mind, but it is not part of the statutory definition of an obscene article that it must induce bad conduct.[9]

I think the dissenting members of the President's Commission on Obscenity and Pornography (1970) were substantially correct when they said:

The government interest in regulating pornography has always related primarily to the prevention of moral corruption and *not* to the prevention of overt criminal acts and conduct, or the protection of persons from being shocked and/or offended.[10]

I think that they were further substantially correct when they said that 'the traffic in obscenity and pornography is a matter of national concern' because 'pornography has an eroding effect on society, on public morality, on respect for human worth, on attitudes toward family love, on culture'[11] (and also when they said that the traffic in pornography is *not* amongst the two or three most serious problems facing the community today).[12] So first I shall identify more precisely what I mean here by 'depraving' and 'corrupting'.

The first way in which obscene and pornographic communications corrupt is by inducing a disposition or state of the imagination

---

[8] Obscene Publications Act 1959, ss. 1(1), 4(1).
[9] *Director of Public Prosecutions v Whyte* [1972] AC 849 at 864 (see also 867) (per Lord Pearson) (see also at 862–3 per Lord Wilberforce; 871 per Lord Cross).
[10] *The Report of the Commission on Obscenity and Pornography—September 1970*, 457.
[11] Ibid., 458.   [12] Ibid., 478.

and sentiments in which it is difficult for people to engage in sexual intercourse otherwise than as a kind of masturbation of one partner on the other, or of both on each other. The privacy, secrecy, or intimacy of sexual intercourse is something to be valued as making it possible for what would otherwise be a mere pleasurable commotion of the senses and relief of tension to be instead a climactic *expression* of the affection, friendship, love between persons, affection which shapes their lives in many public ways but which also, where the context permits it to be offered and taken as such, can be given an expression whose peculiar joy is fully integrated with the meaning of their public lives as partners: husband and wife. Everybody knows how one's fat relentless ego threatens this mutuality. Women particularly are well aware when they are being taken by their husbands or lovers not for the person, unique and uniquely related to that person, but rather as a convenient, available instance of 'desirable woman' whose presence as an appealing figure in the man's aroused imagination impels him towards her until the moment when his biological tension is released, the appealing figure fades in his imagination, and his failure to integrate his insistent words and actions with a common life of friendship becomes evident even to him. The most obvious, but only the most obvious, instance of this form of corruption is willingness to engage in intercourse with a person while imagining that one is engaging in intercourse with *another* person, real or imaginary. This sort of living out a lie seems to me to rob of worth human relationships that should be a principal locus of whatever worth there is in one's conduct of life.

Of course, it is possible for individuals to use, say, the *Song of Songs* as a stimulus or occasion for this sort of quasi-masturbatory intercourse. But it is intrinsic to the artistry of artistic evocations of sexual love that the sensuous symbols which bear the meaning and force of the evocation are so structured as to tend, principally, to present the experience of such love, and of desiring its consummation, as a human reality open to our contemplation and appreciation rather than as a stimulus to feelings or desires calling for gratification. As Strawson has remarked (but it is really a commonplace of aesthetics of every school),

> an aesthetic interest in an individual is not any kind of practical interest, not an interest in anything it can or should do, or that we can do with it, not even an interest in specific responses (say, excitement or stupefaction) which it will produce in us. (If it were this kind of interest, there could indeed be general rules or recipes.)[13]

---

[13] Strawson, 'Aesthetic Appraisal and Works of Art' at 12.

Just as an actor does not vent his own emotions, but conceives and enacts the emotions of the character being played, so creative artists do not so much vent their own emotions as imagine and conceive emotions and feelings in such fashion that their understanding of them can be communicated through the symbolic form of their chosen art.

So aestheticians of many kinds have insisted on the requirement of detachment, 'contemplation,' 'aesthetic' attitude, or attention or objectivity: 'psychical distance' between the work and its public (including the artist). Such distance is obtained by 'separating the object and its appeal from one's self, by putting it out of gear with practical needs and ends'.[14] It does not imply a purely intellectual or impersonal relation between person and work, but a peculiar relation 'filtered' of the 'practical, concrete nature of its appeal'.[15] The ideal in both creation and appreciation is the *'utmost decrease of Distance without its disappearance'*.[16]

Such accounts of aesthetics are not concerned to condemn or even discuss obscenity and pornography. But the accounts enable us to characterize the pornographer as one calculating to avoid all the 'special precautions' with which art must handle certain topics, if the psychical distance necessary for aesthetic appreciation is to be maintained. Some ages and cultures require fewer precautions than others; but whichever are required at any given time and place, the pornographer sets out to defy them. The techniques by which pornographers deliberately destroy the aesthetic attitude include the attribution of male psychology to the female, the arousing of identification with, and the compelling of envy for, the fictional characters in their sexual opportunities and exploits, and many other specifiable narrative and descriptive devices. All such techniques replace aesthetic attention with an attitude in which readers' or viewers' practical concerns with enjoying emotionally aroused states intrude upon and suppress an understanding contemplation of the created symbol.[17]

So the first evil of pornography is that it corrupts the imagination and feeling by stimulating desires and images which conspire with what we can call, compendiously, selfishness—conspire to break into the enclosed garden in which sexual intercourse can be so fine an expression of radically committed friendship. I think the same is true, in differing ways, of advertising which appeals to prurient interest after the fashion of the Sunday magazine supplements, etc. All such publishing would be banned in a society that truly cared for affection between men and women.

---

[14] Bullough, *Aesthetics*, 96.   [15] *Ibid.*, 91; see also Langer, *Feeling and Form*, 49.
[16] Bullough, *Aesthetics*, 100   [17] See essay 17 at nn. 76–89 (1967a at 234–5).

The second way in which pornography depraves and corrupts is by expressing, in powerfully resonant symbols, a profound contempt for people, especially women, as objects to be had, used,—d. With astonishing rapidity what began as desire ends as aggression directed against partner, audience, humanity at large. The finale of *Oh! Calcutta* takes or took the form of the nude cast walking round the stage shouting [harsh, demotic, and obscene words for defecation, copulation, and genitalia]. There is a gradual crescendo. Then they all start making remarks about the show itself; what we in the audience must be thinking, such as 'I wonder what *you* will do when you get home' and 'I bet you're wondering what she does when she has her period' (referring to the naked young women on the stage). Finally they simulate mass copulation, shouting 'Screw on the stage every night' and so forth.[18] Earlier a woman, an actress, kneels naked with her back to the audience, while a man discourses on freedom, saying:

Now let's take another look at Jean. She kneels there—or squats there—in a posture that must be profoundly embarrassing. You might even call it humiliating. However, if the spirit moves her, she is at liberty to get up and go.

[and terminate her employment as an actress]

Jean, the submissive household servant in temporary disgrace, is a free agent... And she is free not only as a parlour maid, but as a human being....

She will formally present herself. She will now arch and offer... It's an outrage to the human spirit... [19]

Ninety per cent of Danish sex films, so it is said, end with an inter-racial fellatio scene of the following form...(described by a young French journalist [quoted by Holbrook, *The Pseudo-Revolution*, 18]). What may shame and disgust us, here in the Philosophy building (12 Merton Street) this evening, is, in its resonant, carefully constructed context, a climax which draws its consenting audience into a world full of violence, hate, racism, apartheid of the race into dominant male and abused female.

Now listen to Jonathan Miller, in his lecture to the British Academy eighteen months ago [October 1971]:

...I cannot fear the harmful effects of pornography, since anyone normal who has been exposed to pornography, hard or soft, far from falling under its pornotopian spell loses interest after a while and returns with pleasure and gusto to the varieties of experience of the world at large. Those who become addicted

---

[18] [At the seminar, several further contemporary examples of obscene and pornographic public spectacles, magazines, Danish sex films, etc. were supplied at this point, as reported by Holbrook, *The Pseudo-Revolution* and other works of Holbrook around 1972.]

[19] Holbrook, *The Pseudo-Revolution*, 145, quoting [the playlet 'Who: Whom'] from Kenneth Tynan's 'Entertainment with Music', *Oh! Calcutta* (1969).

to its characteristic impoverishments are in a mental state close to that of an obsessional neurotic.... [I]t offers for those who for some reason or other *are* impoverished a secure annex of controllable fantasy within which their limited emotional versatility will not show up. For the rest it is a holiday where they are free for a moment to indulge their fantasies and furnish themselves with new images; for fantasy after all plays a vital and nourishing part in maintaining the health and versatility of the imagination. Like dreams, we need fantasies in order to play with emotional conjectures; and a mind unstocked with the variety of alternative conjectures is not equipped to meet the challenges of reality.

...'*the* variety'! Unless your mind is stocked with images and 'conjectures' of bestiality, fellatio, infidelity, promiscuity, and all that Sade's works deploy, you are unequipped to meet reality's challenges. All or nothing. Miller goes on—

He who extracts from pornography an endorsement of his tendency to exploit another as if he [!] had no feelings, is already crippled by some early failure in psychological manufacture and he will exploit his sexual partners just as he does his family or his colleagues in business. At a time in history when our institutions make promiscuous objective use of human beings anyway it seems inappropriate to focus on pornography as a special source of this tendency.

Anyway, I am convinced that the asphyxiated poverty of much pornography arises from the fact that sex and its representation have been quarantined for so long that pornography has fallen into an invalid condition, thereby acquiring the contagious features that we dread. Re-established as part of all the things we consume, it will revert to its normal complexion and proportion.[20]

Miller's remarkable thesis, thus, is that there is a normal level of pornography (last reached, I suppose, in the late Roman Empire before Christianity 'quarantined sex and its representation')—as if there were a normal level of crimes of violence, of bear-baiting and cock-fighting, of slavery, of child abuse... What was the normal level of sadistic-sexual gratification for town- and urban-dwellers who during the centuries-long pagan Roman Empire made weekly visits to the lethal spectacles of the stadium? That there is a normal incidence of such attitudes towards other people is belied by all we know about history, and about the education of attitudes that makes our civilization distinct from others and our society worth distinguishing from and defending against racists and Nazis. Miller[21] goes on to quote and paraphrase extensively from, and heavily rely upon, the anthropological work of Mary Douglas, without a glance at her view that every civilization and society uses the human body to express its attitudes to social organization, interpersonal relations, and self-identification, and that because there is a drive for consonance

---

[20] Miller, *Censorship and the Limits of Permission* at 297–8.   [21] *Ibid.* at 299–301.

between all levels of experience, this is a two-way process in which social organization, interpersonal relations, and self-identification are profoundly affected by the symbols (not to mention the taboos) by which a society mediates to its members their experience of their bodies.[22] A society that allows potent symbols of the bodily degradation of its members to resonate with supreme allure through the media of communication is *teaching* an attitude to people. If people fail to adopt that attitude in their dispositions and actions, it must be at the cost of a profound disintegration and dissociation of their imaginative and emotional life, analogous in its own way to the dissociation paradigmatically exhibited by the gentle home life of some of the Nazi extermination-camp commandants. Someone who thinks that concern over pornography is like trying to adjust one's dress before jumping from a burning building[23] seems to me to be afflicted by the delusion that our attitudes to the human body, to each other, and to ourselves are like pieces of clothing that we can just put on, take off, or 'adjust', bit by bit.

NOTE

The essay ends hastily, running out of seminar time, and fails to articulate, even in outline, a full set of reasons against the use of pornography and against legal or social permission of its publication. The reasons are of two broad types.

Although secondary, I think (see at n. 10 above), one type of reason concerns the causal links between use of pornography and the perpetration of indisputably harmful acts including, at one extreme, rapes and sexual murders, very often associated with heavy use of violent pornography. Evidence about this kind of causal influence was given a sophisticated review in the report of the Attorney-General's Commission on Pornography ('Meese Report') in 1986.

The other type of reason concerns the far-reaching ways in which using pornography wounds one's understanding appreciation of, and responsiveness to, the good of marital commitment, and in so doing not only destroys particular marriages quite directly but also wounds quite pervasively the personal integrity and social culture needed for justice to children (and to all whom dysfunctional children abuse, betray, or neglect) and for the survival of the community in a world which, after all, is

---

[22] Douglas, *Purity and Danger.*
[23] Miller at 302 (last sentence of his lecture):

Our current concern with obscenity and pornography merely delays constructive social action and presents a spectator from another planet with an image as absurd as that of someone trying to adjust his dress before jumping from a burning building.

[Miller had also participated in the Hare-Dworkin seminar earlier in the university term.] [My final comment on Miller's analogy was not very pertinent. It is hard to say what he was suggesting has such great social importance that concern with the evils of pornography is as trivial and senseless as adjusting one's clothing in a supreme emergency. But, whatever it was, his argument was, I think, sophistical in suggesting that because there are or may be problems of greater importance, the availability and use of pornography is not importantly harmful. In significant ways, the beginning of the 'sexual revolution' was the surrender by courts and legislatures, in the late 1950s and early 1960s, of our culture's longstanding resistance to the dissemination of obscene books and pictures; and the sexual revolution has (to speak only of the macro level) left our nations physically and spiritually unmanned in face of the challenge—a burning building certainly beyond Miller's reckoning—of reverse colonization and the prospect of coerced cultural and constitutional transformation with or without civil war of some unpredictable degree.]

not and will not be indulgent to decadent peoples. These reasons are ancillary, then, to those explored and articulated in expounding the ethics of sex and marriage in essays III.20–2 and synoptically in essay IV.5 (2002a), sec. XIX.

See also George, 'Making Children Moral: Pornography, Parents and the Public Interest' in his *In Defense of Natural Law*, 184–95.

BIBLIOGRAPHY OF THE WORKS OF JOHN FINNIS

1962	a		'Developments in Judicial Jurisprudence', Adelaide L Rev 1: 317–37
	b		'The Immorality of the Deterrent', Adelaide Univ Mag: 47–61
1963			'Doves and Serpents', The Old Palace 38: 438–41
1967	a	I.17	'Reason and Passion: The Constitutional Dialectic of Free Speech and Obscenity', University of Pennyslvania L Rev 116: 222–43
	b	IV.8	'Blackstone's Theoretical Intentions', Natural L Forum 12: 63–83
	c		'Punishment and Pedagogy', The Oxford Review 5: 83–93
	d		'Review of Zelman Cowen, *Sir John Latham and Other Papers*', LQR 83: 289–90
1968	a	III.10	'Old and New in Hart's Philosophy of Punishment', The Oxford Review 8: 73–80
	b		'Constitutional Law', *Annual Survey of Commonwealth Law 1967* (Butterworth), 20–33, 71–98
	c		'Separation of Powers in the Australian Constitution', Adelaide L Rev 3: 159–77
	d		Review of Neville March Hunnings, *Film Censors and the Law*, LQR 84: 430–2
	e		'Natural Law in *Humanae vitae*', LQR 84: 467–71
	f		Review of H. Phillip Levy, *The Press Council*, LQR 84: 582
	g		'Law, Morality and Mind Control', Zenith (University Museum, Oxford) 6: 7–8
1969	a		'Constitutional Law', *Annual Survey of Commonwealth Law 1968* (Butterworth), 2–15, 32–49, 53–75, 98–114
	b		Review of Herbert L. Packer, *The Limits of the Criminal Sanction*, Oxford Magazine, 86 no. 1 (new series), 10–11
1970	a	I.6	'Reason, Authority and Friendship in Law and Morals', in Khanbai, Katz, and Pineau (eds), *Jowett Papers 1968–1969* (Oxford: Blackwell), 101–24
	b		'Natural Law and Unnatural Acts', Heythrop J 11: 365–87
	c		i. 'Abortion and Legal Rationality', Adelaide L Rev 3: 431–67 ii. 'Three Schemes of Regulation', in Noonan (ed.), *The Morality of Abortion: Legal and Historical Perspectives* (HUP)
	d		'Constitutional Law', *Annual Survey of Commonwealth Law 1969* (Butterworth), 2–4, 27–34, 37–50, 65–81
	e		Review of H.B. Acton, *The Philosophy of Punishment*, Oxford Magazine, 87 (new series) (13 April)
	f		Review of Colin Howard, *Australian Constitutional Law*, LQR 86: 416–18

1971	a	IV.21	'Revolutions and Continuity of Law', in A.W.B. Simpson (ed.), *Oxford Essays in Jurisprudence: Second Series* (OUP), 44–76
	b		'The Abortion Act: What Has Changed?', Criminal L Rev: 3–12
	c		'Constitutional Law', *Annual Survey of Commonwealth Law 1970* (Butterworth), 2–4, 17–31, 33–42, 51–60
1972	a	III.11	'The Restoration of Retribution', Analysis 32: 131–5
	b	IV.18	'Some Professorial Fallacies about Rights', Adelaide L Rev 4: 377–88
	c		'The Value of the Human Person', Twentieth Century [Australia] 27: 126–37
	d		'Bentham et le droit naturel classique', Archives de Philosophie du Droit 17: 423–7
	e		'Constitutional Law', *Annual Survey of Commonwealth Law 1971* (Butterworth), 2–5, 11–25, 28–41
	f		'Meaning and Ambiguity in Punishment (and Penology)', Osgoode Hall LJ 10: 264–8
1973	a	III.3	Review of John Rawls, *A Theory of Justice* (1972), Oxford Magazine 90 no. 1 (new series) (26 January)
	b	III.18	'The Rights and Wrongs of Abortion: A Reply to Judith Jarvis Thomson', Philosophy & Public Affairs 2: 117–45
	c		'Constitutional Law', *Annual Survey of Commonwealth Law 1972* (Butterworth), 2–8, 23–56, 62–6
1974	a		'Constitutional Law', *Annual Survey of Commonwealth Law 1973* (Butterworth), 1–66
	b		'Commonwealth and Dependencies', in *Halsbury's Laws of England*, vol. 6 (4th edn, Butterworth), 315–601
	c		'Rights and Wrongs in Legal Responses to Population Growth', in J.N. Santamaria (ed.), *Man—How Will He Survive?* (Adelaide), 91–100
	d		Review of R.S. Gae, *The Bank Nationalisation Case and the Constitution*, Modern L Rev 37: 120
1975			'Constitutional Law', *Annual Survey of Commonwealth Law 1974* (Butterworth), 1–61
1976	a		'Constitutional Law', *Annual Survey of Commonwealth Law 1975* (Butterworth), 1–56
	b		Chapters 18–21 (with Germain Grisez), in R. Lawler, D.W. Wuerl, and T.C. Lawler (eds), *The Teaching of Christ* (Huntingdon, IN: OSV), 275–354
1977	a	I.3	'Scepticism, Self-refutation and the Good of Truth', in P.M. Hacker and J. Raz (eds), *Law, Morality and Society: Essays in Honour of H.L.A. Hart* (OUP), 247–67
	b		'Some Formal Remarks about "Custom"', in International Law Association, Report of the First Meeting [April 1977] on the Theory and Methodology of International Law, 14–21
1978	a		'Catholic Social Teaching: *Populorum Progressio* and After', Church Alert (SODEPAX Newsletter) 19: 2–9; also in James V. Schall (ed.), *Liberation Theology in Latin America* (San Francisco: Ignatius Press, 1982)

	b		'Conscience, Infallibility and Contraception', The Month 239: 410–17
	c		'Abortion: Legal Aspects of', in Warren T. Reich (ed.), *Encyclopedia of Bioethics* (New York: Free Press), 26–32
1979		V.18	'Catholic Faith and the World Order: Reflections on E.R. Norman', Clergy Rev 64: 309–18
1980	a		*Natural Law and Natural Rights* (OUP) (425 pp)
			Legge Naturali e Diritti Naturali (trans. F. Di Blasi) (Milan: Giappichelli, 1996)
			Ley Natural y Derechos Naturales (trans. C. Orrego) (Buenos Aires: Abeledo-Perrot, 2000)
			Prawo naturalne i uprawnienia naturalne (trans. Karolina Lossman) Klasycy Filozofii Prawa (Warsaw: Dom Wydawniczy ABC, 2001)
			自然法与自然权利 ([Mandarin] trans. Jiaojiao Dong, Yi Yang, Xiaohui Liang) (Beijing: 2004)
			Lei Natural e Direitos Naturais (trans. Leila Mendes) (Sao Leopoldo, Brazil: Editora Unisinos, 2007)
	b		'Reflections on an Essay in Christian Ethics: Part I: Authority in Morals', Clergy Rev 65: 51–7: 'Part II: Morals and Method', 87–93
	c	V.19	'The Natural Law, Objective Morality, and Vatican II', in William E. May (ed), *Principles of Catholic Moral Life* (Chicago: Franciscan Herald Press), 113–49
1981	a		[*British North America Acts: The Role of Parliament*: Report from the Foreign Affairs Committee, House of Commons Paper 1980–81 HC 42 (21 January) (87 pp)]
	b		'Observations de M J.M. Finnis' [on Georges Kalinowski's review of *Natural Law and Natural Rights*], Archives de Philosophie du Droit 26: 425–7
	c		[Foreign Affairs Committee, *Supplementary Report on the British North America Acts: The Role of Parliament*, House of Commons Paper 1980–81 HC 295 (15 April) (23 pp)]
	d		[Foreign Affairs Committee, *Third Report on the British North America Acts: The Role of Parliament*, House of Commons Paper 1981–82 HC 128 (22 December) (17 pp)]
	e		'Natural Law and the "Is"-"Ought" Question: An Invitation to Professor Veatch', Cath Lawyer 26: 266–77
1982	a		(with Germain Grisez) 'The Basic Principles of Natural Law: A Reply to Ralph McInerny', American J Juris 26: 21–31
	b		Review of Anthony Battaglia, *Towards a Reformulation of Natural Law*, Scottish J Theol 35: 555–6
1983	a		'The Responsibilities of the United Kingdom Parliament and Government under the Australian Constitution', Adelaide L Rev 9: 91–107
	b		*Fundamentals of Ethics* (OUP; Washington, DC: Georgetown University Press) (163 pp)
	c		'Power to Enforce Treaties in Australia—The High Court goes Centralist?', Oxford J Legal St 3: 126–30

	d		'The Fundamental Themes of *Laborem Exercens*', in Paul L. Williams (ed.), *Catholic Social Thought and the Social Teaching of John Paul II* (Scranton: Northeast Books), 19–31
	e		['In Vitro Fertilisation: Morality and Public Policy', Evidence submitted by the Catholic Bishops' Joint Committee on Bio-ethical Issues to the [Warnock] Committee of Inquiry into Human Fertilisation and Embryology, May, 5–18]
1984	a	I.10	i. 'Practical Reasoning, Human Goods and the End of Man', Proc Am Cath Phil Ass 58: 23–36; also in ii. New Blackfriars 66 (1985) 438–51
	b	IV.2	'The Authority of Law in the Predicament of Contemporary Social Theory', J Law, Ethics & Pub Policy 1: 115–37
	c		['Response to the Warnock Report', submission to Secretary of State for Social Services by the Catholic Bishops' Joint Bioethics Committee on Bio-ethical Issues, December, 3–17]
	d		'IVF and the Catholic Tradition', The Month 246: 55–8
	e		'Reforming the Expanded External Affairs Power', in Report of the External Affairs Subcommittee to the Standing Committee of the Australian Constitutional Convention (September), 43–51
1985	a	III.1	'A Bill of Rights for Britain? The Moral of Contemporary Jurisprudence' (Maccabaean Lecture in Jurisprudence), Proc Brit Acad 71: 303–31
	b	IV.9	'On "Positivism" and "Legal-Rational Authority"', Oxford J Leg St 3: 74–90
	c	IV.13	'On "The Critical Legal Studies Movement"', American J Juris 30: 21–42; also in J. Bell and J. Eekelaar (eds), *Oxford Essays in Jurisprudence: Third Series* (OUP, 1987), 145–65
	d		'Morality and the Ministry of Defence' (review), The Tablet, 3 August, 804–5
	e		'Personal Integrity, Sexual Morality and Responsible Parenthood', Anthropos [now Anthropotes] 1: 43–55
1986	a		'The "Natural Law Tradition"', J Legal Ed 36: 492–5
	b		'The Laws of God, the Laws of Man and Reverence for Human Life', in R. Hittinger (ed.), *Linking the Human Life Issues* (Chicago: Regnery Books), 59–98
1987	a	I.9	'Natural Inclinations and Natural Rights: Deriving "Ought" from "Is" according to Aquinas', in L. Elders and K. Hedwig (eds), *Lex et Libertas: Freedom and Law according to St Thomas Aquinas* (Studi Tomistici 30, Libreria Editrice Vaticana), 43–55
	b	II.8	'The Act of the Person' *Persona Veritá e Morale*, atti del Congresso Internazionale di Teologia Morale, Rome 1986 (Rome: Cittá Nuova Editrice), 159–75
	c	III.2	'Legal Enforcement of Duties to Oneself: Kant v. Neo-Kantians', Columbia L Rev 87: 433–56
	d	IV.4	'On Positivism and the Foundations of Legal Authority: Comment', in Ruth Gavison (ed.), *Issues in Legal Philosophy: the Influence of H.L.A. Hart* (OUP), 62–75

	e	IV.12	'On Reason and Authority in Law's Empire', Law and Philosophy 6: 357–80
	f		Germain Grisez, Joseph Boyle, and John Finnis, 'Practical Principles, Moral Truth, and Ultimate Ends', American J Juris 32: 99–151 (also, with original table of contents restored, in 1991d)
	g		*Nuclear Deterrence, Morality and Realism* (with Joseph Boyle and Germain Grisez) (OUP) (429 pp)
	h		'Answers [to questions about nuclear and non-nuclear defence options]', in Oliver Ramsbottom (ed.), *Choices: Nuclear and Non-Nuclear Defence Options* (London: Brasseys' Defence Publishers), 219–34
	i		'The Claim of Absolutes', The Tablet 241: 364–6
	j		['On Human Infertility Services and Bioethical Research', response by the Catholic Bishops' Joint Committee on Bioethical Issues to the Department of Health and Social Security, June, 3–12]
1988	a	V.21	'The Consistent Ethic: A Philosophical Critique', in Thomas G. Fuechtmann (ed.), *Consistent Ethic of Life* (Kansas: Sheed & Ward), 140–81
	b	V.20	'Nuclear Deterrence, Christian Conscience, and the End of Christendom', New Oxford Rev [Berkeley, CA] July–August: 6–16
	c		'Goods are Meant for Everyone: Reflection on Encyclical *Sollicitudo Rei Socialis*', L'Osservatore Romano, weekly edn, 21 March, 21
	d		'"Faith and Morals": A Note', The Month 21/2: 563–7
	e		Germain Grisez, Joseph Boyle, John Finnis, and William E. May, '"Every Marital Act Ought to be Open to New Life": Toward a Clearer Understanding', The Thomist 52: 365–426, also in Grisez, Boyle, Finnis, and May, *The Teaching of Humanae Vitae: A Defense* (San Francisco: Ignatius Press); Italian trans. in Anthropotes 1: 73–122
	f		'Absolute Moral Norms: Their Ground, Force and Permanence', Anthropotes 2: 287–303
1989	a	II.5	'Persons and their Associations', Proc Aristotelian Soc, Supp. vol. 63: 267–74
	b	IV.3	'Law as Coordination', Ratio Juris 2: 97–104
	c	V.11	'On Creation and Ethics', Anthropotes 2: 197–206
	d		'La morale chrétienne et la guerre: entretien avec John Finnis', Catholica 13: 15–23
	e		'Russell Hittinger's Straw Man', Fellowship of Catholic Scholars Newsletter 12/2: 6–8 (corrigenda in following issue)
	f		'Nuclear Deterrence and Christian Vocation', New Blackfriars 70: 380–7
1990	a	I.12	'Aristotle, Aquinas, and Moral Absolutes', Catholica: International Quarterly Selection 12: 7–15; Spanish trans. by Carlos I. Massini-Correas in Persona y Derecho 28 (1993), and in

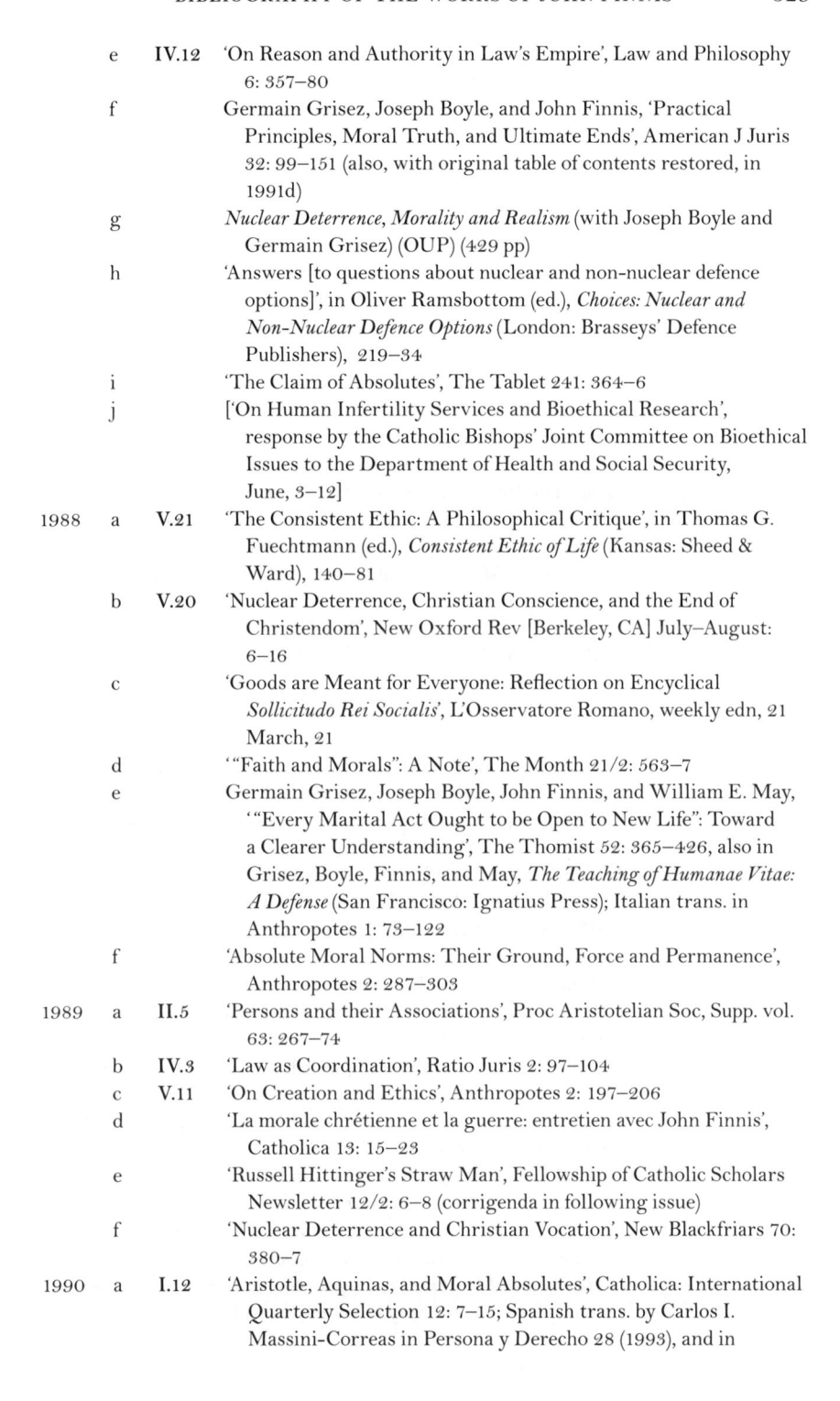

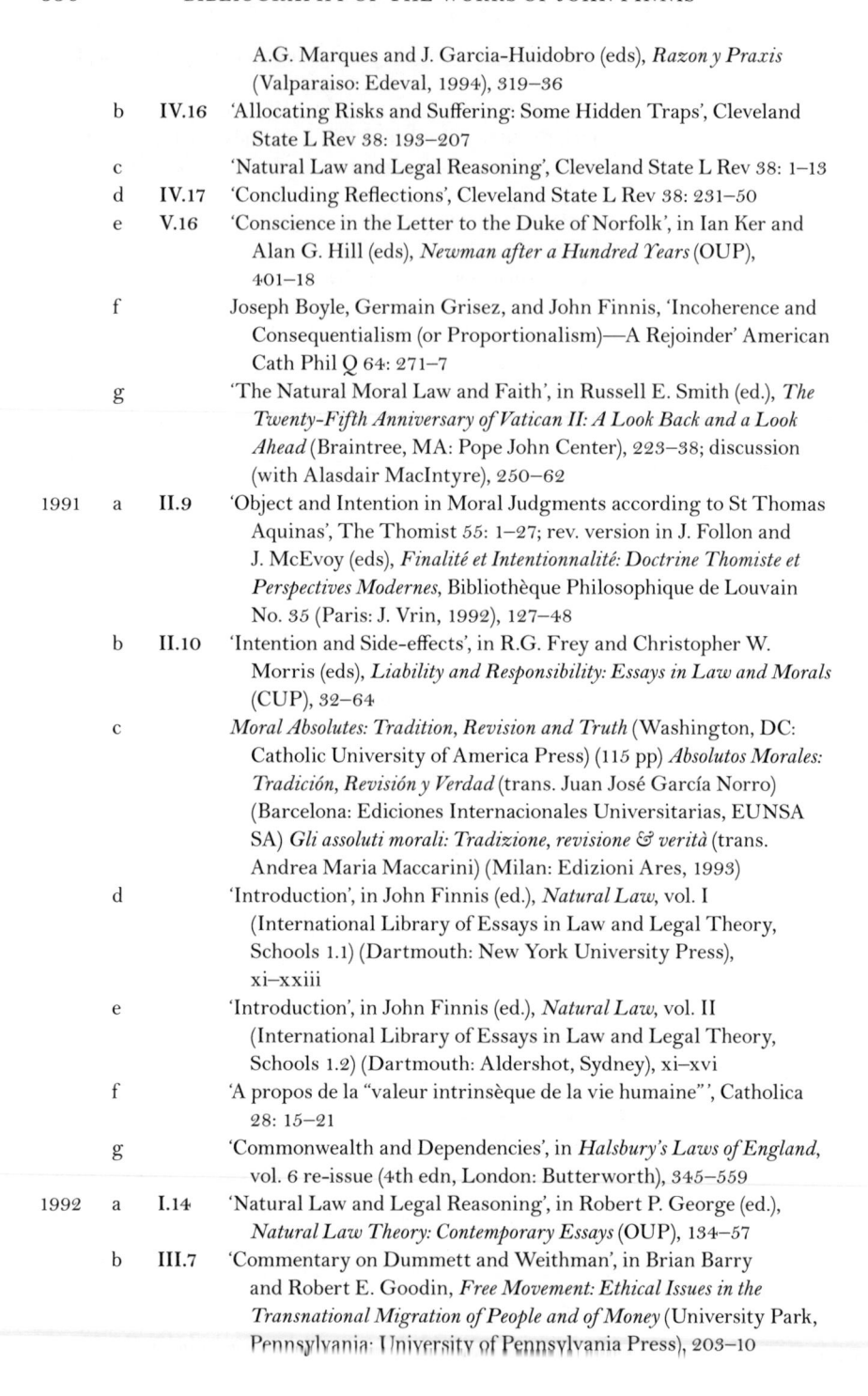

			A.G. Marques and J. Garcia-Huidobro (eds), *Razon y Praxis* (Valparaiso: Edeval, 1994), 319–36
	b	IV.16	'Allocating Risks and Suffering: Some Hidden Traps', Cleveland State L Rev 38: 193–207
	c		'Natural Law and Legal Reasoning', Cleveland State L Rev 38: 1–13
	d	IV.17	'Concluding Reflections', Cleveland State L Rev 38: 231–50
	e	V.16	'Conscience in the Letter to the Duke of Norfolk', in Ian Ker and Alan G. Hill (eds), *Newman after a Hundred Years* (OUP), 401–18
	f		Joseph Boyle, Germain Grisez, and John Finnis, 'Incoherence and Consequentialism (or Proportionalism)—A Rejoinder' American Cath Phil Q 64: 271–7
	g		'The Natural Moral Law and Faith', in Russell E. Smith (ed.), *The Twenty-Fifth Anniversary of Vatican II: A Look Back and a Look Ahead* (Braintree, MA: Pope John Center), 223–38; discussion (with Alasdair MacIntyre), 250–62
1991	a	II.9	'Object and Intention in Moral Judgments according to St Thomas Aquinas', The Thomist 55: 1–27; rev. version in J. Follon and J. McEvoy (eds), *Finalité et Intentionnalité: Doctrine Thomiste et Perspectives Modernes*, Bibliothèque Philosophique de Louvain No. 35 (Paris: J. Vrin, 1992), 127–48
	b	II.10	'Intention and Side-effects', in R.G. Frey and Christopher W. Morris (eds), *Liability and Responsibility: Essays in Law and Morals* (CUP), 32–64
	c		*Moral Absolutes: Tradition, Revision and Truth* (Washington, DC: Catholic University of America Press) (115 pp) *Absolutos Morales: Tradición, Revisión y Verdad* (trans. Juan José García Norro) (Barcelona: Ediciones Internacionales Universitarias, EUNSA SA) *Gli assoluti morali: Tradizione, revisione & verità* (trans. Andrea Maria Maccarini) (Milan: Edizioni Ares, 1993)
	d		'Introduction', in John Finnis (ed.), *Natural Law*, vol. I (International Library of Essays in Law and Legal Theory, Schools 1.1) (Dartmouth: New York University Press), xi–xxiii
	e		'Introduction', in John Finnis (ed.), *Natural Law*, vol. II (International Library of Essays in Law and Legal Theory, Schools 1.2) (Dartmouth: Aldershot, Sydney), xi–xvi
	f		'A propos de la "valeur intrinsèque de la vie humaine"', Catholica 28: 15–21
	g		'Commonwealth and Dependencies', in *Halsbury's Laws of England*, vol. 6 re-issue (4th edn, London: Butterworth), 345–559
1992	a	I.14	'Natural Law and Legal Reasoning', in Robert P. George (ed.), *Natural Law Theory: Contemporary Essays* (OUP), 134–57
	b	III.7	'Commentary on Dummett and Weithman', in Brian Barry and Robert E. Goodin, *Free Movement: Ethical Issues in the Transnational Migration of People and of Money* (University Park, Pennsylvania: University of Pennsylvania Press), 203–10

	c	III.15	'Economics, Justice and the Value of Life: Concluding Remarks', in Luke Gormally (ed.), *Economics and the Dependent Elderly: Autonomy, Justice and Quality of Care* (CUP), 189–98
	d	V.9	'*Historical Consciousness*' *and Theological Foundations*, Etienne Gilson Lecture No. 15 (Toronto: Pontifical Institute of Mediaeval Studies) (32 pp)
	e	V.17	'On the Grace of Humility: A New Theological Reflection', The Allen Review 7: 4–7
1993	a	II.16/ III.19	'Abortion and Health Care Ethics', in Raanan Gillon (ed.), *Principles of Health Care Ethics* (Chichester: John Wiley), 547–57
	b		'The Legal Status of the Unborn Baby', Catholic Medical Quarterly 43: 5–11
	c	II.19	'*Bland*: Crossing the Rubicon?', LQR 109: 329–37
	d		'Theology and the Four Principles: A Roman Catholic View I' (with Anthony Fisher OP), in Raanon Gillon (ed.), *Principles of Health Care Ethics* (Chichester: John Wiley), 31–44
	e		'The "Value of Human Life" and "The Right to Death": Some Reflections on *Cruzan* and Ronald Dworkin', Southern Illinois University LJ 17: 559–71
1994	a	II.12	'On Conditional Intentions and Preparatory Intentions', in Luke Gormally (ed.), *Moral Truth and Moral Tradition: Essays in Honour of Peter Geach and Elizabeth Anscombe* (Dublin: Four Courts Press), 163–76
	b		'Law, Morality, and "Sexual Orientation"', Notre Dame L Rev 69: 1049–76; also, with additions, Notre Dame J Law, Ethics & Public Policy 9 (1995) 11–39
	c		'Liberalism and Natural Law Theory', Mercer L Rev 45: 687–704
	d		'"Shameless Acts" in Colorado: Abuse of Scholarship in Constitutional Cases', Academic Questions 7/4: 10–41
	e		Germain Grisez and John Finnis, 'Negative Moral Precepts Protect the Dignity of the Human Person', L'Osservatore Romano, English edn, 23 February
	f		'Beyond the Encyclical', The Tablet, 8 January, reprinted in John Wilkins (ed.), *Understanding* Veritatis Splendor (London: SPCK), 69–76
	g		Germain Grisez, John Finnis, and William E. May, 'Indissolubility, Divorce and Holy Communion', New Blackfriars 75 (June), 321–30
	h		'"Living Will" Legislation', in Luke Gormally (ed.), *Euthanasia, Clinical Practice and the Law* (London: Linacre Centre), 167–76
	i		'Unjust Laws in a Democratic Society: Some Philosophical and Theological Reflections', in Joseph Joblin and Réal Tremblay (eds), *I cattolici e la società pluralista: il caso delle leggi imperfette: atti del I Colloquio sui cattolici nella società pluralista: Roma, 9–12 Novembre 1994* (Bologna: ESP), 99–114
1995	a	II.11	'Intention in Tort Law', in David Owen (ed.), *Philosophical Foundations of Tort Law* (OUP), 229–48

	b	III.14	'A Philosophical Case against Euthanasia', 'The Fragile Case for Euthanasia: A Reply to John Harris', and 'Misunderstanding the Case against Euthanasia: Response to Harris's First Reply', in John Keown (ed.), *Euthanasia: Ethical, Legal and Clinical Perspectives* (CUP), 23–35, 46–55, 62–71
	c		'History of Philosophy of Law' (465–8), 'Problems in the Philosophy of Law' (468–72), 'Austin' (67), 'Defeasible' (181), 'Dworkin' (209–10), 'Grotius' (328), 'Hart' (334), 'Legal Positivism' (476–7), 'Legal Realism' (477), 'Natural Law' (606–7), 'Natural Rights' (607), in Ted Honderich (ed.), *Oxford Companion to Philosophy* (OUP)
1996	a	III.5	'Is Natural Law Theory Compatible with Limited Government?', in Robert P. George (ed.), *Natural Law, Liberalism, and Morality* (OUP), 1–26
	b	III.13	'The Ethics of War and Peace in the Catholic Natural Law Tradition', in Terry Nardin (ed.), *The Ethics of War and Peace* (Princeton University Press), 15–39
	c	IV.7	'The Truth in Legal Positivism', in Robert P. George (ed.), *The Autonomy of Law: Essays on Legal Positivism* (OUP), 195–214
	d		'Unjust Laws in a Democratic Society: Some Philosophical and Theological Reflections', Notre Dame L Rev 71: 595–604 (a revised version of 1994i)
	e	I.13	'Loi naturelle', in Monique Canto-Sperber (ed.), *Dictionnaire de Philosophie Morale* (Paris: Presses Universitaires de France), 862–8
1997	a		'Natural Law—Positive Law', in A. Lopez Trujillo, I. Herranz, and E. Sgreccia (eds), *'Evangelium Vitae' and Law* (Libreria Editrice Vaticana), 199–209
	b	I.15	'Commensuration and Public Reason', in Ruth Chang (ed.), *Incommensurability, Comparability and Practical Reasoning* (HUP), 215–33, 285–9
	c	III.21	'Law, Morality and "Sexual Orientation"', in John Corvino (ed.), *Same Sex: Debating the Ethics, Science, and Culture of Homosexuality* (Lanham: Rowman & Littlefield), 31–43
	d	III.22	'The Good of Marriage and the Morality of Sexual Relations: Some Philosophical and Historical Observations', Am J Juris 42: 97–134
1998	a	I.16	'Public Reason, Abortion and Cloning', Valparaiso Univ LR 32: 361–82
	b	III.16	'Euthanasia, Morality and Law', Loyola of Los Angeles L Rev 31: 1123–45
	c	V.3	'On the Practical Meaning of Secularism', Notre Dame L Rev 73: 491–515
	d		*Aquinas: Moral, Political, and Legal Theory* (OUP) (xxi + 385 pp)
	e		'Public Good: The Specifically Political Common Good in Aquinas', in Robert P. George (ed.), *Natural Law and Moral Inquiry* (Washington, DC: Georgetown University Press), 174–209

	f		'Natural Law', in Edward Craig (ed.), *Routledge Encyclopaedia of Philosophy*, vol. 6 (London: Routledge), 685–90
1999	a	I.2	'Natural Law and the Ethics of Discourse', American J Juris 43: 53–73; also in Ratio Juris 12: 354–73
	b	III.12	'Retribution: Punishment's Formative Aim', American J Juris 44: 91–103
	c	IV.20	'The Fairy Tale's Moral', LQR 115: 170–5
	d	V.6	'The Catholic Church and Public Policy Debates in Western Liberal Societies: The Basis and Limits of Intellectual Engagement', in Luke Gormally (ed.), *Issues for a Catholic Bioethic* (London: Linacre Centre), 261–73
	e		'What is the Common Good, and Why does it Concern the Client's Lawyer?', South Texas L Rev 40: 41–53
2000	a	II.1	'The Priority of Persons', in Jeremy Horder (ed.), *Oxford Essays in Jurisprudence, Fourth Series* (OUP), 1–15
	b	II.17	'Some Fundamental Evils of Generating Human Embryos by Cloning', in Cosimo Marco Mazzoni (ed.), *Etica della Ricerca Biologica* (Florence: Leo S. Olschki Editore), 115–23; also in C.M. Mazzoni (ed.), *Ethics and Law in Biological Research* (The Hague, London: Martinus Nijhoff; Boston: Kluwer, 2002), 99–106
	c		'Abortion, Natural Law and Public Reason', in Robert P. George and Christopher Wolfe (eds), *Natural Law and Public Reason* (Washington, DC: Georgetown University Press), 71–105
	d		'On the Incoherence of Legal Positivism', Notre Dame L Rev 75: 1597–611
	e		'God the Father', in Peter Newby (ed.), *Occasional Papers from the Millennium Conferences at the Oxford University Catholic Chaplaincy* No. 1 (Oxford), 24–6
2001	a	II.13	'"Direct" and "Indirect": A Reply to Critics of Our Action Theory' (with Germain Grisez and Joseph Boyle), The Thomist 65: 1–44
	b	III.6	'Virtue and the Constitution of the United States', Fordham L Rev 69: 1595–602
	c		'Reason, Faith and Homosexual Acts', Catholic Social Science Review 6: 61–9
2002	a	IV.5	'Natural Law: The Classical Tradition', in Jules Coleman and Scott Shapiro (eds), *The Oxford Handbook of Jurisprudence and Philosophy of Law* (OUP), 1–60
	b	V.22	'Secularism, the Root of the Culture of Death', in Luke Gormally (ed.), *Culture of Life—Culture of Death* (London: Linacre Centre)
	c		'Aquinas on *jus* and Hart on Rights: A Response', Rev of Politics 64: 407–10
	d		Patrick H. Martin and John Finnis, 'The Identity of "Anthony Rivers"', Recusant History 26: 39–74
	e		—— and —— 'Tyrwhitt of Kettleby, Part I: Goddard Tyrwhitt, Martyr, 1580', Recusant History 26: 301–13

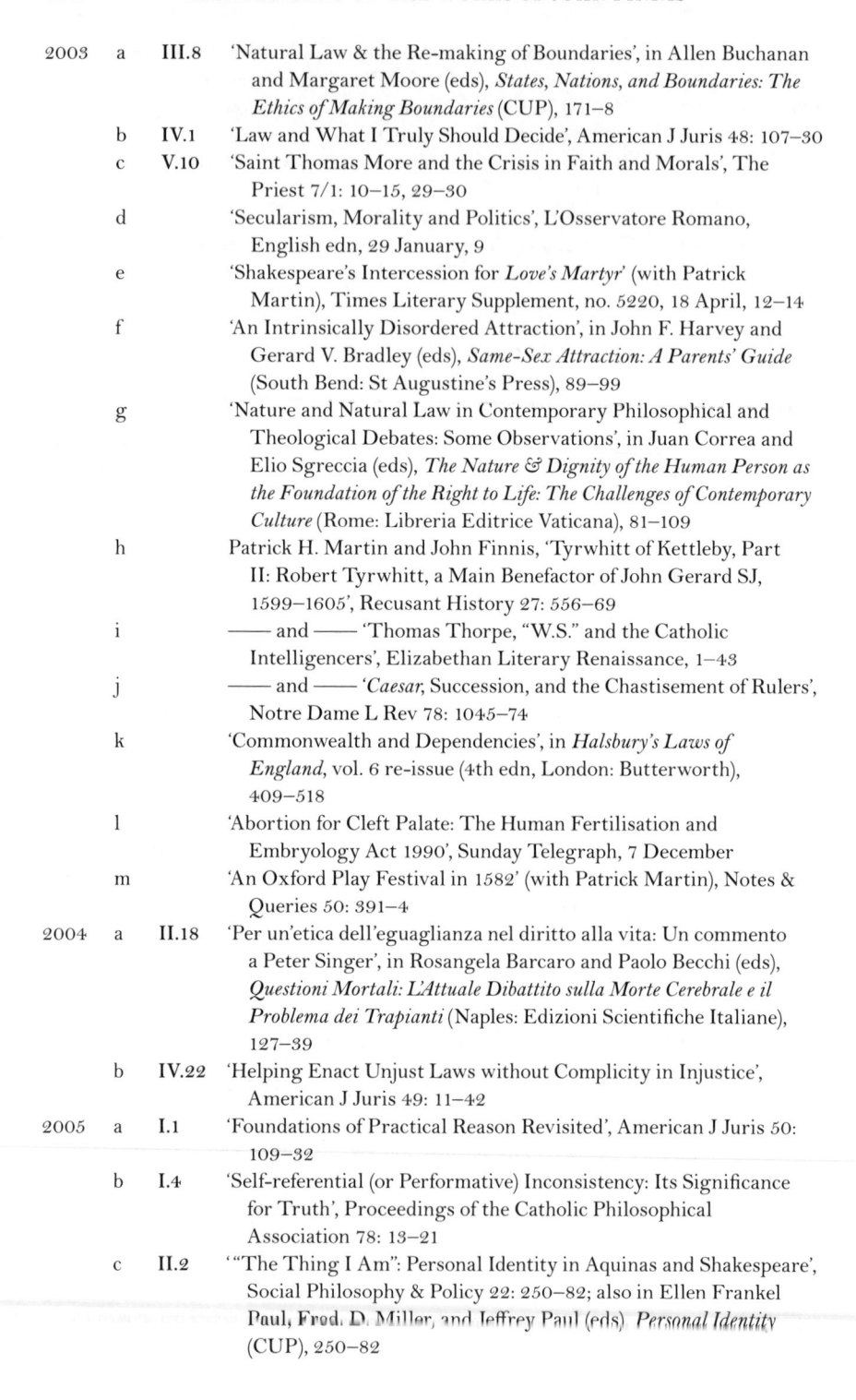

2003	a	III.8	'Natural Law & the Re-making of Boundaries', in Allen Buchanan and Margaret Moore (eds), *States, Nations, and Boundaries: The Ethics of Making Boundaries* (CUP), 171–8
	b	IV.1	'Law and What I Truly Should Decide', American J Juris 48: 107–30
	c	V.10	'Saint Thomas More and the Crisis in Faith and Morals', The Priest 7/1: 10–15, 29–30
	d		'Secularism, Morality and Politics', L'Osservatore Romano, English edn, 29 January, 9
	e		'Shakespeare's Intercession for *Love's Martyr*' (with Patrick Martin), Times Literary Supplement, no. 5220, 18 April, 12–14
	f		'An Intrinsically Disordered Attraction', in John F. Harvey and Gerard V. Bradley (eds), *Same-Sex Attraction: A Parents' Guide* (South Bend: St Augustine's Press), 89–99
	g		'Nature and Natural Law in Contemporary Philosophical and Theological Debates: Some Observations', in Juan Correa and Elio Sgreccia (eds), *The Nature & Dignity of the Human Person as the Foundation of the Right to Life: The Challenges of Contemporary Culture* (Rome: Libreria Editrice Vaticana), 81–109
	h		Patrick H. Martin and John Finnis, 'Tyrwhitt of Kettleby, Part II: Robert Tyrwhitt, a Main Benefactor of John Gerard SJ, 1599–1605', Recusant History 27: 556–69
	i		—— and —— 'Thomas Thorpe, "W.S." and the Catholic Intelligencers', Elizabethan Literary Renaissance, 1–43
	j		—— and —— '*Caesar*, Succession, and the Chastisement of Rulers', Notre Dame L Rev 78: 1045–74
	k		'Commonwealth and Dependencies', in *Halsbury's Laws of England*, vol. 6 re-issue (4th edn, London: Butterworth), 409–518
	l		'Abortion for Cleft Palate: The Human Fertilisation and Embryology Act 1990', Sunday Telegraph, 7 December
	m		'An Oxford Play Festival in 1582' (with Patrick Martin), Notes & Queries 50: 391–4
2004	a	II.18	'Per un'etica dell'eguaglianza nel diritto alla vita: Un commento a Peter Singer', in Rosangela Barcaro and Paolo Becchi (eds), *Questioni Mortali: L'Attuale Dibattito sulla Morte Cerebrale e il Problema dei Trapianti* (Naples: Edizioni Scientifiche Italiane), 127–39
	b	IV.22	'Helping Enact Unjust Laws without Complicity in Injustice', American J Juris 49: 11–42
2005	a	I.1	'Foundations of Practical Reason Revisited', American J Juris 50: 109–32
	b	I.4	'Self-referential (or Performative) Inconsistency: Its Significance for Truth', Proceedings of the Catholic Philosophical Association 78: 13–21
	c	II.2	'"The Thing I Am": Personal Identity in Aquinas and Shakespeare', Social Philosophy & Policy 22: 250–82; also in Ellen Frankel Paul, Fred D. Miller, and Jeffrey Paul (eds) *Personal Identity* (CUP), 250–82

	d	IV.6	'Philosophy of Law' (Chinese trans.), in Ouyang Kang (ed.), *The Map of Contemporary British and American Philosophy* (Beijing: Dangdai Yingmei Zhexue Ditu), 388–413
	e		'On "Public Reason"', in *O Racji Pulicznej* (Warsaw: Ius et Lex), 7–30 (Polish trans.), 33–56 (English original); <http://ssrn.com/abstract=955815>
	f		'Restricting Legalised Abortion is not Intrinsically Unjust', in Helen Watt (ed.), *Cooperation, Complicity & Conscience* (London: Linacre Centre), 209–45
	g		'A Vote Decisive for...a More Restrictive Law', in Helen Watt (ed.), *Cooperation, Complicity & Conscience* (London: Linacre Centre), 269–95
	h		'Aquinas' Moral, Political and Legal Philosophy', Stanford Encyclopedia of Philosophy; <http://plato.stanford.edu/entries/aquinas-moral-political/>
	i		Patrick H. Martin and John Finnis, 'Benedicam Dominum: Ben Jonson's Strange 1605 Inscription', Times Literary Supplement, 4 November, 12–13
	j		—— and —— 'The Secret Sharers: "Anthony Rivers" and the Appellant Controversy, 1601–2', Huntingdon Library Q 69/2: 195–238
2006	a	V.4	'Religion and State: Some Main Issues and Sources', American J Juris 51: 107–30
	b		'Observations for the Austral Conference to mark the 25th Anniversary of *Natural Law and Natural Rights*', Cuadernos de Extensión Jurídica (Universidad de los Andes) no. 13: 27–30
2007	a	III.9	'Nationality, Alienage and Constitutional Principle', LQR 123: 417–45
	b	IV.10	'On Hart's Ways: Law as Reason and as Fact', American J Juris 52: 25–53; also in Matthew Kramer and Claire Grant (eds), *The Legacy of H.L.A. Hart: Legal, Political & Moral Philosophy* (OUP, 2009), 1–27
	c		'Natural Law Theories of Law', Stanford Encyclopedia of Philosophy; <http://plato.stanford.edu/entries/natural-law-theories/>
2008	a	I.5/ II.7/V.8	'Reason, Revelation, Universality and Particularity in Ethics', AJJ 53: 23–48
	b	II.6	'Universality, Personal and Social Identity, and Law', address, Congresso Sul-Americano de Filosofia do Direito, Porto Alegre, Brazil, 4 October 2007; Oxford Legal Studies Research Paper 5; <http://ssrn.com/abstract=1094277>
	c	III.20	'Marriage: A Basic and Exigent Good', The Monist 91: 396–414
	d	[V.13]	'Grounds of Law & Legal Theory: A Response', Legal Theory 13: 315–44
	e		'Common Law Constraints: Whose Common Good Counts?', Oxford Legal Studies Research Paper 10; <http://ssrn.com/abstract_id=1100628>
	f		*Humanae Vitae*: A New Translation with Notes (London: Catholic Truth Society) (31 pp)

2009	a	II.3	'Anscombe's Essays', National Catholic Bioethics Q 9/1: 199–207
	b	IV.11	'H.L.A. Hart: A Twentieth Century Oxford Political Philosopher', American J Juris 54: 161–85
	c	V.1	'Does Free Exercise of Religion Deserve Constitutional Mention?', American J Juris 54: 41–66
	d	V.2	'Telling the Truth about God and Man in a Pluralist Society: Economy or Explication?', in Christopher Wolfe (ed.), *The Naked Public Square Revisited: Religion & Politics in the Twenty-First Century* (Wilmington: ISI Books), 111–25, 204–9
	e		'Endorsing Discrimination between Faiths: A Case of Extreme Speech?', in Ivan Hare and James Weinstein (eds), *Extreme Speech and Democracy* (OUP), 430–41
	f		'Discrimination between Religions: Some Thoughts on Reading Greenawalt's *Religion and the Constitution*', Constitutional Commentary 25: 265–71
	g		'Commonwealth', in *Halsbury's Laws of England*, vol. 13 (5th edn, London: LexisNexis), 471–589
	h		'Why Religious Liberty is a Special, Important and Limited Right', Notre Dame Legal Studies Paper 09–11; <http://ssrn.com/abstract=1392278>
	i		'The Lords' Eerie Swansong: A Note on *R (Purdy) v Director of Public Prosecutions*', Oxford Legal Studies Research Paper 31; <http://ssrn.com/abstract=1477281>
	j		'The Mental Capacity Act 2005: Some Ethical and Legal Issues', in Helen Watt (ed.), *Incapacity & Care: Controversies in Healthcare and Research* (London: Linacre Centre), 95–105
	k		'Debate over the Interpretation of *Dignitas personae*'s Teaching on Embryo Adoption', National Catholic Bioethics Q 9: 475–8
2010	a	II.14	'Directly Discriminatory Decisions: A Missed Opportunity', LQR 126: 491–6
	b		'Law as Idea, Ideal and Duty: A Comment on Simmonds, *Law as a Moral Idea*', Jurisprudence 1: 247–53

OTHER WORKS CITED

Adair, Douglas (1957), '"That Politics May be Reduced to a Science": David Hume, James Madison, and the Tenth Federalist', 20 Huntington Library Q 20: 343–60
Albert the Great ([c. 1250–2] 1968), *Super Ethica Commentum et Quaestiones*, in *Alberti Magni Opera Omnia*, XIV(I) (ed. W. Kuebel) (Münster: Aschendorff)
Alexy, Robert (2002), *The Argument from Injustice* (OUP)
Alkire, Sabina (2000), 'The Basic Dimensions of Human Flourishing: A Comparison of Accounts', in Biggar and Black (eds), *The Revival of Natural Law*, 73–110.
——(2002), *Valuing Freedoms: Sen's Capability Approach and Poverty Reduction* (OUP)
Allen, R.E. (1984), *The Dialogues of Plato*, vol. I (New Haven: Yale University Press)
Ames, James Barr (1905), 'How Far an Act May Be a Tort Because of the Wrongful Motive of the Actor', Harvard L Rev 18: 411–22
Ando, T. (1971), *Aristotle's Theory of Practical Cognition* (3rd edn, The Hague: Martinus Nijhoff)
Anscombe, G.E.M. (1957), *Intention* (Oxford: Blackwell)
——(2005), *Human Life, Action and Ethics: Essays by G.E.M. Anscombe* (St Andrews Studies in Philosophy & Public Affairs, ed. Mary Geach and Luke Gormally) (Exeter, UK and Charlottesville, VA) (Imprint Academic)
Aubenque, Pierre (1966), *Le Problème de l'être chez Aristote* (2nd edn, Paris: Presses Universitaires de France)
Bell, Clive (1914), *Art* (London)
Belmans, Theo G., OPraem. (1980), *Le sens objectif de l'agir humain* (Vatican City: Libreria Editrice Vaticana)
Bentham, Jeremy (1843), *The Works of Jeremy Bentham*, ed. John Bowring (Edinburgh: W. Tait)
Berger, René (1963), *The Language of Art* (London: Thames & Hudson)
Biggar, Nigel and Black, Rufus (2000), *The Revival of Natural Law: Philosophical, Theological and Ethical Responses to the Finnis-Grisez School* (Aldershot and Burlington: Ashgate)
Bourke, Vernon J. (1966), *Ethics: A Textbook in Moral Philosophy* (3rd edn, New York: Macmillan)
——(1982), 'Justice as Equitable Reciprocity: Aquinas Updated', AJJ 27: 17–31
Boyle, Joseph M. (1972), 'Self-Referential Inconsistency, Inevitable Falsity and Metaphysical Argumentation', Metaphilosophy 25: 25–42
——(1984), 'Aquinas, Kant and Donagan on Moral Principles', New Scholasticism 58: 391–408
——(2001), 'Reasons for Action: Evaluative Cognitions that Underlie Motivations', AJJ 46: 177–97
——, Grisez, Germain, and Tollefsen, Olaf (1972), 'Determinism, Freedom, and Self-Referential Arguments', Review of Metaphysics 26: 3–37
—— —— and ——(1976), *Free Choice: A Self-Referential Argument* (Notre Dame: University of Notre Dame Press)

Bradlaugh, Charles and Besant, Annie (1877), *The Queen v Charles Bradlaugh and Annie Besant* (London: Freethought Publishing)
Brennan, William J. (1965), 'The Supreme Court and the Meiklejohn Interpretation of the First Amendment', Harv L Rev 79: 1–20
Brown, Peter R.L. (1967), *Augustine of Hippo* (London: Faber)
Buchler, Justus (1940), *The Philosophy of Peirce: Selected Writings* (London: Routledge & Kegan Paul)
Buckley, Joseph (1949), *Man's Last End* (St Louis and London: Herder)
Bullough, Edward (1957), *Aesthetics* (London: Bowes and Bowes)
Byrne, Robert (1973), 'An American Tragedy: the Supreme Court on Abortion', Fordham Law Rev 41: 807–62
Cahn, Edmond (1956), 'The Firstness of the First Amendment', Yale LJ 65: 464–81
Cairns, Robert B., Paul, James C.N., and Wishner, Julius (1962), 'Sex Censorship: The Assumptions of Anti-Obscenity Laws and the Empirical Evidence', 46 Minn L Rev 1009–41
Calabresi, Guido and Melamed, Douglas (1972), 'Property Rules, Liability Rules, and Inalienability: One View of the Cathedral', Harv L Rev 85: 1089–128
Chafee, Zecharia (1941), *Free Speech in the United States* (HUP)
—— (1947), *Government and Mass Communications: A Report from the Commission on Freedom of the Press* (Chicago: University of Chicago Press)
—— (1949), 'Meiklejohn's *Free Speech*' (Book Review), Harv L Rev 62: 891–901
Chandos, John (1962), *'To Deprave and Corrupt...': original studies in the nature and definition of 'obscenity'* (London: Souvenir Press)
Chappell, Timothy (2000), 'Natural Law Revived: Natural Law Theory and Contemporary Moral Philosophy', in Biggar and Black, *The Revival of Natural Law*, 29–52
—— (2006), 'Bernard Williams', *The Stanford Encyclopedia of Philosophy (Spring 2006)* <http://plato.stanford.edu/archives/spr2006/entries/williams-bernard/>
Chroust, A.-H. (1964), *Aristotle: Protrepticus: A Reconstruction* (Notre Dame: University of Notre Dame Press)
Clark, Stephen R.L. (1975), *Aristotle's Man: Speculations upon Aristotelian Anthropology* (OUP)
Cropsey, Joseph ([1961] 1977), 'The Moral Basis of International Action' in his *Political Philosophy and the Issues of Politics* (Chicago: University of Chicago Press), 172–88
D'Arcy, Eric (1983), 'The Withering Away of Disbelief', Atheism and Dialogue (Secretariat for Non-Believers, Vatican) 18: 158
Destro, Robert (1975), 'Abortion and the Constitution: The Need for a Life-Protective Amendment', California L Rev 63: 1250–35
Dodds, E.R. (1959), *Plato: Gorgias: A Revised Text with Introduction and Commentary* (OUP)
Douglas, Mary (1969), *Purity and Danger: An Analysis of Concepts of Pollution and Taboo* (London: Routledge & Kegan Paul)
Dworkin, Ronald (1970), 'Taking Rights Seriously', New York Review of Books, 17 December, Special Supplement, 23–31
—— (1977, 1978), *Taking Rights Seriously* (rev. edn with Reply to Critics) (HUP; London: Duckworth)
—— (1985), *A Matter of Principle* (HUP)
—— (1986), *Law's Empire* (HUP; London: Fontana)
Edgley, Roy (1969), *Reason in Theory and Practice* (London: Hutchinson)
Engberg-Pedersen, Troels (1983), *Aristotle's Theory of Moral Insight* (OUP)

Finance, Joseph de, SJ (1969), 'Sur la notion de loi naturelle', Doctor Communis 22: 201–23
Fish, Stanley (2003), 'Truth but No Consequences: Why Philosophy Doesn't Matter', Critical Inquiry 29: 389–417
Flippen, Douglas (1987), 'Natural Law and Natural Inclinations', New Scholasticism 60: 284–316
Foot, Philippa (1958), 'Moral Beliefs', Proc Aristotelian Soc 59: 83–104 (cited to her *Theories of Ethics*, 83–100)
—— (ed.) (1967), *Theories of Ethics* (OUP)
—— (1970), 'Comment', in R.S. Khanbai, B.Y. Katz, and R.A. Pineau (eds), *Jowett Papers 1968–1969* (Oxford: Blackwell), 124
—— (1995), 'Does Moral Subjectivism Rest on a Mistake?', Oxford J Legal St 15: 1–14
—— (2001), *Natural Goodness* (OUP)
Forsythe, Clark D. (1998), 'Human Cloning and the Constitution', Valparaiso University L Rev 32: 469–542
Freud, Sigmund ([1927] 1961), 'The Future of an Illusion', in *Sigmund Freud, Complete Psychological Works* (ed. James Strachey) (London: Hogarth Press), vol. 22
Fuller, Lon L. ([1964] 1969), *The Morality of Law* (rev. edn, New Haven and London: Yale University Press)
Gandhi, Ramchandra (1974), *Presuppositions of Human Communication* (OUP)
Gardiner, Harold C., SJ (1955), 'Moral Principles Towards a Definition of the Obscene', Law & Contemp Prob 20: 560–71
Garrow, David J. (1994), *Liberty and Sexuality: The Right to Privacy and the Making of Roe v Wade* (Oxford: Macmillan Maxwell International)
Gauthier, R.-A. (ed.) (1969), *Sententia Libri Ethicorum* in *Sancti Thomae de Aquino Opera Omnia* (ed. Leonine) xlvii, 1 (books I–III) & 2 (books IV–X) (Rome)
—— and Jolif, J.-Y. (1970), *L'Ethique à Nicomaque* (2nd edn, Louvain and Paris)
George, Robert P. (ed.) (1992), *Natural Law Theory: Contemporary Essays* (OUP)
—— (ed.) (1996), *The Autonomy of Law: Essays on Legal Positivism* (OUP)
—— (1997), 'Public Reason and Political Conflict: Abortion and Homosexuality', Yale LJ 106: 2475–504
—— (1999), *In Defense of Natural Law* (OUP)
Gerber, Albert B. (1964), 'A Suggested Solution to the Riddle of Obscenity', U Pa L Rev 112: 834–56
Grant, C.K. (1958), 'Pragmatic Implication', Philosophy 33: 303–24
Griffin, James (1986), *Well-Being* (OUP)
Grisez, Germain (1964), *Contraception and the Natural Law* (Milwaukee: Bruce Publishing)
—— (1965), 'The First Principle of Practical Reason: A Commentary on the *Summa Theologiae*, 1–2, Question 94, Article 2', Natural Law Forum [AJJ] 10: 168–201
—— (1970), *Abortion: The Myths, the Realities, and the Arguments* (New York: Corpus Books)
—— (1974), *Beyond the New Morality: the Responsibilities of Freedom*, with Russell Shaw (Notre Dame: University of Notre Dame Press)
—— (1975), *Beyond the New Theism: A Philosophy of Religion* (Notre Dame: University of Notre Dame Press); reprinted with a new preface: *God: A Philosophical Preface to Faith* (South Bend: St Augustine's Press, 2005)
—— (1978), 'Against Consequentialism', AJJ 23: 21–72
—— (1983), *Christian Moral Principles* (Chicago: Franciscan Herald Press)

—— (1987), 'Natural Law and Natural Inclinations: Some Comments and Clarifications', New Scholasticism 61: 307–20
—— (1988), 'The Structures of Practical Reason: Some Comments and Clarifications', The Thomist 52: 269–91
—— (1993), *Living a Christian Life* (Quincy: Franciscan Press)
Habermas, Jürgen (1993), *Justification and Application: Remarks on Discourse Ethics* (trans. Ciaran P. Cronin) (Cambridge, Mass.: MIT Press)
—— (1995), 'Reconciliation through the Public Use of Reason: Remarks on John Rawls's Political Liberalism', J of Philosophy 92: 109–31
—— (1996), *Between Facts and Norms: Contributions to a Discourse Theory of Law and Democracy* (trans. W. Rehg) (Cambridge, Mass.: MIT Press)
—— (1996), 'Reply to Symposium Participants', Cardozo L Rev 17: 1477–557
—— (1999), 'A Short Reply', Ratio Juris 12: 445–53
Hardie, W.F.R. (1968), *Aristotle's Ethical Theory* (OUP)
Hart, H.L.A. (1964), 'Self-Referring Laws', in *Festskrift till Karl Olivecrona* (Stockholm), 307–16, cited to *Essays in Jurisprudence and Philosophy* (1983), 170–8
—— (1986), 'Who Can Tell Right From Wrong?', New York Review of Books (17 July), 49–52
—— ([1968] 2008), *Punishment & Responsibility: Essays in the Philosophy of Law* (2nd edn, with Introduction by John Gardner, OUP)
Heylbut, G. (ed.) (1892), *Commentaria in Aristotelem Graeca*, vol. 20 (Berlin)
Hintikka, Jaakko (1962), '*Cogito, ergo sum*: Inference or Performance?', Philosophical Rev 72: 3–32
Hobbes, Thomas (1650), *De Corpore Politico*
—— ([1650] 1928), *The Elements of Law* (ed. F. Tönnies) (CUP)
—— ([1651] 1950), *Leviathan* (ed. A.D. Lindsay) (New York: Dutton)
Holbrook, David (1972), *The Pseudo-Revolution: A Critical Study of Extremist 'Liberation' in Sex* (London: Tom Stacey)
Hume, David ([1740], 1978), *A Treatise of Human Nature* (ed. L.A. Selby-Bigge, rev. P.H. Nidditch) (OUP)
—— (1751), *An Enquiry concerning the Principles of Morals* (London: Millar)
Irwin, Terence (1977), *Plato's Moral Theory: The Early and Middle Dialogues* (OUP)
—— (1979), *Plato: Gorgias* (OUP)
—— (1990), 'The Scope of Deliberation: A Conflict in Aquinas', Review of Metaphysics 44: 21–42
—— (1997), 'Practical Reason Divided: Aquinas and his Critics', in Garrett Cullity and Berys Gaut (eds), *Ethics & Practical Reason* (OUP), 189–214
—— (2007), *The Development of Ethics: A Historical and Critical Study*, vol. 1, *Socrates to the Reformation* (OUP)
Isaye, G. (1954), 'La justification critique par rétorsion', Revue philosophique de Louvain 52: 205–33
Jenkins, Iredell (1954), 'The Human Function of Art', Philosophical Q 4: 128–46
Jones, Alexander (ed.) (1966), *The Jerusalem Bible* (London: Darton, Longman & Todd)
Jones, Ernest (1964), *The Life and Work of Sigmund Freud* (abridged ed., Penguin Books)
Kader, David (1980), 'The Law of Tortious Prenatal Death since *Roe v Wade*', Missouri L Rev 45: 639–66
Kalinowski, Georges (1967), *Le Problème de la verité en morale et en droit* (Lyon: Vitte)
Kalven, Harry (1960), 'The Metaphysics of the Law of Obscenity', The Supreme Court Review 1960: 1–45

—— (1964), 'The New York Times Case: A Note on "The Central Meaning of the First Amendment"', in The Supreme Court Review 1964: 191–221
Kant, Immanuel ([1790] 1903), *Analytic of the Beautiful*, in Kant, *Critique of Aesthetic Judgment* (trans. James Meredith) (OUP)
—— ([1785] 1903), *Grundlegung zur Metaphysik der Sitten* (ed. Paul Menzer) (Berlin: Akademie edition 4), 387–463
—— ([1797] 1907), *Die Metaphysik der Sitten* (ed. Paul Natorp) (Berlin: Akademie edition 6), 205–493
—— ([1797] 1991), *The Metaphysics of Morals* (trans. Mary Gregor) (CUP)
Kaplan, Abraham (1955), 'Obscenity as an Aesthetic Category', Law & Contemp Prob 20: 544–59
Kaplow, Louis (1986), 'An Economic Analysis of Legal Transitions', Harv L Review 99: 509–617
Kauper, Paul G. (1962), *Civil Liberties and the Constitution* (Ann Arbor: University of Michigan Press)
Kelsen, Hans (1945), *General Theory of Law and State* (HUP)
—— (1955), *The Communist Theory of Law* (London: Stevens)
—— (1967), *The Pure Theory of Law* (Berkeley and Los Angeles: University of California Press)
Kenny, Anthony (1968), *Descartes: A Study of His Philosophy* (New York: Random House)
—— (1973), *Wittgenstein* (London: Allen Lane; HUP)
Keown, John (ed.) (1995), *Euthanasia Examined: Ethical, Clinical and Legal Perspectives* (CUP)
Kneale, W.M. (1957), 'Aristotle and the *Consequentia Mirabilis*', J of Hellenic Studies 77: 62–6
—— and Kneale, Martha (1984), *The Development of Logic* (OUP)
Koppelman, Andrew (2008), 'Is Pornography "Speech"?', Legal Theory 14: 71–89
Korsgaard, Christine M. (1986), 'Skepticism about Practical Reason', J of Philosophy 83: 5–25
—— (1997), 'The Normativity of Instrumental Reason', in Garrett Cullity and Berys Gaut (eds), *Ethics and Practical Reason* (OUP), 215–54
—— (2009), *Self-Constitution: Agency, Identity, and Integrity* (OUP)
Kramer, Matthew (1999), *In the Realm of Moral and Legal Philosophy* (New York: St Martin's Press)
Kronman, Anthony (1983), *Max Weber* (London: Edward Arnold; Stanford: Stanford Unversity Press)
Lafont, Ghislain (1961), *Structures et Méthode dans la Somme Théologique de Saint Thomas d'Aquin* (Bruges: Desclée de Brouwer)
Langer, Suzanne (1953), *Feeling and Form* (London: Routledge & Kegan Paul)
Lee, Patrick (1981), 'Permanence of the Ten Commandments: St Thomas and His Modern Commentators', Theological Studies 42: 422–43
—— (1996), *Abortion and Unborn Human Life* (Washington, DC: Catholic University of America Press)
—— (2005), 'Comment on John Finnis's "Foundations of Practical Reason Revisited"', AJJ 50: 133–8
—— (2006), 'Interrogational Torture', AJJ 51: 131–47
Lewis, C.I. (1969), *Values and Imperatives* (ed. John Lange) (Stanford: Stanford University Press)
Lockhart, William B. and McClure, Robert C. (1954), 'Literature, the Law of Obscenity and the Constitution', Minn L Rev 38: 295

―― and ―― (1960), 'Censorship of Obscenity: The Developing Constitutional Standards', Minn L Rev 45: 5

Lonergan, Bernard J.F. (1957), *Insight: A Study of Human Understanding* (London: Longmans, Green; New York: Philosophical Society)

―― (1967), *Verbum: Word and Idea in Aquinas* (Notre Dame: University of Notre Dame Press)

―― (1972), *Method in Theology* (London: Darton, Longman & Todd)

―― (1974), *A Second Collection* (London: Darton, Longman & Todd)

Lottin, Odon (1931), *Le Droit naturel chez Saint Thomas d'Aquin et ses predecesseurs* (Bruges)

―― (1955), 'Aristote et la connexion des vertus morales', in *Autour d'Aristote: recueil d'études de philosophie ancienne et médiévale offert à Monseigneur A. Mansion* (Louvain: Publications universitaires de Louvain), 343–64

Luce, D.H. and Raiffa, H. (1957), *Games and Decisions* (New York: Wiley)

MacDonald, Margaret (ed.) (1954), *Philosophy and Analysis* (Oxford: Basil Blackwell)

Mackie, John J.L. (1964), 'Self-Refutation—A Formal Analysis', Philosophical Q 14: 193–203

―― (1973), *Truth, Probability, and Paradox* (OUP)

Magrath, C. Peter (1966), 'The Obscenity Cases: Grapes of *Roth*', in The Supreme Court Review 1966: 7–77

Malcolm, Norman (1968), 'The Conceivability of Mechanism', Philosophical Rev 77: 45–72

Maritain, Jacques (1951), *Man and the State* (Chicago: University of Chicago Press)

―― ([1920] [1935] 1962), *Art and Scholasticism* (trans. Joseph W. Evans) (Notre Dame: University of Notre Dame Press)

―― (1986), *La loi naturelle ou loi non écrite: texte inédit, établi par Georges Brazzola* (Fribourg: Éditions universitaires)

Matthews, Gareth B. (1972), 'Si Fallor, Sum', in R.A. Markus (ed.), *Augustine: A Collection of Critical Essays* (New York: Doubleday)

May, William E. (1984), 'Aquinas and Janssens on the Moral Meaning of Human Acts', Thomist 48: 566–606

McDowell, John H. (ed.) (1973), *Plato: Theaetetus* (OUP)

McInerny, Ralph (ed.) (1993), *Aquinas against the Averroists: On There Being Only One Intellect* (West Lafayette: Purdue University Press)

McShane, Philip (ed.) (1972), *Language, Truth and Meaning* (Dublin: Gill and Macmillan)

Mercken, H. Paul F. (ed.) (1973), *Corpus Latinum Commentarium in Aristotelem Graecorum* VI, 1 (Leiden: Brill)

Mill, John Stuart ([1859], 2003), *On Liberty*, ed. D. Bromwich and G. Kateb (New Haven and London: Yale University Press)

Miller, Henry (1963), 'Obscenity and the Law of Reflection', Kentucky LJ 51: 577–90

Miller, Jonathan W. (1971), 'Censorship and the Limits of Permission', Proc Brit Acad 57: 281–302

Milton, John (1644), *Areopagitica; A Speech of Mr John Milton for the Liberty of Unlicensed Printing* (London)

Moleski, Martin SJ (1977), 'Retortion: The Method and Metaphysics of Gaston Isaye', International Philosophical Q 17: 59–93

Moline, Jon (1983), 'Contemplation and the Human Good', Nous 17: 37–53

Moore, G.E. (1944), 'Russell's Theory of Descriptions', in P.A. Schilpp (ed.) *The Philosophy of Bertrand Russell* (New York: Library of Living Philosophers)

Morrison, J.S. (1958), 'The Origins of Plato's Philosopher-Statesman', Classical Quarterly 8: 198–218
Murphy, Terrence J. (1963), *Censorship: Government and Obscenity* (Baltimore: Helicon)
Nagel, Thomas (1987), 'Moral Conflict and Political Legitimacy', Philosophy & Public Affairs 16: 215–40
Nietzsche, Friedrich ([1882] 1994), *The Gay Science* (trans. Josefine Nauckhoff) (CUP)
—— ([1887], 1996), *On the Genealogy of Morals: A Polemic* (trans. D. Smith) (OUP)
Note (1964), 'Obscenity Prosecution: Artistic Value and the Concept of Immunity', NYUL Rev 39: 1063–86
Nozick, Robert (1974), *Anarchy, State and Utopia* (Oxford: Blackwell)
Nuchelmans, Gabriel (1992), 'A 17th-Century Debate on the *Consequentia Mirabilis*', History and Philosophy of Logic 13: 43–58
Nussbaum, Martha C. (2000), *Women and Human Development: The Capabilities Approach* (CUP)
Owen, G.E.L. (1960), 'Logic and Metaphysics in Some Early Works of Aristotle', in *Aristotle and Plato in the Mid-Fourth Century* (ed. Ingemar Düring and G.E.L. Owen) (Gothenburg: Elanders Boktryckeri), 163–90
Passmore, John A. (1961), *Philosophical Reasoning* (London: Duckworth)
Pildes, Richard H. (1992), 'Conceptions of Value in Legal Thought', Michigan L Rev 90: 1520–59
—— and Anderson, Elizabeth S. (1990), 'Slinging Arrows at Democracy: Social Choice Theory, Value Pluralism, and Democratic Politics', Columbia L Rev 90: 2121–214
Posner, Richard (1990), *The Problems of Jurisprudence* (HUP)
Rawls, John (1971) *A Theory of Justice* (HUP; OUP, 1972)
—— ([1993] 1996), *Political Liberalism* (New York: Columbia University Press)
—— (1997), 'The Idea of Public Reason Revisited', U Chicago L Rev 64: 765–807
Raz, Joseph (1986), *The Morality of Freedom* (OUP)
—— (1994), *Ethics in the Public Domain* (OUP)
Reiman, Jeffrey H. (1997), *Critical Moral Liberalism: Theory and Practice* (Lanham: Rowman & Littlefield)
—— (2000), 'Abortion, Natural Law, and Liberal Discourse: A Response to John Finnis', in Robert P. George and Christopher Wolfe (eds), *Natural Law and Public Reason* (Washington, DC: Georgetown University Press), 107–24
Rolph, C.H. (ed.) (1961), *Does Pornography Matter?* (London: Routledge & Kegan Paul)
Ross, Alf (1969), 'On Self-Reference and a Puzzle in Constitutional Law', Mind 78: 1–24
Ross, W.D. (ed.) (1952), *The Works of Aristotle*, vol. xii, *Select Fragments* (OUP)
—— (ed.) (1955), *Aristotelis: Fragmenta Selecta* (OUP)
Russell, J.B. (1991), *Inventing the Flat Earth: Columbus and Modern Historians* (New York: Praeger)
Santayana, George ([1905] 1924), *Reason in Art* (New York: Charles Scribners)
Schneewind, J.B. (1991), 'Natural Law, Skepticism, and Methods of Ethics', J Hist of Ideas 52: 289–308
Semonche, John E. (1966), 'Definitional and Contextual Obscenity: The Supreme Court's New and Disturbing Accommodation', UCLA L Rev 13: 1173
Sen, Amartya (2009), *The Idea of Justice* (HUP)
—— (2010), 'The Place of Capability in a Theory of Justice', in Harry Brighouse and Ingrid Robeyns (eds), *Measuring Justice: Primary Goods and Capabilities* (CUP)
Simpson, Peter and McKim, Robert (1992), 'On the Alleged Incoherence of Consequentialism', Am Cath Phil 66: 93–8

Slough, M.C. and McAnany, Patrick D. (1964), 'Obscenity and Constitutional Freedom', St Louis ULJ 8: 279–357, 449–532
Smith, J.C. (1989), *Justification and Excuse in the Criminal Law* (London: Stevens)
St John-Stevas, Norman (1956), *Obscenity and the Law* (London: Secker & Warburg)
Strauss, Leo (1953), *Natural Right and History* (Chicago and London: University of Chicago Press)
Strawson, P.F. (1966), 'Aesthetic Appraisal and Works of Art', Oxford Review 3 (reprinted in Strawson, *Freedom and Resentment* (London: Methuen, 1974))
Sylvester, David (1966), 'Tassels, and Other Gadgets', Encounter, June, 36
Thomson, Judith Jarvis (1995), 'Abortion', Boston Review 20: 11
Tollefsen, Christopher (2004), 'Basic Goods, Practical Insight, and External Reasons', in David Oderberg and Timothy Chappell (eds), *Human Values* (Basingstoke: Palgrave/Macmillan), 32–51
Turner, Stephen P. and Factor, Regis A. (1984), *Max Weber and the Dispute over Reason and Value* (London: Routledge & Kegan Paul)
Unger, Roberto M. (1975), *Knowledge and Politics* (New York: Free Press)
Veatch, Henry (1962), *Two Logics* (Evanston: Northwestern University Press)
—— (1974), *Aristotle* (Bloomington: Indiana University Press)
Villey, Michel (1961), 'Abrégé du droit naturel classique', Archives de philosophie du droit 6: 25–72
Voegelin, Eric (1952), *The New Science of Politics* (Chicago and London: University of Chicago Press)
—— (1957), *Plato and Aristotle* (Baton Rouge and London: Louisiana State University Press)
—— (1961), 'On Readiness to Rational Discussion', in Albert Hunold (ed.), *Freedom and Serfdom* (Dordrecht: Reidel), 269–84
Warnock, G.J. (1967), *Contemporary Moral Philosophy* (London: Macmillan)
Weber, Max (1954), *Economy and Society: An Interpretive Sociology* (ed. G. Roth and C. Wittich, from Weber, *Wirtschaft und Gesellschaft* (1922) (Berkeley: University of California Press)
Wiggins, David (1977), 'Truth, Invention and the Meaning of Life', 62 Proc Brit Acad 331–78
Williams, Bernard (1981), *Moral Luck: Philosophical Papers 1973–1980* (CUP)
—— (2002), *Truth and Truthfulness: An Essay in Genealogy* (Princeton: Princeton University Press)
Witherspoon, James (1985), 'Re-examining *Roe*: Nineteenth-Century Statutes and the Fourteenth Amendment', St Mary's L Rev 17: 29
Wittgenstein, Ludwig ([1953] 1958), *Philosophical Investigations*, ed. G.E.M. Anscombe (Oxford: Blackwell).
—— (1969), *On Certainty* (ed. G.E.M. Anscombe and G.H. von Wright) (Oxford: Basil Blackwell)
Wright, Benjamin Fletcher (ed.) (1961), *The Federalist* (HUP)

ACKNOWLEDGEMENTS

The following essays were originally published as indicated:

Essay 1: 'Foundations of Practical Reason Revisited', American Journal of Jurisprudence 50: 109–32

Essay 2: 'Natural Law and the Ethics of Discourse', American Journal of Jurisprudence 43: 53–73; also in 'Natural Law and the Ethics of Discourse', Ratio Juris 12 (Blackwell): 354–73

Essay 3: 'Scepticism, Self-refutation and the Good of Truth', in P.M. Hacker and J. Raz (eds), *Law, Morality and Society: Essays in Honour of H.L.A. Hart* (OUP, 1977), 247–67

Essay 4: 'Self-referential (or Performative) Inconsistency: Its Significance for Truth', Proceedings of the Catholic Philosophical Association 78: 13–21

Essay 5: 'Reason, Revelation, Universality and Particularity in Ethics', American Journal of Jurisprudence 53: 23–48

Essay 6: 'Reason, Authority and Friendship in Law and Morals', in Khanbai, Katz, and Pineau (eds), *Jowett Papers 1968–1969* (Blackwell, 1970), 101–24

Essay 9: 'Natural Inclinations and Natural Rights: Deriving "Ought" from "Is" according to Aquinas', in L. Elders and K. Hedwig (eds), *Lex et Libertas: Freedom and Law according to St Thomas Aquinas* (Studi Tomistici 30, Libreria Editrice Vaticana), 43–55

Essay 10: 'Practical Reasoning, Human Goods and the End of Man', Proceedings of the Amercian Catholic Philosophical Association 58: 23–36; also in New Blackfriars 66 (1985) 438–51

Essay 12: 'Aristotle, Aquinas, and Moral Absolutes', Catholica: International Quarterly Selection 12: 7–15

Essay 13: 'Loi naturelle', in Monique Canto-Sperber (ed.), *Dictionnaire de Philosophie Morale* (Paris: Presses Universitaires de France), 862–8

Essay 14: 'Natural Law and Legal Reasoning', in Robert P. George (ed.), *Natural Law Theory: Contemporary Essays* (OUP, 1992), 134–57

Essay 15: 'Commensuration and Public Reason', in Ruth Chang (ed.), *Incommensurability, Comparability and Practical Reasoning* (HUP, 1997), 215–33, 285–9

Essay 16: 'Public Reason, Abortion and Cloning', Valparaiso University Law Review 32: 361–82

Essay 17: 'Reason and Passion: The Constitutional Dialectic of Free Speech and Obscenity', University of Pennsylvania Law Review 116: 222–43

INDEX

Abbott, Chief Justice (Charles) II: 200, 204; IV: 341–2
Abbott, Thomas Kingsmill III: 55n, 64n
Abbott, Walter M IV: 52n; V: 173, 215n, 266
abduction I: 45n; IV: 11, 394
  explained IV: 1214
Abelard, Peter II: 245, 247; IV: 187n, 328n
abortion III: 15, 279, 282–312; V: 167, 172, 213, 221, 224, 266, 292, 296–7, 306–7, 340, 346–7, 352; and slavery I: 56–8; funding of II: 147, 171; V: 322–3; involvement in II: 170; III: 312–3; legalization of I: 56–8, 209, 256–7, 263–4, 267–74, 276; II: 27, 301; IV: 267n, 436–66; V: 70–2, 110, 121–3, 126, 315, 330–1; 'partial birth a.' II: 250, 252, 268
Abraham V: 86n, 240, 272n, 298
action, act-analysis I.8–14
absolutes, moral, *see* exceptionless
  includes investigations and reflections I: 19
  includes deliberation I: 1
  includes discussion I: 41, 50
Acton, John V: 209n
Adair, Douglas I: 282n
Admiraal, Peter III: 266
affirmative [v negative] moral rules I: 101–2, 189; III: 7, 119; IV: 15, 128, 141, 143, 366, 368, 370, 373; V: 7, 221–2, 267, 285, 293–4, 311–4, 317–22, 324–7
  cannot be absolute I: 226
aggregative theories of right and wrong I: 205, 209–11, 225, 229, 234, 242, 245, 254; III: 32, 196, 242–4, 248, 250; IV: 53–5, 61, 121–2, 356, 368, 371; V: 77
Albert, St. V: 150
Alcibiades IV: 159
Alexander of Hales III: 187, 359–60n
Alexy, Robert I: 85n
Alkire, Sabina I: 10–11, 28
Allen, R.E. I: 41n, 49n, 51n, 186n; III: 100–1, 378n
Alphonsus Liguori, St. V: 216n, 219, 221n
Altman, Denis III: 59n
altruism II: 110; III: 69; IV: 57–61, 68, 75
  not friendship I: 47n
Ames, J.B. I: 228n; II: 209n, 211
Amin, Idi II: 84
analogical reasoning IV.19
analogy, analogical terms IV: 395–6; V: 131
Anderson, Elizabeth S. I: 235n, 253n

Ando, T. I: 160n
Andrews, J.A. III: 30
Angas, George Fife II: xii
Angas, George French II: xi
anima mea non est ego I: 166; II: 40, 42; V: 330
Anscombe, G.E.M. (Elizabeth) embryonic life II: 291–2; friendship between strangers II: 129n; 'I' 93n; intention and double effect: 13–14, 76–7, 159, 189–93, 225n, 268n; III: 235, 296; IV: 236n; V: 366n; marriage and contraception V: 352, 355n, 358–9n, 362, 364–5; mystical value of human being I: 36; moral ought II: 74–5; proposal 3n; spirit 5–6, 8–9, 69–74; III: 4; state authority IV: 85–7; voting paradox III: 22n; IV: 54; *also* V: 116, 162
Anselm of Canterbury, St. V: 179n, 182
Aquinas, Thomas I: 14n; 'a liberal' V: 113
  (*see also* affirmative v negative norms, central-case analysis, *ut in pluribus*)
  on 'act of generative kind' III: 326n, 382–3; IV: 135n; adjudication IV: 127–9; basic good of life I: 34; *beatitudo* and *beatitudo imperfecta* I: 162–72, 185; *bonum ex integra causa malum ex quocumque defectu* II: 172; connaturality I: 205; II: 73; conscience V: 10, 169, 171, 216, 218–20, 222; *consensus* II: 155–7, 231–2; created beings I: 96–7; deliberation as first *de seipso* I: 183; II: 50, 103; IV: 25; *determinatio* needed between reasonable options I: 230; IV: 149, 179, 181–2, 324; V: 318n; discourse opponents I: 44n; divine judgment II: 66; embryonic life II: 39n, 288; V: 307; epistemological principle: object-act-capacity-nature I: 179, 204; II: 7, 128n; IV: 317–8; ethics as practical I: 159; experience of self I: 135–6; II: 41; evil (problem of) V: 13n, 24, 197; first principle of practical reason I: 210; first principles I: 63–4; first principles and inclinations I: 39, 144–7, 150, 176–80, 183, 205; II: 59; first principles or basic reasons for action I: 28, 139, 148–50; IV: 53; V: 58, 120, 245, 268; four orders (and kinds of science) I: 200, 242; II: 36, 261n; IV: 94n, 166; V: 146, 151, 195; free choice and self-determination I: 214n; II: 42; IV: 110; freedom of will and choice II: 6,

348   INDEX

Aquinas, Thomas (*cont.*)
71–2, 103; V: 183–4; friendship I: 112; IV: 432; global government III: 128–9; God V: 23–4, 28–9, 44, 144, 185–7, 226n, 301n; groups II: 95; IV: 214; *habitus* II: 10; harm I: 154; human acts v behaviour II: 133; humility V: 226–7, 230–1; identity and self-determination II: 36–43, 49–50; *imperium* II: 2, 154, 227; *in genere naturae* v *in genere moris* II: 164–9, 250–1; V: 160; 'intention' and 'choice' of 'objects' II: 149n, 151, 152–72, 239n, 245–7, 253n, 273n; IV: 463–5; V: 281, 367; *intrinsece mala* II: 151, 224; V: 298n; *Is v Ought* I: 7, 213n; justice I: 48n; justice and right I: 206; II: 214n; IV: 109–10; knowledge of historical causality V: 144–5, 150; laws' derivation and non-derivation from moral principles or beliefs I: 21; II: 1093; IV: 128, 149n, 177, 179; laws as propositions I: 19; II: 100; IV: 451n; law's alienated subjects I: 90, 108; law's positivity IV: 2n, 31, 76, 109–11, 160–1, 175–85, 323; *lex injusta* I: 209; III: 2–3; IV: 8n, 31, 181–2; limited, non-paternalist government I: 258; III: 10, 65, 83–5, 91; IV: 31, 135, 270; V: 49, 93–4, 112; love of neighbour as self I: 38; marriage as basic good and reason for action I: 154–5; III: 319n, 353n; marital *fides*, 'debt', and sex ethics II: 53–4; III: 110, 320–2, 345–7, 354–65, 372–6, 379–80; IV: 136, 272; V: 355; V: 356n; means as ends I: 180–1; II: 158–61, 201; IV: 238; moral absolutes (exceptionless negative moral norms) I: 188–97; III: 197; natural and eternal law V: 252; natural and positive law II: 102; natural because rational/reasonable I: 258–9; natural reasons accessible to non-believers (in revelation) I: 259, 265n; V: 3, 8, 115; nature and reason in morality III: 365–72; 'necessity knows no law' III: 202n; *per se* v *per accidens* II: 162–3; V: 186; person II: 10; *pietas* and patriotism II: 107; political and legal authority IV: 69; political theory III: 128–9; practical truth I: 170; *praeter intentionem* (side effect) II: 164, 171; V: 186, 341; property II: 120; IV: 145–6; prevalence of folly and evil I: 203; IV: 223n; principles, virtues, and moral norms I: 150–5, 181–2; III: 98; IV: 52, 460; V: 59, 77; promising V: 63; *prudentia* and ends I: 28–31, 173–86; punishment III: 159, 163–5, 173–6, 190; IV: 142–3, 147; V: 309–10; punishment of heretics V: 50n, 117–8; revelation, credibility and pseudo-revelation V: 48, 83–4; rights IV: 116–7; 'secular' 331–2; self-defence (lethal) II: 188, 197; III: 117,

294, 299; V: 308–9, 367; self-refutation I: 46n, 70, 89–90; II: 37; V: 66n, 148; sex for pleasure (only) III: 358–65, 380n; sophists I: 52n; soul as form and act of body I: 35, 54; II: 34, 39; V: 66–7; *synderesis* I: 28–31, 139, 173, 175–6; territorial appropriation III: 130; types of government III: 83–4; IV: 149n; tyrannicide III: 204n; unity of virtues II: 46; war III: 186–8, 190.
Weaknesses in philosophy of I: 208; II: 10; V: 271; (*see also* I: 6, 60, 81, 98, 202; II: 67, 72, 256n, 264n; III: 310; IV: 9n, 10, 93, 157, 163, 208, 219, 328n, 334; V: 14, 140, 154, 361)

Arber, Edward V: 1
Archimedes IV: 331–2
Arendt, Hannah I: 189; IV: 369
Aristotelian
dictum about prudence I: 6
neo-Aristotelian reliance on nature not reason: I: 26
Aristotle (*and see* central-case analysis, focal meaning, nested ends, *orthos logos*, *phronêsis*, *spoudaios*)
on anthropology II: 36; ascent from family to *polis* II: 107, 126; IV: 214, 277; authority IV: 69; 'citizen' and citizenship III: 138n; IV: 240; crime and punishment III: 159, 163–4, 175; definitional Why? II: 82; IV: 23–4, 160; education I: 313, 315; embryology II: 292; ethics and political philosophy as practical reason I: 31, 129, 140, 208; final end of man I: 29, 143, 159–63, 165n, 166; IV: 51–2, 226n; friendship I: 40, 122, 306–7; II: 125; IV: 208, 312, 432; God I: 123, 170, 307; III: 220n; V: 28, 135, 193, 333, 336, 338; good as desirable I: 177n; historical causation V: 144–5; homosexual acts III: 99, 101, 323n, 336, 338, 371–2; identity of the *polis* across revolution IV: 430–1; individual ethics I: 48; insight (*nous*) IV: 124; *Is—Ought* (theoretical v practical) I: 78, 89n, 125, 202; V: 33; justice II: 214n; IV: 150, 337; knowledge of first principles I: 178n; V: 150; justice II: 214n; IV: 150, 337; law and rule of law III: 86; IV: 109, 149n, 157, 218–9, 316, 452n; marriage and sex I: 244n; II: 128; III: 88, 387–8; IV: 138, 272–3; V: 350; moral absolutes I: 187–94; III: 87n; V: 224; natural and legal right I: 201, 214n; III: 159; IV: 161, 176n, 180–2; object-act-capacity-nature: I: 26, 146, 204, 213n; II: 7, 94n; III: 89n; 'philosophy of human affairs' and social theory IV: 110, 214, 265, 318; V: 146; pleasure I: 36; III: 365; practical reasoning and intention II: 14, 160, 201n, 273; III: 186n;

INDEX

IV: 238, 465; V: 77; *praxis* v *poiêsis* I: 240n; II: 104, 140; III: 93; prevalence of error I: 265n; IV: 223n; property IV: 145–6; sacrifice of identity I: 169; self-refutation I: 65n, 70–1, 84, 133, 203; V: 148; social contract III: 91–2; soul and body I: 53n, 54; II: 34, 39, 67n; V: 67, 123; state paternalism IV: 135, 137, 270; V: 107, 112, 118; truth and knowledge I: 43–4n, 63, 97n; types of regime III: 83; virtues I: 283n; weaknesses in I: 30, 59–60; IV: 75, 263 (*see also* I: 81, 90, 92, 138, 230, 303; III: 104n; IV: 9n, 10, 12, 76, 93, 234, 235, 259, 276, 321, 323, 355n; V: 140, 227, 269, 273)
Armstrong, Robert V: 43n
Arrow, Kenneth II: 98n; IV: 54, 55n, 56
Ashbourne, Lord (Edward Gibson) II: 207
Ashley, Benedict II: 288n
Aspasius I: 192n,
Asquith, Lord Justice (Cyril) II: 228
assertion(s) I: 45, 77–9, 85, 93; II: 67, 111, 225; III: 25; IV: 157, 227, 332, 368, 455; V: 149, 159, 164, 167, 173, 205, 372
athanatizein (immortalizing) I: 123; II: 75
atheism V: 1–2, 6–7, 13, 20, 31, 34, 45, 51n, 54, 60–1, 89, 95, 124, 178, 194, 332–4
Atkinson, G.M. II: 287n
Atkinson, Lord (John) III: 137n
Aubenque, Pierre I: 70n
Aubert, J.-M. IV: 187n; V: 253n
Augustine of Hippo, St.
on eternal and natural law IV: 127; V: 216; on final reward and punishment V: 368–9, 372–3, 374n, 375–7; on lying I: 193; on marital good III: 100; on peace and war III: 184, 185n, 188–9; on Plato and revelation, V: 135; on private punishment III: 191n; on self-refutation I: 70–1, 135; V: 148; on sex acts and pleasure III: 321, 359, 365; on two cities I: 312; (*see also* III: 291, 321; IV: 9n, 93, 218, 328n; V: 118, 205, 226n, 301n, 341)
Augustus, Caesar III: 108
Austin, J.L. II: 183n; IV: 258, 260n,
Austin, John I: 19; II: 177, 228n; III: 155; IV: 10, 36, 40, 75, 99, 115–16, 162–3, 400
authority IV.2 & 4
Averroes III: 87n
Averroism
ethical I: 189, III: 87n; Latin I: 89–90
Avicenna III: 364n
Ayer, A.J. V: 130n

baby-making (*see also* IVF) III: 15, 276; V: 158, 213, 224
Bacon, Francis IV: 160; V: 1, 3, 13
Balthasar, *see* von Balthasar
Banner, Michael III: 250

Barker, Ernest II: 94n; IV: 189–90n, 196n, 202n, 205n, 430n
Barnes, Jonathan III: 187–8n
Barnett, Randy IV: 369
Barnhizer, David IV: 354n, 370–1
Bassey, Shirley II: 218n
Batiffol, Pierre V: 142
Baxter, E.L. III: 281n
Bayley, Justice (John) II: 200–2, 204; IV: 345–6
beatitudo
imperfecta I: 29, 163–8; is communal I: 167–8; *perfecta* (*eudaimonia*) I: 149, 160–2, 165–71; V: 93, 228
Beatson, Jack III: 136n
Beauchamp, Tom L. III: 307n
Becanus, Martinus V: 212
Beccaria, Cesare I: 234
Beck, L.W. III: 55–6n, 58n, 63–4n, 69n
Becker, Carl V: 58n, 143–4
Becker, Ernest IV: 354n
Bede V: 189–91
Bell, Carlos A. III: 350n
Belmans, Theo G. I: 169n, II: 149n,
Benedict XVI II: 119, 124n; V: 40–1, 91–2, 289
Benedict, St. V: 225
Bennett, David III: 143n
Bennett, Jonathan III: 298n, 300
Bentham, Jeremy
utilitarian confusions I: 234, 305n; III: 154, 160, 234; IV: 53–4, 75; on definition II: 82; on expository v censorial jurisprudence V: 161, 165, 210; on law IV: 1, 10, 12, 36, 99, 105, 108, 116, 160–2; V: 72; on oblique 'intention' II: 242; III: 215; on responsibility IV: 154; *see also* I: 6; II: 25, 189; III: 168, 173; IV: 132, 147, 190n, 194n, 258; V: 223
Berger, René I: 287n, 291n
Berkeley, George II: 43
Bernard of Clairvaux, St. IV: 328
Bernardin, Joseph V: 291–327
Bertone, Tarcisio IV: 440n
Besant, Annie I: 279, 280n
Best, Justice (William) II: 202n
Bingham of Cornhill Lord (Thomas) III: 133n, 136n, 144–5n; V: 99n
Birkenhead, Lord (F.E. Smith) I: 68–70
Birks, P.B.H. IV: 401n
Bismarck, Otto von V: 209
Black, Justice (Hugo) I: 277, 292, 296; II: 28
Blackburn, Simon II: 74
Blackmun, Justice (Harry) II: 27n; III: 57n, 63n, 252n
Blackstone, William III: 12–13, 139n; IV: 10, 189–210, 320, 410
Blankenhorn, David III: 385n
Blumstein, Philip III: 384n

350 INDEX

Blunt, Anthony III: 378n
Boccaccio, Giovanni II: 45–6, 57; III: 320
Bodenheimer, Edgar IV: 189–90n, 196n
Boethius II: 9, 29n
Bolt, Robert V: 169
Bonaventure, St. V: 222n
bonum ex integra causa, malum ex quocumque defectu II: 172; III: 187, 195–203; *also* II: 167
Boorstin, Daniel IV: 189n
Bork, Robert IV: 327, 331
Boswell, John III: 346, 350n, 356–7, 369–72, 385n
Bourke, Vernon I: 171n-2n; IV: 52n
Bouyer, Louis V: 64
Bowring, John II: 189
Boyle, Joseph M I: 33n, 45n, 66n, 70n, 73n, 84, 90, 153n, 154, 171, 195, 203n, 239n; II: 11, 13, 159n, 177n-8n, 183n, 191, 194n, 235n, 255n, 257n, 267n, 280n, 285n, 293, 302–12; III: 13–14, 66n, 97 , 243n, 250, 310, 357, 359n; V: 46n, 85–6, 96–101, 121, 149n, 150–1n, 186, 278, 303n, 316n, 340, 347n, 364
Bracton, Henry de IV: 191, 193
Bradlaugh, Charles I: 279, 280n,
Bradley, Gerard V. III: 345, 347–9n, 361n, 382n, 387n; V: 28
Brady, Paul IV: 373n
brain life, 'brain death' II.15, II.18–9
Braine, David II: 67n; III: 228n; V: 66
Brandeis, Justice (Louis) III: 63
Brandt, R.B. III: 290
Brasidas IV: 181
Breitel, Charles D. II: 27n
Brennan, Justice (William J.) I: 278, 294, 296, 297n; III: 246, 252n; V: 70
Brewer, Scott IV: 389–9, 392–6
Bridge, Lord (Nigel) II: 174–5n, 274n
Brock, Stephen C. II: 253n, 264n
Broderick, Patrick A. II: 224n
Brody, Baruch III: 303
Brooke, Lord Justice (Henry) II: 196n
Brown, Harold V: 277, 279
Brown, Louise II: 293–4
Brown, Peter R.L. I: 71n; V: 376n
Brown, Stephen II: 314, 318
Browne-Wilkinson, Lord (Nicolas) II: 313, 315; III: 133; IV: 398
Brubaker, Rogers IV: 225n
Buchler, Ira IV: 57n
Buchler, Justus I: 45n; IV: 394–5n
Buckley, Joseph I: 164
Budziszewski, J. V: 35n
Bullough, Edward I: 288–9, 320n
Burgess, Guy III: 378n
Burke, Edmund IV: 154
Burlamaqui, Jean Jacques IV: 197–8
Butler, Joseph I: 195; II: 48n; III: 225n; V: 54n
Butler-Sloss, Lady Justice (Elizabeth) II: 315
Byrne, Robert I: 276n

Caesar, Julius III: 98n, 204n
Cahn, Edmond I: 284n
'Caiaphas principle' I: 188–9; V: 287
Cairns, Robert B I: 278n
Cairo Declaration on Human Rights in Islam III: 149n; V: 39
Cajetan, Thomas de Vio I: 29n, 164n, 183n; II: 164n; IV: 52n
Calabresi, Guido I: 247n; IV: 346n, 350
Callahan, Sidney III: 349, 383
'Callicles' III: 105–6, 198
Callinan, Justice (Ian) III: 143–4n
Campbell, W.E. V: 165n, 167n
Canovan, Margaret III: 148n
Canto-Sperber, Monique I: 199n
capacities (*see also* epistemological principle)
  radical I: 35, 54–5, 272–3; II: 8, 67, 104–5, 286n, 297; III: 219–21, 225, 227–8, 238–40; V: 329, 336–7
Caputo, John V: 197n
Cartwright, J.P.W. II: 222n, 224n
Case, John V: 332, 334–6
cases (principal)
  A v Home Secretary (Belmarsh Prisoners' Case) III: 133, 135, 144–5, 149; IV: 15
  A, B & C v Ireland III: 43n
  A-G for Canada v Cain III: 136
  A-G's References (Nos 1 & 2 of 1979) II: 220
  Al Kateb v Godwin III: 143–4, 149
  Allen v Flood I: 226n; II: 207–8, 211, 219
  Anderton v Ryan III: 135n
  Bancoult (No. 2) IV: 18
  Begum, see R (Begum)
  Bird v Holbrook II: 202–4, 215, 226–7; IV: 344–5, 349–50
  Birmingham City Council v Equal Opportunities Commission II: 269–74
  Bland, Airedale NHS Trust v II: 311–2, 313–21, III: 213
  Bolam v Friern HMC II: 318
  Bradford (Mayor) v Pickles I: 226n; II: 207–8
  Bradlaugh, R v I: 279–81n
  Brown v Topeka Board of Education III: 42
  Burstyn v Wilson I: 285, 290, 292, 295n
  Byrn v NYC Health & Hospitals II: 27
  Calvin's Case III: 135
  Case of Proclamations III: 136
  Chahal v United Kingdom III: 45, 144–6
  Chaplinsky v New Hampshire I: 278, 284, 291
  Charkaoui v Canada III: 149n
  Compassion in Dying v Washington V: 74
  Conjoined Twins (Medical Treatment), Re A II: 196–7, 266–7
  Crofter Harris Tweed v Veitch I: 226n; II: 210, 219
  Croson, City of Richmond v IV: 370–1
  Cruzan v Director V: 76
  Cunliffe v Goodman II: 228–9
  Dred Scott v Sandford I: 275–6; II: 26–7; IV: 16, 153

INDEX

Dudgeon v United Kingdom III: 27n, 29, 41n
Eisenstadt v Baird V: 70, 73
Factortame (No. 2) IV: 18
Frodl v Austria III: 44
Ginzburg v United States I: 277–8, 281n, 285n, 293–4, 296
Griswold v Connecticut III: 94n; V: 70
Hancock, R v II: 174n, 196
Handyside v United Kingdom III: 27n, 30n, 41n
Hardial Singh, ex p. III: 141, 143–4
Haughton v Smith III: 135n
Hicklin, R v I: 279
Hirst v United Kingdom, 30nm (No. 2) III: 41n, 44–5, 179
HJ (Iran) v Home Secretary III: 45, 332–3
Husseyn, R v II: 220
Ilott v Wilkes II: 199–202, 204, 226–7; IV: 341–2, 344–5
James v Eastleigh Borough Council II: 269–74
Januzi v Home Secretary III: 45
JFS (Governing Body), R (E) v, II: 269–75
Johnstone v Pedlar III: 137–8
Kesavananda v State of Kerala I: 68n
Kingsley International Pictures v Regents I: 277, 290, 292
Lawrence v Texas V: 95
Lonrho plc v Fayed I: 226n; II: 2, 41n18
Madzimbamuto v Lardner-Burke IV: 415n, 435
Mannai Investment v Eagle Star Life II: 9, 13, 31–2
McCawley v R I: 68n
Memoirs v Massachusetts I: 277, 288n, 293–7
Meyer v Nebraska V: 70–1
Mogul Steamship v McGregor, Gow II: 209
Moloney, R v II: 174n-5n, 196, 274n
New York Times v Sullivan I: 291–2
OBG v Allan II: 217–9
Paris Adult Theatre v Slaton I: 297
Pierce v Society of Sisters V: 70–1
Planned Parenthood v Casey I: 268; V: 73, 86, 95
Purdy see R (Purdy)
R (Begum) v Denbigh High School III: 3n; V: 98–9
R (Purdy) v DPP III: 46
Refah Partisi v Turkey V: 38–9
Roe v Wade I: 268–9n, 275–6; II: 27–8; III: 21, 23, 42; IV: 16, 324; V: 95
Romer v Evans IV: 16; V: 73
Roth v United States I: 277–81, 284n, 291n, 293
Saadi v Italy III: 45, 136, 145n
Şahin v Turkey V: 99
Sauvé v Canada (No. 2) III: 455
Shaw v DPP III: 28n
Tan Te Lam v Superintendent III: 141–2

Tuttle v Buck II: 211
United Zinc & Chemical v Britt II: 199; IV: 341
Vacco v Quill V: 71, 75
Washington v Glucksberg V: 71
Wheat Case IV: 12–13, 15
Winters v New York I: 292
Woollin, R v II: 196
Zadvydas v Davis III: 142–3, 149
Castañeda, Hector-Neri II: 222n; III: 290n
Castelli, Jim V: 326n
Catechism of the Catholic Church II: 197, 266; III: 173–4, 178n; V: 336n, 340–1
Catherine of Aragon V: 163–4, 170
Cattaneo, Mario A. IV: 407n, 409n
Cavanaugh, J.A. II: 267–8n
Cave, Viscount (George) III: 137n
Centi, T. II: 154n
central case analysis
 explained I: 109–13, 130–7; IV: 108–9, 160, 168, 235; illustrated I: 10, 118, 121, 123, 206, 259; II: 177, 179; III: 2, 183, 212–3, 317, 325, 347; IV: 36, 79–81, 126, 148, 155, 163, 167, 185, 241, 244, 250, 266, 271, 276, 289
'Cephalus' I: 313
certainty I: 130–7
Chadwick, Owen V: 57n, 58, 335
Chafee, Zechariah I: 282n
Chalcidius IV: 174n, 186n
Chamberlain, Neville IV: 256n
Chandos, John I: 289n
Chappell, Timothy I: 9, 100n, 102
Charlton, William V: 153n
Chaucer, Geoffrey III: 320
Childress, James F III: 307n
choice(s)
 free I: 5; lastingness of I: 36, 216–7; phenomenology of I: 223
Chrimes, S.B. IV: 409n
'christendom' V.20
Chroust, Anton-Hermann I: 71n
Churchill, Winston V: 275–6
Cicero, M. Tullius I: 71, 209; II: 5; III: 107, 191, 291; IV: 9n, 93, 157, 159, 177–8, 187, 193, 218–19; V: 3, 8, 265n
civic friendship (*philia politikê*) I: 112, 266–7; II: 125; IV: 50, 432, 434
civic virtue III.6
Clark, Justice (Tom C.) I: 295, 297n
Clark, Stephen R.L. I: 63n
Clark, William P. V: 277–8
Clarke, Samuel I: 125
Clerk, J.F. II: 210n
Clor, Harry M I: 269n
'cluster concepts', (*see also* central-case) IV: 77; V: 57
Cockburn, Alexander JE I: 279–80
Cohen, David III: 337n
Cohen, Lionel II: 228

Cohen, Marshall III: 26n, 31n, 32n, 36n; IV: 100n, 286n
coherence
  not sufficient for rationality I: 80
Coke, Edward III: 84n, 135; IV: 128
Coleman, Jules IV: 41–2, 44, 91, 105n, 112–15
Collingwood, R.G. IV: 232n
commensuration by reason I.14-I5; II: 144–5; IV: 360–4; *see also* incommensurability
common good I: 99–100, 168
complementarity of male and female I: 34; II: 105; III: 328
Comte, Auguste I: 47n; IV: 57n, 75
conceptual clarification II: 305
conditional intention II.12
Confucius III: 281
'connatural' knowledge II: 73; 'non-conceptual' I: 205
connexio virtutum II: 46
conscience V.16; V: 169–70; *also* I: 116; V: 254–6
consensus and truth I: 42
consequentialism I: 13
'consistent ethic of life' V.21
contemplation I: 165, 169
contraception V.23; *also* I: 142, 279–80; II: 70n, 265; III: 94, 281, 311, 324, 328; IV: 278; V: 158n, 272n, 297
conversion I: 60; II: 48, 52, 62–3, 76, 272; III: 4, 38, 328; IV: 274n; V: 91, 98, 111n, 117, 177
Conzemius, V. V: 209n
Coolidge, David Orgon III: 357n
coordination, negative II: 85
  c. problems and solutions IV.2–3
'corporate personality' II: 81
corpore et anima unus II: 42
Cottier, Georges V: 255n
Craig, Thomas IV: 199–200
Cranmer, Thomas V: 164
'Critical Legal Studies Movement' IV.13 & 13, & IV: 327–32
Cropsey, Joseph I: 188n
Cross, Lord (Geoffrey) I: 318n
'culture' V: 138, 146
'culture of death' V: 328–31, 339
Cuomo, Mario III: 263
Curran, Charles E. V: 296–7n
Cuthbert, St. V: 189–92

Dalton, William J. V: 372
D'Arcy, Eric I: 171n; V: 209n
Darrow, Clarence V: 194
Darwin, Charles III: 350n, 356; V: 13, 17, 21–6
Daube, David II: 241n; III: 291–2n
Davidson, Donald II: 225n, 263
Davis, Henry II: 248,
Dawkins, Richard IV: 353–4; V: 6n, 23, 32
Dawson, Christopher V: 140

Decalogue (Ten Commandments) I: 152–4, 190–2, 194; II: 149; III: 98; IV: 176, 460; V: 247–9, 260–8
Delhaye, Philippe IV: 187n; V: 215
deliberation, as action I: 1; and conscience I: 116; *de seipso/meipso* (about oneself) I:183–5; II: 50–2, 103; IV: 25; about ends (as well as means) I: 2, 28–32, 173–86
de Lubac, Henri IV: 52n; V: 58
democracy, democratic I: 53, 262–3, 266; II: 97, 400; III: 21–2, 40, 43, 44–5, 59, 77, 95, 139, 147, 250; IV: 76, 170, 267, 322; V: 8, 37–8, 40, 122; 'militant d.' V: 8, 38; 'People's D.' I: 275
Democritus IV: 188n
De Scala, Peter II: 232n
Descartes, René I: 66, 71, 84, 135; II: 5n, 78, 268n
description, 'under a/the description' II: 76–7, 189–91, 194, 255, 260, 274; *also* I: 76, 164–5, 167, 170, 181, 207, 216, 258, 261–4; II: 13, 137; V: 281, 374n
desirable, as perfective I: 29n
determinatio I: 22; II: 121; III: 3, 179, 331; IV: 2, 12, 123, 128, 131–2, 140, 149, 161, 179, 181, 309, 318; explained I: 208–9; II: 100–3, 106; IV: 182–4, 301–3, 314–5; of purely positive laws I: 22
deterrence, nuclear V.20; *also* V: 11–12; I: 188; II: 86–91; V: 125–6; and punishment III: 13, 67, 91, 93, 154, 157–8, 173–4, 192
Devlin, Lord (Patrick) III: 27–9; IV: 270, 274, 276, 277n
Dewey, John V: 17, 25–6, 32, 183
Diamond, J.J. II: 292n
Diana, Antonius V: 212n
Dias, R.W.M. IV: 378n
Dicey, A.V. III: 136
dignity II: 35; V: 51, 66–8, 338–9; *also* I: 35, 53; II: 320; IV: 170, 349–50; V: 49, 58, 68, 73, 196–7, 247–8, 254–7, 259, 286, 315–6, 365
Dilthey, Wilhelm V: 144
Diplock, Lord (Kenneth) II: 210n; III: 20n, 34–5n
'direct intention' II.13–14
'direction of intention' II: 187
discourse, discussion: ethics of I: 41–7, 50–5; internal (solitary) I: 52; metaphysics of II: 35
discrimination: anti-, new communism II: 126
disparagement, *see* insult
'diversity' III: 109; *also* II: 127; IV: 274
divorce III: 329
Dodd, C.H. V: 152n
Dodds, E.R. I: 49n
Döllinger, Ignaz von V: 209n
Donagan, Alan I: 153n, 227; III: 66n; V: 223
Donaldson, Lord (John) II: 174n
Donceel, Joseph II: 287–9
Donne, John III: 292n

Dorr, Donal III: 121; V: 272n
Dostoyevsky, Fydor II: 74
'double effect' II: 13
Douglas, Justice (William O.) I: 277, 292, 296, II: 28
Douglas, Mary I: 322–3
Dover, Kenneth III: 99n, 337, 385n
droit and *loi* I: 206
Dryer, Douglas P. III: 62n
dualism: body—soul, refuted I: 53–4; II: 8; *see also 'anima mea'*
Duberman, Martin III: 378n
Duff, R.A. II: 174n, 189n, 199n
Duffy, Kevin V: 372
Dummett, Ann III: 116, 118–20
Dummett, Michael II: 74; V: 240, 242–3
Dunedin, Viscount (Murray, Andrew) II: 200n
Durkheim, Emile III: 292
duties to oneself III.2
Dworkin, Ronald I: 220–4; III.1 & 16 & III: 51–3; IV.12; *also* I: 189n, 229, 252n–3n, 298n, 301, 312n, 323n; II: 20–2, 33, 81–4, 86, 103, 108, 110–2, 117, 320; III: 3, 10–12, 14, 20–1, 23–6, 31, 35n, 36, 38n, 48, 95–6, 226n, 228–30, 245–6, 251n, 252, 254–5, 258–9, 261–3, 264n, 266, 268–9, 270; IV: 10–11, 13–14, 32n, 108n, 129, 163–4, 168, 170, 254n, 258, 266, 271n, 280–98, 302, 314, 319, 321, 328–30, 353–4, 360–1, 363, 381–4, 400, 401n; V: 18, 20, 30–1, 51, 71–3, 76, 85, 105, 107–8, 303

Economic Analysis of Law II: 203–6; IV.16
economics III: 242–3; IV: 337–40
Eddy, Mary Baker V: 56
Edgley, Roy I: 127n
Edward IV IV: 429
Edwards, R.G. II: 293–4, 298, 301; III: 280
Eekelaar, John IV: 245
Ehrensing, Rudolph II: 279n
Einstein, Albert V: 23n
Eisenhower, Dwight D. II: 242n
Eisgruber, Christopher L. V: 18, 20, 29–31, 86n, 95
Elders, Leo J. I: 144n
Elias, N. IV: 429n
Elizabeth I V: 91
Elizabeth II IV: 328
Ellenborough, Lord (Law, Edward) II: 202n; IV: 342–4
embryonic life II: 15–17
Empiricism I: 46n, 168–70; critique of I: 88; II: 9
Empiricus, Sextus I: 201
end: last e. of human beings I: 29, 147n, 159–72; basic ends I: 180; are usually also means I: 181; II.9, II.14
Endicott, Timothy IV: 28
Engberg-Pedersen, Troels I: 161

Engelhardt, Tristram V: 316n
Enlightenment I: 60n, 92; IV: 53; V: 118, 140, 143, 217, 372; confusion about value I: 26–7, 211; foundational mistakes of I: 59, 242; IV: 154; V: 152–3, 169, 183, 187, 287
'ensoulment' V: 109
Epictetus I: 141
Epicurus IV: 355n
epistemic conditions, 'under ideal e. c.' II: 101; V: 46–7
epistemological v. ontological I:147–8; II: 7
'e. principle' (object-act-capacity-nature) II: 7, 15
equality basic human I: 48; 'of esteem' III: 327
Erasmus, Desiderius V: 166
Escobar y Mendoza, Antonio V: 212n
Eser, Albin IV: 192n
Essex, Earl of (Robert Dudley) II: 41
ethics, ethical: not soundly distinguished from morality I: 48, 55–8, 92, 101; 'situation ethics' I: 51–2
eudaimonia I: 160–2
Euclid II: 54n
Eugenius IV V: 213n
Euripides IV: 148
European Convention on/Court of Human Rights (ECHR/ECtHR) III: 1–46, 140–1, 144–6; V: 38–9
euthanasia I: 56–8; II.18–19; III.14–16; V.22, V: 68
'evil not to be done for good' II: 143; V: 159–6
evolution III: 350, 356; V: 21–4, 26, 61, 136
exceptionless wrongs, norms, commitments I: 13, 101, 154, 187–98, 226–7; II: 196, 245–7, 252–3, 267; III: 7, 45, 86, 197–8, 200–3, 206, 234, 322; IV: 128, 173, 446, 460–1; V: 121, 172, 221, 224, 261–71, 296, 340, 351
'existential' II: 96
extremity: ethics of I: 187; III: 200–2

Fabro, Cornelio V: 58
'fact of pluralism' I: 42n
'fact v value', *see also* 'Is v Ought' I: 202
Factor, Regis A I: 203n; IV: 224–5n
Fahey, Michael V: 341
faith: as shaped by divine love help II: 52; fundamental option II: 52; V: 173; preambles to V: 162n
falasifa I: 198; III: 87n
family II: 127–8; *also* 123; f. wage III: 324
Fawcett, James III: 43n
feelings, discernment of II: 215
Felix, Marcus Minucius II: 231n
Festugière, A.J. III: 99n
Figgis, John Neville II: 99n
Filliucci, Vincenzo V: 212n
final: good or end I.10, I: 29

Finch, H.A. IV: 34n, 79
Finch, Henry IV: 191
Finlay, Viscount (Robert) III: 137n
Finnis, John I: 39n, 40, 154, 172, 195, 297n; II: 150n, 163n, 244n–5n, 267n; III: 59n, 97, 145n, 243n, 337n, 372n, 380n; IV: 2n, 8n, 71n, 108n, 166, 357–8, 362; V: 195, 224n, 204n, 341–2n
Fisher, Anthony II: 289n–90n; III: 314
Fitzmaurice, Gerald III: 19n, 39n
Flannery, Kevin L. II: 254–6, 267n–8n; V: 341
flat earth: Enlightenment myth of I: 60n
Fleming, John G. II: 183n, 211n
Fletcher, George P. II: 176n, 182n, 185n; III: 61–2n, 64n
Fletcher, Joseph V: 316n
Flew, Anthony V: 23n
Flippen, Douglas I: 146n
focal meaning, *see* central case analysis
Fonda, Henry I: 284n, 301, 305
Foot, Philippa I: 30n, 115, 120–22, 123n, 305–6; II: 14, 191; III: 32, 33n, 295, 296, 300
Ford, John C. V: 270n
Ford, Norman II: 289–90, 292n
Forsythe, Clark D. I: 257n; II: 28n
Forte, David IV: 372–3
Fortescue, John III: 84n; IV: 149n
four kinds of order and science (disciplined knowledge) I: 7, 200, 217–8
Franco, Francisco V: 275
Frankfurter, Justice (Felix) I: 277–8, 282n; III: 22n, 30n
Fraser, Russell II: 44n, 47n
Fredborg, K.M. IV: 187n
freedom: of choice I: 216; II: 4, 7; of speech, I.17–8; threatened I: 14
Freeman, Samuel II: 125n
Freud, Sigmund I: 116, 282n; III: 168
Freund, Julien IV: 34n
Fried, Charles IV: 171, 313
Friedberg, E.A. V: 222n
Friedman, L. III: 22
Friedmann, W. II: 27; IV: 189–90n, 196n, 221n
friendship I: 5, 40, 99; v. altruism I: 47n; types of, central case of I: 111–2; as condition of fruitful discourse I: 43; extends to strangers I: 15; a source of normativity I: 122, 129
Fuchs, Joseph I: 134n; V: 75, 115, 161, 287, 296–7n, 299n, 341n, 360, 365
fulfilment (flourishing)
    integral human f., morality's master principle I: 5
Fulgentius, of Ruspe, St. V: 159
Fuller, Lon L. I: 63, 259; IV: 31, 64n, 170, 281, 284, 324, 418, 419n

Gadamer, Hans-Georg I: 147n; V: 144n
Gaius II: 75, 102; III: 2–3; IV: 117, 183, 218
Gallagher, John V: 173

games: language game(s) I: 104, 123, 133; game theory IV.2 & 4
Gandhi, Ramchandra I: 74n
Gans, Chaim IV: 58–9n, 66, 69
Gardeil, Antoine V: 145n, 150n
Gardiner, Harold C. I: 288n
Gardner, John IV: 6n, 9n, 32, 36–7, 43–5, 188n, 246n, 247
Garet, Ron III: 356
Garrigou-Lagrange, Reginald II: 155n
Garrow, David J. I: 269n; V: 70n
Gauthier, R.-A. I: 159n, 186n; IV: 180n
Gavison, Ruth IV: 74–5
Geach, Mary II: 69, 72, 75, 77; V: 352
Geach, Peter II: 40n, 43n, 233–4; IV: 53n; V: 355n, 374n
Gelasius I: 312
Gellius, Aulus IV: 187–8n
Gemelli, A. III: 298n
George, Robert P. I: 33n, 272n, 324n; II: 286n, 292n, 310n, 313n; III: 87, 89n, 96–7, 324n, 345, 347–9n, 355n, 361n, 373, 378n, 382n, 387n; IV: 120n, 135n; V: 72n
Gerber, Albert B. I: 288
Gerth, H. H. IV: 34n, 224n
Gessert, Robert V: 310n
Gey, Stephen I: 297n
Gibson, JB IV: 197n
Gierke, Otto von II: 94n, 99n; IV: 203n, 208
Gilby, T. G. II: 154n
Gill, S.T. V: xi, 14
Gilson, Etienne V: 141, 143
Gisborne, John IV: 274n
Gladstone, William V: 6–7, 209, 211
Glanvill, Ranulf de IV: 191, 320, 323
Gleeson, Chief Justice (Murray) III: 143n
Glover, Jonathan II: 281–2; V: 316n
God (*see also* atheism, religion, revelation) V: 21–5, 59–62, 80–3, 134, 179–3, 197–8; active I: 169; providence V: 76–7; *also* V: 27, 57, 65, 74, 76–7, 184–6; triune V.15; vision (contemplation) of I: 159, 170
Goff of Chieveley, Lord (Robert) II: 32n, 174n, 182n, 212n, 270–1, 313–4, 316, 321; III: 215n; IV: 399–400
Goldberg, Justice (Arthur) V: 70n
Golden Rule I: 12, 59, 87, 101, 208, 210, 266; II: 183, 194, 213, 298; III: 119, 121, 124, 132, 189, 195–6, 199–200, 218; IV: 15, 29, 101, 253, 351; V: 59, 63, 159, 246, 296, 302, 315, 317; explained I: 59n, 227, 247–53; III: 236; IV: 122
good(s) basic, good for anyone I: 4; desirable: I: 159; as to be pursued I: 3, 100; hierarchy or hierarchies among? I: 63, 80, 140, 196, 244; intrinsic I: 4, 87–8; lists of basic I: 10–12, 140, 145, 213, 244n; III: 88; IV: 98; V: 245, 262, 270, 273; perfective I: 147

Gordley, James IV: 142
Gorer, Geoffrey I: 296n
Gormally, Luke II: 69; III: 249n, 250; V: 352
Gough, John W IV: 196n
Gousset, Thomas-Marie-Joseph V: 216n, 219–20n, 222
grace V: 231
Grant, C.K. I: 74n
Gratian IV: 174n; V: 222n
Gray, Asa III: 356n
Gray, John Chipman II: 27, 81n
Green, Leslie IV: 9n, 56n, 58–9n, 68n, 70n, 247
Greenawalt, Kent V: 51n
Gregor, Mary III: 55–7n, 61–2, 63n, 67n, 104n, 342n
Gregory IX V: 213n
Gregory XVI V: 158n, 218
Grice, H.P. (Paul) I: 74; IV: 395n
Griffin, James I: 245n
Griffin, Leslie C. IV: 446n
Grisez, Germain G. I: 28, 45n, 64n, 73n, 84, 90, 139–42, 146n, 152n–53n, 154, 169, 171–2, 195, 203n, 205n, 218n, 223n–4n, 239n, 272n; II: 3n, 8n, 11, 13, 52n, 66–7, 92n, 118n, 145n, 148n, 155n, 164n, 171n, 177n–8n, 235n, 243n–5n, 252, 254–67, 280n, 285n–9n, 293, 302–12; III: 13–14, 66n, 69n, 87, 97, 194n, 198, 243n, 247n, 249n, 289n, 294n, 296n, 297–8, 305, 310n, 313n, 339, 345, 354–6, 372–3, 377n, 380n, 387n; IV: 52n, 55n, 68n, 293n, 357, 359n; V: 23n, 46n, 60, 76n, 80n, 82n, 110n, 118–19, 123, 148–9, 150–1n, 153, 161n, 179n, 227, 268n, 278, 299–300n, 308n, 316n, 340, 346, 347n, 355n, 360, 364, 370–1
Grosseteste, Robert I: 192
Grotius, Hugo I: 6, 125; III: 131, 191n, 202n; IV: 95, 146n, 337
group existence and action II.4–5, II: 11
Grover, Robinson A. IV: 53n
Gula, Richard M. V: 139–40

Habermas, Jürgen I: 41n–6n, 48n, 50n–3n, 55–60, 61n; IV: 125; V: 99
habitus II: 10
Hailsham, Lord (Hogg, Quintin) II: 174n, 184n; III: 35
Haksar, Vinit III: 32n, 70n
Haldane, John V: 61, 69, 124
Hale, Lady (Brenda) II: 271; V: 99n
Hale, Matthew III: 12, 135n; IV: 191–2
Hallett, Garth L. II: 169n; V: 287
Halsbury, Lord (Hardinge, Stanley Giffard) II: 207–9n
Hamel, Edouard V: 140n, 259n, 261n
Hamilton, Alexander IV: 154
Hampshire, Stuart IV: 235–9, 255
Hampton, Jean V: 52n
Hand, Learned III: 22

Hannen, Lord (James) II: 209n
Hanson, Norwood IV: 394–5
Hardie, W.F.R. I: 110, 191
Hare, R.M. I: 128, 141, 198n, 312n, 323n, II: 281–4; III: 290, 291n
Hargrave, John Fletcher IV: 190n
Häring, Bernard II: 279n
Harlan, Justice (John Marshall) I: 277–8, 281n; V: 70
harm I: 154
Harman, Gilbert IV: 224n
Harrington, James IV: 321
Harris, John III: 211n, 223–41; V: 318n
Hart, H.L.A. IV.10 & 11; *see also* I: 35n, 62, 66n, 69, 92, 102, 104, 106–13; II: 14, 19–22, 30, 81–3, 85n, 99n, 110, 133n, 182n, 267n; III: 10, 48n, 153–60, 163–5, 168, 173, 176–7, 259n, 295; IV: 10–11, 27, 32n, 36–40, 44n, 47n, 50, 53n, 73, 74–5, 76n, 77–82, 87n, 106–8, 119–20, 126, 155n, 162–9, 185, 186n, 188–90n, 198–201, 211n, 221n, 229n, 289, 290n, 388n, 396, 410, 411n, 414, 415n, 416–21, 425–7, 429, 432–3; V: 32, 43, 105n
Hart, Jenifer (née Williams) IV: 257, 273
Harte, Colin IV: 447n, 449n, 455n, 459n, 463n, 466n
Hathaway, R. IV: 51n
Hazeltine, H.D. IV: 189–90n
Heaney, S.J. II: 288n
heaven (*see also beatitudo*) V: 199–202, 206, 249, 371
Hebblethwaite, Peter V: 173
Hegel, G.W.F. IV: 75, 93, 431; V: 144n, 153–4, 183
Hehir, J. Bryan V: 310n
Heidegger, Martin V: 183
Heisenberg, Werner V: 23n
Hekman, Susan J. IV: 79n
hell (*see also* punishment) V.24; V: 171–2, 177–8
Helsinki, Declaration of II: 296
Hemer, Colin J. V: 152n
Henderson, Lynn IV: 360n, 365n
Hengel, Martin V: 141
Henry IV IV: 408
Henry V IV: 408
Henry VI IV: 408
Henry VIII V: 163–4
Henson, Hensley V: 238
Heraclitus V: 143n
'hermeneutical circle' V: 263
Herschell, Farrer II: 207n
Heydon, Justice (J. Dyson) III: 143n
Heylbut, G. I: 192n
Hildick-Smith, Marion III: 249
Hill, Thomas E. III: 55n
Himes, Michael V: 140n
Hindley, Clifford III: 337n
Hintikka, Jaakko I: 135
Hippias of Elis IV: 160

Hippolytus, of Rome, St. V: 159
Hitler, Adolf II: 84
'historical consciousness' V.9
Hobbes, Thomas, on intention as dominant desire I: 23; II: 177, 228–9; on 'public reason' I: 13n, 275; *summum bonum* rejected I: 63; *also* I: 6, 26, 28, 43n, 59, 102, 120, 123n; IV: 10, 55–6, 83, 95–6, 97n, 98, 116, 134, 142, 160, 162, 169, 189n, 239, 255, 264–5; V: 4
Hobhouse, L.T. III: 66–7
Hodgson, D.H. III: 290n
Hoffman, Abbie I: 301
Hoffman, Justice (Julius) I: 301
Hoffmann, Lord (Leonard H.) I: 301; II: 31, 32n, 215n–19n, 318, 320–1; III: 148n; IV: 399–400; V: 99n
Hohfeld, Wesley, N. IV.18; *also* II: 30; III:123n, 137, 283–5, 302; IV: 11, 86, 115–16; V: 36, 90, 94
Holbrook, David I: 321
Holdsworth, William III: 135n; IV: 193
Holmes, G.L. II: 307n
Holmes, Justice (Oliver Wendell) I: 250; II: 199–201, 209n, 211–2; III: 22, 215, 252; IV: 142, 340–2; V: 32
Homer I: 118–19
Honoré, A.M. (Tony) II: 10, 29n, 83, 133n; IV: 166–7, IV: 376n, 409n
Hook, Sidney IV: 156
Hooker, Richard IV: 204, 208
Hooper, Walter III: 274n, 281n
Hope of Craighead, Lord (David) III: 45n, 63n; 144n; IV: 399–400
Hopkins, Gerard Manley V: 374n
Horrocks, John V: xi, 14
Hospers, John IV: 390, 394
Hovenden, John Eykyn IV: 190n, 194n
Howsepian, A.A. II: 286n
Hugh of St Victor IV: 186–7n; V: 115
Hughes, Gerard J. IV: 341n; V: 115, 224n, 258, 261, 262n, 263–4, 272, 280
human rights (*see also* rights) III.1–9
Humboldt, Wilhelm von III: 110, 115n
Hume, Basil V: 289n
Hume, David, denial of practical reason I: 22–3, 26, 33, 38, 234, 283; II: 129; IV: 4, 226n; V: 59, 69; on freedom of the press I: 310; 'genealogical' method I: 93; on *Is* v *Ought* I: 202, 242; IV: 10, 120n; V: 33; on miracles II: 72n; V: 9, 83, 137, 152; self-refuting IV: 131; V: 25, 130; on sympathy and morality I: 125–6, 128–9; *see also* IV: 154, 249, 255, 264, 337; V: 22, 141, 183 *also* I: 59–60, 102, 264; II: 38
Humean (Humeian), Humeanism on desire I: 161n; dogma that reason does not motivate I: 100; II: 4n; III: 320; IV: 252; empiricism I: 43n, 46n, 81; conception of reasons for action I: 96n, 125–9; idea of reason as slave of passion I: 22–3, 30n,

120n, 124; V: 73; misunderstanding of reason and will I: 1, 7, 22; IV: 162, 235, 239 (*see also* Korsgaard)
humility V.17
Hurst, G. II: 287n
Hürth, Francis V: 297n
Hutcheson, Francis IV: 337–8
Huxley, Aldous IV: 231

Iglesias, Teresa II: 284n
immigration II: 118–9; III.7–9; V: 12, 40
impartial spectator, of human arena I: 129
inclinations, and induction of basic reasons for action: I: 38–9, 144–7, 155
incommensurability (*see also* commensuration) I.15; of dimensions of judicial reasoning I: 222–5; of options (proposals for choice) I: 224–7; IV: 357, 360; V: 77
indeterminacy v under-determination I: 228
innate, practical knowledge and principles not strictly I: 177–8; but loosely I: 178–9
Innocent III V: 222n
Innocent XI V: 212
insight(s) I: 45n; into basic goods I: 2–3, 98, 204; non-inferential, non-deductive I: 2–3, 31, 45, 98, 147–8, 178, 204; supervenes on experience I: 2
insult II: 105; V: 30–1
integral directiveness of practical reason's first principles I: 12; human fulfilment I: 12–13, 159–72, 210; II: 122; V: 59
intention II.8–14, III: 213–8; V: 74–5, 158–60
internal attitude I: 108, 112
interpretation II: 32
intransitivity of action II: 10
'intuition' I: 60–1, 99, 148, 186; of feelings I: 237, 254; III: 50; 'of moral propositions' I: 138, 140, 194, 204; V: 264, 268–9; 'our intuitions' III: 368; IV: 35, 124, 422; V: 4
intuitionis: 'official' I: 113, 117, 237; unofficial I: 237, 254; III: 50
Irenaeus, St. V: 115, 247, 260n, 263n
Irwin, Terence I: 28–31, 39–40, 161n, 173–5, 183n; IV: 51n, 226
Is—Ought I.9: no valid inference: I: 50, 78, 126, 202, 206
Isaac V: 272n, 298n
Isaiah V: 203–4
Isaye, G. I: 45n, 72, 84
Isidore of Seville, St. IV: 187n
Islam III: 149; V: 6, 8, 38–41, 53–4, 91n, 96, 98–9
Israel, F.L. III: 22
ius gentium II: 101
IVF II.17, III.17

James I V: 5–7
James, William IV: 124n
Janssens, Louis V: 297n
Jefferson, Thomas I: 275n; V: 4

INDEX

Jenkins, David V: 192n
Jenkins, Iredell I: 288n
Jensen, Joseph V: 264n
Jeremiah V: 135
Jerome, St. V: 56, 225, 331–2
Jerusalem, fall of V: 88, 142
Jesus of Nazareth V: 161–2; *also* III: 319n; V: 48, 50, 54n, 68, 74, 86, 88, 110–11, 116, 118, 125, 136–7, 141–2, 145, 166–8, 171, 175–8, 200–1, 203–6, 228, 230, 240–3, 245–9, 251–2, 253, 260, 262, 264–5, 267, 270, 273–4, 281, 286–9, 295, 300n, 301, 350, 368, 372, 375, 378; resurrection of, 191–2
John XXII I: 207
John XXIII III: 85, 193n; V: 173–4, 254n
John, the Evangelist, St. V: 204, 273
John Damascene, St. II: 163n; V: 159, 187n, 342
John Paul II (*see also* Wojtyla, Karol)
    contraception V: 355, 364–5; double effect II: 251; 'direct' killing V: 299, 341; ethic of life V: 297; exceptionless moral norms V: 281; faith as fundamental option II: 52n; final punishment III: 178n; hope of immortality V: 240–2; human dignity V: 250; 'imperfect laws' IV: 437–49; 'liberation' V: 242; nation II: 12, 123n; nuclear deterrence V: 290; marriage III: 100, 372n; on proportionalism II: 244n; III: 85; solidarity III: 123n; on repentance V: 172
Johnston, Harry III: 126
Jolif, J.-Y. I: 159n
Jones, Ernest I: 121n; III: 168n
Jones, W.T. III: 58n
Jones, William IV: 10, 209
Jonsen, A.R. V: 316n
Jordan, Mark III: 354n, 360n, 364n
Joseph, H.W.B. IV: 258, 274
Josephus V: 142n
Judas Iscariot II: 163n; V: 177, 186, 287
judgment: as prudence (practical reasonableness) I: 31; as bearer of truth I: 44–5, 91
judicial functions and reasoning IV.20
justice I: 47–50; needed in heaven I: 167; distributive III.4
Justinian II: 19, 300; III: 2n; IV: 187n, 218; V: 225–6

Kalinowski, Georges I: 78n
Kalven, Harry I: 279n, 281, 285n, 292n
Kant, Immanuel
    on autonomy III: 54–9; V: 73–4; carnal crimes against nature III: 16, 61–2, 64–6, 104n, 339, 342n; conscience III: 169; V: 60; dualism(s) II: 94; III: 68–70; IV: 136; kingdom of ends I: 245; III: 54–5; IV: 121; liberalism I: 264; IV: 178, 328; V: 183; marriage III: 104n, 342n; philosophy of moral law, right, and law I: 301; III: 10, 47–8, 53–71; IV: 111; punishment III: 161, 163–5; respect for humanity I: 211, 246n; III: 60, 64, 219; V: 246, 267, 270; universalizability and non-contradiction I: 141, 210, 236; III: 60; IV: 53, 97, 142, 164
    inadequate understanding of reason and human good and nature I: 5, 7, 12–13, 24–6, 28, 45n, 55, 59, 102, 128, 147n, 204, 236–7, 242; II: 129; III: 9, 320; IV: 4, 93, 98, 131, 239; V: 59; self-referential inconsistencies in V: 153, 155n
    Neo-Kantian I: 22n, 147n, 202; III: 64, 122; IV: 10, 75, 162, 166–7, 223–4; V: 22; *also* I: 287n; IV: 154, 333, 357; V: 4
Kantorowicz, Ernst H. IV: 410n
Kaplan, Fred I: 287–8n
Kaplow, Louis I: 249n
Kass, Leon R. III: 356n
Kauper, Paul G. I: 277n
Kavka, Gregory II: 233n
Keenan, James F. II: 236n
Keily, Bartholomew V: 305n
Keith, Harry II: 316
Keizer, Bert III: 261n
Kelly, George Armstrong III: 68n
Kelly, Gerald V: 297n
Kelley, J.M. III: 43n
Kelley, Patrick J. II: 211n, 215n; IV: 139, 352n
Kelsen, Hans I: 19, 104–9, 112, 254, II: 24–7; III: 168; IV: 2–3, 12, 36, 40, 79, 99–100, 108, 112, 142, 162–3, 167–8, 186, 211n, 244n, 261, 263, 407n, 408–9, 411–17, 420–3, 426–7, 429n, 433
Kennedy, Duncan IV: 229n, 327–31
Kennedy, John F. II: 5
Kenny, Anthony I: 143n; II: 174n, 183n, 189n, 199n; III: 57n; V: 163n
Kenny, Justice (John) III: 43n
Keown, John I: 57n; II: 312n; III: 253–5n, 260n
Kerr, John II: 272–3
Ketley, M.A. III: 273n
Keynes, J.M. III: 378n
Kingsley, Charles V: 43
Kirk, Marshall III: 349–50n
Kis, Janos V: 103n, 105, 107–12
Kittel, Gerhard V: 261n
Kleinberg, Stanley III: 76–82
Kleinfeld, Andrew III: 256
Knauer, Peter V: 297n
Kneale, W.M. I: 71, 72n; III: 162
knowledge: as basic human good I: 2–5, 47, 62–5, 72–80, 139; is conceptual I: 205; of goods precedes adequate knowledge of nature I: 5; not innate: I: 148; order (epistemological) of coming to know natures I: 5; of possibilities, needed for understanding basic goods I: 5; practical I: 3; warranted, true belief I: 3

Knox, John II: 95n, 230n
koinōnia I: 48n, 123, 312
Koppelman, Andrew I: 297n; III: 326n, 345, 346–7n, 348–9, 350n, 351, 354n, 355–7, 360, 365–9, 372–3, 377–8n, 379–84, 385n, 386, 387n; V: 29
Kornhauser, Lewis IV: 348, 349n
Korsgaard, Christine I: 7, 23–7, 32–3, 101n; IV: 252
Kramer, Matthew I: 85n, 86–88, 91n
Kronman, Anthony I: 22; IV: 211–15, 217–19, 221–8, 315
Kuhn, Thomas IV: 33–4
Kuttner, Stephan IV: 174n, 187–8

Lacey, Nicola IV: 229n, 234, 236–7, 254n, 258–9n, 271n, 275, 278n; V: 32
Lactantius, I: 71n
Ladd, John III: 47n, 61n
Ladenson, Robert IV: 83n
Lafont, Ghislain I: 150n
Lagrange, J.M. V: 142
Lamennais, Hugues-Félicité-Robert de V: 158n
Landes, William M. II: 205–6
Lane, Lord Chief Justice (Geoffrey) II: 174–5n
Lang, Daniel III: 170
Langer, Suzanne I: 286n–8n, 290, 320n
Langholm, Odd V: 157n
langue v parole II: 67
Laplace, Pierre-Simon IV: 177
Larmore, Charles V: 51n
Latham, R.T.E. IV: 414n
Latourelle, René V: 142
Laumann, Edward O. III: 377n
law(s) IV.1–22; and 'bad man' I: 113; contradictory (inconsistent) laws I: 105–6; as cultural object and technique I: 219; foundation of rights (ratio iuris) I: 21n, and friendship I: 123; as means of social control I: 107–8; of nature I: 200; as part of moral life I: 123; primary and secondary rules I: 106–7; as reason for action I: 105; as social phenomenon I: 104–5, 108; sources of I: 19–21; universal propositions of practical reason: I: 19; IV: 449–50 (*see also* sources thesis)
Lawson, Penelope III: 273, 275
Lee, Patrick I: 39, 102, 151n, 154, 190n, 310, 313n; II: 312; III: 355n, 373, 387n; IV: 460; V: 187, 298n, 301n
legal positivism IV.1 & 4 & 7, IV: 99–109
legal reasoning I.14, IV.12–14, IV. 16–20
Legarre, Santiago III: 113n
Leibniz, G.W. II: 7n–8n, 155n; V: 153
Leiter, Brian IV: 32–3, 34n, 35–44, 105n, 112–15; V: 84, 195
Leo XIII II: 85, 126n; III: 186n; V: 253n
Lessius, Leonard V: 212n

Lewis, C.I. I: 72, 84,
Lewis, C.S. III: 16, 273–81
Lewis, David K. IV: 59n, 67n
'liberalism' I: 60–1n; V: 104–5, 113; 'political l.' I: 55–8
Lichtenberg, Judith IV: 366
Lindsay, A.D. IV: 259–60, 263
Line, Anne, St. I: 37; II: 54n
Line, Roger I: 37; II: 55n
Littleton, Thomas de III: 135
Livy IV: 321
Lloyd of Berwick, Lord (Anthony) IV: 398
Lloyd, Dennis IV: 380–1, 383
Locke, John I: 81, 102, 298; II: 38, 43; III: 191, 225n, 239; IV: 10, 12, 93, 95–8, 136, 142, 190n, 200, 208n, 320; V: 141
Lockhart, William B. I: 277n, 279n, 281n, 288n
Lockwood, Michael II: 279–85
Lombard, Peter I: 193; II: 165, 245, 247; III: 353n, 359; IV: 175
Lombardi, Joseph II: 257n
Lonergan, Bernard J.F. I: 71, 84, 88–9, 130n, 134, 137–40, 142, 143n, 168n, 288n; II: 135n, 258; IV: 396; V: 58n, 139–40, 143–8, 149n, 150–2, 155–6, 263n, 272n
Lottin, Odon I: 121; IV: 174n, 180
love: 'hath reason' I: 37–40; of neighbour as self I: 38n; II: 51
Lowry, Robert II: 315, 318
Luban, David IV: 357–69
Lucas, J. R. (John) III: 273n; IV: 378n
Lucas, Paul IV: 189n, 194n, 197–8
Luce, D.H. I: 222n; IV: 56n, 60n, 68, 359n
Luño, Angel Rodriguez IV: 440n
Luther, Martin II: 5; V: 164–5, 171
Lutz, Cora E. III: 99
Lycophron III: 92
lying: I: 50, 151; V: 164; and logic of assertion I: 74

MacCormick, Neil III: 37n; IV: 76n, 77, 163, 211n, 229n, 230, 235, 240, 248n, 390, 394
MacDonald, Margaret I: 74n
Macedo, Stephen III: 92n, 95n, 97–100, 102, 105–6, 110, 114, 326–7n, 340n, 342–3n, 348–9, 351, 380n, 381–2, 384, 386; V: 111n, 116
Machiavelli, Niccolò III: 199, 234; IV: 352; V: 76
Mackie, J.L. (John) I: 45n, 65–6n, 67–8, 71n, 74n, 81, 83, 85, 93n; IV: 133, 224n
Mackinolty, Chips III: 269n
MacIntyre, Alasdair I: 48n; IV: 372; V: 58
Maclean, Donald III: 378n
Macnaghten, Lord (Edward) II: 207n
Madison, James I: 283–4
Madsen, Hunter III: 349–50n
Magrath, C. Peter I: 296n

Maguire, Daniel III: 248n
Mahoney, John (Jack) II: 133n; V: 287
Maimonides, Moses V: 23
Maine, Henry III: 153
Maitland, F.W. II: 99n; IV: 320n
Malawi III: 125–7
Malcolm, Norman I: 73n
Mance, Lord (Jonathan) II: 272
Mandela, Nelson IV: 113
Manuel II, Paleologus V: 91
Marcel, Gabriel I: 210
Maritain, Jacques I: 205, 287n; II: 107n; V: 58, 78n, 243, 275, 285–6, 333
Marius, Richard V: 166
Marmor, Andrei IV: 246n
marriage III.20–22; IV: 135–8; a basic human good I: 9–10, 34, 155; III: 100; an action I: 9; III: 317
Marshall, Justice (Thurgood) III: 252n
Marsilius of Padua IV: 160
Martin, Christopher F.J. II: 43n
Martin, Patrick H. I: 36–7
Marx, Karl IV: 259–60, 332; V: 34, 237
Master, William V: 225, 229–30
Matthews, Gareth B. I: 70n
Matthews, Steven V: 1
Mattison, Andrew W. III: 349
May, William E. I: 154; V: 341
Mazzoni, C.M. II: 296
McAnany, Patrick D. I: 278n
McBrien, Richard P. V: 139–40
McClure, Robert C. I: 277n, 279n, 281n, 288n
McCormick, Richard II: 144–5, 147–9, 152n, 245n, 265; III: 248n; V: 261–2, 265n, 271–2n, 287, 291n, 296n, 299–300n, 303–4n, 306n, 309–10n, 316n, 322n, 360n
McDowell, John H. I: 75n, 81, 186n,
McHugh, Justice (Michael) III: 143n
McInerny, Ralph I: 52–3n; V: 66–7n
McKim, Robert I: 234n
McKnight, Joseph W. IV: 189–90n, 194n, 198n
McKnight, Stephen A. V: 1
McMahan, Jeff II: 307–8, 310
McWhirter, David P. III: 349n
Medeiros, Humberto Sousa V: 291n
Medina, Bartolomé de IV: 52n
Meiklejohn, Alexander I: 282n
Meiland, Jack W. II: 222–4, 226
Melamed, Douglas I: 247n; IV: 346n
Mercken H. Paul F. I: 193n
metaphysics essential to ethics, political theory and law IV: 353; of freely chosen activity (discourse) I: 55, 217; II: 34–5; of persons I: 35, 53, 204; II: 66–7, 70, 93, 105, 283, 302, 307; IV: 142; see also I: 43n, 94, 172, 236; II: 7; III: 370n; IV: 155, 288, 328; V: 17, 42, 149
Meyer, Ben V: 141–2, 152–3

Mill, John Stuart I: 298–9, 304–9, 311n; II: 110n, 124, 126n; III: 2, 51n, 66–7n, 78, 115n; IV: 154, 259–60, 266, 276, 279, 385
Miller, David III: 45n, 148
Miller, Henry I: 287n, 289n
Miller, Jonathan I: 14, 321–3
Mills, C. Wright IV: 34n, 224n
Milton, John I: 13, 274n, 298–9, 309; IV: 385; V: 4
miracles (see also Hume) I: 275; II: 72n; V: 57n, 88–9, 116, 137, 142, 152–3, 167
Moleski, Martin I: 65n
Moline, John I: 165n
Montesquieu, Charles de IV: 12
Montgomery, George R. II: 8n
Moore, G.E. I: 74, 130
Moore, Michael II: 174n, 177n
moral: absolutes I.12; I: 13, 50–2; beliefs, diversity of I: 79; and action I: 115–8; evaluation I: 119–20; ideals I: 118; point of view I: 119; 'morality system' (Williams) I: 102–3; m. philosophy, modern I: 113–23; standards as second level of practical understanding I: 12, 31–2, 140–2, 148–9, 153–5; m. thought as rational thought I: 215
More, Thomas, St. V: 10, 118–19, 163–78, 368
Morris, Harry II: 40n
Morris, Herbert III: 177
Morris of Borth-y-Gest, Lord (John) IV: 435n
Morrison, J.S. I: 314n
Moses V: 136
Moya, Carlos J. II: 199n, 225n
Moya, Matthaeus de V: 212
Mugabe, Robert V: 199–201
Müller, Jan-Werner II: 107
Mulley, Graham III: 249
multi-culturalism (see also 'diversity') II: 12
Munby, James II: 316
Murphy, Jeffrie G. III: 61n, 161–4, 177
Murphy, Mark V: 193, 195–7
Murphy-O'Connor, Cormac II: 266n
Murray, John Courtney IV: 386n, 388n; V: 276, 282
Musonius Rufus I: 244n; II: 128; III: 88, 91, 100, 102, 323n, 338–40, 355; V: 350, 352
Mustill, Lord (Michael) II: 312–3, 315, 318, 320; III: 235n
Muzorewa, Abel V: 199n

Nagel, Thomas I: 259n, II: 84–5; III: 50n, 95n; V: 71, 72n
Namier, Lewis IV: 203n
Napoleon I IV: 395
Nash, John IV: 361
natural law I: 41, 144, 152, 177, 214; n.l. theory I: 199–21; theology of V.19
natures: knowledge of via capacities, acts, and their objects I: 5, 33, 147, 179, 204
Nero V: 203

nested ends and means II: 163
Newman, John Henry: V: 6–7, 9–10, 43, 46n, 54n, 60, 87, 152–3, 162n, 169, 204–5, 209–24
Newton, Isaac II: 8
Nicholls, Lord (Donald) II: 217n–19n; III: 144n
Nicolau, M. V: 153n
Nietzsche, Friedrich I: 22, 28, 41n, 49–51, 69, 88, 94, 96, 118; III: 9, 13, 167–78, 266–7; V: 33–4, 73–4, 183, 194, 197–8, 339
Nietzschian moral theory I: 118
Nigidius, P. IV: 187–8n
Noonan, John T. III: 294n, 298n, 320n, 346n, 356–61, 365n, 366–8, 372; V: 353n
Norman, E.R. V: 235–49
normativ(ity): as ought-knowledge I: 3; of theoretical reason I: 8; source of I: 98–9
Nozick, Robert I: 63, 169, 217; III: 80; IV: 53n, 266; V: 71n
Nussbaum, Martha I: 10–12, 28; III: 16, 99n, 323–4n, 372n, 378n, 385n, 387n

objective/ity: kinds of I: 134–5; certainty I: 130; moral I: 140; of principles I: 64; and truth I: 214; III: 25; of value judgments I: 202
offensiveness (see also insult) II: 117
O'Connell, Daniel P. IV: 407n
O'Connell, Timothy E. II: 133–5, 138, 150n; V: 160n, 257–8n, 261, 262n, 265–6n, 270–1n, 272
O'Connor, James V: 379
O'Connor, John IV: 441n
O'Connor, Justice (Sandra Day) III: 252n; IV: 371
Odo of Dour IV: 174n
Oecolampadius, Johannes V: 165
Olson, Eric II: 292n
omission II: 161
Origen V: 159
Orrego, Cristóbal IV: 262n, 275
Ortiz, Daniel IV: 327–32, 334
others: are like me in basic worth I: 4, 27, 47; III: 172; V: 67
Ottaviani, Alfred III: 191n
ought-knowledge I: 3, 99
Owen, G.E.L. I: 110

Pagden, Anthony III: 130–1n
Pannick, Lord (David) III: 44n
Parfit, Derek II: 150n; V: 305n
Parker, Isaac IV: 391–2
Pascal, Blaise I: 37, 313
passions (emotions): deflect practical reason I: 14, 47; reason's civil rule over I: 14, 211; support practical reason I: 14–15, 213
Passmore, John I: 66, 71n
paternalism II: 109; III: 10–11, 71, III.5; IV: 137n, 268, 270, 276; V: 105, 112, 117–8
Paton, G.W. IV: 189n, 378

patria: one's country II: 107, 118–9, 123; III: 290, 328; heavenly I: 167n
patriotism: I: 40, 253; II: 123, 126–7; IV: 258; V: 11; 'constitutional p.' II: 107
Patterson, Charlotte J. III: 356n
Patterson, Dennis IV: 44n
Paul, St. I: 96, 193, 258, 312; III: 353n, 359n; V: 10, 43, 45n, 115–16, 125, 131, 159–60, 169, 177, 200–1, 227–30, 247, 249, 263, 267n, 273, 302, 350, 372
Paul IV III: 103
Paul VI II: 128, 251; III: 121, 199n; V: 188n, 241–2, 244n, 246, 247n, 274, 299n, 341, 344–67, 371
Paul, James C.N. I: 130, 278n
Paulson, Stanley L. II: 24n
Pearce, Lord (Edward) IV: 435n
Pears, David II: 230n
Pearson, Lord (Colin) I: 318n
Peel, Robert II: 201n; IV: 341n
performative inconsistency, *see* self-refutation
Peirce, Charles Sanders I: 45; IV: 124, 130n, 394–5; V: 26
peoples II: 107
Pericles IV: 157
Perry, Michael III: 383n; V: 194, 197, 198n
person, personal identity I.5, II.1–2; defined II: 9, 98; metaphysics of I: 35; non-fungible I: 40
Peschke, K.-H. II: 153n; V: 75, 187n, 341n
Peter, St I: 258; V: 116, 125, 175, 203, 205–6, 287
Phillimore, Lord (Walter) III: 137n
Phillips of Worth Matravers, Lord (Nicholas) II: 271
Philo Judaeus III: 350n, 385n; V: 159, 187
Philosophers' Brief V: 71, 73
philosophy
  consistency with worth of philosophizing I: 81; of human affairs I: 63, 108
Pijnenborg, Loes III: 254n
Pildes, Richard N. I: 235n, 253n
Pinckaers, Servais II: 154n
Pink, T.L.M. II: 230n
Pius IX V: 218
Pius XI III: 100, 293n; V: 346
Pius XII II: 171n, 237, 249n, 251–2, 303, 306; III: 100–1, 193n, 195n, 199n, 293n, 308n, 310; V: 113, 160n, 215, 254n, 255, 299n, 310n, 341, 346
Planck, Max V: 23n
Plato
  on bad secularisms V: 57–9, 64, 66, 124, 333–4, 342; basic goods I: 161n; 'better to suffer wrong than do it' I: 241–2; III: 201; V: 267; Cave I: 94–7; II: 129; V: 133, 138; cooperation with God III: 9, 189; V: 44n, 133–4, 226–7, 230–1; family II: 13, 126n; friendship I: 41–53, 112; IV: 432; God's

existence and goodness V: 61, 187, 336, 338; good of truth I: 41–53, 63; *Gorgias* I: 41–53, 60; III: 103; IV: 93, 103, 125; law I: 108; IV: [51], 76, 157, 160; method in social theory IV: 80, 235, 265; natural law I: 201; III: 85n, 127; IV: 10, 76, 93, 124–5, 187; V: 33, 267; paternalism III: 27n; IV: 135, 270; V: 105–6, 112, 118; portrait of the philosopher I: 313–5; punishment III: 155, 157–8; V: 13; reason and passions I: 282; *Republic* I: 121IV: 134, 176; self-refutation I: 70, 83–4, 90–1; V: 148; sex ethics II: 128; III: 99–103, 323–4, 336, 338–41, 372n, 378n, 387–8; IV. 137n, 272–4; V: 350; soul II: 34, 40n; *see also* I: 81, 92, 188, 202, 208–9, 265n; II: 5, 38; III: 107, 186n; IV: 9n, 174, 225n, 234n, 258–60, 276, 279; V: 51, 135, 193, 273
play II: 151
Plutarch III: 99n, 102, 104n, 338–40, 342, 355; IV: 137
Pogge, Thomas III: 123–4n
Pollock, Frederick II: 209n; IV: 320n
pornography I.17, I.19
Porter, Jean II: 243n, 256–65; V: 76n, 340–1
positivity of law I: 208
Posner, Richard I: 234n; II: 203–6, 215, 226; III: 170, 242, 243n; IV: 9–10, 53n, 125, 172, 344–7, 349–50; V: 26n, 34
Possidius, St. V: 376
Postema, Gerald J. IV: 66, 73n, 87n, 108n
postmodern(ism) I: 46n, 94; II: 127; IV: 172, 327–34
Pound, Roscoe IV: 189n
Powell, Justice (Lewis) F I: 269n
practical reason I.1, I.6, I.8–11, I.14, IV.17
practical reasonableness: an architectonic basic human good (*bonum rationis*) I: 4, 34, 36, 172, 177, 183; V: 11; inner integrity, outer authenticity I: 14; requirements of II: 139
praxis I: 46, 207, 217, 240; II: 102; III: 93; IV: 283–5; V: 180, 205
Price, Anthony II: 44n, 46n; III: 99n, 103, 337–8n; V: 350
Price, David IV: 320, 321n, 323n, 324–5
Prichard, H.A. I: 237
principle(s): first principle of practical reason I: 29–30, 144–5; first principles of practical reason I: 9–12, 28, 144–50, 177–8, 205; general, of law I: 20; indemonstrable I: 147–8; induction of first principles directing to basic goods I: 5, 32–3, 148; master principle of morality I: 129, 210, 215; moral I: 208, 210, 215–6; of practical reasonableness I: 31–2, 140–2
Proclus IV: 188n
proposal for choice II: 11
propositions I: 65n; concepts and words have full meaning in I: 2; law as IV.22 esp. 449–52 (*see also* assertion, self-refutation)
Prosser, William I: 226n
Protagoras I: 83
Proust, Marcel IV: 230, 251
prudence (*phronēsis, prudentia*, practical reasonableness); concerns ends as well as means I: 26, 173–86; connection with justice I: 120–1; measure of all virtues I: 121; needed in beatitude I: 167; not mere cleverness I: 121
public reason I.15–16, V.2, V.5; Rawlsian restrictions of I: 13, 55; V: 106, 138; straightforward sense I: 13, 58 (*see also* Rawls)
Pufendorf, Samuel von IV: 10, 95–6, 146n, 337
punishment III.10–12; IV: 83–4, 121, 142–4, 179, 381–4; V: 228, 310n, 370–1; capital V: 309
purity III: 387
Putnam, Hilary IV: 223
'pvs' II.18–19
Pythagoras IV: 188n

questioning, significance of V.7; V: 103
Quine, W.V. IV: 33–4, 41
Quinlan, Michael V: 289–90n
Quinton, A.M. I: 302; IV: 259–60, 263, 275

Radbruch, Gustav IV: 221
Radcliffe, Viscount (Cyril) III: 28
Rahner, Karl I: 89; V: 148, 149n, 155, 220–1, 224, 256, 270n, 272n, 373
Raiffa, H. I: 222n; IV: 56n, 60n, 66n, 359n
Ramsey, Paul II: 147n; V: 296n, 299n, 304n, 310n
Raphael, D.D. II: 226n
'rational choice': ambiguity of phrase I: 218–9
rationality norms II: 8; V: 150–4
rationalization II: 13; V: 46
Rawls, John I.16 (*Political Liberalism*), III.3 (*Theory of Justice*); *see also* I: 13–14, 43n, 55, 57–9, 60n, 63, 96n, 141,189, 222; II: 12, 108, 123–7; III: 10, 48–51, 67n, 95 III: 92, 95, 121, 123–4n; IV: 57–8, 155–6n, 264–6; V: 4, 6–8, 11–12, 18, 48, 52–3, 71, 72n, 85n, 87, 113, 116, 138n
Raz, Joseph IV: 2n, 4–9, IV.2–3; *see also* I: 224n, 253; II: 33n, 81n, 112–7, 119n, 123–4n; III: 3, 37n , 50n, 68n, 70n, 95, 147, 148n, 168; IV: 2n, 27–8, 30n, 31, 38, 40, 42n, 100–1, 106n, 108n, 163–5, 169–70, 184, 185n, 188n, 235, 243, 246n, 247, 254n, 258–9, 261n, 278n, 284, 289n, 294–5n, 321n, 324, 414, 421–3, 430, 433; V: 18, 30, 63n, 72n, 105n, 107–8, 110, 111n
Reagan, Ronald V: 278, 280
reason(ing): as action I: 1, 127–8; is to be followed I: 8; judicial I: 221; legal I: 212–30; as motivating I: 22–4, 129; theoretical I: 40

reasonableness *see* prudence I: 128
reasons
  for action I: 1, 10, 212–3; basic I: 24–8, 213–6; 'instrumental' I: 22–3; and law I: 105; 'internal' and external' I: 7
reductionism I: 218
reflection I: 52–2
Reformation, the V: 164–71
Regan, Augustine III: 193n; V: 309n
Reid, Elspeth II: 219n
Reid, Lord (James) IV: 400
Reid, Thomas II: 43n
Reiman, Jeffrey I: 256–7, 261n, 265n, 268n, 272n, 273–6, 275n; V: 330–2
Reinhardt, Stephen III: 253, 256
Reiss, Hans III: 61
religion: basic human good of I: 59; V: 28–9, 85–6n, 92, 117, 180–1; liberty V.4, V: 35–8, 117–8, 158; 'natural religion' V: 27–30, 62, 65, 217; and public reason V.2, V.5, V: 2–9, 84–5, 116; and state V.1, V.4, V: 5–9
repentance III: 373
'respect nature' III: 104
ressentiment I: 118
retorsive argument, *see* self-refutation I: 65, 135–7
revelation V.2, V.8; *also* V: 83–4, 102, 111, 115–6, 175, 218
revolution IV: 8; legal effect III: 203–5; IV.21; IV: 2–3, 16–18, 118, 244–5
Rhonheimer, Martin II: 164n, 166n; V: 160n
Richard III II: 52
Richards, David A.J. III: 10, 48, 53–7, 58–9n, 60, 63n, 66n, 290
Richardson, Alan V: 143
Richardson, Elliot V: 278
Richter, A.L. V: 222n
Rickman, H.P. V: 144n
rights: absolute I: 154, 211; logic of I: 206–7; IV.18, IV: 3
Riker, William IV: 54, 55n
Rinck, Hans-Justus IV: 189n, 196n, 209n
Roberts, Owen I: 278; III: 22–3
Roberts-Wray, Kenneth IV: 414n
Robinson, John A.T. V: 88, 152n
Rodger, Lord (Alan) III: 45n, 144n
Rolland, Romain IV: 251
Rolph, C.H. I: 296n
Roper, Margaret V: 163n
Rorty, Richard IV: 125, 331
Roskill, Lord (Eustace) II: 220n
Ross, Alf I: 66; IV: 415–17, 420–1, 423n, 428–9
Ross, W.D. I: 71n, 237
Rotello, Gabriel III: 384–5n
Roth, Claus IV: 214n
Rousseau, Jean-Jacques I: 13, 275n, II: 196n; V: 4
Royce, Josiah I: 141, 210
Ruff, Wilfried II: 279n

Rule of Law III: 332
rules of law, explained II: 23–4
Russell, J.B. I: 60, 74n

Saeed, Abdullah V: 53
Saeed, Hassan V: 53
Sager, Lawrence G. V: 18, 20, 29–31, 86n, 95
Salaverri, J. V: 153n
Salmond, John IV: 376–7
Santamaria, B. A. III: 114n
Santayana, George I: 289n
sapientia I: 160n
Sartorius, Rolf IV: 47n, 72n, 74–87, 126n
Sartre, J.-P. I: 202; V: 183
Scalia, Justice (Antonin) IV: 153; V: 18n, 76
Scanlon, Thomas V: 71n
Scarman, Lord (Leslie) II: 174n, 220n; III: 23n, 30
scepticism I: 64–5, 70–80, 94, 130–7; critique of I: 201–4
Schauer, Frederick I: 297n; IV: 163
Scheffler, Samuel V: 304–5n
Schelling, Thomas IV: 59n
Schenk, Roy U. II: 279n
Schlesinger, Elliot V: 278–9
Schmitt, Charles B. V: 332n
Schnackenburg, R. V: 260n
Schneewind, J.B. I: 264n
Scholz, Franz V: 297n, 308–9n
Schüller, Bruno II: 144–8, 244n; IV: 75, 187n, 261; V: 187n, 253, 265n, 287, 297n, 300n, 304n
Schwartz, Pepper III: 384n
Scott, James Brown III: 191n
Scott, Lord Justice (Leslie) III: 34
Scott, Richard V: 99n
Scruton, Roger II: 92–8; III: 261n
Searle, John V: 339n
secularism v secularity V.3
Seifert, Josef II: 306
self-constitution II: 196
self-contradiction I: 85
self-evidence I: 64, 77, 133
self-referring laws IV: 230–1, 415–6
self-refutation (self-referential inconsistency, performative inconsistency) I.3–4; V: 148–9; *also* I: 45–7, 127–8, 133–7, 203; V: 32, 66n, 107, 144, 153; kinds of I: 65–8, 81–2
Sellars, Wilfrid II: 222n
Semonche, John E. I: 285n
semper sed non ad semper v semper et ad semper I: 189
Sen, Amartya I: 10; IV: 56
Seneca III: 202n
sex ethics III.20–22; IV: 135–8; V.23
Sextus Empiricus IV: 355; V: 129
Shakespeare, William I: 36, 38
  All's Well that Ends Well II: 42, 44–8, 53, 55–62, 64; V: 334–5; *Anthony & Cleopatra*

I: 31n; *As You Like It* II: 40n, 65, 334;
Hamlet II: 38, 41n, 67, 104; *Henry IV, Part I* II: 63; *Henry V* II: 63; V: 335; *King John* V: 343; *King Lear* I: 33; V: 5n; *Measure for Measure* II: 57, 65; *The Merchant of Venice* II: 40; *A Midsummer Night's Dream* II: 39; III: 324; *Phoenix & Turtle* I: 36–7, 39–40; II: 54–5; *Richard III* II: 49–50, 52; V: 13; *Sonnet XI* IV: 272; *The Tempest* I: 35n
Shand, Lord (Alexander) II: 207n
Shapiro, Scott IV: 91n
Sharswood, George IV: 190n, 194n
Shavelson, Lonny III: 267
Shaw, Russell V: 161n
Shaw of Dunfermline, Lord (Thomas) III: 133n
Shearmur, Jeremy IV: 353–6
Sheehan, Duncan IV: 401n
Shelley, Percy Bysshe IV: 274n
Shewmon, Alan II: 307–9
Shils, E.A. IV: 34n, 79n
Shortt, Edward III: 116–17
side effects II.9–11, II.13–14
Sidgwick, Henry I: 30n, 198n, II: 182n, 212; III: 214–15; V: 74, 265n
Sikkink, David III: 114n
Simmonds, N.E. IV: 245, 250n
Simmons, A.J. IV: 72n
Simon, David II: 175n
Simon, Jürgen II: 300–1
Simon, Viscount (John) II: 210
Simon, Yves IV: 69
Simonds, Gavin III: 36n; IV: 268–9, 429n
Simpson, A.W. Brian IV: 16
Simpson, Peter I: 234n
Singer, Peter I: 57, II: 279n, 281–2, 302–12; V: 68
slavery: and penal servitude I: 59
Slough, M.C. I: 278n, 279n
Smart, J.J.C. V: 61, 69
Smith, Adam IV: 10, 337–40, 348, 352
Smith, Christian III: 114n
Smith, J.C. I: 217n
Smith, M.B.E. IV: 47n
Smith, Stephen W. V: 163n, 169
Smith, Sydney II: 199–202; IV: 342, 344
'social choice' theory IV. 2 & 3
social rules I: 107
social theory I: 205
Socrates I: 41, 43–4, 46, 47n, 49–50, 95, 115, 161n, 241–2, 313, II: 33; III: 4–5, 99–100, 157, 323n, 336–7, 355, 377n; IV: 76, 159–60, 186n, 225n, 226
Sokolowski, Robert II: 43n
Solidarity II: 125
Solon III: 102nm 339n
Sommerville, Margaret R. III: 320n
soul: form and act of body I: 35, 54
'sources thesis' (s. of law only social facts) I: 19
sovereignty: and limitation of self or successors I: 68–70

'speculative' knowledge I: 147n, 168–70
Spender, Stephen III: 378n
Spiazzi, R.M. I: 159n; III: 353n
Spicq, Ceslau V: 186n
Spinoza, Baruch II: 177; IV: 160
spirit(uality) II.3
spoudaios I: 108–13, 122–3, 143, 233n; IV: 80, 433
St. German (Germain), Christopher IV: 199, 200n, 208, 218
St. John-Stevas, Norman I: 279n
Stalin, Joseph II: 84; V: 58
'state of nature' I: 80, 200; IV: 55, 116
  and Blackstone IV: 198–200, 202, 207–9
Staudinger, Hugo V: 142n
Steptoe, Patrick II: 294n; III: 280n
Stevens, Justice (John Paul) III: 245–6
Stevens, Monica V: 170n
Stewart, Justice (Potter) I: 285n, 296
Stone, Julius IV: 376–7, 379–80
Stout, Robert III: 249–50
'stranger in the wilds' I: 15, 99; II: 129
Strauss, Leo I: 187–90; III: 86–7, 89n; IV: 225n; V: 152
Strawson, P.F. (Peter) I: 287n, 319, II: 92n–3n
Suárez, Francisco I: 6, 125, 177n; II: 291n; III: 185n, 188n, 190–2, 193–4, 195n, 198n, 200–1n, 203–4n, 206n; IV: 52n; V: 272, 374n
subjectivity II: 68
substantial change II: 287
sufficient reason, 'principle of' II: 7; V: 183–4
Sugarman, David IV: 274n
Sullivan, Andrew III: 384n
Sullivan, Francis A. V: 115
Sullivan, Thomas D. II: 183n
Sumner, Lord (Hamilton, John) II: 218–19n; III: 137n
survival: as aim I: 63
Sutton, Agneta III: 312n
Swadling, W. IV: 401n
Sylvester, David I: 289n
synderesis I: 28–30, 139, 163, 173, 175–6, 182, 194; V: 179

Tacitus, Publius Cornelius III: 184n
Taney, Roger B. II: 26n
Taylor, Charles III: 323n
Taylor, Gary II: 67–8; V: 335n
Taylor, Harriet IV: 279
Taylor, J. IV: 186n
Teichman, Jenny III: 239n
Teichmuller, Gustav I: 160n
Temple, William V: 243
'temporal' V: 92–3
Thierry of Chartres IV: 187n
Thomas, St. V: 60
Thomas, S. V: 93n
Thomism, Thomist I: 12
Thomson, Judith Jarvis I: 269–70; III: 15, 282–9, 292–3, 295n, 296–305; V: 71–2n, 331

Thucydides, II: 5; IV: 76
Tillyard, E.M.W. II: 46n
Tollefsen, Christopher I: 45n, 73n, 84n, 90, 100n, 203n, 239n; II: 177n, 286n, 292n; IV: 359; V: 149, 150–1n
Tooley, Michael II: 281–2, 287; V: 316n
Torralba, J.M. II: 69n
torts (delict), law of II.11; IV.16, IV: 138–40, 150–1
torture I: 102
transparency for I.8; II: 113; III: 25–6; IV: 255, 286
Tribonian IV: 117
truth I:5; V: 33–4
Tsikata, Fui IV: 429n
Tsikata, Tsatsu IV: 429n
Tubbs, J.W. IV: 149n
Tuck, Richard III: 125, 128–31
Tugwell, Simon IV: 180n
Turner, Stephen P. I: 203n; IV: 224–5n
Turrecremata, Johannes de V: 213n
Tushnet, Mark IV: 352n, 371–2
Twining, William IV: 232n
twinning II: 289–92, 296–7
Twycross, Robert III: 265–8n
Tynan, Kenneth I: 321n
Tyndale, William V: 165, 166–7

Ullmann-Margalit, Edna IV: 56–9n, 67n, 69
Ulpian II: 5; IV: 183, 218
Unger, Roberto M. I: 214; IV: 10, 123n, 299–319, 322, 324–5
usury V: 157–8
ut in pluribus v *ut in paucioribus* I: 189
utilitarian(ism) I: 141, 143

value: aspect of human flourishing I: 137; Lonerganian theory of I: 137–9, 143
'value-free' social science/theory I: 205–6; IV.1, IV.9, IV: 1–4, 7, 17, 106–9, 163–4, 232–5; V: 146
van Beeck, Franz Josef V: 309n
Van den Haag, Ernest I: 289n
Van Reit, Simone V: 84n
Vasquez, Gabriel I: 125; V: 212n
Vattel, Emmerich de III: 139n
Veatch, Henry I: 148n
Vendler, Zeno II: 93
Vermeersch, P. III: 298n
Villey, Michel I: 206–8
Vinogradoff, Paul IV: 409n
virtue I: 120, 150; dependent on rational norm: I: 151–2; end(s) of I: 175–6; to be found again in Kingdom I: 171; V: 288, 366, 371
Vitoria, Francisco de III: 130–1, 190–2, 194, 198n, 200–1n, 206n
Vlastos, Gregory III: 99n, 337
Voegelin, Eric I: 189, II: 14n, 126n; IV: 50n, 259, 278, 321n, 428, 431; V: 34, 58, 146n, 339

von Balthasar, Hans Urs V: 13, 64, 65n, 373–9
von Hildebrand, Dietrich I: 138
von Wright, Georg Henrik I: 130
Vorgrimler, Herbert V: 272n

Wade, F.C. II: 288n
Wade, H.W.R. IV: 415
Waffelaert, J. II: 254n
Walker, Lord (Justice) (Robert) II: 196n; III: 135n, 144n
Waller, Mark III: 23n
Walter, James II: 163n; V: 291n, 298–302n, 304n, 342
Walton, Douglas III: 213n
Walton, Lord (John) III: 211n, 213–16, 222n, 232–3, 262–4, 269, 277n; IV: 277n
Waluchow, W.J. IV: 164
war III.13
Ward, Alan II: 196n
Ward, Keith III: 58n
Warnock, G.J. I: 113–20
Warnock, Mary III: 21n
Washington, George V: 28
Waszink, J.H. IV: 187n
Watson, Lord (William) I: 226n; II: 207–8
Webber, Grégoire III: 45n
Weber, Max I: 22, 37, 202–3, 205–6; IV: 3, 33–4n, 76, 86, 163, 211–29
Wegemer, Gerard V: 163n, 169
Weinberg, Martin S. III: 350n
Weinberg, Stephen V: 194
Weinberger, Caspar V: 277–80
Weinrib, Ernest IV: 123, 163, 395n
Weinstein, Bill II: 81n
Weisheipl, James A. IV: 180n
Weithman, Paul III: 116, 121–2, 123–4n, 383n, 386
Wellman, Carl I: 72n
Wells, Deane II: 279n
Wenham, John V: 88n
Wertheimer, Roger III: 282n, 304
Wheare, K.C. IV: 414
White, Alan R. II: 174n, 199n, 315n
White, Justice (Byron) I: 295, 297n; III: 42n
Whitman, Walt IV: 330, 332–3
Wiggins, David I: 42n, 186n, 260n; II: 43n; III: 225; V: 46n
Wilberforce, Lord (Richard) I: 318n; IV: 256n
will: responsiveness to understood goods I: 1, 33, 38
William of Conches IV: 186–7n
William of Durham V: 189–92
William of Ockham I: 207; IV: 160; V: 150
Williams, Bernard I: 7, 92–7, 100n-1n, 102–3; II: 127–6, 129; III: 239n; IV: 251–3, 275; V: 135n, 305n
Williams, Glanville II: 174n-5n, 177, 182–7, 193, 228n; III: 215; V: 316n
Williams, Gwladys III: 131n
Wilson, George II: 71n

Winch, Peter IV: 211n
Winning, Thomas V: 119
Wishner, Julius I: 278n
Witherspoon, James I: 276n
Wittgenstein, Ludwig I: 71, 80n, 84, 104, 130–7, 142, 143n; II: 5–6, 71; III: 304; IV: 166
Wittich, Gunther IV: 214n
Wojtyla, Karol, (*see also* John Paul II)
    on action II: 136; on choice as lasting V: 78, 303n; II: 104; on nation II: 122–6, 128
Wolsey, Thomas I: 281
Wolff, Robert Paul III: 58n
Wood, Thomas IV: 191
Woolf, Harry III: 141–2
Wootton, Lady (Barbara) III: 156
Woozley, A.D. IV: 72n

words: bearers and manifestations of spirit I: 35
Wright, Benjamin Fletcher I: 284n
Wright, John, J. II: 118n, 123n
Wright, N.T. V: 192n
Wright, Thomas II: 41n, 44n

Xenophon III: 336–7, 340, 355; IV: 159

Yates, Simon II: 321n
Yowell, Maggie II: 108n

Zalba, Marcellino II: 254n; III: 295n, 298n, 310
Zander, Michael III: 19n
Zellner, Harold M III: 290n
Zeno IV: 428
Zipursky, Benjamin C. IV: 150–1n
Zwingli, Huldrych V: 165